PREFACE

In this revision of *Psychology in Human Affairs* the authors have attempted to do three things—include new research that has appeared since the first edition was published, include new fields of application which did not appear in the first edition, and improve occasional roughness in writing which made passages unnecessarily difficult for undergraduate readers. Consequently, only parts of the book have been revised. Changes were made only where they *improved* the material.

Like the first edition, the book is still *factual* and *practical*. Theoretical discussion and "isms" have been kept at a minimum. The book is about the practical applications of psychology in its various fields of usefulness. No apologies are made for its omission of so-called "pure research." Useless facts, no matter how carefully they have been determined, are of interest to the applied psychologist only when they become *useful*.

Like the first edition, the attempt in this revision is to report typical facts about how psychology has been used in more than 20 fields or areas. Sometimes, because of limited space, these facts are reported with a minimum of interpretation. Without guidance they may be confusing to the beginning student. However, this is a classroom textbook and is not intended for the self-educated student or the casual reader of psychological literature. This book needs a teacher to interpret facts and answer questions. The traditional classroom lecture (facetiously designated by one student as "a procedure of transferring ideas from the professor's notebook to the student's notebook without passing through the heads of either") can be eliminated when this book is used as a text. Adequate factual material to give the student a bird's-eye view of the various applications of psychology is included in the following pages. The teaching problem is to explain what this material means.

This book is intended primarily for the beginning student, although it is appropriate for any survey course in applied psychology. A trend in psychology seems to be to devote the first half (or semester) of the beginning course to introductory material and the second half to a survey of the applications of psychology. This book is designed for the second semester of such a course.

The author-editor is again obligated to his coauthors. Some of them have made extensive revisions of material that was already of superior caliber. Because of the death of Dr. Wheeler, the author has written a new chapter on the topic of nutrition and drugs. Because Mrs. Noggle is located in a part of the world where new research in psychology is not readily available, her chapter has been revised by Professor Myles. The contributing authors have all adapted both the content and style of their chapters to the pattern of the rest of the book. For this, the editor is most appreciative.

J. Stanley Gray

McGraw-Hill Series in Psychology
CLIFFORD T. MORGAN, *Consulting Editor*

PSYCHOLOGY APPLIED
TO HUMAN AFFAIRS

McGraw-Hill Series in Psychology
CLIFFORD T. MORGAN, *Consulting Editor*

John F. Dashiell was Consulting Editor of this series from its inception in 1931 until January 1, 1950.

PSYCHOLOGY APPLIED
TO HUMAN AFFAIRS

J. STANLEY GRAY
PROFESSOR OF PSYCHOLOGY
UNIVERSITY OF GEORGIA

With the assistance of ten contributors

SECOND EDITION

NEW YORK   TORONTO   LONDON

McGRAW-HILL BOOK COMPANY, INC.

1954

PSYCHOLOGY APPLIED TO HUMAN AFFAIRS

Library of Congress Catalog Card Number: 53-5164

II

CONTENTS

Chapter 1

INTRODUCTION—ANTECEDENTS OF APPLIED PSYCHOLOGY

Like other sciences, psychology began as mysticism, then became a philosophy, and is now slowly becoming a technique of collecting and interpreting objective data. Unfortunately, it has been difficult for psychology to shake off many characteristics of former stages of development. Purely mystical concepts are yet widely accepted even by psychologists themselves. Philosophical speculation is too often substituted for controlled scientific research. Even with these handicaps, however, psychologists are more and more taking their problems to the laboratory and investigating their data under controlled conditions. As in other scientific fields, the increase in scientific information reduces the amount of armchair speculation. Mysticism and philosophy are not so necessary when facts are known. The fantasies of mysticism and the "isms" of philosophy are significant only when there is ignorance of fact. As psychology becomes more factual, its former techniques of ignorance will be used less and less until they will be remembered only in historical retrospect.

The following pages in this chapter review some of the steps that psychology has taken in its slow rise from mysticism. Subsequent chapters survey facts in various fields that indicate the present scientific status of psychology.

1

SUPERSTITION AND MYSTICISM

The thinking of all primitive people has been patterned by their attempts to explain to themselves two common events—storms and dreams. Theories and later beliefs concerning the universe on one hand, and man's place in the universe on the other, have developed from primitive theories of explanation of the storm and of dreams. The storm was explained by making a basic assumption, which later became a dogmatic belief, that there is some sort of *hidden giant* with human characteristics who can blow his breath and make a hurricane, throw firebrands across the sky, splash the ocean into gigantic waves, roar with thunderous loudness, and pour water over the whole countryside at one time. It was also assumed, and then believed, that this hidden giant with human attributes could be appeased with obeisant expressions of homage and sacrificial offerings. With such appeasement (or worship) he (or it) was less dangerous and could even be protective. Some believed that this giant was a mystical spirit while others said that he was a very real idol. In either case he was feared and had to be appeased.

Attempts to explain dreams also followed a common pattern. There was first assumed and later believed to be in each individual a *hidden self* that could go hunting, for example, while the nonhidden self lay asleep. As time went on, this hidden self, which originally functioned only during sleep, gradually took on functions during the awake state. It was a convenient explanation for implicit language behavior which later became known as "thinking." Because of this alleged function, the hidden self was called the "psyche" or "mind" and as such directed and controlled the individual's behavior.

These theoretical explanations of storms and of dreams soon became accepted not as theories but as *facts*. They became *reified*.[1] The hidden giant became a *great spirit* whose power was not limited to causing storms. He also controlled the universe. As such he was even more effective in social control than verifiable facts of physical existence. The hidden self became the individual's mind, which directed his behavior, and also became his soul, which was assumed to live after death. This thereby satisfied man's desire for immortality. The hidden giant and the hidden self were no longer considered mere postulates but were accepted as facts and affirmed often with zealous fury. The process of reification was now complete.

The transformation of these two postulates (the hidden giant and the hidden self) into accepted beliefs was followed by other postulates and more reifications. For example, in one group culture someone suggested

---

[1] Reify means to assert that a thing exists merely because it is named. For example, witches must exist because they have been named. The fact that we talk about them proves that they exist. Psyche falls into this same category.

that those occasional people who had pink eyes and white hair might be connected somehow with the hidden giant who caused the storm. The suggestion was soon reified, and albinos were worshiped as nonhidden representatives of the hidden storm giant. Conversely, in another group culture someone suggested that those occasional people whose backs were hunched somehow caused harmful events to occur. This assumption too became reified, and hunchbacked people were killed to protect others from the harmful effects now believed to be caused by these unfortunate individuals.

Prescientific man's honest attempts to explain the unknown are even yet accepted as statements of fact instead of statements of theory. Assumptions are mistaken for facts and used as behavior controls. Much superstition and mystical belief today has no justification beyond the fact that it has been believed by generations of ancestors who admittedly had less contact with scientific development and consequently less opportunity to distinguish fact from theory than we have today. Blind and uncritical acceptance of the primitive assumption that a hidden giant causes the storm and a hidden self enables us to dream has led to elaborate ritualistic customs that are effective social controls and often used to attain unscrupulous ends.

The psychologist neither affirms nor rejects any modern version of the hidden giant or of the hidden self. In spite of their reification he considers them to be unproved postulates which are more properly labeled as superstitions. As a scientist his interpretations and explanations go only as far as his facts justify. Beyond that he admits his ignorance and gets little solace from accepting mystical postulates as facts.

PSYCHOLOGY IN THE PRESCIENTIFIC ERA

Man developed methods of recording his progress long before he developed a science of psychology. Consequently, we have a long era of prescientific psychology that has been recorded in considerable detail. The following pages briefly review a small segment of this extensive literature. Just those psychologies are reviewed that, though primitive and fallacious, are still active. Evidence of the fallacies inherent in them is also presented.

ASTROLOGY

It was recently reported that, when a London newspaper omitted its daily horoscope, there were 50,000 protests by personal call, telephone, and telegraph. A California astrologer announced over the radio that he would read the horoscope of anyone who would accompany his request with $4. He is reported to have received 30,000 replies. Evangeline Adams, who would not answer a single question for less than $100, counted among her clients such dignitaries as James J. Hill, the empire builder; J. P. Morgan, the financier; John Burroughs, the naturalist; Caruso, the opera singer; Richard Harding Davis, the writer; and William Jennings Bryan, the politician. She was supposed to have accurately predicted the advent of the First World War, the sex of a New England Hereford calf, the panic of 1907, and the death of the wife of a Southern gentleman. She gave advice on every known problem that concerned human affairs, for which she charged fees that rivaled those of a corporation lawyer.

Astrology began in Babylonia and spread to Greece about the middle of the fourth century. It gradually diminished with the development of science, although in recent years it has regained much of its popularity. Francis Bacon harshly condemned it, and others more recently have subjected it to scientific investigation.

Astrology is a theory that human affairs are controlled by the heavenly bodies. From a study of the stars and their influence, the astrologer believes that human affairs can be predicted. Even the date of birth is supposed to have great influence on one's life because destiny is presumably determined by the zodiac sign under which one is born. What one is to become and the events that occur in his life can be predicted from a study of the zodiac.

In evaluating astrology, it should be noted that astronomers, those scientists who have carefully studied heavenly bodies and know more about the universe of stars and planets than any other group of specialists, agree there is no evidence to support the claims of astrology. If the stars influence human destiny, that influence is so meager that it escapes scientific discovery. Even if there were astral influences, they would change over a period of years because the zodiac is not fixed. True, it changes slowly but fast enough to make the astrological beliefs of the ancients now out of date. (A zodiac circuit occurs every 25,800 years.)

Furthermore, astrologers do not agree among themselves. What signs influence what? How can conflicting opinions about these influences be settled? Astrology has neither subject matter nor methodology of research. Consequently, it can never become a science, and disagreement is inevitable.

A few years ago, Parr[2] had one of his graduate students write to 16 astrologers, located in our own and foreign countries, for horoscope readings. They gave him a total of 60 personality traits, only seven of which were objectionable. Every day in the year was designated as both lucky and unlucky for him by at least one astrologer. Some of them advised him to stay on his present job and some advised him to look for another. Some said that he would soon take a long trip and others said that he would not. Parr concludes that "results of this analysis revealed not only unfulfilled,

[2] Parr, F. W., How's Your Horoscope? *Occupations*, 1937, 16, 236–238.

unrealized, and mistaken predictions but also demonstrated a wide disagreement among astrologers over identical vocational issues."

If the zodiac signs do influence our destinies, a study of the birth dates of eminent men should substantiate this claim. We could expect to find that most great scientists were born under one sign, most great statesmen under another, most great musicians under another, etc. With this in mind, Farnsworth[3] studied the relation of musical and artistic ability to the month of birth, or to the zodiac sign under which eminent musicians and artists are born. He secured his data on the time of birth from three sources—*Musical Who's Who,* by Key; *A Dictionary of Music and Musicians,* by Grove; and the *Cyclopedia of Painters and Paintings.* One would suppose that, if the time of birth makes enough difference to enable astrologers to predict the future development of ability, this evidence would become obvious in Farnsworth's study. However, the data showed that the birth dates of neither musicians nor artists are concentrated under any sign, and certainly not under Libra nor Taurus as claimed by most

Table 1–1. Percentage of Certain Selected Groups Born under Each Zodiac Sign

Zodiac sign	Musicians		Painters	Citizens of	
	Who's Who (N 1,998)	Diction- ary (N 3,257)	Cyclo- pedia (N 2,478)	New York City	Vienna
Aries...............	9.2	9.6	8.8	8.3	9.0
Taurus.............	8.2	7.7	9.5	8.1	8.9
Gemini.............	7.9	8.2	8.2	8.5	8.9
Cancer.............	8.6	7.5	7.6	8.5	8.8
Leo.................	8.1	7.5	7.7	8.4	8.0
Virgo...............	8.3	7.4	8.8	8.3	7.7
Libra...............	7.2	7.7	8.9	8.1	7.7
Scorpio.............	7.2	7.9	6.9	8.0	7.4
Sagittarius..........	8.1	8.2	7.0	8.1	7.5
Capricorn...........	9.9	8.9	8.5	8.5	7.8
Aquarius............	9.0	9.8	8.6	8.5	8.9
Pisces..............	8.3	9.8	9.6	8.6	9.3

astrologers. Farnsworth then took the birth dates of the population of New York City and those of all babies born in Vienna for the years 1925 to 1934, to see if and how the musicians and artists differed in the distribution of their birth dates with these typical populations. All these data are shown in Table 1–1, from which the conclusion is obvious that the time of birth has nothing to do with the development of musical and artistic abilities.

[3] Farnsworth, P. R., Aesthetic Behavior and Astrology, *Character & Pers.,* 1938, **6,** 335–340.

Pintner[4] studied the relation between intelligence and the month of birth of 4,925 New York City school children. (According to astrologers, a majority of intelligent people are born in the month of September.) He found that the month of birth has no influence on intelligence. Held[5] conducted a similar study with college freshmen. He found that the average intelligence of students was about the same regardless of the month of birth. His results are shown in Table 1–2. If zodiac signs were important,

Table 1–2. Average Percentile Rank on Intelligence Test of College Freshmen Born in Respective Months
(N 2,327)

Month of Birth	Percentile Rank on I.Q. Test
January	48.6
February	49.9
March	49.5
April	47.3
May	50.6
June	51.8
July	50.6
August	48.1
September	52.8
October	49.2
November	50.3
December	50.6

we could expect that the intelligence of those students born in September would be significantly higher than those born in other months under other signs.

Goodenough[6] suggests that the better-educated upper-income groups plan parenthood and conceive during the winter months so that their children will be born during the late summer. (Physicians are generally agreed that children born in summer and fall are healthier than those born in the winter and spring.) A survey of 3,275 births indicated that, while births on the lower-income levels occur in about the same proportion throughout the year, those on the higher-income levels are more frequent in summer and fall. Thus, instead of the season's influencing intelligence, intelligence seems to influence the season of birth.

The interpretation of these studies is clear. The month of a person's birth has little significance in his later life. Neither his ability nor his luck is dependent on the month of his birth. The astrologers are wrong in their assumptions and are not justified in making any predictions at all. Astrol-

[4] Pintner, R., Intelligence and the Month of Birth, J. Appl. Psychol., 1931, 15, 149–154.

[5] Held, O. C., Influence of the Month of Birth on the Intelligence of College Freshmen, J. Genet. Psychol., 1940, 57, 211–217.

[6] Goodenough, F., Intelligence and Month of Birth. Psychol. Bull., 1940, 37, 442.

ogy is a hoax from which the uninformed should be protected. Certainly it has no scientific justification.

PHRENOLOGY

Late in the eighteenth century, Franz Joseph Gall wrote a six-volume treatise on cranioscopy, or phrenology. His theory was that man has mental faculties that differ in magnitude or power. He believed that these are located in separate parts of the brain. Then he reasoned that the size of the faculty is correlated with the size of its brain area. If the faculty is large, the brain area will be large and, so Gall believed, will cause the skull to protrude at that place. Then by a study of the protrusions or bumps on the cranium it is possible to predict the size of the mental faculties. For example, if a person's skull protruded immediately above the ears, he was supposed to possess the faculty or trait of destructiveness, since this is the location of that trait. Other traits, 26 in all, were supposed to be located in other specific areas of the brain. Gall even published a map of the brain and showed the location of such traits as cautiousness, imitation, benevolence, self-esteem, parental love, friendship, etc.

Two of Gall's students, Spurzheim and Combe, carried his doctrines to England and America. Phrenology societies were established and journals were published. The theory, or research, phase of the doctrine was soon forgotten and phrenologists diagnosed mental qualities with authoritative dogmatism. Phrenology became a racket.

Evidence to support the extravagant claim of phrenology has never been discovered. On the contrary, investigations soon piled up evidence on the other side. First, it was proved that there is no relation between brain size and intelligence. Some brilliant men have had large brains, and some have had small brains. Thackeray's brain weighed 1,658 g. Daniel Webster's weighed 1,518 g. On the other hand, the brain of Anatole France weighed but 1,017 g. It was found that, while the average human male brain weighs 1,440 g. and the average human female brain weighs 1,360 g., there is no evident difference in intelligence. Certainly brain size is no indication of intelligence.[7]

Second, the shape of the cranium is known to be determined by factors other than the shape of the brain inside. The use of instruments at time of birth often leaves permanent effects on the shape of the cranium. The habitual position in which the infant sleeps during the first years of life often determines the shape of his skull. Furthermore, it is known that the skull is not of uniform thickness. A protrusion may indicate a thick place in the skull and not a development of the brain inside. The shape of the skull is in no way determined by the size or development of mental traits.

---

[7] Of course, abnormally large brains (macrocephalics) and abnormally small brains (microcephalics) are both indicative of limited intelligence.

Table 1-3. Brain-area Functions and Phrenology Claims

Brain areas	Actual function	Phrenology claim
a	Hearing	Destructiveness
b	Vision	Parental love
c	Control of feet and legs	Spirituality
d	Control of arms and hands	Ideality
e	Control of head and face	Constructiveness
f	Body sensations	Cautiousness
g	Speech	Acquisitiveness

Third, it is now denied that mental faculties exist as distinct and recognizable classifications of mental life at all. Memory, for example, is not a discrete trait but a phase of behavior that varies with the material being remembered. No reputable psychologist today believes that the mind is made up of discrete faculties. Instead, he knows mental life is a function of the entire individual in relation to his environment and is difficult to distinguish even from physical behavior. Destructiveness, for example, is not a mental faculty but the way some individuals react to some situations. It is characteristic of that individual only *in that situation.* It is not characteristic of the individual any more than it is characteristic of the situation, because in other situations he does not react in a destructive manner.

Fourth, recent laboratory studies have shown that the various areas of the brain have functions entirely different from those postulated by the phrenologist. For example, it is known that the area just above the ears is the center for hearing and not for destructiveness. The real functions of certain brain areas and the functions claimed by phrenologists are shown in Table 1-3.

The claims of the phrenologists have not been substantiated by experimental results. No studies of brain function afford the slightest evidence for believing the theory that cranial bumps indicate mental traits of any sort. Like astrology, phrenology must be discarded as unscientific and unworthy of serious attention.

GRAPHOLOGY

In 1662, Baldo published in Italy a treatise on the method of analyzing a man's character from his handwriting. This was called "graphology." The theory is that character can be judged from characteristics of handwriting. Somehow, a person's character is supposed to be reflected in his handwriting. Katherine Blackford incorporated graphology in her system of character analysis. She thus popularized it among a large and influential clientele. The more basic writing traits and character traits they are supposed to indicate are shown in Table 1-4.

Table 1–4. Handwriting Traits and the Character Traits They Are Supposed to Indicate

Handwriting Traits	Character Traits
Upward sloping lines	Ambition, pride
Heavy lines and heavy bars over t's	Forcefulness
Fine lines	Bashfulness, timidity
Writing too slanted	Slowness, sluggishness
Closed a's, o's, and d's	Reserve, caution
Open a's, o's, and d's	Dishonesty
Long bars over t's	Perseverance

The validity of handwriting as a means of judging character has been carefully studied. Hull and Montgomery[8] analyzed the handwriting of 17 fraternity brothers who rated each other on the possession of certain character traits. The handwriting was found to possess but little indication of the presence of these traits. The highest relationship was between bashfulness and the lateral narrowness of m's and n's, and this was but 7 per cent better than chance. The results of this study are shown in Table 1–5.

Table 1–5. Correlations of Character with Handwriting

Character traits	Handwriting traits	r^*
Ambition	Upward sloping lines	$-.20$
Pride	Upward sloping lines	$-.07$
Bashfulness	Fineness of lines	$-.45$
Bashfulness	Lateral narrowness of m and n	$.38$
Force	Heavy lines	$-.17$
Force	Heavy bars over t's	$-.06$
Perseverance	Length of bars over t's	$.00$
Reserve	Closed a's and o's	$-.02$

* The coefficient of correlation and other statistical concepts referred to in this book are explained in the appendix.

Brown, as reported by Viteles,[9] followed essentially the same procedure as Hull and Montgomery and found essentially the same low correlations. These results are shown in Table 1–6.

Middleman[10] studied the ability of college students to judge intelligence and age from handwriting. He found a mere chance relationship in the judgment of intelligence from handwriting, and a correlation of but .25 in the judgment of age from handwriting.

[8] Hull, C. L., and Montgomery, R. B., An Experimental Investigation of Certain Alleged Relations between Character and Handwriting, *Psychol. Rev.*, 1919, 26, 63–75.

[9] Viteles, M. S., *Industrial Psychology*, p. 199, W. W. Norton & Company, New York, 1932.

[10] Middleman, W. C., The Ability of Untrained Subjects to Judge Intelligence and Age from Handwriting Samples, *J. Appl. Psychol.*, 1941, 25, 331–340.

Table 1–6. Relation between Character Traits and Handwriting Traits

Character traits	Handwriting traits	r
Bashfulness	Width of down strokes	.11
Ambition	Upward slope of line	.23
Persistence	Width of down stroke	−.05
Persistence	Breaks of line within words	−.03
Personal neatness	Neatness in writing	.23
Personal individuality	Individuality in writing	.15

Consequently, we must conclude that, as far as present knowledge goes, a person's character traits are not revealed in his handwriting. Graphology must also be classified as an unscientific method of personality diagnosis.

PHYSIOGNOMY

Physiognomy is a theory that the physical characteristics of the face and body indicate character and temperament traits. Who has not heard that "red-headed people are hot-tempered," or "fat people are good-natured," or "long fingers indicate artistic ability"? The high forehead, the receding jaw, the short neck, the triangular face, the skin pigmentation, the size of the bones and joints, the texture of the hair, etc.—all have special significance for the physiognomist in character analysis. Personality traits are supposed to be determined by bodily characteristics.

The theory of physiognomy extends back to Galen (A.D. 200). He believed that the universe is composed of four elements—fire, air, water, and earth—which are represented in the body as four biles or humors. These, in turn, determined the temperament of the individual, depending on which one was dominant. Black-bile dominance was supposed to produce a melancholic and sad temperament. Yellow bile caused one to be irritable. Phlegm (bile) produced a dull and listless individual. Blood (bile) brought about vitality and friendliness. While Galen's theory antedates a lot of scientific progress, it is about as reasonable as some of the later modifications of it.

A more recent classification of body types, which has attracted wide attention, was by Kretschmer.[11] He observed (*sic*) that certain types of mentally abnormal patients seem to have certain types of body build. For example, he thought that the manic-depressive patients are usually heavy-set with short limbs, while the schizophrenia patients are more often thin and angular. Between these he placed an intermediate or more normal group. He called the first type "pyknics" and described them as having full faces, short necks and limbs, being overweight, extroverted, good-

[11] Kretschmer, E., *Physique and Character,* Harcourt, Brace and Company, Inc., New York, 1925.

natured, realistic, and relaxed. He called the opposite type "asthenics" or *"leptosomes."* These are slender, tall, sharp featured, introverted, humorless, and phlegmatic. The pyknics tend to range from a gay to a melancholic state, while the leptosomes tend to be "hypersensitive and dull." The in-between group, which Kretschmer called "athletics," are well built and mild-mannered. They are the "cool men of decision, inclined to consistency of thought and general systemization." Kretschmer believed that most individuals fall into one of these three classifications, although he admitted that there are mixed types. This theory has been the subject for a voluminous literature, especially in the German language.

Mention should be made here of the careful study of the relation of body type to temperament by Sheldon and his associates.[12] They have devised a scale for classifying body types and also one for classifying temperaments. They rate a body build on the basis of three characteristics, closely paralleling those of Kretschmer. These are *endomorphy* (soft, flabby, and roly-poly), *mesomorphy* (strong and sturdy), and *ectomorphy* (skinny with long bones and stringy muscles). A physique is rated on a scale of 7 for each of these characteristics. For example, a person who is 6 in endomorphy, 2 in mesomorphy, and 1 in ectomorphy is predominantly soft, fat, and round. Another who is rated 1-7-1 is more of a strong man (or woman). A 3-4-3 person is average in build and cannot be classified into a type.

Another scale has been developed for rating temperaments, also with 7 degrees and 3 characteristics. The characteristics are *viscertonia* (amiable, complacent, enjoys food and relaxation), *somatotonia* (energetic, courageous, loves power and risk), and *cerebrotonia* (restrained, unsocial, does not sleep well). A 7-2-1 individual would be one who is happy, jovial, and likes to eat.

Sheldon rated 200 cases on both scales and found correlations between endomorphy and viscertonia of .79; between mesomorphy and somatotonia of .82; and between ectomorphy and cerebrotonia of .83. Whether these apparently high correlations will be substantiated by further research is a matter for conjecture.

Perhaps the climax of the body-type theories of personality is that of Berman.[13] Because the malfunction of any one of the various endocrine glands will cause certain very characteristic abnormalities in body structure, or in body function, or in both, Berman jumped to the conclusion that at least one of the endocrine glands is malfunctioning in each individual, thus causing a characteristic personality type. "The en-

[12] See Sheldon, W. H., and Stevens, S. S., *The Varieties of Human Physique,* Harper & Brothers, New York, 1940; *The Varieties of Human Temperament,* Harper & Brothers, New York, 1942.

[13] Berman, Louis, *The Glands Regulating Personality,* The Macmillan Company, New York, 1928.

docrine type of an individual is . . . a prediction of his reactions in the future, much as a chemical formula outlines what we believe to be the skeleton of a compound substance." Since an endocrine may either overfunction or underfunction, the personality may be a positive type or negative type. One is usually the opposite of the other. In the following list of personality type characteristics (according to Berman), some are positive and some are negative.

1. The adrenal personality (positive, due to oversecretion)
   Deeply pigmented skin
   Thick, coarse, and dry hair
   Tendency to tuberculosis, diphtheria, and influenza
   Vigorous, energetic, and persistent
   Tendency toward virilism
   "Develops into a progressive winning fighter, who will arrive at the top in the long run every time"
2. The pituitary personality (positive, due to oversecretion)
   Large, spare body frame
   Eyes wide apart
   Broad face
   Teeth large, broad, unspaced
   Square, protruding chin and jaws
   Large feet and hands
   Early hair growth on body
   Thick skin, large sex organs
   Aggressive, precocious, calculating, self-contained
3. The thyroid personality (negative, due to undersecretion)
   Height below average
   Tendency to obesity (toward middle age)
   Complexion sallow
   Hair dry—hairline high
   Eyebrows scanty, either as a whole or in outer half
   Eyeballs deepset, lackluster, in narrow slits
   Teeth irregular, become carious early
   Extremities cold and bluish
   Circulation poor; subject to chilblains
4. The thymocentric personality (positive, due to oversecretion)
   Slender waist, gracefully formed body, rounded limbs, long chest, feminine pelvis
   Skin smooth and velvety
   Little or no hair on face
   Often double-jointed, flatfooted, knock-kneed
   Small heart and fragile blood vessels
   Tendency to homosexuality
   Poor resistance to infections and disease
   Emotionally unstable
5. The gonadcentric personality (negative, due to undersecretion)

Incomplete, irregular, or absent hair development
Skin yellowish, leathery, wrinkled
Voice high pitched
Tall and slender; muscles flabby
Feet and hands small
Straightforward homosexuality

6. The parathyroid centered personality (negative, due to undersecretion)
   Often premature birth
   Hypersensitive, especially affecting visceral organs
   Tendency to hysteria
   Poor teeth
   Body small, health puny
   Tendency to eidetic imagery
   Restless, eternally unsatisfied, and fastidious
   Temporal arteries become hardened early

The trouble with Berman's theory is that it has never been substantiated by research evidence. It is entirely probable that personalities are greatly affected by the endocrine glands, but there is no evidence yet that they can be so classified.

It is the more generally accepted belief among psychologists that personality traits are learned—from parents, from companions, from community ways of doing things. Within hereditary limitations, personality is a product of social conditions. "Tell me the conditions under which a man was reared and I will tell you more about his personality and temperament than any physiognomist can tell from a study of his body dimensions."

Numerous studies have been made of the relation of personality to various other physical characteristics. It is generally believed that skin pigmentation is indicative of a person's temperament traits. A blond or a brunet or a redhead is assumed to have traits which distinguish him or her from people of other complexions.

Paterson and Ludgate[14] studied the scientific justification of Blackford's claim that there are characteristic differences between blonds and brunets in character traits. Their procedure was to have 94 "intelligent and educated adults" rate two blonds and two brunets of their own acquaintance on those character traits alleged by Blackford to distinguish blonds from brunets. The results were then summarized to see if the blonds possessed blond traits and if the brunets possessed brunet traits. The results are shown in Table 1–7. Obviously, complexion is not significant in the possession of character traits. The traits that Blackford claimed were characteristic only of blonds were actually just as characteristic of brunets.

---

[14] Paterson, D. G., and Ludgate, K. E., Blonde and Brunette Traits: A Quantitative Study, *J. Person. Res.*, 1922, 1, 122–127.

Those supposed to be brunet traits were found to an equal degree among the blonds.

Table 1–7. Percentage of 187 Blonds and 187 Brunets Rated as Possessing Each Trait

	Blonds	Brunets
Blond traits (Blackford):		
Positive......	81	81
Dynamic..............................	63	64
Driving...............................	49	50
Aggressive............................	62	56
Impatient.............................	56	51
Active................................	88	82
Quick.................................	70	68
Hopeful...............................	85	85
Speculative...........................	53	51
Changeable............................	53	43
Variety-loving........................	66	62
Domineering...........................	36	36
Brunet traits (Blackford):		
Negative..............................	16	17
Static................................	28	31
Conservative..........................	51	61
Imitative.............................	39	40
Submissive............................	25	26
Cautious..............................	54	60
Painstaking...........................	56	61
Patient...............................	43	52
Plodding..............................	27	31
Slow..................................	20	24
Deliberate............................	47	57
Serious...............................	58	72
Thoughtful............................	67	70
Specializing..........................	52	45

A study was conducted by Garrett and Kellogg[15] in which they obtained a morphological index for each student (male college freshmen) from three photographs in the nude taken by the department of physical education. They then administered the Thorndike Intelligence Test, the George Washington Social Intelligence Test, and the Woodworth Personal Data Sheet (for emotional stability). They also measured the height and weighed each student to obtain a height-weight ratio. The correlations between these various factors are shown in Table 1–8.

Another study of the validity of physiognomy as a method of character analysis was made by Ford.[16] He had character readings made of 18

[15] Garrett, H. E., and Kellogg, W. N., The Relation of Physical Constitution to General Intelligence, Social Intelligence, and Emotional Stability, *J. Exp. Psychol.*, 1928, **11**, 113–129.

[16] Ford, A., A Check on Character Analysis, *Person. J.*, 1930, **9**, 121–123.

Table 1–8. Relation of Personality Traits to Morphological Index and Height-Weight Ratio

Trait	Morphological index		Height-weight ratio	
	N	r	N	r
General intelligence.................	219	.07	219	.10
Social intelligence..................	151	.05	150	.09
Emotional stability.................	123	−.06	122	.05

university students by representatives of a firm of physiognomists, operating under the trade name of "Vitosophy." These readings were then correlated with university grades, psychological tests, and the student's self-estimates. To compare the results with chance, he also made character readings by a lottery procedure. The results are shown in Table 1–9.

Table 1–9. Correlations between Measures of Ability and Vitosophy Scores and Lottery Scores

	Vitosophy	Lottery
Mathematics grades...................	−.16	−.24
Written English grades...............	.32	−.10
Science grades.......................	.10	.15
Scholarship (all grades)..............	.23	−.38
Intelligence (Army Alpha)............	−.21	.24
Mechanical ability (self-estimate).......	−.55	.16
Musical ability (self-estimate)..........	−.31	.07
Average..........................	−.08	−.01

Note that all correlations are low and the Vitosophy method is no better than the lottery method (pure chance).

A very extensive study of the validity of physiognomy was made by Cleeton and Knight.[17] They made 28 careful physical measurements of a group of college fraternity and sorority students to see if any physical characteristic is correlated with any character trait. The degree of the possession of a character trait was determined by the judgment of both close and casual acquaintances. Needless to say, no physical measurement was significantly correlated with any character trait. The average of all correlations was exactly zero. The average of the correlations of physical measurements with eight character traits is shown in Table 1–10. Note that all the correlations indicate but slight variations from chance.

[17] Cleeton, G. U., and Knight, F. B., Validity of Character Judgment Based on External Criteria, *J. Appl. Psychol.*, 1924, 8, 215–231.

Consequently, it would seem that the claims of physiognomy are no more justified than those of astrology, graphology, and phrenology. It is another psychological "gold brick." It constitutes a part of the psychological underworld. Character analysis on the basis of physical characteristics is no better than lottery.

Table 1–10. Average Correlations between Physical Measurements and Character Traits as Judged by Close Associates and Casual Observers

Trait	r for close associates	r for casual observers
Judgment	−.005	.145
Intelligence	.027	.051
Frankness	.055	.155
Will power	.074	.036
Friendliness	.110	.195
Leadership	−.041	.066
Originality	.095	.079
Impulsiveness	.100	−.067

PSYCHOLOGICAL STEPS TOWARD SCIENCE

While the preceding pages review a fragment of that prescientific psychology which still has a considerable following, the following pages will review some of the steps psychology has taken toward becoming a science. Again, only a few highlights that now seem to be significant will be mentioned. Psychology's struggle from mysticism to its present approach to science has been slow and long. To review it in detail would take a book in itself.[18] The following high spots are suggestive, however, of some of the difficulties encountered, the techniques developed, the information obtained, and the progress yet to be accomplished.

STUDIES IN PSYCHOPHYSICS

Early in the last century (about 1829) Ernst Weber, professor of comparative anatomy in the Medical School of the University of Leipzig (Germany), performed a series of experiments to discover the relation of stimulation (physical) to sensation (psychical). These culminated in the discovery of Weber's law, which stated that the increase of stimulation necessary to be sensed as such is not absolute, but proportionate to the stimulation already present. For example, if a weight of 10 lb. is already being lifted, the addition of an ounce will not be sensed. But if only 10 oz. is now being lifted, the addition of an ounce can be sensed. Weber found that, for a given sense, the proportionate increase in stimulation necessary to be sensed as an increase is a constant fraction of the stim-

[18] See Boring, E. G., *History of Experimental Psychology,* Appleton-Century-Crofts, Inc., New York, 1950.

ulation already present. This fraction for the judgment of weight (the kinesthetic sense) is $\frac{1}{30}$. In other words, to be sensed as an increase, the present stimulation must be increased by $\frac{1}{30}$. If 10 lb. is being lifted, $5\frac{1}{3}$ oz. ($\frac{1}{30}$ of 10 lb.) must be added before an increase can be sensed as such. On the other hand, if only 10 oz. is being lifted, an increase of $\frac{1}{3}$ oz. ($\frac{1}{30}$ of 10 oz.) can be sensed. This constant fraction, or ratio, of the increase in stimulation to the stimulation already present was designated as the "just noticeable difference" or the j.n.d.

This fraction, or ratio, or j.n.d., was found to be different for each sense. Weber found that the constant fraction for vision was approximately $\frac{1}{50}$. When a subject is asked to judge the difference in length of two lines, one line must be $\frac{1}{50}$ longer than the other before it is sensed as being longer. (This is true when they are presented simultaneously. If they are presented successively, the increase must be at least $\frac{1}{20}$.)

Weber also began the experimental study of thresholds, or sensory limens. The lower threshold refers to the amount of stimulation necessary to arouse sensitivity at the lower limit. The upper threshold refers to the upper limit of sensitivity beyond which the addition of more stimulation will not be sensed. The differential threshold refers to the amount of stimulation necessary to enable one to distinguish one sensation from another. It is the j.n.d. For example, 18 vibrations per second is the lower threshold of pitch sensitivity; 25,000 vibrations per second is the upper threshold of pitch sensitivity. Vibrations above and below these thresholds cannot be heard by humans, although some of the lower animals can hear both higher and lower sounds than can man. The differential threshold is the number of vibrations between two tones recognized as different. People with absolute pitch can sense the difference in tones when the real difference is only a few vibrations. They have low differential thresholds.

Another experiment by Weber, which is now standard in any course in experimental psychology, was the "compass test." Its purpose was to discover how far apart two points must be on the skin to be recognized as separate. This was called the cutaneous two-point threshold. Weber found that different areas of the body differed in the two-point threshold. For example, in the middle of the back, two points of pressure a wide distance apart are still sensed as one point. The hands or the tongue are very sensitive in this respect. Two points do not need to be very far apart until they are sensed as two points. The two-point threshold is much less on the hands than on the back.

One of Weber's students was Theodore Fechner, who became interested in the relation of the sensed world to the physical world—psychophysics. Fechner assumed that all j.n.d.'s were equal and therefore were the units of sensation. A large sensation was assumed to be composed of a certain number of j.n.d's. Therefore, he reformulated Weber's law as follows: When stimulation is increased by a constant ratio, the sensations aroused are increased by equal steps. Figure 1–1 illustrates this law in psychophysics. The increment in sensation is an arithmetical progression, while the increment in stimulation is a geometrical progression. In terms

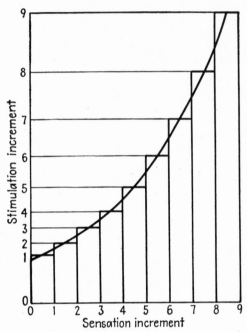

FIG. 1–1. The relation of simulation increase to sensation increase. (Constant fraction ¼.)

of mathematics, we would say that stimulation is a logarithmic function of sensation. Table 1–11 shows the same data as Fig. 1–1 but stated differently. Fechner could now state Weber's law as follows: Sensations are in proportion to the logarithms of the stimulation.

Table 1–11. The Logarithmic Relation of Stimulation to Sensation
(Constant fraction, ¼)

Sensation Increment	Stimulation Increment (Lower Threshold)
1	10
2	12.5
3	15.6
4	19.5
5	24.4
6	30.5
7	38.1
8	47.6
9	59.5

The methods of research that were used in the study of psychophysics are worth our attention. Not only were Weber and Fechner very careful and objective in their work but they were pioneers. It is easier to modify and improve a method than it is to originate it. The three methods of research in psychophysics were not only good when considered in light of the time in which they originated, but they are good research methods even when compared with present-day standards. These were the method of minimal change, the method of constant stimuli, and the method of average error.

The Method of Minimal Change. This is essentially the method of just noticeable differences by which Weber discovered the constant fraction. The procedure is to start with a given stimulus as a base (the standard stimulus) and then slowly increase it, or slowly decrease it, until the subject is able to notice a difference. Thus, the minimum change necessary for recognition is discovered. Sometimes, two stimuli are used—a fixed or standard stimulus and a changing stimulus. Whenever the changing stimulus is just barely recognized as different from the standard stimulus, a differential threshold, or a sensory unit (j.n.d.), or a constant fraction, is discovered. For example, suppose that subject A is able to recognize the difference in weight between 10 lb. and 10 lb. $5\frac{1}{3}$ oz., or between 10 lb. and 9 lb. $10\frac{2}{3}$ oz. However, he could not recognize the differences in weight when they were less than $5\frac{1}{3}$ oz., either above or below 10 lb. We would then say that with 10 lb. as the standard stimulus, the j.n.d. was $5\frac{1}{3}$ oz. Then, suppose that we repeat the same procedure with 10 oz. as the standard stimulus. Here we find that the j.n.d. is $\frac{1}{3}$ oz. We then use 6 lb. as the standard stimulus and find the j.n.d. to be 3.53 oz. In each case, we compute the ratio of the j.n.d. to the standard stimulus and find that it is 1:30, or expressed as a fraction is $\frac{1}{30}$.

It is important in the method of minimal change that the changing stimulus be both increased from equality with the standard stimulus and decreased to equality with the standard stimulus. Results from the two approaches are not identical. Sometimes it is easier to tell when a different stimulus becomes equal to a standard than it is to tell when an equal stimulus becomes different from a standard. Both approaches are necessary to find the true j.n.d.

The Method of Constant Stimuli. With this method, fixed stimuli, rather than gradually increasing and decreasing stimuli, are used. The subject judges over and over again whether a stimulus is more than, less than, or the same as a standard stimulus. For example, a subject may judge that a weight of 10 lb. 5 oz. is the same as a standard stimulus of 10 lb. in 80 per cent of his judgments and as more than the standard stimulus in the remaining 20 per cent. On the other hand, a weight of 10 lb. 6 oz. may be judged to be more than the standard weight of 10 lb. in 95 per cent of his judgments. A weight of 10 lb. 5⅓ oz. may be judged to be heavier than the standard weight in 50 per cent of his judgments and the same as the standard weight in the remaining 50 per cent of his judgments. This latter weight, then, is said to be the upper threshold of that j.n.d. Whatever weight is found to be judged as less than the standard in 50 per cent of the judgments is said to be the lower threshold. The percentages used vary, of course, with the experimenter. Sometimes 75 per cent of accurate judgments is used instead of 50 per cent. Often a threshold is designated as "the 75 per cent threshold," or "the 50 per cent threshold."

The Method of Average Error. The procedure of this method is to establish a fixed or standard stimulus and then provide the subject with a variable one which he can adjust to equal the standard stimulus. His error is then recorded and the procedure repeated. For example, suppose that we ask a subject to pour enough water in a bucket to make its weight equal to a 10 lb. standard weight. We then actually weigh the bucket to find his error. A record of his errors for a hundred trials would provide us with an average error. This method is quite like the method of minimal change except that the subject regulates the changes himself.

The relative value of these three methods of research in psychophysics depends on the sensitivity that is being studied. The method of constant stimuli is most often used to measure tactual and kinesthetic sensitivity. The method of minimal change seems to be best adapted for visual measurements. Modifications of all three methods have been used in psychological research since the time of Fechner. Problems in learning, problems in mental testing, problems in heredity, etc., have all been studied by techniques suggested, at least, by these pioneer methods of psychophysics. But more important than their methods of research, Weber and Fechner left psychology with an attitude of research. They put psychology into the laboratory and thus paved the way for the next step in its approach to becoming a science.

THE FIRST PSYCHOLOGICAL LABORATORY

Weber was a professor of anatomy and Fechner was a professor of physics. Their experiments in psychophysics were performed in their own laboratories. They put psychology in a laboratory, but not in a psychology laboratory. This step remained for Wilhelm Wundt at the University of Leipzig. While Wundt's title was professor of philosophy, he was primarily a psychologist. He believed that psychology is a science and should be studied by experimentation in a laboratory designed for such study. Consequently, he established the world's first psychological laboratory, in the year 1879.

Soon there began a steady stream of students from all over the world to study psychology by experiment in the Leipzig laboratory. Outstanding among the Americans who studied under Wundt and later became prominent psychologists were Hall, Cattell, Scripture, Angell, Witmer, Titchener, Warren, Stratton, Judd, Arps, and many others. Most of them later became professors of psychology in American universities and, in turn, established psychological laboratories. The first one was established by G. Stanley Hall, Wundt's first American student, at John Hopkins University in 1883. This was followed by one at the University of Pennsylvania in 1888 by Cattell, and another at Toronto in 1889 by Baldwin. Today, there is a psychological laboratory in every college and university of any significance in the United States.

The psychological laboratory at Leipzig was but the next step in a long line of events that pointed to this culmination. If it had not been Wundt, certainly someone else would soon have put psychological experiments in a separate room. Experimental psychology was developing an identity of its own. The work of Weber and Fechner has already been mentioned as characteristically psychological. Perhaps Hermann von Helmholtz did as much as anyone else in laying the foundation for an experimental laboratory in psychology. He was an army physician who attracted academic attention by stating in a paper, on the conservation of energy, that the human body is no exception to nature's laws of causation. He soon became professor of physiology at the University of Königsberg. While here he measured the rate of a neural impulse, invented the ophthalmoscope, and wrote the first volume of his famous book, *Physiological Optics*. He then went to the University of Heidelberg where he was most prolific in research and writing, principally in the field of sense perception. He finished the three-volume book on *Optics*, which is still the basic reference text in this field, and wrote another almost equally famous book on hearing. This was based on extensive laboratory research. At the age of fifty he went to the University of Berlin where he continued writing and research. Few other scientists have ever written a book that was published 60 years after it first appeared. (*Physiological Optics* was first published in 1856 and again in 1925.)

Another man who helped to set the stage for Wundt's laboratory was Sir Francis Galton. He was a distant relative of Darwin and also interested in quantitative studies in heredity. Galton's investigations were exceedingly varied. He studied such diverse problems as the geographical distribution of female beauty, the efficacy of prayer, the experimental induction of paranoia, the heredity of genius, the measurement of mentality, the extent and type of mental imagery, the measurement of sense perception, the function of one sense through another (synesthesia), etc. His contributions in psychology come under three categories. First, he originated the study of *individual differences*. As research techniques he invented the mental test (association test) and the pedigree method (used by Dugdale in his study of *The Jukes*). Second, Galton studied *mental imagery*, using the questionnaire method. Here, he was chiefly interested in establishing hereditary resemblances. Third, and perhaps his greatest contribution to psychology, was his study of *statistics*. He originated the idea of the coefficient of correlation, although the technique was extended by one of his students, Karl Pearson. The Galton whistle for the study of hearing, the Galton bar and the angle disk for the study of vision, the odor bottles for the study of smell, the color discrimination test, and many other pieces of Galton apparatus are still found in psychological laboratories. It is also interesting that in 1884, five years after the laboratory at Leipzig, Galton opened a laboratory of Anthropometric Measurement at the International Health Exposition. This was later transferred to a museum in London. Measurements were made of 9,337 persons.

There are many others who helped to prepare the way for the first psychological laboratory. Darwin, Spencer, Romanes, Hering, J. Muller, Kulpe, and Lotze were a few of those who helped to make psychology an experimental science.

The First Psychological Test

As mentioned above, in 1884 Galton administered psychometric measurements in sensory discrimination and "quickness of blow." In 1890 Cattell used the term "mental testing" and, soon after, administered tests in reaction time and free and controlled association to students of Columbia University.[19] Jastrow published a "set of mental tests" in the same year.[20] Munsterberg exhibited mental tests at the World's Fair at Chicago in 1893. Ebbinghaus invented the completion test in 1897. Kirkpatrick compared school children on the basis of mental tests in 1900,[21] and Kelley compared normal with abnormal children in 1903.[22] However, all these tests were of simple sensorimotor functions, such as rote memory, attention span, speed and accuracy of perception, sensory acuity, etc. There were no tests to measure the higher mental processes, such as reasoning, imagination, and judgment.

In 1905, Alfred Binet, Director of the Psychology Laboratory at the Sorbonne, constructed a test to distinguish between children who were really feeble-minded and those who were merely lazy in school. By the use of fairly complex tasks this test measured attention, imagination,

[19] Cattell, J. McK., and Farrand, L., Physical and Mental Measurements of Students of Columbia University, *Psychol. Rev.* 1896, 3, 618–648.

[20] Jastrow, J., Some Anthropometric and Psychologic Tests on College Students, *Amer. J. Psychol.*, 1892, 4, 420–427.

[21] Kirkpatrick, E. A., Individual Tests of School Children, *Psychol. Rev.*, 1900, 7, 274–280.

[22] Kelley, T. L., Psychological Tests of Normal and Abnormal Children, *Psychol. Rev.*, 1903, 10, 345–372.

reasoning, judgment, and memory. It thus enabled Binet to make a more accurate estimate of intelligence than did any of the mental tests already in use. His test consisted of 30 carefully selected questions that were arranged in order of difficulty. He had tried them out on normal school children and knew what scores normal children should make. He revised the test in 1908 and again in 1911. In these revisions, he arranged the questions, or tasks, in age groups. When a question could be answered by 60 to 90 per cent of normal children of that chronological age, Binet considered it was appropriate for that age group. The following extracts from the 1911 revision will illustrate the nature of the test.

From Binet's 1911 Mental Test

Age 3:
1. Point to nose, eyes, and mouth.
2. Repeat two digits.
3. Enumerate objects in a picture.
4. Give family name.
5. Repeat a sentence of six syllables.

Age 6:
1. Distinguish between morning and afternoon.
2. Define familiar words in terms of use.
3. Copy a diamond.
4. Count thirteen pennies.
5. Distinguish pictures of ugly and pretty faces.

Age 15:
1. Repeat seven digits.
2. Find three rhymes for a given word in one minute.
3. Repeat a sentence of twenty-six syllables.
4. Interpret certain pictures.
5. Interpret certain given facts.

If a child of ten could not pass the tests for higher than age eight, let us say, Binet considered him to have a mental age of eight. This concept of mental age, as distinguished from chronological age, proved to be a very useful one. Then, Stern conceived the idea of dividing the mental age by the chronological age and getting a "mental quotient," which Terman later called the "intelligence quotient" or I.Q.

Binet's new idea of mental testing was enthusiastically accepted in America. Goddard made the first English translation in 1908. In 1916 Terman published the famous Stanford Revision, which was again revised in 1937 by Terman and Merrill. Kuhlmann published three revisions of Binet's test—in 1912, 1922, and 1939. There have been many other revisions.

Mental tests have been put to a greater variety of uses than perhaps any other tool ever developed by the psychologists. They are now used wherever human ability is appraised. They are used in industry, business, education, penal institutions, psychiatric institutions, military affairs, propaganda efforts of all sorts, vocational guidance, etc. The mental test is the most frequently used of all psychological techniques.

But more than contributing merely a tool in psychology, the early test makers, especially Binet and Ebbinghaus, contributed an objective method that has been applied with equal effectiveness to the measurement of many other forms of human ability. Using the same technique as for the measurement of mental ability, the psychologists have devised tests for mechanical ability, interest, sociability, art appreciation, musical ability, neurotic tendencies, temperament, honesty, common sense, dexterity, etc.

A direct outgrowth of the testing movement has been the development of statistics. Psychologists are now able to calculate how good a test is and how much confidence should be placed in its use. A statistical evaluation of a test is now considered to be a part of its construction.

The contributions to psychological knowledge made by the mental test have been of inestimable value and almost as varied as its uses. For example, the distribution of intelligence among various groups—distinguished by age, race, socioeconomic level, ancestry, nationality, occupation, amount of schooling—is now known. The relation between intelligence and such factors as labor turnover, annual income, left-handedness, age at puberty, sex, etc., has been studied. The mental-test movement has certainly been a major step in the progress of psychology.

THE LAWS OF LEARNING

Back in 1897, in the basement of William James's home at Harvard University, a young graduate student was initiating two research movements—controlled animal experimentation and experimental studies in learning. This was Edward Lee Thorndike, who later went to Columbia University where he had access to better laboratory facilities and better direction (under J. McKeen Cattell). However, Thorndike's work, while of a pioneer nature, was preceded by other excellent scientific work in both of these fields. In animal studies, Darwin was the "voice in the wilderness," followed closely by Lubbock, who studied ants, bees, and wasps (1882); Romanes, who collected anecdotes regarding animal behavior; Lloyd Morgan, who insisted that the anthropomorphic error (reading "higher psychic faculties" into lower animal behavior) violated a fundamental scientific principle (usually called the "law of parsimony"); Jacques Loeb, who explained that animal behavior is tropistic, like that of plants; Spalding, who studied the flying instinct of swallows; and many others whose works constituted a basis for Thorndike's strictly quantitative study of animal behavior.

In the field of learning, the monumental work of Ebbinghaus ante-
dated that of Thorndike. However, Ebbinghaus was interested principally in memory. His development and use of the nonsense syllable was,
nevertheless, as quantitative as any of Thorndike's work.

Thorndike's first problem was the "nature of the learning curve in animal behavior." (Later on he became more interested in human learning.) He invented a puzzle cage from which the animal could escape only
by pushing a button, pulling a string, depressing a release mechanism, or
pulling a wire. (Of course, only one of these methods was used on each
box.) The procedure was to place a hungry cat or dog inside the cage
and a piece of fish or meat just outside. The animal then tried various
ways to get out of the cage. He would claw at the bars, try to push
through between the slats, pace back and forth, and finally, by accident,
would operate the release mechanism. He was allowed to eat a bit of food
and then was returned to the cage for another trial. Again the hit-or-miss,
or trial-and-error, behavior resulted accidentally in pushing the button,
or stepping on the pedal, or pulling the string, or whatever the release
mechanism was. As time went on, the attempts at release became less
varied and more concentrated on the area where the release mechanism
was located. This reduced both the errors made and the time taken for
release. Finally the animal learned to operate the release mechanism immediately and without error.

Thorndike found that the dog learned somewhat more readily than
the cat, but both were far inferior to monkeys. However, he observed
some interesting characteristics in the learning of all his animals. He
called these the "laws of learning." First, he observed that there is a
gradual drop in both the number of errors as well as in the time necessary
for the animal to get out of the cage. Learning increases as the number of
trials increases. Thorndike said this was evidence of the "law of exercise."
Stated simply, this law says that an animal learns to do a thing by doing
it. The more often he does it, the more rapidly he learns it.

Second, Thorndike observed from his studies of animal learning that
the amount and rate of learning seem to depend on the satisfyingness of
the reward. If the cat is hungry and if he gets good food when he escapes
from the cage, he will learn faster than when these factors provide less
satisfaction. Thorndike called this the "law of effect," and stated it as follows " . . . other things being equal, the greater the satisfyingness of a
state of affairs which accompanies or follows a given response to a given
situation, the more likely that response is to be made to that situation in
the future."

These two laws were later supplemented by two other laws—the law of
readiness and the law of belonging. The law of readiness was a sort of
corollary to the law of effect. It concerned the conditions under which

satisfaction could be produced and thus, indirectly, affected learning. Thorndike explained that "the activities of the neurones which cause behavior are by original nature often arranged in long series involving all degrees of *preparedness* for connection-making on the part of some as well as *actual* connection-making on the part of others. . . . Then *for a conduction unit ready to conduct to do so is satisfying, and for it not to do so is annoying*."[23]

The law of belonging is of more recent development. Thorndike found that, when a group of 10 short sentences are repeated 10 times, the memory of word sequences depends on the degree to which they belong to each other. For example, if these sentences are repeated three times,

Alfred Dukes and his sister worked sadly.
Edward Davis and his brother argued rarely.
Francis Bragg and his cousin played hard.

the word that comes after "sister" will be remembered more easily than the word that comes after "sadly." The reason is that the word that comes after "sister" belongs to "sister." They are both in the same sentence. The word that comes after "sadly" is not remembered so easily because it belongs in another sentence. Consequently, the effectiveness of the other laws of learning depends on the degree to which the acts to be learned belong to each other or are related. The greater the degree of relationship, the less exercise necessary to produce learning.

Thorndike's laws of learning as well as his experiments were criticized by Wolfgang Koehler, of the University of Berlin. Koehler believed that "insight" is an indispensable factor in learning. He argued that Thorndike's cats appeared to learn gradually and to "discover" the solution over and again because the puzzle box problems were too difficult for them. If the problems had been within the comprehension limits of the animals, all errors would have been immediately eliminated as soon as the solution was discovered. The learning would not be the gradual effects of exercise but the sudden and immediate result of insight. To prove this contention, Koehler used chimpanzees as subjects and devised problems that seemed to be within the insight limits of the animals. The following experiment is typical of a large number that Koehler tried out on his animals.

In one experiment, a hungry chimpanzee was placed in a cage where a basket of bananas was hanging suspended from the ceiling. Also in the cage was a box that, if placed under the bananas, would make them easily accessible. Some animals were unable to solve this problem, but others discovered the solution—not by accident, but by insight. One chimpanzee held the box above his head and tried to knock the bananas

[23] Thorndike, E. L., *Educational Psychology* (Briefer Course), p. 54, Columbia University Press, New York, 1914.

down with it. When this was unsuccessful, he reversed the process, climbed up on the box, and solved the problem. The problem was then made more difficult by putting the bananas higher and putting two boxes in the cage. Now it was necessary to pile the boxes on top of each other to reach the bananas. Other variations were to place a jointed pole in the cage instead of the boxes. The intelligent animals learned to fit the joints together and knock the bananas down. In all cases, the animals solved the problems by insight behavior rather than by the hit-and-miss method used by Thorndike's cats. The attempts were often failures due to wrong insight, but they were not just blind trials.

Koehler's experiments were, no doubt, largely responsible for Thorndike's law of belonging. Insight is merely the perception of a state of belonging. The animal learned when he perceived that the box belonged to the banana problem. Since the cats in the puzzle cage could not perceive how the release mechanism belonged to the door, this factor did not enter into the problem. Thorndike obviously overgeneralized from his earlier experiments.

The influence of Thorndike and Koehler has been most obvious in the field of educational psychology. Most of our present information about learning is based on their experiments. Thorndike's later experiments with human subjects have almost completely dominated progress in educational psychology. Certainly, he has made one of the major steps toward establishing psychology as a science.

THE CONDITIONED RESPONSE

About the turn of the century, two Russian scientists were experimenting with learning, or the conditioned response, in relation to various conditions of stimulation. One was a physiologist, Ivan Petrovitch Pavlov, who was awarded the Nobel prize in medicine in 1904. The other was Vladimir Bekhterev who wrote a book—*Objective Psychology*—in 1907, describing a system or point of view in psychology which five years later was "originated" in America under the name of "behaviorism." Because these men both published in Russian, they did not immediately attract American attention. However, their work was so quantitative, so carefully done, and so significant for the new American behaviorism, that it was soon acclaimed.[24]

Pavlov's studies began with the observation that a dog's mouth will water at the sight or odor of food. He observed that the same reaction

[24] Whether Pavlov's "conditioned reflex" or Bekhterev's "associated reflex" antedates the other is unknown. Evidently they collaborated in much of their research. However, because Pavlov was honored by the Nobel Prize, and because his works have been translated into English (Bekhterev's writings are in Russian, French, and German), we shall follow the American pattern of crediting the discovery of the conditioned response only to Pavlov.

often took place when the master appeared with the food dish but without the food. The food dish would cause the saliva to flow even in the absence of either the sight or odor of food. Pavlov then began to experiment to see if he could bring about the same results by using some stimulus which had nothing to do with the food except that it would be experienced at the time of feeding.

He called food the biologically adequate, or the unconditioned, stimulus. He decided to use a bell for the biologically inadequate stimulus. The problem was to see if he could make the bell become a biologically adequate, or conditioned, stimulus; if so, how many experiences are necessary to bring this about (see Fig. 1–2).

Pavlov was very thorough. He put the dog in a harness and connected his saliva ducts to a tube.[25] This enabled him to count the drops of saliva flow. He then rang a bell at the same time food was given to the dog. The procedure was repeated until the dog formed a saliva flow reaction to the bell alone. This was the conditioned response.

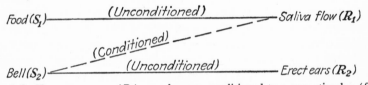

Fig. 1–2. How a response (R_1) may become conditioned to a new stimulus (S_2).

Pavlov found that it was important for the conditioned stimulus (bell) to precede or accompany the unconditioned one (food). If it followed so much as 1 second after the unconditioned stimulus, there was no learning. He found that he could ring the bell 5 minutes before the food was brought in and a conditioned response was established. But if the food appeared even 1 second before the bell rang, there was no conditioning.

The conditioned-response technique has led to research on a wide variety of problems, using both the lower animals and humans as subjects. For example, the procedure of unconditioning (experimental extinction) has been studied and applied in the treatment of phobias and stuttering, in eliminating errors in typewriting and piano playing, and in correcting various bad habits in rearing children. Inhibitory responses have been studied, especially in connection with experimentally induced neurosis. Sleep has been conditioned to a sound loud enough to prevent it under ordinary circumstances. Even involuntary reactions, like the pupillary reflex and the knee jerk, have been conditioned to various forms of inadequate stimulation.

[25] This was done by means of a small incision in the dog's cheek, which readily healed and did not interfere with eating.

One of the most interesting and useful applications of the conditioned-response technique has been in the study of children's fears. Watson and his students were pioneers in this research. They observed that very young children are not afraid of those animals that older children often do fear —such as snakes, rabbits, dogs, cats, bugs, worms, etc. The theory was that these fears are acquired by social conditions, or the conditioned-response technique in a social rather than an experimental setting. To test this theory, Watson induced the fear of white rats in a boy, Albert by name, by using a loud noise as the unconditioned stimulus for fear. Albert was first tested to make sure that he had no fear of white rats already. He obviously enjoyed playing with them. He was next tested to make sure that he had a fear reaction to a loud noise produced by striking a steel bar with a hammer. Now, could the fear reaction to the noise be transferred, by the conditioned-response technique, to the white rat? The procedure was to strike the steel bar every time Albert attempted to play with the white rat. After 10 experiences of this nature, Albert showed unmistakable signs of fear when the rat was presented alone. The rat had become the conditioned stimulus for the fear reaction. This soon spread to other furry objects. The child showed fear of a rabbit, a dog, a fur coat.

The next step was to discover if the fear reaction could now be eliminated by the conditioned-response procedure, or could still another conditioned response be formed to the rat stimulus as a substitute for the fear response? What would happen if the rat, now a stimulus for fear, was experienced with food, which is a biologically adequate stimulus for enjoyment? Another child, Peter by name, who had a strong fear of rabbits, was used for this experiment. The procedure was to bring a rabbit into the room when the child was eating but it keep it too far away to produce fear. (The conditioned stimulus must always be weaker than the unconditioned one, or there will be no learning.) Gradually, the animal was brought closer and closer until the child could reach it. Finally the rabbit became a conditioned stimulus to the enjoyment reaction. It was then possible to present the rabbit without the food and still get the food reaction of enjoyment. The fear reaction to the rabbit had dropped out.

It would be difficult to overemphasize the importance of the conditioned response as a technique of experimental research in psychology. As Garrett has said, "Pavlov's contribution to experimental psychology lies in his having provided a precise technique, machinelike in its accuracy and subject directly to laboratory control. The possibilities (for further research) of the conditioned reflex methods have by no means been exhausted."[26] The conditioned-response technique lends itself to the study of problems that would otherwise be impossible. For example, as early

[26] Garrett, H. E., *Great Experiments in Psychology,* rev. ed., Appleton-Century-Crofts, Inc., New York, 1941.

as 1912, Pavlov had found that dogs can discriminate between tones of 1,000 vibrations per second and tones of 1,012 vibrations per second. (This is approximately twice as fine pitch discrimination as has ever been found in a human.) No other method of research now known could possibly solve such a subtle problem.

THE FIRST WORLD WAR ARMY TESTS

Binet's mental tests had two characteristics that limited their usefulness for the Army: they could be given to only one person at a time, and their administration necessitated careful training. Consequently, when the war broke out in 1917 psychologists could offer the Army no practical tools for classifying great numbers of men. A committee was appointed by the American Psychological Association, with Robert Yerkes as chairman, to prepare a test that (1) could test large groups of men at one time; (2) would be as independent of school information as possible; (3) would be sharply graded in difficulty so that it would measure superior and inferior, as well as average, mental abilities; (4) could be scored quickly and easily; and (5) could be administered by those without professional training as psychologists. As a result, two tests were developed —one for those who could read and write, the Alpha, and one for illiterates and those who could not speak English, the Beta.

The Alpha test consisted of eight types or kinds of test material arranged in subtests. These were (1) following directions; (2) arithmetic problems; (3) practical judgment; (4) synonyms and antonyms; (5) disarranged sentences; (6) number series completion; (7) analogies; and (8) general information. Within each test the items were of increasing difficulty.

The Beta test consisted of seven subtests, all of which could be administered orally or by pantomime. These were (1) pencil maze; (2) block counting; (3) X-O sequence; (4) number sequence; (5) number error checking; (6) missing part (picture); and (7) figure design. Here, too, the items within each test were of increasing difficulty.

The world's first group intelligence test, the Army Alpha, was used to measure 1,750,000 men. Of these, 8,000 were discharged because of low intelligence, 10,000 were put in special development battalions, and hundreds of thousands were assigned to Army jobs most appropriate for their intelligence levels. After the war, the results were carefully tabulated and published by Yerkes,[27] Yoakum and Yerkes,[28] and Brigham.[29]

However, the usefulness of the Army tests continued after the war.

[27] Yerkes, R. M. (Ed.), Psychological Examining in the United States Army, *Mem. Nat. Acad. Sci.,* 1921.

[28] Yoakum, C. S., and Yerkes, R. M., *Army Mental Tests,* Henry Holt and Company, Inc., New York, 1920.

[29] Brigham, C. C., *A Study of American Intelligence,* Princeton University Press, Princeton, N.J., 1923.

While other group tests were soon published, the Army tests (especially the Alpha) were widely used for many years. The fact that large groups could be tested at low expense, in comparison with the cost of the Binet tests, added to their popularity. The Army tests were used to classify school children, to compare groups (such as race and occupational groups) with each other, to guide in vocational selection, to select men for employment, to study sex differences, to evaluate treatment of the feeble-minded—in short, to promote every phase of human engineering. Undoubtedly, the postwar mental-testing fever ran too high. Tests were administered by those who were inadequately trained, especially in interpreting the results. They were used in situations for which they were not designed and for which they were inappropriate. They were often used as the only basis for decisions, instead of along with other factors that ordinarily would determine decisions. They were also handicapped by inadequate statistical procedure for their evaluation and interpretation.

But, regardless of their misuse, the Army tests marked a forward step in the progress of psychology. First, as suggested above, they popularized the possibilities of psychological tests in a wide variety of applications. While psychology tests had been used in many practical ways before the First World War, their usefulness was largely unknown to the general public. Now the public wanted to be tested.

Second, the Army tests initiated a prolific group-test construction movement. Otis, who had furnished much of the material for the Army tests, published an intelligence test in 1918. Pressey published one designed for high schools. Haggerty's Delta I (nonverbal) and Delta II appeared in 1919. The National Intelligence Test was the result of the cooperative efforts of a committee. There were many others.

Third, statistical techniques for the validation and standardization of tests developed rapidly, although much in the wake of the progress of test construction. Courses in statistics soon became a part of the curriculum of every college where psychology and education were taught.

A fourth effect of the Army tests was the rapid spread of the technique of group testing to the measurement of other traits. Tests to measure progress in every form of learning were patterned after the Army Alpha. Classroom teachers became objective-test conscious. A voluminous literature soon developed on homemade objective tests. Standardized tests were constructed to measure musical aptitude, art appreciation, mechanical aptitude, personality traits, attitudes, beliefs, dexterity, knowledge of all sorts, psychoneurotic tendencies, etc. A national test movement was initiated by the Army tests of the First World War.

APPLIED PSYCHOLOGY

Psychology really attained status when it became useful. Soon after the First World War psychologists began to apply their meager facts and immature methods to practical human problems in business, industry, psychiatric hospitals, schools, prisons, and wherever the need could not wait for a slowly developing science. Many mistakes were made, and often the practicing psychologist was but one step removed from his charlatan predecessor. However, the usefulness of psychology motivated greater research efforts, and soon verified facts and methods were coming from psychological laboratories at an astounding rate. New tests were developed, new techniques were devised, new psychologists were trained, new uses were discovered—and with it all, more careful and accurate interpretations and remedial procedures were developed. The long-needed scientific psychology was emerging rapidly.

To promote the continued development of scientific psychology and to repress the occasional outcropping of prescientific charlatans, a number of societies and associations developed. Each was composed of members interested in a limited field of psychology. In 1944 they all combined with the American Psychological Association and became "divisions." Each division has officers and convention programs, and some publish division journals. There are also geographical-area associations (state, city, region) of psychologists which have officers, conventions, and semi-publications. All these promote research and disseminate it among both psychologists and other interested persons.

A further indication of the mature status of psychology is the adoption of license laws in various states. The state of Georgia, for example, has a law which provides for issuing a license to any properly trained psychologist and makes it a misdemeanor for anyone to charge fees for psychological services without such a license. A state board of examiners composed of psychologists determine who is qualified for licensing. The law states in part:

Any person wishing to obtain the right to practice applied psychology in this state, who has not heretofore been licensed to do so, shall, before it shall be lawful for him to practice applied psychology in this state, make application to the State Board of Examiners of Psychologists through the joint-secretary, State examining boards, upon such form and in such manner as shall be adopted and prescribed by the board, and obtain from the board a license to do. . . . A candidate for such a license shall furnish the board with satisfactory evidence that he (a) is of good moral character; (b) is a citizen of the United States or has legally declared his intention of becoming one; (c) has received a degree of doctor of philosophy in psychology from an accredited educational institution recognized by the board as maintaining satisfactory standards, or, in lieu of said degree, a doctorate degree in a closely allied field if it is the opinion of the board that the training required therefor is substantially similar; (d) has had at least one year of experience in applied psychology of a type considered by the board to be qualifying in nature; (e) is competent in applied psychology, as shown by passing such examinations, written or oral, or both, as the board deems necessary; (*f*) has not within the preceding six months failed an examination given by the board: Provided that the board may at its discretion accept satisfactory substitute training and experience in lieu of that prescribed in subsections (*c*) and (*d*).

SUMMARY

A number of prescientific psychologies, still functioning in American life, have been discussed in light of scientific studies that have been made of their value. All of them—astrology, phrenology, graphology, and physiognomy—are theories that have been proved erroneous. Human character traits cannot be discovered by such procedures. Those who claim to be able to diagnose human personalities on the basis of any of these theories are charlatans. The predictions of none of them are better than chance. The oracles of the ancients were no less mystical and unreliable than the "gold bricks" of these modern "professors" of character reading.

Some of the more significant steps psychology has taken in its slow progress toward becoming a science have been reviewed. Unfortunately, mention could not be made of hundreds of other experiments that were necessary foundations on which these front-page experiments were based. Significance is so frequently built on insignificance. But whether these are truly the great experiments in psychology or not is unimportant. They serve to impress the reader with the fact that psychology is becoming objective and experimental—the necessary prerequisites to science.

RECOMMENDED SUPPLEMENTARY READINGS

Boring, Edwin G.: *A History of Experimental Psychology,* Appleton-Century-Crofts, Inc., New York, 1950.

Garrett, Henry E.: *Great Experiments in Psychology,* Appleton-Century-Crofts, Inc., New York, 1949.

Hall, G. Stanley: *Founders of Modern Psychology,* Appleton-Century-Crofts, Inc., New York, 1924.

Murphy, Gardner: *An Historical Introduction to Modern Psychology,* Harcourt, Brace and Company, Inc., New York, 1949.

Pillsbury, W. B.: *The History of Psychology,* W. W. Norton & Company, New York, 1920.

Valentine, W. L., and Wickens, D. D.: *Experimental Foundations of General Psychology,* Rinehart & Company, Inc., New York, 1949.

Chapter 2

PSYCHOLOGY IN COLLEGE LIFE

The typical college student has only an academic interest in the applications of psychology in industry, business, education, and war. He is profoundly interested, however, in the application of psychology to his daily problems of college life. He wants to know how to study more efficiently, how to rest more effectively, how to think more clearly. This chapter will review some of the facts regarding the first two of these problems, and Chap. 6 will discuss the third one.

HOW TO STUDY

Psychological research on problems of study is now adequate to justify some conclusions. While only typical examples of this research can be reviewed in the following pages, the references listed at the end of this chapter contain more details.

REASONS FOR STUDY

The first problem that confronts college students in relation to study is: How much study is advisable? Are good grades worth the effort necessary, or is it better to devote more time to extracurricular activities and be satisfied with lower grades? This problem has been the subject of considerable research. In general, it has been found that good grades are closely related to two factors—intelligence and consequent success in life.

Scholarship and Intelligence. Held[1] found that there is a definite relation between grades and intelligence, as measured by the Thorndike Psychological Examination. Those students who made high scores on that examination also made high grades in the university, as indicated by their high quality point average (see Table 2–1).

Table 2–1. Relation of Thorndike's Psychological Examination to Quality Point Average of 678 Students

Percentile Score	Quality Point Average
100	1.48
90	1.38
80	1.27
70	1.15
60	1.04
50	.93
40	.82
30	.71
20	.59
10	.48
00	.37

The relation between intelligence and college grades, as indicated by the coefficient of correlation, in various studies ranges from .30 to .70, the average being around .50. The Ohio State University Psychological Test correlates with the grades of 1,030 university freshmen .68. The Carnegie Mental Abilities Test correlations with scholastic grades range from .50 to .70. In other words, good grades usually indicate superior intelligence, and, when the effort factor remains constant, superior intelligence is usually an accurate means of predicting good grades.

Scholarship and Success in Life. The relationship of good grades to success in life after schooling is over has been studied by a number of investigators. Gifford[2] found that, when he compared the salaries of the employees of the American Telephone and Telegraph Company, who were college graduates, with their scholarship record, there was an obvious relationship. Those who made the best grades in college were now receiving higher salaries than those who made low grades (see Table 2–2).

After investigating the success of a group of university graduates, Smith[3] concluded, "If a student belongs to the highest tenth of his class, his chances of achieving a career in life, distinguished by the approval of his fellowmen, are forty times as great as they are if he belongs to the lower nine-tenths."

In a study of the relation of scholarship to inclusion in *Who's Who in*

[1] Held, O. C., *An Attempt to Predict the Success of College Freshmen in Their Adjustment to Scholastic Work,* Ph.D. Dissertation, University of Pittsburgh, 1933.

[2] Gifford, W. S., Does Business Want Scholars? *Harper's Magazine,* 1928, 156, 669–674.

[3] Smith, H. A., College Records and Success in Life, *Education,* 1927, 27, 513–529.

Table 2–2. Relation of Salary to Scholarship

Scholarship in college	N	Per cent of median salary
Upper one-tenth............	498	155
Upper one-third............	1554	120
Middle one-third...........	1468	96
Lower one-third............	784	79

America, Gambrill[4] found that 5.9 per cent of those who made Phi Beta Kappa (a national scholarship fraternity) were later included in Who's Who. In two colleges she found that 5.4 per cent of those who graduated in the highest tenth of their class in scholarship were in Who's Who, whereas the percentage decreased with each tenth down in scholarship. (The second tenth was 2.9 per cent, the third was 2.5 per cent, the fourth was 1.8 per cent, etc.) Smith (quoted above) found that students graduating in the highest tenth of their class in scholarship have 50 times as great a chance of being later listed in Who's Who as those graduating in the lowest tenth.

Unquestionably, good grades are significant. In general, they indicate that a student has ability and has formed those habits that are useful in making a success in life after graduation. However, as the above data indicate, grades are not always accurate in these indications and must be interpreted with care. Teachers vary greatly in their evaluations of student accomplishments, and the grades they give are not always comparable. A low grade from one professor often represents more accomplishment than a high grade from another. Nevertheless, regardless of their inaccuracy, grades are significant goals and must be so considered by college students.

This conclusion is substantiated by Magoun's study[5] of the relation between scholarship and later distinction attained by the graduates of Massachusetts Institute of Technology (1868 to 1910). However, note in Table 2–3 that the lowest decile in scholarship is well represented in all the directories of men of distinction. Undoubtedly this variation from the trend in the rest of the scholarship distribution is due to other factors.

Scholarship and Extracurricular Activities. While scholarship is more important, extracurricular activities also afford excellent training for success in life. They are significant indices of personal qualifications. A leader in college life will usually become a leader in postcollege life. After studying the success of college men in business, Bridgman[6] con-

[4] Gambrill, B. L., College Achievement and Vocational Efficiency, Columbia University Press, New York, 1922.

[5] Magoun, F. A., Scholarship and Distinction, Technology Review, Massachusetts Institute of Technology, 1935, 37, No. 8.

[6] Bridgman, D. S., Success in College and Business, Person. J., 1930, 9, 1–19.

Table 2–3. Scholarship Standing and Later Recognition of Eminence

Scholarship (deciles)	Who's Who in America (N 442), per cent	Who's Who in Engineering (N 795), per cent	American Men of Science (N 515), per cent	In all three (N 91), per cent
1	15.3	16.1	23.8	22
2	13.5	13.6	16.5	14.3
3	10.2	10.9	13	17.6
4	11.1	11.7	12	12.1
5	5.9	7.9	7.6	6.6
6	4.3	5.7	5.1	3.3
7	5.2	5.8	4.5	3.3
8	6.8	6.8	4.5	6.6
9	5.9	6.7	4.5	5.5
10	21.8	14.8	8.5	8.8

cludes that "men who are outstanding in campus activities, and who are also good students, win greater success in life than those who are merely good students, or merely outstanding in campus affairs."

The question now arises: Since both extracurricular affairs and study take time, to what extent should one be sacrificed for the other? The answer is not a "one or the other" (or an "either or") one. Scholarship and leadership do not seem to interfere with each other. Remmlein[7] studied the relation of scholarship to extracurricular activities by comparing the "mean leadership score" of a group of students whose scholarship level was above their intelligence level, with another group whose scholarship level was below their intelligence level. She found very little difference. Those students who get better grades than would be expected from their intelligence level apparently are just as active in extracurricular activities as are those students whose grades are lower than would be expected.

These results are substantiated by Williamson,[8] who found a positive relationship between scholarship and intelligence, but a negative relationship between intelligence and the number of hours studied per week. (His data are shown in Table 2–4.) In other words, intelligent students make good grades with but little study. The low correlations (both positive and negative) between scholarship and the hours of study indicate that good grades are due to other factors than long hours of study.

From these two studies we conclude that, since both good grades and leadership in extracurricular activities are significant in postschool life, and since they do not interfere with each other, they are both desirable goals in education.

[7] Remmlein, M. K., Scholastic Accomplishment as Affected by Intelligence and Participation in Extra-curricular Activities. *J. Appl. Psychol.*, 1939, 23, 602–607.

[8] Williamson, E. G., Relation of Number of Hours Study to Scholarship, *J. Educ. Psychol.*, 1935, 26, 682–688.

Table 2–4. The Correlation of Scholarship, Intelligence, and Hours of Study

	Four studies			
	A (*N* 450)	B (*N* 221)	C (*N* 105)	D (*N* 130)
Correlations between:				
Scholarship and intelligence............	.60	.28	.65	.69
Scholarship and hours studied..........	.32	.00	−.06	−.28
Intelligence and hours studied..........	.35	−.15	−.20	−.41
Partial correlations between:				
Scholarship and intelligence (hours studied partialed out)....................	.80	.28	.65	.66
Scholarship and hours studied (intelligence partialed out).................	.70	.04	.11	.00
Intelligence and hours studied (scholarship partialed out)..................	−.72	−.15	−.22	−.32

The Nature of Scholarship. Granted that good scholarship is desirable, how can it be attained? What is done to become a good scholar and what are the characteristics of poor scholars? The answers to these questions have been the object of two special investigations. Pressey[9] compared superior students with failing students on a number of details of study. The differences in the two groups are shown in Table 2–5. While some good students obviously have poor study methods and some poor students have some good study habits, the typical good student and the typical poor student are different in many respects. These different study habits account for much poor scholarship. Poor students would become better students if they followed the procedures practiced by good students.

Bird[10] investigated the frequency of study difficulties as reported by 171 freshmen and sophomores in the University of Minnesota. He found that inability to concentrate was believed by the students themselves to be their greatest difficulty. The frequencies of the difficulties reported are shown in Table 2–6.

Laycock and Russell[11] made an analysis of 38 how-to-study manuals and found that 517 study skills and habits were considered important enough for discussion. Of course, no one manual covered all of them. The student whose scholarship indicates that his present methods of study are inadequate should read the following pages carefully. Then,

[9] Pressey, S. L., *et al., Research Adventures in University Teaching,* Public School Publishing Company, Bloomington, Ill., 1927.

[10] Bird, C., and Bird, D. M., *Learning More by Effective Study,* p. 24, Appleton-Century-Crofts, Inc., New York, 1945.

[11] Laycock, S. R., and Russell, D. H., An Analysis of 38 How-to-study Manuals, *Sch. Rev.,* 1941, **49,** 370–379.

Table 2–5. Percentage of Failing Students Answering Each Question Wrong in Excess of the Percentage of Superior Students

Question	Answer	Per cent
A. Study environment and general routine of study		
1. Do you usually study every day in the same place?	No	36
2. Do you have a daily plan of work?	No	24
B. Reading		
1. Do you frequently skip the graphs or tables in your text-books?	Yes	40
2. Do you frequently make simple charts or diagrams to represent points in your reading?	No	40
3. When you find a word that you do not know, do you usually look it up in the dictionary?	No	32
4. Do you usually skim over a chapter before reading it in detail?	No	28
5. Do you usually have trouble in getting the meaning of a chart or table?	Yes	28
C. Note taking		
1. Do you keep your notes from one subject together?	No	32
2. Do you usually take your notes in class just as rapidly as you can write?	Yes	32
3. Do you usually take your notes in outline form?	No	28
D. Self-expression		
1. Do you usually have difficulty in expressing yourself in written work?	Yes	56
2. Do your teachers frequently complain that you do not make sentences when you write?	Yes	28
E. Examinations and reviews		
1. Do you sit up late the night before an exam studying?	Yes	40
2. Do you often write the answer to a question, only to find that it is the answer to some other question on the examination?	Yes	32
3. In preparing for an examination do you try to memorize the text?	Yes	28
F. General attitudes		
1. Do you frequently try to analyze your work and try to find out just where you are weak?	No	36
2. Do you frequently use what you have learned in one course to help you in some other course?	No	28

he should get some of the books listed at the end of this chapter and read them. There is considerable evidence that attention to good study methods is needed by the good student as well as by the one who is making poor grades. Brown[12] found in a survey of the study habits of 120 successful students and 211 failing students that both were deficient in good study habits. His results are shown in Table 2–7.

[12] Brown, C. W., Study Habits of Failing and Successful Students in the First Two Years of College, *J. Exp. Educ.,* 1941, 9, 205–208.

Table 2-6. Frequency of Study Difficulties Reported by 171 College Freshmen and Sophomores
(In per cent)

Difficulties	First-term freshmen	Second-term freshmen and sophomores
Concentration	81.6	84.0
Taking notes	40.0	34.0
Lack of interest	36.5	30.4
Slow reading	25.2	26.8
Study interruptions	24.4	17.9
Outside activities	24.4	10.7
Outside work	18.3	5.4
Procrastination	17.4	17.9
Selecting important ideas	11.5	19.6
Scheduling time	7.0	35.7

Table 2-7. Percentages of Successful and Failing Students with Good Study Habits

Habits concerning	Successful	Failing
Concentration	34	40
Reading	58	61
Critical evaluation	66	67
Note taking	50	54
Preparation for examinations	50	55
Promptness in preparation	33	38
Reviewing	50	51
Average	48.7	52.1

EFFICIENT STUDY METHODS

Good scholarship is not entirely a matter of ability and hard work. There are methods of study that can be learned and without which even a capable student will do work below his intellectual level. The following pages review some of the more important factors that affect good scholarship. Efficient study, like efficiency in industry, depends in part on methods of work. Both good students and poor students can become better students by improved methods of study.

Planning. In almost any intelligent behavior, planning is essential. Study is no exception. High school students have their study periods, as well as their class periods, planned for them. Sometimes, the study is even supervised and directed. However, the college student must schedule his own study. Except for his class periods, nothing is planned for him. Until a student learns to plan his study periods intelligently, he is likely to squander a lot of time and then find that his work has piled up and he cannot complete it. One writer estimates that the average college student wastes enough time to enable him to hold down a half-time job. Evidence that this is not a mere conjecture is shown in Heilman's[13] study. He compared the grades of employed freshmen with those of unemployed freshmen and found that employed students are not handicapped in scholarship. The results are given in Table 2–8. These data are substantiated by

Table 2–8. The Relation of Employed to Unemployed Freshmen in Terms of Grades

Women	Employed N 92		Unemployed N 60	
	Mean	S.D.	Mean	S.D.
Average grades......................	3.18	.72	3.07	.83
Intelligence.........................	7.72	1.38	7.48	1.49
Class load...........................	16.24	1.36	16.87	1.05
Employed, hr. per week..............	3.02	....	000	
Men	**N 70**		**N 49**	
Average grades......................	2.86	.83	2.58	.79
Intelligence.........................	7.54	1.57	7.05	1.23
Class load...........................	15.73	1.91	16.57	1.99
Employed, hr. per week..............	3.2	....	000	.

Shaffner[14] in a study of 610 college students. She compared three groups —the nonworkers (those who worked less than 4 hours per week or none), the moderate workers (those who worked 6 to 21 hours per week), and the hard workers (those who worked 24 or more hours per week). The moderate workers were highest in scholarship, with the hard workers a close second, but there was not a statistically reliable difference between them. The nonworkers were lowest in scholarship, and this difference was statistically reliable.

College students who work or engage in extracurricular activities are forced to use their time very carefully. This means that they must plan and schedule all activities as well as class recitations. Some students, who try to get as much out of college life as possible, even schedule such activities as eating, loafing, exercise, reading the newspaper, etc. A time schedule of this nature is shown in Table 2–9. This schedule would perhaps fit

[13] Heilman, J. D., Student Employment and Class Load, *J. Educ. Psychol.*, 1939, **30**, 527–532.
[14] Shaffner, Martha, The Effects of Part Time Employment on the Scholarship Ratings of College Students, *Kan-as Teach.*, October, 1939.

Table 2–9. Time-distribution Sheet for John Doe

Hours	Monday	Tuesday	Wednesday	Thursday	Friday
7–8	Dress and breakfast	Dress and breakfast	Dress and breakfast	Dress and breakfast	Dress and breakfast
8–9	English	Chemistry lab	English	*Chemistry*	English
9–10	*Psychology*	Chemistry lab	*Psychology*	*Chemistry*	*Psychology*
10–11	Psychology	Chemistry lab	Psychology	*	Psychology
11–12	*French*	Chemistry lab	*French*	*	*French*
12–1	Lunch and newspaper	Lunch and newspaper	Lunch and newspaper	Lunch and newspaper	Lunch and newspaper
1–2	French	Chemistry lecture	French	Chemistry lecture	French
2–3	Economics	*French*	Economics	*French*	Economics
3–4	*English*	*Psychology*	*English*	*Psychology*	*English*
4–5	Athletics	Athletics	Athletics	Athletics	Athletics
5–6	Athletics	Athletics	Athletics	Athletics	Athletics
6–7	Dinner and rest	Dinner and rest	Dinner and rest	Dinner and rest	Dinner and rest
7–8	*Chemistry*	*Economics*	*Chemistry*	*Economics*	*Chemistry*
8–9	*Chemistry*	*Economics*	*Chemistry*	*Economics*	*Chemistry*
9–10	*Economics*	*English*	*Economics*	*English*	*Economics*
10–11	*	*	*	*	*
11–	Retire	Retire	Retire	Retire	Retire

NOTE: Mr. Doe worked on Saturday and did not study on Sunday.

* These hours are for extra study purposes, such as examinations, term papers, special assignments, etc.

Italicized subjects indicate study hours.

no other student, and it was frequently altered to fit unexpected events in the life of this student. Time schedules must be custom-made.

While a time schedule should be used constantly, it should be flexible enough to permit alterations for unexpected emergencies. Football holidays, visits of parents, illness, field trips, etc., are examples of unexpected events that may upset a time schedule. However, note in Table 2–9 that only 45 hours per week are scheduled for schoolwork. This student still has 7 hours per week for emergencies, not counting Saturday and Sunday. Even with athletics and outside work, only the most extraordinary events would justify this student's getting behind in his schoolwork for more than a few days.

A time schedule must also fit the learning ability of each student. The student in Table 2–9 spends but 5 hours per week in the study of French.

For another student, 10 hours per week may not be enough. Even the total hours spent in study per week will vary greatly with the ability of the student. Bird[15] found that students in a how-to-study course ranged from 7 hours per week to 53 hours per week in time devoted to study (see Fig. 2–1).

Bird also found that students who spent more than 35 hours per week in study did not receive high grades. They are usually students of less than average college ability and must study long hours in order to pass their courses. On the other hand, those who study less than 15 hours per week "typify most often the capable student who earns average grades. In a larger sense, he is the real college failure."

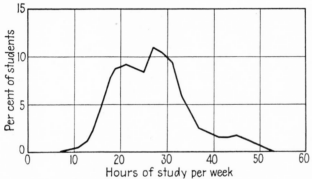

Fig. 2–1. Hours of study for 108 students.

The fact that the average college student spends but 26.29 hours per week in study certainly is evidence that college students are not being overworked. If the average classroom hours are added to this, the average student's week becomes but 41.29 hours. Hutchinson and Connard[16] found that 503 college women (at a college for women) spent but 38.3 hours per week in both study and classroom. We must conclude, then, that the average college student could do more work if he would plan his time more intelligently.

Reading. The amount of reading varies greatly from course to course but, on the whole, it is the most usual technique of study. In fact, reading is the only method of study for such courses as history, economics, sociology, etc. A student who is not proficient in reading is handicapped at the college level.

The degree to which college students are deficient in reading is indi-

[15] Bird, Charles, *Learning More by Effective Study,* Appleton-Century-Crofts, Inc., New York, 1945.

[16] Hutchinson, R. G., and Connard, M. H., What's a College Week? *Sch. & Soc.,* 1926, 24, 768–772.

cated in a number of studies. Arnold[17] found that 7 per cent of a group of college students were below the eighth-grade average in reading comprehension and 30 per cent were below the same norm in reading speed. Pressey[18] found that 20 per cent of university freshmen read less efficiently than the eighth-grade level. Bird[19] found that only 89.6 per cent of university students exceeded the eighth-grade level in reading comprehension and less than half of the group (47.5 per cent) reached the senior high school level. Cole[20] concludes that "the average degree of skill in reading shown by unselected freshmen is clearly not sufficient for the needs of college students." The data on which she bases this conclusion are shown in Table 2–10.

Table 2–10. Percentage of Freshmen Able to Read with Tenth-grade Comprehension

Directions for experiments, writing themes, carrying out projects, etc... 61
Presentation of theories, rules, or laws with illustrations.............. 70
Description of apparatus, processes, or organisms.................... 57
Discussion of developments or causal relationships.................. 67
Narratives.. 82
Diagrammatic drawings...................................... 69
Linear graphs... 72
Cross-section drawings...................................... 42
Maps.. 73

Now the question is: Can students who are poor readers learn to read well enough to earn grades equal to their mental levels? Book[21] answers this question as follows, "Experiments have shown that with a moderate amount of practice, speed in reading may be increased from 50 to 100 per cent if one's attention is directed sharply enough toward this particular point." Pressey[22] gave remedial reading training to a group of freshmen who were low in reading ability and compared their resulting grades with a matched untrained control group at the end of the term. The trained group received an average of 1.68 grade honor points, while the control group received but 1.41 honor points. This is equivalent to at least one letter grade difference. About half the experimental group improved in reading to equal or surpass the median for the entire freshman class. (This group received an average of 1.97 grade honor points.) Lauer[23] studied the effects that 20 practice periods in improving the rate of read-

[17] Arnold, H. J., Disabilities of College Students in Certain Tool Subjects, *Phi Delta Kappan,* 1929, **11,** 169–174.
[18] Pressey, L. C., Training College Freshmen to Read, *Ohio Col. Assn. Bull.,* 55.
[19] *Op. cit.*
[20] Cole, Luella, *The Background for College Teaching,* Rinehart & Company, Inc., New York, 1940.
[21] Book, W. F., *How to Succeed in College,* Warwick and York Incorporated, Baltimore, 1927.
[22] *Op. cit.*
[23] Lauer, A. R., An Experimental Study of the Improvement in Reading by College Students, *J. Educ. Psychol.,* 1936, **27,** 662–665.

ing had on a group of 367 college students. The average initial rate was 247 words per minute. The improvement ranged from 0 to 249 per cent —the average being 35.3 per cent. He found that fast readers made more improvement than slow readers and that, in general, college students do not improve in reading unless some "regular remedial program is carried out." Consequently we can conclude that both reading speed and reading comprehension can be learned, and these will result in improved scholarship.

There are three factors involved in improving reading ability. First, a student should learn to read more rapidly. He should force himself to read just as fast as possible without loss of comprehension or meaning. He should break the habit of dawdling when he reads. It is best to practice easy material, like the newspaper, every day for 15 or 20 minutes. Some students keep a weekly record of the time it takes to read 10 inchs of newsprint with satisfactory comprehension. After a few weeks, a graph can be made to show the increase in reading speed.

Reading speed is frequently handicapped by lip movements. Silent reading should be free from any kind of silent speech. Huey[24] found as long ago as 1908 that good silent reading is approximately twice as fast as oral reading. When the vocal organs are used, they slow up the speed of the eye in seeing and the brain in comprehension.

The second factor involved in reading ability is word knowledge. Obviously, it is impossible to understand the meaning of a sentence if the words in it are not understood. Some students look up the meaning of all unfamiliar words in the dictionary and then write an abridged definition in the margin of the book in which the word is found. While this is an excellent habit for books which are personally owned, it is not recommended for borrowed and library books. Another good practice is to write new words and their definitions in a special section of a notebook. If a separate notebook is used for each course, there should be a new-word section in each one. Douglass and Barrow[25] found that at all levels of intelligence students who have the habit of looking up new words in the dictionary make higher grades than those who do not.

Whatever method is used in remembering word meanings, a good dictionary is a necessity. The G. & C. Merriam Company and the Funk & Wagnalls Company both publish excellent collegiate dictionaries. No textbook is more important to a college student than a dictionary.

The third important factor in reading ability is analysis for thought content. The purpose of reading is to get ideas. Each chapter, each section, each paragraph, contains a central idea. The reader should get the

[24] Huey, E. B., *The Psychology and Pedagogy of Reading*, The Macmillan Company, New York, 1908.

[25] Douglass, H. R., and Barrow, H. C., The Study and Practice of 395 High School Pupils, *J. Educ. Psychol.*, 1938, **29**, 36–43.

central idea and the supporting ideas from his reading. This requires analysis.

There are a number of techniques, or procedures, or rules, for reading to facilitate analysis. While they are all beneficial, they are not "musts" because they are not used by all good readers. However, poor readers will find that they are helpful. A procedure widely recommended is first to look over the reading assignment hurriedly to see what it is about, or find the trend or progress, before reading more carefully. This hurried overview will reveal the plan of the chapter and constitute a background for more thorough reading. It enables one to avoid becoming lost in the details. It helps one to understand how details are related to each other. Sometimes a preliminary survey is given at the beginning of chapters in the form of an outline (as in this book), or a synopsis. Sectional and topic headings facilitate a preliminary survey of the important features of a chapter. If neither of these aids is given in a book, sometimes there is a summary at the end of the chapter that will assist the reader in getting this overview.

Table 2–11. Relation of Reading Time to Recitation Time in Recall

Proportion	Immediate recall	Delayed recall
Reading with no recitation......	100 (Base)	100 (Base)
Reading with 1/5 recitation.....	112	115
Reading with 2/5 recitation.....	119	146
Reading with 3/5 recitation.....	122	162
Reading with 4/5 recitation.....	120	152

Another important technique for improving the effectiveness of reading is self-recitation, or the practice of mentally reviewing important ideas in the material read. Experiments indicate that, when a student spends part of his study time reciting (to himself) the important facts in material he has read, he remembers them much better than when he spends his whole study time in reading alone. Years ago, Gates[26] investigated the effectiveness of various proportions of study time to recitation time. He found that recitation was more effective than mere reading in all proportions. His results are summarized in Table 2–11.

Germane[27] compared a group of students who spent their entire study time in reading with another group who spent half the time in reading and half in answering (to themselves) questions about the material read. The advantages of the second procedure were 30 per cent for college sophomores and 50 per cent for grade school pupils.

Reading effectiveness is also improved by the procedure of deliberately

[26] Gates, A. I., Reciting as a Factor in Memorizing, *Arch. Psychol.*, 1917, No. 40.
[27] Germane, C. E., The Value of the Controlled Mental Summary as a Method of Studying, *Sch. & Soc.*, 1920, 12, 591–593.

looking for the keynote of each chapter, each section, each paragraph. Tables, graphs, and charts contain valuable information that can be obtained only by looking for it. Too many students pass these up without notice. Some students find it helpful, when they have found a keynote idea, to underscore it in the book or make a check mark in the margin. Of course, this is recommended only when the book is owned by the reader. To make the important things more noticeable, it is effective to use a red lead pencil for underscoring. Marshall[28] trained one group of students in underlining important words and ideas and then compared their progress with another equated group not so trained. The results (see Table 2–12) on two units of subject matter indicate a superiority

Table 2–12. Effects of Special Training in How to Study

	Control group mean	Experimental group mean	Difference in favor of experimental group
Otis S-A Intelligence Test......	47.9	49.7	1.8
Test on first unit..............	58.4	68.0	9.6
Test on second unit..........	62.9	67.2	4.3

of the experimental group. Some students take notes in the form of outlines, summaries, or synopses. Certainly some method of distinguishing the important from the unimportant should be used. It is a waste of time to read unless facts and ideas are being communicated from the writer to the reader. Unless these are recognized and identified by some method, they are missed and there is no communication.

Note Taking. Whether a student takes notes on his textbook reading or not, he must use this procedure of retaining facts and ideas that he gets from his library reading and his classroom lectures. The notebook should be a depository into which are constantly being poured facts and ideas from various sources. It thus becomes the student's most valuable source of information. If he makes his notes in a clear, concise, and classified manner, he will have immediately available concentrated information ample for passing all tests that he may confront. In fact, a good notebook is often useful years after the student has graduated. It is a very important factor in the education of any student.

Notes for each course should be kept together, either in a separate notebook or in a separate part of a large notebook. Systematic classification is a basic fundamental for all useful notebooks. When notes are taken in a haphazard manner, they are of little value. Of course, class notes must be taken quickly and are usually poorly organized. For this reason, it is better to rearrange and copy them in a more careful man-

[28] Marshall, M. V., Guided Study with College Juniors, *Sch. & Soc.,* 1938, 48, 28.

ner. Elaboration and reinterpretation of class notes before they "get cold" is an excellent procedure for getting the most out of a course.

The form, or pattern, of note taking varies with students. Some take their notes in outline form, in which each item is subordinate to, superordinate to, or coordinate with every other item. Main items are designated by Roman numerals, subitems by capital letters and indentation, and more subordinate items by Arabic numerals and small letters. Other students take notes in the form of synopses and summaries. This requires less organization and weighting of items than does the outline method. Consequently, notes can be taken more quickly without sacrifice of content. There is, of course, a loss of perspective and relationship. Another plan of note taking is to record just those important items that should be remembered. Notes are not taken on everything read or heard in a lecture, but just those facts and ideas that are worth while are recorded. This means that there are gaps and lack of relationship between facts as they appear in a notebook. Each item is discrete and significant for its own sake. The notebook then becomes a storehouse of significant, though not carefully organized, items. Consequently, it is of less value at a later time when relationships are no longer remembered. Also, it is more difficult to find a specified item of information when notes are taken in this fashion.

However, most any method of note taking is better than none at all. Too many students do not take notes in any manner. One of the best studies of the value of note taking was made by Barton.[29] He compared the school progress of an experimental group of high school students specially trained in note taking with a control group that was equal in all other respects except that it was not trained in note taking. The experiment was performed in three different schools and involved 94 pairs of students. The results were definitely in favor of the group trained in note taking. (See Table 2–13 for a summary of the results.)

Table 2–13. Comparison of Pupils Trained in Note Taking with Control Group

	Experimental group	Control group	Difference	S.D. of the diff.	C.R.
Mean.......	37.7	27.3	10.4	2.2	4.7

Crawford[30] studied the relation of note taking to school marks and found correlations ranging from .36 to .66 with a median of .50. "The

[29] Barton, W. A., Outlining as a Study Procedure, Teachers College, Columbia University Press, New York, 1930.

[30] Crawford, C. C., A Correlation between College Lecture Notes and Quiz Papers, J. Educ. Res., 1925, 12, 282–291; also, An Experimental Study of the Results of College Note Taking, J. Educ. Res., 1925, 12, 379–386.

immediate value of notes is less than the delayed-review value," but, "when results are measured by a general quiz after a period of days and weeks and after there has been opportunity to review the notes which were previously taken, the note-takers showed marked superiority over those who do not take notes." These results are indicated in Table 2–14.

Table 2–14. Comparative Value of Note Taking Immediately and after Interval of Time

Type of test	Interval after learning	Score with notes	Score without notes	Difference in favor of notes
Essay...........................	Short	10.70	10.32	.47
True-false......................	Short	7.96	7.45	.51
Essay...........................	Long	12.89	5.06	7.83
True-false......................	Long	15.33	12.62	2.71
Both types*....................	Long	19.33	16.93	2.40

* This was a library reading only.

While Bird[31] regrets that there does not yet exist "convincing evidence to prove the value of notes to a student," yet he ventures the opinion that "it is probable that the greatest advantage to learning lies in the process of making notes."

Review and Examination. Frequent review and examination are exceptionally valuable aids in learning. The teacher who gives but one or two examinations during a course is putting a great handicap on the learning of his students. There are a number of reasons why this is true. First, frequent examination enables the student to keep informed of his progress. Numerous studies indicate that when a student knows the amount and rate of his progress he will learn more than when he does not know how well he is doing. Years ago, Book and Norvell[32] compared the learning of a group of university students who were informed of their learning progress with a control group who were not so informed. The results were so obvious that at the end of the tenth practice period the groups were reversed and the control group was informed of their progress while the other was not. These results are shown in Fig. 2–2.

Second, frequent examination means frequent review, more study, and more learning. Review for examination must not be confused with "cramming." Review is checking up and refreshing that which has already been learned, while cramming is original learning at the last minute. Review enables the student to get a bird's-eye view of the course and see

[31] Bird, *op. cit.*
[32] Book, W. F., and Norvell, L., The Will to Learn, *Ped. Sem.*, 1922, 29, 303–362.

each part in perspective. It enables the student to get out from among the trees and see the woods. Consequently, students should welcome examinations. Ross[33] found that weekly examinations have a definite positive

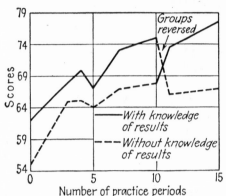

Fig. 2–2. The effects of knowledge on performance.

value to college students in psychology courses. (See his results summarized in Table 2–15.) This value is especially obvious with weaker students.

Table 2–15. Gains Made by Students Tested Weekly Over a Control Group Tested Only at End of Term

	Experimental group	Control group	Difference	P.E. of diff.	C.R.
Instructor R..	49	37.88	11.12	2.31	4.8
Instructor H..	49	44	5	2.56	1.9

The best preparation for examinations is daily study. The student who keeps up with his courses needs no long all-night review. He merely reviews his notebook and the underscored parts of his textbook, and he is ready for any examination. He does not cram; he reviews.

If the examination is the essay type, each answer should be carefully planned before it is written. In fact, the essay test asks for a short essay on each question. Answers should not be a series of hodge-podge ideas that are written down just as they occur to the student. A good essay test paper is written after an outline has been constructed at the expense of precious examination time. However, it should be noted that as a measuring device the essay examination is condemned for its low reliability

[33] Ross, C. C., and Henry, L. K., The Relation between Frequency of Testing and Progress in Learning in Psychology, *J. Educ. Psychol.*, 1939, **30**, 604–611.

(*i.e.*, different instructors give it different scores). Ashburn[34] found that, when several teachers graded the same essay test papers, the passing or failing of 40 per cent of the students examined depends on *who* grades the papers. Also, 10 per cent of the students will pass or fail depending on *when* the papers are graded. Not only do instructors disagree as to the value of a paper but they do not agree with themselves when they grade papers at different times. Nevertheless, the essay test is still widely used.

In objective examinations, the important thing is to read the statements carefully. A wrong answer because of misinterpretation is just as wrong as though it were due to ignorance. Some students and even some instructors have developed the foolish belief that an objective examination should be taken hurriedly and with but little deliberation. They believe that it should represent the student's first impression. This is utterly wrong. Each statement should be studied carefully and answered only after careful deliberation. If time permits, the test should be gone over again and those answers that appear wrong on more deliberate thought should be changed. Objective examinations are usually carefully prepared and should be just as carefully answered. Berrein[35] found that students improve their scores on objective tests by going back over them and changing answers that appear to be wrong. His results are shown in Table 2–16.

Table 2–16. Effects of Changing Answers on Objective Examinations

	Number	Per cent
Lowered score........................	34	22
Raised score..........................	99	64
Score unaffected......................	15	10
Made no changes......................	6	4

There are three widely used types of objective test questions—the completion, the multiple choice, and the true-false—that have been carefully studied for reliability (consistency) and validity (whether or not the test measures the factor it purports to measure). In general, the multiple-choice type of question has been found to be the most reliable, and the completion type to be the most valid. Kinney and Eurick[36] have summarized a number of these studies; their results are shown in Table 2–17.

Themes, Term Papers, and Reports. There are two stages in the preparation of a theme or term paper or report—first, collecting or develop-

[34] Ashburn, R., An Experiment in the Essay Type Question, *J. Exp. Educ.*, 1928, **7**, 1–3.

[35] Berrein, F. K., Are Scores Increased on Initial Tests by Changing the Initial Decision? *J. Educ. Psychol.*, 1940, **31**, 64–67.

[36] Kinney, L. B., and Eurick, A. C., A Summary of Investigations Comparing Different Types of Tests, *Sch. & Soc.*, 1932, **36**, 540–544.

Table 2–17. Rank of Examination Types in Reliability and Validity as Shown by Various Studies

Study by	Test type			
	Comple-tion	Multiple choice	True-false	Essay
In reliability:				
J. S. Kinder	3	1	2	4
A. C. Eurick	2	1	4	3
In validity:				
S. G. Brinkley	1	2	3	4
E. P. Wood	1	2	3	4
A. C. Eurick	2	1	4	3
Summary rank	2	1	3	4

ing the information and ideas, and second, stating it in written form. Many students sit down to write a theme and, because they have not performed the first stage (preparation), they conclude that they are not in the mood. Writing is impossible without something to write about. It is a means of communication. If there is nothing to communicate, obviously there can be no writing. The procedure of getting ideas or facts to communicate varies with the nature of those ideas or facts. Sometimes they are best obtained from books in the library. If so, a notebook is all the equipment necessary. However, facts and ideas are sometimes best obtained from an inspection trip, or an experiment, or an interview, or a survey, or a session of good hard thinking. If so, specialized training, financial expenditure, time, travel, and the assistance of others may be necessary. Whatever the nature and the requirements of this fact-getting stage, it is fundamental.

The second stage is to record, or communicate, the information amassed in written form. This is a skill step and can be acquired in no other way than by practice. The only way to learn to write is to write and rewrite. The more practice, other things being equal, the more perfect the skill. But writing, like any other intelligent behavior, must follow a plan, or an outline. Otherwise, even the best writing is ineffective. This book, for example, was carefully planned long before a single word of manuscript was written. Of course, the plan may change as writing progresses and relationships become more clear. Even the plans for a building are often changed during construction. However, the plan of a theme or a term paper is usually determined by the teacher or department making the assignment, so the student need only follow instructions.

There has been much argument among educators about the learning value of themes and term papers in courses on the college level. (Of course, their value in written English classes is admitted.) Some think they impose mere busy work upon the student for which he receives but little value. They believe that the time would be better spent in textbook study and assigned library readings. Bird[37] disagrees with this point of view. "The term paper challenges thinking and the assembling of pertinent information; it offers an opportunity to develop the skills required in undertaking original investigations; and it has an educational significance beyond that of almost all other forms of course assignments."

McClusky[38] studied the value of the term paper as a learning procedure by ascertaining its effect on objective examinations. He equated two groups of college students on the basis of their scores on the Army Alpha Intelligence Test and the Chapman-Cook Reading Test. He assigned a term paper to one group and announced an approaching examination to the other. Three weeks later, he gave the test to both groups (unannounced to the term paper group). Ten days later he repeated the same test without notice. The results are shown in Table 2–18. The

Table 2–18. Effect of Writing a Term Paper on Examination Grades

Group	Number	Intelligence score	Reading score	First test score	Second test score	Time spent on term paper or review
Term paper....	42	157	22.9	31.3	33.1	10.9
Review	38	153	22.7	32.5	32.3	5.8

author comments as follows, "Writing a term paper is far superior to the customary direct preparation for an examination because, without involving the disadvantages of direct preparation, the paper achieves the same factual material and carries with it the exercise of the higher mental processes of organization and creative expression."

HOW TO REST

Equally as important as how to study, for college students, is how to rest. Being young and energetic, students often do not realize that the efficiency of the human body is affected by its operating condition. Perhaps the most significant factor in the maintenance of good bodily condition is *rest*. Habits of rest are formed during youth. Consequently, it is important for college students to realize what sort of rest habits they may now be forming. There are two important aspects of this problem—relaxation and sleep.

[37] *Op. cit.* 64.
[38] McClusky, H. Y., An Experimental Comparison of the New Type Test and the Term Paper, *J. Appl. Psychol.*, 1933, **17**, 621–627.

Relaxation

The rest cure is being prescribed more and more by physicians for more and more different reasons. It has long been recognized as an essential part of the treatment of neurasthenia and other nervous disorders. Due in part to the increased *tempo* of modern civilized living and in part to clinical research, muscular and nervous tensions are now considered to be important causes of peptic ulcers and other gastrointestinal disorders, various cardiac maladies, hyperthyroidism, arthritis, pulmonary tuberculosis, etc.

Jacobson[39] lists five values of rest that indicate its importance both in medical practice and in maintaining health.

1. It repairs fatigue or exhaustion, thereby increasing the general resistance of the organism to infection and other noxious agents.
2. It decreases the strain on the heart and the blood vessels.
3. It diminishes the energy output and thus also the required calorie intake.
4. It quiets the nervous system, thus tending to relieve excitement, heightened reflexes, and often spastic states.
5. It diminishes the motion of affected body parts, thereby averting possible strain and energy.

There is less energy being consumed during rest than during activity. (Of course, the number of calories used by an individual depends on his size and other factors, as well as on his activity.) Langworthy and Barrott[40] found that while sitting in a chair an individual uses about 60.7 calories per hour, or less than 1,000 per day (16 hours). Sewing requires about 70 calories per hour and sweeping the floor about 100 per hour. In vigorous exercise, like playing football, an individual may use as much as 1,200 to 2,000 calories per hour. This is more than some other person will use in an entire day.

However, rest is more than merely sitting down and becoming inactive. It is *relaxation,* or freedom from unnecessary muscular and nervous tensions. The human body is so constructed that every muscle has an opposite. The contraction, or tension, of a muscle will move an arm or a leg, but the opposing muscle must contract to move it back again. Muscles have only the power to contract. They cannot expand. In a repetitive movement, like walking, a muscle must contract and then quit contracting, or relax, as soon as its opposite begins. Otherwise, they will interfere with each other. If both contract at the same time, there is no movement. However, there is a state of tension. Both muscles are working although nothing is being accomplished. Such tension states are necessary for body

[39] Jacobson, E., *Progressive Relaxation,* University of Chicago Press, Chicago, 1938.
[40] Langworthy, C. F., and Barrott, H. C., Energy Expenditures in Household Tasks, *Amer. J. Physiol.,* 1920, 52, 400.

posture. It is impossible to sit or stand unless the muscles hold the body in position.

Thus, the two functions of muscles are to move the body and to hold it in position. If a muscle is not necessary for either function, it should then be in a state of relaxation. A muscle should not contract unless that contraction is useful.

There are two faults a person may develop in using his muscles. First, he may contract too many muscles when he moves his body or any part of it. Skill and gracefulness in muscle movement depend on whether or not he is able to use just the muscles necessary and no others. Awkwardness results from the use of more muscles than necessary for the movement desired. The golfer who does not learn this does not become a good golfer or a graceful one. Skill in anything exists only after all unnecessary muscular contractions have been eliminated.

Second, a person may use too many muscles in maintaining his body posture. When a soldier learns to maintain posture with a minimum of muscular tension, he is able to stand at attention for hours without serious fatigue. When the public speaker learns to stand before an audience without contracting more muscles than necessary to give him good posture, he is not likely to experience the trembling knees so characteristic of the overtense speaker.

It is obvious that a person who uses more muscles than are necessary for movement and posture, or who contracts them more vigorously than necessary, will become fatigued more quickly than another who uses just the right muscles to the right degree. Young people should learn to move and to hold posture with as many muscles relaxed as possible. In other words, they should learn to rest as many muscles as possible for as much of the time as possible.

Muscular contractions and tensions produce so many fatigue products and damage the bodily mechanism to such an extent (catabolic processes) that major rest periods for rehabilitation and recovery are necessary. These enable the body to throw off accumulated waste products and make anabolic repairs. Such periods are usually accompanied by a cessation of those sensorimotor processes located in the higher center (cerebral cortex). These will be discussed in the next section of this chapter. Of course, minor rest periods are always interspersed throughout the awake period and enable the body to make partial recovery. The efficiency of the human body depends on these minor rest periods (see Chap. 15 for further discussion of this point).

It is now obvious that the most complete rest or relaxation can take place only when the body is in a reclining position. In any upright position, muscle tension is necessary for posture. The sitting position requires less tension than the standing position (and therefore permits more rest), but both require more tension than the reclining position. This is the position the human body takes for those major rest periods, called sleep. However, the mere fact that a body is in a reclining position does not prove that it is relaxed. Some people have difficulty in relaxing in any position. Activity and posture have become so habitual and rest periods have become so infrequent in the lives of many people that they have lost the ability to relax. How to regain the ability to relax and how to form the habit of relaxing will be the objective of the rest of this discussion.

Jacobson has found that it is possible to reacquire the ability to relax. The first step is to learn what relaxation feels like. A person may recline and think that he is relaxed, yet may have residual tension. Often he is not able to recognize the difference between real relaxation and this state of partial tension. Or, he may realize that he is not relaxed but be unable to locate the muscles that are yet partly tensed. Jacobson's procedure is for the patient to recline and practice tensing and relaxing isolated muscles. For example, practice may begin with tensing and relaxing just the muscles of the right arm. This is done over and over again until the patient learns to recognize the feel or experience of those muscles in tension and in relaxation. From here on the practice is in relaxation only. This initial practice is to enable the patient to learn what he should not do. Relaxing is not doing something but doing nothing. It is refraining from doing something. Obviously, the first step is to learn what not to do and how to avoid doing it.

After the patient has learned to relax his biceps and knows what it feels like when they are not relaxed, he then follows the same procedure with another muscle, and then another, until all the muscles of his body can be relaxed individually. This often takes a long time and diligent practice. He must learn to tense the muscles of the third finger of his left hand, for example, and then relax them in isolation from other related muscles. The object is to teach him to recognize and locate feelings of tension in any part of his body.

The same procedure then extends to muscle combinations. All muscles in the right arm, for example, are relaxed together. By this time he will be able to recognize if a muscle in his arm is not relaxed and to locate it. When the relaxation of the muscles of the right arm is mastered, he then extends his training to the left arm and then to all other parts of the body. Finally, after much practice, he learns to relax all parts of his body together. He is then ready for the next step in his training.

There are degrees of relaxation. A muscle is seldom either tense or relaxed. It is usually only partly relaxed even when the patient is reclining and feels relaxed. The instructions Jacobson gives his patients are, "You are to continue on and on, past the point where the part seems to you perfectly relaxed." It may take 15 minutes to relax completely a single muscle. Even the person who has learned to relax and has practiced it for years can lie down and feel a muscle relax more and more and more, even for as long as 5 minutes. This is progressive relaxation.

Relaxation cannot be learned quickly. It takes conscious practice and then more practice. Over and over again, separate muscles must be relaxed more and more completely. It takes the average individual weeks to learn how to lie down, or sit down, and do nothing.

After one has learned to relax the large skeletal muscles of the arms, legs, and trunk—completely or deeply—the next step is to learn to relax the delicate muscles of the eye, ear, throat, viscera, etc. This is definitely more difficult. However, the procedure is exactly the same. For example, the patient is asked to close his eyes tightly and then to relax them without opening his lids. Then, he is asked to turn his eyes to the right and relax; then to the left and relax. He is then instructed, "Just let your eyes go. Do not look in any direction." After a while the patient learns to relax his eyes until, even with the lids open, the eyes are not seeing.

The most difficult relaxation to learn is that of the muscles of speech. It is difficult to relax the processes of implicit speaking. First, the patient must realize that he talks to himself (or thinks) with implicit or subvocal muscle tensions. Whether he identifies thought processes with this implicit speech or not is unimportant, as long as he realizes that there is a relationship. He must learn to recognize the experience of implicit speech muscle tensions. Then only can he learn to relax them. When accompanied by the relaxation of other muscles, the relaxation of the implicit speech muscles produces a state of borderline sleep which is about the last stage of progressive relaxation.

Relaxation must not be confused with the hypnotic state. In fact, there is but little in common. Hypnosis is produced by suggestion, and the patient becomes more and more suggestible. Relaxation has nothing to do with suggestion. The patient is no more suggestible when he is relaxed than when he is tense, nor does suggestion promote relaxation.

The therapeutic value of relaxation in the treatment of various afflictions cannot be overemphasized. Some of Jacobson's results along this line are shown in Table 2–19. However, being able to relax is just as important to the healthy as to the afflicted. Perhaps relaxation will become a significant part of health and physical training in the future.

Another phase of Jacobson's work that interests the applied psychologist is the function of relaxation while on the job. If training in relaxation will enable us to perform our daily activities with less effort, it is certainly worth attention. For example, with relaxation these words are written with less effort than might be used ordinarily. Driving a car can be very fatiguing unless the driver is relaxed and handles the wheel with a minimum of effort. A soldier can stand at attention with no more effort than he can stand at ease if he knows how to maintain posture while partially relaxed. As the golfer improves his score and the singer improves his

Table 2–19. The Value of Relaxation in the Treatment of Various Afflictions
(After Jacobson)

Improvement as reported by	Disorders					
	Nervous hyper-tension	Insom-nia	Anxiety states	Cyclo-thymic depres-sion	Stutter-ing	Phobias
	(*N* 82)	(*N* 34)	(*N* 5)	(*N* 14)	(*N* 2)	(*N* 5)
The physician:						
1. None.............	0	0	0	2	0	0
2. Doubtful.........	4	1	0	1	1	0
3. Slight............	7	6	2	0	0	0
4. Marked..........	33	12	0	2	0	1
5. Very marked.....	38	15	3	9	1	4
The patient:						
1. None.............	1	0	0	2	0	0
2. Doubtful.........	1	0	0	2	0	0
3. Slight............	4	4	2	2	0	0
4. Marked..........	27	13	0	0	1	1
5. Very marked.....	49	17	3	8	1	4

resonance by proper relaxation, so can the day laborer, or the man at the bench, or the one at the desk, perform his work with less effort if he learns how to relax. This is a phase of fatigue that has too long escaped the attention of the efficiency expert.

SLEEP

Sleep is the natural cessation of those complex sensorimotor processes by which the organism adjusts itself to its environment. It is distinguished from unnatural cessations of adjustment—such as coma, trance, anesthesia, etc.—in that the subject can be awakened or returned to an adjusting state by ordinary procedure. During sleep there is a decrease in pulse and metabolic rates, a fall in blood pressure, and a change in the rhythm of brain waves. While sleep is more or less regular and periodic, it can be induced at irregular times by fatigue, monotony, relaxation, suggestion, etc. Sleep is a natural state of highly reduced sensorimotor activity that is distinguished from the awake state principally by the absence of consciousness.

The function of sleep is to enable the body to repair the damages done to it by the activity and tensions of the awake state. Fatigue poisons are thrown off, tissues are built up by anabolic processes, sugar is stored in the liver and fat in the tissues. In fact, the whole body is rehabilitated for another state of awake activity. Sleep is a period in which the body reconstructs itself and thus minimizes the wearing-out effects of living.

The Duration of Sleep. A common topic of discussion among college students is—how much sleep is necessary? Edison is supposed to have averaged but 3 or 4 hours sleep in each 24-hour period, yet health authorities commonly advise at least 8 hours sleep. What are the minimum

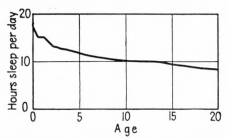

FIG. 2–3. Decrease in total hours of sleep with increase in age.

sleep requirements for good health? Beyond what time does sleep become a waste of time, or perhaps a luxury?

Kleitman[41] claims that standard sleeping-hour schedules, especially for children, have always recommended too much sleep. "Since from birth to adulthood the actual observed sleep-duration values are consistently and evenly lower by 1 hour than the prescribed, it is time to discard the theoretical scale in favor of the empirical one." The truth of this statement is suggested in Fig. 2–3, which shows the time actually slept by American children. To force a child to stay in bed for longer periods, merely because the Children's Bureau booklets recommend more sleep, is to invite him to form nonsleeping habits in bed.

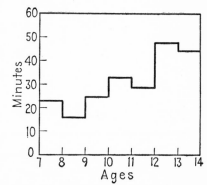

FIG. 2–4. Minutes superior children sleep each day above the average for unselected children.

Some studies show, however, that superior people sleep more than the average. Terman[42] found in his studies of superior children that they sleep longer on an average than do unselected children. (That is, from ages seven to fourteen. Below the age of seven there were no differencs.) These data are shown in Fig. 2–4. Laird[43] reports that men who have attained distinction in life

[41] Kleitman, N., *Sleep and Wakefulness,* University of Chicago Press, Chicago, 1939.
[42] Terman, L. M., *Genetic Studies of Genius,* Stanford University Press, Stanford, Calif., 1925.
[43] Laird, D. A., A Survey of the Sleep Habits of 509 Men of Distinction, *Amer. Med.,* 1931, **26**, 271–275.

sleep on an average of 8 hours per night. This is almost an hour more than the average. Moore, Jenkins, and Barker[44] administered some 1,500 dynamometer tests to 26 women after varying amounts of from 6 to 9 hours sleep. They found that muscular performance is better with 9 hours than with 6 hours sleep. Barry and Bousfield[45] reported that students feel better (euphoria) the next day after 8 to 8.75 hours sleep than they do when they sleep less than 6 hours or more than 9. Jenkins and Dallenbach[46] found that subjects can retain memorized material better after 8 hours sleep than after 4, 2, or 1 hour of sleep.

There seem to be great individual differences in the duration of sleep, however. Kleitman found a range of variation of more than 3 hours in the average sleep duration of 25 subjects. After a series of experiments with 170 institutional children on factors affecting sleep motility, Renshaw, Miller, and Marquis[47] conclude that "the optimal amount of sleep for a child of a given age is an undetermined value." Whether necessary or not, some people certainly do sleep much more than do others.

It has been suggested that the duration of sleep is dependent on the depth of sleep. Deep sleep is supposed to have more recuperative effects than shallow or fitful sleep. One of the oldest studies of the depth of sleep was by Kolschütter who plotted a dept-of-sleep curve by determining the amount of noise necessary to waken a person after various periods of sleep. By this method, the greatest depth of sleep seemed to come during the first 3 hours of sleeping. However, Kleitman found that the intensity of a sound necessary to waken a sleeper depends on "the period of immotility immediately preceding the test." If a subject has just recently moved in his sleep (*i.e.*, within 5 or 10 minutes), he is more easily wakened than after he has slept in the same position for a longer period of time (20 or 30 minutes). Because the average person moves more frequently during the latter part of the night, he would therefore be more easily wakened by noise at that time.

Many other methods have been used in the attempts to measure the depth of sleep. On the assumption that it is indicated by the ease of being wakened, pain, tactile, olfactory, and auditory stimulation have been used. These all give different depth-of-sleep curves. Based on still different assumptions regarding depth of sleep, brain waves, electrical skin resistance, body temperature, heart rate, blood pressure, the size of the pupil of the eye, have all been measured during sleep to determine its

[44] Moore, L. M., Jenkins, M., and Barker, L., Relation of the Number of Hours Sleep to Muscular Efficiency, *Amer. J. Physiol.*, 1922, 59, 471.

[45] Barry, J., and Bousfield, W. A., A Quantitative Determination of Euphoria and Its Relation to Sleep, *J. Abnorm. Soc. Psychol.*, 1935, 29, 385–389.

[46] Jenkins, J. G., and Dallenbach, K. M., Oblivescence during Sleeping and Waking, *Amer. J. Psychol.*, 1924, 35, 605–612.

[47] Renshaw, S., Miller, V. L., and Marquis, D. P., *Children's Sleep*, The Macmillan Company, New York, 1933.

depth. There is no consistent agreement between these different methods of measurement. Consequently, no conclusions can be drawn regarding what part of the sleeping period is characterized by the greatest depth of sleep.

Another factor that is claimed to affect the rest value of sleep is continuity. Edison is reported to have slept but 4 hours during each diurnal cycle. However, as reported, this was in several short periods. The general opinion is that the best sleep is unintermittent. Husband[48] attempted to study this problem with, unfortunately, but one subject. The subject slept uninterruptedly for 8 hours every night for 1 month. During this time, and also during the following month, he was tested every Saturday with a battery of mental and physical tests. Then, for a month, the subject slept from 11:00 P.M. to 2:00 A.M. and again from 5:00 A.M. to 8:00 A.M.—in all only 6 hours. There were no consistent differences between the two sleeping patterns in intellectual, motor, or physiological functions. Unfortunately, no conclusions can be drawn from this study because of its limitations.

So, in answer to the question—how much sleep is necessary?—we must conclude by saying that it is an individual matter and cannot be answered categorically. An Edison may need but 4 hours sleep, but John Doe may need 9 hours. Individual differences are too great to justify any generalizations regarding the necessary duration of a sleeping period or how frequently those periods should occur.

The Necessity of Sleep. Can a person get along without any sleep at all and for how long before behavior and health are impaired? In 1896 Patrick and Gilbert[49] kept 3 subjects awake for 90 hours. Every 6 hours they were given simple tests (reaction time, tapping, memory of digits, memory of nonsense syllables, addition, and visual, auditory, and kinesthetic sensitivity). Observations were made of pulse rate, temperature, body weight, and urine composition. It was found that visual acuity improved during the awake period, although there was considerable eye pain. There was much less deterioration on the other tests than was expected. Complete normality, as indicated by the tests, was restored after 16 to 35 per cent of the lost sleep was made up.

Robinson and Hermann[50] studied the effects of the loss of sleep for a period of 60 hours on 3 subjects. The tests used were tapping, steadiness, hand grip, naming letters, and mental multiplication. They found no ill effects whatsoever. The authors themselves suggest, however, that the tests

[48] Husband, R., The Comparative Values of Continuous Versus Interrupted Sleep, *J. Exp. Psychol.*, 1935, 18, 792–796.

[49] Patrick, and Gilbert, On the Effects of Loss of Sleep, *Psychol. Rev.*, 1896, 3, 469–483.

[50] Robinson, E. S., and Hermann, S. O., Effects of Loss of Sleep, *J. Exp. Psychol.*, 1922, 5, 19–32.

may have tapped "capacities comparatively uninfluenced by insomnia." Furthermore, because of a feeling of lowered capacity, the subjects may have compensated by expending more effort. After a single night's sleep the subjects reported that all feelings of "consequences of the insomnia had disappeared."

Robinson and Richardson[51] used a control group of 39 college students with which to compare the effects of the loss of 1 night's sleep on another group of 25 college students. Various forms of the Army Alpha test were administered before the sleepless period, after the sleepless period, and after 8 hours of sleep. The scores of both groups increased slightly because of the effects of practice, but there was no advantage in favor of the control group. Again, they suggest that the insomnia group may have compensated by expending extra effort. "The insomnia group, working under experimental conditions, took interest in the experimental situation after the sleep group, unaffected by the loss of sleep, had become relatively bored." The results of this study are shown in Table 2–20.

Table 2–20. The Effects of Sleep Loss on Intelligence Test Scores

Group	Preceding sleep loss	After sleep loss	After one night's sleep
Control................	161.00 ± 2.00	170.5 ± 1.7	171.5 ± 1.7
Insomnia................	160.2 ± 3.2	168.1 ± 3.0	168.4 ± 3.7

One of the most recent studies of the effects of experimental insomnia was made by Edwards.[52] Seventeen college students were in the experiment group and 10 in the control group. Both groups were given a battery of 18 standardized psychological tests and six measures of physiological functions, 2 days before the loss of sleep, during the experiment, and 2 weeks after the sleepless period. In general, the results corroborate those of earlier investigations that the loss of sleep has but little detrimental effect though accompanied by obvious increase in effort.

There were no detrimental effects of the loss of sleep in reaction time, hand steadiness, hand grip, blood pressure, oral temperature, pulse rate, height, weight, vision, or patellar reflex. In static ataxia (maintaining upright balance) the experimental group swayed more as the loss of sleep increased. On the intelligence test (American Council on Education Test) after 24 hours without sleep, 13 did better (than 2 days before the experiment started) and 3 did worse; after 48 hours, 6 did better and 11 worse; and after 96 hours, 2 did better and 14 did worse. After 2 weeks

[51] Robinson, E. S., and Richardson, R. F., Effects of Loss of Sleep, *J. Exp. Psychol.,* 1922, 5, 93–100.

[52] Edwards, A. S., Effects of the Loss of One Hundred Hours Sleep, *Amer. J. Psychol.,* 1941, 45, 80–90.

of normal sleep, 16 did better and 1 did worse. There was also a deterioration of memory after 72 hours of sleep loss.

Twelve clinical symptoms appeared in the experimental group which, of course, were not obvious in the control group. They were as follows: dozing and falling asleep, irritability, inability to sustain attention, increasingly great effort required to perform various tasks, difficulty in maintaining equilibrium, alternate feelings of being very sleepy and then wide awake, increasing restlessness, extreme desire to be left alone, reduced ability to read and study, memory loss for very recent happenings, pseudohallucinations, and headaches. Other less common symptoms were irrelevant remarks, dizziness, speech difficulties, incorrect dressing, and seeing double.

There were four women in the experimental group and no sex differences were observed. However, the larger and more athletic individuals seemed to be affected by the loss of sleep more than the smaller and apparently weaker ones.

Conclusions from these and other comparable studies seem fairly clear. The human body can take a lot of punishment, as far as loss of sleep is concerned, and still function efficiently. However, the long-time effects on the body of prolonged insomnia are still in doubt. It is known that young puppies cannot withstand the loss of sleep longer than a week, even when fed artificially. There is "fatty degeneration in ganglion cells, capillary hemorrhages, and an increase of leucocites." Crile[53] found that the loss of sleep produces changes in the central nervous system quite similar to those produced by starvation. After keeping rabbits awake for 96 to 118 hours he found lesions in the liver, the adrenal gland, and in the central nervous system. Perhaps the apparent freedom of detrimental results from the loss of sleep in human subjects is due to crude methods of measurements. At any rate, these experiments should not be interpreted as meaning that the college student can go without sleep for long periods of time without unknown (though unproved) detrimental results.

Motility during Sleep. How often the statement is made—"I slept like a log. I didn't move all night. I was in the same position when I wakened this morning as I was when I went to sleep." This problem of motility during sleep has been rather extensively studied. Johnson[54] and his associates at Mellon Institute found, in some 15,000 measurements made on 11 students, that the average sleeper moves about once every 11.5 minutes during the night. They found that he moves every 5 minutes (or less) for 1.5 hours, every 10 minutes (or less) for 2.5 hours, and every 15 minutes (or less) for 3.5 hours. The frequency of the moves varies

[53] Crile, G. W., *A Bi-polar Theory of Living Processes*, the Macmillan Company, New York, 1926.

[54] Valentine, W. L. (Ed.), Johnson, H. M., *Readings in Experimental Psychology*, Chap. 23, Harper & Brothers, New York, 1931.

with the sleeper but not much from night to night. Some sleepers are habitually more active in sleep than are others. Also, some are more active during certain parts of the night than others. "Some sleepers tend to rest more during the first half of the night; others during the last half; and others during the middle."

Kleitman[55] found that there is much more motility during the second half of the night than during the first, and that there is a relation between body temperature and motility during sleep. When the temperature is below normal, there are fewer movements than when the temperature is above normal. This would suggest that eating before retiring, drinking stimulants (coffee, tea, etc.), intense excitement, or anything that would increase metabolism and hence body temperature would increase sleep motility.

Renshaw, Miller, and Marquis[56] studied the effects of moving pictures, change in season, experimental insomnia, and coffee on the motility of institutional children during sleep. The results are shown in Table 2–21.

It is now obvious that sleep is not motionless. No one position seems to afford maximum rest for all parts of the body. Movement is necessary to relieve the body of position tensions. While there is no rest value in the motion itself, the new position is more restful than the old one. Body rest seems to be a progressive affair. Thirty-five to 50 positions each night are necessary to afford the average sleeper rest for every part of his body.

The Control of Sleep. From a practical standpoint, the college student is interested in two phases of the sleep problem—how to go to sleep and how to stay awake. There are times when he wants to sleep and cannot and other times when he wants to stay awake and cannot. If he has insomnia, he wants to be able to sleep without counting sheep, and if he has an examination, he wants to stay awake and study without that drowsy feeling which reduces his efficiency.

The fact that sleep can be induced is as old as civilization itself. The rocking cradle and the lullaby to induce sleep in children have been practiced by mothers for generations. However, modern mothers have learned that sleep is a habit that can be learned. They teach their children to go to sleep when put to bed. No special inducements are necessary other than those physical and physiological conditions that nature has decreed are conducive to sleep. These conditions produce sleep naturally and no supplemental methods are necessary. First is the need for sleep. No child will go to sleep immediately after he has awakened. Sleep comes naturally only when it is needed. Second, other physiological needs should be satisfied. A child will not go to sleep if he is hungry or thirsty or needs

---

[55] Kleitman, *op. cit.*

[56] Renshaw, S., Miller, V. L., and Marquis, D., *Children's Sleep*, The Macmillan Company, New York, 1933.

to go to the toilet. Third, the sleeping room should be darkened and as free from immediate noise as possible. There should be no sleep distractions. When these conditions are provided for the child, he soon forms a sleeping habit.

Table 2–21. The Effects of Various Factors on Sleep Motility

Factor	Effects
Temperature and humidity......	No effects
Age.............	Sleep motility increases with age
Sex.............	Boys are more active during sleep than girls after the age of 10
Seasons*........	Winter is least active season for both boys and girls. Sleep motility is greater for other seasons

Season	Boys, per cent	Girls, per cent
Winter............................	100	100
Spring............................	104	124
Summer...........................	110	140
Autumn...........................	121	121

Factor	Effects
Moving pictures..	Motility increased for some children (60.5 per cent) and decreased for others (39.4 per cent) Young children (below ten) are less affected
Sleep deprivation (up to 33%)	Decreased motility. Extends into several nights following deprivation Effects are greater for young children Boys are affected more than girls
Coffee..........	Individual differences too great to permit generalization. (Motility increased for some children, decreased for others, and unaffected for others.) Double dosage does not double effects. Kaffee Hag causes more motility than coffee for some children

* Working with 12 adult subjects over a period of 4 years, Kleitman found that sleep motility is least in the spring (100 per cent), more in the winter (111 per cent), more yet in the summer (130 per cent), and most in the autumn (150 per cent).

Now, what about the adult who has well-formed habits of sleeping and yet sometimes is unable to do so? He tosses and turns and counts sheep and still cannot sleep. The first step in treating insomnia is to discover and remove the cause. Sleeping pills may produce sleep, but they will not remove the cause for sleeplessness. Insomnia is due to a wide variety of causes. Among them are the overuse of tobacco or coffee; overwork and overtension; overeating; disease; unusual physiological conditions (such as upset stomach, aching teeth, infection, etc.); sleeping room too hot or too cold; indigestion; eyestrain; pregnancy; tuberculosis; liver ailments; worry, etc. Whatever the cause, it must be removed in order to restore the person to his normal sleeping habits.

Even if the cause of insomnia is not removed, the person can lie in bed with deep relaxation and get almost as much value from his rest as he would from sleep. Cases have been reported of people who have lived for years without sleeping. Kleitman quotes Benon as reporting a case of insomnia of 17 years duration that "showed no dementia but only a melancholic depression." The loss of consciousness in sleep merely brings about the relaxation of a few speech muscles and sensory centers in addition to those that may be relaxed while still awake. Learning how to relax is not only important in getting the maximum values out of rest, but it is a good method of inducing sleep even when the cause of sleeplessness still exists. Relaxation always produces beneficial results, whether with sleep or without it. The importance of developing the technique of relaxation cannot be overemphasized as a means of promoting rest. This is becoming even more important with the ever-increasing tempo of our modern civilized living.

There are a number of ways of inducing sleep, even when the causes for staying awake still exist, in addition to those already mentioned (rocking cradle, lullaby, pills, relaxation). Immotility, or lying perfectly still, is often effective. Many years ago, Sidis[57] was able to induce sleep in guinea pigs, cats, dogs, and children by limiting their movements and keeping their eyes closed. A monotonous sound will often induce sleep. The continuous tick of a clock, or the running of a motor, or the hum of electrical apparatus, acts somewhat as the mother's lullaby of the last generation. A drink of lukewarm milk or water is sometimes effective. (This does not mean hot coffee, or anything that will increase metabolism and body temperature.) Some people read themselves to sleep. This is very effective if the individual is already in a sleeping position. While a reclining position produces eyestrain, yet that very fatigue may be all that is necessary to induce sleep.

Much has been written about the importance of the bed, and especially the mattress, for restful sleep. There is no evidence that the type of mattress, whether hard or soft, has anything to do with the type of sleep. Some people form habits of sleeping on inner-spring mattresses, some on the ground, and some in swinging hammocks. As Kleitman says, "It is all a matter of individual likes and dislikes, and, except through suggestion, is of little importance in the quality of sleep produced."

Perhaps the most important factor in controlling sleep is regularity. If each day follows essentially the same pattern, the habit of going to sleep

[57] Sidis, B., An Experimental Study of Sleep, *J. Abnorm. Psychol.*, 1908, **3**, 1–32, 63–96, 170–207.

at a certain time is inevitable. Kleitman has found that a person's diurnal body temperature follows a definite pattern. His efficiency drops off as his temperature goes down. Consequently, his day should be patterned. He should eat at regular intervals, work during certain hours, eliminate waste products at definite times, and go to bed at a specified hour every night. Nature will then take care of the formation of habits. Then, when insomnia occurs, it will be due to unusual causes that can be discovered and eliminated.

The problem of how to stay awake is not so difficult as the one of how to go to sleep. Of course, both are products of nature and do not constitute problems in the normal healthy individual. If the student sleeps when he is tired and studies when he is rested, he does not have a problem of either insomnia or sleepiness. But, sleepiness sometimes comes even when the body is rested. A student who sleeps 8 hours per night may still be unable to stay awake to study for an examination in psychology. Experimental insomnia, with both humans and animals, indicates that activity or movement is most effective in keeping subjects awake. A brisk walk will brighten up a puppy even when it is near death from the effects of insomnia. Sleep is a cessation of the function of the higher cerebral centers. Obviously, it cannot occur while these centers are kept in a state of function.

Practical devices often used by students to stay awake are many and varied. A short walk around the block, vigorous calisthenics, drugs (including coffee), lowered temperature of the study room, maintaining an upright position, etc., are all used to repress sleep and induce wakefulness. Some students do better work, or so they think, by getting up early in the morning instead of studying late at night. If drowsiness is difficult to control, this is probably a better procedure. However, it would seem to be a better method yet to plan work so that the regular routine schedules of sleeping and studying do not interfere with each other. Then the law of nature—to sleep when tired and work when rested—will not be violated.

SUMMARY

Good scholarship and leadership in extracurricular affairs were found to be worth-while objectives in college life. Both are highly correlated with success after college. While scholarship depends largely on native intelligence, it also depends on study habits that can be learned. These are

1. Intelligent planning and budgeting of time
2. Rapid reading with satisfactory comprehension
3. Intelligent note taking
4. Frequent review, whether for examination or not
5. Planning, organizing, and writing ideas in the form of themes, term papers, and reports

The problem of proper rest was found to consist of relaxation and sleep. Few people know how to relax and thus avoid much of the fatigue from being awake. Procedure for learning how to relax was explained. Sleep was found to be a complex problem that is not well understood, but on which there has been wide research. Some of this was reviewed and conclusions made when justified.

RECOMMENDED SUPPLEMENTARY READINGS

How to Study

Bird, C., and Bird, D. M.: *Learning More by Effective Study,* Appleton-Century-Crofts, Inc., New York, 1945.

Cole, L., and Ferguson, J. M., *Student's Guide to Effective Study,* Rinehart & Company, Inc., New York, 1946.

Frederick, H. W., Kitchen, P. C., and McClure, A. R., *A Guide to College Study,* Appleton-Century-Crofts, Inc., New York, 1947.

Robinson, F. P., *Effective Study,* Harper & Brothers, New York, 1946.

How to Rest

Jacobson, E.: *Progressive Relaxation,* University of Chicago Press, Chicago, 1938.

Jacobson, E.: *You Must Relax,* McGraw-Hill Book Company, Inc., New York, 1942.

Kleitman, N.: *Sleep and Wakefulness,* University of Chicago Press, Chicago, 1939.

Chapter 3

CHILD DEVELOPMENT

"What you are to be, you are now becoming," was the admonition a college president of the last generation gave to all entering freshmen. While the implications of this statement are trite and obvious, it is too often the trite and obvious that are ignored. Certainly, the child is growing into an adult. Certainly, he is now becoming what he is later to be—so what? A subtle implication of the above statement, which probably escaped its author, is that the character and personality of the child are *determined* by his present and past actions. What the child becomes as an adult is positively and irrevocably produced by his childhood experiences. He is caused to be what he becomes. Adults cannot lift themselves by their bootstraps into desirable personalities by any hocus-pocus of will power, system of character formation, or religious experience— regardless of traditional and popular beliefs. What the child is to be, he is now in the process of becoming. When he arrives, there is nothing he can do about it. He cannot go back and live his childhood over again. Human character is the product of determining causes.[1]

[1] Fortunately, character is always in the process of formation and can be altered constantly. The adult can change his personality by the same process by which it was formed—experience. The child forms personality habits through experience; the adult can change personality habits through experience. However, there is one significant difference. The child starts with nothing, or, as John Locke said, with a *tabula rasa*. He forms a new personality. The adult must alter an old one. He cannot start new.

69

No other principle of child guidance is quite as significant as this one. Society molds its childhood into citizens—both good and bad. It is now forming its statesmen, educators, scientists, artists, engineers, and other constructive leaders of the next generation, as well as its murderers, drunkards, vagabonds, thieves, and criminals of various types. Both the good and bad citizenship of the future is now being molded side by side in our homes, schools, churches, and communities. Whether we like it or not, we are now making the bad citizens of the next generation as well as the good ones. Society is responsible for the nature of its citizenship.

ORIGINAL NATURE

One of the most difficult problems that science has ever attempted to solve is that of inheritance. However, speculation about the mechanisms of heredity has always been abundant. Even primitive people have ideas about how parents transmit certain characteristics to their children. But until the beginning of the present century, there was little scientific knowledge about the actual process of inheritance. Gregor Mendel published the results of his careful studies of crossbreeding different varieties of garden peas in 1866, but it was not until 1900 that his work received any attention in the scientific world. Since 1900, Mendel's laws of heredity have been carefully proved, and the processes by which they function have been discovered. Under the leadership of Thomas H. Morgan, hundreds of experiments have been performed in crossbreeding various plants and animals (especially a small insect called the fruit fly) which have led to a remarkably clear understanding of the details of heredity. This field of scientific investigation is called "genetics."

How the Child Inherits

The geneticists have discovered that the egg (the ovum) of the female and the sperm of the male unite (at conception) and form a single cell, which is the beginning of a new organism. They have found that these two germ cells (the egg and the sperm) contain only half of the usual content of other body cells. In other words, the first cell of a new individual is formed by the union of two half-cells, one half-cell coming from the father and the other half-cell coming from the mother. The father and the mother each contributes exactly half of the heredity of the new individual. That is, all other cells in a human body contain 48 chromosomes while the egg and the sperm cells contain only 24 chromosomes each. When they unite, they then form a new cell of 48 chromosomes, 24 of which come from the sperm (the father) and 24 from the egg (the mother) (see Fig. 3–1).

When this process of fertilization has taken place (when the sperm and the egg have united) and the first cell of the new baby has been formed, the process of growth begins. There are four necessities for all organic growth—food, oxygen, water, and normal temperature. In birds, the food and the water are stored up in the egg, the oxygen is supplied through the porous shell, and normal temperature is furnished by the mother's sitting on the eggs. In human beings, however, the growth or development of the new baby takes place inside the body of the mother where food, oxygen, and water are absorbed from her blood, and her

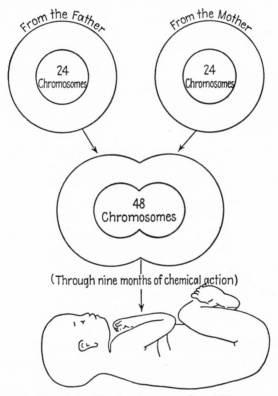

FIG. 3–1. The development of a child.

temperature makes this factor normal. In other words, the human mother furnishes the four necessities for the growth of the new individual without interfering with her own usual behavior.

The process of growth consists of changing food and water into living matter through chemical processes. The chromosomes are made up of very small chemical packets called "genes" that work in pairs, one of each pair originally coming from the father and the other from the mother. It is through the chemical action of the genes that the raw products—food and water—are changed into body tissue. Oxygen and normal temperature are necessary conditions for this change.

When a certain amount of growth has taken place and the original cell has increased in size, it then divides into two cells. Each gene also divides so that there are exactly as many genes in each new cell as there were in the original cell. More growth takes place (*i.e.,* food and water are changed into living matter through the chemical action of the genes) and these two cells each divide again. This process is continued throughout the life of the individual. However, the cells soon begin to differ from each other, some of them becoming bone cells, some nerve cells, some blood cells, etc. These different kinds of cells become arranged after a certain pattern that is characteristic of the human organism. After about nine months, sufficient growth and development have taken place for the new baby to live outside the body of the mother. It is then expelled from her body, or it is born.

Before birth, the child received the four necessities for life—food, oxygen, water, and normal temperature—directly from the body of the mother. After birth, however, it gets oxygen through its own lungs, food and water through its own mouth (usually from the breast glands of the mother), and temperature from its own bodily processes. Birth is in no sense the beginning of life. The born child is essentially the same as it was before birth. About the only difference is that it is no longer inside the body of the mother. It is approximately 268 days old when it is born and is in no sense a new baby. Birth is merely an incident that takes place in the life of the child when he is about nine months old.

Now, just what does a child inherit? He inherits 24 strings of genes (called chromosomes) from his father and 24 strings of genes from his mother. Whether he has blue or brown eyes depends on whether he has the genes that produce blue eyes or the genes that produce brown eyes. He will be tall or short, dark or light, bright or dull, male or female, etc., depending on what genes he has received from his parents. Children do not inherit physical characteristics but only the genes that may produce those characteristics. However, the genes produce normal characteristics only if food, oxygen, water, and temperature are normal. The inherited genes of a child may be normal but if any one of these four necessities for life is abnormal, the child will be abnormal. Genes that would produce blue eyes may produce some other color, or no eyes at all, if the food, oxygen, water, or temperature of prebirth life is not normal.

Interesting experiments have been performed with some of the lower organisms such as flies, frogs, fish, and salamanders, which do not develop inside the body of the mother. The food, oxygen, water, and temperature have been varied from the normal, with the result that abnormal development has taken place. For example, when the temperature of the room in which fruit-fly eggs are being hatched is lowered, a queer abnormality develops. The flies have extra legs. When the humidity or moisture of the room is increased above normal, the shape of both the stomach and the eyes is abnormal.

A Mexican salamander or lizard lives normally in water. It has gill slits, paddlelike feet, and a flat tail suited for swimming. If a proper amount of iodine is placed in the water where this lizard lives, it undergoes great bodily changes, similar to those which a tadpole undergoes when it becomes a frog. The lizard loses its gills and develops lungs. Its paddlelike feet become adapted for crawling on land. Its flat swimming tail becomes round, and the animal ceases to live in the water and lives on land.

The number of eyes in both fish and frogs can be changed by bringing about certain changes in the environment. When the eggs of sea minnows are hatched in water containing magnesium chloride, the fish have only one instead of two eyes. When frog eggs are turned over at a certain stage of their development the tadpoles develop with two heads instead of one. Such partial twin formations may also be brought about in young fish by reducing the normal supply of oxygen.

All these experiments show that normal heredity will produce normal organisms only under normal prebirth environment. The inherited genes may be normal, but the new organism will be abnormal if the water, oxygen, food, and temperature are not supplied in a normal manner.

This means, then, that as far as the organism is concerned heredity and environment are so interconnected and interrelated that they are both necessary and equally important in producing physical characteristics. Heredity cannot function without environment and environment cannot function without heredity. Both are essential in producing the organism (see Fig. 3–2).

Herediviron

Color blindness	Temperament	Citizenship
Hemophilia	Strength Stubbornness	Delinquency
Height	Weight Cheerfulness	
Eye color	Intelligence Reasoning ability	Character
Blood type	Special aptitudes Ambition	
Sex	Tendencies Emotional stability	
	Propensities Interests	Good manners
Basic motives	Likes and dislikes	

Entirely heredity ... *Entirely environment*

FIG. 3–2. The interrelation of heredity and environment in producing personality traits. (Traits near the left extreme are influenced most by heredity and those near the right extreme most by environment.)

However, mammillary organisms (*i.e.*, those that suckle their young) are free from most of these extreme environmental changes during embryonic development because their young develop within the body of the mother. Food, oxygen, water, and temperature conditions are usually

normal for this reason. When mammals are born with abnormal characteristics it may mean that they have received abnormal genes from the
parents. But this is not always true. James X has an abnormally formed
lower arm because before birth the umbilical cord became twisted around
his arm and prevented its normal development. He did not inherit the
abnormal arm, but it was produced by abnormal environment before
birth. What we humans inherit depends on the conditions that exist while
we are being formed.

Commenting on this close relation of heredity and environment, Professor Jennings has said,

With the same set of genes, different environmental conditions may induce the production of diverse characteristics. And with the same environmental conditions, different genes may induce the production of diverse
characteristics. The same difference in characteristics that may be produced in some cases by diversity of genes is in other cases produced by diversity of environment. There is then no thorough-going distinction in
kind between diversities producible by gene differences, and those producible by environmental differences. Characteristics do not fall into two
mutually exclusive classes, one hereditary, the other environmental. A given
characteristic may be altered by changing the genes; and this is the ground
on which it is called hereditary. But the same characteristics may be altered
by changing the environment; and this is the ground on which it is called
environmental. The genes supply one set of conditions for development,
the environment another set, and there is no necessary difference in kind
between them. The characteristic produced may be changed by adequate
alteration of either set. From the nature of a distinctive characteristic, it
is not possible to decide whether it is due to diversity of genes or to diversity
of environment, since the same peculiarity may be due in different cases to
either set of causes.[2]

This amalgamated relationship of heredity and environment has been
described in one of the author's publications as follows:[3]

In the light of modern science, it now becomes necessary for us to modify
the traditional conception of heredity and environment as being two distinct
and separate forces, or sources, and think of them as amalgamated into *one*
influence. No trait, either of behavior or of structure, can be attributed to
inheritance exclusive of environment, or to environment exclusive of inheritance. The genes, or workmen, come by way of inheritance, but the environment, or the engineers and bosses, immediately assumes control of
their behavior. There is a single rather than a dual source of organic
structure. There is neither heredity nor environment, but the two in
closest amalgamation—let us call it *herediviron*.

[2] Jennings, H. S., *The Biological Basis of Human Nature,* p. 134, W. W. Norton
& Company, New York, 1930.

[3] Gray, J. S., *Psychological Foundations of Education,* pp. 67ff., American Book
Company, New York, 1935.

However, the gene explanation of the formation of organic structure should not be interpreted to apply only to embryonic life. The process of body development before birth is fundamentally no different from the process of growth after birth. An organism's life begins at the moment of fertilization, and birth is only an episode in life. Cell mitosis, metabolism, gene behavior—all begin at fertilization and end only at death. Before birth, the organism gets its food (or raw cytoplasm) from the mother and is subjected only to her environment; after birth, the source of food supply changes and the environment becomes more diverse. However, the process of the genes transforming cytoplasm into body structure is the same throughout the life of the organism, and in no sense is birth the beginning of that life.

Now, what is original nature from the standpoint of this biological explanation of organic growth? It is quite evident that there is no original nature in the sense of body structure. What is the original nature of an automobile? The iron ore (food) is transformed by factory workmen (genes) into the type of a machine (organic structure) which is determined by the factory draftsmen, engineers, foremen, machinery, and working conditions (environment). An automobile does not have an *original* nature. Neither does an organism. It would be better to ask, What is the physical *status quo* of an organism at birth, or at any other time in its life span? The answer would be, It is what its inherited genes have been able to make it under the control of its environment up to that time. Never should the question be asked, What is innate? Nothing is innate. No trait, physical or otherwise, is exclusively inherited. Inheritance and environment become amalgamated in organic life and each loses its identity. The influence of environment begins long before birth, in fact at the very moment of fertilization. The mother herself is only an environmental factor after conception. Her hereditary influence ceases, with the father's, when the ovum and spermatazoon unite. After that, she is merely a host to a distinct and organically separate individual. After birth, that host-parasite relationship is altered but not fundamentally changed.

So we can say that the organism has no original nature any more than it has an "acquired" nature. It is at any time in its life span a product of both heredity and environment in amalgamation. What an organism is, even before birth, is determined jointly by heredity and environment— *herediviron.*

THE NATURE OF THE CHILD AT BIRTH

Unquestionably, heredity sets certain limitations beyond which no amount of environmental training can go. Human genes cannot produce an organism that can live under water, nor one that can fly (without mechanical apparatus), nor one that can hibernate. Just being human carries certain hereditary limitations in comparison with other organisms. Then, within those hereditary limitations are all sorts of individual variations. Some of these are characteristic of races, some of families, and some of individuals. The genes of one race produce men of 70 in. in height, while those of another seldom produce men of over 65 in. in height. The genes of one family produce children of high intellectual aptitude, while those of another produce children of low intellectual capacity. The genes of one man may produce a body structure that can compose and play great music, while those of another produce structure that cannot discriminate harmony from discord. All environmental influence on human development is confined to the limitations of the inherited genes.

However, environment sets additional limitations. Inherited aptitudes are seldom developed to their fullest extent. In fact, it is doubtful if even the best environment offers sufficient opportunity for the fullest development of any innate capacity. In ordinary environment great innate apti-

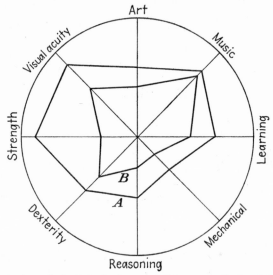

Fig. 3–3. The relation of the inherited potentialities or aptitudes (A) to the developed abilities (B) of John Doe.

tudes are often almost entirely undeveloped. Men with great musical capacities often spend their lives at menial labor, and potential artists greater than da Vinci are never discovered. The great function of vocational guidance is to analyze a person's innate capacities and then guide him into work that makes use of those native advantages (see Chap. 5 for further discussion of this). In Fig. 3–3 the circle represents the greatest possible human inheritance. The outer polygon indicates the inherited capacities of John Doe. The inner polygon represents the abilities of John Doe as they have been developed up to the present time. Whether inherited aptitudes are great or small, their development depends on the opportunities of environment.

Because the human child develops within the body of his mother and therefore is subjected to a fairly stable prebirth environment, we can assume that the differences in children at birth are largely due to differences in inherited genes. Furthermore, if we are careful to keep the postbirth environment of two or more children the same as far as possible, we can assume that differences that develop are due largely to different genes. Likewise, if we vary the postbirth environment of two children known to have identical genes, such as identical twins, we can assume that differences that develop are due to environment. In other words, even though heredity and environment are amalgamated in human structure, the relative influence of each can be studied in three ways—by studying neonates, or babies at birth; by studying identical twins reared apart; by studying unrelated children reared together. Space permits only a brief introduction to the research on these topics.

The Baby at Birth. The study of human neonates is limited by their frailness and restricted behavior. They do little but vegetate and in this respect are not essentially different from neonates of other species, especially those that are also undeveloped at birth. (The human neonate has undergone a lower percentage of his mature development than that of any other animal. He also has a longer period of infancy.) Jordan[4] has listed a set of traits that he labels as "probably inherited." He recognizes that "heredity and environment cooperate in producing any and all structure which appears."

I. Traits which appear at birth or soon thereafter.
   A. Reflexes
      1. Those which are aroused by stimuli within the organism itself.
         a. Sneezing
         b. Crying
         c. Hiccoughing
         d. Yawning
         e. Urination and defecation
      2. Those which are aroused by stimuli from outside the organism.
         a. Withdrawing and defense movements
         b. Rejecting—such as unpleasant tastes
         c. Grasping
      3. Those which are aroused by stimuli sometimes within the body and sometimes outside the body.
         a. Head movements
         b. Hand movements
         c. Arm movements
         d. Leg and foot movements
         e. Smiling

[4] Jordan, A. M. *Educational Psychology*, pp. 44*ff*., Henry Holt and Company, Inc., New York, 1942.

    B. Sources of language and skill
      1. Vocalization
      2. Manipulation
      3. Visual exploration
    C. Organic responses
      1. Food getting—begins with sucking
      2. Thirst
      3. Emotion—both pleasant and unpleasant
II. Traits which appear after maturation of nerve, gland, or muscle.
    A. Those much dependent on heredity
      1. Blinking
      2. Walking
      3. Sex behavior
    B. Those less dependent on heredity
      1. Mastery—desire to control one's environment
      2. Rivalry—desire to surpass another or one's own past record
      3. Fighting—often an effect of the desire for mastery

However, regardless of what is inherited and what is not, it is more important to the psychologist to know which human wants and desires are immutable and which can be altered by training. For example, is the want to own property an innate and immutable want or is it the product of social training? Is mother love somehow innate in the germ plasm, or is it a cultural pattern? The following classification of human wants is based on wide research which cannot be reviewed in limited space.

  I. Basic or primary wants—those that are present in all humans regardless of variations in culture
    A. Organic needs—wants for food, water, air, comfortable temperature, etc.
    B. Sex pleasure—becomes more intense at puberty
    C. Maternal love—due to hormones produced by the physiological condition of motherhood
    D. Activity—want to release stored up energy
    E. Rest—want to recuperate from activity
    F. Regurgitate or vomit—due to disgusting sensations
    G. Avoid pain, illness, and death
    H. Avoid interference
  II. Derived or secondary wants—those that are learned but vary little with culture, due perhaps to certain common characteristics in human cultures
    A. Emotional excitement
    B. To be with others
    C. To be liked by others
    D. To control one's environment—includes ownership
    E. To follow leaders

F. To explore

G. To compete with others

H. To worship

III. Individualistic wants—those that have been learned and are peculiar to individuals. These are too numerous to list.

The strength of a want does not depend on whether it is basic, derived, or individualistic. A learned individualistic want may become stronger than an unlearned basic want.

Basic wants should be recognized and accepted as inevitable. It is foolish to try to change them or to ignore them. Any derived wants can be changed, although when they are approved by cultural standards change is difficult. Information as to which human wants, or motives, are changeable and which are instinctive has a determining effect on child training.

Identical Twins Reared Apart. Identical twins always develop from the same original cell. After the first mitosis, for some unknown reason, the two cells become separated and two children develop instead of one. Their heredity is therefore identical, they are of the same sex, and develop before birth in the same chorion. They usually grow up together and are very much alike in both looks and actions.

Since identical twins have identical heredity, when they are reared in separate homes any differences that appear are then properly attributed to environment. Such cases are few and are reported in the literature as case studies. Muller[5] reports the case of identical twin girls who were reared apart from the time they were two weeks old. At the time of the study they were thirty years old. One completed the twelfth grade and had taught school. She was married and had one child. The other attended school only four years, was unmarried, and at the age of thirty was actively engaged in a minor business. Both were energetic, popular, and active in community affairs. On intelligence tests the twins obtained very similar scores. They made raw scores of 156 and 153 on the Army Alpha, and 64 and 62 on the Otis Advanced Test of Intelligence. "Marked differences were found, however, on personality tests, speed of free association, and tests of motor speed and coordination. The differences were in general such as would be expected from the variations noted in their environments."

Newman[6] has studied 19 pairs of identical twins reared apart and compared them with 50 pairs of identical twins reared together. He was very careful to establish the fact of identity by comparing finger prints, shape of teeth, and general appearance. A comparison of the differences between the identical twins reared together and those reared apart is shown in

[5] Muller, H. J., Mental Traits and Heredity, *J. Hered.*, 1925, 16, 433–448.

[6] Newman, H. H., Freeman, F. N., and Holzinger, K. J., *Twins: A Study of Heredity and Environment*, University of Chicago Press, Chicago, 1937.

Table 3–1. Note that differences in weight, I.Q., and educational achievement are significant whereas other differences are not.

Table 3–1. Mean Differences for Two Groups of Identical Twin Pairs

Traits	Reared apart	Reared together	Diff.	P.E.d	$\dfrac{\text{Diff.}}{\text{P.E.}d}$
Height........................	1.8	1.61	0.19	0.31	0.6
Weight........................	9.9	4.03	5.87	1.22	4.8
Head length....................	2.2	2.59	−0.39	0.42	0.9
Head width....................	2.85	2.25	0.6	0.4	1.5
Binet I.Q.....................	8.21	5.35	2.86	0.95	3.0
Otis I.Q......................	8	4.54	3.67	0.89	4.1
Stanford Achievement...........	16.26	6.38	9.88	1.91	5.2
Woodworth-Mathews...........	5	5.48	−0.48	0.93	0.5

In many cases one twin was reared in an environment that was vastly superior to that of his mate. Newman tried to discover the relation of the magnitude of the differences in traits to the magnitude of differences in environment. He rated each separate environment on three factors—educational, social, and physical characteristics. Differences in these ratings

Table 3–2. Correlation of Twin Differences on Certain Traits with Estimated Differences in Three Environmental Ratings

Traits	Environmental difference rating		
	Educational	Social	Physical
Height.................................	−.015	−.005	−.175
Weight.................................	−.095	.226	.599
Head length............................	−.139	−.256	−.102
Head width............................	−.024	.15	−.352
Cephalic index.........................	.105	.154	−.375
Binet I.Q..............................	.791	.509	.304
Otis I.Q...............................	.547	.533	−.225
International Test.......................	.462	.534	−.026
American Council Test..................	.57	.321	.082
Stanford Educational Age................	.908	.349	.139
Woodworth-Mathews....................	.044	−.075	−.291
Kent-Rosanoff:			
Common reaction.....................	−.218	.102	−.342
Frequency of response.................	−.272	.014	−.128
Pressey Emotions:			
Number crossed out...................	.249	−.418	.124
Number deviations....................	.221	.349	−.183
Downey Will-Temperament:			
Total score...........................	.411	.271	.465
Pattern difference....................	.435	.021	.142

were then correlated with twin differences on traits. These results are shown in Table 3–2. Note that educational and social factors in environment are very significant in mental and educational tests but most other correlations are too low to be significant.

It is obvious from these tables that environmental differences affect some traits more than others, and, from data not here shown, it is obvious that these differences affect some twins more than others. The small number of cases, however, makes any conclusions tentative.

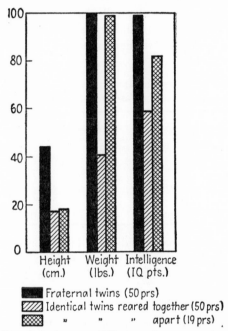

Fig. 3–4. Average differences between twins.

It is interesting to compare the differences of these 19 pairs of twins reared apart with the differences of identical twins reared together and fraternal twins reared together. Identical twins reared together are more alike in weight and intelligence than are identical twins reared apart. Height seems to be unaffected by whether they are reared together or apart. Fraternal twins reared together are more different in all three respects (height, weight, and intelligence) than identical twins. These differences are shown in Fig. 3–4.[7] If the data were available, it would be interesting to compare the differences of fraternal twins reared apart with the differences shown in this figure.

[7] The data for this graph are found in Newman, Freeman, and Holzinger, *op. cit.;* and Woodworth, R. S., Heredity and Environment, *Social Sci. Res. Counc. Bull.,* 1941, No. 47.

Foster Children Reared Together. When unrelated children are reared together any increase in similarity above the average (*i.e.,* correlation greater than zero) may properly be attributed to environment. Burks[8] studied a group of 214 adopted children in comparison with a control group of 105 children who were living with their natural parents. The control group was matched with the foster group in age of children; age, occupation, education, and social status of parents; and the cultural level of the home. The Stanford-Binet Intelligence Test was given to the parents and children of both groups and correlations computed between parents and children. Another study that followed the same pattern was performed by Leahy.[9] He used 194 children in each group, experimental and control. His results were quite similar to those of Burks. The data of both are given in Table 3–3.

Table 3–3. Correlations between the Intelligence of Children and That of Their Parents

	Burks data		Leahy data	
	Foster	Control	Foster	Control
Father and child..................	.07	.45	.19	.51
Mother and child..................	.19	.46	.24	.51
Cultural index of home.............	.25	.44	.26	.51

Both authors conclude that heredity is much more important than environment in determining the ability to do well on our intelligence tests. Burks says, "The maximal contribution of the best home environment to intelligence is apparently about 20 points, and almost surely lies between 10 and 30 points."

Freeman[10] studied three groups of foster children to find the effects of home culture on intelligence. The children in Group I were given intelligence tests before adoption and again several years after adoption. Forty-one of them were placed in homes of low cultural levels and 33 were placed in homes of higher cultural levels. The children in the better homes gained 5.3 I.Q. points while those in the poorer homes made no gain at all. However, it was found that children who were adopted into better homes after the age of twelve made no gains.

Group II consisted of 125 pairs of siblings who were adopted into different foster homes. They were found to correlate only .25 on intelligence

[8] Burks, B. S., The Relative Influence of Nature and Nurture, *27th Yearb. Nat. Soc. Stud. Educ.,* 1928, Part I, 219–316.

[9] Leahy, A. M., Nature-Nurture and Intelligence, *Genet. Psychol. Monogr.,* 1935, **17,** 236–308.

[10] Freeman, F. N., Holzinger, K. J., and Mitchell, B. D., The Influence of Environment, *27th Yearb. Nat. Soc. Stud. Educ.,* 1928, Part I, 103–217.

tests whereas siblings in natural homes correlate .50. Those sibling pairs who were adopted in homes of similar cultural levels correlated .30 while those who were adopted into homes of significantly different cultural levels correlated only .19.

The third group studied were children adopted into homes where there were other children, either natural or also adopted. There were 112 pairs of such foster siblings. The correlation here was .35 as compared with .50 for natural siblings in the same home.

For the entire group of children studied, there was a correlation of .48 between I.Q. and the cultural level of the home, of .37 between the foster child and the foster father, and of .28 between the foster child and the foster mother.

What, then, is the nature of the child at birth? He is a developing organism that has certain hereditary limitations beyond which development cannot go, and he has certain hereditary potentialities that may be developed *if* his environment (home, school, neighborhood, etc.) is appropriate for that development. Consequently, any test of his ability (either mental or physical) will be affected by both his hereditary potentialities and the degree to which his past environment has nurtured those potentialities. Obviously, the proper function of the home, the school, and the neighborhood is to provide for the greatest development of the native potentialities of every child.

MATURATION

It is characteristic of the human neonate (like that of any other newborn organism) that he functions as a coordinated mass of protoplasm, or as a whole. This is called "organic function," as distinguished from inorganic "elementalistic function" where each unit or part is capable of functioning alone. The neonate cannot move a finger or toe alone; he must move his entire body. This movement is head-centered and diffuses to other parts of his body.[11] As he grows older he becomes able to localize this behavior into a certain part of his body. Localized leg movements develop into walking, localized hand movements develop into writing, localized tongue movements develop into talking, etc. Maturation is a process of localizing and differentiating movements from immature gross total patterns into specific and more delicate patterns.

Maturation should be distinguished from learning. The end result of both is the establishment of behavior patterns, but maturation patterns are somehow inherent in the germ plasm while learning patterns are definitely inherent in environmental conditions. Maturation follows certain patterns regardless of environmental variations. Learning follows those

[11] See Irwin, O. C., The Amount and Nature of Activity in New Born Infants, *Genet. Psychol. Monogr.*, 1930, 8; and Coghill, G. E., *Anatomy and the Problem of Behavior*, The Macmillan Company, New York, 1929.

patterns that are determined by environmental variations. A child will become adolescent, or attain the same height, or see with the same acuity, whether he lives in the torrid or the frigid zones, whether he lives in the city or the country, whether his parents are rich or poor, whether he goes to school or works in a factory, in short, regardless of his environment. But, a child will learn to speak English, or French, or Russian, depending on early environment. He will learn to operate a typewriter, or play the piano, or drive an automobile, or draw the plans for a building, if his environment trains him in such behavior patterns. Therefore, it is important in rearing children to know which behavior patterns are the result of maturation and which ones are learned.

PHYSICAL MATURATION

When a behavior pattern develops, or matures, it may involve any one or any combination of the following factors—accuracy or precision, speed, steadiness, and strength. A certain degree of development in all four factors is necessary for any behavior but the amount of each varies greatly with the type of behavior. Piano playing requires considerably more accuracy and speed but less steadiness and strength than working as a steeple jack, for example. Billiard playing requires great precision, speed, and steadiness but not much strength. Torch welding requires steadiness and precision but neither speed nor strength. Then, individuals differ greatly in their propensities in these four behavior factors. Some are naturally strong but lack the factors of accuracy, speed, and steadiness. Others are highly accurate, others are very fast, and others excel in steadiness.

Psychologists have developed apparatus for measuring each of these factors. Dynamometers measure strength, tracing boards measure steadiness and accuracy, a telegraph key and Veeder counter measure speed, and various pegboards and assembly tests measure all these factors in combination. Tables of norms for each of these factors have been developed for children of different ages.[12]

Physical maturation is not uniform in the developmental life of the child, nor is it uniform between children. Figure 3–5 illustrates the patterns of maturation of three children. Note that they are all equally mature at the age of eighteen, but at any previous age A is precocious and C is retarded. All three children develop rapidly during a period between childhood and adulthood, although they vary in the age boundaries of this period. At age six, for example, A has undergone 34 per cent of his maturity, B has undergone 25 per cent of his maturity, and C has undergone but 17 per cent of his maturity. It is always difficult to determine whether an atypical child is maturing atypically or has atypical heredity.

[12] See Brace, D. K., *Measuring Motor Ability,* A. S. Barnes and Company, New York, 1927.

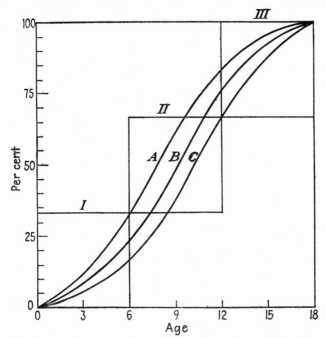

FIG. 3–5. Showing accelerated (*A*), normal (*B*), and retarded (*C*) patterns of maturation.

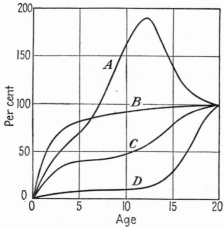

FIG. 3–6. Maturation patterns of various body organ systems: (*A*) Lymph, (*B*) neural, (*C*) muscles and bones, (*D*) sex.

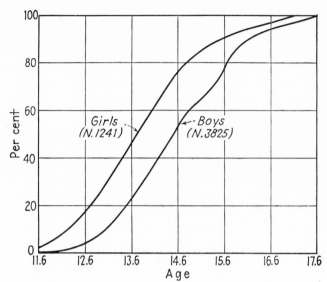

Fig. 3–7. Age of pubescence of boys and girls.

Table 3–4. Normative Summary for Walking

Activity	Normal Age Range, Weeks
Lifts head momentarily when on stomach	4– 8
Raises upper chest when on stomach	16–36
Sits with body erect, supported	20–28
Sits with slight or no support	20–32
Sits one minute or more	32–40
Rolls from back to stomach	32–40
Sits for indefinite period	40–56
Crawls	40–52
Creeps	44–56
Stands only when both hands are supported	36
Pulls to standing position	48–56
Stands independently without support	56
Walks using support	48–56
Walks independently	56

Note that Fig. 3–5 tells the entire story of maturation from fertilization to complete maturity. Often only segments of maturation are studied. Suppose that the maturation of A is studied between the ages of six and nine. Only that part of the curve contained in box II would then be shown. A complete maturation curve is always S-shaped.

Physical maturation also varies greatly between bodily organs within the child himself. Figure 3–6 shows the average pattern of maturation in the average child for four divisions of body organs, or organic systems. Note that the lymph system reaches greatest maturity at the age of twelve, which is 190 per cent of its maturity at the age of twenty. On the other hand, the sex system is still relatively dormant at the age of twelve. Of course, there are accelerated and retarded patterns of development for each of these organic divisions. Some children begin sex maturation (puberty) at the age of ten and others at the age of sixteen. Individual differences between children, as suggested in Fig. 3–5, also exist in each of the four patterns of maturation shown in Fig. 3–6.

Patterns of maturation vary between the sexes. Girls mature more rapidly after the age of eight than do boys. Figure 3–7 shows the age at which boys and girls become pubescent. At the age of twelve, for example, 30 per cent of the girls and only 10 per cent of the boys are pubescent. At the age of fifteen, 84 per cent of the girls and 66 per cent of the

Table 3–5. The California Infant Scale of Motor Development

Activity	Age, Months
Head erect—vertical	1.9
Head erect and steady	2.9
Turns from side to side	3.4
Sits with support	3.5
Holds head steady	3.6
Beginning thumb opposition	4.1
Sits with slight support	4.6
Turns from back to side	5
Partial thumb opposition	5.1
Sits alone momentarily	5.7
Pulls to sitting position	6.2
Rolls from back to stomach	7
Complete thumb opposition	7.6
Partial finger prehension	7.8
Sits alone with good coordination	8.5
Fine prehension with pellet	9.3
Raises self to sitting position	9.4
Pulls to standing position	10.5
Stands up	10.6
Walks with help	11.6
Sits down	12.5
Stands alone	12.5
Walks alone	13
Walks upstairs with help	20.3
Walks downstairs with help	20.5
Walks upstairs alone; marks time	24.3
Walks downstairs alone; marks time	24.5
Jumps off floor; both feet	28
Stands on one foot alone	29.2
Walks upstairs alternating forward foot	35.5
Walks tiptoe 3 meters	36.2
Jumps from height of 30 cm	37.1
Distance jump, 36–60 cm	39.7
Hops on right foot less than 2 meters	49.3

boys have become pubescent. When weight and height are plotted in terms of percentage at age eighteen, the curves are quite like those in Fig. 3–7.

Norm tables of physical maturation have been constructed from studies of the development of large groups of children. Two of these are reproduced in Tables 3–4[13] and 3–5[14]. Variation from these norms does not always mean that a child is innately handicapped. As indicated in Table 3–4, a child may be retarded in physical development for a few years and yet be perfectly normal at the adult level. However, variations from normal physical development should be watched carefully for other indications of hereditary handicap. Children with inferior heredity do mature more slowly than do normal children.

MENTAL MATURATION

The pattern for mental maturation is much like that for physical maturation. Normal variations occur similar to those shown in Fig. 3–4.

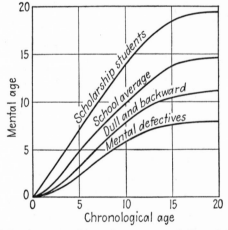

FIG. 3–8. Mental development of superior, average, dull, and defective children.

Also, variations occur within the child himself in the patterns of maturation of the various mental traits, similar to the variations of physical traits illustrated in Fig. 3–5. When a large number of mental traits are taken together, such as those measured by intelligence tests, the pattern of maturation is then an average of that for all those traits. Figure 3–8 shows the patterns of mental development for children of superior, average, and

[13] From Gesell, A. and Thompson, H., *The Psychology of Early Growth,* The Macmillan Company, New York, 1938.
[14] From Bayley, N., The Development of Motor Skill during the First Three Years, *Nat. Res. Council Monogr.* I, 1935.

inferior mental aptitudes. Note that mental differences become more pronounced as the children get older. The reason is that mental tests measure the effects of an aptitude functioning in its environment. These effects are cumulative so that a limited aptitude in a limited environment or a superior aptitude in a superior environment becomes more obvious in measurement. This same effect is apparent when an individual child is tested successively over a period of time. Figure 3–9 shows the results of successive tests given approximately a year apart to a child who was two

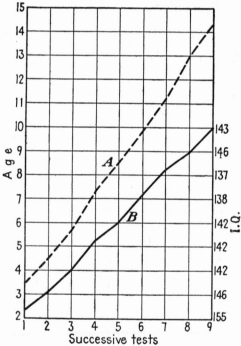

FIG. 3–9. Mental age (A) of a child at successive chronological ages (B).

years old at the first test and ten at the last one. The distance between his mental age and his chronological age becomes ever greater. However, note that the I.Q. remains fairly constant.

The two problems suggested in the preceding paragraph—the distribution of intelligence and the constancy of intelligence—are of sufficient significance for further attention.

The Distribution of Intelligence. Like any other trait in nature, intelligence is distributed in a normal manner if enough cases are considered. Bradley[15] measured the intelligence of some 1,500 junior and senior

[15] Bradley, W. A., Correlates of Vocational Preferences, *Genet. Psychol. Monogr.*, 1943, 28.

high school pupils in the Philadelphia region and found that even in such a select group there is a fairly symmetrical distribution. These data are shown in Table 3–6.

Table 3–6. Distribution of Intelligence and A Grades of 1,500 High School Pupils

I.Q.	Per cent	Per cent of A grades	Ratio
140–149	0.2	3.2	16.0
130–139	1.3	10.6	8.1
120–129	7.5	25.5	3.4
110–119	22.5	35.1	1.6
100–109	32.5	18.1	0.6
90–99	25.3	4.3	0.2
80–89	9.7	3.2	0.3
70–79	1.0	0.0	0.0

Incidentally, Bradley also found that the pupils with the higher I.Q.'s also made the highest grades in high school. This is shown in the last column of Table 3–6. Intelligence is closely related to vocabulary size.

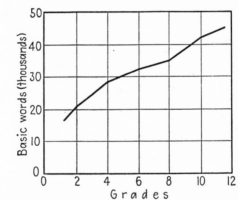

FIG. 3–10. Growth of vocabulary through elementary and high school.

Figure 3–10 shows the average increase in vocabulary through the grades and high school.[16]

Pressey and Robinson[17] summarized a mass of research and interpreted it in a table showing the distribution of children at each I.Q. level, the adult mental-age equivalent, the more popular classification terminology, and the academic and vocational possibilities. This summary is reproduced in Table 3–7.

[16] Smith, Mary K., Measurement of the Size of General English Vocabulary, *Genet. Psychol. Monogr.*, 1941, 24, 311–345.

[17] Pressey, S. L., and Robinson, F. P., *Psychology and the New Education*, p. 89, Harper & Brothers, New York, 1944.

Table 3–7. Intelligence Levels and Their Significance

I.Q.	Per cent	Adult M.A.	Classification	Academic possibility	Vocational possibility
140 up	.6	21 up	Very superior	Graduate	Professional, executive
120–139	9.9	18 –21	Superior	Technical	Professional, technical
110–119	16	16.5–18	High average	College	Technical, business
90–109	47	13.5–16.5	Average	High school	Clerical, skilled
80– 89	16	12 –13.5	Low average	9th grade	Semiskilled
70– 79	7.5	10.5–12	Inferior	7th grade	Routine work
60– 69	2.4	9 –10.5	Borderline deficient	5th grade	Unskilled labor
50– 59	.5	7.5–9	Deficient	3rd grade	Simplest labor
Below 50	.1	Below 7.5	Very deficient	Special class	Unemployable

The Constancy of the I.Q. Mental age is obtained by giving a child a mental test and then comparing his score with that made by a large number of other children. If his score is the same as that made by children who are seven years and six months old (ninety months), let us say, he is then considered to have a mental age of seven years and six months. Now, if his chronological age is also seven years and six months, a quotient obtained by dividing his mental age by his chronological age will be exactly 100. (The decimal point is always dropped.) It is obvious that if his mental age had been greater than his chronological age, the quotient would have been greater than 100. Or, if his mental age had been less than his chronological age, the quotient would have been less than 100.

If the child develops mentally at exactly the same rate as other children tested (from which a table of norms has been constructed by which all test scores are interpreted into equivalent mental ages) his I.Q. will remain constant. However, if his mental development is faster than that of other children, his I.Q. will increase. Likewise, if his mental development is slower than that of other children, his I.Q. will decrease.

Thorndike[18] has found that in 1 year the average variation in I.Q. is 5.32 points and in 9 years it is 9.34 points. Therefore, variations of no greater than these averages, regardless of the conditions, must be expected.

Cattell [19] found that the average median difference in I.Q. was only 1.7

[18] Thorndike, E. L., The Effects of the Interval between Test and Retest on the Constancy of the I.Q., *J. Educ. Psychol.*, 1933, **24**, 543–549.

[19] Cattell, P., Constant Changes in the Stanford-Binet I.Q., *J. Educ. Psychol.*, 1931, **22**, 544–550.

I.Q. points when 1,383 children were measured at intervals of from three months to six years. These data are shown in Table 3–8.

Table 3–8. Constancy of the I.Q. of 1,383 School Children

Time between Tests	Median Difference in I.Q. Points
3 months	5.0
6 months	3.8
1 year	0.2
1½ years	2.0
2 years	0.5
3 years	0.2
4 years	2.7
5 years	1.0
6 years	0.1

Wellman and a group of her associates at the University of Iowa, however, have amassed a body of data indicating that in *atypical* environment the I.Q. will vary significantly more than the average. The longer the child remains in that environment the more its I.Q. will become typical of that cultural level. Gordon[20] found as long ago as 1923 that English children living on canal boats and gypsy children apparently become less intelligent as they grow older. He found a correlation of —.75 between intelligence and age for canal-boat children and —.57 for gypsy children. Speer[21] found that this is likewise true of the children of feeble-minded mothers. The older the children of feeble-minded mothers, the nearer they approach their mothers in I.Q. Speer's data are shown in Table 3–9.

Table 3–9. The I.Q. of Children of Feeble-minded Mothers

Age of child	N	Median I.Q.
– 2	12	100.5
3– 5	19	83.7
6– 8	12	74.6
9–11	9	71.5
12–15	16	53.1

Barrett and Koch[22] studied the effects of nursery-school environment on a group of orphanage children in comparison with a control group (matched as to age, sex, and mental age) that did not attend nursery school. The mean I.Q. of the nursery-school group increased 20.9 I.Q.

[20] Gordon, Hugh, Mental and Scholastic Tests among Retarded Children, *London Bd. Educ. Pamph.* 44, 1923.

[21] Speer, G. S., The Mental Development of Children of Feeble-minded and Normal Mothers, *39th Yearb. Nat. Soc. Stud. Educ.*, 1940, Part II.

[22] Barrett, H. E., and Koch, H. L., The Effects of Nursery School Training upon the Mental Test Performance of a Group of Orphanage Children, *J. Genet. Psychol.*, 1930, **37**, 102–122.

points, whereas that of the control group increased only 5.1 points. Wellman's series of studies[23] substantiate these results.

Studies of children in restricted environments all report that there are progressive decreases in I.Q. with advancing chronological age. The results of three of these studies are shown in Table 3–10.[24]

Table 3–10. The I.Q.'s of Children Reared in Restricted Environments at Various Ages

	Ages				
	7	9	11	13	15
Kentucky Mountains (Asher)	83	74	66	63	61
Tennessee Mountains (Wheeler)	..	95	87	79	73
Underprivileged homes (Skeels)	92	80	83	80	

On the other hand, McNemar and others disagree that the I.Q. is so subject to environmental variations. Much of the confusion is due to the use of the term "intelligence." When intelligence means mental limitations as determined by innate germ plasm, it is obvious that no environmental condition can affect it. Heredity is fixed from the moment of fertilization. However, when intelligence means the results on mental tests and is interpreted by tables of norms established by testing other children, it is obvious that environmental variations will affect the results. The need for further research and more careful thinking about this problem is obvious.

PERSONALITY DEVELOPMENT

Personality is the sum total of the ways a person affects other people. The rating of a personality is determined by what acquaintances think about a person's habits, ideas, ideals, appearance, etc. If they are attracted by a person, he is said to have a good personality. If they are affected adversely, he is said to have a poor personality. "How to win friends and influence people" is another way of saying "How to develop a good personality."

The child is constantly forming habits of doing things that eventually will affect other people favorably or unfavorably. He is forming his personality. Of course, he does not realize this, and seldom do his parents.

[23] These are reviewed in the 39th Yearb. Nat. Soc. Stud. Educ., Chap. 26, 1940, Part II.

[24] Asher, E. J., The Inadequacy of Current Intelligence Tests for Testing Kentucky Mountain Children, J. Genet. Psychol., 1935, 46, 480–486. Wheeler, L. R., The Intelligence of East Tennessee Mountain Children, J. Educ. Psychol., 1932, 23, 351–370. Skeels, H. M., and Fillmore, E. A., Mental Development of Children from Underprivileged Homes, J. Genet. Psychol., 1937, 50, 427–439.

Personality is the by-product of living. It is constantly developing and more and more becoming fixed. The pattern of adult personality is usually fairly well fixed by the age of ten. Even in the first two years, behavior patterns are formed that are recognizable on adult levels.

Some personality factors are definitely learned (habits, ideas, ideals, attitudes, interests, etc.) and others are more limited by heredity (complexion, stature, physiological reactions, limits of learning, etc.) However, within hereditary limitations any child can develop a good or a poor personality depending on his cultural environment (home, school, neighborhood, etc.)

EMOTIONAL DEVELOPMENT

The word *emotion* refers to almost any kind of behavior that is caused by overstimulation. Routine experiences of daily living are not usually emotional. They provoke neither enjoyment nor annoyance. There is no overstimulation nor consequent feeling of pleasure or displeasure. How-

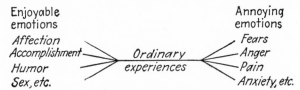

FIG. 3–11. Opposing types of emotion.

ever, episodes arise that cause the person to experience emotion, even though there may be no outer manifestation of it. Emotion is always accompanied by an inner feeling and usually by some sort of outer or overt expression of it.

Emotions are of two opposing types—enjoyable and annoying. The young child indicates the presence of the former by laughing and the latter by crying. As he grows older he modifies this behavior as determined by his experience and training. Figure 3–11 illustrates these two opposing classifications.

Children (and adults) differ greatly in their susceptibility to emotional stimulation. Some become emotional easily, and therefore frequently, while others are more stable. Some feel more often and more intensely than others. They are more emotional. Children also differ in emotionality at different times. A hungry child is more emotionally sensitive than he is after he has been fed. This is illustrated in Fig. 3–12. Note that 11 A.M., 5:30 P.M. (before meals), and 8:30 P.M. (before bedtime) are times of greatest anger outbursts.[25]

There is likewise a great difference between children in their ways of

[25] Goodenough, F. L., *Anger in Young Children,* University of Minnesota Press, Minneapolis, 1931.

expressing emotion or in their behavior while in the emotional state. Some are very expressive and their emotional states are quite obvious. Others are apparently calm and unemotional although they may be "boiling inside." They repress their emotions. (More is said of this in Chap. 6.)

The physiological factors in emotion are not too well known but some things seem fairly clear. The pleasant emotions (sometimes called positive) are accompanied by the function of the cranial and sacral sections of the autonomic nervous system. The organs of the upper viscera are connected to the cranial section, which promotes digestion and other vegetative processes. The sacral section is connected with the organs of the

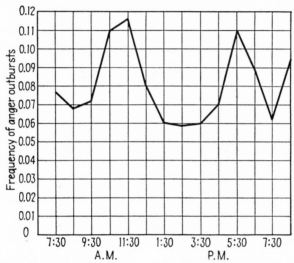

FIG. 3–12. Diurnal variations in frequency of outbursts of anger among young children. (*From Goodenough.*)

lower viscera and promotes the elimination of waste products (bladder and bowels) and sex behavior. The unpleasant emotions are accompanied by the function of the sympathetic section of the autonomic nervous system. This is connected to all organs of the viscera and inhibits the functions promoted by the cranial and sacral sections. Digestive processes are interrupted, heartbeat and blood pressure are increased, glycogen is converted to glucose and poured into the blood stream at an increased rate, muscles become tense, and the body is set for action. The body is in a state of annoying emotion. Obviously, the physiological processes of the enjoyable emotions promote bodily welfare, while those of the annoying emotions are debilitating. However, these physiological processes during both the enjoyable and the annoying emotions are more intense than in ordinary experiences.

The scientific study of emotion began with the research of John B. Watson to find, first, which emotions are original, or unlearned, and second, how emotions are learned. He studied newly born babies to find what stimuli would produce emotion. He discovered that the pleasant emotions are produced (in addition to satisfying the child's vegetative needs) by fondling or gently stroking the baby's body. He found that the unpleasant emotions are produced by loud noises, falling, and restraint of movement. He called these the "unlearned emotions." Then, he found that, when the baby experiences an inadequate emotional stimulus at the same time as the unlearned adequate emotional stimulus, this too became adequate to produce the emotion. For example, in one of Watson's experiments, a baby was accustomed to playing with a rabbit without fear. (It was an inadequate emotional stimulus.) Then, a loud noise (an adequate emotional stimulus) was produced at the same time the baby played with the rabbit. Soon the baby reacted to the rabbit in the same way he did to the loud noise. The new emotional stimulus became a substitute for the old one.[26]

Watson then concluded that most of our loves, fears, hates, etc., are learned. We do not instinctively fear snakes, or hate other races, or love our own flesh and blood, or enjoy the praise of other people. We (perhaps) inherit emotionality, or the equipment for emotional behavior, but the objects or stimuli that arouse these emotions are definitely learned.

Annoying, or negative, emotions should be avoided whenever possible. Any environmental condition that arouses the child's dissatisfying emotions is bad for the child. Both the home and the school should be so regulated that the child is protected, as much as possible, from unusually intense overstimulation.

Avoidable Conditions in the Home That Cause Annoying Emotions. Children often become emotional by observing other members of the family who are emotional. Peculiar fears, such as fear of the dark, and unusual antagonisms, such as race hatreds, are often learned from other members of a family. A child learns to be hot-tempered by associating with others who are hot-tempered. Emotional parents produce emotional children by training as well as by heredity "Like father, like son."

In some families, a child is often the "goat," or "butt end" of jokes. This irritates him and soon ruins even a good disposition. Teasing should never be allowed in any form.

Parents often create emotional situations by wishy-washy discipline. Some orders are allowed to be violated and others are enforced. The child never knows whether to resist or to obey. This lack of regularity usually carries over to other things. There is no certainty about anything. Unstable living promotes unstable emotions.

[26] This process is called "conditioning" and is more adequately explained in the next chapter. Watson's experiment is described on p. 29.

Pressey and Robinson[27] report that, in a certain city having 1,800 blocks of single-family residences, there were but 86 emotionally unstable, or maladjusted, school children per 1,000 enrolled. In 750 city blocks of multiple-family dwellings in the same city, there were 183 emotionally unstable school children per each 1,000 enrolled. Other factors associated with maladjuted children are shown in Table 3–11.

Table 3–11. Factors Related to Maladjustment in School Children

Factor	Per Cent
Fathers—unskilled laborers	67
Fathers—semiskilled	22
Fathers—clerical	8
Fathers—professional	3
Inadequate family income	90
Living with neither parent	15
Living with stepparent	20
Living with mother only	62
Homes rated very poor	66
Child underweight	35

Avoidable Conditions in the School and Neighborhood That Cause Annoying Emotions. Perhaps the greatest cause of emotional tension in school is "goose-stepping," or regimentation. All children are poured through the same mold, given the same courses, treated in the same way. This discourages originality and promotes submerged resentment. Perhaps the most basic principle of the progressive-education movement is that of individualized education. The mass-production methods of the average American schoolroom are undoubtedly the worst aspect of our educational system.

Another frequent source of emotional irritation in the schoolroom is the teacher herself. Intellectually, teachers are usually well trained. They know their subject matter. They know the best methods of teaching. They know the advantages and weaknesses of various methods of discipline. But they are not always emotionally stable. They have not learned how to behave intelligently when they become irritated. Consequently, they create situations that bring about emotional stress in their pupils. Hart[28] reports a survey of 3,725 high school seniors to find the traits of best-liked and those of least-liked teachers. His results are shown in Table 3–12.

Then, too, the content of the curriculum itself is often so anachronistic and impractical that it is irritating to the child. Little of it has any value in his life outside of school. (We adults know that much of it has no value even in adult life.) Consequently the child lacks motivation and the teacher uses threats of punishment to force him to learn. This not only

[27] Pressey and Robinson, op. cit. p. 167.
[28] Hart, F. W., Teachers and Training, The Macmillan Company, New York, 1934.

Table 3–12. Four Most Frequently Mentioned Traits of Best-liked Teachers and of Least-liked Teachers

Best-liked Teachers	Times Mentioned
Helpful with schoolwork, explains lessons clearly	1,950
Cheerful, jolly, can take a joke	1,429
Human, friendly, companionable, "one of us"	1,024
Interested in and understands pupils	1,024
Least-liked Teachers	
Cross, crabby, nagging, sarcastic, loses temper	1,708
Not helpful with schoolwork, work not planned	1,025
Has favored students and picks on others	859
Haughty, overbearing, does not know you out of class	775

causes him to develop a dislike for schoolwork but also to develop constant nervous tension, which makes him even more emotionally sensitive. Schoolwork should be made to fit the child instead of trying to force him to fit a course of study that has doubtful value anyhow. This is the point of view of progressive education.[29]

INTERESTS AND ATTITUDES

Interest refers to that behavior which an individual may persist in manifesting because it gives him a feeling of enjoyment. Referring to the graph, Fig. 3–11, interesting behavior is located left of the center of the straight line designated as "ordinary experiences." When ordinary experiences are enjoyable, the individual tries to prolong them. This is called interested behavior.

Whether or not behavior is interesting depends on a number of conditions. First, if the individual has an aptitude for the behavior he is likely to perform it more successfully and therefore derive more enjoyment from it. Second, if there are no annoying factors, whether primary or secondary, in the behavior situation the enjoyment is greater than when these interfere. There is more interest. Third, if other people approve of the behavior, this additional enjoyment supplements the natural enjoyment and the tendency to prolong and repeat the behavior is greater.

It should be noted that interest is not an innate and immutable factor. Its permanence depends on the continued satisfaction derived from the behavior. If the three conditions mentioned above—innate aptitude for the behavior, freedom from annoying factors, and social approval—are all present, interest will then persist.

Attitude is a predisposition to respond to a situation with approval or disapproval. It is closely related to interest, except that it may also be

[29] See Dewey, John, *Democracy and Education,* The Macmillan Company, New York, 1916; Rugg, H., and Shumaker, A., *The Child Centered School,* World Book Company, Yonkers, New York, 1928; Gray, J. S., *Psychological Foundations of Education,* American Book Company, New York, 1935; Kilpatrick, W. H., *The Educational Frontier,* Appleton-Century-Crofts, Inc., New York, 1933.

Table 3–13. The Most Popular Play Activities of 26,058 Boys and Girls at Four Age Levels

Boys	Age	Girls
Playing with a ball Playing with blocks Playing with a wagon Playing house Playing horse Hide-and-seek Playing tag Drawing Playing school Playing in sand pile	5	Playing house Playing with dolls Playing with a ball Playing school Drawing Mulberry bush Playing with blocks Skipping Making things Jumping rope
Football Baseball Boxing Just playing catch Riding a bicycle Basketball Wrestling Roller skating Marbles	10	Playing the piano Going to the movies Looking at the "funny paper" Playing with dolls Roller skating Riding in an automobile Reading books Jacks Listening to the victrola
Basket ball Football Baseball Driving an automobile Tennis Watching athletic sports Hunting Going to the movies Boxing Reading books	15	Reading books Going to the movies Social dancing Playing the piano Riding in an automobile Having dates Watching athletic sports Going to parties, picnics Basketball Doing gymnasium work
Having dates Watching athletic sports Football Basketball Listening to the radio Going to the movies Driving an automobile Reading the newspaper Tennis Baseball	20	Social dancing Playing the piano Having dates Going to entertainments, etc. Just hiking or strolling Going to the movies Reading books Watching athletic sports Card games Riding in an automobile

negative. (Interest can be only positive; it varies only in degree.) An attitude may be strongly negative, or strongly positive, or not exist at all. For example, an individual may have a strong negative attitude (disapproval) toward one nation, a strong positive attitude (approval) toward another, and no attitude at all toward another. Like interest, an attitude is formed from experience. Enjoyable experience usually results in positive attitudes while enjoyable experiences result in negative attitudes.

A strong attitude does not necessarily indicate a strong interest. One may approve of baseball and yet not be interested in playing or seeing it. One may disapprove of socialism and yet be greatly interested in how it works. Interest is closely associated with one's desires, likes, and wants; attitude refers to one's appraisal of evaluation of an idea or situation.

Children's Interests. The major interests of children center around different forms of play. In the early years this is largely manipulative and individualistic. Later, it becomes more complex and socialized. Lehman and Witty[30] studied the play activities of some 26,000 children and youth to find the trend of play interests. They found that play becomes more vigorous, more complex, more socialized, and more sex discriminative as the child grows older. However, as he passes adolescence and reaches the adult level (age twenty) he becomes less active himself and more interested in watching activity. These results are shown in Table 3–13.

Children's reading interests also undergo major changes as they become older. Younger children are interested in fairy stories and highly illustrated

Table 3–14. Percentages of Children Interested in Various Types of Books

Type of book	Ages							
	Boys				Girls			
	9–11	12–13	14–16	17–18	9–11	12–13	14–16	17–18
Adult fiction.........	4	6	18	30	15	33	45	58
Juvenile fiction.......	27	19	11	9	67	44	30	13
Adventure...........	56	64	59	49	12	17	18	22
Miscellaneous........	13	11	12	12	6	6	7	7
Number of children...	59	253	846	283	87	336	1,195	414

reading, such as the comic strips. Later, adventure stories and juvenile fiction become more popular. Jordan[31] surveyed the books read by several thousand school children and found results as shown in Table 3–14.

[30] Lehman, H. C., and Witty, P. A., *The Psychology of Play Activities*, A. S. Barnes and Company, New York, 1927.

[31] Jordan, A. M., *Educational Psychology*, p. 160, Henry Holt and Company, Inc., New York, 1942.

Johnson[32] made a study of the parts of the newspaper read by the school children in Duluth (grades 5 to 11). He found the comic page at the head of the list for both boys and girls at all ages. The front page was relatively high for both sexes (it increased with age), and the sport page was high for the boys. All other parts of the newspaper were read by less than 50 per cent of the children. Even the children's page was read by only 30 per cent of the boys and 44 per cent of the girls.

An interesting study of the vocational interests of children was made by Lehman and Witty.[33] They gave a vocational attitude test to 27,000 school children ranging in age from eight to sixteen years. Changes in the vocational interests of boys with increase in age is shown in Table 3–15.

Table 3–15. Rank of Occupations Liked Best by Boys of School Age

Occupations	Ages					
	8½	10½	12½	14½	16½	18½
Aviator	2	1	1	1	1	1
Cowboy	1	2	2	16		
Lawyer	6	10	7	10	4	3
Civil engineer	..	8	3	2	3	7
Physician	11	10	11	11	6	6
Army officer	14	3	6	24	21	8
Musician	20	14	10	7	9	5
Electrical engineer	..	20	5	3	2	4
Architect	..	..	17	4	5	2
Physical director or coach	..	..	..	23	11	4
Soldier	3	4	20			

Fleege[34] studied the topics of conversation of some 2,000 high school boys. While he found that there was some change of interests as indicated by the topics they discussed (especially regarding girls, social events, and sex), there was little indication that high school boys are much interested in world happenings or future vocation. These data are shown in Table 3–16.

Children's Attitudes. An attitude is the part of a situation that an individual carries with him. A child responds to his teacher, for example, not as the teacher really is but as she is when combined with the predisposition toward her that the child carries within himself. The teacher may be aided or handicapped by this attitude, but she cannot escape from it.

[32] Johnson, B. L., Children's Reading Interests as Related to Sex and Grade in School, *Sch. Rev.*, 1932, **40**, 257–272.

[33] Lehman, H. C., and Witty, P. A., One More Study of Permanence of Interest, *J. Educ. Psychol.*, 1931, **22**, 481–492.

[34] Fleege, U. H., *Self-revelation of the Adolescent Boy*, The Bruce Publishing Company, Milwaukee, 1945.

Table 3–16. Topics Discussed Most Frequently by High School Boys
(Data in per cent)

Topic	Year in high school			
	First	Second	Third	Fourth
Sports.................................	62.0	80.2	75.0	75.1
Girls..................................	53.6	76.6	70.6	80.0
School, studies, etc......................	27.0	27.2	29.0	27.3
Social activities.........................	9.6	16.0	20.0	24.2
Sex...................................	11.2	12.4	16.4	20.1
Movies................................	16.4	10.4	9.0	7.6
World happenings.......................	7.6	7.9	7.1	10.6
Autos, airplanes, etc.....................	5.4	8.2	7.4	7.0
Personal experiences.....................	6.0	3.2	2.0	1.6
Hobbies...............................	2.5	3.2	4.4	2.0
Money................................	1.2	2.8	3.0	3.1
Future vocation.........................	1.2	1.4	1.6	4.7
Miscellaneous: religion, home, food, clothes, etc.	4.0	2.2	3.2	4.3

Attitudes are formed as soon as the child begins to learn, and they may last as long as he lives. Obviously, the home is fundamentally important in the development of attitudes. This is shown in a study that measured the attitudes of parents and children on religion, war, and communism.[35] Table 3–17 shows the correlations between the various members of the families studied.

Table 3–17. Parent-child Correlations in Attitude

	Church	War	Communism
Mothers—sons...........................	.57	.45	.58
Mothers—daughters......................	.69	.43	.49
Fathers—sons...........................	.64	.45	.54
Fathers—daughters......................	.64	.43	.62
All siblings.............................	.59	.36	.47
Mothers—fathers........................	.75	.43	.57

Attitudes are also affected by reading material. Annis and Meier[36] studied the effects of favorable and unfavorable editorials on the attitudes of two groups of college students concerning a visiting politician. One group read the favorable editorials and the other read the unfavorable editorials. The results of this study are shown in Fig. 3–13. Perhaps the

[35] Newcomb, T. M., and Svehla, G., Intra-family Relationships in Attitude, *Sociometry*, 1937, 1, 180–205.
[36] Annis, A. D., and Meier, N. C., The Induction of Opinion through Suggestion by Means of Planted Content, *J. Soc. Psychol.*, 1934, 5, 65–81.

reason there is so little overlapping between the two groups is that the politician was relatively unknown to both groups before the editorials were read.

Voelker[37] conducted an experiment to evaluate the effects of boy-scout training on attitudes toward trustworthiness. Two groups of scouts and

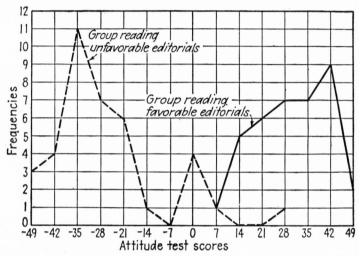

FIG. 3–13. Attitude scores toward a visiting politician as affected by editorials.

two groups of boys who were not scouts were given two trustworthiness tests within a 7-week interval. During the interval the scouts were given regular scout training in trustworthiness. The tests were practical life situations in which the boys were given an opportunity to be dishonest

Table 3–18. The Effects of Boy Scout Training on the Attitude of Trustworthiness

Group	First test, per cent	Second test, per cent	Gain, per cent
Scouts I............................	63.5	77	13.5
Scouts II...........................	64.5	74.4	9.9
Control I...........................	75	67.4	− 7.6
Control II..........................	58.2	48	−10.2
Average difference favoring scout groups........................			20.6

with money, to tell an untruth, to retain borrowed property, etc. There were 10 such items on each test. During the 7-week interval the scouts gained almost 21 per cent in trustworthiness over that of the control group. The results are shown in Table 3–18.

[37] Voelker, P. F., The Function of Ideals and Attitudes in Social Education, *Teach. Coll. Contr. Educ.*, 1921, No. 112.

Motion pictures have been found to have lasting effects on the attitudes of children. Peterson[38] tested children's attitudes toward certain topics and then showed the children moving pictures dealing with those topics. She tested them again immediately after the picture and again after intervals of varying length. She found that significant changes in attitudes were produced by motion pictures and that a large percentage of these changes remained after several months time. Her results are shown in Table 3–19.

Table 3–19. Effects and Permanence of Motion Pictures on Attitudes

Picture	Attitude	Change (raw score)	Difference P.E.d	Permanence remaining after	
				Mo.	%
Sons of the Gods	Pro-Chinese	1.31	17.	19	60
Birth of a Nation	Anti-Negro	1.53	25.	5	62
Four Sons	Pro-German	.47	5.37		
The Criminal Code	Prison reform	.50	. . . . .	9	78

It is now obvious that children's attitudes are produced by experience and they can be changed by controlling that experience. The success of Nazi Germany in producing a generation of fanatics by controlled education (both in school and out) indicates how effectively attitudes can be molded under totalitarian conditions.

SUMMARY

Children live within the confines of three limitations—heredity, immaturity, and environment. Every child is born with *hereditary* limits beyond which no development and training will enable him to go. These limits may be greater than those of the average child, less than those of the average child, or equal to those of the average child. Whatever the degree, they are immutable. Then, the child is also limited by his *immaturity*. Growth expands these limitations. The child is more able to learn as he grows and matures. Learning that is impossible at one age may become easy at a later age. However, the limitations of immaturity are also immutable except as the age factor varies. The third limitation is *environment*. The child with superior musical aptitude (hereditary limits less than those of the average child), for example, may or may not develop musical ability depending on whether or not his environment stimulates his interest in music and provides the facilities for training him.

[38] Peterson, R. G., *et. al., Motion Pictures and the Social Attitudes of Children,* The Macmillan Company, New York, 1933.

With the progress of culture, educational opportunities for the development of an ever-increasing range of aptitudes are augmented.

It has been found that adult personalities are largely determined by the experience of childhood. In other words, they are formed during the years of maturation. Emotions and interests constitute the major habits of personality and have been studied carefully. Certain factors in the home, school, and neighborhood have been found to be closely associated with emotional instability, whereas other factors seem to produce emotional stability. Likewise, children's interests and attitudes are determined by factors in their environments. Consequently, it is fundamentally important to control the child's environment if his personality development is to be controlled.

RECOMMENDED SUPPLEMENTARY READINGS

Barker, R. G., Kounin, J. S., and Wright, H. F.: *Child Behavior and Development,* McGraw-Hill Book Company, Inc., New York, 1943.

Carmichael, L.: *Manual of Child Psychology,* John Wiley & Sons, Inc., New York, 1946.

Garrison, K. C.: *Growth and Development,* Longmans, Green & Co., Inc., New York, 1952.

Jersild, A. D.: *Child Psychology,* Prentice-Hall, Inc., New York, 1947.

Merry, F. S., and Merry, R. V.: *From Infancy to Adolescence,* Harper & Brothers, New York, 1940.

Olson, W. C.: *Child Development,* D. C. Heath and Company, Boston, 1949.

Thorpe, L. P.: *Child Psychology and Development,* The Ronald Press Company, New York, 1946.

Tyler, L. E.: *Psychology of Human Development,* Appleton-Century-Crofts, Inc., New York, 1947.

Chapter 4

EDUCATIONAL PSYCHOLOGY

In no other field has psychology been so widely used for so many years as in the field of education. Children were tested and placed in school according to those test results within a few years after tests were first developed. In fact, the first psychological test was constructed by Binet for use in a school for retarded children. Educators always make every possible use of the tools psychologists develop for them. Education has long been psychology's greatest consumer.

The use education has made of psychology has been in two major areas —learning and testing. The following pages will review some of the ways in which psychology has been useful to the educator in each of these areas.

LEARNING

In Chap. 1 a brief review was given of the development of the laws of learning by Thorndike and the method of the conditioned response by Pavlov. Any discussion of learning must be based on these two significant developments. (It is advised that the student read these sections in Chap. 1 again at this time.)

Also, in Chap. 3 a fundamental distinction was made between learning and maturation. Both learning and maturation involve the alteration of patterns of physical structure by metabolic processes. The difference is that some pattern changes are somehow innate in the germ plasm and occur largely irrespective of environment, while others are completely dependent on environment. The development of innate patterns is called "maturation"; the development of those patterns controlled by environment is called "learning." Learning is the process of forming behavior patterns while adjusting to environmental conditions. It is the inevitable result of the process of behavior. It can be controlled only by controlling behavior.

Conditions That Affect Learning

Learning may be fast or slow, permanent or temporary, continuous or intermittent, depending on the presence or absence or combination of a large number of affecting factors. Some of these are not yet well understood. Others have been studied with sufficient care to justify conclusions. The following pages review some of the more significant factors which affect learning.

Maturation. Learning is not the same as maturation, but it is very definitely limited by it. Maturation is independent of learning, but learning is not independent of maturation. The limits maturation places on learning are illustrated by various co-twin experiments. The procedure is to give one of a pair of identical twins extensive training at an early age. Both are then given limited training at a later age. The amount of learning in each is then compared to see the effect of the premature training. All such studies show that limited training *after* proper maturation is superior to extensive training *before* proper maturity.

Gesell and Thompson[1] studied the effects of maturation on the learning of a certain pair of identical twins—T and C. Beginning at the age of forty-six weeks, twin T was given 6 weeks training in climbing steps. At the age of fifty-two weeks, she could climb the steps in 25 seconds. Beginning at the age of fifty-three weeks, twin C was given 2 weeks of similar training. At the age of fifty-five weeks, she could climb the steps in 10 seconds. "The climbing performance of twin C at fifty-five weeks was far

[1] Gesell, A. G., and Thompson, H., Learning and Growth in Identical Infant Twins, *Genet. Psychol. Monogr.,* 1929, **6**, 1–123.

superior to the climbing performance of twin T at fifty-two weeks, even though twin T had been trained seven weeks earlier and three times as long. The maturation advantage of three weeks of age must account for this superiority."

Morphett and Washburne[2] studied the effectiveness of teaching reading to children of various mental ages. They found that less than 10 per cent of children with a mental age of six can make satisfactory progress in reading. However, at the mental age of seven, more than 70 per cent of them can make satisfactory progress. Obviously, the educator should wait for maturation before he should attempt to teach the child to read.

Premature learning is sometimes even detrimental to the child. First, he learns *wrong* habits that are difficult to correct later on. For example, if he is too young to learn to write properly he learns to write improperly. It is then more difficult to unlearn the wrong habits and learn the right ones than it is to learn the right ones without any previous learning. This is likewise true of all school subjects. Second, premature learning is so difficult that the child forms a dislike for the subject matter. This is most unfortunate because the subject matter may be in the area of the child's greatest aptitudes. Third, premature learning brings about unnecessary nervous and emotional tensions. The average schoolroom produces too many emotional tensions at best, and the difficulties of premature learning add to these greatly.

Learning Aptitude. If a mental age of seven is necessary for satisfactory progress in learning to read, it makes but little difference whether a child with a mental age of five, for example, is immature or innately mentally handicapped. In either case he cannot make satisfactory progress in reading. All learning requires a degree of learning aptitude—the more difficult the learning, the more aptitude necessary. As indicated in Fig. 3–3, all aptitudes are inherited and constitute limits beyond which no amount of training will enable an individual to go. Consequently, the educator must be able to recognize the degree of the child's native potentialities as well as his degree of maturation. Later on in this chapter, methods of measuring native aptitudes will be reviewed.

However, a low I.Q. does not mean that a child is handicapped in all learning. Low intelligence usually means only that the individual is inferior in abstract learning. Table 4–1 shows the relation between intelligence and various types of academic learning. Note that drawing and handwork have but little relation to intelligence.

Emotion. In considering the relation of emotion to learning it is necessary to distinguish between intense emotion and mild emotion or emotional tone. Mild emotion aids the learning process while intense

---

[2] Morphett, M. V., and Washburne, C., When Should Children Begin to Read? *Elem. Sch. J.*, 1931, **31**, 496–503.

Table 4–1. Correlations between Intelligence and Proficiency in School Subjects*

Subject	r
Composition	.63
Reading	.56
Arithmetic	.55
Spelling	.52
Writing	.21
Handwork	.18
Drawing	.15

* After C. Burt, *Mental and Scholastic Tests.*

emotion, especially if annoying, interferes with it. Carter[3] studied the ability of sixth- and seventh-grade children to learn to associate pictures with pleasant, unpleasant, and indifferent words. He found that 2,200 errors were made on the pleasant words, 2,724 errors on the unpleasant words, and 3,106 errors on the indifferent words. Both the pleasant and the unpleasant associations were made with fewer errors than the indifferent ones.

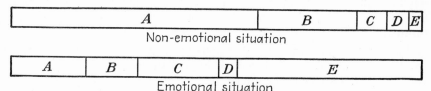

Non-emotional situation

Emotional situation

Fig. 4–1. Effects of emotion on quality of response in learning.

However, the effect of intense emotion on learning is a different story. Patrick[4] studied the effects of emotion on the ability of adults to discover the way out of a problem room. Their responses were rated on a quality scale from *A* ("tendency to make rational inferences") to *E* ("automatisms, unadaptive, preservative"). Emotion was aroused by cold water, electric shock, and loud noise. The results are shown in Fig. 4–1. Note the decrease in *A* quality (rational) behavior and the increase in *E* quality (unadaptive) behavior during emotion.

Motivation. One cannot learn more or faster than his hereditary limitations permit. However, whether one learns as much or as fast as he can depends on how much he wants to learn. Getting children to want to learn is the problem of *motivation.*

Modern education has attempted to secure *derived motivation* by relating learning to the things children already want to do. For example, children like to explore. Consequently, as a part of the educational program, field trips are conducted that involve exploration and useful learn-

[3] Carter, H. D., Emotional Correlates of Errors in Learning, *J. Educ. Psychol.,* 1936, **27,** 55–67.

[4] Patrick, J. R., Studies in Rational Behavior and Emotional Excitement, *J. Comp. Psychol.,* 1934, **18,** 153–195.

ing. A small college recently sponsored a sociology field trip to Chicago, a distance of some 600 miles. The students enjoyed the trip and, incidentally, learned a lot of sociology that otherwise would have been dull and uninteresting. Another method of derived motivation is called the "project," in which children perform some interesting task involving the desired learning. Most laboratory experiments are of this nature. In such derived motivation the child performs the behavior for its own sake, but the educative values are by-products.

The great difficulty in motivating children to learn what is called their "social heritage" is the lack of its present usefulness. Education is preparation for a future that seems to the child to be a long way off. Why learn something now that will not be needed for 5, 10, or 15 years yet? One great educator (John Dewey) suggested that the best education is not preparation for the future but the most adequate adjustment for the present. The difficulty with this idea is that too much learning would then pile up at the late adolescent levels. Either the child would not be prepared, or the future would have to be postponed. The method of civilization, as distinguished from that of primitive society, is to prepare for the future.

A number of methods are used by the modern educator for motivating children to learn that which has no immediate usefulness. They are all very effective when skillfully used.

Adjustment Needs. It is common knowledge that information actually needed to make an adjustment will be learned in much less time and with much less effort than is possible with any other sort of motivation. A boy may be failing a course in Spanish, for example, until he learns that his father is planning a trip to some Spanish-speaking country and will take his son along only on condition that he first learn to speak and read the language. Or a girl may find chemistry very difficult until she falls in love with the teacher or gets a job in which chemistry is a prerequisite. Any learning that is necessary to satisfy an adjustment need will occur with relative ease. This is the principle on which much modern and so-called "progressive education" is based. The project curriculum is an attempt to create a need for the information being taught. The "cooperative curriculum" in colleges of engineering is an attempt to intensify and make vivid the usefulness of the complex facts and techniques necessary to learn in an engineering course. Space is not available here to review the research evidence of the superiority of this form of motivation.

Competition and Cooperation. Certainly the child is not born with an instinct for either competition or cooperation. He merely finds both to be enjoyable and soon acquires a desire to compete with other children at some times, to cooperate with them at other times, and to compete with some while cooperating with others at still other times. Competition and cooperation are both involved in a large part of the child's play activities.

The traditional school encourages competition more than it does co-operation. In fact, some teachers discourage cooperation in schoolwork. When the writer's daughter was in grade school she was reprimanded by a teacher for helping her girl friend on an assignment in which both girls were interested. The teacher considered it dishonest. Perhaps one reason why so many people insist on a competitive economic system is that our schools have fostered that type of thinking.

The relative effectiveness of competition and cooperation as a means of motivating schoolwork was studied by Maller.[5] His subjects were 1,538 children in grades 5 to 8. The work was in arithmetic. The control group studied in the usual manner with no special motivation. In one experimental group, the pupils competed with each other for class rank and individual prizes. In another group, they cooperated with each other within their classes but competed with other classes for class honors and prizes. Both the competition and the cooperation groups were superior to the control group but competition was more effective than cooperation when these two forms of motivation were compared. When the children were allowed to choose for themselves whether they would compete for individual prizes or cooperate for class prizes, 74 per cent chose to compete.

Sims[6] performed a similar experiment with college students. He compared the relative effectiveness of competition and cooperation as a means of motivating his subjects to increase their reading speed. Progress was measured after 12 practice periods distributed over 4 weeks. The control group practiced as directed but was not otherwise motivated. In the competition group each student was paired with another of equal initial ability and then urged to surpass him. Each knew the score of the other. The cooperative group was divided into competing sections with group scores posted. The results of both studies are shown in Table 4–2.

Hurlock's frequently quoted study[7] also shows the value of competition as a means of motivating progress in arithmetic. She paired 155 children (73 boys, 82 girls) of grades 4 and 6, using one of each pair for the control group and one for the experimental group. The control group was encouraged to do the best they could on the tests. The experimental group was divided into subgroups that competed with each other. Her results are shown in Table 4–3.

Success and Failure. Success in learning may be indicated in many ways—reaching a goal, being praised by others, getting high grades, get-

[5] Maller, J. B., Cooperation and Competition: An Experimental Study in Motivation, *Teach. Coll. Contr. Educ.*, 1929, No. 384.

[6] Sims, V. M., The Relative Influence of the Two Types of Motivation on Improvement, *J. Educ. Psychol.*, 1928, 19, 480–484.

[7] Hurlock, Elizabeth B., The Use of Group Rivalry as an Incentive, *J. Abnorm. Soc. Psychol.*, 1927, 22, 278–290.

Table 4–2. Competition and Cooperation Compared as a Means of Motivation

Groups	Maller study	Sims study (gain)
Control: unmotivated	41.2	14.6
Individual competition	46.3	58.3
Intraclass cooperation (interclass competition)	43.6	24.4
Superiority of:		
Competition over control	5.1	43.7
Cooperation over control	2.4	9.8
Competition over cooperation	2.7	33.9

Table 4–3. Competition as a Motivating Factor in Arithmetic

Tests	Groups		Superiority of competition
	Control	Competition	
First	7.43	7.24	−.19
Second	8.12	11	2.88
Third	8.19	11.26	3.07
Fourth	7.99	11.17	3.18
Fifth	8.06	11.39	3.33

ting material rewards (money or otherwise). Likewise failure may be indicated in many ways—not reaching a goal, being reproved by others, getting low grades, being punished. The value of these and other forms of success and failure in motivating schoolwork has been the subject of many studies. Some of the more representative of these are briefly reviewed in the following pages.

Hurlock[8] compared the learning of four equivalent groups of grade-school children in arithmetic under four different forms of motivation. The children in the "praised" group were named individually and praised for their good work before the rest of the class. The children in the "reproved" group were named individually and reproved for their poor work before the rest of the class. The children in the "ignored" group were in the room and heard the others being praised and reproved but their names were not mentioned in either praise or blame. The children in the control group were in another room under ordinary school conditions. Table 4–4 shows the progress made by all four groups on five successive daily tests.

Flügel[9] studied the effects of a constantly increased money reward on

[8] Hurlock, Elizabeth B., An Evaluation of Certain Incentives Used in School Work, *J. Educ. Psychol.*, 1925, 16, 145–159.
[9] Flügel, J. C., Practice, Fatigue and Oscillation, *Brit. J. Psychol. Monogr. Suppl.*, 1928, No. 13.

Table 4–4. Average Daily Scores Made in Arithmetic by Groups Working under Four Types of Motivation

Days	Motivation groups			
	Control	Praised	Reproved	Ignored
First	11.8	11.8	11.8	11.8
Second	12.3	16.6	16.6	14.2
Third	11.6	18.8	14.3	13.3
Fourth	10.5	18.8	13.3	12.9
Fifth	11.4	20.2	14.2	12.4
Average	11.52	17.24	14.04	12.92
Average gain	−.28	5.44	2.24	1.12

the behavior of 46 English schoolgirls (ages nine to thirteen) in adding numbers. Each girl received a "flat rate" in money plus a constantly increasing bonus each time she broke her own previous week's record. The records of the girls were posted and they worked in groups. The curve of their constantly increasing improvement is shown in Fig. 4–2. Unfortunately, Flügel did not compare these results with a control group of girls

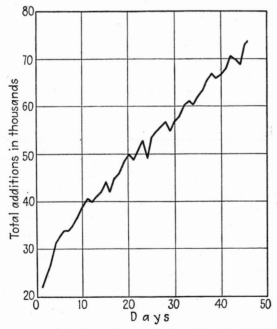

Fɪɢ. 4–2. Effects of constantly increasing motivation with schoolgirls in solving simple problems in addition.

with the same qualifications and under the same conditions except for the constantly increasing motivation.

Various other forms of motivating schoolwork have been studied. Frequent examinations have been found to be an effective motive in learning (see Chap. 2). Jones[10] studied the effects of a short test each day on the retention of the content of classroom lectures. He found that a group tested daily was 21 per cent superior to a control group of students on factual material and 18 per cent superior on "thought" material.

An interesting study was made by Leuba[11] to determine the relative motivation values of (1) no incentives, (2) chocolate bars, (3) rivalry for social prestige (captaincy and class rank), and (4) incentives (2) and (3) combined. The work consisted of practice exercises in multiplication. The subjects were 35 children in grade 5A. The procedure was to vary the nature of the motivation at each practice period. The results are shown in Tables 4–5.

Table 4–5. Average Number of Multiplication Problems Solved in 10-minute Practice Periods with Different Forms of Motivation

Form of motivation	Mean	Superiority over no incentive	
		Increase	Per cent
(1) No incentive...........	23.6		
(2) Chocolate bars........	35.9	12.3	52
(3) Social prestige........	34.6	11.	47
(4) Combined incentives...	38.9	15.3	65

TRANSFER OF LEARNING

One of the most mooted problems in the field of educational psychology has been that of the transfer of mental learning. In what way and to what extent will the knowledge, attitudes, and understandings learned in one situation be useful in another? There are at least three problems involved in this controversy: (1) How does the transfer of mental learning take place? (2) What sorts of mental learning transfer more effectively than what other sorts of learning? (3) When, or under what conditions, does the transfer of mental learning take place?

How Learning Transfers. Before experimental investigation began in educational psychology it was believed that the mind was made up of powers, or faculties, which could be developed by exercise. The power of memory, for example, could be developed by exercise in memorizing—

[10] Jones, H. E., Experimental Studies in College Teaching, *Arch. Psychol.*, 1923, No. 68.

[11] Leuba, C., The Measurement of Incentives and Their Effect, *J. Soc. Psychol.*, 1932, **3**, 107–114.

hence the study of Latin, Greek, etc. The power of reasoning could be developed by exercise in reasoning—hence the study of geometry. The power of concentration could be developed by exercise in concentrating —hence the study of any subject that was uninteresting. Then, when a mental power became developed it was supposed to function on that level in all situations, regardless of similarity to the situation of development. For example, the power of memory developed in the study of Latin would function just as well in the study of any other subject. Consequently, education in itself did not need to be useful as long as the mental powers it developed were useful.

It was known that muscular skill and muscular strength acquired in one situation would transfer to another. For example, Davis[12] had proved that training the right hand improved the left-hand performance. He found that skill acquired by hitting a target with a fencing foil in the right hand transferred to the left hand and improved its performance by 75 per cent. He also found that strength developed in the right arm by swinging dumbbells transferred to the left arm and increased its strength. Consequently it was assumed that mental training would transfer in a like manner.

However, a little scientific investigation soon revealed that mental powers are not so generalized as is muscular power. Instead, they are specific and varied abilities that are *identified with the situations in which they are developed.* There is not a generalized power of memory, for example, but many memory abilities varying with the situations in which they function. A child who can easily memorize a large Latin vocabulary may have difficulty memorizing chemical formulas, or historical dates, or the names of the bones of the cranium. There does not seem to be a generalized power of memory or of any other mental faculty.

The first experiment in the transfer of mental learning was performed by William James.[13] He tested his own memory ability by noting the time and the repetitions necessary for him to memorize 158 lines from Victor Hugo's *Satyr.* He then trained his memory by practicing 20 minutes daily for 38 days memorizing Milton's *Paradise Lost.* Then, he again tested his memory ability on 158 more lines from the *Satyr.* He found that there was no transfer. His memory ability was not improved. He repeated the experiment on four of his students but found no transfer.

Then, scientific investigation also revealed that the future usefulness (transfer) of any type of mental learning (whether knowledge, understanding, or attitude) depends on the similarity of the two situations—the learning situation and the later situation of application. The more the

---

[12] Davis, W. W., Researches on Cross Education, *Yale Psychol. Lab.,* 1898, **6,** 6–50.
[13] James, William, *Principles of Psychology,* Vol. I. pp. 666–668, Henry Holt and Company, Inc., New York, 1890.

two are alike, other things being equal, the more easily transfer can take place. This means that the content of school learning should be governed by the child's needs after he leaves school. There is no value in school learning if it has no use after school days are over. Latin is valuable in the preparation for life only to the extent that it is used in life. Geometry should be studied in school only if it is used outside of school. No school subject matter can be justified by the claim that it trains a hypothetical mental power. Schoolwork that is not valuable for its own sake in life outside of school cannot be justified.

Furthermore, it was found that even though learning has useful applications it must not be assumed that the child will make those applications unless he is trained to do so. Transfer of training cannot be left to chance. Subject matter must not be studied in the abstract but *in use.* Haskell[14] compared two equated groups of pupils on gains in English vocabulary. One group had been taught Latin by the conventional method, while the other was taught Latin as it is related to English. The second group gained twice as much as the first in knowledge of English words of Latin derivation and surpassed the first group in knowledge of other English words. The results are shown in Table 4–6.

Table 4–6. Gains Made in English Vocabulary of Pupils Studying Latin Per Se and Those Studying Latin in Relation to English

Group	N	Gains made in English vocabulary	
		Latin derivatives	Non-Latin derivatives
Conventional Latin.............	118	4.05	2.77
Latin in application...........	118	8.12	3.49

Consequently, two conclusions may be made as to how mental learning obtained in one situation transfers to another—(1) maximum transfer takes place when the learning itself has maximum future usefulness, provided, (2) a representative sampling of those uses has also been learned. In other words, the *transfer of learning is greatest when useful material has been learned in use.* Both the content of education and the method of educating are important for greatest transfer of mental training.

What Learning Transfers. The educator is always interested in the practical problem of *what* school learning transfers most. From the above discussion it could be assumed that school learning which is of most worth in after-school life will have the greatest transfer value. While this is true, there is still the question of what school learning has the greatest

[14] As quoted by S. L. Pressey and F. P. Robinson, in *Psychology and the New Education,* p. 579, Harper & Brothers, New York, 1944.

after-school value. It is a very mooted question. Every school subject has been studied from this point of view. Some research has dealt with the problem of the transfer of learning in a certain subject to other school subjects (such as the effects of the study of Latin on learning in English), and other research has been concerned with the more practical problem of the relation of learning in a certain subject to life situations after school (such as the effects of studying agriculture on the management of a farm in later years). Typical studies of both types will be briefly reviewed.

The Transfer of Mental Learning within School. Thorndike[15] studied the transfer value of various high school subjects on 8,564 pupils in grades 10, 11, 12. A battery of intelligence and achievement tests was given in May, 1922, and again in May, 1923. The relation of the relative gains made on these tests to the school subjects the pupils had studied in the meantime was carefully noted. Allowances were made for such variables as intelligence, age, sex, other subjects studied, etc. Thus, weighted gains for each school subject were computed. While differences were found, they were not great (see Table 4–7). The author concludes, "The ex-

Table 4–7. Differences in Test Gain between Pupils Taking Certain Subjects and Other Equated Pupils Not Taking Those Subjects

School Subjects	Weighted Gains
Arithmetic and bookkeeping	2.92
Chemistry, physics, and general science	2.64
Geometry, algebra, and trigonometry	2.33
Latin and French	1.64
Physical training	.66
Civics, economics, psychology, and sociology	.27
History, music, shop, Spanish, English, drawing, and business	.00
Dramatic art	−.29
Stenography, cooking, and sewing	−.47
Agriculture and biology	−.90

pectation of any large differences in general improvement of the mind from any one study rather than another seems doomed to disappointment. The chief reason why good thinkers seem superficially to have been such by having taken certain school studies is that good thinkers have such subjects, becoming better by the inherent tendency of the good to gain more than the poor from any study."

The same author with two collaborators[16] extended this study to discover what effects the various high school subjects have on the ability to think. They used a battery of 14 tests of various phases of thinking. Again the "differences are so small and the unreliabilities are relatively so large

[15] Thorndike, E. L., Mental Discipline in High School Studies, *J. Educ. Psychol.*, 1924, 15, 1–22; 83–98.

[16] Broyler, C. R., Thorndike, E. L., and Woodyard, E., A Second Study of Mental Discipline in High School Studies, *J. Educ. Psychol.*, 1927, 18, 377–404.

that the influence of the subject studied seemed unimportant." (See Table 4–8.)

Table 4–8. Differences in Thinking Ability between Pupils Taking Certain Subjects and Other Equated Pupils Not Taking Those Subjects

School Subjects	Weighted Gains
Algebra, geometry, trigonometry, etc.	3.0
Civics, economics, psychology, sociology	2.9
Chemistry, physics, general science	2.7
Arithmetic and bookkeeping	2.6
Physical training, athletics	.8
Latin, French	.8
Business, drawing, English, history, music, shop, Spanish	.0
Cooking, sewing, stenography	−.1
Biology, zoology, botany, physiology	−.2
Dramatic art	−.5

The Transfer of School Learning to Practical Situations. After all, the principal value of any school subject is the extent to which it affects the behavior of the pupil to his advantage in practical life situations as well as academic situations. Hamlin[17] studied the effects of training in vocational agriculture on the farming habits of students after they left school. As shown in Table 4–9, there was not only a transfer effect on those trained but the ideas learned were also passed on to their neighbors.

Table 4–9. Effects of Instruction in Agriculture on the Percentage of Farm Land Sown in Legumes

Groups	First survey	Second survey	Gain
Uninstructed neighbors	6.7	8.1	1.4
Ex-agriculture students	11	16.4	5.4

Scharff[18] studied the transfer effects of special training in health education to the selection of food in a school cafeteria. Her results, shown in Table 4–10, indicate that children selected food more intelligently after the health education than before.

Consequently, two conclusions would seem to be justified: First, school subjects do not have significantly different values in their transfer to other school subjects. Academic knowledge does not seem to depend on the subjects studied but rather on the caliber of the student himself. Second, those school subjects having vocational usefulness seem to have significant transfer value to practical situations. By implication this would

[17] Hamlin, H. M., Measuring the Effects of School Instruction through Changes in Community Practice, J. Educ. Res., 1928, 18, 315–317.

[18] Scharff, Ruth, The Health Education Program in Connection with the Cafeteria, Prac. Home Econ., 1934, 12, 197.

Table 4–10. Transfer Effects of Instruction in Health on Choice of Food Items in a School Cafeteria

Food	Before	After	Per cent gain
Milk (half-pints).........................	4,624	5,697	23
White bread sandwiches.................	10,064	8,704	−14
Brown bread sandwiches................	1,020	2,212	117
Salads.................................	680	901	33

seem to suggest that the so-called "cultural" subjects have more doubtful transfer value to practical situations.

What Conditions Promote Transfer? In Haskell's study, quoted above, the amount of transfer depended in part on whether or not Latin was taught for transfer. When Latin is taught in relation to English, its usefulness in understanding English is then greater than when it is merely taught as Latin. Too much schoolwork is taught for its own sake and not for its future value. Useful learning must be acquired in use. Children must be taught not only useful learning but also how to use it.

A second condition that affects the transfer of learning is the intelligence of the learner. Werner[19] compared pupils with low, medium, and high intelligence who had studied a foreign language to pupils with low, medium, and high intelligence who had not studied a foreign language

Table 4–11. Comparison of Pupils of Varied Intelligence Who Have Studied a Foreign Language with Those Who Have Not on Tests of English Usage

Tests	Superiority on tests		
	Low I.Q.	Medium I.Q.	High I.Q.
Reading speed.........................	11.2*	7.8*	12.2
Reading comprehension.................	3.1	1.7	8.9
Punctuation...........................	1.8*	.1*	.1*
Sentence structure.....................	1.1*	.2*	.6*
Grammar..............................	1.2*	1.5*	3
Language usage.......................	4.8*	1.4*	3.7

* Indicates superiority of the nonlanguage group.

on a series of tests in English usage. He found that, while superior pupils did better on English tests because of the study of a foreign language, pupils of average and inferior ability apparently were handicapped by it. In other words, the study of a foreign language apparently has positive transfer value for superior pupils and negative transfer value for average and inferior pupils. Werner's results are shown in Table 4–11.

[19] Werner, O. H., The Influence of the Study of Modern Foreign Languages, *Stud. Mod. Lang. Teach.,* 1930, **17**, 97–145.

Third, the transfer of learning depends on the method of teaching. Overman[20] compared the transfer effects of four methods of teaching simple addition to four equated groups (112 pupils in each) of second-grade pupils. Group I was shown how to add but no explanation was given. Group II was aided in developing general methods of procedure. They were encouraged to draw conclusions and use them in solving subsequent problems. Group III discussed reasons and principles but were left free to make their own generalizations. They were given explanations but not generalizations. Group IV was taught by both generalizations and explanation. They formulated rules of procedure and were given explanations and reasons. All four groups were taught to solve the same problems during training. Then, tests of new material (in addition) were given to see the comparative transfer value of the four methods of teaching. The results are given in Table 4–12.

Table 4–12. Percentage of Transfer Produced by Four Methods of Teaching Addition

Method of Teaching	Per Cent of Transfer
I. Demonstration	46.6
II. Generalization	67.6
III. Explanation	53.8
IV. Generalization and explanation	63.8

Another experiment that illustrates the importance of the method of teaching on the amount of learning transfer was performed by Woodrow.[21] He compared two groups of college students, on memorizing tests after they had been given two different types of memory training, with a control group that had received no special training. The three groups were first equated on initial tests in memorizing. The control group was given no memory training. The practice group devoted eight periods (a total of 177 minutes) to memorizing poetry and nonsense syllables. The training group spent only a part (101 minutes) of their eight periods on memorizing, and the rest of their time (76 minutes) was devoted to a study of the rules for memorizing. They learned about the "whole" method, about the value of self-testing and grouping, about secondary associations, etc. Then, each group was again tested. The results are shown in Table 4–13. The practice group was but little better than the control group, but the training group was vastly superior.

Shuttleworth[22] found that "failure to see the need" was given by college

[20] Overman, J. R., The Problem of Transfer in Arithmetic, 10th *Yearb. Nat. Counc. Teach. Math.*, 1935, pp. 173–185.
[21] Woodrow, H., The Effects of Type of Training upon Transference, *J. Educ. Psychol.*, 1927, **18**, 159–172.
[22] Shuttleworth, F. K., The Adolescent Period, *Monogr. Soc. Res. Child. Developm.* 1938, **3**.

Table 4–13. Comparison in Percentage Gain or Loss of Three Groups of College Students after Different Types of Intervening Memory Training

Type of test	Per cent gain or loss(−)			Advantage over control	
	Control	Practice	Training	Practice	Training
Poetry..................	−32.8	−29.1	−10.6	3.7	20.2
Prose...................	28.7	25.5	50.7	− 3.2	22
Facts...................	− 4.9	− 4.7	12.8	.2	17.7
Dates..................	29.	37.5	87.7	8.5	58.7
Vocabulary.............	− .6	3.4	55.2	4	55.8
Memory span...........	6.7	− 5.7	20.3	−12.4	13.5
Average..............				.13	34.65

students as one of the major reasons for lack of interest in high school subjects. Their reaction to Latin, history, and mathematics is shown in Fig. 4–3.

Certain conclusions regarding the transfer of learning would seem to be justified from this rather extensive research.

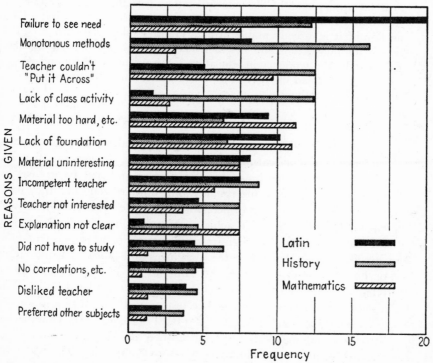

Fig. 4–3. Frequency of reasons given by college students for disliking three high school subjects.

ıg will transfer from the learning situation to later situations of
tion if it is useful in itself. There is no justification for the old
that learning develops mental powers that can function irrespective of the content of the learning. If the content of learning is not useful,
there is but little future value in it. The more closely learning is related
to situations of future use, the more that learning will transfer to those
future situations.

2. Learning transfers more readily when the learner has superior mental
capacity than when he has average or inferior mental capacity. The implication of this is that pupils of average and inferior mental capacities
should be given more lifelike education and less of the so-called "cultural" kind. Unless children are taught "culture in use" it is largely
wasted time.

3. The transfer of learning in American education has been affected adversely by two influences—first, the traditional curriculum, which has
cultural prestige but is ineffective in transfer value, and second, a branch
of the progressive-education movement, which promotes the idea that
education is not preparation for the future (which they insist cannot be
predicted) but enjoyable adjustment to the present. Regardless of the
philosophical justification for these points of view, neither produces a
type of education that has transfer value comparable to the more practical laboratory and lifelike education that gets the pupils ready for a
future that is near enough to guide the content of learning so that a large
portion of it is directly usable in life. Transfer takes place when education is for life as it is and not as it may be envisaged by some idealist.
Fortunately, the tendency in education is toward more useful and practical training instead of the idealistic cultural training that was originally
designed for gentlemen.

TESTS AND MEASUREMENTS

Tests are used in education for measuring aptitudes (or native capacities), achievement (or learning), and personality. In general they are
objective (*i.e.*, they have but one right answer and can be graded by
different people with the same results) and standardized (*i.e.*, they have
been given to a large number of people so that tables of norms, or answer
frequencies, are available). To achieve objectivity, test items are usually
stated in some manner that requires no writing. For example, true-false
items are statements that the testee recognizes and labels as being either
true or false. (Columbus discovered America in 1607.—True, False.)
Multiple-choice items are statements that may be completed by any one
of a number of alternate answers. The testee must recognize and choose
the right one. (The sum of 5 and 8 is—10, 17, 23, 13, 14.) Completion
items are those statements that are not finished and the testee must fill in
the missing concepts. (Columbus discovered America in————.)
Matching items are usually arranged in two lists (*viz.*, a list of dates and a

list of battles) and the testee must connect the items in one list with their mates in the other list.

Tests are standardized by being given to a large number of people. Then, tables of frequencies are constructed so that a score can be compared to the scores made by others. In fact any test, whether published or homemade, must have some sort of norms or the scores are meaningless. This is likewise true with data in any field. A child weighs 36 lb. This is meaningless unless we know how much other children of his age and height weigh. To standardize a test is to find out what scores other people make on it. A high score is high only when compared with the scores made by other people.

Also, published tests usually have satisfactory (or, at least, known) *reliability* and *validity*. A high reliability means that a test can be repeated with the same results. If a pupil makes a high score on a test one day and a low score on the same test the next day, it is then unreliable. The reliability of a test may be computed in various ways. It may be given to the same pupils on different occasions. However, so many other variables (physical condition, intervening experiences, etc.) may cause differences in scores that it is unwise to condemn a test on this basis. It is better to compare the score made on a part of the test, usually the even-numbered items, with the score made on another part of the test, the odd-numbered items. If half the test gives relatively the same score as the other half, it is judged to be reliable. Some tests have two forms, which are equated, and either form may be used. When pupils make the same score on both forms, taken at different times, the test is then said to be reliable.

The validity of a test refers to its worth or value in doing what it is supposed to do. If a history test measures historical knowledge, it is then said to be valid. The validity of a test is usually determined by comparing it with some other (presumably better) measure of the same characteristic. If the scores made on a history test compare closely with the grades pupils make in a history course, this is evidence of validity.

Both reliability and validity of a test are expressed in coefficients of correlation. A reliability correlation indicates the relation of a test in comparison with itself. A validity correlation indicates the relation of a test in comparison with some criterion measurement of the same factor.

THE MEASUREMENT OF APTITUDES

An aptitude may be defined as a native or inherited capacity to learn. Musical aptitude is the capacity to learn music. Mechanical aptitude is the capacity to learn mechanical skill. Intellectual aptitude is the capacity to learn to think and to solve abstract problems. Aptitude must be distinguished from ability. Ability is the actual amount of one's learning, while aptitude is the limit of one's possibility to learn. Ability is what one has already learned to do; aptitude is what one can learn to do.

Intelligence Tests. The aptitude most commonly measured in the field of education is intelligence, or mental capacity. The tests used are of two types—individual and group. Individual intelligence tests (originated by Binet) are given orally by the examiner to a single subject. The answers are recorded by the examiner. Group tests are usually given to a large number of subjects at the same time. Each subject records his own answers on either the test or an answer sheet. (See discussion of the first psychological test and the Army tests in Chap. 1.)

There are a number of ways of interpreting the raw score made on an intelligence test. One way is to translate it into mental age. This is done by comparing it with the raw scores made by average children of various chronological ages. For example, suppose that the average nine-year-old child makes an average raw score of 156 on a certain test. Then, any child making a score of 156 on that test may be said to have a mental age of nine regardless of his chronological age. A mental age of nine is indicated by a test score like that made by normal children of the chronological age of nine.

Then, if a child's mental age is divided by his chronological age, the resulting quotient is indicative of variation above or below normal and may be compared with other quotients obtained in the same way regardless of the ages involved. This is called the "intelligence quotient," or the I.Q. For example, if a child has a mental age of eight years and a chronological age of nine years his intelligence quotient would be .88 or, expressed without the decimal, 88. Since the quotient is less than 100, it indicates inferior intelligence. Suppose that another child has a mental age of 10.6 years and a chronological age of 12 years; his intelligence quotient will also be 88. Merrill[23] suggests that when the 1937 revision of the Binet test is used the I.Q.'s obtained should be given the following interpretation:

140–169	Very superior
120–139	Superior
110–119	High average
90–109	Average
80–89	Low average
70–79	Borderline defective
30–69	Mentally defective

The percentile is also used to express intelligence level. Suppose that a test is given to 1,000 people. Then suppose that the scores are divided into 100 percentiles of 10 scores each, ranging from lowest to highest. The

[23] Merrill, Maud A., I.Q.'s on the Revised Stanford-Binet Scale, *J. Educ. Psychol.*, 1938, **29**, 641–651.

lowest 10 scores would be the first percentile, the next 10 scores would be the second percentile, etc. Each of the 100 percentiles would have a score range and an average score. Suppose that 156 is the average score for the 25th percentile. Then anyone subsequently taking the test and making that score would be in the 25th percentile, or less intelligent than 75 per cent of all those who have taken the test.

Raw scores on intelligence tests are often translated into standard scores, or unit distances, from the average (or mean) score. A standard score is an indication of the degree a raw score may deviate from the average. It is calculated from the standard deviation and always indicates plus or minus fractions of standard deviations from the average or mean.

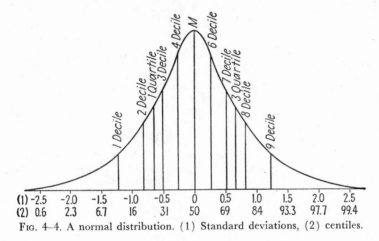

(1)	-2.5	-2.0	-1.5	-1.0	-0.5	0	0.5	1.0	1.5	2.0	2.5
(2)	0.6	2.3	6.7	16	31	50	69	84	93.3	97.7	99.4

Fig. 4–4. A normal distribution. (1) Standard deviations, (2) centiles.

Often 50 is arbitrarily assigned to the mean and each standard deviation above or below is given a value of 10. A standard score of 35 would then indicate 1.5 standard deviations below the mean, or approximately the 7th percentile. Standard scores are comparable regardless of the differences in raw scores (which are not comparable). For example, a student may make a raw score of 156 on one test and 287 on another. The first score may have a standard value of 62 while the second may have a standard value of only 47. Since standard scores are comparable, they can be added and the average score computed (which in the above case is 54.5).

The meaning of these various ways of interpreting raw scores and their relation to each other are shown in Fig. 4–4.

It has been found that scores made on intelligence tests are highly indicative of subsequent success in schoolwork. Pupils who make high scores usually do well in school while those who make low scores usually do poorly in school. For example, Terman[24] quotes a study by Dickson show-

[24] Terman, L. M., *Intelligence of School Children*, p. 46, Houghton Mifflin Company, Boston, 1919.

ing a correlation of .72 between mental age and school grades (See Table 4–14). However, this relationship varies with such factors as age, mental level, school level, and school subjects. The correlation is lower with older pupils, in the higher grades, and in nonacademic subjects (such as home economics, manual arts, etc.).

Intelligence tests were originally developed by Binet to distinguish between children with limited intelligence and normal children. They are still used for this purpose. Some schools put mentally handicapped children in the same class with normal children and teach them by methods that are not so appropriate for normal children. This is called "homogeneous grouping."

Mentally superior children are likewise often isolated in special classes and allowed to progress at a much faster rate than is possible with average children. Intelligence tests are used to select these superior children.

Perhaps the greatest value of intelligence tests in education is in pupil guidance. Proper advice in problems of vocational choice, rate of school progress, school-subject selection, learning proficiency, etc., depends on the intellectual level of the pupil being advised. No teacher can give a child proper guidance without knowing something of the child's intellectual level. Even guidance in disciplinary problems depends on the intellectual caliber of the pupil involved. The value of tests of intelligence in educational guidance cannot be overemphasized. This use of intelligence tests is discussed at length in Chap. 5.

Table 4–14. Relations of Mental Age to the Quality of Schoolwork in the First Grade (*N* 149)

Mental age	Grades				
	A	B	C	D	E
9.5 up	3				
9 to 9.4					
8.5 to 8.9	1	1			
8 to 8.4	2	1		1	
7.5 to 7.9		1	5		
7 to 7.4	3	7	10	6	
6.5 to 6.9		3	18	9	
6 to 6.4		1	14	6	
5.5 to 5.9			7	7	3
5 to 5.4			4	6	4
4.5 to 4.9			2	7	8
to 4.4				2	7

Mechanical Tests. Tests of mechanical aptitude are often used in education to predict success in industrial arts. Correlations between scores made on these tests and school progress in various courses in industrial arts are equally as high as those between intelligence test scores and school progress in academic subjects. (These correlations range between .30 and .70 with the central tendency around .50.) Tests of mechanical aptitude may be samples of actual performance or pencil and paper tests of information.

Performance tests of mechanical aptitude are of various kinds. The assembly tests consist of articles that have been disassembled, and must be put together accurately in the shortest possible time. In the Minnesota Assembly Test there are four boxes with 10 articles to be assembled in each box. For example, box B consists of a safety razor, a monkey wrench, a thumbscrew clamp, a jar clamp, a spark plug, calipers, an electric plug, a pair of pliers, an iron handle, and a mousetrap. There is a time limit and the score consists of the total number of proper connections made in assembling the various articles.

Spatial relations tests, sometimes called "form board" tests, usually consist of boards with a number of peculiarly shaped holes or recesses in them. Then there are pieces of wood that fit exactly into these recesses. The test consists of placing these pieces in their proper recesses in the shortest possible time.

Manipulation tests are of various kinds. Many of them are of the pegboard nature. Here, a board has a number of small, round holes drilled in it. There are a number of pegs, usually metal, that fit into these holes. The test consists of placing as many pegs as possible in the holes in a given time, first with one hand and then with the other. Another manipulation test consists of packing wooden blocks in a box, and another of sorting ordinary playing cards.

Other Aptitude Tests. The measurement of musical aptitude has been the lifetime interest of Professor Seashore[25] at the University of Iowa. His tests are widely used and are probably the best in this field. By the use of phonograph records various factors in musical aptitude are measured. Scores are obtained for tonal memory and the discrimination of differences in rhythm, timbre, time, intensity, and pitch. It has been found that training in music has very little effect on one's ability to pass these tests.

Tests have also been developed for the measurement of art aptitude, which, like musical aptitude, is composed of a number of factors. There is no one test that measures all these factors. Various tests measure color sensitivity, sense of balance, sense of proportion, sense of perspective, richness of imagery, motor coordination and control, judgment of nuances of light and shade, etc. The Meier Art Judgment Test consists of a num-

[25] Seashore, C. E., *Psychology of Music,* McGraw-Hill Book Company, Inc., New York, 1938.

ber of pairs of pictures of the same subject differing only in some minor respect that can be perceived only by those who have art aptitude. The McAdory Art Test consists of four pictures of the same subject differing in some essential art factor. Each picture has a score value that indicates the degree of art aptitude. (See Chap. 12 for further discussion of both music and art tests.)

ACHIEVEMENT TESTS

The most common form of test used in education is the achievement test. The purpose of these tests is to find out how much the pupil has learned so that (1) further learning can be more intelligently directed and (2) rewards in the form of grades can be given more fairly. Consequently commercial tests, which can be purchased from publishing companies, have been developed in almost every subject-matter field. These are more satisfactory than homemade tests when accuracy of measurement is desired. They are usually more objective and more adequately sample the field covered than do homemade tests. They have been revised to improve reliability and validity. They have been given to other students so that norms are available and raw scores become meaningful. In other words, they are standardized. The use of standardized achievement tests is now a common practice in the field of education at all levels.

However, accuracy of measurement is not always the paramount factor in classroom testing. Often the main purpose in testing is to motivate pupils to greater learning effort. For this, the homemade test is just as good as the standardized commercial test. In fact, most teachers who use commercial tests limit their use to midterm and final examinations. At other times they construct their own tests.

Homemade Tests. No test can do more than sample a block of learning. It is impossible to make a test all-inclusive. Consequently it is important to sample adequately all learning. Important learning must be sampled in proportion to its importance. When unimportant learning is oversampled it then carries more weight on a test than is justified. Ruch[26] advises that a table of specifications be set up before a test is constructed. Each area of learning should be listed and the percentage of items on the test predetermined. Next, again according to Ruch, the test items should be drafted in preliminary form. These items should first concern the high spots, or important factors, and then the less important factors. An item should be stated in the form (multiple choice, completion, matching, true-false) most appropriate for the time. Then, the test should be edited and cut to desired length.

Many instructors keep a file of old test items and use them in the con-

[26] Ruch, G. M., *The Objective or New-type Examination*, p. 151, Scott, Foresman & Company, Chicago, 1929.

struction of new tests. If a record is kept of the difficulty of each item (*i.e.,* the percentage of those who marked it right) and of complaints regarding its interpretation, so that it can be altered accordingly, the use of old items in a test has the effect of partial standardization. They make a better test than new and untried items.

Authors of textbooks in some fields, including psychology, construct objective tests on each chapter and publish them at the time the book is published. Sometimes norms are given. These are better than homemade tests, just as appropriate, less expensive, and may be altered and reproduced in mimeograph form. Sometimes they are printed in a workbook with learning exercises and projects. Students can then use them as self-checks on learning progress.

The essay type of homemade test is no longer seriously considered by teachers who know testing limitations. In fact it is doubtful if essay exercises should be called tests at all. The principal difficulty is that they cannot be graded. Teachers do not agree as to what constitutes a good test paper or a poor one. Monroe[27] quotes a study in which facsimile copies were made of a geometry paper and submitted to 116 geometry teachers for grading on a percentage basis. The grades ranged from 28 to 91. Approximately half of them were failing (below 70). There was very little agreement among these specialists in evaluating student efforts.

Standardized Tests. When a homemade test has been tried out, revised, tried again, and then given to enough students to make the scores meaningful, it becomes standardized. Its reliability and validity have been calculated. Like the homemade objective test, it is easily administered, easily scored, and easily interpreted. Unlike the homemade test, it is published and therefore available in any quantity.

The first standardized test, published by Stone in 1908, was in arithmetic; and the second, published by Thorndike in 1910, was in handwriting. Today there are published standardized tests for every phase of school learning. Some tests cover a wide range of school subjects and are called "survey tests," or "test batteries." One such test is the Cooperative General Culture Test, and another is the Graduate Record Examination. Both of these have norms for undergraduate and graduate levels. Survey tests on the grade school level are sometimes called "placement tests" because they are used to indicate the grade in which the child tested should be placed. Sometimes they are called "diagnostic tests" because they are used to indicate the subjects in which more learning should take place. They locate areas of inferior learning.

Again, the advantages of the standardized test over the homemade

[27] Monroe, W. S., *Measuring the Results of Teaching,* p. 9, Houghton Mifflin Company, Boston, 1918.

achievement test should be emphasized. The standardized test is more carefully constructed (items are in ascending order of difficulty), less ambiguous (and therefore more objective), more reliable, more valid, more easily interpreted (because it has been given to more people and the norms are more adequate), more available (because it is published), and more accurate in measurement. Standardized test results are comparable with those from other parts of the country, because the norms are usually national in scope.

PERSONALITY TESTS

Personality is the sum total of all those factors that affect the adjustment of an individual to his environment. It is not intangible. However, it is broad and difficult to measure in its entirety. It is composed of physical factors, habits, attitudes, feelings, likes and dislikes, hereditary qualifications and limitations, socioeconomic-cultural status, etc. The word "personality" is used to designate any factor about an individual that affects or may affect the reaction or attitude of other people toward him.

It is obvious why personality is important in education. Young people are in the process of forming their personalities, and a large part of that formation is determined by what takes place in the schoolroom. Habits of relationships with others, countless attitudes toward both a world of objects and a world of ideas, patterns of emotional behavior, feelings of self-sufficiency, and other phases of personality are constantly in the process of formation and alteration. A child is not born with a personality. He develops it. It is the product of his living. Because so much of a child's living is in the schoolroom, a large part of his personality is there formed.

Personality measurement is yet in its infancy, and consequently its accuracy is limited. We are hardly yet removed from an age of charlatans, when personality was diagnosed by reference to the stars, or palm lines, or face contour, or cranial protuberances (see Chap. 1). However, though present methods of personality measurement are crude, they are the best available. When properly interpreted, personality-measurement data increase the accuracy of human judgment. Personalities are better evaluated when all available data are used.

Acquaintance Ratings. When personality is defined as those factors about an individual that affect the reaction or attitude of other people toward him, acquaintance ratings become a significant method of measurement. If a personality is good or bad depending on how it affects other people, it is then necessary to measure other people. Perhaps the most accurate description of a personality is the consensus of a number of close acquaintances.

The most common method of acquaintance rating is to describe a trait and then ask the raters to classify the rated personality as superior, average, or inferior. The following example illustrates this simple procedure:

What is the usual condition of this individual's health and physical vigor?
_____Superior _____Average _____Inferior

It has been found that the reliability of acquaintance rating is increased by describing the degrees of variation more completely than by the use of single words. The following example illustrates this more detailed practice:

Is he tolerant of new ideas; is he open-minded and receptive to progressive suggestions?

_____He eagerly welcomes ideas and suggestions.
_____He is open to ideas and suggestions.
_____He is usually open-minded.
_____He frequently objects to new ideas.
_____He usually objects and opposes new suggestions.
_____I am not acquainted with this individual in regard to this trait.
Please record here a specific instance to support your judgment.

An interesting method of acquaintance rating was developed by Scott for use in officer's training schools during the First World War. Personality traits were described and each rater was then directed to select from his own personal acquaintance some individual who possessed the trait in the highest degree, another who possessed the trait in the lowest degree, another who was just average, another who was between the highest and average, and a fifth who was between lowest and average. The names of these individuals were written on the rating sheet. Then, the one to be rated was compared man to man with these individuals. Values were assigned to each degree and a personality score was thus obtained. The following extract from this rating scale will illustrate the method used:

Physical qualities.
Physique, bearing, neatness, voice, energy, and endurance. (Consider how this man impresses you in the above respects.)

Highest	John Brown	(15)
High	Richard Black	(12)
Average	Samuel Green	(9)
Low	William White	(6)
Lowest	James Gray	(3)

Another procedure is to rate a number of people in comparison with each other on some single trait. If a teacher is rating the children in her classroom, she will roughly rank them in comparison with each other on some trait. Then at a later time, she will similarly rate them on another trait. By considering only a single trait and by comparing children with each other the accuracy of rating is greatly increased. This method is illustrated as follows:

Qualities of leadership. Consider the extent to which others seek to follow the person being rated. (List your pupils in order of merit on this trait.)

_____

_____

_____

_____

No trait should be included in a rating scale if it can be more accurately measured in some other way. It is foolish to ask raters to estimate a person's intelligence, for example, when that trait can be better measured by tests for that purpose. Acquaintance-rating procedure is inaccurate at best and should be used to evaluate only those traits that cannot be more accurately evaluated in some other manner.

Trouble Questionnaires. These are sometimes called "psychoneurotic inventories." During the First World War a list of 116 questions, which could be answered by "yes" or "no," were prepared by Woodworth to distinguish between those personalities that had a well-adjustment history and those that were psychoneurotic. The following extract illustrates the nature of this questionnaire:

2. Do you usually sleep well?	Yes No
19. Have you ever had fits of dizziness?	Yes No
23. Do you have a great many bad headaches?	Yes No
43. Do you make friends easily?	Yes No
61. Are you troubled with the idea that people are watching you on the street?	Yes No
66. Does it make you uneasy to sit in a small room with the door shut?	Yes No
84. Do you ever feel a strong desire to steal things?	Yes No
100. Did you ever have a strong desire to commit suicide?	Yes No
114. Can you stand the sight of blood?	Yes No

Many other trouble questionnaires of this nature have been developed in recent years. Perhaps the best, and certainly the most extensive, is the Minnesota Multiphasic Test. More than 500 questions in this test are printed on separate cards. The procedure is to classify the cards in "true," "untrue," and "cannot say" groups. The questions are similar in nature to those listed above. The minor troubles revealed by this test indicate not only psychoneurotic tendencies but also the nature of these tendencies.

An interesting variation of the trouble questionnaire is the X-O, or cross-out, test developed by Pressey. This test consists of a number of words in separate lists. The testee is instructed to cross out every word that suggests anything wrong, or every word that for any reason may have caused him to worry, or every word that is or suggests something unpleasant.

Tables and norms permit the calculation of an idiosyncrasy score, or the number of responses that are not usually made by normal people. The following extract suggests the nature of this test:

Directions—Read through the twenty-five lists of words given just below and *cross out everything that you think is wrong*—everything that you think a person is to be blamed for. You may cross out as many or as few words as you like: in some lists you may not wish to cross out any words. Just be sure that you cross out everything you think is wrong.

1. Begging, smoking, flirting, spitting, giggling;
2. Fear, anger, suspicion, laziness, contempt;
3. Dullness, weakness, ignorance, meekness, stinginess;
4. Fussiness, recklessness, silliness, nagging, fibbing

Trouble questionnaires are perhaps more valuable as guides to interviews than as measuring devices. Reliability correlations are usually low because of the effect the mood of the testee has on the way he answers questions. They are valuable means of uncovering symptoms but not too accurate in measurement.

Experimental Tests. Some tests put the subject in an experimental situation and then judge his personality by what he does in that situation. For example, Howells[28] devised a test of persistence, in which the testee was subjected to a series of graduated pain stimulations. The test had a reliability coefficient of .87 and correlated with intelligence .09 and with university grades .37.

Cushing[29] attempted to measure perseverance in small children by assigning them difficult or impossible tasks (inserting a bent key into a lock, dropping marbles through a hole in a box, etc.) and then observing how long they continued to try to accomplish the task.

Downey[30] devised a test in which the subject was asked to perform a number of tasks under certain conditions on the assumption that he would reveal certain personality traits in so doing. For example, to measure coordination of impulses the subject was asked to "write on a short line (3 cm.), just as rapidly as you can, the words 'United States of America.' There are two things you must do: write very rapidly, and keep from running over the line." To measure flexibility the subject was asked to "write 'United States of America' in a style very unlike your own. Change your writing so that none of your friends would know it." However, the test was found to be so low in reliability that it was never more than an interesting oddity.

[28] Reported in *Proceedings of Ninth International Congress of Psychologists,* p. 229, Psychological Review Co., Lancaster, Pa., 1930.
[29] Cushing, H. M., A Perseverant Tendency in Pre-school Children, *Arch. Psychol.,* 1929, No. 108.
[30] Downey, June E., *Downey Group Will-temperament Test,* World Book Company, Yonkers, New York, 1929.

A well-known battery of experimental personality tests was devised by Hartshorn and May.[31] They measured cheating, stealing, and lying by setting up situations where the child could choose between honesty and deceit. For example, to measure stealing children were given small boxes in which there was one quarter, four dimes, four nickels, and four pennies. Problems were given in counting money to cover up the real purpose of the test. The children were then directed to "pass the boxes to the middle aisle" where they were collected in a basket. Each pupil had an opportunity to steal if he wished. Each box was secretly numbered so that those who stole could be identified. Cheating and lying were measured in similar ways.

Free association tests to locate emotional complexes (and to detect lying) are also examples of experimental tests of personality. The individual being tested is given a list of words and asked to respond to each with the first word he thinks of. If his response is a variation from a list of normal responses, already discovered by having given the test to people known to be normal, the conclusion is that the individual has abnormal tendencies.

Perhaps most interesting of the experimental types of personality tests are the projective techniques. In one such test (by Rorschach) the subject is shown a series of ink blots and asked to tell what he sees in each blot and what it reminds him of. His responses are then compared with norms to discover the atypical ones. A somewhat similar test (Thematic Apperception Test) uses both ink blots and music, to arouse fantasies, and an assortment of toys that are to be used in the creation of a dramatic scene.

These fantasy tests attract more and more attention in the psychological world and are slowly becoming more objective and more adequately standardized. They are used more carefully by those who are more carefully trained and consequently they are less and less tools of charlatans. Projective techniques are discussed more fully in Chap. 9 in this book.

SUMMARY

Learning is affected by many conditions. Some can be controlled to facilitate it (motivation, emotion, methods of study) and others are immutable (stages of maturation and aptitude). The real value of learning is usually not its immediate use but its future use. This transfer depends on whether or not the learning is for future use, the intelligence of the learner, and the method of learning.

Testing is an essential part of the educational process. It is used to measure aptitudes, the amount of learning (abilities), and personality traits. Psychological measurements are in the developmental stage and must be

[31] Hartshorn, H., and May, M. A., *Studies in Deceit,* The Macmillan Company, New York, 1928.

interpreted with caution. They indicate variations from the average and not absolute amounts. Tests are useful in providing data for more intelligent judgment but are not answers in and of themselves. They are of most value when used by those who understand the basic mechanics of their construction, use, and interpretation.

RECOMMENDED SUPPLEMENTARY READINGS

Cole, L. E., and Bruce, W. F.: *Educational Psychology,* World Book Company, New York, 1950.

Crow, L. D., and Crow, A.: *Educational Psychology,* American Book Company, New York, 1948.

Davis, R. A.: *Educational Psychology,* McGraw-Hill Book Company, Inc., New York, 1948.

Ellis, R. S.: *Educational Psychology,* D. Van Nostrand Company, Inc., New York, 1951.

Gutherie, E. R., and Powers, F. F.: *Educational Psychology,* The Ronald Press Company, New York, 1950.

Pressey, S. L., and Robinson, F. P.: *Psychology and the New Education,* Harper & Brothers, New York, 1944.

Sorenson, H.: *Psychology in Education,* McGraw-Hill Book Company, Inc., New York, 1948.

Stephens, J. M.: *Educational Psychology,* Henry Holt and Company, Inc., New York, 1951.

Stroud, J. B.: *Psychology in Education,* Longmans, Green & Co., Inc., New York, 1946.

Tilton, J. W.: *An Educational Psychology of Learning,* The Macmillan Company, New York, 1951.

Trow, W. C.: *Educational Psychology,* Houghton Mifflin Company, Boston, 1950.

Woodruff, A. D.: *Psychology of Teaching,* Longmans, Green & Co., Inc., New York, 1951.

Chapter 5

VOCATIONAL GUIDANCE

Plato said, in the *Republic,* "I am myself reminded that we are not all alike; there are diversities of nature among us that are adapted to different occupations." A more recent writer has observed, "Our present educational system is better equipped to give eight years of the wrong kind of education to its pupils than eight hours of competent psychological guidance in the choice of the right type of education."[1] In other words, children are better fitted by nature for some occupations than for others, but our schools (for lack of adequately trained counselors) are unable to advise each child individually about his qualifications and the occupation that is most appropriate for him. The ineffectiveness of our schools in vocational guidance is illustrated in the results of a *Fortune Magazine* poll on the question: "If you could go back to the age of eighteen and start life over again, would you choose a different career or occupation?" The results are shown in Table 5–1.[2]

However, it is erroneous to conclude that no vocational counseling is being done in our schools. Some schools have well-trained counselors and make a specialized study of the qualifications of each pupil and of the appropriate vocational opportunities. Leonard and Tucker[3] made a survey

[1] Link, H. C., Wheat and Chaff in Vocational Guidance, *Occupations,* October, 1934.

[2] *Fortune Magazine,* January, 1938.

[3] Leonard, E. A., and Tucker, A. C., *The Individual Inventory in Guidance Programs in Secondary Schools,* Voc. Div. Bull. 215, U.S. Office of Education.

136

Table 5–1. Percentage Who Would Change Career If Life Could Be Lived Over Again (*N*, 5,000)

	Change	Satisfied	Depends
Men..	43	37.9	19.1
Women.....................................	37	43.5	19.5
Professional people.......................	29	53.3	17.7
Factory laborers..........................	61.3	21.3	17.4

of the extent of ,vocational counseling in 870 American high schools. Their results are shown in Table 5–2.

Table 5–2. Vocational Counseling in High Schools (*N*, 870)

By whom	Per cent of schools	
	Regularly	Occasionally
Principal...........................	27	41
Counselor..........................	64	7
Home room teacher..................	18	36
Teacher............................	13	42
Vice-principal......................	15	20
Dean of girls.......................	20	11
Dean of boys.......................	12	7
Vocational coordinator..............	14	4
Others.............................	8	5

Most colleges give courses to train vocational counselors, and many states require such specialized training for certification in vocational counseling. However, there is a difference between vocational counseling based on scientific individual analysis and scientific occupational analysis, and vocational counseling based on opinions. Even states that require certification for vocational counselors often do not require enough scientific training to enable them to do careful work. Perhaps no other phase of educational work is done so glibly by teachers who are so poorly trained, and on the basis of such inadequate information, as is vocational counseling.

It is now obvious that two factors are involved in vocational guidance —the individual and the vocation. Two questions must be answered: What special aptitudes does the individual have? What special aptitudes does the occupation require? Two techniques must be developed—how to analyze the individual and how to analyze the occupation. Consequently, this chapter is in two parts—one concerning the analysis of the aptitudes of the individual and the other concerning the analysis of the requirements of the occupation.

ANALYZING THE INDIVIDUAL

It was pointed out in Chap. 1 that an individual's aptitudes cannot be determined by astrology, phrenology, graphology, or physiognomy. In spite of their popular appeal and general usage, they are the "gold bricks" of psychology. They constitute the psychological underworld. In Chap. 4 it was emphasized that aptitudes are innate limitations beyond which abilities cannot go. They cannot be measured directly but must be inferred or predicted from a measurement of an individual's abilities in comparison with the same abilities of other people. For example, intelligence can be predicted with fair accuracy when scores on tests of vocabulary size, speed of learning, comprehension, numbers calculation, etc., are compared with the scores of other individuals of the same age and experience. Consequently, ability analysis consists of giving an individual tests, which have been standardized on other people, and then comparing his scores with the norms. For example, if he makes a score on a musical aptitude test equal to that made by the highest 1 per cent of all those who have taken the test, it can be assumed that he has very superior musical aptitude.

CATEGORIES OF QUALIFICATIONS

There is considerable disagreement among psychologists regarding the basic aptitudes, or primary mental abilities. Thurstone[4] has used a procedure of factor analysis, on the results of a battery of 57 different tests, and has concluded that there are eight basic mental factors. These are briefly stated as follows:

1. The *space* factor, or the ability to judge space and form accurately.
2. The *perceptual* factor, or the ability to pick out detail quickly, even when it is buried in irrelevant material.
3. The *number* factor, or the ability to perform the simple arithmetical processes (addition, subtraction, multiplication, and division) quickly and accurately.
4. The *verbal relations* factor, or the ability to read and interpret sentence meanings.
5. The *word* factor, or the ability to spell and define simple words.
6. The *memory* factor, or the ability to memorize.
7. The *induction* factor, or the ability to discover some basic principal that is common in a classification of items.
8. The *deduction* factor, or the ability to apply a general principle to specific cases.

In the Minnesota Occupational Rating Scales, only six human abilities are listed and named according to their function. (This scale also designates the amount of each ability necessary for success in some 430 occupations.) They may be defined as follows:

[4] Thurstone, L. L., Primary Mental Abilities, *Psychometr. Monogr.*, 1938, **1**, No. 1.

1. *Academic*—the ability to understand and manage ideas and symbols.
2. *Mechanical*—the ability to manipulate concrete objects and to deal mentally with mechanical movements.
3. *Social*—the ability to understand and manage people.
4. *Clerical*—the ability to do rapidly and accurately detailed work, such as checking, classifying, and filing.
5. *Musical*—the ability to discriminate musical sounds and to give some form of expression through them.
6. *Artistic*—the ability to create artistic forms of merit and to evaluate forms already created.

TESTS OF QUALIFICATIONS

In vocational guidance there are never too many significant data. Any test that will provide accurate and relevant data can be used appropriately. The limit is only the cost in time and money. However, if a boy has always wanted to be a lawyer, if his interest tests substantiate these wants, if his intelligence tests show him to be in the upper centiles, if his personality tests show no traits that would obviously interfere, and if he has the money to finance a law education—there is but little point in testing him further in irrelevant qualifications, such as dexterity, music, and art. Tests afford a qualification picture of an individual; but all items in such a picture are not significant for all occupations. In other words, neither the presence nor absence of some traits is significant for success in some occupations.

The real worth of a test in vocational guidance is determined by using it on both successful and unsuccessful members of an occupation. If it distinguishes between them, it is of worth. If not, the data it would provide are insignificant for that use. The fact that an intelligence test, for example, is found to be valuable in selecting successful candidates for an engineering school does not prove that it will be equally valuable in selecting candidates for a medical school, even though intelligence is known to be a significant trait in both vocations. A test should always be tested for its worth in the specific use to which it is put. Some tests have been evaluated for selecting candidates for specific occupations; others have not.

Fortunately, psychological tests are constantly being developed and improved. They are ever being used and evaluated in new situations. As a result, they are sometimes discarded, sometimes modified, and sometimes used further with more intelligent interpretation. However, until psychological tests have improved far beyond their present status, it will be necessary for vocational counselors to be especially well trained in their use. A human trait must be measured with many tests and the data must be very cautiously interpreted. This can be done only by an expert.

It should be noted that the amount of testing in vocational counseling depends somewhat on the age of the person being counseled and the experience he has already had. An older person will have eliminated many occupational possibilities by actual experience and loss of interest. He will have certain other marked vocational interests and will want to know if he has the necessary qualifications. Testing will be limited, therefore, to the specific qualifications involved. There will be no necessity for exploratory testing.

On the other hand, a younger person usually has no stable vocational interests and no background of occupational experience. He is, vocationally speaking, virgin territory with no signposts to guide the counselor. Obviously, the testing done will have to be exploratory and general. A survey will have to be made of all his possible qualifications. All data will have possible significance. Overtesting will be impossible. Not until trends begin to point to certain occupational fields can any possible ability be neglected.

This suggests that vocational guidance is really a continuous affair. It begins with a test survey of undeveloped and immature aptitudes and unites with this a wide study of all the occupational fields. As the pupil grows older, his aptitudes become more pronounced and his interests more localized. All this should be verified by test data as well as by opinion. The counselor should be sure that the pupil himself is getting a more detailed and accurate picture of his own qualifications, as well as of the jobs in an appropriate occupational field. As the pupil becomes older, he becomes more of a specialist concerning his own vocational problem. He learns what data are significant and what data are still needed. He helps plan the further solution of his own problem. The counselor becomes less and less essential as the pupil (who by now has become a young man) learns more and more about himself in relation to the occupational world into which he must fit.

Interpreting Test Scores

As was pointed out in Chap. 4, a test score has no meaning except in relation to the scores of other people on the same test. Suppose that a student makes a score of 390 on a test that has 500 possible points. Is this score high, low, or average? Now suppose that we give the same test to 100 classmates of this student. They make scores ranging from 300 to 400 with an average of 350, let us say. It is now obvious that the score 390 is above the average. Suppose that we rank all the scores from highest to lowest and find that 390 is third from the highest. We now know what the score means.

When hundreds of scores on a test are arranged in order from highest to lowest, they are often divided into 100 groups called "centiles," or into ten groups called "deciles," or into four groups called "quartiles." A new score is then interpreted in terms of quartile, decile, or centile (also called "percentile"). Highest scores are located in the 99th centile, or the 10th decile, or the 4th quartile. Scores are usually distributed on each side of the average in a fairly symmetrical manner and with steadily decreasing frequency. This means that the score difference between the 41st and 50th centiles is not so great as that between the 1st and the 10th centiles.

Now suppose that the student mentioned above takes another test, which has only 80 possible points, and makes a score of 67. How does this score compare with the score on the first test? Obviously, it is impossible to compare the scores directly. Again it is necessary to interpret this score in relation to other scores on the same test. By referring to a table of scores made by students who have already taken the test, we find that 50 is the average score and 67 is in the 95th centile. Since the score on the first test was in the 97th centile, we can now conclude that the student made high scores on both tests.

It should be observed that in psychological measurement the base line is the average score, rather than zero as in most other forms of measurement. A psychological test score has meaning in terms of its distance above or below the average, instead of above or below an absolute zero. When a number of tests are given to the same individual and a composite picture of his qualifications is desired, a graph can be made that shows all his scores in relation to each other. Figures 5–1 and 5–2 show the profiles of two students in relationship to the average scores made on the various tests.

A table of scores made on a test (usually called a table of "norms") is often misleading unless proper recognition is made of the other qualifications of those whose scores are so listed. For example, the table of norms used for interpreting the score of John Doe in Fig. 5–1 on the Ohio State Psychological Examination was constructed from scores of college freshmen. John Doe was a senior. His centile, if compared with seniors, would probably be considerably lower than that indicated in the profile. In fact his centile on the American Council on Education test, which he took as a freshman, indicates that he is overrated by the Ohio State test. Another illustration is the Crawford-Bennett Point Motion Test. The norms here were scores made by engineering students. John Doe was a liberal arts student. Certainly he would have ranked higher if his score had been compared with those of liberal arts students. If the norms for either of these tests had represented the general population, of course John Doe would have ranked much higher.

The point cannot be overemphasized that the use of tests is fundamental in good vocational guidance, yet they cannot be interpreted by one who has not had specialized training in their use. The average school teacher cannot give the child intelligent vocational guidance without the

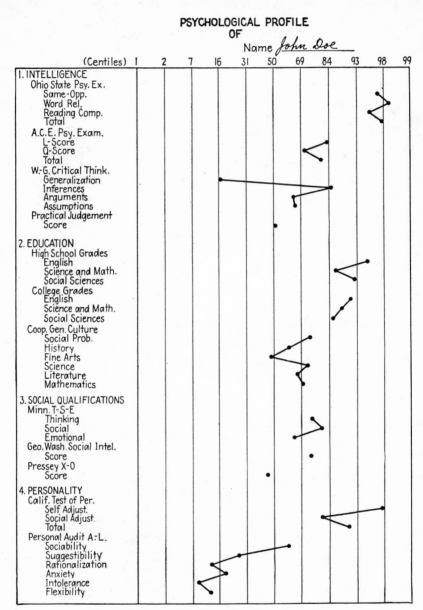

FIG. 5–1. Test profile of a university male student.

PSYCHOLOGICAL PROFILE
OF
Name *Mary Roe*

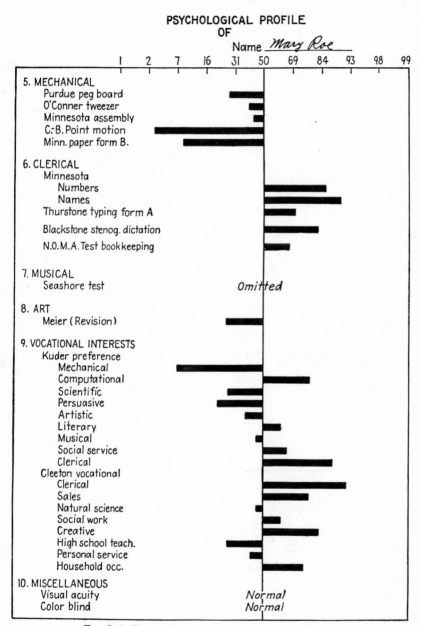

FIG. 5–2. Test profile of a university female student.

information afforded by psychological tests, but neither can she use tests and interpret them accurately enough to be of guidance value. Good vocational guidance necessitates specialized training in the use of psychological techniques of measurement.

COURSES IN VOCATIONAL GUIDANCE

There are two kinds of vocational guidance courses—those that have the primary purpose of helping the student to analyze his own qualifications and to choose an appropriate occupational field, and those that have the primary purpose of teaching the student to become a vocational counselor himself. Enrollment in courses of the latter type is limited to psychology students who have had the necessary prerequisite courses in testing techniques. Such courses are concerned with guidance techniques and need not concern us here. Courses of the former type are designed to make vocational guidance available to a larger number of students than is possible by the usual individual guidance procedures. Tests of those abilities that are significant in all occupations (such as intelligence, personality, interests, etc.) can be given to individuals in groups with but little more time and effort than is necessary to test individuals singly. Group vocational guidance, supplemented by individual guidance, is no less effective and much more economical than is individual vocational guidance.

The subject matter in a vocational guidance class differs considerably from that of the usual class. There is no cultural heritage to be learned and there are no skills to be formed. There is no textbook to be followed and there are no examinations to pass. Instead, the subject matter is the student himself. The problems dealt with are his own problems. He literally follows the old adage that "the proper study of mankind is *man*." The content of a course of this nature is rather interestingly described in the preface to the term paper of one of the writer's students. It is quoted literally.

This term paper is part of the semester's work in the course Vocational Psychology. The title of the paper—MYSELF—is all that it implies. It is all about me and how I am fitted for my chosen occupation. It is about me, by me, and for me. The paper is in three parts—first, a statement of test results and their interpretation; second, an analysis of the requirements of the occupation (social work) in which I am most interested; and, third, an attempt to predict how I will succeed in this occupation.

I have noticed that most books are dedicated to someone who presumably is deserving. I feel it fitting that I should dedicate this paper to someone who is deserving. I hereby dedicate it to *myself*. After all, I have been the subject matter, I have done the work, and I hope I will get the benefit.

S. S.

There is, of course, danger that undergraduate students who have had little or no training in psychology will misinterpret test results in spite of all an instructor can do to prevent it. However, frequent individual conferences on the significance of individual profiles, emphasis on the importance of vocational plans being constantly adjusted to fit new developments, and the requirement of a very careful summarizing statement (such as term paper) that meets the approval of the instructor will reduce misinterpretations to a minimum. But certainly a scientific study of vocational qualifications, even assuming errors, will not increase a student's misconceptions about himself. He has already made an evaluation of his vocational qualifications and on the basis of but little objective evidence. A course in vocational guidance will motivate additional study of a problem that may remain yet unsolved but can hardly become more unsolvable.

ANALYZING THE OCCUPATION

Just as individuals are analyzed to discover what qualifications they possess, so are occupations analyzed to discover what qualifications are needed. Some people have more intelligence, for example, than 98 per cent of other people, and some occupations need more intelligence than 98 per cent of other occupations. The scarcity of human superiority in certain traits is often matched by the limited need for those traits in the occupational world. Likewise, the abundance of certain other traits is matched by the abundant need for those traits. Almost any pattern of human traits possessed by an individual has a counterpart in the need of some occupation. The problem of vocational counseling is to fit peculiar patterns of individual qualifications into correspondingly appropriate occupational needs.

OCCUPATIONAL ABILITY PATTERNS

The original attempts at occupational analysis were subjective opinions that could not be, or were not, substantiated by metrical data. For example, Munsterberg analyzed occupations by armchair procedure (illustrated in Table 5–3) and then by similar "expert judgment" tried to select individuals to fit. Theoretical individuals were fitted to theoretical occupations. One wonders just what is meant by some of the traits and if the analysis is always accurate. Is "beauty" a necessary personal motive of a domestic worker?

The most recent procedure is to analyze occupations by a careful enumeration of the duties performed, the training and experience required, the conditions of work, the dangers involved, the human traits found to be necessary, etc.[5] The *human* traits essential on a job are often discovered by testing the qualifications of successful workers in compari-

---

[5] For a more complete discussion of the technique of job analysis, see Chap. 2 in *Psychology in Industry* by J. S. Gray, McGraw-Hill Book Company, Inc., New York, 1952.

Table 5–3. Munsterberg's Analysis of Two Occupations

Occupation	Abilities required	Duties performed	Personal motives	Social interests
Journalist	Sociability Energy Memory Accuracy Judgment Observation	Typewriting Quick expression Forceful style	Honor Truth Influence Salary Progress	Politics Education Information Entertainment
Domestic worker	Joyful work Energy Patience Teaching Economy Physique	Housekeeping Sewing Cooking Nursing House furnishing	Morality Beauty Position Home life Family welfare	Comfort of community Family comfort

son with the qualifications of the unsuccessful, or mediocre, workmen on the same job. Sometimes workers on one job are compared in qualifications with workers on other jobs. Both these methods were used by Dvorak[6] in her study of differential ability patterns. She compared the ability patterns of the employees of various occupations, as indicated by scores on a battery of tests, with each other. Typical results are shown in Figs. 5–3 and 5–4. She also studied the relation of superior groups of

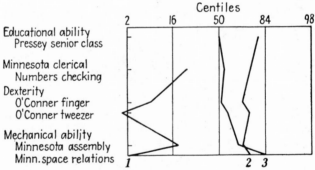

Fig. 5–3. Ability patterns characteristic of (1) common laborers, (2) manual-training teachers, and (3) garage mechanics.

employees to inferior groups in the same occupation. Figure 5–4 shows the relation of the ability pattern of superior women office workers to that of inferior women office workers. Then she compared the ability patterns of selected groups of employees in the same occupation but in

[6] Dvorak, Beatrice J., Differential Ability Patterns, *Univ. Minn. Bull. Emplyt. Stab. Res. Inst.,* Vol. 3, No. 8.

different locations and under different conditions. For example, Fig. 5–5 shows the ability pattern of private-duty nurses as compared with that of nurses in institutions.

Data obtained by Dodge[7] substantiate Dvorak's study in that he also found "significant differences between average scores of the various occu-

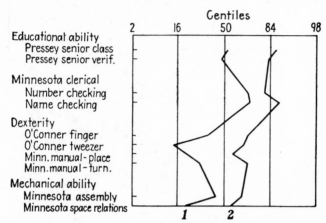

Fig. 5–4. Ability pattern characteristics of (1) inferior women office clerks, and (2) superior women office clerks.

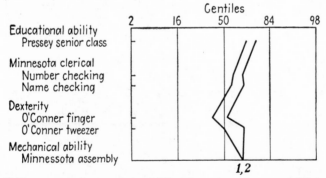

Fig. 5–5. Ability pattern characteristic of (1) private-duty nurses and (2) institutional nurses.

pational groups." However, both authors warn that all occupational groups have such wide distributions of scores on all tests and overlap with each other to such an extent that conclusions for use in individual vocational counseling must be made with caution. As suggested by the overlapping of score distributions on the Minnesota Clerical Test, illustrated in Fig. 5–6, individuals of almost any pattern of abilities are found to be employed in almost any occupation. Perhaps the proper conclusion to

[7] Dodge, A. F., Occupational Ability Patterns, *Teach. Coll. Contr. Educ.*, No. 658.

draw from such studies is that significant inferiority to the occupational average on any ability constitutes a handicap that at least should be recognized by the individual concerned.

It is obvious from the data here presented, which are typical of what data exist, that too few occupations have been studied by too few tests to make occupational ability patterns useful in vocational guidance. In addition, patterns overlap; they are not constant for all locations of the

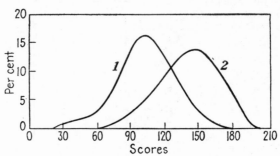

Fɪɢ. 5–6. Distribution of scores on Minnesota clerical (number checking) for (1) salesmen (retail) and (2) office clerks (women).

same occupation (see Fig. 5–5); and they change with variations of labor supply. The vocational guidance counselor must look elsewhere for a more helpful means of vocational analysis.

Tʜᴇ Mɪɴɴᴇꜱᴏᴛᴀ Occᴜᴘᴀᴛɪᴏɴᴀʟ Rᴀᴛɪɴɢ Sᴄᴀʟᴇꜱ

The fact that a sufficient number of occupations has not been scientifically analyzed does not reduce the practical need in vocational counseling for a knowledge of the specific requirements of a wide range of occupations. Relatively, in general terms, how much intelligence is required to be a draftsman, for example? How much clerical ability is required to be a successful small business executive? How much mechanical ability should a landscape gardener have? So far, these and similar questions can be answered only by the "polled judgments of vocational psychologists." *The Minnesota Occupational Rating Scales* list the minimum levels of six human abilities necessary for success in 430 occupations. The six human abilities have been stated earlier in this chapter. There are four levels described for each of the six abilities. The four levels of academic ability, for example, are described as follows:

Level A (Professional, Semiprofessional, and Executive Occupations) Requires superior abstract intelligence with training equivalent to college graduation from a first-class institution, or to two or three years of college, or to that of an executive of a moderately large business. Ability for creative and directive work is implied. Includes top decile in general population.

Examples: Lawyer, college president, president of a large manufacturing concern, executive of a moderately large business, veterinary doctor, high-school teacher, etc.

Level B (Technical, Clerical, Supervisory Occupations) Requires high average abstract intelligence equivalent to high-school graduation and/or technical school or junior college. Includes 76 to 90 percentile.

Examples: Minor executive (foreman, department heads) or highly technical work often involving dealing with abstract classifications and details, such as railroad clerks, some retail dealers, photographers, telegraphers, shop foremen, stenographers, etc.

Level C (Skilled Tradesmen and Low Grade Clerical Workers) Requires average abstract intelligence with training equivalent to vocational high school. Work demanding specialized skill and knowledge; tasks mostly of a complicated but concrete nature requiring specialized training. Includes 26 to 75 percentile.

Examples: Auto mechanic, stationary engineer, file clerk, typist, etc.

Level D (Semiskilled and Unskilled Occupations) Requires low average or slightly below average abstract intelligence with training equivalent to eighth grade or less. Work demanding a minimum of technical knowledge or skill but may involve special abilities, such as dexterity in the performance of repetitive and routine work. Includes 1 to 25 percentile.

Examples: Packer in factories, operatives in factories (operate machines but do not understand principles and are unable to repair or set up the machine), lowest grade of clerical work (numbers sorters, deliverymen), or routine manual work under supervision requiring no skill or technical knowledge (day laborers, railroad section hands, etc.).

The other five abilities (mechanical, social, clerical, musical, and artistic) are similarly analyzed. Then, each of 430 occupations is analyzed and the "minimum level of ability required for job competition" is indicated by the appropriate letter symbol. Table 5–4 illustrates the procedure.

Since there are six abilities considered and four levels of each, there are 360 possible ability patterns. Actually, but 155 were found and 85 of these were for single occupations. That means that in the 345 remaining occupations there were but 70 ability patterns. Sometimes a single ability pattern was found in as many as 34 occupations. As illustrated in Table 5–5, many occupations are "sisters under the skin."

The authors claim that three uses can be made of the occupational rating scales: to supplement other teaching methods in counselor training classes; to assist students, in courses about occupations; to learn facts that are significant in making wise occupational choices; and to aid personnel workers in counseling individual cases regarding their most appropriate occupational selections. They warn against the mechanical use of the scales by those who are inadequately trained for scientific vocational counseling.

Table 5–4. Minnesota Occupational Rating Scales

Occupation	Abilities					
	Aca-demic	Me-chan-ical	Social	Clerical	Musi-cal	Artis-tic
19. Auctioneer, general.....	C	D	A	C	D	D
25. Banker and bank officer, small town...........	A	D	B	A	D	D
51. Cartoonist, newspaper or magazine............	B	C	B	D	D	B
88. Day laborer............	D	D	D	D	D	D
92. Dentist, great, in city...	A	A	B	C	D	D
124. Engineer, electrical, college training.........	A	A	D	B	D	D
158. Hairdresser, manicurist, employed in shop.....	D	C	C	D	D	D
192. Laundry owner and manager, of average laundry.................	B	C	B	C	D	D
249. Oil well driller..........	D	B	D	D	D	D
277. President, college.......	A	D	B	B	D	D
313. Retail dealer, florist.....	C	D	C	C	D	C
339. Salesman, auto.........	B	C	A	C	D	D
384. Teacher, high-school (college graduate)........	A	D	B	C	D	D
405. Undertaker, funeral director..............	B	C	B	C	D	D

Perhaps the additional criticism should be given that the scales analyze occupations on the basis of some abilities that are unimportant (music and art) in most occupations and omit other abilities that are important (personality and sensory acuity) in most occupations. This is due in part to the ease and accuracy of measuring music and art and the difficulty of measuring personality. However, sensory acuity is easily measured and social intelligence is very difficult to measure.

The authors warn, and rightly so, that "use [of the scales] assumes an understanding of the theory of aptitudes, current thinking and counseling practices in regard to special and general abilities, backgrounds in measurement and techniques, job description and job analysis work, and the professional vocabulary of the educational personnel worker." In other words, the Minnesota Occupational Rating Scales should be used only by those who are well trained in the scientific techniques of vocational counseling, although in that case, the scales are unnecessary. A well-trained counselor becomes so familiar with the human requirements of the various occupations that he does not need to refer to a scale of

Table 5–5. Ability Patterns and Related Occupations

Patterns						Occupations
Aca-demic	Me-chan-ical	Social	Clerical	Musi-cal	Artis-tic	
A	C	B	B	D	D	Land owner, operator, large scale Manager or superintendent, average size factory Officer, army Official manufacturing, head of large company Professor, university, A.M. or Ph.D.
B	D	C	B	D	D	Agent, express and freight Appraiser, taxes, insurance, etc. Conductor, railroad Retail dealer, department store Stenographer, shorthand, typing
C	D	C	C	D	C	Clerk in art store Retail dealer, candy, confec-tionery Retail dealer, florist

"pooled judgments of vocational psychologists." A part of his training is a wide knowledge of vocational requirements. However, the value of these scales in training future vocational counselors, as well as in teaching a counselee, is not overemphasized by the authors.

A "counseling profile set of disks" is devised to accompany the Occupational Rating Scales. They are colorful, suggest the accuracy of the circular slide rule, and thus are impressive to the naïve client. Perhaps they also suggest a professional dignity to vocational counseling, but as a tool for the trained counselor, they are worthless.

THE GOVERNMENT PROGRAM OF OCCUPATIONAL RESEARCH

The Wagner-Peyser Act (passed by Congress in 1933) created a national Employment Service that provided for the registration of workmen according to their occupational characteristics. (Twelve-and-a-half million workmen were registered during the first year.) It soon became obvious that an enormous amount of research would be necessary to create proper tools and methods for employment service. In 1934 the Secretary of Labor appointed a Technical Board to guide the research program of the Employment Service. This research progressed along two lines—collection of occupational information and development of techniques of selecting workmen. The job information research was broken down into three phases—a definition of jobs (*Dictionary of Occupational Titles*), a classification of jobs at various levels of combination according to their human requirements (the *Occupational Code*), and detailed information about the essential content of each occupation (*Job Description*). The selection technique research was broken down into two phases—the measurement of work proficiency (*Trade Question,* and *Work-sample Tests*) and tests to measure aptitudes or capacities to learn (*Potentiality Predictors*). These two phases of research were integrated (really a third phase) in the attempt to discover what jobs are sufficiently alike (*Job Equivalents*) to permit the transfer of workmen from one job to another without too great a handicap.

The results of research in selection techniques have not been published for general circulation. They are available for use only in the 1,600 offices of the United States Employment Service. Obviously, the general dissemination of information of this type would soon render it useless for the purpose for which it was intended. However, it is known that wide use was made of commercial tests as well as of new tests that were developed. Perhaps the major contribution of research in selection techniques was the development of appropriate norms for each occupation for which a test was used. General population norms are of little value when applicants are being selected for a highly specialized job. The U.S.E.S. has developed norm tables for various tests on a large number of occupations.

The research in job information is available to the public in a number of outstanding publications, which will be described in the following pages.

The Dictionary of Occupational Titles. The original research work of the U.S.E.S. in the field of occupational information was an exhaustive analysis of certain occupations and the publication of detailed job descriptions (such as a five-volume study of the construction industry and a three-volume study of the retail trade). However, it soon became evident that a more immediate need was for a condensed description of jobs in all occupations and in all parts of the country—a job dictionary. This project was begun in 1936. Then it became evident that a revised classification of jobs was fundamental. Consequently, a new system of job coding developed concurrently with the definitions of some 17,452 jobs (known by some 29,744 different titles) from some 54,189 separate job analyses. The Dictionary of Occupational Titles was published in 1939. It defined at least 75 per cent of all the jobs in the United States, in which are employed at least 90 per cent of all workers. "The job definitions in the Dictionary are short statements of the work performed in the various jobs found to exist in those industries and types of work listed and defined." There are six sections of the book: (1) a description and explanation of the definitions and titles and of the code system; (2) directions for using the book; (3) the book proper, jobs and their definitions; (4) a glossary of technical terms used in the dictionary; (5) a list of commodities sold in retail and wholesale with the job titles of their vendors; and (6) definitions of all industries and lists of jobs found in each. Needless to say, all definitions were verified by referring them to trade associations, labor unions, and other authorities.

Soon after the Dictionary of Occupational Titles was published in 1939 its limitations began to become evident. A great many jobs had been omitted. The first year after its release some 1,400 new definitions and 800 new code numbers were added. Consequently a new supplement was published in 1942 with 3,064 new definitions, another in 1944 with 1,137 definitions, and a third in 1945 with 1,906 definitions. In 1949 a new edition of the Dictionary of Occupational Titles was published which contains 22,028 defined jobs known by 40,023 different titles, and identified by 8,983 code numbers.

In both editions of the dictionary each code number consists of three parts—a single digit, followed by a dash, two digits followed by a decimal point, and then two or three additional digits. For example, a matcher operator in the woodworking industry is identified by the following code number, 6-33.463. This occupation includes such closely related jobs as matcher man; matcher-machine operator; side-matcher man; tongue-and-groove machine operator.

Each of the three parts of a code number indicates a major occupational group. The first digit indicates the following major classifications:

0—Professional and managerial occupations
1—Clerical and sales occupations
2—Service occupations
3—Agricultural, fishery, forestry, and kindred occupations
4 and 5—Skilled occupations
6 and 7—Semiskilled occupations
8 and 9—Unskilled occupations

The second part of the code number (those digits between the dash and the decimal) indicates major subdivisions of the above groups. Some of these are as follows:

Professional and Managerial Occupations

0–0 through 0–3	Professional occupations
0–4 through 0–6	Semiprofessional occupations
0–7 through 0–9	Managerial and official occupations

CLERICAL AND SALES OCCUPATIONS

1–0 through 1–4   Clerical and kindred occupations
1–5 through 1–9   Sales and kindred occupations

SERVICE OCCUPATIONS

2–0 through 2–09   Domestic service occupations
2–2 through 2–5   Personal service occupations
2–6   Protective service occupations
2–8 through 2–9   Building service workers and porters

AGRICULTURE, FISHERY, FORESTRY, AND KINDRED OCCUPATIONS

3–0 through 3–4   Agricultural, horticultural and kindred occupations
3–8   Fishery occupations
3–9   Forestry (except logging) and hunting and trapping occupations

SKILLED OCCUPATIONS

4–0 through 5–18   Occupations in manufacturing activities
5–2 through 5–61   Occupations in nonmanufacturing activities
5–63 through 5–89   Occupations in miscellaneous activities
5–91 through 5–99   Foremen

SEMISKILLED OCCUPATIONS

6–0 through 7–18   Occupations in manufacturing activities
7–20 through 7–61   Occupations in nonmanufacturing activities
7–63 through 7–89   Occupations in miscellaneous activities
7–93 through 7–99   Apprentices

UNSKILLED OCCUPATIONS

8–0 through 9–18   Occupations in manufacturing activities
9–20 through 9–61   Occupations in nonmanufacturing activities
9–63 through 9–89   Miscellaneous

The significance of each step in a specific code number is illustrated as follows:

2–   Service occupations
2–2   Personal service occupations
2–26   Cooks, except private family
2–26.0   Chefs and cooks, large hotels and restaurants
2–26.01   Executive chef

The value of the Dictionary of Occupational Titles in vocational counseling cannot be overemphasized. No counselor, regardless of his breadth of experience and scope of training, can be familiar with 17,000 jobs and 9,000 occupations. Whether the counselor is in the personnel department of an industry or on the staff of an educational institution, the Dictionary of Occupational Titles is an indispensable handbook. It gives him a vertical view of more than 22,000 jobs and a horizontal view of jobs of the same general level. By interpreting the code numbers and reading the definitions, a counselor can get a working understanding of a job with which he is completely unfamiliar. Certainly the use of this dictionary should be the first step in the study of any job.

Job Descriptions. The first industry to be thoroughly analyzed by the U.S.E.S. was the laundry industry. This was soon followed by the cotton textile industry and later by automobile manufacturing and construction industries. By March, 1942, fourteen industries had been analyzed and all jobs therein carefully described. These industries employ approximately 45 per cent of all wage earners and salaried workers in the country. More than 65,000 copies of these job descriptions have been distributed to libraries, schools, employment offices, industries, and the general public.

These job descriptions are vastly more detailed and complete than the job definitions in the Dictionary of Occupational Titles. Consequently, they are of more value in vocational counseling. They supply both the counselor and the counselee with a complete picture of each job in an industry—the work performed, the equipment used, the material which is processed, the physical conditions under which the job is performed, the dangers or safety hazards involved, the physical or mental effort required, etc. Neither the vocational counselor nor the person whom he counsels need be "in the dark" about any job covered by these job descriptions.

In training courses for vocational counseling these job descriptions are second only to firsthand information about the various jobs in American life. It is best for a counselor to have worked at a job himself and know it firsthand; it is next best for him to know a great deal about a job, even if he gets the information out of a book. Students of vocational counseling should use both methods extensively. One should supplement the other. Job descriptions enable the counselor to become familiar not only with the details of jobs themselves, but also with human requirements of the job. A part of every description is a detailed analysis of the human traits and abilities that are important in job success.

Job Equivalents. It is very important, both to the worker and to the industry in which he is employed, that each employee be capable of performing several jobs. If a worker is fitted to perform but one job and that job is abolished, he is no longer useful to that company. On the other hand, if he can perform several related jobs he is assured of steady employment and the company has the advantage of a steady workman. (The cost of labor turnover varies in different industries but ranges from $30 to $500 per man.)

As jobs were analyzed for the Dictionary of Occupational Titles and for Job Descriptions, records were also kept of the amount of some 47 human traits or worker characteristics estimated to be needed on jobs. These included such traits as strength, dexterity, perception of form, visual acuity, memory, adaptability, initiative, oral expression, etc. A worker-characteristic form was made out for each job analyzed. In 1937 the processing of these data began and jobs were classified into related groups or job families. By 1940 the worker-characteristic data for some 8,000 jobs had been analyzed and 49 job families had been discovered. Each job family consisted of a list of jobs requiring approximately the same human abilities. A workman who was successful on one of the jobs of a job family could with a minimum of effort and training perform any other job of the family with equal or nearly equal success.

The procedure used to determine how much of a worker characteristic is required by an occupation was the rating method. After analysts were carefully trained they simply judged whether a job required A, B, or C amount of each of the 47 characteristics. An A amount of a characteristic was a very great amount—that possessed by not more than 2 per cent of the general population. A B amount of a characteristic was also a superior amount but less than that indicated by A. It was more than that possessed by 70 per cent of the general population but less than that possessed by 2 per cent. A C amount of a characteristic was that possessed by the lowest 70 per cent of the population. Studies indicated that the reliability of the ratings was sufficiently high to justify the method.

It was found that job families were larger on those levels that require short or no training periods. Jobs with long training periods were not found in large job families. For example, there were a large number of jobs on the unskilled levels that required the same worker characteristics. On the other hand, there were relatively few jobs on the professional levels that required the same worker characteristics. The range of job families, and the consequent range of transferability, may be illustrated by a pyramid of occupations arranged on levels as determined by the length of the training period (see Fig. 5–7).

Information about job families has a number of significant uses in vocational counseling. First, workmen can be transferred (for reasons of seasonality, shortage of material, war necessities, changes in consumer demands, etc.) to other jobs that are most like the jobs that they now perform. Consequently, there is a minimum of loss in additional training, waste of material, reduced production, etc. Second, new workmen can be placed in the appropriate job family even when it is impossible to place them on a specific job for which they have had training and experience. Third, workmen can be upgraded to jobs that are near the border line of a job family and just across the line from another job family that carries a higher pay rate. In short, information about job families enables a counselor to manage his manpower in a more intelligent manner.

Such information is also useful to the school counselor. Both he and the student can see a job in its functional relationship to other jobs. Opportunities and blind alleys are more clear. The worth of various human characteristics is more obvious. A job can better be evaluated when it is judged with other jobs in its job family.

Information about job families is released to the various offices of the

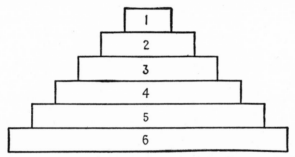

FIG. 5–7. Relation of levels of training to size of job families. (1) Professional occupations, (2) semiprofessional and managerial occupations, (3) crafts and skilled occupations, (4) clerical occupations, (5) semiskilled occupations, (6) unskilled occupations.

U.S.E.S. as it becomes available. However, it is not restricted information and may be obtained by others from the Department of Labor, Washington, D.C.

RELATING INDIVIDUAL ANALYSIS TO JOB ANALYSIS

It would seem that, when the qualifications of an individual have been carefully evaluated and the requirements of various occupations are known, the next step of getting the individual into the proper occupation would follow automatically. Actually the problem is not so simple. There are a number of difficulties. First, analyses of both the individual and the occupation are so inaccurate that conclusions can be drawn only with the utmost caution. Analyses furnish the individual with more information, but his vocational problem is yet to be solved. Second, there are always degrees of occupational success, and happiness is often as great at the lower levels as at the higher ones. An individual may be better qualified for a certain occupation but he may prefer more limited success in another field. Third, abilities are always dependent on effort and opportunity. Even a genius cannot succeed without trying and having an opportunity.

In practical vocational guidance there are a few key factors to be considered after the individual's abilities have been analyzed and occupations have been studied. They are practical considerations that may outweigh or supplement the data on individual and job profiles.

OCCUPATIONAL TRENDS

The 1950 census showed that there were approximately 150,000,000 people in the United States (see Fig. 5–8). More than 60,000,000 of

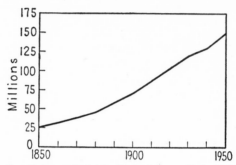

FIG. 5–8. Population gain in the United States from 1850 to 1950.

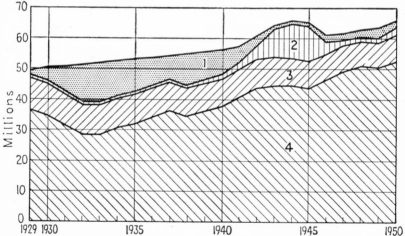

FIG. 5–9. Labor force and unemployed—annual averages. (1) unemployed, (2) armed forces, (3) agricultural employees, (4) nonagricultural employees.

these were gainfully employed. (In April, 1950, there were 63,000,000 employed, or 57 per cent of the total population over fourteen years of age.) Of these, 7,200,000 were engaged in agricultural work, 51,500,000 were in nonagricultural work, and the rest were in the armed services. These proportions are shown in Fig. 5–9. As would be expected, more men were employed than women and more of both sexes between the ages of twenty and sixty-five. Figure 5–10 gives the percentages of employment of both sexes and of each age level.

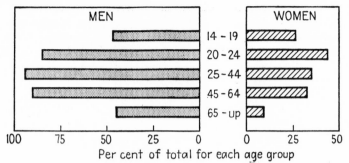

FIG. 5–10. Labor force for 1950 for age and sex.

The trends in various fields of occupations are shown in Table 5–6 and Fig. 5–11. The table shows the percentage of the total labor force in each occupation while the figure shows the number of employees in each occupational field. Some fields are increasing, some are decreasing, some are more sensitive to depression than others, some are more sensitive to war, and some are constant and apparently but little affected by conditions.

So much for occupational trends as they have occurred in the past. Now, what of the future? Which occupational fields can be expected to increase and which ones will probably decrease? There are a number of fairly obvious trends that will probably carry into the future. First, the trend to develop machines to take care of more and more crude, unskilled work is probably only in its infancy. We shall need fewer unskilled laborers and more trained mechanics and machine operators. Second, the trend toward more and more govern-

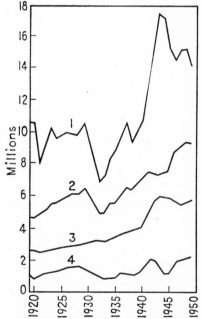

FIG. 5–11. Trend of employment in (1) manufacturing, (2) retail and wholesale trade, (3) government service, and (4) construction work.

mental function (in both service and regulation) will probably increase regardless of the political party in power. Most of these jobs are cler-

Table 5–6. Occupational Trends for 1940 and 1950 in Per Cent of Total Employed*

	1940	1950
Professional, technical, kindred..........	7.9	8.9
Farmers and farm managers.............	11.5	8.0
Managers, officials, proprietors..........	8.3	9.0
Clerical and kindred...................	9.8	12.1
Sales workers.........................	6.5	6.7
Craftsmen and foremen................	11.4	13.7
Operatives and kindred................	18.2	19.8
Private household workers..............	4.6	2.6
Service workers.......................	7.2	7.4
Farm laborers........................	6.7	4.5
Laborers (other than farm).............	6.9	6.0
Unreported...........................	0.8	1.4

* From bulletin dated Apr. 11, 1951, U.S. Bureau of Census.

ical in nature, but many of them are pioneering research and investigation. Third, the slowly developing trend toward the more efficient distribution of goods (through various forms of cooperative agencies) and the elimination of the parasitical and functionless middleman will probably become more pronounced in the future. In fact, all occupations that are not essential in the cooperative life of our people will probably decline.

In Table 5–7 there are a number of occupations and occupational

Table 5–7. Probable Occupational Trends in the Future

Increase	Decrease
Scientific farming	Unskilled labor
Industrial chemistry	Sales (other than across counter)
Aviation	Domestic service
Engineering (all kinds)	Subsistence farming
Electrical	Lumbering
Mechanical	Animal husbandry
Chemical	Railroading
Agricultural	
Lighting and heating	
The professions of	
Medicine	
Nursing	
Teaching	
Personnel management	
Mechanical repair and operation	
Clerical jobs (all kinds)	
Governmental work	
Welfare work	
Skilled and semiskilled labor	

fields that may be expected to increase in the future and a number that may be expected to decrease. These predictions are based on obvious trends in the 1940 census, developments since 1940, and the predictions of specialists in occupational development.[8]

INTELLIGENCE IN OCCUPATIONS

The most fundamental aptitude to be considered in vocational guidance is mental activity. There are two reasons for this: first, occupations vary in the amount of intelligence they require, and second, individuals

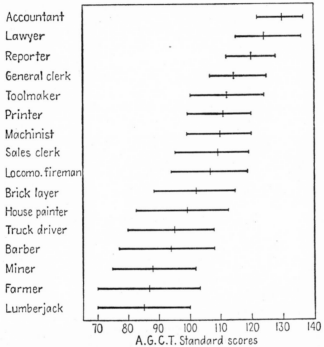

FIG. 5–12. Army General Classification Test scores for sixteen representative occupations showing the range of the two middle quartiles.

vary in the amount of intelligence they possess. Because there is a scarcity of intelligence on the higher levels it is important for every man to be engaged in an occupation that just fits his intellectual level. The intellectual hierarchy of occupations was long assumed but definitely proved by the Army Alpha Test of the First World War and the Classification Tests of the Second World War. By far the greatest mass of data ever collected on the relation of intelligence to occupational status was during the Second World War when almost 10,000,000 American soldiers were given classification tests. Figure 5–12 shows the standard scores of the middle quartiles of 16 occupations. Note that the average accountant

[8] An excellent source of material on occupational trends is the *Occupational Outlook Handbook*, Bull. 998, U.S. Department of Labor, 1951.

ranks one and one-half sigmas (score 130) above the mean for the general army population (score 100) while the average farmer ranks more than a half sigma (score 87) below the general population mean.

The significance of intelligence in relation to occupational status is also indicated in a follow-up study of 4,184 citizens of Cincinnati, Ohio, who had taken an intelligence test in the sixth grade 12 years previously. The results are shown in Table 5–8. In general, those who were in the higher

Table 5–8. Relation of Intelligence in the Sixth Grade to Various Factors 12 Years
Later (N 4,184)
(In per cent of total)

Intelligence test percentile	Graduated from		Delinquent	Vocational status					
	High school	College		Professional	Clerical	Sales	Skilled	Unskilled	Housewife and unemployed
80–100	74	28	0.3	16	24	14	4	9	27
60–79	54	15	4	9	23	16	5	13	31
40–59	34	6	6	6	18	13	8	16	37
20–39	14	2	9	3	13	12	9	22	39
1–19	6	1	10	1	6	8	9	31	44

levels on the test went to college and were in the higher occupations. Those in the lower levels on the test were more frequently delinquent and engaged in unskilled work.

Hartson[9] reports a study of the relation of intelligence to the occupational choice of some 1,100 graduates of a small college. The average centile rank of each occupational group on an intelligence test taken while in college is shown in Table 5–9. This merely indicates which occupations appeal to the various intellectual levels.

However, the vocational counselor is not so much concerned with the average intelligence of those who are now in the various occupations as he is with the level of intelligence necessary for success in the various occupations. As suggested earlier in this chapter, the Minnesota Occupational Rating Scales indicate the intelligence level necessary for success in some 430 occupations. The Barr Scale of Occupational Status is another attempt to arrange occupations into an intellectual hierarchy. This was also constructed by pooling the judgments of 20 experts concerning the minimum intellectual requirements of 121 occupations. Sample occu-

[9] Hartson, L. D., Intelligence and Scholarship of Occupational Groups, *Person. J.,* 1928, **7**, 281–285.

Table 5-9. Intelligence and Occupational Choice of College Graduates

Occupation	Intelligence Centile	Occupation	Intelligence Centile
College teaching (women)	77	Business (men)	50
College teaching (men)	65	Engineering	49
Secretarial work	59	Business (women)	49
Journalism	57	Library work	46
High school teaching (men)	57	Salesmanship	44
Medicine	54	Social work	41
High school teaching (women)	53	Y.M.C.A. and Y.W.C.A.	39
Religious work	51	Physical education (women)	35
Law	51	Art	27
Music	51	Physical education (men)	20

Table 5-10. Extracts from the Barr Scale of Occupational Status

3.38	Circus roustabout	Does heavy, rough work about a circus
6.42	Switchman	Tending switch in railroad yards
7.54	Policeman	Average patrolman
10.11	Telegraph operator	In small town
12.02	Librarian	In small institution or public library
15.14	High school teacher	College or normal graduate. Not the most progressive
16.59	Consulting engineer	In charge of corps of engineers
17.81	University professor	Has A.M. or Ph.D., writes, teaches, and does research
19.45	Research leader	Like Binet or Pasteur

pations and P.E. values are shown in Table 5–10. Terman[10] used this scale in his study of the fathers of gifted children and found that their mean score was 12.77 as compared with 7.92 for the general population.

Fryer[11] studied the intelligence test data from the First World War and attempted to modify them to fit occupational requirements. His list is similar to the Barr list but arranged in groups of occupations having essentially the same intellectual requirements. The professions are in the A group and the common-labor jobs in the C and D groups.

Lorge and Blau[12] used both the Barr and Fryer scales to estimate the intellectual demands of the major occupational groups in the Dictionary of Occupational Titles. They first classified all the occupations listed in both scales into the major groups as listed in the dictionary. They then computed the mean scale value for each group. These values are shown in Table 5–11. On the basis of this they recommended that the dictionary groups be given values, as indicated in the last column in Table 5–11.

However, if the mean Barr values and the mean Fryer values are added for each group, a relationship is indicated that does not quite conform to

[10] Terman, L. M., et al., Genetic Studies of Genius, Vol. I, Stanford University Press, Stanford, Calif., 1925.

[11] Fryer, D., Occupational Intelligence Standards, Sch. & Soc., 1922, 16, 273–278.

[12] Lorge, I., and Blau, R. D., Broad Occupational Groupings by Estimated Abilities, Occupations, 1942, 21, 288–295.

Table 5–11. Barr Scale and Fryer Scale Values for Major Occupational Groups of the Dictionary of Occuptional Titles

Occupational groups	D.O.T. codes	Mean Barr value	Mean Fryer value	Lorge-Blau value
Professional..........	0–0 through 0–3	14.62	6.05	10
Managerial and official	0–7 through 0–9	13.75	5.5	9
Semiprofessional.......	0–4 through 0–6	11.58	5.68	8
Clerical and kindred...	1–0 through 1–4	10.13	5.38	7
Sales and kindred.....	1–5 through 1–9	10.45	4.76	6½
Protective service.....	2–6	8.58	5.17	6
Skilled...............	4– and 5–	8.54	4.9	5½
Agricultural..........	3–0 through 3–4	7.62	4.9	5
Personal service.......	2–2 through 2–5	8.03	4.64	4½
Semiskilled..........	6– and 7–	6.67	4.72	4
Unskilled............	8– and 9–	3.93	3.73	3
Domestic service......	2–0	1.54	4.0	2
Fishery..............	3–8	.....	3.68	1

Table 5–12. Sum of Barr and Fryer Scale Values and Interpretation in Approximate Intelligence Meanings

Occupational groups	Sum of Barr and Fryer values	Approx. M.A.	Approx. I.Q.
Professional............................	20.67	18 up	120 up
Managerial and official.................	19.25	17	113
Semiprofessional.......................	17.26	16	107
Clerical and kindred....................	15.51	15	100
Sales and kindred......................	15.21	15	100
Protective service......................	13.75	14	93
Skilled................................	13.34	14	93
Personal service.......................	12.67	13.5	90
Agricultural...........................	12.52	13.5	90
Semiskilled............................	11.39	13	87
Unskilled..............................	7.66	11	73
Domestic service.......................	5.54	10	67
Fishery................................	.....	9.5	63

the Lorge-Blau recommendations (see Table 5–12). If these sums are taken as a basis for comparing the intellectual demands of each group, an approximate estimate can be made of the mean mental age and I.Q. for each group. This is indicated in Table 5–12.

THE WORTH OF VOCATIONAL GUIDANCE

Vocational guidance has been widely adopted and practiced by those who are qualified and by those who are not. Undoubtedly its use by qualified counselors has been beneficial to thousands of individuals at all levels of development. The junior and senior high schools, the colleges, the army, industry, business, are all scenes of vocational counseling —both good and bad. Any study of the effects of vocational counseling is affected by whether or not the counseling was done by well-trained counselors or by those who were in counseling positions.

Webster[13] made a follow-up study of a group of advisees from 2 to 5 years after they had been given a battery of tests and vocationally advised. He found that 52.8 per cent of them had followed recommendations, 29 per cent had ignored recommendations, and 18.2 per cent could not be classified in this respect. For those who followed recommendations, the ratio of vocational success to vocational failure was 28 to 1; for those who did not follow recommendations, this ratio was but 1 to 1.

Failor and Isaacson[14] questioned 658 veterans about the worth of army vocational guidance and found enthusiastic approval. Veterans believed that they were definitely benefited by the army guidance although they were dissatisfied with the paucity of information about occupations. They would have liked to learn about a wider variety of occupations.

Anderson[15] studied the effects of vocational counseling based on carefully collected information regarding personal and family data, previous employment experience, work record on the present job, medical examination, and data from a rather elaborate psychological testing program. She found that young employees seemed to benefit more than the older ones, the educated more than the less educated, and those with superior ability more than those with low ability. More than 82 per cent believed that the counseling was of personal value. Many suggested that the counseling was too brief. The same author checked the opinion of 444 veterans who were counseled for placement in postwar jobs; 82.4 per cent considered that they were well placed and their employers concurred in this opinion.

Barnette[16] did a mail questionnaire study of the opinion of 890 veterans in the New York area who had been completely counseled, *i.e.,* including vocational counseling. Exactly 75 per cent reported that the counseling had been helpful, 19 per cent considered it of doubtful value, 3 per cent thought it was impractical, and 3 per cent had no opinion.

A study of 639 vocational advisees of the National Institute of In-

[13] Webster, E. G., A Follow-up of Vocational Guidance, *J. Appl. Psychol.,* 1942, **26,** 285–295.

[14] Failor, C. W., and Isaacson, L. E., The Veteran Evaluates Counseling, *Occupations,* 1949, **28,** 18–24.

[15] Anderson, Rose G., Reported and Demonstrated Values of Vocational Counseling, *Jr. Appl. Psychol.,* 1949, **33,** 460–473.

[16] Barnette, W. L., Jr., Reactions of Veterans to Counseling, *Jr. Appl. Psychol.,* 1950, **34,** 399–405.

dustrial Psychology in England revealed that the ratio of success to failure was 15 to 1 for those who had followed recommendations and but 2 to 1 for those who had not. Of those who completed their formal schooling and followed recommendations, 79 per cent were considered to be vocationally well adjusted.[17]

Perhaps the most complete study of this nature was made by Thorndike.[18] Eight years after 1,807 New York school children (ages thirteen to fifteen) had been given intelligence, clerical, and mechanical tests, they were interviewed concerning the kind of work they were doing, their annual wages, their interest in their work, and the frequency of job changes. In general, the correlations were all extremely low. The author concludes that "no combination of the facts gathered by us at the age 14 would have enabled a vocational counselor to foretell how well a boy or girl would do in mechanical work six to eight years later, or how happy he would be at it." Critics have suggested that if these young people had been vocationally counseled as well as merely tested, the correlations would have been much higher. Then, the original testing for the study was done in 1921 when vocational tests were less adequate than they have become in more recent years. However, it is worth noting that, while low, the correlations in this study were positive. They indicated some relationships. The test data were not entirely insignificant. A well-trained vocational counselor could have used these data to supplement other data about these young people, and the picture for making an inevitable vocational choice would have been more clear. Test data are not infallible but they help.

The point cannot be overemphasized that test data in the field of psychology are yet crude and must be used with intelligent caution by those who are properly trained for their interpretation. Vocational guidance counselors must be more than teachers who are merely interested in young people and their problems. They must be professionally trained psychologists who are willing to limit their work to this special field. Vocational guidance is a profession that must be as carefully and thoroughly prepared for as medicine or law or engineering.

The future of vocational guidance would seem to be especially alluring. Monumental steps have been made in the last 5 years in developing scientific techniques in individual and occupational analysis. The experience of the analysis and placement of 10,000,000 soldiers will soon be made available to us. New tools already exist for more accurately solving the problem of a boy's or girl's vocational choice. The need is for those who are adequately trained in using these new devices.

[17] Report on a Follow-up of Vocationally Advised Cases, *Hum, Factor, Lond.,* 1937, **11**, 16–26.

[18] Thorndike, E. L., *et al., Prediction of Vocational Success,* Oxford University Press, New York, 1934.

SUMMARY

Vocational guidance consists of two steps—analyzing the individual and analyzing the occupation. Both are technical procedures that require the services of those who are professionally trained. However, even with all the technical data possible and the clarity of its interpretation, the human element is still involved and the individual concerned makes the final decision. All the vocational specialist can do is counsel. He must sell his conclusions to the counselees.

This suggests that in addition to being a specialist in analyzing the qualifications of individuals and the requirements of occupations the counselor must also be a teacher. The individual whose vocational problem is being solved must learn why one occupation is more appropriate than another. He must understand his qualifications and their significance in the occupational world. He must be taught to become a specialist concerning his own problem.

RECOMMENDED SUPPLEMENTARY READINGS

Bingham, G. V.: *Aptitudes and Aptitude Testing,* Harper & Brothers, New York, 1937.

Cronbach, L. J.: *Essentials of Psychological Testing,* Harper & Brothers, New York, 1949.

Myers, G. E.: *Principles and Techniques of Vocational Guidance,* McGraw-Hill Book Company, Inc., New York, 1941.

Paterson, D. G., *et al.: Student Guidance Techniques,* McGraw-Hill Book Company, Inc., New York, 1938.

Paterson, D. G.: Analysis of the Individual, *Occupations,* 1934, **12,** 1–91.

Ruch, G. M., and Segal, D.: *Minimum Essentials of the Individual Inventory in Guidance,* Voc. Div. Bull. 202, U.S. Office of Education, 1939.

Shartle, C. L.: *Occupational Information,* Prentice-Hall, Inc., New York, 1952.

Stead, W. H., *et. al.: Occupational Counseling Techniques,* American Book Company, New York, 1940.

Strong, E. K.: *Vocational Interests of Men and Women,* Stanford University Press, Stanford, Calif., 1943.

Super, D. E.: *Appraising Vocational Fitness,* Harper & Brothers, New York, 1949.

Chapter 6

PERSONALITY ADJUSTMENT

Personalities are the product of adjustments which are made to the ordinary incidents that occur in our lives. If these adjustments are successful, the effect on the personality is then beneficial. Too often unsuccessful and partially successful adjustments are made and personalities are warped accordingly. Habits, attitudes, predispositions, prejudices, beliefs, and emotional patterns are formed as a result of these adjustment experiences. The following three examples illustrate how experiences mold personalities.

Professor X taught music in a small Middle Western denominational college and had a very maladjusted personality. He was negativistic and over-sensitive to criticism (had ideas of reference). At the same time he was egotistical and arrogant. He overemphasized two things—his doctor of philosophy degree and his disdain for correspondence schools. He had worked his way through college and made very poor grades. After graduation he taught in high schools for four years (at four different places) and was frequently embarrassed by his inadequate knowledge of the subjects he tried to teach. He was a fairly good church organist and decided to specialize in music at an Eastern school. After several years he somehow acquired a doctor of philosophy degree. He then returned to the Middle West and with added prestige was able to secure a college position. (It was later learned that he had secured his doctor of philosophy degree from a second-rate correspondence school.)

Mary X was thirty-one years old and had stuttered since she was eleven. She was unmarried and rather obviously an introvert. Her mother, whom she had supported since she graduated from high school, had recently died. Mary consulted a speech clinician about her stuttering and he uncovered the following facts. At the age of eleven Mary was completely ignorant about sex and its significance. Her mother, who was a widow, was very religious and very strict in discipline. In discussing sex with an equally naïve preadolescent neighbor boy, Mary suggested that they remove their clothing to see how each other looked. This was done in the garage just back of Mary's home. Entirely by accident, the boy's mother discovered them displaying themselves to each other. Both were severely punished (physically) and Mary was made to feel that somehow she was doomed to a lifetime of disgrace. She was very much ashamed of the affair and feared that every one knew her secret. Night after night she cried herself to sleep. She had nightmares. She began to stutter.

Susan Y was a senior in high school. She had studied hard and ranked high in her class but as commencement neared she had two disappointments. First, she was not chosen for a part in the senior play. Second, she was neither valedictorian nor salutatorian. The morning before the class play, Susan awakened to find herself unable to see. She was functionally blind. The family physician was called and after examining Susan remembered that when she was younger she had had an eye affliction that kept her out of school several days.

An old saying that "life is just one darn thing after another," when properly interpreted, is literally true. Life is a continuous process of overcoming difficulties, or of making adjustments. No sooner is one adjustment made than another arises. Successful adjustment is necessary for continued living. *Adjust or die* is the law of life.

In making these adjustments, habits are formed that become the pattern for making future adjustments. Individuals become identified by their habits of adjustment. For example, one individual may habitually approach his adjustment problems slowly and calmly. He does not become excited and impatient with life. He is persistent and tenacious in his habits. He does not solve many adjustment problems but he never side-steps a problem and he never leaves one half-solved. Another individual lives "fast and furious." He disposes of problems quickly. If they are easily solved, well and good; if not, they are avoided, by-passed, ignored. He is a man of action. Both these men have identifying habits of adjustment. Both learned them in the same way—by making adjustments.

The habits that people form in adjusting themselves to the ordinary problems of living constitute their *personalities*. Personality may be defined as the sum total of those habits a person has formed in adjusting himself to life situations. A good personality is a set of habits that are successful in adjustments; a poor personality is a set of habits that are relatively unsuccessful. Personality, then, is learned. It is the aftereffect of making adjustments. Successful adjustments result in good personalities; unsuccesful adjustments result in poor personalities. Personality is constantly being formed and changed.

There are a number of factors about an adjustment situation that have psychological significance. First, a *want* must exist. If there is no want there is no need for adjustment. Second, adjustment is the *satisfaction* of a want. When a want is satisfied an adjustment has been made. Even the sudden cessation of a want constitutes an adjustment. Third, *difficulties* that interfere with the satisfaction of wants constitute adjustment problems. If adjustments could be made easily, habits of adjustment would be relatively unimportant. These three fundamental factors in making adjustments are represented graphically in the following diagram.

It must be recognized that the satisfaction of all *human wants* is impossible. The difficulties that stand in the way of satisfying some wants are too great to be controlled. After all, human beings are mortal with all the limitations of mortality. When human wants are beyond human limitations they must be recognized as impossible to satisfy. To continue to want the moon is to create a permanent adjustment problem. Human wants must be restricted to the limits of possible satisfaction.

However, some people have more limitations than others and yet their wants are equally ambitious. For example, a person with a low intellectual aptitude may want to become a physician; or a physical weakling may want to become a prize fighter; or an untalented girl may want to become a movie actress; or a sexually unattractive woman may want to become a wife and mother. Such wants are within human limitations but not within certain personal limitations. For some people, they are simply impossible to satisfy. Again, human wants must be restricted to the limits of possible satisfaction.

Frequently wants that could be satisfied under certain conditions cannot be satisfied under other conditions. A boy might become a physician, but he does not have enough money to enable him to pay for the prerequisite education. A woman might become a school teacher, but she cannot control her temper long enough to hold a job beyond the probationary period. A girl might become a movie actress, but she does not have enough "pull" to enable her to get a screen test. Again human wants must fit the limits of possible and probable satisfaction.

In other words, human adjustments are often difficult to make because wants are too often impractical and unintelligent. They do not fit the peculiar limitations of the individual concerned.

The *difficulties* that may stand in the way of satisfying human wants are sometimes characteristic of the external environment—such as distance, time, social requirements, and other people—and sometimes characteristic of the individual himself—such as low ability, conflicting attitudes, and emotionality. Whatever the nature of adjustment difficulties, they constitute problems that must be studied carefully and solved in such a manner that consequent maladjustments are not created. The fundamental distinction between good and bad habits of adjustment is found in the consequences. Good habits result in successful adjustment with no consequent maladjustments; poor habits result in limited or no adjustment with consequent adjustment problems often greater than the original one. Problems of adjustment must be solved intelligently, with foresight of consequences.[1]

The *state of adjustment,* or satisfaction of wants, must meet two criteria —it must remove the organic tensions caused by the want, and it must not violate social custom. No adjustment is made until the individual himself is satisfied. It may be a peculiar adjustment and not acceptable

[1] All human problems deal with the difficulties of satisfying wants. Some are problems of relationship to other members of the family, some of relationship to the other sex, some of vocational adjustment, some of religious adjustment, some of cultural interpretations, some of scientific research. Whatever the nature of human problems, they are all problems of adjustment.

to others, yet if it relieves his state of tension and satisfies the want of the individual concerned, it constitutes an adjustment. However, if an adjustment violates a social custom it creates consequent maladjustments often greater than the original. Social customs are often foolish but it is always dangerous to violate them (unless the violation is in secret and is not consequently discovered). Social disapproval is in itself an adjustment problem that is often most difficult to solve.

The consequences of an individual habitually making successful adjustments to his varied problems of living are beneficial. He enjoys the experience of satisfying his wants; he forms a set of adjustment habits (personality) that are effective; he has a feeling of being integrated with his physical and social environment (of belonging); and he develops an attitude of personal importance and significance. The consequences of an individual habitually making unsuccessful adjustments to his varied problems of living are not beneficial. He experiences a constant state of physical tension due to unsatisfied wants; he forms adjustment habits (personality) that are ineffective; he has a feeling of not fitting in with either his physical or social environment. When human wants are extremely intensive and adjustments are extremely ineffective, one of the three following alternatives must eventuate:

1. Adjustment somehow becomes more effective so that want tensions are relieved.
2. Death intervenes.
3. The nervous system takes a vacation from such an intolerable condition of tension. (In other words, a state of insanity occurs.)

Individuals vary greatly in their tolerance of an unadjusted state. Some are able to endure it without showing symptoms of the condition, and others become quite psychoneurotic.

Few individuals form personalities that are composed only of successful adjustment habits. Likewise, few individuals form personalities that are composed only of unsuccessful adjustment habits. Most personalities are composed of some habits that are effective in satisfying wants and some that are relatively ineffective. Personality improvement consists of breaking, or discarding, the ineffective habits and forming more effective ones. This is called *mental hygiene*. The process, as would be expected, is largely one of identifying the ineffective habits (diagnosis) and establishing the more desirable and effective ones in their stead (therapeutics).

There are two major difficulties in the practice of mental hygiene— *understanding* what habits are ineffective and why, and *wanting* to substitute more effective ones. The first difficulty, more closely associated with diagnosis, is largely a matter of education; the second, more closely associated with therapeutics, is largely a matter of motivation. The mental hygienist must do two things—(1) diagnose his patient and instruct him about both his effective and ineffective habits; (2) plan a remedial program and motivate his patient to put it into practice.

Both adults and children need assistance in making the ordinary adjustments of living. Rogers[2] found in a sampling of elementary school children that 12 per cent had serious adjustment problems, 17.5 per cent had moderate adjustment problems, and 70.5 per cent were relatively well adjusted. Fenton[3] found in a study of the mental health of 241 teachers that 15.4 per cent were seriously maladjusted, 7.1 per cent were moderately maladjusted, and 77.5 per cent were well adjusted.

In a survey of the mental health of 600 teachers Hicks[4] found that men were better adjusted than women. While 20 per cent of the women were in poor mental health only 8 per cent of the men were so classified.

Ackerson[5] made a statistical study of the 5,000 children examined at the Illinois Institute for Juvenile Research. He found that adjustment problems were more frequent among boys than among girls and that frequencies increased for both up to about the age of twelve years. He divided adjustment problems into (1) personality problems and (2) conduct problems. The frequencies of these two types of adjustment problems are shown in Table 6–1. However, other investigators have

Table 6–1. Comparative Frequencies of Certain Behavior Problems

Personality Problems	Per Cent	Conduct Problems	Per Cent
Mental conflict................	4	Stealing.....................	26
Hyperactive (restless)..........	23	Lying........................	24
Inferiority feelings.............	6	Truancy (from school).........	19
Daydreaming.................	7	Disobedience.................	17
Egocentric...................	11	Truancy (from home).........	18
Seclusive....................	10	Fighting....................	10

found greater frequencies of mental conflicts and inferiority feelings. Paynter and Blanchard[6] found 45 per cent of a group of Los Angeles children with mental conflicts and 54 per cent of a group of Philadelphia children with inferiority feelings.

The 10 most frequent adjustment problems found by Ackerson are

[2] Rogers, C. R., A Study of Mental Health in Three Representative Elementary Schools, Ohio State Univ. Educ. Res. Monogr., 1941, 25, 130–161.

[3] Fenton, N., Mental Health in School Practice, Stanford University Press, Stanford, Calif., 1943.

[4] Hicks, F. R., The Mental Health of Teachers, Peabody Contributions to Education, 1934.

[5] Ackerson, L., Children's Behavior Problems, University of Chicago Press, Chicago, 1931.

[6] Paynter, R. H., and Blanchard, P., A Study of Educational Achievement of Problem Children, Commonwealth Fund, Division of Publication, New York, 1929.

Table 6–2. Comparative Frequencies of Behavior Problems in Boys and Girls

Problems	Boys (*N* 2,853)	Girls (*N* 1,739)
1. Nervous, restless, overactive, irritable, high strung, impatient, excitable............................	44	39
2. Disobedient, incorrigible, stubborn, contrary, defiant	42	37
3. Temper display, emotional, temperamental..........	34	27
4. Dull, slow, listless, lack of initiative...............	30	28
5. Fighting, quarrelsome............................	28	20
6. Sensitive, worries...............................	19	18
7. Egocentric, selfish...............................	17	15
8. Lacks interest, inattentive........................	18	11
9. Swears, profane, obscene language.................	11	6
10. Depressed, unhappy.............................	9	6

shown in Table 6–2. While the frequencies are relatively the same for both boys and girls, note that the boys exceed the girls in all 10 classifications of adjustment problems.

While there is evidence that youth have more adjustment problems than older people, there is also evidence that they can take it without serious

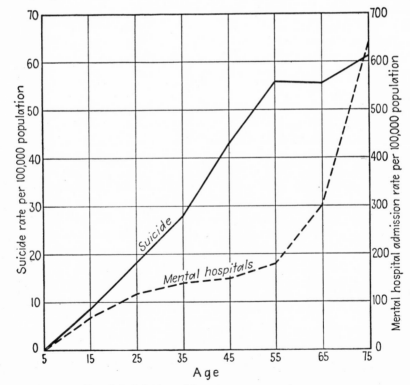

Fɪɢ. 6–1. Suicide and insanity rates at various ages.

immediate consequences. They have more "frustration tolerance" than do older people. The two most common manifestations of the effects of inability to solve adjustment problems are suicide and insanity. These are unusual at early ages but increase steadily with age. Figure 6–1 shows both suicide rate and insanity rate for various ages.[7]

Adjustment habits are usually not either good or bad, effective or ineffective, even in the same individual. More often they are somewhere between these two extremes. Some are effective and result in adjustment; some are partly effective and result in limited adjustment; some are neutral, neither effective nor ineffective; and some are actually harmful and increase the maladjustment. It is important to know the classification to which each adjustment habit belongs so that one can either foster or correct it in his own personality. The following pages discuss each of these classifications.

HABITS THAT PRODUCE ADJUSTMENT

A want for food may be satisfied by the simple process of going to the kitchen icebox to get it. The want is not unusual and has been foreseen. Food has been placed in the icebox. Even the individual's food likes may have been recognized and his personal satisfaction is assured. However, a food want may give rise to a problem of much greater magnitude. Jean Valjean (in Hugo's *Les Miserables*) wanted food also but the difficulty of obtaining it constituted a problem that he was unable to solve in a satisfactory manner. He spent 20 years as a galley slave because his solution resulted in subsequent maladjustment. Obviously, some adjustments are easy to make and are taken care of by routine habits. Other adjustments, sometimes to the same want, are difficult to make and require the most careful consideration. The method of solving an adjustment problem depends on its difficulty.

TRIAL-AND-ERROR BEHAVIOR

Fisher[8] points out that trial-and-error behavior, sometimes called "varied response," is "the most universally adjustive of all modes of reaction to difficulties. . . . A considerable part of the activity of the normal (adjusted) human individual, child or adult, which is concerned with adjustment to baffling situations, is of this type." Trial-and-error behavior on the human level implies *persistence* and *insight*. Unless there are repeated adjustment attempts there is not likely to be success. "If at first you don't succeed, try, try again," is more than a mere copybook

---

[7] The suicide data are taken from the U.S. Bureau of Census, Suicide—Vital Statistics, *Special Reports*, 1942, **16**, 157–660. The mental hospital admission data are taken from Kaplan, O. J. (Ed.), *Mental Disorders in Later Life*, Stanford University Press, Stanford, Calif., 1945.

[8] Fisher, V. E., *An Introduction to Abnormal Psychology*, p. 76, The Macmillan Company, New York, 1937.

exercise. It is the secret of adjustment when trial-and-error behavior is used.

However, unless the trials are to be blind, there must be a degree of insight or understanding so that each trial will be a little nearer to the goal than the preceding one. Each must be built on the lessons learned from the preceding failures. Thorndike's cats in the problem box (discussed in Chap. 1) used trial-and-error behavior but the adjustment, or solution, came by chance. Koehler's chimpanzees (also discussed in Chap. 1) were able to use insight and profit from each mistake. Consequently, they made fewer trials, fewer errors, and depended less on chance.

On the human level, trial-and-error behavior may be vicarious or mental; that is, a trial can be tried out in imagination and its success or failure foreseen. If it appears to be a failure, it is discarded without further attention; but if it is foreseen to be a success, it is actually tried out overtly. The accuracy of one's ability to foresee, or to predict, the success or failure of a trial depends on his level of intelligence. The greater the intelligence, the more accurate the prediction of the success or failure of a method of solving an adjustment problem.

So we may conclude that trial-and-error behavior is a good method of satisfying certain wants when these conditions are met—first, the trials must continue until one of them succeeds; second, each one must be based on lessons learned from the preceding ones; and third, they must be implicitly tried and predictions of overt results made with a degree of accuracy.

THE SCIENTIFIC METHOD

Simple problems can be solved by simple methods but difficult problems necessitate more refined methods. The most difficult problems of human adjustment, which lend themselves to solution at all, have been solved by the scientific method. This procedure varies considerably with the nature of the problem and the person using it, but it is essentially a method of tested thinking. It is a refinement of the trial-and-error method just discussed. The steps listed below are those used by the Mellon Institute of Industrial Research. They have enabled this institution to solve its problems and to adjust to its wants. However, the application of these steps to the more personal problems of individual adjustment is equally appropriate.

1. Understand the Problem. This means that the specific nature of the want must be exactly stated; the difficulties that may interfere with adjustment must be specially described; the conditions that probably will satisfy the want must be accurately predicted. An adjustment problem is always less difficult if it is clearly understood. This is the first step in the intelligent approach to any difficult adjustment.

2. Collect Information. How has the problem been solved by other individuals on other occasions? (Perhaps there is a readymade solution if it could just be found.) What are the conditions that are significant? What are the aptitudes and abilities of the individual concerned? What is his background? What social standards must be met? What emotional habits and prejudices may interfere? Is the want an appropriate one for this individual?

It is impossible to determine, at this early stage in the solution of a problem, just what information is significant. The usual procedure is to go on to later steps in the process and then to return and collect more information as it is needed. However, time is often wasted in the evaluation of possible solutions that a little more information would have made obvious.

3. Discovery of Possible Solutions (hypotheses). As information is collected, with the nature of the specific problem in mind, theories of solutions are suggested. In fact, the purpose of collecting information is to find a solution to the problem. If a "hunch" appears to be especially promising, it is then followed up immediately and the collection of information is temporarily dropped.

4. Evaluation of Possible Solutions. The essential difference between intelligent and unintelligent behavior is the degree of accuracy of the foresight of consequences. Intelligent behavior is that which proceeds according to accurate predictions. It is in accordance with events that have not yet occurred. If Napoleon had acted in accordance with an accurate prediction of the nature of the Russian winter of 1812, the history of Europe might have been much different. Intelligent people predict accurately and behave accordingly.

When adjustment attempts can be accurately evaluated before they are made, many harmful effects can be avoided. Jean Valjean could have avoided 20 years as a galley slave if he had acted more in accordance with a correct prediction of consequences. Mistakes in vocational choice, marriage, and social relationships can be reduced in frequency with a more careful preevaluation of adjustment attempts.

5. Test of the Best Solution. The armchair speculator is satisfied to rely on his evaluation of problem solutions without experimental investigation. He does not care to test his theories. He is convinced that he is right and is dogmatic in his conviction. The scientist never relies on an untested opinion. True, he often finds out "what everybody else already knows," but at any rate he knows for sure. He can prove his opinions.

In human adjustments, especially to problems of social relationships, there are so many variables that conclusions are difficult to draw even when scientific testing has been done. Accurate predictions of human behavior, apparently due to certain conditions, are often but little better than chance. There are always exceptions. What can be said with certainty about a group of individuals can be said with but relative certainty about any one member of the group. For example, it can be predicted accurately that X street in a city will produce more delinquent children than Y street. However, it cannot be predicted accurately that Johnny Jones from X street will be more of a behavior problem than Billy Brown from Y street. The chances are greater that he will, but the prediction may be entirely wrong.

When a theoretical solution is tried out and found to be wrong, it is then necessary to go back to Step 2 and collect more information and, if possible, get another "hunch." Insight into the meaning and implications of information about a problem is the only source of possible solutions. Adequate information properly interpreted is a prerequisite to the solution of any adjustment problem. When another promising theory appears, it is followed through Steps 4 and 5 and discarded or accepted as results justify.

6. Conclusion. It is important that every experience in making adjustment be beneficial in making future adjustments. One should always profit from his mistakes as well as from his successes. Certain information that turned out to be wrong, certain principles that were found to be true, certain methods that were very effective, certain people who were very helpful, all become valuable information for making future adjustments. This transfer is possible only if conclusions are made and implications are specifically stated. Conclusions are not automatic. They are the products of careful study.

The application of the scientific method to the solution of a problem of university adjustment is illustrated by the case of Donald Jones.

Donald Jones graduated from high school at the age of eighteen and decided to go to college because his father wanted him to go and several of his friends were going. He decided to go to X University, because it was near and his friend was going there. He enrolled in the School of Engineering because that was the course his roommate was taking and he had a vague notion that it might enable him to see the world.

At the end of the first semester Donald's grades were so low that he was put on probation. He studied hard, or so he thought, during the second semester but again received low grades and was called to the dean's office and advised to drop out. This worried him a great deal. He did not wish to drop out and admit failure and he did not wish to continue and be kicked out. Entirely unlike any other adjustments he had ever faced, there did not seem to be a solution into which he could drift. The problem did not solve itself nor did any of his friends solve it for him. His past habits of drifting and relying on others would not work.

Donald was advised to confer with a professor of psychology, which he did. A careful study was made of his problem and the various factors that seemed to be related to it. When the diagnosis indicated that the solution was rather obvious, Donald was encouraged to apply the scientific method to his difficulty. The following analysis is quoted from Donald's own report.

Problem: How can I avoid becoming a failure in the School of Engineering?

Subproblems:

Do I really want to become an engineer?
Do I have the necessary ability?
Am I better qualified to go into some other vocation?
Do I know how to study?

Data:

Tests showed that I am interested in engineering, I have adequate ability to become an engineer, I am not fitted better for any other vocation, and my mental ability is superior to that of the average college student. However, I do not know how to study effectively. My case history indicates that my past grades were better than I deserved. My father was on the school board and cashier in the bank, which probably influenced some of my teachers. I was an athlete and the school emphasized sports.

Plan for solution:

I will study under the psychology professor's supervision for a summer term and learn how to study properly.

Evaluation of the plan:

This ought to work because I floated through high school and did not even try to study. I came from a small town where it would have been unpopular for a teacher to flunk me. It will be cheaper to pay this professor for tutoring than it will be to scrap the year I have already spent in school.

Test of the plan:

I was first required to make out a schedule of what I planned to do every hour of the day. I was not allowed to deviate from this plan, unless it was approved in a conference with the professor. I then learned to read carefully and take notes on the important ideas. This was harder work than I had ever done before and I was putting in more hours than I had ever put in before. At first I got behind. I could not cover as much material as was assigned. After about a month things began to be easier. I gradually learned to concentrate and it did not take as long to get the ideas from a page. At the end of the six weeks summer term I had learned what to do but was yet unskilled in doing it. The next fall I was on my own but reported to the professor occasionally. The plan worked.

Conclusion:

Since I have learned how to study my courses are more interesting and I am making satisfactory grades. My greatest benefit was learning how to solve problems of adjustment.

CHARACTERISTICS OF THE ADJUSTED PERSONALITY

Aside from the fact that a good personality is made up of effective adjustment habits, and so has no unsatisfied wants of long duration, what other characteristics are important enough to mention? What are the symptoms of being well adjusted?

Happiness. A happy person is never in bad psychological condition. He may be economically broke, he may have no social standing, he may be physically deformed, he may be ignorant, but if he is happy he is probably in good mental health. As Morgan[9] says, "The degree of happiness which you experience is as accurate an indicator of mental balance as the temperature of your body is of your physical health."

Self-honesty. "To thine own self be true." A person who is realistic, who sees things as they are regardless of how they may appear, who distinguishes between what he knows to be true and what he may wish were true, who may put his best foot forward for social reasons but is never dishonest with himself, has already acquired one of the hardest-to-learn characteristics of good mental health. It is so easy to pretend, even to one's self, and so hard to face cold facts, especially if they are unpleasant. *Events occur in this world as they are caused* whether or not they fit into the theological faiths and philosophical beliefs.

Emotional Control. According to Cannon,[10] emotion has had a survival value in the past and still has an "emergency" value. Be that as it may, emotion is a psychological handicap to good mental health. It causes an individual with superior intelligence to act like one with inferior intelligence. Foolish adjustments are made when one is emotionally aroused. Fortunate is he whose emotions never rule his intelligence.

Enjoyable Occupation. The nature of a man's occupation is unimportant as long as it is interesting to him. Years ago John Dewey pointed out the fallacy of labor and leisure.[11] He argued that if a man is vocationally adjusted and working conditions are as they should be, he will get leisure values out of his labor. Leisure can be useful enjoyment as well as useless enjoyment. Certainly enjoyable work is a major characteristic of an adjusted personality.

Harmonious Habits and Ideas. It is mentally unhealthy for an individual to conflict with other people, but it is worse for him to conflict with himself. When a man disagrees with himself he is not well adjusted. The integrated personality has no self-conflicts. It may conflict with social custom, but it does fit with itself. It is a harmonious structure. Ideas and habits agree with each other. There are no postbehavior feelings of guilt because personal principles have been violated. The adjusted personality is adjusted to itself.

[9] Morgan, J. J. B., *Keeping a Sound Mind,* p. 6, The Macmillan Company, New York, 1934.

[10] Cannon, W. B., *Bodily Changes in Pain, Hunger, Fear, and Rage,* Appleton-Century-Crofts, Inc., New York, 1929.

[11] Dewey, J., *Democracy and Education,* The Macmillan Company, New York, 1916.

Physical Health. Personality is not something apart from the body; it is the body in action. If the body is in poor health, it is almost impossible for it to have normal wants and to satisfy them in a normal manner. Good physical health is almost a prerequisite to good personality.

Evidence of this close relationship is shown in a study by Laird[12] and his associates. They investigated the effects of only 2 weeks of special school feeding on nervous children (as determined by the Olson Behavior Check List). A control group of 10 children received no special feeding and improved but 2.3 per cent in nervousness. Another group of 17 children received plain milk at 9:30 each morning. They improved 8.2 per cent in nervousness. A third group of 21 children received milk plus food concentrate at 9:30 each morning. They improved 15.6 per cent in nervousness.

Social Status. Fundamental to the adjustment of any individual is his adjustment to his companions. It is not enough for him to approve of himself; he must also be approved of by his friends. Social adjustment is a prerequisite to good mental health. A physical or economic handicap is not so very serious in personality development until it becomes condemned by acquaintances. Even the slightest social stigma attached to a handicap will make adjustment doubly difficult.

This factor functions in the adjustment of nations to each other as well as in the adjustment of individuals to each other. Diplomats sometimes jeopardize world peace to save face or avoid humiliation. Often diplomacy is handicapped by instances of humiliation long past. It is important for human beings in all their relationships to maintain social status.

Importance of Having an Adjusted Personality

The importance of being well adjusted is too obvious for extended comment. However, the effect of a maladjusted person on his associates is sometimes overlooked. A whole group of individuals is often thrown out of adjustment by the influence of a single psychoneurotic member. A nervous parent or child will soon affect the adjustment of other members of a family. This is also true in a schoolroom, especially if the nervous person is the teacher.

Boynton[13] compared the effect of a group of emotionally unstable teachers with that of a group of emotionally stable teachers on the pupils of their respective classrooms. The fifth- and sixth-grade teachers of Nashville were given a modified form of the Woodworth-Mathews Personal Data Sheet and classified into quartiles according to their scores. Then the pupils of the teachers in the fourth quartile, the adjusted teachers, were

[12] Laird, D. A., Levitan, M., and Wilson, V. A., Nervousness in School Children as Related to Hunger and Diet, *Med. J. & Record,* 1931, **134,** 494–499.

[13] Boynton, P. L., *et al.,* The Emotional Stability of Teachers and Pupils, *J. Juv. Res.,* 1934, **28,** 223–232.

given the same test and compared with the pupils of the teachers in the first quartile, the unadjusted teachers. These data are shown in Table 6–3. The authors conclude that "if a teacher is of a hyperemotional type,

Table 6–3. Differences in Emotional Stability of Pupils in Rooms of Stable and Unstable Teachers

	Boys' medians	Girls' medians
Unstable teachers................	15.33	18.75
Stable teachers..................	13.75	16.63
Difference in favor of stable teachers	1.58	2.12
Index of reliability..............	3.59	3.59

she tends to disturb her pupils emotionally, but if she is emotionally stable she tends to bring about emotional stability among her pupils."

Hattwick and Stowell[14] found that children who are well adjusted at home are usually well adjusted at school. They compared a group of fifth-grade children who were well adjusted at home with a group who were babied and another group who were pushed or nagged at. The adjusted group were approximately three times superior to the other two groups in both social adjustment and work habits at school. This was true on both the second- and fifth-grade levels.

HABITS THAT PRODUCE PARTIAL ADJUSTMENT

Few individuals are able to make adjustments that are always complete. Even a good personality has some wants that are only partly satisfied. This may be due to conditions that make complete adjustment impossible. Wants may not fit limitations. (Such inappropriate wants were discussed earlier in this chapter.) At such times, halfway adjustments are unavoidable and justified. However, ineffective adjustments may also be due to ineffective adjustment habits. Better methods of adjustment are possible but have not been learned. In such case, there is no excuse for partial adjustments. There is need for personality reformation. Ineffective habits should be eliminated and more effective ones learned in their stead. The first step is to be able to recognize habits that afford but limited adjustment.

One of the greatest difficulties in making adequate adjustments to problems of living is the almost universal want to "save face," or to avoid being considered inferior by other people. Every human being wants other human beings to think he is at least normal in his ability to adjust to living problems. Perhaps it is caused by our competitive culture but it

[14] Hattwick, L. W., and Stowell, M., The Relation of Parent Overattentiveness to Children's Work Habits and Social Adjustment, *J. Educ. Res.*, 1936, **30**, 169–176.

is a general human trait to hide inferiorities from other people. Consequently habits are formed of denying, concealing, ignoring, and even justifying our own feelings of inferiority, whether real or imagined. These habits are called "defense mechanisms." Many of the adjustment habits described in the following pages are defense mechanisms which attempt to conceal or justify inferior ability to make adjustments.

There are three general patterns of reaction which thwarted wants may elicit—aggression or hostility, withdrawal or fugue, and compromise. Some individuals become hostile and antagonistic when the satisfaction of their wants is thwarted. The objective of the hostility may or may not be the cause of their frustration. The hostility of the Germans (under Hitler) toward the Jews was largely unjustified but nonetheless a result of a nationwide feeling of frustration. When a troubled businessman comes home and kicks his cat (or his wife), it is a substitute for his feeling toward his boss or his competitor or perhaps for his own feeling of incompetence. Thwarted wants may cause aggressive behavior which may be misdirected.

Sometimes thwarted wants cause a withdrawal from the thwarting situation. An individual may avoid situations which contain, or are thought to contain, problems of adjustment. This is sometimes called a "fear reaction" and consists of psychological withdrawal as well as physical avoidance. Some people become nonsocial and introverted because they feel thwarted in the presence of other people. Some people avoid music situations because they are, or were, thwarted in their own musical wants or ambitions. An unfortunate love affair may cause either a man or a woman to avoid the preliminary steps toward marriage. It is a common human reaction to avoid those situations which are associated with earlier experiences of thwarted wants and frustrations.

A third and usually more intelligent pattern of reaction to difficulties of adjustment is compromise. Wants are modified to fit blocks, ethical standards are revised, symbolic satisfactions are accepted, and substitute goals become the objects of ambition. Wish fulfillments are compromised. The soldier's pin-up pictures, the old maid's devotion to teaching first-grade children, the starving man's willingness to eat worms and snakes, the zealous faith that some dogma is true, the druggist who flunked out of medical school—all are examples of compromise reactions to thwarted goals. They are examples of the adage that "half a loaf is better than no bread."

Habits of Substitution

When the satisfaction of a want is thwarted by a difficulty of considerable magnitude, partial relief of the resulting tensions may be accomplished by indirect substitute satisfaction. Direct adjustment is not made but some other adjustment is substituted that affords partial satisfaction. It is better than nothing but not as good as a direct adjustment to the specific want.

Daydreaming. Daydreams may be good, or they may be bad. When they are the forerunners of future action, they are good; when they are substitutes for future action, they are bad. Daydreams can be plans, predictions, blueprints. They can be ideals for guiding the most complete and satisfying adjustments. But they can also be ends in themselves. They can be substitutes for adjustments.

The daydreamer is often one who has found that desired adjustments are too costly in effort. He feels that the satisfaction of adjustment is not worth the cost of its accomplishment. So he retreats from the outside world of reality with its difficult adjustments into the world of his own imagination. Here difficulties are easily eliminated and successful adjustments are achieved without effort. Of course he knows that his dreams are not real but he enjoys them anyhow. They partly relieve the tensions of his unsatisfied wants, and they do him no harm. Daydreaming is an enjoyable pastime.

Identification. It is sometimes pleasant to identify oneself with those who have made adjustments that we would like to make. For example, it is difficult to become an athlete, but it is not difficult to join an athletic club and associate with athletes; it is difficult to become wealthy, but it is not difficult to join a country club and associate with the wealthy; it is difficult to graduate from college, but it is not difficult to attend college functions and become quite "collegiate." There is some satisfaction in being identified with those who have satisfied the wants we would like to satisfy if we were not thwarted in doing so.

Identification begins early in the life of the child. He is small, weak, and unimportant, so he identifies himself with his father. He reacts to any criticism of his father as a personal affront. Also, he enjoys the reflected glory of his father's achievements. Likewise, he identifies himself with his dog and enjoys as a personal adjustment any credit or admiration that goes to the dog. Some boys identify themselves with inanimate objects such as airplanes, locomotives, automobiles. The power and beauty of these objects give the boy who owns them (a form of identification) a feeling of satisfaction, even if they are but pictures pasted on the walls of his room. Any criticism of his objects of ownership is taken as personal. He has formed a habit of identification.

Identification is better than nothing if direct adjustment is impossible, but it should not become a habit that interferes with more complete adjustment. A boy gets limited satisfaction from shaking hands with Joe DiMaggio, but he will get more satisfaction from becoming a big-league player himself. Identification is at best but a substitute for the real thing.

Overemphasis. A little man would like to be influential with his fellows, but he is so short that they seldom notice him; so he develops a loud voice. This tends to detract attention from his size to his voice. An unattractive woman would like to be attractive, but her physical charms are below average; so she develops a habit of wearing spectacularly attractive clothing. This tends to detract attention from her physical limitations to her clothing superiorities. A boy would like to be appreciated by his teacher and his fellow pupils, but he has a low I.Q. and no other traits of superiority; so he joins a back-alley gang. These fellows treat him as an equal, and, after the first raid on a fruit stand, they admire his bravery. They pay no attention to his inferiority in schoolwork.

Well-adjusted people do not overemphasize anything. They do not need to. They are not trying to cover up anything and they do not feel the need for undue attention. Overemphasis of a trait or adjustment is usually to detract attention from some other trait or adjustment regarding which the individual feels inferior.

Miss A was a fourth-grade teacher who was very critical and unfair in her treatment of a little illegitimate colored boy in her room. It was later learned that Miss A herself had an illegitimate child who was being reared by a married sister.

Delinquency. It is characteristic of all individuals, regardless of age, to desire the approval of others. Human beings want other human beings to think well of them. (This is a derived want.) Every child wants to secure and maintain desirable social status. If he does not attain it, he seeks for some substitute satisfaction (*i.e.,* he compensates).

Children who do inferior schoolwork, and thus lose social status, may compensate for it by exhibiting superior bravery in acts of delinquency. Students of delinquency have found that the factor that correlates most highly with delinquency among school children is low grades. This does not prove that low grades cause delinquency but only that they are both factors in the same situation. However, the implication is that, if the child could have his want for social approval satisfied in the school, he would not seek for it elsewhere. Children who are socially accepted in school do not need to seek for social acceptance with the delinquent gang (see Chap. 11 for discussion of delinquency).

Sublimation. When conditions beyond control make the satisfaction of wants impossible, partial satisfaction can be attained by changing the want to one that is closely related but more "sublime." As Wallin[15] explains, "Sublimation in its general connotation refers to the indirect expression of primitive urges in ethically and socially acceptable and useful

[15] Wallin, J. E. W., *Personality Maladjustments and Mental Hygiene,* 2d ed., McGraw-Hill Book Company, Inc., New York, 1949.

behavior patterns." Everyday life is full of illustrations of sublimation. The good teacher is often the motherly type who was never asked to marry and now sublimates her wants by mothering other people's children. The boy who manages school traffic so well was the school bully in the lower grades. His want to control others is now sublimated into a useful channel. The local druggist really intended to be a physician but his school grades were too low to enable him to get into medical school so he has compromised on a related but what is to him a sublime occupation. Sublimation is a socially approved alternate when the real want cannot be satisfied.

Habits of Rationalization

Rationalization is a term in psychology that suggests a desirable type of behavior. One would suppose that it is derived from "rational," meaning to reason. It is not. It means self-deception. It is a process of fallacious thinking intended to justify an adjustment that is emotionally desirable but not intellectually justified (and often socially disapproved as well). It is a procedure of fooling oneself into believing something that was originally recognized as false. An inferior adjustment with emotional appeal is always defended against a superior adjustment with intellectual appeal.

Projection. A common form of rationalization is to project the blame for the consequences of one's own behavior to something else, or to someone else. A poor golfer fools himself into believing that the fault is not with himself but with his clubs, or with the course, or with the ball, or even with the caddy. Projection is a misplacement of blame. The woman who has made an unsatisfactory marriage is likely to condemn her husband, or his family, or her children, or the neighborhood, or the marriage institution itself. She fools herself into believing that circumstances beyond her control were responsible for the failure of her marriage. She projects the cause of her failure from herself to someone else.

Projection may also take the form of excusing some fault, or socially disapproved motive, by pretending to see it in others. The woman who is unattractive is likely to see the same fault in many other women. The boy who is intellectually inferior takes pride in pointing out the inferiority of others. The man who is secretly dishonest is likely to suspect that everyone else is also dishonest. It is easy to project one's own faults into others. In fact, when one is oversensitive to the presence of some fault in others, the chances are that he also possesses the same fault.

Sour Grapes. The fox reasoned that the grapes that were too high to get were too sour anyhow. They were unattainable and *therefore* undesirable. Many people engage in the same sort of rationalizing. A man whose party was defeated in the 1944 election expressed the opinion that the winning party was most unfortunate. The war and all its attending problems, he said, made office holding at this time extremely undesirable. He even opinionated that the losing party in some cases had deliberately chosen weak candidates so as to be sure to lose the election. A rival who loses a girl's affections to a competitor can see all sorts of faults in her. He tries to fool himself into believing that he is really the lucky man.

James C was recently refused admission to a certain medical school and was accepted by one of definitely inferior standing. He elaborately explained to the writer why he had "chosen" the latter. He was really trying to make himself believe that the good school that he could not attend was inferior to the poor school that he could attend.

Habits of Evasion

Another method of partial adjustment is to avoid or to evade the scene of a difficulty. Problems that can be avoided do not need to be solved. A difficult school adjustment can be partly accomplished by being absent from school on the day when the adjustment must be made. The problem of fitting into a disagreeable employment situation can be partly solved by getting another job. All the difficulties of securing a college education can be side-stepped by not going to college. Sometimes such avoidance is justified but there is danger of forming a habit of avoidance and then using it when a more complete adjustment could be made. When people habitually avoid problems, they become timid and seclusive. To avoid problems, they become unsocial, selfish, individualistic, and suspicious. They withdraw more and more and live within a shell of personal interests.

The habit of avoiding adjustment problems is more serious in mental health than is usually apparent. Children who avoid problems are seldom as much of a nuisance around adults as those who face adjustments and struggle with them. Consequently, avoidance habits usually become well formed before they are recognized as such. In fact, teachers do not usually recognize those behavior traits associated with avoidance as undesirable. Wickman[16] asked 13 groups of elementary school teachers (500 in all) and 30 mental hygienists from child guidance clinics to rank a list of 50 behavior problems, common among children, as to seriousness. "Whereas the teachers considered shyness, sensitiveness, unsocialness, fearfulness, dreaminess, among the least serious of all problems, the mental hygienists ranked them, together with unhappiness, depression, easy discouragement, resentfulness, cowardliness, suggestibility, and overcriticalness, at the very top of the list of the most serious problems." This is indicated in Table 6–4.

[16] Wickman, E. K., *Teachers and Behavior Problems,* Commonwealth Fund, Division of Publication, New York, 1938.

Table 6–4. Rankings of Teachers and Mental Hygienists on Seriousness of Certain Behavior Traits

Behavior traits	Mental hygienists' rankings	Teachers' rankings
Unsocialness.....................	1	40
Suspiciousness...................	2	37
Unhappy, depressed.............	3	22
Resentful.......................	4	29
Fearfulness.....................	5	36
Cruelty, bullying................	6	8
Easily discouraged..............	7	23
Suggestible.....................	8	28
Overcritical of others............	9	45
Sensitiveness...................	10	48
Domineering....................	11	33
Sullenness......................	12	35
Stealing.......................	13	2
Shyness........................	14	50
Physical coward.................	15	31

While evading adjustment is usually accomplished by withdrawal and introverted habits, it may be attained by what Wickman calls "active attack." A problem may be evaded by defiantly attacking the difficulty. Instead of the individual adjusting to the difficulty, the difficulty is forced to adjust to the individual. For example, a boy may avoid learning a school assignment by militantly denouncing it. If it is then changed to fit him, the evasion is successful. Of course, if he fails to change the difficulty, he is in a greater state of maladjustment than ever. His behavior has not afforded even partial adjustment.

HABITS THAT PRODUCE NO ADJUSTMENT

Those people who have formed habits that produce complete adjustment are in good mental health. They enjoy the satisfaction of accomplishment. Those who have formed habits that produce but partial adjustment are in corresponding states of tension. They are not in mental ill health, and yet the happiness of living is definitely limited. They are handicapped. Still other individuals form habits that result in no adjustment. Their problems are neither increased nor diminished. Their tensions are not reduced. In time they become maladjusted personalities.

The question arises: Why are completely useless adjustment habits ever formed? The answer depends somewhat on the type of habit, but in general, useless habits are carry-overs from childhood days. They indicate that an individual's personality has not kept pace with his years. An adult in age is not always an adult in conduct.

WORRY

If a person should accidentally step on a tack, or sit on a pin, or touch his hand against a hot stove, and then should remain in that position without moving except to talk about it to anyone who would listen, he would be worrying. Worry is a constant nonadjustive verbal reaction (either explicit or implicit or both) to an adjustment situation. It is a state of grumbling and enduring. Worrying is not a process of adjustment. It is not even planning for adjustment. It is an utterly useless waste of time.

Worry usually occurs only when a person does not know how to make a successful adjustment. Therefore, it is an indication of ignorance. People do not worry about problems concerning which they have adequate knowledge. They may make continuous solution attempts, but they do not worry. The worrier does not try to solve his problems; he just talks about the fact that they exist. He continues to be irritated by his problems, yet he makes no attempt to reduce the irritation.

The worrier is often emotionally unstable. His wants are beyond his capacity and then he is irritated because he cannot realize his ambitions. He becomes oversensitive. He worries about problems that should not concern him at all. He creates his own maladjustments.

Worry is perhaps the most common symptom of mental ill health. Hicks[17] surveyed a group of 600 school teachers from all geographical sections of the United States, to find the frequency of symptoms of nervous instability. He found that worry ranked first. "Worry, disturbed sleep, shyness, indecision, absent-mindedness, fatigue, and headache were problems of greatest number."

The remedy for worry is to become so occupied with wants that can be satisfied that there is no time to worry about wants that cannot be satisfied. Active, successful people do not worry. A successful mother does not need to worry about her children, and she is too busy to worry about not being elected president of the local chapter of the A.B.C. A successful farmer has no farm problems to cause worry, and he does not have time to worry about problems that do not concern him directly. Women without family responsibilities, or men without occupational obligations, who have not learned how to spend leisure time intelligently, become interested in problems that are beyond their intellectual and educational limitations. They do not know how to make the first steps toward solution. So they worry. Worry is often about events that have occurred in the past and cannot possibly be corrected. A woman worries because her husband has died; or a man worries because he has lost money in an investment. The remedy, as stated above, is to become so occupied with making useful adjustments that there is no time left to worry about events that are past.

[17] *Op. cit.*

Only a child, either in age or intelligence, cries because he cannot reach the moon.

The importance of correcting the habit of worrying cannot be over-emphasized. It always leads to something worse. Unfortunately, the mental capacity of the worrier is limited, and he usually needs help to correct his bad habit. The worrier should see a psychologist, a psychiatrist, or a mental hygienist of some sort, for assistance in substituting habits of adjusting to more sensible problems. Worry is senseless reaction to in-appropriate problems.

NEGATIVISM

Children frequently develop patterns of anti-behavior. They refuse to do what they are told to do, just because they are told. They have formed habits of violating direction and advice regardless of the adjustive value of such behavior. This is called "negativism" and is a common character-istic of child behavior. It is a child's way of asserting his independence and protesting against adult control. It is a crude way of proving to him-self that he is independent and able to get along without the help of others.

Studies show that negativism occurs most frequently in children at the age of three. Levy and Tulchin[18] found in a study of a thousand children that the maximum frequency (30 per cent of all children) of completely negativistic children was between thirty and forty months of age. This agrees with Ackerson's study (quoted above) except that he found that negativism increased again at age sixteen.

Negativistic behavior is not serious in the child, but it too frequently appears on the adult level. The adult who is negativistic is, like the child, rebelling against his own feeling of inferiority. He objects to the advice of others, not because it is bad advice, but because it implies that he is inferior to the one who gives the advice. In order to prove (to himself) that he is not inferior, he not only ignores the advice but acts in an opposite manner.

Such behavior is more popularly known as stubbornness. It is supposed to be a characteristic of some of the lower animals. The expressions, "stubborn as a mule," "bullheaded," "contrary as a hog," refer to this type of behavior. It is frequently emotional and seldom intelligent.

Negativism in the adult is not limited to opposition to the advice of other individuals. It may be directed against social customs. Social non-conformity is an example of such behavior. Even criminality may be an expression of negativism. Laws and customs are often violated, not to effect an adjustment, but to enable some immature person to prove to himself that he is important. Individuals who have such negativistic be-havior patterns are jealous of any limitations of personal freedom. If a

[18] Levy, D. M., and Tulchin, S. H., The Resistance of Infants and Children, *J. Exp. Psychol.*, 1923, **6**, 304–322.

custom or a law forbids an act of behavior, the negativistic person is not satisfied until he has performed the act. By prohibiting the use of intoxicants the Eighteenth Amendment caused many people who would never have tasted liquor to begin to patronize the bootlegger. Wartime price control was sabotaged by the black market, not because price regulation was wrong, but because there were so many negativistic people in our society.[19] In other words, laws and customs are often violated, not because they are wrong and inappropriate, but because those who violate them are trying to prove to themselves that they are not weak and unimportant but stronger than society itself.

Such behavior is not even partly satisfying. As a means of adjustment it is a complete failure. It does not relieve the tensions of a want, nor does it relieve the feelings of personal inferiority. Negativism is a childish way of reacting to adjustment difficulties.

The remedy for negativistic habits, similar to that for all inadequate attempts at adjustment, may be stated as follows:

1. Identify the negativistic habits.
2. Identify the wants and difficulties that bring about the negativistic reaction patterns.
3. Learn how to make complete adjustment to these wants by
   a. Modifying the want to fit the limitations of the wanter.
   b. Practicing the methods suggested above (trial and error, and scientific method) for producing complete adjustment, until they become habits.

It is not necessary to break negativistic habits after the more adjustive habits have been learned. They were formed for want of better adjustments and will naturally drop out when the better methods are learned. However, they will continue to function in those situations that are not adequately and promptly relieved by the newer habits.

REGRESSION

Successful adjustment is enjoyable. It is a pleasure to satisfy wants. Consequently, human beings attempt to enjoy such pleasure as often and as long as possible. Not to satisfy wants is annoying and produces organic tensions that are detrimental to health and happiness. It is natural to try to avoid such states as much as possible. When the enjoyment of successful adjustment is more limited and more seldom than usual, there is a temptation either to recall former adjustments and live them over again in memory, or to use the adjustment procedures over again that were successful on former occasions, whether they are now appropriate or not. This is

[19] Being defeated in a series of elections creates a feeling of inferiority in some people that is not unlike that of the child. "New deal" policies were violently opposed, not on their merits, but to demonstrate that anti-forces were still powerful. Such opposition is not constructive but destructive and negativistic.

called "regression." The individual returns to states of former adjustment and attempts to experience them over again in memory, or he actually uses the methods that he found to be successful on former occasions.

The old man who tells of the successful adjustments of his earlier years, or the woman who cries when her wants are thwarted, or the man who angrily strikes another who disagrees with him, or the boy who is homesick when he goes away to college, or the woman who pretends she is ill when her husband refuses to buy her a new dress—these are examples of regression.

Harold C was a very successful college athlete. Because of this, his professors made college especially easy for him. After graduation he became a road construction contractor, work he knew but little about. He failed at this and lost most of the money he had borrowed to get started. He is now employed in a cheap pool hall and entertains everyone who will listen with stories of his college days. He ignores the present as much as possible because he is unadjusted. He lives over and over his college days because he was then more enjoyably adjusted.

Regression explains most of the infantile behavior of adults. When they face difficult adjustments, they simply regress to forms of behavior that worked when they were children. As judged by adult standards, this behavior is completely nonadjustive. It is no better than negativism and worry. It does not reduce tensions of maladjustment, and it does not lead to a state of happiness.

Regression explains many of our inadequate social customs. We regress to more primitive methods of adjustments when we face difficult adjustment problems. War is perhaps the best example of such regression. Many of our ritualistic customs are regressions to infantile and primitive forms of behavior. Codes of morality, legal procedures, forms of religious worship, patterns of education, precedents of government, mores of property ownership, customs of human justice, all contain elements of primitive and infantile carry-over that now have little or no adjustive value. To suggest that the scientific method be used in making some of these adjustments is to invite popular scorn and ostracism.

Whether in the individual or in society, regression is a procedure that leaves the adjustment problem unchanged. Fortunately, regression is not usually harmful either to society or to the individual. It is just a waste of time as far as making an adjustment is concerned.

TANTRUMS

The word "emotion" is used to designate two entirely different types of behavior—intense enjoyment and intense annoyance. (See Chap. 3 for further explanation of this distinction.) Intense enjoyment is not usually detrimental to personality development, but intense annoyance is. The emotions of annoyance are anger and fear, in various degrees and combinations. Psychologically, the greatest effect of these emotions is that they handicap the intelligence. Behavior is unrestrained and without benefit of intellectual inhibitions. Primitive wants are dominant and cultural restrictions are ignored. In addition to the fact that annoying emotion interferes with adjustment, it is detrimental to the body mechanism. It increases metabolic rate, interferes with digestion, steps up the production of blood sugar beyond that of actual need, increases muscular tension, and prepares the body for attack or flight whether or not either is justified.

Some people form habits of emotional release instead of emotional restraint. When they are thwarted, they become very angry or very much afraid. In either case, they behave like animals without intellect instead of like human beings with the power of intelligence. If the emotional release is relatively much greater than the restraint, the resulting behavior is called a "tantrum." It may take almost any form, but it is always characterized by lack of restraint.

Emotion is a physiological condition brought about by action of the autonomic nervous system and is not subject to voluntary control. When adequate stimulation brings about this condition, there is no way to avoid it. It just goes with being human.

However, there are three ways an intelligent person can make the best of his handicap of becoming emotional. First, he can avoid the conditions that stimulate emotion. If he is afraid of snakes, he can stay away from them. If he becomes angry when others disagree with him, he can avoid arguments. Second, he can recondition his emotional reaction to the significant conditions. He can learn to like snakes. He can learn to argue without becoming angry. With few exceptions, any emotion-producing stimulation can be reconditioned. Third, he can learn to act "like a gentleman" even when he is emotional. Gentlemen do not have tantrums, though they do become angry.

Tantrum habits are usually formed in homes where an adjustive value is given to such behavior. To relieve a child's tantrum a parent will rescind a rule of discipline. Thus the child learns that if he can make the tantrum intense enough he will get what he wants.

Georgie B was a little three-year-old boy who frightened his mother into granting all his wishes. When she denied him anything, he would fling himself on the floor, become rigid, hold his breath, and grit his teeth. One day the writer observed one of these episodes and quickly threw a glass of cold water in Georgie's face. The tantrum was never repeated.

Childhood tantrums must never succeed if adult tantrum habits are to be avoided.

HABITS THAT HAVE HARMFUL CONSEQUENCES

The habits of adjustment that have been discussed so far in this chapter are those that we commonly see all around us. We possess some of them ourselves and we observe others in our friends. They are not the most effective habits and we try to correct them, but they are not harmful. The rest of this chapter will be devoted to habits that lead to something worse. Psychoneuroses and insanities (discussed in Chap. 8) are often caused by habits that were intended to aid the individual in overcoming his difficulties and satisfying his wants. The habits discussed in this section not only fail to effect an adjustment but they increase the maladjustment.

PHOBIAS

A phobia is an intense, morbid, unreasonable, uncontrolled fear. Its origin is in the forgotten past and usually so unpleasant that it is remembered only with great effort. It is frequently aroused by some symbolic representation of the original primary stimulation. It is an unpleasant, maladjustive reaction to a usually harmless situation. Perhaps a specific example will make its nature more clear.

Miss B had a mouse-plus phobia. She was intensely afraid of both mice and basements, which she associated with mice. Her phobia was comparatively mild because she could talk about it without visible evidence of her feeling or emotional panic. However, it was a nuisance. The sight of a mouse made her "weak and faint for an hour afterward," and she had not been in her basement at home for seven years. She was thirty-two years old, principal of a grade school, and thoroughly ashamed of her phobia. If she were at home alone, and the house was cold, she would go to bed rather than go to the basement to fix the furnace fire.

The remedy for a phobia, like that for all other bad personality habits, is diagnosis and re-education. What caused the phobia in the first place? How can habits of adjustment be learned instead? To illustrate this personality reformation, let us return to the case of Miss B.

Investigation revealed that Miss B's phobia originated from being playfully frightened by her brother with a dead mouse when she was in the first grade. Other boys soon found that it was fun to chase her with mice, sometimes real and sometimes pretended. Fortunately, when she was ten years old her parents moved to another town and the new schoolmates did not know about her fear. However, the damage had already been done. She had acquired a phobia that was to last more than 20 years. The basement attachment seemed to have originated from seeing mice in the basement at various times.

The re-education procedure began with the basement. First, the brother, who was now married and thoroughly ashamed of his childhood prank, made sure that Miss B's basement was cleared of mice. Next, Miss B went to the basement door and experienced the phobia for one-half minute every day until it was "worn out" for that location. She then went down a step and wore the phobia out there. This took another week. After several months, she could stand before the furnace without experiencing the phobia. Of course, she felt uneasy but it was not the phobia.

She then began on the mouse phase of her phobia. First, she read about mice and looked at pictures of them. She learned about how white mice are used to advance medical knowledge. She learned that mice never attack and never bite unless they are caught and held. Next, she bought a white mouse and kept it as a pet, in a cage of course. It was several weeks before she could feed it without experiencing the emotional panic. However, her persistent efforts were rewarded, and she was finally able to take the mouse to school and show it to the children. Today, the phobia is entirely gone although her fear of mice is still "healthy."

There are many kinds of phobias and they have been given impressive names. A fear of high places is called acrophobia; of open places, agoraphobia; of closed places, claustrophobia; of darkness, nyctophobia; of crowds, ochlophobia; of disease, pathophobia; of fire, pyrophobia; of poisoning, toxophobia; and of animals, zoophobia. Whatever the nature of the phobia, it is a bad habit of attempted adjustment that leads to harmful results. It should be corrected under the guidance of a mental hygienist before it has done more serious psychological damage.

OBSESSIONS AND COMPULSIONS

An obsession is a persistently recurring idea that may be recognized as irrational but cannot be avoided. A compulsion, which results from an obsession, is a persistently recurring act that may be recognized as irrational but cannot be avoided. For example, John Brown, of Harpers Ferry fame, had the obsession that he was divinely commanded to free the slaves. This compelled him to try to seize the arsenal at Harpers Ferry. Adolf Hitler was obsessed with the idea that he should rule the world. This compelled him to perform acts that are unparalleled in all history.

Compulsions are usually called "manias" (not to be confused with manic conditions discussed in Chap. 8). The compulsion to steal is kleptomania; the compulsion to start fires is pyromania; the compulsion to alcoholic indulgence is dipsomania; the compulsion to count everything, such as steps, is numeromania.

Shakespeare gives us one of the most famous illustrations of a compulsion. After the murder of Duncan, Lady Macbeth is obsessed with the idea that "these hands will ne'er be clean." Even in her sleep she says, "Here's the smell of blood still: all the perfumes of Arabia will not sweeten this little hand."

The hand-washing compulsion is a common symbolic expression of an obsession of guilt for some immoral or unconventional act. Masturbation by one who believes it to be wrong often leads to excessive hand washing. In fact, hand washing is even found in religious rituals as symbolic of purification.

Obsessions and compulsions do not usually occur in those personalities that have developed the characteristic mentioned above—self-honesty. Realistic people seldom have obsessions. They recognize facts for their worth and check the truth of their ideas. Obsessions and compulsions do not necessarily indicate low intelligence, or even the lack of education, but they usually do indicate the lack of realism and of self-honesty.

ANXIETY

When worry is accompanied with a constant fear of impending disaster, a condition of anxiety exists. Often worry becomes so intense that it arouses a state of fear. There is a continuous feeling of approaching doom and disaster. This is anxiety. It is one of the most harmful habits a person can form. It is a tremendous strain on the nervous system and cannot be endured for long. Either the difficulties that interfere with want satisfaction must be eliminated, or one of two tragic results will follow—death or insanity.

There are a number of characteristics of anxiety that make it easily identified. These may be listed as follows:

1. There is a feeling of insecurity, of inadequacy, of personal inability to cope with a situation.
2. There is the continual presence of morbid fear, fear that is intense and debilitating.
3. The object or condition of fear is in the future and intangible. It is some sort of impending doom.
4. There are resulting psychophysical tensions that interfere with digestion and even with sleep. It is almost impossible to relax. The individual is hypersensitive and irritable.
5. The difficulty that is at the base of these anxiety states may be either of the following:
   a. Real and recognized by others. (Death is an example. However, healthy personalities do not worry about inevitable difficulties.)
   b. Imagined and not recognized by others. (Personal ill health is an example.)

The remedy for anxiety states (sometimes called anxiety neurosis) is twofold. First, it is necessary to remove the difficulty that interferes with satisfying the want involved. Often this is not easy to determine (especially if the want is related to sex). Even the patient himself does not know exactly what his want is. Sometimes it is easier to remove the patient from the scene of the difficulty than it is to remove the difficulty. A vacation trip, or a visit, or a change of jobs, will often correct a bad anxiety state.

Second, it is important for the individual to be in good physical health. Healthy people do not worry easily, and when they do they seldom carry it to a state of anxiety. Good mental health and good physical health usually go together.

The bad effects of anxiety cannot be overemphasized. As Wallin[20] states so effectively, "Nervous anxiety may precipitate a vicious circle of disturbances, including hyperacidity, which may lead to duodenal ulcer, and dyspepsia, which, in turn, may lead to gastric atony (lack of tone) and dilation. These lead to visceroptosis (downward displacement of the visceral organs), to intestinal stasis, to toxic absorption, to endocrine disorder, and back to nervous anxiety."

REPRESSIONS

Society disapproves of the satisfaction of some human wants. In fact, it disapproves of having some wants at all. For example, sex wants in unmarried people are regarded as indecent. Even in married people they are often regarded as base and carnal. This is likewise true of the want to wear clothing that is not in fashion. A college professor would be severely reprimanded if he should appear before his class in a swimming suit, or even in slacks and sweatshirt. Consequently, when a person has wants of which society disapproves, he either represses them or keeps them secret. If he has been trained to "keep his mind clean," he dares not have "evil" wants even in secret. The other alternative is to repress them.

The repression of a strong want does not eliminate it. The want for food, for example, might be ignored for a time, or called by another name, or even denied, but it does not cease to exist for these reasons. It may vary in intensity or even disappear for some other reason, but it is not eliminated by repression.

To repress a socially disapproved want is really to drive it under cover. It becomes known by another name and treated as another want. Consequently it is not satisfied and tensions of maladjustment are not relieved. Psychologically, a repressed want is much worse than the evil of admitting that it exists.

Society has the approval of religious teaching in declaring many wants to be taboo. Children are taught, not that these wants are merely unconventional, but that they are forbidden by God. Consequently, when the want arises there is a conflict between the want itself and the want to satisfy God. This becomes a major psychological problem. The individual now has two opposing wants—the unconventional or "evil" want, and the want to act in accordance with his training, which he now calls his "conscience." The stronger the wants are, the greater the conflict and the greater the state of maladjustment.

[20] *Op. cit.*

It is always difficult to bring a conflict between a repressed want and a strong conscience out into the open. The reason is that the individual has unconsciously tried to pull a fast one on himself. He has tried to satisfy both wants without appearing to do so. The "evil" want has been changed and replaced by more decent ones. He has deceived himself into believing that the evil want no longer exists. Consequently, the individual himself does not know what wants are involved in a conflict.

Mary R was a school teacher who was becoming worried and nervous because "life was slipping by so fast." She took a summer course in mental hygiene and was required to write a paper analyzing some problem of adjustment. She analyzed her own sex adjustment and stated the following facts as significant.

She was taught by her mother that sex was evil and interest in it should be repressed. "Nice little girls do not even think of sex." Consequently, she never masturbated, never listened to sex discussions even in college, and never was interested in boys except on an intellectual basis as fellow students. As a school teacher, she ignored sex but now wonders if sex has ignored her. She was shocked to learn from her textbook in mental hygiene that sex is a physiological drive and no more evil than hunger if it is satisfied in an approved manner. She realized now that her own sex wants have been entirely repressed by the idea that they were evil.

The recognition and fairly detailed description of her problem was as far as her analysis went, at least in the paper submitted in class.

A prominent procedure of diagnosing personality conflicts is called *psychoanalysis*. It has changed somewhat since Freud originated it about the close of the last century, but it is still too complicated to attempt to explain here.[21]

FANTASY

Planning is a process of imagining how a proposed adjustment will work out when it is tried. It is a preparatory step to further adjustment. Daydreaming is a process of imagining that an adjustment has already been made. It is an end in itself and does not lead to further adjustment. Fantasy is a process of imagination that has nothing to do with adjustment at all. It is an end in itself. In fact, fantasy is a means of escape from the thought of disagreeable adjustment problems. It is not a substitute for adjustment, as are daydreams; it is a substitute for life itself. A world of fantasy is substituted for a world of reality. Fantasy is an escape from a real world with all its limitations to a world where there are no limitations.

[21] Brief explanations of psychoanalysis may be found in Chap. 14 of L. F. Shaffer's book, *The Psychology of Adjustment,* Houghton Mifflin Company, Boston, 1936; or B. Hart's *The Psychology of Insanity,* Cambridge University Press, London, 1920; or R. S. Woodworth's *Contemporary Schools of Psychology,* Chap. 5, The Ronald Press Company, New York, 1931.

Fantasy is dangerous because it is but one step to delusion and hallucination. Exaggerated imagery may become so real that voices are heard or visions are seen that do not exist. Imagined beliefs may be accepted as true regardless of evidence to the contrary. When ones lives too much in a world of fantasy, it is easy to confuse the imagined world with the world of reality. (Such a confused state of mental illness is discussed more fully in Chap. 8.) Excessive fantasy is usually an indication that a serious mental breakdown is not far off.

The individual may picture himself as a conquering hero who performs mighty deeds of valor, acquires the things he most desires, and is acclaimed by all his acquaintances. However, this is more frequently on the level of a compensation daydream and not as serious as other types of fantasy.

The suffering-hero type of fantasy pictures the individual as a victim of discrimination, abuse, and mistreatment. He imagines that others are plotting against him and planning to harm him. Even nature is unjust and unfair to him. He is an innocent victim of enemies and conditions. Actually there is no factual basis for such fantasy at all.

The most frequent type of fantasy is a sort of reverie that runs on and on in a storybook fashion. The individual himself is the leading character. His experiences are enjoyable and exciting. Thus, he is able to escape from real life into a more enjoyable life of fantasy.[22]

The remedy for fantasy is to establish the characteristics of good mental health mentioned earlier in this chapter. No one wants to escape from the real world to a world of fantasy unless the real world is becoming intolerable. The person who spends his time in fantasy needs help in making his real world adjustments. Then, an occasional flight into fantasy will do him no harm.

DRUG ADDICTION

A very immediate and easy, though temporary, escape from difficult problems of adjustment is to take small doses of those drugs which produce depressant and torporous states. Opium, for example, will relieve tensions produced by troubles and cause temporary disorientation in both time and space. It causes one to feel that he is floating through space and existing in some nebulous age when past experience is transcended. Alcohol, cocaine, marijuana, all produce similar states. A few experiences with such trouble-free existence cause an individual to seek its repetition. He becomes a drug addict. (See Chap. 10 for a more detailed discussion of drug addiction.)

It is true that drug addiction is sometimes due to a continued use of

---

[22] If he can record his fantasies in writing, he may be able to market them as literature. More than one novel has been a by-product of an unhealthy mental adjustment. Thus an attempt to escape adjustment may lead to adjustment.

some pain-relieving drug. Physicians appropriately prescribe narcotics and barbiturates in routine medical practice. The resultant state of euphoria is more enjoyable than the pain it is prescribed to relieve. When the pain state and need for the drug no longer exist, the average patient will return to his normal pattern of living. However, if he has difficult adjustment problems—such as unpaid debts, family frictions, vocational difficulties—he is likely to remember his experience with the pain-relieving drug. He may then prescribe for himself further use of the drug to relieve his mental pain. Drug addiction is usually indicative of some personality maladjustment.

SUMMARY

This chapter has briefly reviewed one of the most important fields of applied psychology. No one ever forms such adequate habits of adjustment that there is no need for improvement. Mental hygiene can profitably be used by everyone. No other phase of psychology is applicable to so many people as is mental hygiene.

Habits that produce adequate adjustments were reviewed briefly. It was recommended that easy and less important adjustments be effected by trial and error and that more difficult adjustments be made by the scientific method. Many of the characteristics of good mental health were mentioned.

Then, habits that are only partly effective were discussed. These are habits of compensation (such as daydreaming, identification, overemphasis, delinquency, sublimation), habits of rationalization, and habits of evasion. We all make partial adjustments by these methods, but if we are well adjusted we do not use them habitually when other methods would be more appropriate.

The habits that produce no adjustment are worry, negativism, regression, and emotional tantrums. They do not relieve the tensions of maladjustment, and they produce no satisfaction.

Five categories of harmful adjustment habits were discussed. They all lead to psychoneuroses and more serious maladjustments. Phobias, obsessions, anxieties, repressions, and fantasies are all habits to be avoided. They increase the state of maladjustment and lead to some of the abnormal conditions discussed in Chap. 8.

RECOMMENDED SUPPLEMENTARY READINGS

Coleman, J. C.: *Abnormal Psychology and Modern Life,* Scott, Foresman & Company, Chicago, 1950.

Fisher, V. E.: *An Introduction to Abnormal Psychology,* The Macmillan Company, New York, 1937.

McKinney, F.: *Psychology of Personal Adjustment,* John Wiley & Sons, Inc., New York, 1949.

Morgan, J. J. B.: *How to Keep a Sound Mind,* The Macmillan Company, New York, 1946.

Shaffer, L. W.: *Psychology of Adjustment,* Houghton Mifflin Company, Boston, 1936.

Thorpe, L. P.: *Psychological Foundations of Personality,* McGraw-Hill Book Company, Inc., New York, 1938.

Tiegs, E. W., and Katz, H.: *Mental Hygiene in Education,* The Ronald Press Company, New York, 1941.

Travis, L. E., and Baruch, D.: *Personal Problems of Everyday Life,* Appleton-Century-Crofts, Inc., New York, 1941.

Wallin, J. E. W.: *Personality Maladjustments and Mental Hygiene,* McGraw-Hill Book Company, Inc., New York, 1949.

Chapter 7

SPEECH CORRECTION

Man's superior behavior over that of the lower animals is most characterized by his superiority in language, or in his ability to use a complex system of signals by which he communicates with his fellow men. In every other type of behavior, he is surpassed by some of the lower animals. Some of them are stronger than man, some are faster, some see better, some hear better, but none of them can use predicative language. To be sure, the lower animals have language of a simple interjectional nature. An animal can announce a dangerous situation, for example, but he cannot describe details. Only man, with his ability to use sentence language, can describe situations that are remote in both time and space. Only man can communicate information about events that occurred in the past and at places beyond present sensory range.

This ability to use predicated language has many values.[1] It has enabled man to cooperate with his fellow men and *together* they have been able to control the lower animals in spite of inferiority in speed, sensory acuity,

---

[1] These values are discussed in more detail in Gray, J. S., *Psychological Foundations of Education,* Chap. 5, American Book Company, New York, 1935.

strength, etc. Without language, cooperation is impossible. Plans and directions for regulating cooperative behavior can be communicated only by sentence language. Another value of language is in thinking. Without discussing the thesis that language *is* thinking, we can at least agree that thinking is greatly aided by language. Some people can think better if they talk aloud, some if they write, and some if they merely speak implicitly to themselves. Without language of any sort, it would be impossible to communicate the results of thinking to others, assuming that it could take place at all. A third value of language is the pleasure of its use. Language is a delightful form of behavior—whether spoken or written. The poet enjoys expressing himself in poetry, while the lady across the street enjoys expressing herself to anyone who will listen. As Jespersen[2] says, language is "an instrument that one loves to play on."

In this chapter, however, we are interested in that form of language, known as speech, that can be produced without the use of tools. It may be gesture (including the sign-speech of the deaf) but it usually is vocal in nature. The signals are produced by the speaker manipulating certain parts of his own body. Gestures are made by the hands, face, head, etc., and are used to communicate feeling-tone or emotional attitude, while voice is made by the breath, larynx, jaws, tongue, lips, etc., and is used to communicate ideas. In comparison with other types of behavior, vocal speech is very rapid and requires precision movements of a large number of very delicate muscles. No other behavior is so exacting and necessitates such fine muscular coordination. Obviously then, some people whose neuromuscular endowment is somewhat limited will develop difficulties in the use of speech. Some will be unable to learn it readily, while others will acquire difficulties in its control after learning. Because these speech difficulties are behavior problems, they have been widely studied by the psychologists. The following pages review some of this research.

THE EXTENT OF SPEECH DISORDERS

Perhaps the most outstanding, and certainly the most quoted, survey of the extent of speech problems was made by the Federal government in 1931.[3] The data were collected from 48 cities with more than 10,000 population each. The percentage of school children with speech defects in these cities ranged from 1 to 21.4 per cent (the mean was 6.9). "There are in America 1,000,000 school children between the ages of five and eighteen so defective in speech as to require remedial treatment and training." This number does not include those who stopped their schooling before reaching eighteen, or those who may have been in special

[2] Jespersen, O., *Language, Its Nature, Development and Origin,* Henry Holt and Company, Inc., New York, 1922.

[3] White House Conference on Child Health and Protection, *Special Education, The Handicapped and the Gifted,* Appleton-Century-Crofts, Inc., New York, 1931.

schools for speech defectives. The relative frequency with which the various speech defects were distributed in this report is shown in Table 7–1.

Table 7–1. Relative Frequency of Speech Defects in Each 10,000 Cases
(White House Conference data)

Disorders	Frequencies
Oral inactivity	4,851
Articulatory disorders (structural)	1,059
Stuttering	1,029
Sound substitution	1,014.3
Voice disorders (functional)	1,014.3
Dialectal	470.4
Voice disorders (structural)	441
Articulatory disorders (paralytic)	58.8
Aphasic disorders	29.4
"Hard-of-hearing" speech	14.7
Voice disorders (paralytic)	14.7

Louttit and Hall[4] investigated the frequency of speech defects among 199,839 public school children in the state of Indiana. They found more defects in rural schools than in city schools and more in the lower grades than in the upper grades. Their results are shown in Table 7–2.

Table 7–2. Percentage of School Population in Indiana with Speech Defects

Grade	Rural			Urban			Rural and urban
	Articulation	Stuttering	Total	Articulation	Stuttering	Total	
K	9.5	1.2	10.7	8.49	0.73	9.2	9.85
1	10.5	1.2	11.5	6.41	0.64	7.1	9.07
2	6.9	1.5	7.9	5.15	0.92	6.1	7.0
3	4.3	0.86	5.2	4.18	0.76	4.9	5.02
4	4.07	1.14	5.2	2.62	0.75	3.4	4.2
5	2.6	1.01	3.6	1.93	0.79	2.7	3.0
6	2.33	0.95	3.3	1.44	0.67	2.1	2.5
7	1.64	0.89	2.5	1.31	0.75	2.1	2.24
8	1.62	0.83	2.5	0.82	0.5	1.3	1.72
9	0.74	0.39	1.1	0.4	0.85	1.2	1.21
10	0.71	0.58	1.3	0.43	0.69	1.1	1.18
11	0.42	0.39	0.8	0.32	0.38	0.7	0.75
12	0.47	0.51	1.0	0.25	0.35	0.6	0.8
Average	3.47	0.88	4.3	2.6	0.75	3.37	3.7

Morley kept records of the incidence of speech defects among University of Michigan students for a 10-year period (1941 to 1951).[5] Of the

[4] Louttit, C. M., and Hall, E. C., Survey of Speech Defects among Public School Children of Indiana, *J. Speech Disorders*, 1936, **1**, 73–80.

[5] Morley, D. E., A Ten Year Survey of Speech Defects among University of Michigan Students, *J. Speech & Hearing Disorders*, 1952, **17**, 25–31.

more than 33,000 students examined, 3.6 per cent had some sort of speech disorder. This frequency, however, varied from 1.3 per cent in 1949 to 8 per cent in 1941. See Table 7–3 for these results. Perhaps a part of this

Table 7–3. Speech Defects among Students of University of Michigan

Year	Number examined	Articu- lation	Stutter- ing	Voice	Miscel- laneous	Total
1941	3,220	119	31	67	40	257
1942	3,095	94	35	32	0	161
1943	2,264	76	20	18	7	121
1944	2,251	30	26	6	6	68
1945	2,836	82	29	16	24	151
1946	4,432	49	22	20	10	101
1947	3,469	64	37	11	6	118
1948	4,357	36	24	10	5	75
1949	3,706	19	16	8	5	48
1950	3,362	51	25	28	3	107
1951	353	7	4	0	2	13
Total.............	33,339	627	269	216	108	1,220
Per cent...........	......	50.7	25.5	15	8.8	

variation from year to year was due to the subjective nature of the test. While one examiner would class a borderline case as a defect, another would not. There is no objective speech defect test.

Carhart[6] surveyed 405 schools in Illinois and found that "more than 20 per cent" of the 144,570 pupils represented have articulatory, voice, or rhythmic difficulties of speech. Burden[7] found slightly fewer serious speech defects in the Indianapolis schools (2.9 per cent) but estimates that perhaps one-third of the children in the primary grades need corrective speech work. Voelker[8] found that 12 to 18 per cent of the students of a liberal arts college need corrective speech attention.

THE EXTENT OF CORRECTIVE PROCEDURES

It is now obvious that the speech-correction problem is more extensive than indicated by the attempts often made to solve it. While some cities have employed trained speech correctionists to help these afflicted children, others have made no provision whatever to help them. Even the cities employing speech-correction teachers often give them such large

[6] Carhart, R., A Survey of Speech Defects in Illinois, *J. Speech Disorders*, 1939, 4, 61–70.
[7] Burden, L. G., A Survey of Speech Defectives in the Indianapolis Primary Grades, *J. Speech Disorders*, 1940, 5, 247–258.
[8] Voelker, C. H., Two Surveys of Defective Speech in a Cultural College, *J. Amer. Ass. Colleg. Registr.*, 1938, 14, 39–42.

Table 7–4. Number of Speech Defective Children and Provision for Their Rehabilitation in Certain American Cities

City	Number of defectives	Number of teachers	Pupils per teacher
Population over 100,000:			
Los Angeles.............	3,662	17	215
San Francisco...........	2,247	7	321
Washington, D.C.........	3,321	9	369
Chicago................	5,330	23	232
New Orleans............	3,250	6	541
Baltimore..............	1,260	8	157
Boston.................	3,613	23	157
Detroit................	7,868	38	207
Minneapolis............	1,586	12	132
St. Louis..............	1,931	10	193
Buffalo................	4,584	9.5	482
New York..............	27,153	38	714
Philadelphia...........	7,708	26	296
Pittsburgh.............	4,566	6	761
Milwaukee.............	2,342	6	390
Population under 100,000:			
Stockton (Calif.)........	227	1	227
Kokomo (Ind.)..........	305	1	305
Dubuque (Iowa)........	65	5	13
Lansing (Mich.)........	18	1	18
Butte (Mont.)..........	300	1	300
Schenectady............	1,413	1	1,413
Johnstown (Pa.)........	558	1	558
Waco (Tex.)...........	10	1	10
Roanoke (Va.)..........	206	1	206
Holland (Mich.)........	160	1	160
Mankato (Minn.).......	168	1	168
Manitowoc (Wis.).......	277	2	138
Redwood (Calif.).......	253	1	253
Caldwell (Idaho)........	5	1	5
Beaver Dam (Wis.)......	121	1	121

numbers of defectives to train that their efforts are futile. Table 7–4 is made up of data taken from a publication of the Office of Education in Washington.[9] These data are selected from the reports of 144 city school systems with 438 specially trained speech-correction teachers on their staffs. There are 126,146 children with speech defects in these cities. This averages 288 children per teacher. (Note the variations from this, however, in the table.) Even if a teacher should hold but one lesson per week for each pupil in classes of 10, she would have a large teaching load. How

[9] Martens, E. H., and Foster, E. M., *Statistics of Special Schools and Classes for Exceptional Children, 1939–1940*, Bull., U.S. Office of Education, 1942.

teachers with twice this load can be of much assistance to children with speech defects is difficult to understand.

It is obvious that there is a great need for teachers with special training in speech disorders. This training is afforded at many colleges and universities where speech clinics are located and prospective teachers work with speech defectives under expert supervision. In some places this training is given in the English and speech departments, but most often it is given in the psychology department. Here research similar to that reviewed in this chapter is constantly being performed so that the prospective speech teacher develops a research attitude toward his pupils. Then, national conferences on speech correction are held in conjunction with the American Psychological Association, the National Association of Teachers of Speech, and the American Speech Correction Association. However, as indicated in Table 7–4, there is still great need for well-trained speech correctionists. Too often the speech-correction teacher is improperly trained. He takes a few courses in public speaking and then poses as an authority in all phases of speech and language. Speech correction should be attempted only by those who have been trained at reputable institutions. Quackery in this field is especially deplorable.

The success of speech-corrective work on 16,213 cases is reported by Rogers[10] and shown in Table 7–5. It is obvious that the correction of

Table 7–5. Percentage of Effectiveness in 16,213 Speech-correction Cases

Speech Defect	Corrected	Improved
Stuttering	27	60
Lolling	36.5	4.8
Lisping	35	55
Defective phonation	50	40
Foreign accent	30	60
Dialect	30	66
Nasality	21	42
Others	6	40

speech disorders is a difficult matter. It is estimated by one speech authority that improperly trained correctionists do patients about as much harm as they do good. The fact that a person is the head of a school for speech correction, or that he is a physician on the staff of some hospital, or that he is a professor in a university, is not evidence that he is a qualified speech correctionist.

If, as estimated above, there are 1 million school children in the United States with speech disorders and if a speech teacher can direct the cor-

[10] Rogers, J. F., *The Speech Defective School Child*, Bull. 7, U.S. Bureau of Education, 1931.

rection of 250 cases at one time, simple arithmetic indicates that we need 4,000 speech correction teachers. Since membership in the American Speech Correction Association is less than 500, and this is perhaps a near accurate indication of *qualified* correctionists, it is obvious that children with this handicap are being unfairly neglected. We have special institutions and spend millions of dollars, and rightly so, on children with other types of defects (such as deafness, blindness, etc.) while speech defects are too often ignored completely.

DISORDERS IN LEARNING SPEECH

We have defined speech as an organized, or systematized, group of symbols used for the purpose of communicating ideas and feelings to other people. These symbols are conditioned stimuli that are learned, like any other conditioned stimuli, by being associated with natural or unconditional stimuli (see discussion of the conditioned response in Chap. 1).

When the child is born he uses the muscles of his body in a random fashion. There is not much control or coordination. We say that he makes random movements. As he matures, he learns to control his muscles and his behavior becomes more intentional. His fists no longer punch him in the face by accident and he can reach for an object without having his hand go somewhere else. He has learned a degree of muscular control and coordination.

How Words Are Learned

The same procedure of development occurs in the child's speech muscles. At first, there are random movements producing random sounds or babbling. These slowly give way to controlled movements and controlled sounds. The child reaches a stage in maturation when he can make a desired sound rather than some other unintentional one. He is then, and only then, ready to learn language. Up until now, all babies are alike. The Japanese, the Indian, the Eskimo, the English, the French, the Greek children—all make the same prelanguage sounds. It is estimated that the normal child makes every possible sound sometime during his prelanguage babbling. Certainly he makes all the sounds that are later preserved for language purposes.

As Allport[11] explains, "The chief significance of the vocal play of babies seems to be in establishing circular reflexes between the sound of the syllable and the response of speaking it." This means that the child may say "da" by accident, but he *hears* the sound as well as *feels* the muscles used in its production. After a few random repetitions, the hearing of the sound becomes the stimulus for the muscular action of producing it and a conditioned response is formed. After that, another person may say

[11] Allport, F. H., *Social Psychology*, Chap. 8, Houghton Mifflin Company, Boston, 1924.

"da" and the child responds by the muscular action that produces "da." The child can now make a particular sound in response to particular stimulation. Random behavior has now become localized and the child is ready for the next stage of speech development.

After the child has learned to make specific sounds and to recognize these sounds when they are made by others, he next learns what they mean or what they stand for. This again is a conditioned response. Suppose, for example, that a parents says "da" only when a particular object, let us say a ball, is present. He says "da" as he hands the child the ball. This stimulates the child to say "da" as he grasps the ball. The ball and "da" are experienced together. Soon the ball alone will stimulate the muscular action of producing the sound "da" and likewise the sound "da" will stimulate the manipulative reactions to the ball. Each becomes a symbol or a substitute for the other.

Now suppose that the child utters the sound "da" some day when the ball is not present. The mother hears this and immediately produces the ball. After this is repeated a few times, the child learns, again by the conditioned response process, that the sound "da" can be used to bring about a specific reaction in another person. "Da" is now a sound that he can make to cause the mother to get the ball for him. He now has learned language.

Thus words are first made by accident, or as a result of random muscle movement. With maturation and learning, they are next repeated by intention, or as the specific reaction to specific stimulation. Finally, they are uttered to produce a specific reaction in others. They are used to communicate ideas and feelings and wants and aversions. They are tools for human cooperation.

Vocabulary Growth

The increase in words or vocabulary of children has been carefully studied. Many authorities consider vocabulary growth to be an excellent indication of mental development. While there are wide individual differences even among normal children, due to environmental variations, it has been found that when the environmental factor is constant an inferiority in vocabulary is a fairly reliable indication of inferiority in mental development.

Smith[12] found that the average child of one year has a vocabulary of only three words, but at the age of six it has increased to more than 2,500 words. His results are shown in Table 7–6.

Buckingham and Dolch[13] give an estimated vocabulary for children

[12] Smith, M. E., An Investigation of the Development of the Sentence and the Extent of Vocabulary in Young Children, *Univ. Ia. Stud. Psych.*, 1926, 3, No. 5.

[13] Buckingham, B. R., and Dolch, E. W., *A Combined Word List*, Ginn & Company, Boston, 1936.

Table 7–6. Increase in Vocabulary with Age

Age	Number	Words	Gain
1	52	3	3
2	25	272	269
3	20	896	624
4	26	1540	644
5	20	2072	532
6	9	2562	490

Table 7–7. Estimated Vocabulary of School Children

	Words	Increase
Beginning of grade 1......................	2,000	
Beginning of grade 2......................	2,800	800
Beginning of grade 3......................	3,600	800
Beginning of grade 4......................	4,500	900
Beginning of grade 5......................	5,400	900
Beginning of grade 6......................	6,400	1,000
Beginning of grade 7......................	7,500	1,100
Beginning of grade 8......................	8,700	1,200
End of grade 8..........................	10,000	1,300

Table 7–8. Average Word Length of Verbal Responses of Children of Various Ages

Age, years	McCarthy study		Smith study		Young study	
	Boys	Girls	Boys	Girls	Boys	Girls
1.5	1.0	1.3				
2	1.4	2.1	1.3	2.2		
2.5	3.2	3.1	2.2	2.4	3.1	3.3
3	3.1	3.8	3.3	3.5	3.3	3.9
3.5	4.2	4.4	4.4	3.8	4.2	4.6
4	4.3	4.4	4.1	4.4	4.6	4.8
4.5	4.6	4.7	4.8	4.7	4.7	5.0
5	...	...	4.7	4.6	4.9	5.5

at each school grade. This is shown in Table 7–7. The age six vocabulary, or the beginning of grade 1, is somewhat lower than that found by Smith, but the average I.Q. of the 9 six-year-olds in the Smith study was 108.

Even more important than vocabulary size in early speech development is sentence length. There have been a number of studies of the number of words used in each verbal response. Three of these are shown in Table 7–8 as reported by McCarthy.[14] In general, girls are superior to boys of the same age and children from higher socioeconomic levels are superior to those from lower levels.

VARIATIONS FROM NORMAL SPEECH DEVELOPMENT

Now, what is the significance of variation either above or below the normal pattern of speech development? First, such variations may indicate corresponding variations in intelligence. There are exceptions, but, in general, the child who is superior in speech development is also superior in mental development. Likewise, although there are many exceptions, the child who is slow in speech development is likely to be mentally retarded. Terman[15] reports that, while speech begins in the child of superior mental ability at 12 months, it does not begin until 15.8 months in the child of average mentality, and not until 34.4 months in the feeble-minded child. He found a correlation of .91 between vocabulary size and mental age and concluded that "children of a given mental age have approximately the same vocabulary regardless of chronological age."

Second, variations from normal speech development may merely indicate that the child is not maturing in all his traits in a uniform manner. Few children follow the same pattern of development in all traits. If a child is slow in speech development and apparently normal in other respects, he should not be urged to improve his speech. Leave him alone and let nature take its course. Urging will be of no value and it may create a social adjustment problem that is harmful. Some speech-correction authorities insist that few speech problems should be considered as such until the child is at least five years old. Normal maturation often takes care of what at one stage in the child's development seems to be a serious speech disorder.

DISORDERS OF PHONATION

Contrary to popular opinion, caused perhaps by the misleading name, the voice is produced not by the vibration of cords but of bands. The voice producing vibrators are two flat pieces of muscular cartilage extending out from the walls of the larynx or "Adam's apple." Both ends and one side are attached to the larynx so that only one side is free to vibrate. If a flat piece of rubber is tied across the end of a tin can, and then a slit made through the middle of it, we have an analogy to the vocal vibrators in action. In ordinary breathing they relax and leave a wide air passage, but when in vibration they come very close together with only a narrow slit between.

Pitch in sound depends on the number of vibrations per second. Change

[14] McCarthy, D., Language Development in Children, in L. Carmichael (Ed.), *Manual of Child Psychology*, John Wiley & Sons, Inc., New York, 1946.

[15] Terman, L. M., *Genetic Studies of Genius*, Vol. I, Stanford University Press, Stanford, Calif., 1925.

in the length or the thickness or the tensity of a vibrator will cause a change in pitch. . . . Vocal pitch is changed by activity of the vocal muscles, which are attached to the vocal bands. They can change the length, the thickness and the tensity of the bands, thus giving them a wide pitch range.

Resonance is the reenforcement of the fundamental tone, produced by the vibrator, with the sympathetic vibrations of other agents. The sound board on a piano, the pipes on a pipe organ, the body of a violin, are examples of resonance agents. Their sympathetic vibrations add quality to the fundamental tone. The bones and cartilages of the chest, the neck, and the head, all send out sympathetic vibrations as does the piano sound board. Place the hand on the chest and speak in a low tone. Immediately you feel sympathetic vibrations. The air cavities of the chest and head likewise produce sympathetic vibrations which reenforce the fundamental sound of the vocal bands. These reenforcements make the voice much stronger and more pleasing than it would be if it came directly from the larynx without resonance.

Vocal force, or loudness, is caused by wider vibrations of the vocal bands brought about by greater breath pressure. Breath pressure is caused by greater and more powerful contraction of the muscles which force the air out of the lungs. In proper diaphragmatic breathing, these are the abdominal muscles. They contract, pushing the abdominal organs up against the diaphragm which becomes more arched into the chest cavity, and thus forces the air out. Observe a dog barking and notice the action of his abdominal muscles. The loudness of his bark will depend upon the force of contraction of those muscles. Thus, the degree of vocal force depends on the degree of contraction of the abdominal muscles.[16]

It is now obvious that disorders of phonation are all in some manner asociated with these three characteristics of the voice—pitch, resonance (or quality), and loudness.

Disorders of pitch are associated either with the vocal bands directly or with the muscles that control them. Often the vibrating edges of the vocal bands become irregular. This causes a hoarse voice and is very noticeable after football games. Often auctioneers, public speakers, and newsboys speak with a pinched throat and thus become hoarse. More muscles than necessary are contracting to position the vocal bands for producing the desired pitch. The bands may be pulled so close together that they interfere with each other in vibration. This causes the edges to become cracked and then swollen. The remedy for this condition is to speak with a minimum of muscular effort in the larynx. The speaker must learn to relax all laryngeal muscles except those necessary to produce the desired pitch. Directions for relaxation discussed in Chap 2 are appropriate for use here.

[16] The above quotation concerning phonation is taken from J. Stanley Gray, *Communicative Speaking,* Expression Company, Boston, 1928.

Another common disorder of pitch is the lack of variation, or speaking in a mono-key. When the mono-key is unusually high the voice is especially displeasing.

The high piercing tones of my neighbor who at this moment is screeching, "Ma-r-ee!" prompts me to put the error of too high a pitch at the top of the list. Marie now has answered, "I'm coming; can-tcha hea-r-rrr?" in unconscious mimicry of her mother. The pitch is not only inappropriate to the age and sex of the individual; it is inappropriate to anything called human. The tensions in extrinsic as well as intrinsic muscles of the neck and larynx have become a fixed habit in the mother and become as well the general bodily configuration of nervous excitability and strain. Through imitation Marie is certain to be known as the girl with the "squeaky voice."[17]

Fortunately, most problems of pitch control respond readily to corrective procedures. The books listed at the end of this chapter describe these in detail.

Disorders of resonance are usually due either to malformations in the resonance mechanisms (such as adenoids, cleft palate, enlarged tonsils), or to maladjustments in voice production. Remedy of the first type of difficulty is obviously surgical attention. However, remedy of maladjustments in voice production depends on the nature of the maladjustment.

There are three kinds of maladjustment which produce three characteristic kinds of impure quality in the voice.

First, there may be unnecessary contraction or tensity in the muscles of the throat, causing characteristic "throaty" quality.

The remedy is proper relaxation, which can best be attained by the procedure outlined in Chap. 2.

The second type of maladjustment is "voice misplacement" or misdirection. As the voice comes up from the vibrators, it should be directed against the hard palate, just back of the upper front teeth. This is the bony part of the mouth roof and reflects the sound out of the mouth. If it is directed further back it hits the soft palate and loses much of its force. This part of the mouth roof is soft and deadens sound, just as velvet curtains do. . . . The third type of maladjustment is lack of breath conservation. The use of too much breath gives a "breathy tone" which is always hard to hear. Hold a mirror close to the mouth and try to speak so that moisture does not collect on the mirror. Do not try to increase the capacity of the lungs. Remember that the only function of breath in voice production is to cause the vibration of the vocal bands.[18]

Disorders of loudness are almost always associated with faulty breath control.

[17] Quoted from Berry, M. F., and Eisenson, J., *The Defective in Speech*, p. 158, F. S. Crofts & Co., New York, 1942.
[18] Quoted from Gray, *op. cit.*

Voice can be produced only by outgoing breath. Consequently, in continuous talking the inspiration must be quick so the talk will not be broken, and the expiration economized so the talk will be continuous. In other words, the speaker must spend a minimum of time in breathing in and a maximum of time in breathing out. This requires that the breathing muscles be well developed and well controlled.

These are the muscles of the diaphragm, an arched partition between the lung cavity and the abdominal cavity. This may

. . . be pulled downward by contracting the fan-shaped muscles which are attached to the walls of the body and spread out over the diaphragm. This action forms a vacuum in the lower part of the chest where the lungs have greatest capacity. There is no weight to press on them and hasten expiration, as in the case of shoulder breathing. The expansion comes where there is least limitation. These muscles are used for no other purpose and evidently were intended by nature to be used for breathing. They are very powerful and easily controlled.

The diaphragm method of breathing can be developed with practice. Lie down on a bed and completely relax. Notice that breathing now seems to center in the abdominal region below the chest cavity. This is because the diaphragm is arched upward, and when pulled down to increase the capacity of the chest it presses on the abdominal organs. These in turn, push the abdominal walls outward. Expansion in the abdominal region is a test of proper diaphragm breathing. Now, stand up and try to breath in the same way. Learn to read and speak while breathing properly. Learn first while lying down, and then go through the same process while standing.[19]

Mastery of diaphragm breathing will soon take care of all ordinary disorders of loudness.

A fourth disorder of phonation is *aphonia,* or loss of voice. This may be due to congestion in the larynx, as with a bad cold, or to psychological reasons (hysteria) that cannot be discussed here. The remedy must, of course, depend on the cause.

DISORDERS OF ARTICULATION

When vocal sound leaves the phonation mechanism in the larynx it moves with the breath to the oral and nasal cavities where it is modified by the soft palate, the tongue, the teeth, and the lips into words, or speech. Voice is the raw product out of which speech is made. The process of converting voice into speech is called "articulation."

Vowel and Consonant Sounds

There are two classifications of elementary speech sounds—vowels and consonants. The vowel sounds, or continuants, are made by altering the voice passageway without interfering with or interrupting the voice pas-

[19] *Ibid.*

sage. Vowels are continuous in flow and made by positioning the organs of articulation, especially the tongue and lips. On the other hand, consonant sounds are made by regulating the free escape of the voice. This is done by contact, or near contact, of the soft palate, the tongue, the teeth, and the lips across the voice passageway. Some consonants (v, f, l, w, h, s, and r) are "open" and made by the voice or breath passing through the mouth or nose with no complete stoppage. Some (b, d, g, p, t, and k) are "explosive" and made by the complete interruption of the voice passage and then its sudden release. Three (m, n, and ng) are made in the nasal cavity.

In general, all articulation disorders center around the formation of vowels and consonants. The vowel disorders are due either to an inadequate passageway for the voice sound or to an improper position of the tongue and lips for forming the desired sound. However, vowel sounds are comparatively easy to make and cause the average speaker but little difficulty. If the phonation itself is not defective in pitch, resonance, or strength, it is easy to learn to place the tongue and lips in proper positions for making the various vowel sounds.

The proper formation of consonant sounds is not so easy. Most consonant sounds are hard to make and necessitate very precise and prompt action of the muscles of the palate, tongue, jaw, and lips. Few other muscles in the body must be so well trained and well controlled.

Consonant sounds vary greatly in the frequency with which they appear in spoken language. Travis[20] checked more than 46,000 sounds in the speech of children, university adults, and common laborers. He found that the four consonant sounds made most frequently by children (t, n, r, and s) are made most frequently by adults. Also, the four sounds made least frequently by children (sh, ch, j, and wh) are made least frequently by adults (see Table 7–9 for these results).

Lisping is a common articulation disorder in which the patient substitutes the sound th for the sound s. It may be due to bad front-teeth formation, or to inactive muscles in the tip of the tongue, or to a bad habit. Malformation of the incisors can usually be corrected by dental attention. The inactive genioglossus muscle and the bad habit can both be corrected by exercise. Any book on speech correction contains exercises for remedying this sound substitution.

Lolling is a speech disorder characterized by articulatory inactivity. The tongue, especially, is too slow, and the speech is thick and unfin- ished. The sounds r, l, t, d, k, and g are especially indistinct. Lolling is often due to deficient mentality, but muscular incoordination resulting from a childhood disease and defectively formed speech organs (such as short frenum, large tongue, defective nerve control) may cause such lazy

[20] Travis, R. C., *Speech Pathology*, Appleton-Century-Crofts, Inc., New York, 1931.

Table 7–9. Relative Frequency of Consonant Sounds in the Conversational Speech of Children and Adults

Sound	Frequencies in per cent		
	Children	University adults	Common labor adults
t (to)	12	13.4	12.5
n (no)	10.4	10.3	10.8
r (ride)	9.3	8.8	8.8
s (see)	8.9	7.4	7.2
l (lady)	6.3	6	5.5
d (do)	6.3	7	6.8
m (me)	5.2	4.9	6.8
k (kite)	5.1	4.8	5.4
z (zero)	4.3	4	3.6
w (we)	4.2	4.3	4.6
th (these)	4	4.3	4.5
h (he)	3.9	4.2	4.3
b (be)	2.9	2.6	2.8
p (pail)	2.8	2.3	2
g (go)	2.7	2.5	2.5
f (fight)	2.4	2.7	2.7
v (vine)	2.4	2.6	2.6
ng (ring)	1.9	1.9	1.9
y (yes)	1.7	2.4	2.1
sh (she)	1.3	1.6	1.4
ch (church)	.7	.6	.9
j (joy)	.7	.7	.6
wh (white)	.6	.5	.3

speech. Exercises are essential, but the correction is a long slow process and sometimes impossible.

Dialects constitute a large percentage of speech defects. Foreign dialects are difficult because many English speech sounds are not found in some other languages. Provincial dialects are not considered very important unless they represent a lower socioeconomic status. A Bostonian dialect is not usually a problem for the speech correctionist, but an East Side dialect or a Texas drawl or "Minnesota skol talk" are all speech problems. The remedy for any sort of a dialect is to determine which sounds are difficult and then drill on those alone and in combination with other sounds. The remedy is corrective practice.

There are certain directions for correcting dialects which have been widely used. They are:

1. The learner should be made acutely conscious of the acoustical difference between the sound that he should produce and the one he does produce.

He should be able to recognize the difference between the right sound and the wrong one.

2. He should develop both a visual image and a kinesthetic feeling of the positions his speech mechanisms should take to make the proper sound.

3. He should develop muscular control so that his speech apparatus can assume the positions necessary for producing the desired sounds.

4. The final step is to habitualize the behavior just described. Like other forms of habit learning, the behavior should be slow and accurate. Speed should never be attained at the sacrifice of accuracy.

DISORDERS OF SPEECH RHYTHM (STUTTERING)

Rhythm is just as important in speech as in any other type of behavior. Those who are unable to speak rhythmically are said to "stutter." Because of intense excitement or physical fatigue or prolonged anxiety, anyone may stutter. Most children go through a stuttering stage before their speech habits are well established. But some people habitually experience intense muscular cramps and spasms when they try to speak. They may repeat the initial sound of a word over and over again, or they may experience a complete sound blockage and for a time are unable to make any sound at all. At any rate, the rhythm of speaking is definitely blocked.

There are a number of facts concerning stuttering that most authorities accept because they have been established by research methods.

1. There are about 1,400,000 stutterers in the United States, or approximately 1 per cent of the population stutters.

2. The stutterer can speak normally on some occasions. This indicates that his trouble is not a defect in structure but a defect in function. There is neuromuscular incoordination, hypertension, and, usually, emotional disturbance.

3. Stuttering occurs from three to five times as often among boys as among girls.[21]

4. There is no relation between mental ability and stuttering, although this handicap does cause an average school retardation of about one year.[22]

5. There are three age peaks at which stuttering begins: (a) the language learning age, two to four years old; (b) the starting-to-school age, six to seven years old; (c) the puberty age, twelve to fourteen years old.

6. Other neuromuscular functions, especially breathing, may be included in the stuttering spasm syndrome. Even when not speaking, stutterers do not usually have proper breathing rhythm. The ratio of inspiration time

[21] In the Louttit and Hall study referred to above, the ratio of stuttering among boys to that among girls was 2.76 to 1 in the rural areas and 3.09 to 1 in the cities. In the Morley study, Michigan boys exceeded the girls in stuttering by 4 to 1, and in articulation problems by 3 to 2.

[22] Evidence for this statement is found in studies by Travis, West, and Wallin. Louttit has summarized these data in his book *Clinical Psychology*, Harper & Brothers, New York, 1936, from which the following data are taken.

to expiration time is considerably less with stutterers than with non-stutterers.[23]

I.Q. Distribution of Stutterers

I.Q.	Travis data	West data
Above 120	9.6	7.2
110–119	16.4	13.1
100–109	37.	20.7
90–99	19.	25.7
80–89	12.	19.9
70–79	2.7	10.3
60–69	1.4	2.5
Below 60		.77

School Retardation of Stutterers
(Wallin data)

Years retarded	Number	Per cent
0	90	17.7
½	5	1
1	185	36.4
2	134	27.5
3	55	10.8
4	24	4.7
5	6	1.2
6	2	.4
7	1	.2

HEREDITY

It is a generally accepted fact that stuttering runs in some families. However, whether it is due to heredity, or to habits learned from association with a stuttering parent, is not so clear. Nelson[24] studied the incidence of stuttering among 6,600 ancestors of 204 stutterers and compared the results with those of a similar study of 6,266 ancestors of 204 control nonstuttering subjects. She found 210 stutterers (143 males, 67 females) in the ancestry of the stutterers, but only 37 stutterers in the ancestry of the controls. There were 56 cases among the ancestry of the stutterers where the father, son, and grandson all stuttered. In the ancestry of the controls, there were but 4 such cases. Of the stutterers, 75 (37 per cent)

[23] Murray, E., Disintegration of Breathing and Eye Movements in Stutterers during Silent Reading and Reasoning, *Psychol. Monogr.* 1932, **43**, 218–275; Hendrikson, E. H., Simultaneously Recorded Breathing and Vocal Disturbances of Stutterers, *Arch. Speech,* 1938, **9**, 79–96; and Travis, V., A Study of Horizontal Distintegration in Breathing during Stuttering, *Arch. Speech,* 1936, **1**, 157–169.

[24] West, R., Nelson, S., and Berry, M. F., The Heredity of Stuttering, *Quart. J. Speech,* 1939, **25**, 23–30.

had associated with stutterers; but 60 (29 per cent) of the controls had also associated with stutterers. In reporting this study, West concludes that a very large percentage of stuttering is due to heredity alone.

Wepman[25] made a similar comparative study of 250 stutterers and 250 nonstuttering control subjects, matched as to age, sex, and social environment. He checked the frequency of stutterers (other than the subject) in the families of both stutterers and nonstutterers. He found that 68.8 per cent of the families of stutterers contained other stutterers whereas only 15.6 per cent of the families of the control nonstutterers contained other stutterers.

Some evidence has been found that stuttering and twinning are inherited together. At any rate, they are both found in the same families more often than chance would account for. Berry[26] found in a study of 250 families containing twins that there is one stutterer for each 18 children. (In unselected samples, there is one stutterer for each 100 children.) Considering just twins alone, she found the ratio of stutterers to nonstutterers to be 1 to 11.

CEREBRAL DOMINANCE

A right-eyed, right-handed, and right-footed person is said to be bilaterally right-sided. This means that he has left cerebral-hemisphere dominance, since the nerves cross over and one side of the brain controls the opposite side of the body. The bilaterally left-sided person has right cerebral dominance. However, some people are right-eyed, left-handed, and right-footed. This means that they have no cerebral dominance. In such cases, the sides of the brain are equipotential. After a study of cerebral lesions in 92 patients, Weisenberg[27] concludes that handedness is a criterion of the dominant brain hemisphere in at least 95 per cent of the cases. The dominant side of the brain also controls speech. Evidence for this fact is given by Chesher[28] who found in a study of 157 patients that brain lesions on the side opposite that of the preferred hand interfere with speech; while lesions on the same side as the preferred hand do not affect speech, except with those people who have no brain dominance. In such cases, lesions on either side affect speech.

There is some evidence that stuttering is more frequent among people who do not have cerebral dominance than among those who do. In 1912 Ballard[29] observed in a study of 11,939 school children that stuttering

[25] Wepman, J. M., Familial Incidence of Stammering, *J. Hered.*, 1939, **30**, 207–210.

[26] Berry, M. F., A Common Denominator in Twinning and Stuttering, *J. Speech Disorders*, 1938, **3**, 51–57.

[27] Weisenberg, T. H., A Study of Aphasia, *Arch. Neurol. Psychiat.*, *Chicago*, 1934, **31**, 1–33.

[28] Chesher, E. C., Some Observations Concerning the Relation of Handedness to the Language Mechanism, *Bull. Neurol. Inst. N.Y.*, 1936, **4**, 556–562.

[29] Ballard, P. B., Sinistrality and Speech, *J. Exp. Pedagogy*, 1912, **1**, 298–310.

occurred with greater frequency (25.8 per cent) among those who had been changed from left- to right-handedness. (It is now known that left-handed people are less bilaterally sided, *i.e.*, do not have cerebral dominance, than right-handed people. A change in handedness may not change brain dominance but may merely equalize it.) Oates[30] found that 2.01 per cent of 4,176 schoolboys who had clear cerebral dominance also had speech defects, whereas 11.8 per cent of those who did not have cerebral dominance had speech defects. After a study of 600 cases, Quinan[31] estimates that stuttering occurs in left-handed men from three to seven times as frequently as in right-handed men.

Bryngelson[32] compared a group of 78 stutterers with a group of 78 control subjects, matched for sex, age, mental ability, and social status. He found that 58 per cent of the stutterers had had shifts in handedness and perhaps lacked definite brain dominance. His results are shown in Table 7–10.

Table 7–10. Comparison of Stutterers with Control Subjects in Handedness

	Stutterers, Per cent	Normals, Per cent
Now right-handed......................	69	94
Now left-handed.......................	6	6
Now ambidextrous......................	29	0
Handedness was shifted.................	58	1
Left-handedness in family...............	49	42
Stuttering in family....................	54	6

Bryngelson claims that he has been unusually successful in correcting stuttering by "building up a dominant gradient in one cerebral hemisphere."[33] He says that "the success of the dominance technique is so marked that we have come to feel that a differential diagnosis, which usually considers other causal factors in treatment, though valuable is not absolutely essential." In building up cerebral dominance, he believes that sometimes it is necessary to shift handedness from right to left, where it was originally and should have remained, and sometimes it is merely necessary to make a right-, or left-, handed child more definitely right-, or left-, handed. The bilateral dominance may not be great enough and needs development. In 127 cases treated "with the cerebral dominance

[30] Oates, D. W., Left Handedness in Relation to Speech Defects, Intelligence and Achievement, *Forum Educ.*, 1929, **7**, 91–105.

[31] Quinan, C., Sinistrality in Relation to High Blood Pressure and Defects of Speech, *Arch. Intern. Med.*, 1921, **27**, 257–261.

[32] Bryngelson, B., A Study of Laterality of Stutterers and Normal Speakers, *J. Soc. Psychol.*, 1940, **11**, 151–155.

[33] Bryngelson, B., Treatment of Stuttering, *Symposium on Stuttering*, Madison, Wis., 1931.

therapy," 42.5 per cent of them were cured and 47.5 per cent were "markedly improved." Only 13 of the 127 showed no improvement. Of these, seven should have been changed in handedness but because of parental objection the attempt was made to establish left brain dominance. During the summer, four of the cured cases went back to right-handedness and again began to stutter. In September they were shifted back again and by December were cured.

Stutterers show other indications of the lack of cerebral dominance. Travis[34] found that there is a definite lack of coordination and synchronization between the two sides of the body in the breathing of stutterers. She estimates that at least 90 per cent of stutterers do not have bilateral synergy in breathing. Sometimes there is a complete lack of breathing movement on one side of the body, and sometimes an inspiration will be interrupted for an expiration. There is poor rhythm. Cross[35] compared a group of 42 stutterers (31 right-handed, 11 left-handed) with an equated group of nonstutterers and found that the stutterers were decidedly inferior to the controls in bimanual activity. Right-handed controls were superior to stutterers in the rate of movement of the right hand, the left hand, lips, jaw, tongue, and diaphragm. Left-handed controls were superior only on left-hand movements.

However, all studies do not substantiate the data given above. In fact, some evidence indicates that there is no relation between cerebral dominance and stuttering. Daniels[36] gave handedness tests to 1,548 college students and found data that "lend little or no support to many relationships commonly reported as existing between handedness and stuttering." There were 138 ambidextrous students, four of whom stuttered. The rest (1,376) were right-handed and 15 stuttered.

Spadino[37] studied a group of 70 stutterers in comparison with a control group of 70 nonstutterers, matched as to age, race or language of parents, and mental ability. He found no significances between the two groups in any phase of cerebral dominance. His results are shown in Table 7–11. The author concludes, "This study has found little evidence to corroborate the theory that stuttering is often associated with lack of unilaterality."

In face of this conflicting evidence regarding the relation of cerebral dominance to stuttering, any conclusion must be postponed until further research clears up the matter. Why different studies using essentially the

[34] Travis, V., A Study of Horizontal Disintegration in Breathing during Stuttering, *Arch. Speech,* 1936, 1, 157–169.

[35] Cross, H. M., The Motor Capacities of Stutterers, *Arch. Speech,* 1936, 1, 112–132.

[36] Daniels, E. M., An Analysis of the Relation between Handedness and Stuttering with Special Reference to the Orton-Travis Theory of Cerebral Dominance, *J. Speech Disorders,* 1940, 5, 309–326.

[37] Spadino, E. J., Writing and Laterality Characteristics of Stuttering Children, *Teach. Coll. Contr. Educ.,* 1941, No. 837.

Table 7–11. Comparison of 70 Stutterers with 70 Controls on Various Phases of Bilateral Dominance

	Stutterers		Nonstutterers		Critical ratio of difference
	Number	Per cent	Number	Per cent	
Handedness:					
Right...................	59	84	62	89	.86
Ambidex...............	0	0	1	1	.83
Left...................	11	16	7	10	1.05
Eyedness:					
Right...................	39	56	45	64	.96
Ambidex...............	5	7	3	4	.77
Left...................	26	37	22	32	.38
Footedness:					
Right...................	53	76	56	80	.57
Ambidex...............	7	10	7	10	.00
Left...................	10	14	7	10	.73
Laterality:					
Right...................	56	80	58	83	.45
Ambidex...............	5	7	5	7	.00
Left...................	9	13	7	10	.56

same methods of investigation should find opposing results is not now understood. However, it has happened before in science and will happen again. There are many problems in all fields of science about which there is conflicting evidence.

MENTAL ADJUSTMENT

Fletcher[38] argues that, because the stutterer can speak perfectly on certain occasions but stutters on others, his real difficulty must lie in his relationship to those stuttering occasions. "All communication demands a social adjustment, either intellectual or emotional, or else both at once. . . . Stuttering represents a morbidity of these adjustment processes, . . . a pathological social response." In other words, stuttering is merely a symptom of a social maladjustment, or a psychoneurosis. It is not a speech problem per se at all. When the mental adjustment problem is taken care of, the stuttering symptom disappears. "We are forced to conclude that the speech instrument of the stutterer is normal, and that its malfunction is due to a state of mind which appears to be subject to some degree of control."

From this point of view, the treatment of stuttering becomes psychological. If the individual learns to become adjusted to his social environ-

[38] Fletcher, J. M., *The Problem of Stuttering,* Longmans, Green & Co., Inc., New York. 1928.

ment, his speech problem is taken care of. The real treatment, then, is mental hygiene. Fletcher warns that this must be done by "providing an environmental situation in which he can function normally until his speech processes have become properly fixed and his emotional attitude reconditioned." The environment must be molded to fit the stutterer instead of trying to mold him to fit an environment that has already caused him to develop a psychoneurosis. Then, as he becomes more successful and confident in his adjustments, he will become more proficient in speech.

Most of the medical authorities on stuttering agree with Fletcher. They believe that stuttering is a mental problem and must be treated accordingly. Dr. Smiley Blanton believes that "the fault is not with the organs used in speech but with the emotional difficulty in the unconscious. . . . Psychoanalysis is the preferred method for assisting in readjustment, for discovering the difficulty." However, since this is "open only to a limited number because of the time and expense involved," Blanton approves of "a practical application of good mental hygiene." He believes that "when the emotional reeducation is accomplished the speech difficulty will take care of itself."[39]

Dr. Coriat believes that "stammering is a psycho-neurosis caused by persistence into later life of early pregenital oral nursing, oral sadistic, and anal sadistic components. . . . Because stammering is a neurosis, psychoanalysis is the therapy of choice.[40]

There is some test evidence to justify the view that stutterers are maladjusted personalities. Bender[41] compared a group of 249 male stutterers with a control group of 303 male nonstutterers on the Bernreuter Personality Inventory. He found that "the stuttering group was significantly higher neurotically, more introverted, less dominant, less self-confident, and less sociable" than the control group.

Stinchfield[42] administered the Thurstone Personality Schedule to 46 girls in the speech-correction classes at Mount Holyoke College. (They were not all stutterers.) She found that 60 per cent of the items listed by Thurstone as indicating psychoneurotic tendencies were in her list of high frequency items. She believes that "this in itself is a strong argument for the need of mental hygiene as well as corrective speech work with these students."

---

[39] These quotations are from Blanton's statement of his own theory of stuttering as found in E. F. Hahn, *Stuttering—Significant Theories and Therapies,* Stanford University Press, Stanford, Calif., 1943.

[40] *Ibid.*

[41] Bender, J. F., *The Personality Structure of Stuttering,* Pitman Publishing Corp., New York, 1939.

[42] Stinchfield, S. M., *Speech Disorders,* Harcourt, Brace and Company, Inc., New York, 1933.

Schroeder and Ackerson[43] studied the relation of stuttering to a large number of behavior factors. They found low but positive correlations between stuttering and psychoneuroticism, mental conflict, lack of initiative, inefficiency in study, inferiority complex, unpopularity, nervousness, and being teased by other children. They found negative correlations between stuttering and bad companions, running with a gang, heterosexuality, truancy, contrariness, stealing, and destructiveness. The authors suggest that, while stuttering is associated with psychoneurotic unaggressive behavior, there is a question as to which is cause and which is effect, or perhaps both are "symptoms of some deeper lying causal complex."

BIOCHEMICAL FACTORS

Starr[44] found that stutterers are "overloaded with carbon dioxide far in excess of normal speakers." He believed that breathing exercises and a decrease of carbohydrates in the diet would improve the stutterer's condition. Travis[45] admits that stutterers have an excess of carbon dioxide in the blood stream, but he believes it to be "a result of the faulty breathing of the stutterer in his attempts at speech."

Kopp[46] has found a series of abnormal serological ratios in the blood stream of stutterers. Inorganic phosphate and sugar are excessive in quantity, while protein and calcium are below normal. More serious than the abnormal amount of these chemicals, however, is the abnormal ratio they hold to each other in the blood of stutterers. This is summarized in Table 7–12.

Table 7–12. Comparison of the Blood Serum Ratios of Stutterers and Normals

Blood serums	Normals	Stutterers
Calcium and inorganic phosphate........	Negatively correlated	Positively correlated
Calcium and protein..................	Positively correlated	Negatively correlated
Potassium and inorganic phosphate......	Positively correlated	Negatively correlated
Potassium and protein................	Negatively correlated	Positively correlated

West[47] believes that, while these chemical differences are unimportant in ordinary living processes, they may "affect speech disastrously." Some

[43] Schroeder, P. L., and Ackerson, L., Relationship of Personality and Behavior Difficulties to Disorders of Speech, *Symposium on Stuttering*, Madison, Wis., 1931.

[44] Starr, H. B., The Hydrogen Ion Concentration of the Mixed Saliva, *Amer. J. Psychol.*, 1922, **33**, 394–418.

[45] *Op. cit.*

[46] Kopp, G. A., Metabolic Studies of Stutterers, *Speech Monogr.*, 1934, 1, No. 1.

[47] West, R., Kennedy, L., and Carr, A., *The Rehabilitation of Speech*, Harper & Brothers, New York, 1937.

people are of the "normal biochemical type and never stutter." Others have a blood chemical unbalance "so marked that they stutter even when reading or speaking to themselves in complete privacy." Then, there are borderline people whose blood chemical balance depends on "changes in their social medium." When these unfortunate conditions of poor social adjustment occur they cause a temporary blood chemical unbalance that produces the stuttering syndrome—bilateral incoordination, constriction of peripheral blood vessels, irregular breathing, etc.

Berry and Eisenson[48] suggest that there may be some connection between basal-metabolism rate and stuttering. They have observed in a few cases that a high basal-metabolism rate is accompanied by stuttering. "Two months after W.B.'s operation for exophthalmic goiter (BMR, plus 35), his wife reports that the stuttering which appeared with the illness was no longer noticeable." Obviously, there is need for more data.

HABIT

Some authorities (Dunlap and McDowell) believe that stuttering is merely "a habit which can be broken." Children who stutter do so because of associating with others in the home who stutter or because they have never formed that rhythmic flow of speech characteristic of the normal person. The remedy is merely a process of breaking an undesirable habit and forming a desirable one in its stead. Dunlap suggests his "beta hypothesis" as the best means for this procedure.[49]

It is undeniable that children who stutter have a habit of doing so. The cause may be heredity, or the lack of cerebral dominance, or poor mental adjustment, or something else, but the result is a stuttering habit. However, to say that all stuttering is merely a bad habit without any underlying cause is to ignore the research in stuttering, which now indicates that there are various causes. The correction of stuttering is more than a process of breaking one habit and forming another. The first step is to remove the cause.

It is true that after the cause of stuttering has been removed, there often remains a residual stuttering habit. Perhaps this can best be broken by negative practice, or some other simple procedure. Dunlap advises that the stutterer study "his specific type of involuntary spasm, copy this as nearly as possible, and then stutter voluntarily." At any rate, it is now a speech problem per se and can be taken care of by speech drills.

McDowell[50] advises that the first step in correcting the speech of stutterers is the "recognition of the habit to be acquired by the person who

[48] Berry, M. F., and Eisenson, J., *The Defective in Speech*, F. S. Crofts & Co., New York, 1942.

[49] Dunlap, K., *Habits, Their Making and Unmaking*, Liveright Publishing Corp., New York, 1932.

[50] McDowell, E. D., Some Interpretations of Recent Researches in the Correction of Stuttering, *Symposium on Stuttering*, Madison, Wis., 1931.

must acquire it," then to "apply many exercises and activities for setting up connections." Unfortunately, this advice is worthless if the original cause of stuttering has not been taken care of. The stutterer's difficulty is not that he lacks good speech habits but that he cannot use them at critical times. When he talks to himself or to his dog, or when he whispers, his speech is perfect. He does not need new speech habits; he merely needs to be able to use his habits without being blocked by neuromuscular spasms.

It is obvious that modern research has not yet solved the problem of why children stutter or of how to cure them of it. But it has indicated rather definitely that they stutter for various reasons and can be improved by various procedures. Also, it has revealed enough of the causes and conditions of stuttering to cast doubt on the claims of the "specialist" who has developed a "revolutionary" technique for curing all stuttering (provided the patient pays a liberal fee).

Treatment of Stuttering

It is obvious from the preceding discussion of causes of stuttering that the treatment must depend on the diagnosis. A procedure that will help (it is doubtful if a "cure" is ever possible) a stutterer who has a bad habit will be of little value to another stutterer who lacks cerebral dominance. Nevertheless, there are some *don'ts* as well as some *do's* that should be followed until better corrective methods are available.

1. Do not:
    a. Call attention to the problem by "free advice." You really do not know what he should do.
    b. Show by facial expression or action that you disapprove of the stuttering.
    c. Praise him for his occasional periods of fluency. He knows well enough what good speaking is.
    d. Apologize to others in his presence for his poor speech.
2. Do:
    a. Observe the conditions under which he is fluent. Try to reproduce those conditions as often as possible. Stuttering is often outgrown if situations fostering it are not cultivated.
    b. Praise his efforts along other lines. He needs self-confidence.
    c. Attend carefully to *what* he is saying, not how he is saying it.
    d. Keep him in good physical condition.

SPEECH DISORDERS DUE TO DEFECTIVE HEARING

Hearing is just as necessary in learning to speak as seeing is in learning to write. In general, those who cannot hear cannot speak. There is nothing wrong with their speech mechanism. They are mute, or dumb, because they are deaf. It was believed, until in comparatively recent years, that people who are completely deaf cannot learn to talk at all. Then, it was discovered that by using the phonetic method deaf people can be taught to talk; and by lip reading they can learn to understand what is being said to them. Now, the most up-to-date institutions for the deaf teach phonetic speaking and lip reading, instead of the ancient sign language.

There are degrees of hearing loss, from normal hearing to complete deafness. Those who can hear well enough to learn vocal speech in the ordinary course of events and yet have a hearing handicap are classed as *hard-of-hearing*. Those who do not hear well enough to develop vocal speech, unless they are given special phonetic training, are classed as *deaf*. The normal person hears frequencies (pitch) between 20 and 20,000 and intensities from the hearing threshold up to the feeling threshold, *i.e.*, when the sound is so loud that it is felt by other body tissues. (Of course, when sound becomes so loud that it can be felt, the deaf person is at no disadvantage.) However, speech usually occurs within a much narrower range of frequencies (100 to 8,000). Tests to determine the percentage of hearing loss generally include the range from 64 to 8,192 vibrations. As they are generally used in speech, phonetic sounds vary in pitch from those of low frequencies (such as b, d, m, n, ng, j) to those of the highest frequencies (such as th, s, z, f, ch).

THE HARD-OF-HEARING

It is estimated by Phillips and Rowell[51] that there are 3 million school children in the United States who have a hearing loss great enough to handicap them in schoolwork, but not great enough to prevent them from learning vocal speech. After a survey of the New York City schools, Caplin[52] estimates that at least 4.5 per cent of the school children in that city need otological diagnosis and 3.5 per cent need special instruction in lip reading. (He found that training in lip reading reduced the percentage of school retardation of a group of 4,566 hard-of-hearing children from 41.9 before lip reading to 5.6 after lip reading.)

The hard-of-hearing child misses many things in schoolwork because of his handicap. Sometimes this makes him appear mentally dull. However, studies show that, excluding the effects of his sensory handicap, the hard-of-hearing child is normal in intelligence. Pintner and Lev[53] compared a group of normal children with a group of hard-of-hearing children and another group of extremely hard-of-hearing children on a

[51] Phillips, W. C., and Rowell, H. G., *Your Hearing, How to Preserve and Aid It,* Appleton-Century-Crofts, Inc., New York, 1932.
[52] Caplin, D., A Special Report of Retardation of Children with Impaired Hearing in the New York City Schools, *Amer. Ann. Deaf.,* 1937, 82, 234–243.
[53] Pintner, R., and Lev, J., The Intelligence of the Hard of Hearing School Child, *J. Genet. Psychol.,* 1939, 55, 31–48.

verbal intelligence test. As was to be expected the hard-of-hearing groups showed the effects of their handicap. Then, they compared normals with hard-of-hearing and extremely hard-of-hearing children on a nonlanguage intelligence test. Here the handicapped children showed no significant inferiority. These results are shown in Table 7–13. Some hard-

Table 7–13. Comparison of Normal with Hard-of-Hearing Children on Mental Ability Tests

Group	*N*	Mean I.Q.	Sigma	Mean diff.	Sigma diff.	Mean diff. / Sigma diff.
Verbal test:						
Normals...............	1,286	99.75	24.55			
Hard-of-hearing........	1,186	94.67	24.12	5.08	.98	5.2
Extremely hard-of-hearing...............	462	92.47	24.57	7.88	1.33	5.5
Nonverbal test:						
Normals...............	372	102.16	21.5			
Hard-of-hearing........	315	99.29	20.5	2.86	1.6	1.8
Extremely hard-of-hearing...............	140	99.26	21	2.89	2.09	1.4

of-hearing children were tested on both the language and the nonlanguage tests. They showed a higher I.Q. on the latter test than on the former.

The effect of hearing loss is especially obvious when the educational achievement of hard-of-hearing children is studied. Pintner[54] and others have studied the effects of hearing loss on personality. In general, the effects are slight but obvious. The hard-of-hearing groups (those with 15 decibels loss and those with 30 decibels loss) are not quite so well adjusted as the normals, and the differences are statistically significant. This is likewise true of emotional stability. The greater the hearing loss, the less the degree of emotional stability. However, as indicated by the low correlations in Table 7–14, this negative relationship is not great. The traits of ascendance-submission and introversion-extroversion show no significant relation to hearing loss.

The handicap from partial loss of hearing can be largely overcome by two procedures—hearing aids and lip reading. Hearing aids are portable and can be worn inconspicuously. The type of device most appropriate depends on the nature of the hearing loss, *i.e.*, the part of the auditory anatomy that is deficient. Stationary hearing aids are sometimes furnished

[54] Pintner, R., An Adjustment Test with Normal and Hard of Hearing Children, *J. Genet. Psychol.*, 1940, 56, 367–381; Some Personality Traits of Hard of Hearing Children, *J. Genet. Psychol.*, 1942, 58, 143–151.

Table 7–14. Mean Scores on Personality Tests for Groups of Various Degrees of Hearing

Personality test	Normal hearing	Hard of hearing	Extremely hard of hearing	Correlation of hearing-loss and trait
General adjustment:				
Boys......................	79.5	77.4	75.4	
Girls......................	84	84.6	81.9	
Ascendance-submission:				
Boys......................	18.31	18.64	18.71	.05
Girls......................	16.37	16.65	17.45	.08
Introversion-extroversion:				
Boys......................	21.79	21.13	21.71	.004
Girls......................	20.82	20.54	19.36	−.08
Emotional stability:				
Boys......................	25.34	23.87	22.24	−.07
Girls......................	26.35	25.37	21.03	−.14

by the school. Of course, the function of all hearing aids is to amplify sound so that it can be heard. Lip reading is especially valuable as a supplement to impaired hearing. What the ears do not hear, the eyes can often see. When a sound is not quite audible, the slight additional cue of seeing it being articulated is all that is necessary for its perception. Lip reading is often limited by the fact that some sounds are made by the same action of the articulating organs as some other sounds. For example, the sounds b and p, d and t, l and n, and g and k look alike to the lip reader. However, training develops unusual skill in perceiving speech just from watching its production.

THE DEAF

Because deaf children are unable to learn vocal speech, they get but little value out of attending the public schools. Consequently the state provides institutions for the education of deaf children. Except for the accumulating effects of being unable to hear, deaf children are no different from other children. They are mute, not because there is anything wrong with their speech mechanism, but because they are deaf and cannot imitate the sounds of other people. Their intelligence is no higher and no lower than the average, although they are handicapped on verbal tests. They are retarded educationally, as would be expected.

Two things about the training of deaf children in modern institutions for this purpose seem almost miraculous—they are taught to speak, and they are taught to understand the speech of others. Deaf children can be taught to speak by the phonetic method. This consists of patiently learning to make each elementary sound separately and then in word combinations. Both sight and feeling are used to enable the children to learn the slight differences between some of the sounds. They watch the teacher to see how to place the articulating organs, and then they feel her throat with their fingers to get the feel of the proper vocal action. It is a slow tedious process that requires endless patience.

To learn how to understand the speech of others, deaf children are taught lip reading. This does not mean, however, that they observe only the lips. The rest of the face and the hands indicate the emotional content of speech. The articulating organs indicate only the ideational content of speech. The greatest difficulty of lip reading is to distinguish between those words that *look* alike, such as, nine and dine, new and dew, labor and neighbor, etc. Another difficulty in lip reading is the great differences between people in articulating speech. Some speak with a masklike facial expression and a minimum of lip and jaw movement. Even hearing people cannot understand them easily. But with proper training, the deaf person can learn to understand speech with amazing accuracy.

SUMMARY

One of the most neglected fields of human affliction is that of speech disorders. Charlatans flourish as in no other field. Well-trained speech correctionists are too few to take care of the needs of more than a small fraction of those who need help. Even the public schools all but ignore this major human handicap.

Fortunately research is beginning to accumulate, and scientific diagnosis and therapy are now possible. A sampling of such research was reviewed in this chapter to indicate that many data already exist. Except for the disorders of speech rhythm, almost every kind of speech defect can now be properly diagnosed and improved by treatment. Even stuttering is well enough understood to be diagnosed with a degree of accuracy and treated with some success.

However, speech correction is a field where specialization and scientific training are essential. Not only must the correctionist understand speech but he must be a psychologist as well. Courses in public speaking and voice improvement are of but little value in the scientific treatment of speech disorders. Speech correction is a field of applied psychology and has but little in common with the descendants of elocution.

RECOMMENDED SUPPLEMENTARY READING

Bender, J. F., and Kleinfeld, V.: *Principles and Practice of Speech Correction,* G. P. Putnam's Sons, New York, 1938.

deLaguna, Grace: *Speech, Its Function and Development,* Yale University Press, New Haven, 1927.

Eisenson, J.: *The Psychology of Speech,* Appleton-Century-Crofts, Inc., New York, 1938.

Eisenson, J., and Berry, M.: *The Defective in Speech,* Appleton-Century-Crofts, Inc., New York, 1945.

Johnson, W.: *Speech Problems of Children,* Grune & Stratton, Inc., New York, 1950.

Pintner, R., Eisenson, J., and Stanton, M.: *The Psychology of the Physically Handicapped,* Appleton-Century-Crofts, Inc., New York, 1941.

Van Riper, C.: *Speech Correction, Principles and Methods,* Prentice-Hall, Inc., New York, 1947.

West, R., Kennedy, L., and Carr, A.: *The Rehabilitation of Speech,* Harper & Brothers, New York, 1947.

Chapter 8

MENTAL ILLNESS[1]

[1] This chapter was written by Dr. Paul A. Brown, Associate Professor of Psychology at the St. Lawrence University.

The description and understanding of behavior that is out of the ordinary are matters of absorbing interest to the student who is beginning the study of psychology. This interest becomes even more intense when it is realized that the symptoms of abnormal behavior are simply symptoms of normal behavior carried to an exaggerated degree and are best understood in terms of the same causal relationships that underlie the activities of the average man. Actually, the major value of the study of abnormal psychology consists in the insight the student acquires into his own behavior. Some of this has been presented in Chap. 6. It is the purpose of this chapter to describe the symptoms of mental illness, the major psychoses, and some of the recent advances in the treatment of such conditions.

HISTORICAL CONCEPTS OF MENTAL DISEASE

It is quite probable that human beings have always been susceptible to mental illness. Even in very early written records we find mention of its existence. The Ebers Papyrus (1550 B.C.) gives evidence that the deterioration of old age, alcoholic reactions, and melancholia were recognized in ancient Egyptian medicine.[2] In the Bible we find frequent references to conditions we would today term as insane. One of the earliest is in Deuteronomy 28:28, "The Lord shall smite thee with madness, and blindness, and astonishment of heart." Similar references are occasionally found in the early writings of the Hindus and the Persians. The ancient Chinese described diseases as being due to the influence of evil supernatural factors. There can be little doubt that all the conditions recognized today as psychotic have always existed. The lack of adequate diagnostic techniques kept many of them from being recognized during the early days of civilization.

In their efforts to understand unusual and often spectacular behavior disorders, men, in those ancient days, resorted to superstition. A diffused demonology was presupposed, and evil spirits were believed to inhabit

[2] Lewis, N. D. C., *A Short History of Psychiatric Achievement,* p. 26, W. W. Norton & Company, New York, 1941.

the bodies of afflicted persons. Treatment consisted in driving out such malevolent influences by the techniques of exorcism and torture, and it was a matter of religion rather than medicine. As time went on, this concept crystallized into one of an archdemon, Satan, who struggled with the individual for the possession of his soul. The unfortunate person was considered as in league with, or possessed by, Satan. Treatment was in the hands of priests and inquisitors. Witch scares were common and persisted into more modern centuries. The treatment was to purify the body by burning. Hollingworth[3] reports that in one European principality alone there were, within a few years time, the execution of over 6,000 witches!

With progress in medical knowledge, such a naïve approach became untenable, save in isolated areas. Instead, among the uninformed, mental illness was considered to be the result of a life of sin. The road to mental health was a life of piety. Such a belief, of course, is not widely held today, but it has resulted in an unfortunate carry-over. Many educated individuals who are objective in their approach to other matters still adopt a hush-hush attitude in discussing insanity as it affects their own circles. This is unfortunate, for many of the insanities are actually less vicious in their effect and more easily cured than many purely physical ailments.

Concomitant with the development of these popular approaches toward an understanding of insanity, there has always been a painfully slow, but encouraging, progress of medical science toward a more materialistic interpretation. Through the centuries, there have always been men with a gift for observation and description who, with great patience, have attempted to understand man in terms of his body. Even as early as the sixth century B.C., Alcmaeon is believed to have performed a human dissection.[4] In spite of frequent setbacks and the opposition of popular superstition, a growing accumulation of facts and a knowledge of diagnostic techniques gradually intruded into medical science, from which it infiltrated into popular sophistry. As education spread and people became more literate, the popular beliefs became more and more similar to those of the doctor, and the mysticisms and superstitions were gradually discarded. Today, it is recognized by all educated peoples that a man termed "insane" is a sick man and that his care and treatment are best when in the hands of a competent psychiatrist. People no longer resort to exorcism. They go to the hospital.

Modern Concepts of Mental Disease

Modern psychology attempts to understand abnormal behavior in non-mystical terms. However, so many factors are pertinent to the background

[3] Hollingworth, H. L., *Abnormal Psychology*, p. 25, The Ronald Press Company, New York, 1930.

[4] Zilboorg, G., *A History of Medical Psychology*, p. 38, W. W. Norton & Company, New York, 1941.

of each condition that the importance of any one is often obscured. Two individuals may react in entirely different ways to the same physical situation or as a result of injuries to the same general brain area. This indicates that our approach must be of a clinical nature and that each case must be considered in terms of the whole life history of the person concerned.

There are, however, two major interpretations of abnormal conditions, both of which are helpful and both of which should be grasped by the beginning student. They are not to be thought of as antithetical viewpoints, but rather as complementary to each other. They are usually referred to with the descriptive labels of "functional" and "organic" psychoses.

Functional Psychoses. The psychologist is interested in the manner in which an individual reacts to an environmental situation. These reactions, directed in part by the person's past experiences, determine to a large degree what his future reactions to somewhat similar situations will be. We say that such behavior is learned behavior. The schoolboy may learn to give the wrong answer because of misunderstanding. Similarly, individuals may learn to give wrong reactions on such a broad scale that their behavior sets them apart from their fellow men. These people become objects of interest to students of abnormal psychology.

The writer has an acquaintance who believes all lawyers are either incompetent or dishonest. He will defend this belief with considerable vehemence. Such a false belief is termed a *delusion*. In this case, it is due to a series of unfortunate experiences with lawyers of both varieties. Some individuals maintain delusions so vigorously that it affects their entire behavior. They may believe that, because of their superior abilities, they are persecuted by a jealous society; or that they fail in the business world because of office politics; or that their enemies are poisoning their food or are directing death rays against them. Such individuals are termed *paranoiacs*. Examination fails to reveal either an organic lesion or a toxic condition. It is not impossible that they have suffered from life experiences of such a nature that they have learned to rationalize their failures with bizarre delusions. Or, it may be in many cases that some obscure physical condition is operative but has eluded all diagnostic techniques. Nevertheless, the fact remains that there are a variety of mental illnesses, similar to paranoia, in which *no organic or toxic condition has been demonstrated as a dominant factor. Such insanities are termed the functional psychoses.*

Organic Psychoses. The behavior of an individual may be altered because of a change in the physical condition of his body. A man may lose his ability to write because of fatigue in the muscles of his hand, or because he breaks his arm, or because of an injury to certain motor areas in the brain, or because of alcoholic intoxication or the delirium of fever, or simply because he is sleeping at that particular time. We cannot say he has learned an inability to write—though such a functional condition is not impossible—because here the source of trouble is patently a bodily condition.

Certain changes in the body sometimes bring about such vast changes in behavior that they fall within the subject matter of abnormal psychology. Long-continued overindulgence in alcoholic beverages (see also Chap. 10), the degenerative changes in the brain that may occur in old age, damage to the central nervous system by infectious diseases, changes in endocrine balance, particularly at certain critical periods, damage to the brain as the result of injury—all seriously affect the individual's behavior. These conditions—some of which will be considered later—differ in point of origin from the functional interpretation *only in that the body's condition is a dominant factor in determining the total behavior picture*. Without such a structural change, such abnormal behavior would probably not have made its appearance. Actually, the past experience of the patient may be a predisposing factor and must always be taken into consideration.

Insanities best understood in terms of demonstrable organic pathologies are referred to as the *organic psychoses*.

MENTAL DISEASE IN THIS COUNTRY

The beginning student is, naturally enough, interested in just how widespread mental illness is in the country in which he lives. He may have known, in his own circle of acquaintances, cases of the nature to be described in this chapter. He is interested in the expectancy of such conditions among the general population and in how their frequencies compare with the incidences of other types of ailments. It is necessary, however, that the student be reminded of certain difficulties in the way of presenting a clear picture of the field. Any discussion of such questions must be based on available statistics, and such do not always tell the whole story. In the first place, many mental conditions are never detected. The presence of a systematized delusion, a depression, or a withdrawing, shut-in personality may never be brought to the attention of a doctor, simply because the behavior may not run afoul of the law or become annoying to other individuals. Secondly, even in the best hospitals, it is frequently difficult to distinguish one kind of insanity from another, so that an analysis of statistics within the general picture may become somewhat confusing. In the third place, many cases are cared for at home or in private hospitals. Statistics for such cases are not available for public scrutiny. Finally, many analyses are based on first-admission figures. Such figures make no allowance either for changes in diagnosis or for cases that represent a recurrence of an old condition. Figures based on total admissions per unit time somewhat remedy the latter difficulty. These cautions must be borne in mind in interpreting the following section.

PREVALENCE

Landis and Page,[5] in a thorough analysis of the available data, indicate that in any one year approximately 0.5 per cent of the population of the United States is at some time part of the resident population in our mental hospitals. That this does not give the complete true picture is evident when it is realized that in such states as New York and Massachusetts, where mental-hospital facilities are more adequate, the figure is somewhat higher. Also, it must be remembered that the figures are based only upon those who are in mental institutions and do not include those in general hospitals, homes for the aged, or those who are cared for at home. As hospital facilities are increased, the total number of patients grows larger. As an example of this, the number of patients on the books of state hospitals increased between 1926 and 1938 from 272,716 to 424,-118.[6] Thus, it would seem that a greater prevalence exists than the published hospital figures indicate. It has been estimated for New York State that, in 1917, 1.5 per cent of the male population was mentally ill.[7]

Those who do enter the hospitals occupy approximately half the available beds. However, this does not mean that there are as many mental cases as nonmental cases. About half of the mentally ill remain in the hospital for more than a year. In the general hospitals, however, the average bed occupancy is only about 2 weeks. During 1935, only 2 per cent of hospital admissions were for cases of mental illness. The principal functional conditions (schizophrenia, manic-depressive, and paranoia) account for approximately one-third of these hospital cases. A breakdown of first admissions with respect to the kind of psychoses is presented in Table 8-1.

The above figures do not include those individuals who have been discharged or cured or those who may at some future time develop a psychosis. Thus, they fail to give the answer to questions concerning the statistical probability that an individual member of the population will become incapacitated by mental disease. Several analyses of available statistics bearing on this problem have been reported. After examining many of these reports, Landis and Page conclude that "while 1 out of every 20 born alive will eventually be admitted and spend some part of his life in a mental hospital, in all probability 1 out of 10 will be incapaci-

[5] Landis, C., and Page, J. D., *Modern Society and Mental Disease*, pp. 19–26, Rinehart & Company, Inc., New York, 1938.

[6] Maslow, A. H., and Mittelmann, B., *Principles of Abnormal Psychology*, p. 623, Harper & Brothers, New York, 1941.

[7] Landis and Page, *op. cit.*, p. 22.

Table 8–1. First Admissions to Hospitals for Mental Disease in the United States, by Psychosis, 1937*

	Number	Per cent
Total..	110,082	100.0
With psychosis...............................	93,236	84.7
General paresis..............................	7,517	6.8
With other forms of syphilis of the C.N.S.............	1,629	1.5
With epidemic encephalitis.........................	373	.3
With other infectious diseases......................	639	.6
Alcoholic....................................	5,639	5.1
Due to drugs and other exogeneous poisons............	653	.6
Traumatic..................................	586	.5
With cerebral arteriosclerosis......................	11,543	10.5
With other disturbances of circulation................	742	.7
With convulsive disorders.........................	1,952	1.8
Senile......................................	8,530	7.7
Involutional psychoses............................	3,677	3.3
Due to other metabolic, etc., diseases................	1,393	1.3
Due to new growth..............................	174	.2
With organic changes of nervous system..............	875	.8
Psychoneuroses................................	3,795	3.4
Manic-depressive...............................	12,626	11.5
Schizophrenia.................................	20,658	18.8
Paranoia and paranoid conditions....................	1,812	1.6
With psychopathic personality......................	1,252	1.1
With mental deficiency...........................	3,099	2.8
Other, undiagnosed, and unknown.	4,072	3.7
Without psychosis..............................	16,846	15.3

* From Maslow, A. H., and Mittelmann, B., *Principles of Abnormal Psychology*, p. 624, Harper & Brothers, New York, 1941.

tated, though not sent to a mental hospital, by mental disease at some time during his life."[8] These figures are high, but they should not be applied indiscriminately by the unwary student. As we shall see later in the chapter, there are many factors that affect mental disease, and, to some extent, those afflicted represent a select group of the population.

SYMPTOMS OF MENTAL DISORDER

A man who is mentally sick is quite apt to reveal the fact, and the nature of his sickness, in his behavior. It is important, however, to realize that his behavior differs from normal behavior more in *degree* than in *kind*. All the signs of a sick individual are possessed by the healthy person, but to a lesser extent. Bearing this in mind, the beginning student should avoid stressing the significance of these symptoms in applying them to

[8] *Op. cit.*, p. 25.

himself. Abnormal behavior is merely exaggerated normal behavior. All of us possess at times all the symptoms that are to be described. They are, however, incidental to our personality integration. In the psychotic individual, the symptom frequently becomes a dominant factor in the control and regulation of his behavior.

A list of symptoms may be classified in various ways. The scheme used here roughly divides the characteristics of mental illness into four major groups. An individual may have a distorted awareness of the world about him. This may reveal itself in unusual interpretations of his *sensory* experiences. As a result, he may react in an unusual fashion, and his illness may be reflected in his *motor* responses. Or his abnormalities may be primarily *intellectual*. He may have false ideas, fits of forgetfulness, an inability to think clearly, or a rigidity of his thought processes. Finally, insanity may show itself through the *emotional* behavior. The patient may be dejected to the point of suicidal attempts or so excessively elated that he must be restrained. The symptoms will be discussed in terms of these four groups.

Sensory Disorders

Illusions. An illusion is a false perception, an incorrect interpretation of a stimulating situation. The student who fancies a dark shadowy mass in the corner to be an animal, only to discover it later to be a carelessly thrown overcoat, is experiencing an illusion. The mental patient in the hospital may interpret the creaking of a door or howling of wind as the shrieking of a voice carrying threats or insults to his person. He, too, is experiencing an illusion with somewhat more severe personal implication.

Hallucinations. Hallucinations are perceptions in the absence of an adequate stimulus. They may affect any of the senses. Even though no real external sounds are present, the patient may hear voices shrieking imprecations in his ear. The victim of a delirium may see strange animals moving about the room, may feel insects crawling over his skin, or may smell unusual odors—and interpret them as poison gases sent by his enemies to kill him! Many patients will describe electric "radio" vibrations they feel passing through their bodies. Normal individuals experience hallucinations when they dream.

Perceptual Insufficiency. The patient pays but little attention to the surrounding environment and fails to grasp adequately everything that occurs. He may not know what is said to him; he may not realize where he is or how he got there. He may be bewildered, showing poor orientation with respect to space and time. In cases of extreme degree he may be in a wild and undirected state of excitement or almost in a state of coma, and the condition is known, descriptively, as *clouding of consciousness*.

MOTOR DISTURBANCES

Overactivity. In this condition the patient is in a constant state of excitement, always "on the go." He cannot lie or sit, nor can he relax. He is restless, sleepless, engaged in continuous activity. He will not take time out for eating or sleeping; he may jump about, breaking furniture, discarding his clothes, shouting, and dancing. In a mild state, the individual may carry on his everyday activities, but with tenseness and great pressure. In severe states he must be restrained.

Retardation. Here, a condition opposite from the above prevails. The patient may be able to carry on his work, but only with great difficulty. His every action is delayed and slow. He drags his feet, his speech is sluggish, and he prefers inactivity. In extreme cases he is apparently unable to do anything and must be washed, fed, and cared for by attendants.

Stereotopy. This term refers to a tendency found in some patients to carry on mechanically the repetition of a certain act or of certain phrases or sentences. Just as a small child will repeat over and over some short combination of words or a bit of doggerel, so will these patients dwell endlessly on a theme that is meaningless to the listener or repeat continually some simple gesture. It is usually supposed that such stereotopy possesses some symbolic meaning to the patient.

Negativism. A patient exhibiting this symptom refuses to perform acts that are appropriate to the situation. In extreme cases the patient will do nothing at all. He will not talk or pay any attention to things done or said to him. Food can be placed in the mouth, but it will not be swallowed. In less extreme cases the negativism may be shown only in certain kinds of actions. For example, a patient may carry on all regular activities but refuse to talk (*mutism*).

Suggestibility. This symptom pertains to an abnormal tendency found in some patients to yield to suggestion. The patient may retain his body in even the most awkward of positions, once it is placed in that position by someone else (*waxy flexibility*), or he may repeat everything that is said to him (*echolalia*) or mimic the actions of those around him (*echopraxia*).

INTELLECTUAL DISTURBANCES

Amnesia. By amnesia is meant a total or partial loss of memory. This memory loss may be either for the events preceding a shock or disturbance or for the events immediately following. It may be localized to the extent that it refers only to certain incidents, times, or places; or it may be so complete that the patient has forgotten his name, where he is, or how he got there.

Retrospective Falsification. When events are remembered not as they really occurred but in a changed and distorted fashion, we say the individual has retrospectively falsified his account. This is not the same as conscious lying. The patient will defend his story stoutly and with full belief. Normally, this happens in all individuals, because none of us have perfect memories and we are influenced by motives of which we are not conscious. However, our accounts are not as obviously distorted as are those of a mental patient.

Associational Disturbances. Normally, our thought processes consist of a continuous succession of associations, whether they are controlled (as in solving a problem in calculus) or random (as in ordinary day-dreaming). As would be expected, we find peculiar distortions of this activity among mental patients. Some show a stereotopy, their conversations all revolving around some simple theme. Others are excessively and morbidly preoccupied with some more complicated idea (such as the thought that one is about to die). Such symptoms are termed "obsessions." At times obsessive associations are carried into action. The individual feels an almost irresistible urge to perform an act that is irrelevant to the situation. Such an urge is a "compulsion." Still others relate all their thinking to their own emotional conflict (or *complex*). Often, associations given verbally by patients are symbolic of deep-rooted, unconscious problems.

Dearth of Ideas. Some patients have considerable difficulty in forming associations or at least in giving expression to them. They may find it difficult to concentrate on a problem or to think of things to say. They reply to simple questions only after a long interval and often with the answer, "I don't know." They may even refuse to talk at all, staring dully at the doctor as if not comprehending him. These symptoms are highly characteristic of those psychoses in which a depression is a prominent feature.

Flight of Ideas. Some patients show an abnormal tendency to jump from one topic to another. There is an apparent lack of ability to keep to the subject under consideration. Any stimulus, whether relevant or not, is incorporated into the associational chain. The individual may talk on for hours and exhibit neither selective control nor normal inhibition in his rambling. This symptom is prominent in cases where a mild mania is prevalent.

Delusions. A delusion is a false belief. All normal individuals have some delusions as the result of misinformation, overgeneralization, or emotional or intellectual bias. In mental patients, delusions are often exaggerated to the point of absurdity. One will tell you he is the savior of the world; another, that he is the worst sinner that has ever lived. A patient may say that his food has been poisoned by his enemies —and go right on eating it! Another may say that his internal organs have rotted away, or that he has been dead for years and is just a phantom. When delusions are logically organized, with all facts co-ordinated into the scheme in a plausible fashion, we say they are *systematized*. When delusions are loosely organized, fragmentary, and rather weakly woven, we refer to them as *unsystematized*.

Disturbances of Judgment. Sometimes an individual may lose normal control over ordinary judgment. He will squander all his money in an unnecessary fashion, such as buying several cars when he already has one; or he may write large checks when he has no bank account. He may become excessively careless in his dress, his conversation, his ordinary activities. He may become uninhibited to the point of embarrassing his friends and family. He may lose the ability to foresee the consequences of an act. He has lost a sense of balance in his judgment.

Dementia. By this is meant a condition of intellectual deterioration, usually permanent and frequently progressive. The patient becomes less able, mentally. He experiences difficulty in concentrating his attention upon a problem, and is less flexible in his attack upon its solution. Interest in new experiences, and even in familiar situations, is dulled. It is hard for him to remember, the forgetfulness sometimes extending to his most intimate affairs, such as the place of his birth or the names of his relatives.

EMOTIONAL DISTURBANCES

Apathy. By apathy, we mean emotional indifference. The apathetic individual apparently just doesn't care. Regardless of how you stimulate him, it is almost impossible to bring forth the normal emotional reactions of anger, fear, or joy. He seemingly has divorced himself from the surrounding world and is out of emotional contact with the objective environment. For this reason, emotional apathy is usually considered a very serious condition.

Depression. The depressed patient presents an attitude of dejection, often accompanied by feelings of anxiety and hopelessness, even in the absence of situations that should normally call forth such attitudes. He may refuse to eat, may moan constantly and ask for the forgiveness of imaginary sins. Such patients must be constantly watched, for there is an ever-present threat of suicide.

Emotional Instability. Some patients have little or no control over their emotional reactions. At the slightest provocation they will exhibit violent anger leading to excess in behavior. Just as quickly, they will "snap back" to normal. They may become quickly enthusiastic about a project or cast down into sorrow at the least setback, swinging from high ambition to the depths of despair in a comparatively short time.

Fears. Morbid fears are frequently found in mental patients. They may be obsessed with the idea of committing suicide or of sudden death from heart failure. They may fear the designs of unspecified enemies;

or they may simply have an unlocalized anxiety that they cannot justify nor explain but which is, nevertheless, troublesome. Violent, panicky fears are often encountered among those suffering from the hallucinations of *delirium tremens* (see below). Fears are also not uncommon among depressed conditions.

THE MAJOR PSYCHOSES

Within the space limits of the present chapter it is impossible to give an extended discussion of the psychoses, nor is it possible to give illustrative case material. The student is urged to supplement his reading with the use of one of the standard texts in the field such as that of Dorcus and Shaffer.[9]

It must be kept in mind that no two cases with the same diagnosis present identical pictures. The symptoms in any one case may vary strikingly from time to time. Diagnosis, at its best, is a somewhat precarious task. Nevertheless, certain common denominators are found that justify classification within certain limits. It is with these common denominators that we will concern ourselves.

Organic Psychoses

Alcoholic Psychoses. The problem of alcoholism is of very great importance, whether the point of view adopted be that of the sociologist, economist, or psychiatrist. Over 5 per cent of first admissions to our mental hospitals (see Table 8–1) and between 10 and 15 per cent of total admissions each year are alcoholic psychoses. In addition, it has been estimated that over 750,000 persons in our country suffer from alcoholism.[10] We will describe the most common kinds of these unfortunate disorders. A more extended discussion of conditions due to alcoholic excess is given in Chap. 10.

Delirium tremens, as is suggested by the name, is characterized by a state of delirium accompanied by generalized tremors, principally in the facial muscles, fingers, and tongue. It occurs in the course of chronic alcoholism (see below), usually after a period of heavy drinking with little food. The patient is sleepless and restless, is disoriented in both time and space, and experiences almost constant hallucinations. The emotional component of the condition is almost uniformly an intense and irrational fear. Suicidal or homicidal attempts may be present. The delirium usually lasts 3 to 6 days, the patient sinking into a heavy sleep from which he awakens in a lucid state, though with an amnesia for the period of delirium. More than 85 per cent of the cases recover

[9] Dorcus, R. M., and Shaffer, G. W., *Textbook of Abnormal Psychology,* 3d ed., The Williams & Wilkins Company, Baltimore, 1944.

[10] Coleman, J. C., *Abnormal Psychology and Modern Life,* p. 441, Scott, Foresman & Company, Chicago, 1950.

fully.[11] The most common immediate cause of death for the remainder is a complicating pneumonia.

Chronic alcoholism is a term referring to the condition of an individual who drinks habitually and heavily. Such a condition is not to be confused with that of periodic drunken sprees separated by relatively long periods of sobriety (*dipsomania*). The individual characteristically suffers from loss of memory, some degree of dearth of ideas, an inability to concentrate, with poor judgment and unclear thinking. Delusions sometimes develop, and these are apt to be of self-accusation and unworthiness. Physically, he exhibits mild tremors and is apt to have circulatory and gastrointestinal disorders. The best treatment for chronic alcoholics seems to be complete abstinence (see Chap. 10).

Korsakow's psychosis develops most frequently in late middle age and is found more frequently among women than men. The essential features are amnesia for recent events with a tendency to confuse these with remote events; disorientation in space and time; retrospective falsification; fair memory for events preceding the illness; and absence of cloudy consciousness, the patient being lucid and understanding. The patient may develop an insight into his condition and complain of his poor memory. He may spend several months or longer in the hospital, and chances of recovery are poor.

Psychoses Associated with Syphilis. *General paralysis of the insane,* frequently called *paresis* and *dementia paralytica,* accounts for the largest proportion of the syphilitic mental conditions, which comprise approximately 10 per cent of our hospitalized mental patients (Table 8–1). Of the approximately 4 individuals per 1,000 population in the United States who contract syphilis, about 5 per cent, or 2 per 10,000, develop the condition. It occurs among men more commonly than women in a ratio of nearly 4 to 1, and the majority of patients are between the ages of thirty and sixty years. It is found nearly twice as frequently among Negroes as Whites, and nearly 4 times as often in urban as in rural populations.[12]

Beginning 10 to 20 years after the first infection, the disease develops slowly, usually manifesting three general stages. In the first stage, the mental symptoms include poor memory, impairment of judgment, and a reversal of mood and character. Neatness is replaced with slovenliness, efficiency with carelessness, caution with recklessness. There is frequently overindulgence in alcohol and sex activity. The individual may feel in good health and refuse to see a doctor, though medical examination would detect neural involvement through reflex disturbances. If

---

[11] Rosanoff, A. J., *Manual of Psychiatry,* p. 387, John Wiley & Sons, Inc., New York, 1938.

[12] *Ibid.,* pp. 339–343.

left untreated, the second phase gradually develops and the symptoms are now quite marked. The voice is thick and words are slurred. There is frequently difficulty in controlling the muscles used in walking, and the patient walks with a trembling gait. There is much mental confusion, disorientation, and frequent unsystematized delusions. These latter may be expansive, and the patient may talk glibly of his great wealth or power; or they may be melancholy or depressed in nature. If the disorder progresses into the third stage, the patient is helpless and bedridden. He becomes completely disoriented, suffers from tremors and convulsions, the condition becoming progressively more severe, with death as the terminal point.

Cerebrospinal syphilis develops rather soon after the initial syphilitic infection (6 months to 5 years). The onset is rapid, only a few weeks being required for full development of the symptoms. The patient suffers from severe headache, a feeling of dizziness, will vomit, is unable to sleep, and yet may present a somewhat lethargic picture to the examiner. Normal reflexes are disturbed; the Argyll-Robertson sign is usually absent, *i.e.*, pupillary reaction is present to far and near accommodation but is absent to light. Any of the cranial nerves may be involved. Diagnosis of the condition is made by means of both clinical and laboratory tests.

Tabes dorsalis with psychosis occurs in some cases of syphilitic infection, where the posterior roots of the spinal column are involved preventing proprioceptive impulses from the muscles from reaching the brain. The patient becomes unable to control adequately such motor activities as walking, talking, and writing. Tremors and disturbances in these activities are pronounced. The individual can stand with his eyes open but will fall if they are closed; walks, aided by a cane, with a trembling gait; slurs his words, and the like. Double vision and dimness of vision frequently occur. When definitely psychotic, the patient is agitated, may suffer from delusions of a persecutory nature and from fear-producing hallucinatory experiences.

Senile Psychoses. The most frequently occurring psychosis associated with old age is *senile dementia*, one of the commonest of psychiatric conditions. Its incidence in the general population of all ages for the year ending June 30, 1935, was 6.9 per 100,000. For the year 1920, in New York State, its incidence for only that portion of the population over sixty years of age was 80 per 100,000; for persons aged seventy years or more, the rate was 180.2. It occurs more frequently among women than men in a ratio of about 10 to 6.[13] While associated with old age, the exact cause of the condition is unknown.

The chief symptom is an impairment of memory with pronounced

[13] *Ibid.*, pp. 513–514.

tendencies to retrospective falsification and pseudoreminiscence. Memory failure is most marked for recent events. As the condition progresses, there is a pronounced narrowing of interests, a general apathy, and, frequently, irritability and depression. Delusions of a persecutory nature are also quite apt to appear. The patient may become self-centered and demanding in the satisfaction of his comfort. As little is known of the prevention of the condition, the treatment consists in institutional or home care. The duration is usually less than 5 years and is invariably terminated in death.

Presbyophrenia is a type of senile dementia somewhat resembling, in its clinical picture, Korsakow's psychosis. The patient is unable to remember recent events and lacks insight into his present condition. He appears to be mentally more alert than the simple senile patient. There is considerable confabulation and contradiction in his conversation. Frequently he is restless and unable to continue long in simple tasks. The prognosis and treatment are about the same as for cases of senile dementia.

Cerebral arteriosclerosis, while it can occur at earlier ages, is found most frequently among people in late middle age or older. For the year ending June 30, 1935, of 2,281 cases in the New York state hospitals, 1,342 were sixty-five years or over in age, 688 were between ages fifty-five and sixty-four, 228 were between ages forty-five and fifty-four, and the remaining 23 were all over thirty-five years old.[14] It is reported more frequently among men than women. It is not always accompanied by a psychosis. High blood pressure coupled with the hardening of the arteries of the brain may result in the bursting of cerebral blood vessels. As a result of this stroke, the individual may suffer from the loss of ability to concentrate, yet retain an insight into this decreased efficiency. Frequently there are found depressions, confused states, clouding of the consciousness, irritability, and emotional instability.

FUNCTIONAL PSYCHOSES

Schizophrenic Disorders. These conditions represent the most commonly encountered group of all the major psychoses. Malzberg presents data showing that in New York State mental hospitals, during the years 1929 to 1931, schizophrenia accounted for 26.3 per cent of total first admissions, and Dayton's data for first admissions in Massachusetts between 1917 and 1933 for the same condition are 19.46 per cent.[15] The term schizophrenia literally means "split mind." It refers to a dis-

[14] *Ibid.,* p. 509.
[15] Cameron, Norman. The Functional Psychoses, in J. McV. Hunt (Ed.), *Personality and the Behavior Disorders,* Vol. II, p. 872, The Ronald Press Company, New York, 1944.

integration of the individual's personality structure that is so characteristic of the disease. Since it was once believed that young people were particularly prone to develop this insanity, it is sometimes called *dementia praecox,* a "deterioration of youth." Actually, cases can be found at all ages, the greatest number occurring between ages twenty and thirty.

No other psychosis presents so baffling and varied an array of symptoms, nor is any other psychosis so little understood. All the symptoms do not appear in any one patient, and an individual clinical picture may change strikingly in a very short time. There are, though, certain basic common denominators running through the behavior of these patients. The outstanding characteristic is an emotional apathy or indifference, coupled, frequently, with a disharmony between intellectual and emotional reactions. Normal anger- or fear-producing situations fail to bring forth the appropriate response. There is also evidence of withdrawing behavior, as if the patient retreats from the external world and has trouble distinguishing fact from fancy. The result of such social retreat is to place a psychological barrier between the patient and other people. He becomes socially inaccessible. Attainment of rapport on the part of the physician is quite difficult and at times impossible. There is increasing personality deterioration, the patient becoming careless in behavior and appearance. Mental deterioration may also occur. Ideas of reference and a self-centeredness of attitude are often found.

For purposes of classification, it has been found convenient to describe four special types of schizophrenia. This does not mean that we have to contend with separate and distinct conditions. It only means that at the time of diagnosis a particular group of symptoms predominated. These types have the common characteristics of schizophrenia plus other particular symptoms. All schizophrenic cases cannot be classified into any one definite type. Many are mixed cases possessing symptoms of more than one type.

Simple schizophrenia is one of these types. The outstanding characteristics are emotional apathy, indifference, a loss of ambition, and general listlessness with some intellectual deterioration. The individual may become asocial and seems to be increasingly preoccupied with his own daydreams or fantasies. The onset is so gradual it is frequently not noticed. Many cases are never hospitalized but manage to take care of themselves. It is quite possible that cases of this type are found among tramps, prostitutes, and the unemployed. It can occur at any age but is found most frequently among young adults.

Hebephrenic schizophrenia is the classification given to a rather large and varied group. The condition has a more sudden onset than the simple type, and much greater disintegration is shown. The behavior is usually pointless and incongruous with respect to the situation. There is apt to be inappropriate smirking and laughter. Many bizarre notions are held by the patient, and we frequently find unsystematized delusions. There may be occasional hallucinations. Hebephrenic literally means "child mind," but the behavior is really not so childish as it is irrelevant and inappropriate.

Catatonic schizophrenia refers to those cases where the dominant symptoms involve disturbances of motor behavior. The chief characteristic is motor stereotopy, but the behavior may range from violent excitement to deep stupor. Between these ranges we may find less dramatic mannerisms of posturing, gesturing, repetitive stereotyped grimacing, and the like. It is believed that these mannerisms may have a symbolic meaning, best understood in terms of some inner emotional conflict. In the case of stupor, the patient is completely negativistic and must be cared for as if an infant, although he is frequently aware of happenings in his vicinity. When in a state of catatonic excitement, the patient's behavior is unpredictable. For that reason, such cases are potentially dangerous and require great care in handling.

When delusions of either the persecutory or grandiose type are predominant symptoms, the case is diagnosed as *paranoid schizophrenia.* Other symptoms (particularly of the hebephrenic variety) are also present but are subordinate to the delusional picture. The delusions are not as well systematized or as firmly defended as those of true *paranoia* (see below). Additional symptoms include apathy, disintegration, and withdrawing behavior. This form of schizophrenia responds to treatment even less readily than the other forms.

Affective Disorders. Under this heading we group those functional conditions characterized chiefly by abnormal manifestations of mood and emotion. Principally, these refer to the elated and depressed conditions where, most frequently, no deterioration of intelligence has occurred. There are two important psychoses found in this group: *manic-depressive* disorders and *involutional melancholia.* In the report of Malzberg referred to above,[16] the manic-depressive group made up 13.4 per cent of the first admissions to New York State mental hospitals during years 1929 to 1931, and involutional melancholia accounted for 2.8 per cent. Dayton's figures for Massachusetts (1917 to 1933) give 9.66 per cent manic-depressives and 2.17 per cent involutional disorders.

Extremes of emotion are the chief characteristics of the manic-depressive psychosis. An individual who has previously exhibited quite normal behavior may develop, either gradually or quite suddenly, a state of great elation and pronounced motor overactivity and suggesti-

[16] *Ibid.*

bility, exhibit flight of ideas in conversation, and present a picture of markedly happy contact with the environment. Emotional instability is present, as irritation appears at any thwarting or restraint. The patient does not want to take time for eating, sleeping, or elimination and is constantly "on the go" and in pronounced good humor. In extreme cases (*acute mania*) these symptoms are all exaggerated, and delusions of grandeur or achievement may appear. There may be transitory hallucinations. Behavior is recognized, even by the uninformed, as definitely pathological. Occasionally the behavior may develop to the point of wild delirium (*hyperacute mania*). Here there are complete disorientation, frequent hallucinations, and continual activity that throws a strain on the cardiorespiratory system that may have fatal consequences.

The reverse of all this may occur. The attack may result in a state of depression, considerable motor retardation, a dearth of ideas, and a general picture of unhappy dejection. The patient is blue without understanding why. He may rationalize his sadness with delusions of sin or unworthiness. The depression may become more severe (*acute melancholia*) with an exaggeration of the above symptoms. The patient apparently gives up and will sit motionless for hours, sometimes mumbling to himself phrases indicative of self-accusation. In some cases the patient will fail completely in establishing environmental rapport. He will lie without moving, must be tube-fed and cared for, usually suffering physical impairment. This state is known as *depressive stupor*.

Manic-depressive psychosis occurs most frequently in middle life, and either, or both, of the above states may be present. The patient recovers, usually in less than a year, but there is always danger of recurrence. A manic state may be followed by a period of normal behavior or may change overnight to a depression. Attacks are frequently brought on by a precipitating cause. They may be separated by days or years, or there may never be another attack. Any combination in sequence of the states of normality, mania, and depression may be found with any time interval separating them. The prognosis of recovery from any single attack is good, but more than half the patients will have another attack.

Involutional melancholia is most apt to occur at that time of life when the sex glands cease to function. Although it may occur in either sex, it is found more frequently among women and at an earlier age than in men. The patient becomes quite depressed and anxious. Life apparently has no future, and there is a dissatisfaction with the past. Apprehensiveness and irritability are commonly present. The patient experiences feelings of unreality and may develop delusions that he doesn't exist. Ideas of sinfulness and unworthiness are also common. Motor and intellectual retardation are often found, but in some cases there is considerable agitation with restless fearfulness. Recovery from involutional melancholia is normally to be expected.

Paranoid Psychosis. A not very common, but interesting, psychosis, in which the only symptom of any importance is a well-systematized delusion, dominating the entire attitude of the patient and subordinating all his activities, is the condition known as *paranoia*. Since the only abnormal phase of behavior is the rigid and vigorously defended delusion, many paranoics probably are not hospitalized. It is only when, in conformity with their false belief, they infringe on the rights of others or run afoul of the law that they are noticed. Hence, the reported hospital incidence of between 1 and 2 per cent[17] is probably not representative of the true figure, which is appreciably larger.

The patient who develops paranoia is apt to have had, most of his life, a somewhat rigid type of personality. He is apt to have been the sort of person who cannot easily accept correction or make concessions; who has been oversensitive and unduly concerned with what others are thinking of him; who has had a tendency to brood and has been inclined to self-isolation. He has usually been suspicious of the goals and motives of others, with a tendency to ascribe special meanings with relation to himself to the indifferent activities of acquaintances. From such a background the delusional system develops slowly but with increasing strength. When it has become recognizably pathological, it is usually so firmly systematized and so logically organized that little can be done toward the patient's re-education. The delusion may be persecutory or of the compensatory variety of grandeur. It may also take other forms, such as religious, amorous, jealous, inventive, litigious, or reformatory paranoia. When well developed, paranoia has a very poor prognosis.

FACTORS AFFECTING MENTAL DISEASE

AGE

One of the most important facts that we can know about a patient is his age; and about a group of patients, the age distribution of the group. The care and treatment of the patient and his chances of recovery will very largely depend upon his age. Knowing the age distribution of the group enables us to predict with considerable accuracy the sex distribution, the number in each group of diseases, the years of expected life, and other pertinent problems with respect to the group.

Although the actual number of first admissions of patients under

[17] *Ibid.*

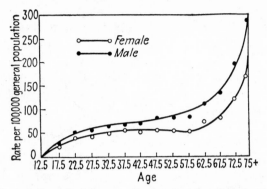

FIG. 8–1. Number of first admissions to state mental hospitals in the United States during 1933, by age and sex, expressed as rates per 100,000 of the corresponding general population as of 1933. (*From Landis, C., and Page, J. M., Modern Society and Mental Disease, p. 28, Rinehart & Company, Inc., New York, 1938.*)

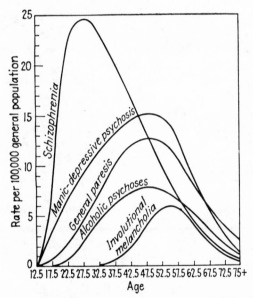

FIG. 8–2. Number of first admissions to state mental hospitals in the United States during 1933, by age and psychosis, expressed as rates per 100,000 of the corresponding general population of 1933. (*From Landis C., and Page, J. M., Modern Society and Mental Disease, p. 28, Rinehart & Company, Inc., New York, 1938.*)

fifty years of age is greater than of those aged over fifty, it must be remembered that the proportion of the total population under fifty is also greater. When first admissions are expressed in rates per 100,000 of the general population *of the same age*, it is found that the incidence of mental disease increases with age. This is not a constant relationship.

There is a sharp increase in incidence between ages fifteen and thirty and another beyond age sixty. During the years forty-five to sixty the rate does not vary greatly. At all ages, the rate is consistently higher for males than for females.[18] These facts are presented in Fig. 8–1. Evidence has also been presented that the median age at first admission has increased markedly for all psychoses with the exception of schizophrenia and involutional melancholia.[19] The reasons for this are obscure, and no explanation is offered.

In studying the factor of age with respect to specific psychoses, we find, in a broad way, that each psychosis has its own age span.[20] Mean ages for the various conditions may differ as much as several years. The distributions for most conditions are bell-shaped and are presented in Fig. 8–2. Curves for the senile conditions are not presented, since the tendency for census and hospital reports to combine all patients older than seventy years in one group would result in the highest rates being found at the upper age level.

URBAN AND RURAL ENVIRONMENTS

A commonly held belief is that the complexity of life in a large city places increasing strain on a human being's adjustive capacity and leads to a greater frequency of mental breakdown. It will be profitable to consider the facts bearing on this belief. The United States census arbitrarily classifies communities with less than 2,500 inhabitants as rural; all others are urban. Comparing these two groups, very real differences do appear. The average rural rate of first admissions per 100,000 population in 1933 was 44.6 for women, 69.5 for men, a combined rate of 58.0. These are to be compared with urban rates of 94.1 for women, 134.8 for men, a combined rate of 113.5.[21] But it must be remembered that large centers of population have more hospitals and better medical facilities. Cases that might go undetected or be cared for at home in a small town are more apt to be hospitalized in the city. Thus, to really examine the problem, it is necessary to compare the incidences in cities of different sizes. When this is done, it is found that the most marked difference is found between communities of less than 2,500 population and those between 2,500 and 10,000. This is illustrated in the data[22] below showing the incidence rates per 100,000 population. Thus, it is probable that the increased urban incidence is

[18] Landis and Page, *op. cit.,* pp. 27–31.

[19] Landis, Carney, and Farwell, J. E., A Trend Analysis of Age at First-admissions, Age at Death, and Years of Residence for State Mental Hospitals: 1913–1941, *J. Abnorm. Soc. Psychol.,* 1944, **39,** 3–23.

[20] Landis and Page, *op. cit.,* pp. 36–38.

[21] *Ibid.,* p. 46.

[22] *Ibid.,* pp. 50, 164.

at least partly explained in terms of improved and more easily obtainable medical facilities.

Population	Incidence Rate
2,500 or less	61.6
2,500 to 10,000	87.6
10,000 to 25,000	87.7
25,000 to 100,000	98.2
100,000 to 200,000	106.6
New York City	105.4
Total urban	102.7

HEREDITY

A popular belief of "the man in the street" is that insanity is inherited. The statement, of course, is too indefinite to have any real meaning. There are many different kinds of insanity and each specific psychosis has its own complex of etiological factors. The role of heredity may not carry the same import in one disease that it does in another. Also, it must be remembered that to say heredity is a factor does not mean that the children of a patient will necessarily acquire the disease. It simply means that, statistically, there is a greater probability that the psychosis will appear among close relatives than in the general population. Also, in considering the problem, we must bear in mind that much of the evidence is not very reliable. We cannot be sure of the accuracy of diagnosis, for in the past many of these conditions were simply grouped together under one heading. Also, available figures do not include those relatives who were unhospitalized and undetected, and yet were mentally ill.

The actual significance of the factor of heredity is by no means as yet settled. Among the psychoses considered in this chapter, inheritance seems to play an important role in the schizophrenic disorders and in manic-depressive conditions. It has been reported[23] that the children and relatives of patients with these diseases have a greater expectancy of themselves becoming patients than is found in the general population. When one parent is schizophrenic, the expectancy rate for children is around 16 per cent; when both parents have the disease, the rate is close to 68 per cent. Siblings of the patient have an expectancy rate of from 8 per cent to 24 per cent. These figures should be contrasted with the fact that less than 1 per cent of the general population can be expected to develop schizophrenia. Children of manic-depressive patients have a mental-illness expectancy rate of from 10 per cent to 24 per cent. If neither of the parents has had the disease, siblings have an expectancy rate of 7.4 per cent; but if one of the parents has been a

[23] *Ibid.*, pp. 81–87.

mental patient, the figure is close to 24 per cent. These data all clearly indicate that the factor of heredity is important in any consideration of mental illness.[24]

MARITAL STATUS

Another popular belief is that mental disease is in some way related to marriage. As Fig. 8–3 shows, this popular belief is borne out by the reported facts.[25] The incidence of first admissions per 100,000 general population during 1933, when corrected for age differences between the

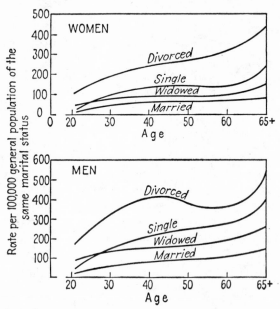

FIG. 8–3. Number of first admissions to state mental hospitals in the United States during 1933, by marital status, expressed as rate per 100,000 of the general population.

groups, was 73 for married men, 161 for widowers, 221 for bachelors, and 362 for divorcees. The corresponding figures for women were 59, 92, 130, and 263. Among the women, there were two exceptions to this general trend. Female alcoholic patients and female paretics (general paralysis) had a slightly smaller group of single members than the general population. Probably such women are less inhibited and have greater opportunities for marriage. In all the organic conditions there

[24] Heredity is also important in the consideration of mental deficiency with psychosis and epilepsy. However, this group of patients make up only about 5 per cent of the first admissions.

[25] Landis and Page, *op. cit.*

was a larger percentage of widowed patients than is found in the general population. The high rate of divorced individuals would be expected, as such people do not tend to have a happy married life.

AMERICAN POPULATION GROUPS

All available figures indicate a greater prevalence of mental disease among immigrant groups than among native-born citizens of the United States, but such figures are usually presented in a manner uncorrected for such factors as age, sex distribution, economic status, and urbanization. As Landis and Page point out,[26] an earlier study had shown mental disease occurred more frequently among native Americans who had migrated from the east to California than among native-born Californians. It would appear that people who make up a migratory group have a larger than average proportion of potential psychotics. Uncorrected figures indicate two to three times as great an incidence among immigrants as among native citizens. When the admission rate is based, however, upon the general population over fifteen years in age (immigrant groups contain few children), the foreign-born rate is only 20 per cent higher than that of natives. When further correction is made for urbanization (most immigrants live in cities), the rate becomes only 8 per cent higher. Although there are many factors complicating the total picture, it is quite possible that, with the application of more thorough statistical analysis, there will be found very little, if any, difference between the two groups.

It is widely believed, even among the medical profession, that among the Jewish people an unduly large amount of mental illness occurs. Early studies that bore this out and that have been much quoted failed to correct for the factor of urbanization.[27] For example, in Germany, in 1926, the incidence of mental disease among the Jewish population was one-third higher than among either Catholics or Protestants. When however, the figures are limited to the city of Berlin, the rate per 10,000 for Jews was actually lower than that of either of the two other groups (26 as contrasted with 29 and 28 per 10,000). Similar findings have been presented concerning Jews and non-Jews in New York City. The evidence also indicates that with respect to the old-age insanities, paresis, and the alcoholic psychoses, the Jewish group has an appreciably lower rate.

Clear-cut statistical differences seem to exist between Negroes and Whites. A representative example of these differences is presented in Table 8–2. That urbanization is not a factor is evident from the fact that these differences are not reduced when the state populations out-

[26] *Ibid.,* pp. 92–97.
[27] *Ibid.,* pp. 97–100.

Table 8–2. Average Annual Number of Negro and White First Admissions to All Institutions for Mental Disease in New York State, 1929–1931, Expressed as Standardized Rates per 100,000 of the Corresponding General Population as of 1930*

Diagnosis	Rates per 100,000 general population		
	White	Negro	Negro-White ratio
Manic-depressive........................	13.3	20.0	1.5
Senile dementia..........................	27.6	52.1	1.9
Dementia praecox........................	25.7	51.1	2.0
Cerebral arteriosclerosis..................	41.1	119.6	2.9
Alcoholic psychoses......................	6.5	22.2	3.4
General paresis..........................	9.3	37.9	4.1
Total................................	97.4	224.7	2.3

* Landis, C., and Page, J. M., Modern Society and Mental Disease, p. 101, Rinehart & Company, Inc., New York, 1938.

side of New York City are compared.[28] This, however, must not be taken to indicate an actual difference in susceptibility between the Negro and the White. The Negroes in New York City are migratory individuals, and we have already seen that migratory groups have more than their share of psychopathic material. The differences are, in fact, considerably reduced when we compare the incidence rate of first admissions between native New York Whites (45 per 100,000) and native New York Negroes (40 per 100,000). For immigrant whites the rate is 157, and for immigrant Negroes, 186. Also, it should be remembered that Negroes, living on a lower economic scale, may not achieve hospitalization as frequently as do whites. However, the differences that have been published are too large to be argued away, and further investigation of this problem is certainly needed.

The various geographical areas of the United States show marked differences in the incidence of hospitalized patients.[29] In New England, in 1935, for example, the rate per 10,000 for the population over fifteen years of age was 53 as compared with a rate of only 28 in the South Central states, a rate of 36 in the North Central states and a similar rate in the South Atlantic states. The rate in the Middle Atlantic states and along the Pacific coast was 43. Roughly, our seaboard states present the highest incidences, and the South Central states the lowest incidences. This is due to the larger number of available hospital beds

[28] Ibid., pp. 97–100.
[29] Ibid., pp. 107–109.

in the industrialized and urbanized areas in our coastal districts. Many cases in the South were probably undetected or not hospitalized.

TREATMENT OF MENTAL DISEASE

In addition to such necessary precautions as are essential for physical health, such as clean living conditions, an adequate and palatable diet, exercise, rest, and medical care, certain special modes of treatment are applied to mental patients. Some of these involve the prescription of certain drugs and medicines under specified conditions (*chemotherapy*); others involve the application of certain physical principles (*physiotherapy*); and some techniques are purely psychological in nature (*psychotherapy*). The purpose of this section is to describe and evaluate some of the more prominent of these techniques. It must be remembered that treatments, while they apply the findings of experimental science, represent a clinical approach and cannot always be understood from the experimental point of view. Lacking adequate controls, when patients recover, we cannot be sure that they might not have recovered even though the treatment had not been applied. Some of these techniques are the results of many years of clinical application and are well established. Others are promising but still in the trial-and-error stage.

Psychotherapy

A psychotherapeutic technique often used is that known as "suggestion." This consists largely in reassuring the patient, who, not understanding his symptoms, gradually has his faith in the ability of the physician built up to the point where active cooperation is secured. In no other branch of medicine is such active cooperation as essential. Occasionally, direct *hypnosis* is resorted to as a therapeutic measure. Such suggestive measures may be direct, once rapport is established, or they may be indirect. In the latter case spectacular apparatus or procedures are used that are superficially quite convincing, though actually useless and harmless. Here, the patient is convinced largely because of an ignorant awe of such an apparently scientific setup. To the extent that such suggestive techniques effect a reorientation of the patient's general attitude toward his life problems, they are wholesome and desirable. Unfortunately, such measures lend themselves too easily to an eradication of the symptoms rather than to an attack on the basic causative factors.

Because many mental patients are troubled with problems that they are afraid of or ashamed to face, a sincere effort is made, in talking with them, to draw them out and to get them to verbalize their basic difficulty. Such attempts are known as methods of "catharsis." It is sometimes possible for the patient, in talking of his troubles, to make the adequate emotional response he had so long inhibited. Also, it is frequently possible for the patient to acquire an objective perspective of his condition that, through enabling him to evaluate the situation, aids in effecting a more adequate personality integration. Only after rapport has been established and the patient's reserve has been broken down and confidence obtained can this method be applied.

A technique for producing this, one that achieved some popularity during the Second World War, is known as "narcosynthesis." An injection of sodium pentothal or sodium amytal is introduced intravenously into the patient and continued until his speech becomes thickened and confused. At this stage he is more talkative and, presumably, more suggestible than is usually the case. Under the influence of the drugs he is questioned and in many cases is found to give the emotional response which he normally inhibits.

In the course of treatment, an attempt may be made to train the patient to the point where he can accept life situations without experiencing the disturbing emotions (*e.g.*, fear) that have accompanied them. This is known as "desensitization." When the treatment further consists in the building up of adequate habits of adjustment, the process is referred to as "re-education." Essentially, all psychotherapy is re-educative. In the functional conditions, it is frequently found that the emotional response has become a habit response. If, however, the

Table 8–3. Prognosis in Mental Disease before Newer Therapies Were Developed
(Based on outcome after 5 years)

	No. cases	Recovered		Improved		Unimproved		No. dead	No. lost
		No.	%	No.	%	No.	%		
Dementia praecox	116	12	10	25	21.5	66	56.8	10	3
Manic-depressive	171	86	50.2	19	11.1	30	....	24	12
Paresis	38	13	....	8	....	5	....	12	
Involutional melancholia...	47	12	25.5	10	21.2	10	....	13	2
Somatic disease	60	22	....	8	....	3	....	23	4
Senile	50	2	....	4	....	8	....	31	5
Alcoholic	10	1	....	....	....	3	....	2	4
Psychoneuroses	37	21	56.7	7	16.9	4	10.8	3	2
Paranoid conditions	9	3	....	3	....	2			
Unclassified	72	27	....	13	....	11	....	8	13
Psychopathic	8	....	....	4	....	2	....	1	1
Encephalitics (adult)	8	1	....	1	....	2	....	2	2
Total	626	200	....	102	....	146	....	129	48
Per cent	100%	35%	....	18%	....	25.5%	....	22%	

treatment has enabled the patient to attain an objective insight into his condition, with no ill effect, such an emotional response becomes, under repetition, dulled. With the gradual disappearance of the undesirable habit, the treatment aims to introduce, as a substitute, the positive, aggressive habits of thought and action that are consonant with good mental hygiene. Obviously, the success of this depends, as it should, upon the patient's active cooperation. Also, it is evident that it presupposes a level of intelligence on the part of the patient sufficient to acquire such insight.

How successful are these techniques? They are difficult to evaluate, for, when a patient recovers, we cannot be sure that it is due to the treatment. Also, the standards for recovery vary from investigator to investigator, and it is not always possible to distinguish between various degrees of recovery. Appel[30] presents a table based upon the work of Bond and Braceland (see Table 8–3) that is representative of the situation before some of the newer therapies came into use. This can serve as a standard by which some of these new techniques can be evaluated.

CHEMICAL SHOCK TREATMENT

The schizophrenic disorders are sometimes treated by the repeated production, usually daily, of a hypoglycemic shock in the patient by an intramuscular injection of insulin. The dosage is regulated to the patient and given in bed in the early morning. The patient feels weak and hungry, perspires quite a bit, and gradually enters a stage of progressive somnolence. He must be attended constantly. The actual coma occurs 2 to 4 hours after injection and is allowed to continue from a few minutes to an hour, depending upon the patient's condition. It is terminated by tube or mouth feeding, depending upon the severity of the shock. The treatment should not be used with patients showing signs of myocardial damage, tuberculosis, or severe arteriosclerosis. It is based upon the theory that the schizophrenic will experience an interruption in his delusional or withdrawn thinking and may be reoriented in the process. Certainly some patients are improved, and the improvement becomes better as the treatment continues. The effectiveness evidently depends upon how soon the treatment is begun. Malzberg's figures, as reported by Shipley and Kant,[31] were based on 1,039 insulin-treated cases and 1,039 matched noninsulin-treated controls. He reported 13 per cent recovery and 54 per cent improvement in treated cases and 3.5 per cent recovery and 19 per cent im-

[30] Appel, K. E., Psychiatric Therapy, in J. McV. Hunt, (Ed.), *Personality and the Behavior Disorders*, Vol. II, p. 1151, The Ronald Press Company, New York, 1944.

[31] Shipley, W. C., and Kant, F., The Insulin-shock and Metrazol Treatments of Schizophrenia, with Emphasis on Psychological Aspects, *Psychol. Bull.*, 1940, **37**, 259–284.

provement among the controls. In terms of psychosis duration before treatment the figures were:

	Treated group, per cent	Control group, per cent
Up to 1 month..................	43	8
1 to 3 months..................	33	7
7 to 12 months.................	16	0
1 to 2 years...................	12	.6
3 to 5 years...................	4	.0

Metrazol-shock treatment is sometimes administered in schizophrenia and in the affective disorders in the case of severe depressions, particularly in involutional melancholia. The treatment is given in bed. Attendants are necessary for the protection of the patient. An initial dose of 3 to 5 cc. of a 10 per cent metrazol solution is given intravenously. Within a few seconds the patient becomes bewildered and restless and experiences pronounced fear. He goes into a convulsion of the epileptiform type after which he lapses into a state of coma for several minutes. This is followed by a short period of clouded restlessness, after which he goes to sleep. Convulsions are evoked two or three times a week, the treatment continuing for from 1 to 3 months. This treatment is gradually becoming supplanted by electro-shock treatment (see below), but published figures indicate that it, like insulin-shock, has some merit. The report of Meduna and Friedman, based on 2,937 cases, as discussed by Shipley and Kant,[32] indicates 19.86 per cent full remissions and 38.43 per cent improved cases. Its value also depends upon how soon it is begun, for when the figures are analyzed in terms of the duration of the psychosis, they show:

Less than 6 months....	60.9% recoveries	20 % improved cases
6 months to 1 year....	36.8% recoveries	23.1% improved cases
Over 1 year..........	8.4% recoveries	37.7% improved cases

ELECTRO-SHOCK TREATMENT

The technique of introducing convulsions in the affective disorders by means of the electro-shock method has largely supplanted the use of metrazol in recent years. The treatment is more humane, since fatalities and complications are relatively rare and, since the patient becomes unconscious before the shock, the element of fear is minimized. Electrodes are placed on the temples and an electric current, usually not

[32] *Ibid.*

more than 600 milliamperes, is passed through the cortex for a fraction of a second. The patient becomes immediately unconscious and his body jerks into a pronounced state of tonus. Attendants are necessary to prevent dislocations or fractures. The tonic phase breaks down into a series of clonic contractures, and the seizure is usually terminated in less than a minute. The patient may awaken immediately but usually remains in a state of coma for some time. The treatment may be administered daily for several days, followed by a rest period and then a repetition of the series; or it may be given only two or three times a week for several weeks. While it seems of little effect in the schizophrenic disorders, published reports indicate that it may have merit as a treatment of the affective psychoses. This seems particularly true with respect to involutional melancholia. Dorcus and Shaffer[33] reporting on the work of Smith and coworkers summarize their findings in Table 8–4.

Table 8–4. Effects of the Use of Electro-shock Therapy

Diagnosis	No. cases	Per cent recovered	Per cent improved	Per cent unimproved	Per cent relapsed
Involutional melancholia........	20	85	15	0	5
Manic-depressive, manic.......	10	70	0	30	0
Manic-depressive, depressive....	49	72	10	18	0
Schizophrenia.................	16	0	7	93	0
Undiagnosed.................	8	37.5	0	62.5	12.5
Psychoneurosis................	5	60	0	40	0

PREFRONTAL LOBOTOMY

Brain surgery has been applied to the treatment of the functional disorders in recent years in what may be a promising technique. The aim of the operation, known variously as prefrontal lobotomy, leucotomy, and psychosurgery, is to sever the connections between the thalamus and the prefrontal cortex. Freeman and Watts, who are the chief proponents in this country of the technique, believe that these connections mediate the affective component of ideational activities.[34] When the patient's condition is characterized by anxiety, depression, or agitated fearfulness, the operation is performed. It consists in the severance of the long fibers of the white matter of the cerebrum in the plane of the coronal suture anterior to the corpus callosum. A modification of this technique, known as transorbital lobotomy, consists in in-

[33] Dorcus and Shaffer, *op. cit.*, p. 431.
[34] Freeman, W., and Watts, J. W., The Frontal Lobes and Consciousness of the Self, *Psychosom. Med.*, 1941, 3, 111–119.

serting the surgical instrument into the frontal lobes of the brain through the bony part of the eye socket. In another technique, thalectomy, the surgeon lowers an electric needle into the thalamus. As a result of the operation, it is claimed the patient loses many aspects of inhibited behavior, much anxiety and fearfulness, becomes more cheerful and comfortable, with little, if any, loss in intelligence.

Differences of opinion with respect to a technique as recently advanced and radically new as prefrontal lobotomy are bound to exist. Many claims in its favor were rushed into print too soon after the performance of the operation to justify statements in terms of the permanence of its effect. A summary of many evaluative studies is presented in tabular form by Schrader and Robinson.[35] For the student's benefit, this is reproduced in Table 8–5.

Table 8–5. Results of Prefrontal Lobotomy in Representative Studies

Investigators	No. of cases	Results			
		Good	Fair	Poor	Deaths
Moniz............................	20	7	7	6	0
Cohen, Noric and Ettelson..........	6	2	3	1	0
Strecker, Palmer, and Grant.........	22	14	4	2	2
Peterson and Buckstein.............	29	16	11	1	1
Heilbrunn and Hletko..............	11	0	2	7	2
Rees.............................	30	9	13	6	2
Strom-Olsen, Last, Brody, and Knight	30	7	13	9	1
Dax and Smith....................	50	16	15	16	3
Cook.............................	20	9	6	4	1
Kisker............................	20	6	4	7	3
Watts and Freeman................	136	82	22	21	11
Porteus and Kepner................	20	6	5	9	0
Schrader and Hoctor...............	207	108	39	54	6
Totals........................	601	282	144	143	32
Percentages...................		47	24	24	5

SUMMARY

Man's earliest attempts to understand abnormal behavior sprang deep from the lore of the supernatural and were couched in the language of ignorance. As people became more literate, the concepts of medical science became more widely understood and a more objective attitude was attained. Today, those who are mentally ill are considered sick. This sickness may be due to an organic lesion or a toxic condition or to faulty habit formation. Whatever the cause, it is wide-

[35] Schrader, P. J., and Robinson, M. F., An Evaluation of Prefrontal Lobotomy through Ward Behavior, *J. Abnorm. Soc. Psychol.*, 1945, **40**, 61–69.

spread, approximately 10 per cent of our population having an expectancy of being sometime incapacitated by such conditions.

These disorders show themselves in exaggerated behavior manifestations known as symptoms. The symptoms may be disorders of sensation and perception, aberrations of motor activity, disturbances of intelligence, or changes in emotion. The most prominent of the organic psychoses are those due to alcohol, syphilis, and old age. The functional psychoses include the schizophrenic conditions, the affective disorders, and the systematized delusions of the paranoid.

Mental disease occurs most frequently among older individuals, though it can occur at almost any age. Although a larger number of patients are found in urban areas, this is probably due to better diagnoses and more ample hospital facilities. Heredity seems to play an important, if not thoroughly understood, role in schizophrenia and manic-depressive conditions. Psychoses occur in decreasing frequency among individuals who are divorced, single, widowed, and married, in that order. They are noticed more frequently among men than women. The greater incidence among foreign-born immigrants is due partly to the factors of age and urbanization and partly to the fact that migratory groups apparently contain more psychopathic material. The seaboard areas of our country, with better hospital facilities, report a larger number of cases than other areas. We also find a greater frequency among Negroes than among Whites.

In recent years, the techniques of psychotherapy have been supplemented by chemical-shock and electro-shock methods that apparently have some merit. The art of the brain surgeon has contributed the operation of prefrontal lobotomy, which is still in the process of being evaluated.

RECOMMENDED SUPPLEMENTARY READINGS

Burton, A., and Harris, R. E.: *Case Histories in Clinical and Abnormal Psychology,* Harper & Brothers, New York, 1947.

Cameron, Norman: *The Psychology of Behavior Disorders,* Houghton Mifflin Company, Boston, 1947.

Coleman, J. C.: *Abnormal Psychology and Modern Life,* Scott, Foresman & Company, Chicago, 1950.

Dorcus, R. M., and Shaffer, G. W.: *Textbook of Abnormal Psychology,* 4th ed., The Williams & Wilkins Company, Baltimore, 1950.

Guilford, J. P. (Ed.): *Fields of Psychology,* Chaps. 9, 10, 11, D. Van Nostrand Company, Inc., New York, 1940.

Hunt, J. McV. (Ed.): *Personality and the Behavior Disorders,* Chaps, 18, 29, The Ronald Press Company, New York, 1944.

Landis, C., and Bolles, M. M.: *Textbook of Abnormal Psychology,* rev. ed., The Macmillan Company, New York, 1950.

Landis, C., and Page, J. D.: *Modern Society and Mental Disease,* Rinehart & Company, Inc., New York, 1938.

Morgan, J. J. B., and Lovell, G. D.: *The Psychology of Abnormal People,* Longmans, Green & Company, Inc., New York, 1948.

O'Kelly, L. I.: *Introduction to Psychopathology,* Prentice-Hall, Inc., New York, 1949.

Page, J. D.: *Abnormal Psychology,* McGraw-Hill Book Company, Inc., New York, 1947.

Rosanoff, A. J.: *Manual of Psychiatry and Mental Hygiene,* 7th ed., John Wiley & Sons, Inc., New York, 1938.

White, R. A.: *The Abnormal Personality,* The Ronald Press Company, New York, 1948.

Chapter 9

CLINICAL PSYCHOLOGY[1]

The first psychological clinic was established at the University of Pennsylvania under the direction of Professor Lightner Witmer in 1896. *The Psychological Clinic,* a journal edited by Dr. Witmer, records many studies made in the early years of clinical practice. The history of the first clinic, published in a memorial symposium[2] commemorating its thirty-fifth anniversary, and papers[3] read at a symposium in honor of 50 years of clinical psychology, at the University of Pennsylvania, Sept. 3, 1946, indicate that this clinic maintained a very close working relationship with schools and physicians and dealt primarily with the problems of children. Although the work of clinical psychologists has expanded to include adjustment problems of people of all ages, and in many fields of human affairs, it is noteworthy that some of the fundamental concepts developed in the early years of the first psychological clinic have changed very little. For example, the analysis of the individual's behavior, the study of the environmental forces that impinge upon him, and the use of these data to bring about better adjustment in behavior are still among the basic aspects of clinical practice.

The essence of all clinical practice in psychology lies in the identification and study of the influences that are related to maladjustment of behavior, whether the influences come from within the individual or from the environment, and in the modification of these influences to

[1] This chapter was written by Dr. Carroll A. Whitmer, Chief, Clinical Psychology Service, VA Hospital, Fort Douglas, Utah.

[2] Brotemarkle, Robert A., *et al., Clinical Psychology:* Studies in Honor of Lightner Witmer, University of Pennsylvania Press, Philadelphia, 1931.

[3] *J. Consult. Psychol.,* 1947, 11, 1–20.

achieve a better adjustment. It is obvious that the clinical psychologist cannot work alone.[4] He uses techniques developed through psychological research, but he must also depend upon other professional disciplines to carry out procedures which their training prepares them to contribute. For example, a behavior maladjustment may arise from defective physical condition, onset of psychosis, friction within the family, or maladjustment in school. In these situations the clinical psychologist works in collaboration with physician, psychiatrist, social worker, or teacher, respectively, or with more than one of these related professions if the problem so indicates.

A clear distinction between the work of the clinical psychologist and that of related professions is not entirely possible. Clinical practice in the application of psychology overlaps every other field considered in this book as well as the practice of related professions. In fact, wherever problems of adjustment in human behavior are considered the clinical psychologist may have a role. The tendency toward more practice of psychotherapy by clinical psychologists has increased the overlapping of the work of psychiatrists, psychologists, and social workers.[5]

During the years since the founding of the first psychological clinic, the work of many psychologists in clinical practice has continued the core of diagnosis and treatment described by Witmer. The term "clinical practice" has been subject to various emphases so that there has been much disagreement in the definition of clinical psychology. The definitions summarized by Louttit[6] indicate a range from emphasis on comprehensive diagnosis and therapy to the simple administration of psychometric tests. Perhaps a description of the training of clinical psychologists and their work in various settings will give a better understanding of psychology in clinical practice than can be given in any definition.

TRAINING AND CERTIFICATION FOR PRACTICE IN CLINICAL PSYCHOLOGY

There was little uniformity in the training of clinical psychologists in American universities before the Second World War. A committee of the American Association for Applied Psychology[7] proposed a program[8]

---

[4] Raimy, Victor C. (Ed.), *Training in Clinical Psychology,* Chap. 13, Relation with Other Professions, Prentice-Hall, Inc., New York, 1950.

[5] Symonds, Percival M., New Trends in Clinical Psychology, *Amer. J. Orthopsychiat.,* 1948, **18,** 153–162.

[6] Louttit, C. M., The Nature of Clinical Psychology, *Psychol. Bull.,* 1939, **36,** 361–389.

[7] This organization was started in 1937 to promote professional development of applied psychology and in 1944 was merged with the American Psychological Association.

[8] Proposed Program of Professional Training for Clinical Psychology, *J. Consult. Psychol.,* 1943, **7,** 23–27.

in 1943 for training in clinical psychology. Revision and extension of this report[9] were made in 1947 by a Committee on Training in Clinical Psychology appointed by the American Psychological Association. The report made by this committee has provided the basis for increasing uniformity in graduate training of clinical psychologists. A 4-year graduate program, including 1 year of internship, leading to the doctorate degree is now generally accepted. The recommended program is comprehensive, and in this chapter only the major points of emphasis can be indicated.

The report enumerates personal characteristics considered desirable for the clinical psychologist. The basic undergraduate program recommended includes a broad background in the biological, physical, and social sciences, mathematics, education, history of culture and languages in addition to about 20 semester hours of courses in psychology. The graduate professional program should include general fundamental training in psychology rather than specialization in any technique or system. The recommended instructional areas are general psychology, dynamics of human behavior, related disciplines, diagnostic methods, therapy, and research methods. Training should emphasize integration of theory and practice and the development of professional responsibility.

A year of supervised practical experience in various types of clinical settings is a generally accepted part of training in clinical psychology. A growing number of hospitals and institutions have provided internship opportunities.[10]

Following the report of the Committee on Training in Clinical Psychology, arrangements were made by the American Psychological Association to have universities offering doctoral training visited by evaluating committees. The universities offering approved doctoral training programs in clinical psychology appear in a published list.[11]

The training programs sponsored by the Veterans' Administration,[12] the United States Public Health Service, and the United States Army[13] have all given impetus and support to raising the standards of training in clinical psychology. The details of these programs are given in the references indicated.

[9] Recommended Graduate Program in Clinical Psychology, Amer. Psychol., 1947, 2, 539–558.
[10] Wolfle, Helen, Available Internships in Psychology, 1949–1950, Amer. Psychol., 1949, 2, 43–47.
[11] Approved Doctoral Training Programs in Clinical Psychology, Amer. Psychol., 1951, 6, 171.
[12] Miller, James G., Clinical Psychology in the Veterans Administration, Amer. Psychol., 1946, 1, 181–189.
[13] The U.S. Army's Senior Psychology Student Program, Amer. Psychol., 1949, 4, 424–425.

A conference on graduate education in clinical psychology sponsored by the American Psychological Association under a grant from the U.S. Public Health Service was held in Boulder, Colo., in 1949 to review and discuss training problems. This conference was attended by representatives from universities offering doctoral training in clinical psychology, representatives of the government agencies and institutions employing clinical psychologists, and representatives from allied professions. The conference served to point up similarities and differences in training programs and to provide an opportunity to develop better understanding of problems involved. The conference report[14] has served as a reference for further improvement of training.

The public demands for psychological service and a growing consciousness of a young profession concerning its own competence have brought about an increase in the consideration of the problem of protecting the public from the misguided or poorly trained person who professes to be a clinical psychologist. The enactment of legislation presents many difficult problems for a profession as young as clinical psychology. Thoughtful consideration of these complex problems appears in an article[15] by the executive secretary of the American Psychological Association in 1950. A few states have enacted some legal control of the practice of clinical psychology. The first licensing law for psychology was passed in Kentucky in 1949. Other states[16] have passed certification laws which prevent the unqualified practitioner from using the title "certified psychologist." A number of states have license provisions for school psychologists.[17] The training requirements for school psychologists have generally been below those considered for certification or licensing for individual private practice.

State psychological associations and the American Psychological Association have been active in considering professional qualifications. The requirement for fellowship in the clinical sections of these associations is a doctorate degree plus qualifying experience. However, membership does not necessarily indicate competence in clinical practice. The American Board of Examiners in Professional Psychology, Inc.,[18] was organized to give professional recognition to clinical, counseling, and industrial psychologists who meet very high qualifications. The layman may reasonably use the following criteria to judge the

[14] Raimy, op. cit.

[15] Wolfle, Dael, Legal Control of Psychological Practice, Amer. Psychol., April, 1950, 5, 651–655.

[16] Miles, Walter R., A Year of State Certification of Psychologists, Amer. Psychol., 9, 393; The Certification of Clinical Psychologists in Virginia, Amer. Psychol., 9, 395.

[17] Horrocks, John E., State Certification Requirements for School Psychologists, Amer. Psychol., 1946, 1, 399–401.

[18] The Work of the American Board of Examiners in Professional Psychology, Amer. Psychol., 1950, 5, 577–584.

responsibility and competence of a clinical psychologist: first, diplomate of the American Board of Examiners in Professional Psychology; second, licensed or certificated by a state for private practice; and third, recommended by a department of psychology in a university offering an approved training program in clinical psychology.

DIAGNOSTIC AND TREATMENT METHODS IN CLINICAL PRACTICE

The methods and procedures used in clinical practice vary with the training and background of the clinician, but general acceptance of basic procedures determines some uniformity in practice in similar cases under similar conditions.

Diagnostic procedures in clinical psychology are aimed toward understanding the individual and his behavior problems. In order to approach this goal the psychologist may make a detailed study of the individual and his environment. Such studies often include family background, birth conditions, infancy and early training, health history, personal relationships in the home, school, and community, and the particular characteristics of the behavior maladjustment.

Most of the data of a case study are obtained through skillfully conducted *interviews*. The interview procedures vary with the nature of the individual and the problem. For example, if a retarded child is being studied, most of the case history is obtained from adults who know the child, and the interview may be essentially a fact-finding procedure. On the other hand, if an adult is being studied, most of the information about him and his problem is obtained from the person himself. An interview of this type may actually contribute much to the individual's understanding of his own problem and be therapeutic for him as well as helping the clinician to understand the nature of the problem.

The *psychological examination* is a second method used in the diagnostic study of the individual. In this part of the study psychological tests[19] are used to make an appraisal of the quantity and quality of the individual's performance in response to a standardized stimulus. The test performance is used as an index, along with other information, to estimate probable level of development, amount of deterioration, and various modes of reaction which characterize the individual's behavior or reveal relationships between his experiences and his present behavior.

Tests which measure quantity of intellectual performance scored in a numerical figure are commonly called "objective-type tests." The Binet scale is the original test in this category. It is an age scale, so called because it presents a number of test items that have been stand-

[19] There are many comprehensive books on mental tests. Psychodiagnostic use of tests is well presented in Rosenzweig, S., and Kogan, K. L., *Psychodiagnosis*, Harper & Brothers, New York, 1949.

ardized for each age level of mental growth. This test, first published in 1905, has undergone successive revisions. One scale of this type in common use is the Terman-Merrill Revision of the Stanford-Binet.[20]

The items on this scale are scored in months of credit, and the sum of credit in years and months is called the "mental age" of the individual on that test. The mental age is divided by the child's chronological age, and the resulting quotient times 100 is the intelligence quotient. This quotient, within the limitations of the test, indicates the relative rate of a child's mental growth. The Terman-Merrill Revision of the Binet test has been extended beyond the average age of mental maturity so that intelligence quotients may be obtained from the test performances of superior adults, although the test is most appropriate for children.

The Wechsler Bellevue[21] scale of intelligence tests is the most widely used individual test for adults. This scale provides point values for responses on tests of verbal and nonverbal or performance type and a total point value so that an intelligence quotient evaluation of two types of abilities may be made.

Performance tests are useful indicators of ability to comprehend and perform tasks that do not involve language. One of the more commonly used scales of this type for children is the Grace Arthur Scale of Performance tests.[22] Such tests are particularly useful in clinical practice with children who are deaf or who have a language handicap. Tests of the performance type are valuable not only for their quantitative scores but also because they present a situation in which qualitative aspects of behavior such as how the child reacts to a puzzling situation may be observed.

In addition to tests of general mental ability the clinical psychologist uses objective-type tests and questionnaires to investigate social maturity,[23] educational achievement,[24] and school-subject disabilities.[25] In the study of late adolescence and adulthood when vocational adjustments are part of the problem, the investigation of aptitudes[26] and

[20] Terman, L. M., and Merrill, M., *Measuring Intelligence,* Houghton Mifflin Company, Boston, 1937.

[21] Wechsler, David, *The Measurement of Adult Intelligence,* The Williams & Wilkins Company, Baltimore, 1941.

[22] Arthur, Grace, A Point Scale of Performance Tests, Vol. I, *Clinical Manual,* Commonwealth Fund, Division of Publication, New York, 1943.

[23] Doll, Edgar A., *Vineland Social Maturity Scale, Manual of Directions,* Minneapolis, Educational Test Bureau, 1947.

[24] Remmers, H. H., and Gage, N. L., *Educative Measurement and Evaluation,* Harper & Brothers, New York, 1943.

[25] Fernald, G. M., *Remedial Techniques in Basic School Subjects,* McGraw-Hill Book Company, Inc., New York, 1943.

[26] Bingham, Walter V., *Aptitudes and Aptitude Testing,* Harper & Brothers, New York, 1937.

interests[27] may be indicated. Although the questionnaire type of procedure has generally been supplanted by projective methods (described below) in the clinical study of personality characteristics the Minnesota Multiphasic Personality Inventory[28] is widely used as a diagnostic device.

The general use of projective methods in the study of personality is one of the more recent developments in clinical practice. Projective methods make use of relatively unstructured situations or stimuli to permit the individual to reveal various aspects of his personality that he would not or could not verbalize.

The Rorschach method of personality diagnosis[29] is one of the most widely used projective techniques. This method of diagnosis employs a series of 10 standardized ink blots to elicit responses that can be analyzed to determine many aspects of personality. The responses are what the individual sees in the blot and are studied on the basis of the meaning to him rather than from any right or wrong criterion.

Pictures are frequently used in projective tests. The Thematic Apperception Test devised by Murray[30] is a series of 20 pictures depicting people in various relationships. The response to this test is in the form of a story indicating what the person thinks the picture shows, including what led up to this scene, the feelings of the people in the picture, and the outcome. By systematic analysis of the themes in the stories it is possible to find, for example, how an individual meets the stresses in his own life. The Thematic Apperception Test is equally applicable to the study of children and of adults.

In addition to ink blots and pictures a wide variety of stimulus situations have been used as projective methods in clinical practice. Drawings of the human figure,[31] finger painting,[32] and play with dolls[33] are used as projective methods.

Since the Second World War the clinical psychologist has taken an increasingly active part in treatment procedures. Although therapeutic methods, particularly those concerned with the personality disorders,

[27] Strong, E. K., *Interests of Men and Women,* Stanford University Press, Stanford, Calif., 1943.

[28] Hathaway, Stark R., and Meehl, Paul E., *An Atlas for the Clinical Use of the M M P I,* University of Minnesota Press, Minneapolis, 1951.

[29] Klopfer, B., and Kelly, D. M., *The Rorschach Technique,* World Book Company, Yonkers, N.Y., 1942.

[30] Murray, H. A., Techniques for a Systematic Investigation of Phantasy, *J. Psychol.,* 1937, **3**, 115–143.

[31] Machover, Karen, *Personality Projection in the Drawings of the Human Figure,* Charles C Thomas, Publisher, Springfield, Ill., 1949.

[32] Napoli, P. J., Finger-painting and Personality Diagnosis, *Genet. Psychol. Monogr.,* 1946, **34**, No. 2.

[33] Levy, D. M., Studies in Sibling Rivalry, *Amer. Orthopsychiat. Ass., Res. Monogr.,* 1937, No. 2.

have generally been practiced by the medical profession, it has been increasingly recognized that diagnosis and therapy are in many cases inseparable. It is not within the scope of this chapter even to mention all types of *treatment methods* that psychologists have practiced or to which they have contributed.

One outstanding contribution to therapeutic method has been made by Dr. Carl Rogers[34] and his students. This method has been the subject of much controversy,[35] and its advocates have been unique in the promotion of research in therapy. Rogers and his students have centered their attention upon aiding the self-growth of the client. A basic assumption in their system of therapy is that the individual who seeks help for his problems has within himself the strength to make an adjustment. In order to make use of his own inner resources he needs help to achieve insight and to begin effective action to meet his problems. The client-centered therapist uses only the interview method in dealing with the client. He uses no diagnostic tests nor does he make any suggestion or recommendation to the client. The interview in the client-centered method has been studied and refined to avoid direction by the therapist and to achieve the goal of permitting the self-growth of the client.

A first impression might be that the client-centered therapist does very little and therefore needs little training. Actually the practice of client-centered therapy demands extensive training if the therapist is prepared to be skilled in understanding the client's reactions and to be able to take the role which will be most effective in promoting the client's self-growth.

The neuropsychiatric hospital and out-patient setting have favored the development of *group psychotherapy*,[36] and psychologists have participated in this clinical activity. Some group psychotherapy had been practiced in child guidance clinics and in a few hospitals before the Second World War but because of the need for therapy and the shortage of trained personnel it was expedient to treat men in groups in many army situations. The effectiveness of group psychotherapy has been recognized so that the practice has become a very common one in many neuropsychiatric hospitals and neuropsychiatric out-patient clinics. In group psychotherapy the patients are encouraged to discuss their problems. The group interaction makes possible the release of

[34] Rogers, Carl R., *Client-centered Therapy*, Houghton Mifflin Company, Boston, 1951.
[35] Critical Evaluation of Non-directive Counseling and Psychotherapy, *J. Clin. Psychol. Monogr. Suppl.* 4, 1948.
[36] Kaplan, J. W., *Group Psychotherapy, Theory and Practice*, Grune & Stratton, Inc., New York, 1946.

emotional tensions and increases the patient's insight into his own personality characteristics through group discussion. The interpersonal relationships which develop in group therapy give the therapist an opportunity to observe the patients' personality in action.

The role which the clinical psychologist plays in therapy depends greatly upon the situation in which he works. In the remainder of this chapter we shall attempt to describe some of the work done by the psychologist in clinical practice in various settings.

THE PRACTICE OF CLINICAL PSYCHOLOGY

UNIVERSITY CLINICS

The first psychological clinic was part of a university department of psychology at the University of Pennsylvania. Since that time departments that have trained clinical psychologists have maintained clinics in which the student may practice, under supervision, the theories he has learned in course work. Many university clinics encourage referrals from the community so that a wide variety of psychological problems may be available for the experience of the student. In many communities, away from large population centers, the only psychological service available is in the nearest university clinic. A survey of psychological service centers conducted by a committee of the American Psychological Association[37] shows 139 of 548 service centers connected with universities or colleges.

Clinic practice in university clinics varies from one staff psychologist working more or less independently to very elaborate training clinics in which psychiatrists and social workers are regular staff members. In the training clinics a wide variety of diagnostic and treatment procedures are used to acquaint the student in practice with values and limitations of various techniques. Referrals to university clinics are made by parents, schools, physicians, courts, business and industrial organizations, and in fact any institution in the community that does not maintain independent psychological services.

CLINICAL PSYCHOLOGY IN SCHOOLS

The application of psychology in education was one of the first fields of applied psychology, and the first psychological clinic dealt with the problems of children in schools. A symposium[38] on the school psychologist in the *Journal of Consulting Psychology* in 1942 describes the many and varied functions of psychologists who practice in schools.

[37] Trow, W. Clark, A Survey of Psychological Service Centers, *Amer. Psychol.*, 1950, **5**, 412–421.

[38] The School Psychologist, *J. Consult. Psychol.*, 1942, **6**, No. 4.

This symposium indicates that the type of work done by the school psychologist depends upon the organization of the psychological services in the schools and may be primarily educational rather than clinical. In this chapter we shall limit our discussion to the practice of clinical psychology in the school.

Work with the mentally retarded and slow-learning children occupies a large portion of the school psychologist's time. The psychologist is concerned with the study of the child's abilities and helps in planning appropriate educational treatment so that the child can develop his limited capacities in practical ways and gain the self-confidence that comes through successful performance. The psychologist is concerned with the interpretation of the abilities and behavior of the retarded child to teachers and to parents. If the child's limitations are recognized he may be relieved of stresses which come from pressures to make him comprehend and achieve beyond his capacity. Many retarded children develop personality disorders engendered by environmental pressures that arise because the children are misunderstood. Understanding the child is important as the basis for correcting his maladjustment and preventing further maladjustment.

The development of a well-adjusted personality in the child who has a crippling physical handicap is often a difficult problem which needs psychological study. Frustrations arising because the crippled child cannot lead a normal-child life can, if neglected, lead to distorted personality developments. The clinical psychologist, working with teachers and parents as well as with the child, can aid in the development of good mental hygiene in spite of physical handicaps.

The problem of estimation of ability in some types of crippling conditions is difficult because the child's speech and muscular control are impaired. This is true of the child handicapped by cerebral palsy (commonly called the "spastic child"). Some children who have this crippling condition are very intelligent and may develop to the extent of being able to live quite normal lives if early training is possible. If the intelligent cerebral palsied child is understood and proper training facilities are provided it is possible for him to achieve normal emotional adjustment.

The analysis and correction of school-subject disabilities is a clinical practice field of growing importance in modern schools. Crowded classrooms with less time for individual instruction of each pupil result in the failure of some children to develop correct habits in the basic school subjects. It is now recognized that all children in the same intelligence range do not have the same aptitudes for accomplishment in school subjects. Studies of special disability in reading have led to the conclusion that there are numerous factors associated with reading disability.[39] For example, emotional handicaps, short attention span, lack of environmental opportunities, low sensory capacity, as well as factors of motivation may all operate as hindrances in learning to read even though the child has high general intelligence.

The clinical study of reading disabilities includes a comprehensive examination of general and specific abilities, analysis of the reading performance if the disability is partial, check of general physical condition and sensory acuity and functioning, and the determination of the child's attitude toward school and especially toward reading. In some cases diagnostic teaching may be necessary in order to determine the faulty habits that impede reading. No longer are nonreaders dismissed with a diagnosis of "word blindness." Case histories of particularly difficult reading problems are given by Fernald.[40] These case histories show the complexity of behavior relationships involved in the case of the nonreader. The most effective remedial treatments are those that follow comprehensive study of the child's disabilities. Additional assignments in reading are not a remedy for reading disabilities.

The diagnosis and treatment of behavior problems form a very important area of clinical practice in schools. Conduct problems in general, truancy, nervous habits, sudden changes of personality and, in fact, almost any form of antisocial behavior appear on the list of referrals for psychological study. Relatively few schools have an adequate staff or time to study and treat all behavior problems. Some of the more complex behavior problems and particularly very disturbed children may necessarily be referred to clinics where facilities for treatment are better.

The school psychologist who practices with limited allied clinic services in the school frequently has a working relationship with clinic services outside the school. If such services are available the school psychologist often refers complex problems involving out-of-school relationships to the cooperating specialists or clinic, along with his preliminary investigation. He also cooperates in the treatment insofar as the school is involved in the treatment plan. A working relationship saves duplication of service and concentrates the available service on the phase of the problem where it will prove most effective.

The future for the clinical psychologists in schools is bright. Such service is available only to a small proportion of school children in the United States. As the public becomes better acquainted with the practice of clinical psychology more service will probably be made available to schools.

[39] Monroe, Marion, *Children Who Cannot Read*, University of Chicago Press, Chicago, 1932.
[40] *Op. cit.*, pp. 273–318.

CLINICAL PSYCHOLOGY IN CHILD GUIDANCE AND COMMUNITY MENTAL HEALTH CLINICS

The psychologist who works in a child guidance clinic or community mental health clinic sees many children whose problems are similar to those referred to a school clinic. The community clinic is likely to receive more seriously disturbed children and problems which are too complex for the school clinic to treat.

Child guidance clinics under sponsorship of the National Association for Mental Health are directed by psychiatrists. The psychologist works as a member of a team whose other members are the psychiatrist and the social worker. The psychologist's unique contribution in the guidance center is the psychological testing, analysis of school-subject disabilities, and qualitative observations of the patient in the testing situation. The information contributed by each member of the professional team is pooled to determine the diagnosis and the treatment program.

The treatment program in the guidance clinic may involve one or all of the members of the professional team. The psychologist's part in the treatment program consists of diagnostic and remedial teaching and therapy under the direction of the psychiatrist. Special observations of the child through play interviews may contribute to diagnosis and therapy[41] through better understanding of the child. Play therapy[42] is a very commonly used diagnostic and treatment procedure in guidance clinics. In play therapy the child is treated in a room equipped with many toys. He may use any toy in any way that he chooses while the therapist observes his use of the toys and his conversation. A set of dolls to represent a family often gives the child an opportunity to release his emotional tensions and display his attitudes toward members of his family through manipulation of the dolls.

Community mental health clinics partially supported by the National Mental Health Act of 1946 not only serve the functions of child guidance but also accept adult problems involving marital relationship and general problems of adult mental health. In these clinics the duties of the clinical psychologist, as described in the recommended qualifications for state mental health personnel, include diagnostic and treatment functions at a level consistent with his training and experience. The wide variety of problems and patients of all age levels makes practice in the community mental health clinic a most challenging situation for the practice of clinical psychology.

[41] Frankl, Anni Weiss, Play Interviews with Nursery School Children, *Amer. J. Orthopsychiat.*, 1941, 11, 33–39.
[42] Axline, V. M., *Play Therapy: The Inner Dynamics of Childhood,* Houghton Mifflin Company, Boston, 1947.

Some guidance clinics are primarily psychological rather than psychiatric, and the leading role in the interpretation and treatment program in such clinics is taken by psychologists. One of the older community guidance clinics in America, The Wichita Guidance Center,[43] is of this type. This center was organized in 1930 by Dr. Edwina Cowan. The following services are listed among those offered by this agency: study and treatment of persons with such difficulties as poor schoolwork, truancy, antisocial habits, fears, worries, and personal problems. The agency is supported by the Community Fund and offers its services to other agencies to aid in understanding and planning for their clients. The Wichita clinic aims to serve normal individuals with normal problems. Applicants with major personality disorders are referred elsewhere.

INSTITUTIONS FOR THE MENTALLY DEFICIENT

The psychologist who practices in the *institution for the mentally deficient* has a long historical tradition and well-known predecessors in his field. Among the best known names of psychologists who have practiced in institutions for the mentally deficient are Seguin, Goddard, Huey, Porteus, Kuhlmann, and Doll. Each of these men has made significant contributions to the understanding of the feeble-minded. There are relatively few institutions for the mentally deficient in which significant psychological contributions have been made. Unfortunately many institutional administrators have been satisfied to emphasize their custodial responsibilities. It is in the training institution that the clinical psychologist can make a distinct contributon toward the most effective treatment of the mentally deficient.

Letchworth Village at Thiells, N.Y., is one of the more progressive institutions for the treatment of the mentally deficient. This institution uses psychological service in its clinical function as well as in training and research. Kinder[44] has described the clinical service at Letchworth Village in terms of three objectives—first, to meet the needs of the institution, second, to furnish clinical material for students in training, and third, the provision of data for research studies. The major load of work is described as the examination of new admissions and presentation of the psychological data to the various departments that are concerned with the child in the institution. The psychiatrist, neurologist, and psychologist make a diagnosis of the patient at the staff consultation clinic. In addition to the clinical work with new admissions, the psychologist continues study with retests to determine the special

[43] Carter, Jerry W., Jr., The Wichita Guidance Center, *J. Consult. Psychol.*, 1944, 8, 27–30.

[44] Kinder, Elaine F., Psychological Work at Letchworth Village, Thiells, New York, *J. Consult. Psychol.*, 1937, 1, 76–80.

abilities of higher grade patients. The information obtained from these studies is pertinent to the general understanding of the child and aids the staff, who actually carry out the child's training.

The extensive study of the mentally deficient that has been carried on during the past half century has contributed much to the general understanding of children's behavior. Institutions for the mentally deficient have provided excellent settings for research because of the continuity of residence, making possible the study of individuals over long periods of time. Much of the research in these institutions has contributed to the basis of information and techniques underlying clinical psychology.

PENAL AND CORRECTIONAL INSTITUTIONS AND COURTS

Many juvenile courts and some criminal courts use the services of clinical psychologists. In these institutions psychologists work with psychiatrists and social workers to help diagnose the personality problems of offenders so that the courts can make better decisions concerning the type or length of treatment.

The practice of clinical psychology in penal and correctional institutions is, according to Corsini,[45] a relatively new field, having grown since the First World War. The work of the prison psychologist has in some cases been primarily psychometric; *i.e.,* he collects test data for the records or research. This is a very limited function of the clinical psychologist. The most valuable function of the prison psychologist is his work in personal guidance of the inmate. If the function of the institution is to become more corrective and less punitive the clinical practice of the prison psychologist is an important contribution. Corsini[46] points out that the personality and experience background of the prison psychologist are most important because the success of his work depends upon his ability to establish rapport with the prisoners, who may be from sixteen to eighty years of age, of any race, and of any social or economic status.

The prison psychologist works with other members of the professional staff and contributes information about the inmate's ability, personality, and aptitudes so that his treatment in the institution will be most effective and his success on parole more probable. Giardini has been a leader in the study and prediction of success on parole. He has shown[47] that it is possible to make relatively accurate predictions of the success of prisoners on parole.

[45] Corsini, Raymond, Functions of the Prison Psychologist, *J. Consult. Psychol.,* 1945, **9,** 101–140.

[46] *Ibid.,* p. 103.

[47] Carter, A. C., and Giardini, G. I., Reliability of Psychological Prognosis in Western Penitentiary of Pennsylvania, *J. Crim. Law Criminol.,* 1935, 26, 556–560.

A survey[48] of psychological work in institutions for delinquent boys and girls was reported by Giardini in 1942. Replies to a questionnaire were received from 84 superintendents and 43 psychologists. The replies from the superintendents indicated that every superintendent who had a qualified psychologist on his staff regarded psychological work in the institution as essential and generally expected that the psychologist would contribute more than the results of mental testing. The order of frequency of psychological services listed was (1) to help the administrator understand the inmates, (2) to aid in the treatment of behavior problems, (3) to recommend and aid in training programs, (4) to aid in selection of parolees, and (5) to help train the staff in understanding and handling the inmates. Case reports indicate that the primary treatment technique used was that of guidance interviews with directed activities.

HOSPITALS

A few hospitals, notably Worcester State Hospital and Boston Psychopathic in Massachusetts, have employed well-qualified clinical psychologists since early in the present century. Many state hospitals for mental diseases have employed psychologists at the technician level, i.e., primarily to do mental testing. A symposium[49] presented in 1944 indicated at that time that there was a trend toward more clinical practice as opposed to mental testing in hospitals. The emphasis on practice at a professional level was indicated in the division of the hospital psychologist's time recorded by Schott[50] as follows: interviewing 40 per cent; therapy 30 per cent; testing 25 per cent; and miscellaneous 5 per cent, including general participation in hospital staff problems.

The discussions in the symposium indicate that the psychologist practicing in the hospital is likely to be recognized on the staff at a level in keeping with his training and professional ability. That is to say, if he is prepared to participate in the functions of the hospital at the professional level his activities will not be confined to the technical level.

Following the Second World War the need for psychological services in Veterans' Administration and Army hospitals was acute. The Veterans' Training Program for Clinical Psychologists and the Army Surgeon General's senior psychology training program prepared many well-trained psychologists for work in these hospitals. The psychologists who were trained for these positions in programs which met the high

[48] Giardini, G. I., Report of the Committee on Psychological Work in Institutions for Delinquent Boys and Girls, *J. Consult. Psychol.*, 1942, **6**, 157–162.
[49] Psychologists Function in Hospitals, *J. Consult. Psychol.*, 1944, **8**, 267–322.
[50] Schott, Emmett, L., The Psychologist in the General Hospital, *J. Consult. Psychol.*, 1944, **8**, 302.

standards set by the VA and the Army were prepared to give professional service in clinical practice and took positions in keeping with their training. The psychologists in VA and Army hospitals work with the other professions in diagnostic and treatment programs and have contributed significant research which has served to increase the understanding of the neuropsychiatric patient.

CHILD WELFARE ORGANIZATIONS

The clinical psychologist in the Child Welfare Organization is likely to do more diagnostic work and less treatment than does his professional counterpart in the guidance clinic. The fact is that the welfare agency frequently refers difficult problems involving mental disturbance to mental hygiene clinics for treatment. There are some large welfare organizations which maintain psychiatric clinics in which the duties of the psychologist are quite similar to his duties in a community mental health clinic. In most welfare organizations the psychologist studies the child for the purpose of interpreting his abilities and behavior characteristics to the social worker, parent, and foster parent. Treatment programs are suggested by the psychologist, but the actual carrying out of the treatment is usually done by the parents or foster parents through the direction of the social worker. One of the most important services of the psychologist in the welfare agency is accurate diagnosis and prognosis of the child's abilities and characteristics when he is offered for adoption. Through this type of service the probability of successful adjustment in adoptions is greatly increased.

The child welfare agency frequently stands in the place of parents, and the psychologist can offer many suggestions that will help in the home adjustment as well as the educational and vocational guidance of the child. Many children who first come under the care of social welfare agencies are disturbed and need various types of therapeutic treatment. The responsibility for the treatment program falls primarily upon the social worker, but the psychologist contributes much toward the understanding of the child through the interpretation of his behavior and the measurement of effects of treatment.

THE PRACTICE OF CLINICAL PSYCHOLOGY IN THE SECOND WORLD WAR

During the Second World War many clinical psychologists practiced in military sections and subsequently wrote concerning their experiences. Common assignments were in general and convalescent hospitals, induction centers, personnel centers, rehabilitation centers, and disciplinary barracks. Even a brief summary of the literature describing this work is impossible within the scope of this chapter. The analysis made by Hutt and Milton[51] indicates the widespread use of psychologists in clinical practice during the war and the type of duties they performed. Clinical psychologists were first commissioned in the Army in 1944 when almost 300 were elevated from the ranks. Others were assigned to the program after that date.[52] The study by Hutt and Milton was based upon the reports of 50 commissioned clinical psychologists who were on active duty in 1946 and concerned their activities from September, 1944, to April, 1946. At the beginning of this period these officers estimated 30.8 per cent of their time spent in giving individual psychological examinations and 12.8 per cent in guidance and therapy as compared with 34.9 per cent and 24.4 per cent, respectively, in those activities at the end of the period. It is considered significant that more than half of the time of these officers was devoted to two major professional responsibilities and that the trend was toward more guidance and therapy.

PRIVATE PRACTICE

For many years clinical psychologists have engaged in private practice apart from their regular employment using the diagnostic and treatment procedures appropriate for the type of case accepted. Some psychologists have worked in collaboration with physicians, particularly pediatricians and psychiatrists. In some large population centers, notably New York and Los Angeles, there has been an increasing number of psychologists who devote full time to private practice. The psychologist in private practice faces the difficult problem of determining whether treatment of the problems which come to him is within his area of competence. Therefore, only psychologists with a wide experience background should attempt private practice. They should maintain professional contacts with allied professions so that referrals of problems outside the psychologist's competence may be facilitated.

RESEARCH IN CLINICAL PSYCHOLOGY

Psychology in clinical practice is dependent upon continuous research[53] for the improvement and validation of diagnostic and treatment methods.[54] Training programs and job specifications for clinical psychologists at the professional levels have emphasized the responsibilities of the clinical psychologist in the research area.

[51] Hutt, Max L., and Milton, Emmette O., An Analysis of Duties Performed by Clinical Psychologists in the Army, *Amer. Psychol.*, 1947, 2, 52–56.
[52] *Ibid.*, p. 52.
[53] Schofield, William, Research in Clinical Psychology: 1949, *J. Clin. Psychol.*, 1950, 3, 234–237.
[54] Zubin, Joseph, Personality Research and Psychopathology as Related to Clinical Practice, *J. Abnorm. Soc. Psychol.*, 1949, 44, 14–21.

There is great public demand for the services of the clinical psychologist; and continued attention to problems of training, ethical practice, and research make a bright future for the practice of clinical psychology.

SUMMARY

Clinical practice in psychology deals with problems of behavior adjustment. The work of the clinical psychologist involves a combination of art and science. The basis for clinic practice lies in the use of scientifically proved techniques, but the effectiveness of the service rendered to the individual is dependent upon the experience and judgment of the clinician. Professional practice entails a cooperative relationship with other professional fields, such as psychiatry, medicine, education, and social work.

The training necessary for practice in clinical psychology consists of basic courses in psychology and the techniques of applied psychology. Internship under supervision is particularly important in the training of the clinical psychologist.

The diagnostic methods in clinical practice are interviews and standardized psychological tests that give quantitative and qualitative information about behavior. These techniques are used to obtain the individual's developmental history, present environmental influences, the present status of mental development, personality structure, aptitudes, interests, and abilities. Treatment techniques vary with the behavior problem at hand, the age, and the emotional status of the individual. Common treatment techniques include individual interview and group therapy, play therapy, and environmental manipulation. The latter procedure is primarily applicable to children and requires cooperation of parents, teachers, and others in carrying out a planned program.

Practice in clinical psychology began with children, and work with children continues to be one of the most extensive areas of practice. Child guidance clinics and school and community mental health clinics are concerned with both the correction of behavior problems and the prevention of behavior maladjustment by the encouragement of environmental circumstances which promote good mental hygiene.

Clinical psychologists are employed in penal and correctional institutions, hospitals, and out-patient clinics. The need for treatment facilities for neuropsychiatric patients during and following the Second World War created a great demand for clinical psychologists. Professional practice in neuropsychiatric service involves cooperation with psychiatrists, physicians, and psychiatric social workers in a diagnostic and treatment program.

The tendency to expand the treatment phase of clinical practice is evident in the literature describing psychological practice. The need for research to continue a sound basis for clinical practice is receiving increasing attention.

RECOMMENDED SUPPLEMENTARY READINGS

Bingham, Walter V.: *Aptitudes and Aptitude Testing,* Harper & Brothers, New York, 1937.

Brotemarkle, Robert A., *et al.: Clinical Psychology,* University of Pennsylvania Press, Philadelphia, 1931.

Fernald, G. M.: *Remedial Techniques in Basic School Subjects,* McGraw-Hill Book Company, Inc., New York, 1943.

Kelly, E. Lowell: Current Trends in Clinical Psychology, in W. Dennis (Ed.), *Current Trends in Psychology,* University of Pittsburgh Press, Pittsburgh, 1947.

Louttit, C. M.: *Clinical Psychology,* Harper & Brothers, New York, 1947.

Pennington, L. A., and Berg, Irwin A.: *An Introduction to Clinical Psychology,* The Ronald Press Company, New York, 1948.

Raimy, Victor C. (Ed.): *Training in Clinical Psychology,* Prentice-Hall, Inc., New York, 1950.

Rapaport, D.: The Future of Research in Clinical Psychology and Psychiatry, *Amer. Psychol.,* 1947, **2,** 167–172.

Richards, T. W.: *Modern Clinical Psychology,* McGraw-Hill Book Company, Inc., New York, 1946.

Rogers, Carl R.: *Client-centered Therapy,* Houghton Mifflin Company, Boston, 1951.

Rogers, Carl R.: *The Clinical Treatment of the Problem Child,* Houghton Mifflin Company, Boston, 1939.

Rosenzweig, Saul, and Kogan, Kate Levine: *Psychodiagnosis,* Grune & Stratton, Inc., New York, 1949.

Sears, Robert R. (Ed., special number): Clinical Psychology in the Military Services, *Psychol. Bull.,* 1944, **41,** No. 8.

Symposium: The Rorschach Method, *J. Consult. Psychol.,* 1943, **7,** No. 2, 63–126.

Thorne, F. C.: *Principles of Personality Counseling,* University of Vermont, Brandon, 1950.

Watson, Robert I: *Readings in the Clinical Method in Psychology,* Harper & Brothers, New York, 1949.

Chapter 10

PSYCHOLOGICAL EFFECTS OF
DIET AND DRUGS

It is not inaccurate to say that we are a product of what we eat and drink. Certainly behavior is affected by the chemical condition of the body which, in turn, is affected by the food we eat and the drugs we imbibe. When an individual is malnourished, he is psychologically a different person from when he is adequately nourished. It is more obvious, however, that an intoxicated individual is psychologically a different person from when he is sober. The psychologist is interested in both diet and drugs as factors which affect human behavior.

DIET

It is the usual practice in employment, in taking out life insurance, and in joining the armed forces to examine the physical condition of the applicants. Health is considered vitally important in almost every walk of life; yet little attention is given to one of the most fundamental factors in health—diet. Improper diet will soon produce poor health. Proper nutrition is too often neglected by those who recognize the importance of good health.

FACTS ABOUT DIET

Human behavior (both mental and physical) is possible only because a chemical process called "metabolism" transforms food into energy or muscular action. The unit of this energy transformation is the large calorie (the amount of heat required to raise the temperature of a kilogram of water one degree centigrade). Different foods contain different amounts of potential energy or calories, and different behavior requires different amounts of calorie consumption.

Table 10–1. Vitamins and Minerals, and Their Characteristics

Vitamins and minerals	Foods in which found	Deficiency symptoms
A Antibacteria Stored in body Destroyed by cooking	Milk fats, cream, butter Fish-liver oils Egg yolk Raw green vegetables (carrots, kale, spinach tomatoes, cheese, liver)	Infections of mucous membrane Sore eyes Sinus difficulties Kidney trouble Frequent colds Retarded growth Shortens life span Diarrhea
B (B₁) (thiamin) Antineurotic Must be eaten daily Not destroyed by cooking	Dried yeast Wheat germs Whole-grain foods Leafy vegetables Dried beans, peas Bran, spinach, egg yolk Whole milk, tomatoes Asparagus, liver	Poor appetite Poor digestion Constipation Nervousness Retarded growth
C (ascorbic acid) Antiscurvy Must be eaten daily Destroyed by cooking and drying	Citrus fruits (grapefruit, oranges, lemons) Raw green vegetables Fresh raw fruits (strawberries, pineapple) Tomatoes	Sore mouth Sore joints Retarded growth Bad teeth Anemia
D Antirickets Stored in body Not destroyed by cooking	Fish-liver oils Egg yolk Sunshine Viosterol Liver	Bowlegs Knock-knees Poor teeth
E Antisterility Stored in body Not destroyed by cooking	Most foods—especially in whole grains Leafy vegetables Fresh meats	Deficiency seldom occurs
G (B₂) (riboflavin) Essential for tissue respiration Not destroyed by cooking	Green vegetables Sea foods Dairy products Liver	Loss of hair Loss of weight Bodily weakness
P-P (nicotinic acid) Antipellagra Must be eaten daily Not destroyed by cooking	Dried yeast Liver Lean meat Wheat germs	Skin irritations and infections Poor appetite Red tongue Diarrhea Vomiting

Table 10–1. Vitamins and Minerals, and Their Characteristics (*Continued*)

Vitamins and minerals	Foods in which found	Deficiency symptoms
Calcium Required for bone development Not destroyed by cooking	Beans, oysters Cheese, cream, egg yolk Turnip tops, nuts, cauliflower, celery Kale	Poor development of bones Bad teeth Nose bleeding
Phosphorus Essential elements in all cells and in all body chemistry Not destroyed by cooking	Cheese, egg yolk Whole-grain meals Milk, lean meats Nuts, fish, carrots Spinach, tomatoes Cabbage	Retarded growth Poor appetite Loss of weight
Iron Essential for tissue respiration and formation of hemoglobin	Egg yolk, heart Oatmeal, kidney Whole wheat Dried beans	Low vitality Retarded growth Anemia
Iodine Necessary for normal function of thyroid gland	Cod-liver oil Sea foods Broccoli Iodized salt	Susceptible to infections Cretinism Myxedema

OTHER VITAMINS AND MINERALS

Vitamin B_6—Found in seed oils, lard, egg yolk, etc. Essential to skin health.

Vitamin K—Found in leafy vegetables, egg yolks, liver, etc. Important for blood coagulation.

Chlorine—Found in bread, cheese, oysters, etc. Essential for digestion and tissue retention of water.

Magnesium—Found in beans, raisins, whole grains, etc. Important for muscle action, bowel movement, etc.

Potassium—Found in dairy products, sea foods, liver, etc. Important in growth, digestion, and heart action.

Copper—Found in bran, cocoa, nuts, sea foods, etc. Important in growth of red blood cells and utilization of iron.

Foods contain three basic elements—carbohydrates (about 4 Cal. per g.), proteins (about 4 Cal. per g.), and fats (about 9 Cal. per g.). Milk, for example, contains 4.9 per cent carbohydrates, 3.5 per cent protein, and 3.9 per cent fats. One hundred grams of milk (about 3.5 oz.) contain 19.6 Cal. of carbohydrate food value, 14 Cal. of protein food value, and 35 Cal. of fat food value—a total of 68.6 Cal. of food value in 3.5 oz. of milk.

Food experts recommend that 10 to 15 per cent of food intake should consist of proteins, 60 to 75 per cent of carbohydrates, and 15 to 25 per cent of fats, depending on the work being performed, the size of the person, the season of the year, etc.

Another important consideration in determining food value is the vitamin content. The function of each vitamin and the foods that contain each are shown in Table 10–1.

It is obvious that a restricted diet soon has a detrimental effect on some phase of body function. Good diet is not merely eating what taste preferences indicate but rather eating those foods that contain the food elements necessary for health.

Many people have foolish ideas about food which lead them to restricted diets. The following list of statements corrects some of these more common misconceptions regarding food.

1. Nuts do not possess all the essential food elements.
2. Whole-wheat bread supplies more vitamins and minerals but less energy than white bread.
3. Raw vegetables should be taken in moderate quantity. Excessive amounts are injurious.
4. Salt improves food value as well as taste and is very essential in hot weather.
5. Acid (sour) fruits cause an alkaline reaction.
6. It is not harmful to eat sea foods with dairy products. Fish and milk do mix.
7. Aluminum, iron, and tin cooking utensils do not cause food poisoning.
8. Canned food is not contaminated by being left in the can if kept cool.

To maintain life, it is necessary to eat enough food to supply 1500 to 1800 Cal. per day, depending on the size of the individual and his basal metabolism. Any activity he may engage in requires more calories. The first 1500 to 1800 Cal. are sometimes called "life calories," and those beyond are called "work calories." While a shoemaker can get along on 800 to 1000 work calories per day, a carpenter needs 1200 to 1500. The calories necessary for various types of work are shown in Table 10–2.

Table 10–2. Calories per Hour per Pound Necessary for Various Types of Activity

Activity	Calories per Hour per Pound	Activity	Calories per Hour per Pound
Sleeping	0.43	Walking, 2.6 miles per hour	1.56
Awake, lying still	0.50	Walking, 3.75 miles per hour	1.95
Sitting at rest	0.65	Walking downstairs	2.36
Reading aloud	0.69	Sawing wood	3.12
Standing at attention	0.74	Swimming	3.25
Dressing and undressing	0.77	Running, 5.3 miles per hour	3.70
Typewriting rapidly	0.91	Walking, 5.3 miles per hour	4.22
Sweeping (38 strokes per minute)	1.09	Walking upstairs	7.18
Shoemaking	1.17		

A man weighing 150 lb. engaged in shoemaking would need 1400 work calories for an 8-hour day in addition to his 1500 life calories ($150 \times 1.17 = 175.5 \times 8 = 1404.$)

FACTS ABOUT DEFICIENT DIETS

Almost any investigation of the food habits of a group of people will show diet deficiencies. Table 10–3 summarizes 10 such surveys and

Table 10–3. Ten Typical Studies Showing the Percentage of Workmen Getting Adequate, Borderline, and Inadequate Food Content

Studies	Nature of food content		
	Adequate	Borderline	Inadequate
1	8	21	71
2	14	22	64
3	9	36	55
4	4	21	75
5	20	58	22
6	2	11	87
7	14	46	40
8	26	48	26
9	39	42	19
10	52	45	3
Average....	18.8	35.0	46.2

gives the percentages of the people studied who ate foods containing adequate, borderline, and inadequate food count. Judging from this, not more than one-fifth of the population eat proper foods and almost one-half are being starved by eating foods which do not contain the proper elements.

An excellent study of the relation of calorie intake to work output was made of slave labor by Krout and Fuller[1] in Germany during Hitler's regime. When workmen were fed 820 work calories (in addition to the basal life calories) per day, they averaged 1.5 tons per day in a shoveling operation. When they were fed 1300 work calories, they averaged 2.2 tons per day. Also, their body weight increased 8.8 lb. per man. Then, with the same food (1300 work calories) cigarettes were offered as bonus beginning only at 3 tons per day. The work output was increased to an average of 3.4 tons per day but at a loss of 7.7 lb. per man in body weight.

The same authors verified this study by another study using coal miners as subjects. With 1200 work calories per day, 7.0 tons of coal were mined. This was 170 work calories per ton. When the work

[1] Kraut, H. A., and Fuller, E. A., Calorie Intake and Industrial Output, *Science*, 1946, **104**, 495–497.

calories were increased to 1600 per day, the work output increased to 9.6 tons per day. This was only 155 work calories per ton. However, there was a loss in body weight which was corrected by adding 400 more calories to the daily food intake. It was thus determined that 2000 work calories are necessary for efficient coal mining and the maintenance of body weight.

The authors concluded:

As a result of our investigations, it is clear that every professional activity requires a fixed amount of calories. No activity can be continuously greater than in accordance with the calorie intake; otherwise, loss of weight is induced and this lowers capacity, finally stopping work entirely. A regular control of body weight in industrial workers is, therefore, a good measure of their calorie supply. The output on varying rations is unconsciously adapted to the available work calorie by the worker himself, the body weight being kept constant.

Borsook[2] studied the relation of vitamin food supplement to absenteeism and merit rating with a group of aircraft workers in California during the Second World War. The experimental group was given vitamin capsules 5 days a week for 1 year. A control group was given placebo capsules, and a third group was checked to determine the effects of the placebo. The groups were equated in age, seniority, and merit.

As the year progressed, the vitamin group became superior to both the placebo and the base control groups in every respect. Absences were reduced 18.6 per cent, nonmilitary terminations reduced 38 per cent, and merit ratings increased. The gain of the vitamin group over the other two was 10.5 working days per man-year. Some of these results are shown in Fig. 10–1.

It is obvious from these data that deficient diet is not only an insufficient amount of food but an insufficient amount of the proper food elements. Both the amount of food and the composition of food are important in nutrition.

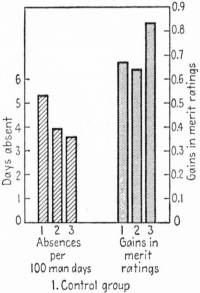

FIG. 10–1. Effects of vitamins on absenteeism and work merit.

[2] Borsook H., Nutritional Status of Aircraft Workers, *The Milbank Memorial Fund Rept.* 23, 1945.

ADEQUATE DIET

An adequate diet consists of 1800 base calories per day plus the work calories necessary for the activities performed. It should be composed of 10 to 15 per cent proteins, 60 to 75 per cent carbohydrates, and 15 to 25 per cent fats. There should be 3000 international units of vitamin A, 300 units of vitamin B_1, 1000 units of vitamin C, 500 units of vitamin D, 450 of vitamin G (or B_2), 15 mg. of nicotinic acid, and 70 kg. of various minerals. This can be obtained by eating daily

1 egg
1 serving of meat
2 servings of potatoes or rice, two or three cooked vegetables, and one green or raw vegetable or salad
1 serving of fruit
1 pint of milk

The U.S. Department of Agriculture[3] has listed seven basic food groups which should be represented in the daily diet of everyone. They are as follows:

Group 1—Green and yellow vegetables
Group 2—Citrus fruits, tomatoes, salad greens
Group 3—Potatoes and fruits
Group 4—Milk
Group 5—Meats, fish, eggs, nuts
Group 6—Breads and cereals
Group 7—Butter or margarine

A practical division of a food budget may be stated as follows:

One-fifth for vegetables and fruits
One-fifth for milk and cheese
One-fifth for meats, fish, and eggs
One-fifth for bread and cereals
One-fifth for sugar and other food supplements

A food budget that spends equal amounts for fruits, dairy products, and meats can then vary other food expenditures according to taste and still not be far wrong. Another good rule is to eat a wide variety of foods and trust to nature's wide distribution of food elements to provide an adequate diet.

There are two problems in putting a proper food diet across. First, it is necessary to get the housewife (who cooks most of the food eaten in this and other countries) to prepare a proper diet; and, second, it is necessary to get people to develop taste likes for proper foods. This

[3] Goodhart, R. S., *Industrial Feeding Management,* U.S. Department of Agriculture, War Food Administration, April, 1945.

is a problem of education which is taking place too slowly but with considerable effort on the part of the government, schools, and others who are sensitive to the importance of diets which include all the essential food elements. Literature on nutrition is dispensed free by many organizations including the following:

U.S. Department of Agriculture
U.S. Public Health Service
The National Research Council
American Institute of Banking
American Meat Institute
American Red Cross
H. J. Heinz Co.
Metropolitan Life Insurance Co.
National Association of Manufacturers
Westinghouse Electric Corp.

DRUGS

A drug is any chemical that is used as a medicine or in the composition of a medicine. Unfortunately, many chemicals that have beneficial medical uses also are used in ways that are harmful. Alcohol, for example, may be prescribed by the physician for the benefit of the patient. It may also be taken without need and in such quantities as to produce a toxic state. Many drugs, such as alcohol, are habit-forming and lead to states of addiction. The proper use of drugs is beneficial to mankind while the improper use of them is harmful.

While some drug addiction (including that to alcohol) is due to environmental circumstances, such as being prescribed by a physician, most drug habits are compensation for some unrelated maladjustment which keeps the subject in a constant state of tension. He then uses the drug because it gives him temporary relief from his troubles. (This has been discussed in Chap. 6.)

ALCOHOL

The wide nonmedical use of alcohol in various forms among all people and at all levels of culture is due to its effects on the nervous system and the resultant feelings of euphoria. The mild toxic state produced by alcohol releases those inhibitions demanded by our social standards and creates a temporary state of amnesia for any unsolved problems of adjustment. Alcohol enables one to go on a short psychological vacation. While these vacations become habitual and often harmful, they are widely practiced in the United States. It is estimated that at least 50,000,000 are regular in their drinking—perhaps half of these to a harmful degree. At least a million people could be classed as confirmed alcoholics, and a half million of these are alcoholic psychotics. They make up about 10 per cent of the first admissions to our mental hospitals.

Alcohol is not a stimulant (except for some individuals and for short periods not exceeding 30 minutes) but a depressant. While it makes the drinker feel better, he is actually less efficient both mentally and physically than he is without alcohol. Even small amounts (an ounce of whisky or a bottle of beer) produce muscular incoordination, reduce sensory discrimination, and increase errors in judgment. Whatever may be said for or against the use of alcohol, it is not a stimulant and it does not increase efficiency.

While different individuals are affected in different ways and in different degrees by given amounts of alcohol, an over-all picture of the effects of alcohol is facetiously indicated in Fig. 10–2.

2 oz. of whiskey or 2 btls. beer	6 oz. of whiskey or 6 btls. beer	Excessive amounts of alcohol in any form				
Not legally influenced	Influence varies	Everyone is influenced				
Dry and decent	Delighted and devilish	Delinquent and disgusting	Dizzy and delirious	Dazed and dejected	Dead drunk	Dead — period
0.05% or less	0.10%	0.18%	0.22%	0.32%	0.4%	0.5% or more

FIG. 10–2. Effects of various amount of alcohol in the blood.

Alcohol has a high food value (about 200 Cal. per oz.), but the body can use it at the rate of only about ⅓ oz. per hour. This means that, if alcohol is limited to 1 oz. every 3 hours, the body could use it as food. However, it is so deficient in vitamin content that it could have value only as a food supplement.

Overuse of Alcohol. Alcoholism has four major effects—pathological intoxication, delirium tremens, alcoholic hallucinosis, and Karsakow's psychosis.

1. *Pathological intoxication* is an extreme reaction to alcohol characterized by disorientation and/or homicidal rage. Crimes of violence and sex crimes are frequently committed while in this state. Individuals with such low tolerance for alcohol may not be habitual alcoholics, but rather occasional drinkers whose physiological condition sometimes reacts acutely even to a small amount of alcohol. Pathological intoxication frequently terminates in a period of deep sleep followed by amnesia for happenings while intoxicated.

2. *Delirium tremens* is a condition of muscle tremor and a state of delirium which usually occurs in the older person who has long been an alcoholic. Hallucinations are vivid and disorientation is frequently complete. Delirium tremens is usually preceded by a period of restlessness and apprehension which causes the subject to "quit drinking" temporarily. The state of delirium may last for several days and terminates with a long sleep. The subject is then weakened and scared and may temporarily reform.

3. *Alcoholic hallucinations* are usually auditory (hearing voices) and center around the subject's repressed adjustment problems. He fears punishments of an imagined nature for his own violations of his personal code of ethics. He may become terror-stricken and attempt suicide. Alcohol is usually but an incidental factor in the struggles of a maladjusted personality. After days and even weeks of hallucinations, the subject slowly becomes oriented and objective, though remorseful and often without insight into his real problems.

4. *Karsakow's psychosis* is more prevalent after the age of fifty and with women. There is loss of memory, especially for recent events, and apparent hallucination due to errors in attempts to fill in memory gaps. There is reduced ability to form new associations and to relate new happenings with past happenings. Again, alcohol is incidental to another condition. There is a definite deficiency of vitamin B_1, due perhaps to the long use of alcohol in substitution for a balanced food diet. There is usually poor recovery from this affliction.

No discussion of the overuse of alcohol would be complete without mention of Alcoholics Anonymous. This is an organization of ex-alcoholics and others who are attempting to break their habits of using alcohol in excess. It operates as a form of group psychotherapy in which members try to help each other. There are social activities and entertainments to fill the time of those who drink when they have nothing else to do. Problems that drive men to drink are diagnosed and discussed. Each member is made to feel that he is among understanding friends who have been through similar experiences themselves.

About half of those who join are cured of alcoholism within a few weeks; about half of those remaining are helped but relapse; and 25 per cent remain alcoholic. Fundamental to Alcoholics Anonymous is the admission by the subject that he is licked and needs help. The cure is then the cooperative effort of the subject himself and his new friends.

NARCOTICS

The earliest drugs referred to in primitive records were the narcotics, especially opium. Just as today, they were used both for medical purposes and also for the pleasant state of intoxication they produced. Addiction to the narcotics accounts for over half of all drug habituation.

The physician properly prescribes their use when necessary to deaden pain and produce relaxation and sleep.

The narcotic drugs that are most frequently taken in excess are opium (morphine, heroin, codeine) cocaine, and the hemp derivatives (marijuana and hashish).

Opium (Morphine, Heroin). In his *Confessions of an Opium Eater,* DeQuincey described the intoxicated state of dream as follows:

I seemed every night to descend literally into chasms and sunless abysses, depths below depths, from which it seemed hopeless that I could ever reascend. . . . Buildings, landscapes, etc. were exhibited in proportions so vast as the bodily eye is not fitted to receive. Space swelled and was amplified to an extent of unutterable infinity. . . . I seemed sometime to live for 70 or 100 years in one night; nay, sometimes had feelings representative of a millennium passed in that time or of a duration far beyond the limits of any human experience.

This opiate state lasts from 4 to 6 hours and constitutes the psychological reason for craving the drug after the habit is formed. Usually, opium addiction begins as a means of escape from some intolerable adjustment problem which has literally "driven" the subject to opium (see Chap. 6).

The opium addict needs the drug daily or he experiences marked symptoms of mental and physical distress. He becomes nonsocial, depressed, irritable, apprehensive, and may even develop hallucinations. He refuses to eat or sleep; he becomes tense and even violent. After 4 or 5 days, this condition passes and the subject returns to a more normal state. However, these periods of intense craving for the drug are recurrent.

Continued use of opium results in both mental and physical deterioration. Because its possession is illegal, the addict soon becomes associated with criminals and is regarded as a physical and mental degenerate.

In treatment, two factors must be considered—the opium habit and the maladjustment that caused the person to begin the use of the drug. The effects of opium are apparently not permanent, and reformed addicts are able to return to normal patterns of living.

Cocaine. Like opium, cocaine produces a state of euphoria but, unlike opium, it is a sexual excitant. The subject does not become physically addicted to it as with opium, but he has all the psychological symptoms of drug deprivation. Because sexual promiscuity usually accompanies its use, cocaine is often considered to be a more dangerous drug than opium. Like opium addiction though, some personality maladjustment is usually at the basis of its use.

Hemp Derivatives (Marijuana, Hashish). It is doubtful if marijuana should be called a drug since it has no value in the practice of medicine. It is a product of the flowering top of the hemp plant (otherwise used for making rope) and a resin called "cannabine" is its active principle. It is usually smoked, although it may be chewed or drunk as a tea. The neural synapses are affected by its use, producing feelings of elation and illusory enchantment. It was erroneously thought to be a sex excitant, but authorities now believe that its reduction of inhibitions results in increased sex freedom with no increase in the sex drive. There is marked loss of orientation in both space and time, and a pleasant feeling of floating or drifting.

Probably the widest use of marijuana is among young people in the form of cigarettes called "reefers." Because of the feelings of self-confidence and personal adequacy produced by the drug, sex advances are made, cars are driven recklessly, conversation is loud, those in authority are insulted, and behavior in general is inconsistent with usual personality patterns. In fact, personality habits are permanently affected by continued use of marijuana and changes in personality are sometimes marked.

There are no harmful physical aftereffects of even a continued use of marijuana and no addiction as there is with opium. A psychological habit of want for its use is built up but no physiological need for it.

The remedy for marijuana addiction would seem to be to make the drug impossible to attain.

THE BARBITURATES

There are many derivations of barbituric acid which vary only in the trade name. Phenobarbital, luminal, veronal, differ from each other only in minor respects. Even the sodium salts of this group (sodium amytal, dilantin sodium) have essentially the same function as the parent acid.

In general, they are depressants or sleep-producing. The physician prescribes them to reduce nervousness and tension. Large dosage produces coma and even death. They are sometimes used with mental patients to break down inhibitions and facilitate psychoanalysis. They are used with epileptics to reduce the frequency and intensity of seizures. One study[4] of 118 patients with *grand mal* attacks found that 58 per cent were completely relieved by dilantin and 27 per cent showed marked improvement. Of 74 patients with *petit mal* attacks, 35 per cent were completely relieved and 49 per cent showed reduction of attacks.

[4] Reported by C. Landis and M. M. Bolles, *Abnormal Psychology*, p. 371, The Macmillan Company, New York, 1950.

DRUGS THAT STIMULATE

The drugs so far mentioned are depressants, although the release of inhibitions often makes the individual appear to be stimulated. Alcohol especially is often erroneously considered to be a stimulant. Some commonly used stimulating drugs are benzedrine sulphate, coffee, tea, and cocoa.

Benzedrine sulphate has an effect on the body very similar to that of adrenalin (a secretion of the medulla of the adrenal gland) except that it does not dilate the vascular system. Heart action is increased and blood pressure goes up. The nervous system especially is stimulated and feelings of fatigue are eliminated. An oral dosage of 10 to 30 mg. of benzedrine increases alertness, elevates mood, reduces fatigue, and restores self-confidence and mental alertness. It is useful when long periods of wakefulness are essential.

Carl and Turner[5] compared the effects of 10 mg. of benzedrine with a control dose of lactose on 143 adults. Benzedrine increased mental and psychomotor efficiency for 4 hours, although larger amounts (20 mg.) did not have a favorable effect. It is probable that benzedrine increases alertness and effort without affecting ability. Barmack[6] found that scores on the Otis Mental Ability tests were not affected by a dose of 10 mg. of benzedrine.

It is a non-habit-forming drug and does not have uniform effect on all individuals. It is used by the Air Force when long periods of wakefulness are important. It has doubtful value except to inhibit feelings of fatigue and sleepiness. It has much the same effect as coffee except that taking it (usually in tablets or capsules) is not such a pleasurable experience.

The *beverages*—coffee, tea, and cocoa—all have about the same effect on those who have formed habits of their use. The caffine of coffee, the theophylline of tea, and the theobromine of cocoa, are in such small amounts in a cup of beverage that the habit of their use is harmless. It is generally agreed that they are all stimulants and increase feelings of euphoria. Most experimental studies indicate that performance, both mental and physical, is improved, although it is doubtful if ability is increased. The subject just feels more like expending effort and accomplishing the job. He is neither stronger, quicker, nor more intelligent. He is just more awake, feels less fatigued, and expends more effort to achieve his goods.

If the habitual use of these stimulants (benzedrine sulphate, caffine, theophylline, and theobromine) is harmful to the human body, it is

[5] Carl, G. P., and Turner, W. D., The Effects of Benzedrine Sulphate on Performance in Psychometric Examinations, *J. Psychol.*, 1939, 8, 165–216.

[6] Barmack, J. E., The Effects of Benzedrine Sulphate on Boredom and Other Factors, *J. Psychol.*, 1933, 5, 125–133.

certainly a very slowly acting harm. They do not produce toxic states as do most other drugs. They do not release inhibitions and so are not used as psychological compensations. Their overuse may cause sleep deprivation, but even this is unusual and remedied by a reduction in their use. The beverage habit is not so much a need for the effects of the drugs as it is an enjoyment of social contacts and relaxation while they are being taken. Drinking coffee or tea affords a psychological justification for a short rest and conversation with friends.

TOBACCO

Tobacco is not used as a medicine or in the composition of medicine, although its active principle, *nicotine,* is appropriately classed as a drug. Nicotine is a poisonous alkaloid and makes a very effective insecticide. However, in the use of tobacco—whether smoked, chewed, or snuffed —a negligible amount of nicotine enters the system. In fact, nicotine is destroyed in smoking and even traces of it can be found only in the smoke of very rapidly burning cigarettes. Whatever the detrimental effects of smoking may be, they cannot be attributed to nicotine.

Table 10–4. Per Cent Gain or Loss in Various Functions as an Effect of Pipe Smoking

	Smokers	Non-smokers
Pulse rate..............................	+ 6.62	+ 5.81
Hand steadiness.........................	−21.8	−28.1
Fatigue.................................	0.2	+16.2
Reading reaction time....................	+ 0.7	+ 0.55
Rate of learning........................	+ 2.2	+ 2.8
Adding, speed...........................	+ 4.71	− 3.11
Memory span............................	− 3.66	− 5.12
Adding, accuracy (doubtful differences).....	− 1.5	−22.66

One of the most carefully controlled studies of the effects of smoking was made by Hull.[7] He investigated the effects of smoking a pipe on both physical and mental reactions of nine nonsmokers and ten habitual smokers. He first constructed a nontobacco control pipe which electrically heated the bowl so that warm air could be drawn through the stem. The subjects were all blindfolded and "smoked" either an already lighted pipe with tobacco or the experimental pipe with heated air. After "smoking," various tests were made and the tobacco-smoking days were compared with the "hot-air" days. Table 10–4 gives the results of this study.

[7] Hull, C. L., The Influence of Tobacco Smoking on Mental and Motor Efficiency, *Psychol. Monogr.,* 1924, **33,** 150.

For both smokers and nonsmokers, pipe smoking increases pulse rate and reduces hand steadiness. It increased muscular fatigue for the non-smokers and probably diminished accuracy in adding numbers. The speed of adding numbers was somewhat increased for the smokers but diminished for the nonsmokers.

The effect of smoking cigarettes on finger tremor was studied by Edwards.[8] He found that smoking without inhaling had little effect on

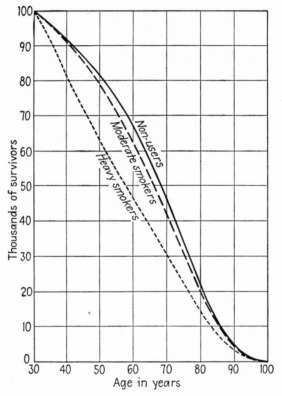

FIG. 10–3. Survivals per hundred thousand after the age of thirty for smokers and nonsmokers; (a) nonusers (solid line), (b) moderate smokers (dash line), (c) heavy smokers (dotted line).

hand steadiness, while inhaling and even breathing cigarette smoke in a smoke-filled room increase finger tremor.

Maris[9] reports a study in which six habitual smokers were given a battery of tests after smoking regular cigarettes, after smoking corn-silk cigarettes, and after having intravenous injections of nicotine. The corn

[8] Edwards, A. S., The Effects of Smoking on Tremor, *J. Appl. Psychol.*, 1948, **32**, 150–158.

[9] Maris, R., The Facts about Smoking, *Hygeia*, 1944, **22**, 740.

silk produced negligible results. The tobacco cigarettes and the injections of nicotine caused an increase in heart rate (36 beats average), blood pressure (14 points), and basal metabolism.

Pearl[10] studied the longevity of heavy and light smokers with that of nonsmokers. His results are shown in Fig. 10–3. Note that life expectancy at all ages from thirty to sixty is greater for both nonsmokers and moderate smokers than for heavy smokers. Pearl recognized that the heavy smokers are probably nervous personalities who are usually tense and would not live long even if they did not smoke.

SUMMARY

Good nutrition is more than eating enough food to satisfy hunger. In fact, the satisfaction of hunger is unimportant if the body has an adequate supply of essential food elements. Stock farmers now feed their animals according to intelligently planned diets. In fact, they are so fertilizing their pastures that grasses will contain proper amounts of the various food elements. Unfortunately, those same farmers are not so carefully and intelligently feeding their children. As a nation, we do not recognize that enough food may not be adequate nutrition. A small balanced menu is better than great amounts of foods that omit essential elements. The chemical needs of the body are not satisfied by civilized man any better than they were by his primitive ancestors. How and what to eat is still an unsolved problem in so-called "civilized cultures."

Drugs are the chemical elements in medicines which, if used properly, reduce disease and prolong human life. They are the products of civilization. However, because they produce psychological states of unreality, many people who are unable to enjoy life as it is take drugs to escape from their troubles if only in unreality. Alcohol is the drug most commonly used for this purpose. Unfortunately, the continued use of most drugs is harmful to the body. Physical condition deteriorates with the duration of addiction. Drugs are another product of civilization, the uses of which "both bless and burn."

RECOMMENDED SUPPLEMENTARY READINGS

Coleman, J. C.: *Abnormal Psychology and Modern Life,* Chap. 10, Scott, Foresman & Company, Chicago, 1950.

Poffenberger, A. T.: *Principles of Applied Psychology,* Chap. 11, Appleton-Century-Crofts, Inc., New York, 1942.

Quarterly Journal of Studies in Alcohol.

Sherman, H. C.: *Chemistry of Food and Nutrition,* 6th ed., The Macmillan Company, New York, 1941.

[10] Pearl, R., The Search for Longevity, *Sci. Mon., N.Y.,* 1938, **46,** 462–483.

Chapter 11

CRIME AND CRIME DETECTION[1]

Nearly everyone is interested in crime. There are those who deliberately make a career of it; those who are forced into it; and those who live by the attempt to suppress it. The newspapers, the movies, and the radio commercialize its dramatic appeal. Businessmen and politicians are accused of compromising with it. The rest of us, when our attention is directed to crime by some highly publicized offense or one that strikes close to home, fear or resent the criminal. Few, however, understand the social behavior we call crime or the psychological mechanisms that operate to produce the criminal and crime.

CRIME DEFINED

Crime is essentially a legal term. Briefly stated, it signifies "an act forbidden and made punishable by law."[2] Unlawful intent, or *mens rea*,

[1] This chapter was written by Dr. David B. Rogers, Professor of Sociology in the University of Pittsburgh.

[2] Taft, Donald R., *Criminology*, pp. 4ff., The Macmillan Company, New York, 1942.

300

is frequently an important condition to the establishment of guilt. On the other hand, the desire to do wrong is not an essential condition. While in some crimes specific intent is necessary, many minor crimes do not require that the lawbreaker shall have maliciously or willfully or knowingly violated the law. This is true of a growing class of technical violations of laws ordering our economic activities, the use of the automobile, and legal controls over activities related to our growing technological culture.

The criminal is a convicted person "whose behavior does not follow the general pattern approved by law-abiding society."[3]

The criminal code does not operate as an effective social control apart from certain individuals and groups who enforce or interpret it. The police decide whom to arrest and which laws shall be enforced. The prosecuting attorneys, for reasons that may have to do with political or personal ambitions, select the cases that are to be tried, and the courts, by their interpretations, give the written law its meaning and effectiveness. Exerting influence on all of these is public opinion. In our type of society, officials, responsive to the popular will, are most energetic in enforcing those laws that, when neglected, create public resentment. Since our legislatures are constantly enacting new laws and rarely repeal an outmoded law, it follows that the American community can, and does, get from the resulting confusion only the kind of law enforcement it demands. Actually, then, crimes are violations of those laws that are enforced.

CAUSES OF CRIME

The behavior of the criminal is unique for only one reason. It is done in violation of the law. A general psychological explanation of *criminal* behavior is equally applicable to *all* human behavior. Any causal explanation must be found, then, in (1) the selective factors operating to produce the personality of the criminal as it is *at the moment the crime is committed*, and (2) the *specific combination of factors* that constitutes the stimulating situation to which he responds. No two personalities are identical, nor is the personality of the same individual identical from moment to moment. Neither is the same environment the same in its effect on any two individuals. Obviously, then, no two crimes are the same, and, contrary to the historic approach to the study of crime and the theoretical assumptions that underlie our contemporary methods of dealing with crime, we should concentrate on *studying and treating criminals, not crimes.*

While a summary of the literature on the causes of crime leaves the critical student without the kind of answers he would like, it is useful

[3] Vold, George V., in Emerson P. Schmidt (Ed.), *Man and Society*, p. 258, Prentice-Hall, Inc., New York, 1938.

to show how "many definite and foolish notions have been accepted." Among such theories are attempts to establish as the cause of crime the machinations of Satan, atavism, heredity, and such single-factor explanations as imitation, psychological obsessions, emotional instability, feeble-mindedness, epilepsy, degeneracy, and particularistic biological, economic, and social causes. The very profusion of theories suggests that an understanding of crime must be sought in the study of specific cases.

Modern attempts at the objective study of crime are usually said to have begun with the work of the Italian military physician, Cesare Lombroso (1836–1909).[4] Basing his study on the anthropometry and physiognomy of 5,907 convicts, he concluded that the typical criminal could be identified by certain physical stigmata such as a low, retreating forehead, heavy superorbital ridges, a heavy jaw and an atavistic chin, and in extremes in body hairiness or its absence and sensitivity to pain. These he thought indicated an atavistic hereditary type. In 1913, Dr. Charles Goring, Physician of His Majesty's Prisons, published a refutation of Lombroso's theory in *The English Convict*. Using Lombroso's methods, but checking the measurements of 3,000 convicts, who were all recidivists, against various other groups, he demonstrated that there is no set of physical characteristics of criminals that is not equally characteristic of the general population, except that (in his sample) the convicts were not so tall, weighed less, and had poorer school records than his sample of noncriminals. These last observations suggest traits of the criminal that may be the result of a criminal career as well as its cause.

An important contribution of the Italian school, especially the work of Enrico Ferri (1856–1928), was that, for students of criminal causation who wish to be realistic, it shattered the fallacy of free will and moral responsibility. But even today, in the light of modern psychological research, most laymen and public administrators see no reason for discarding our present methods of treating criminals—methods that are rooted in this discredited doctrine.[5]

This kind of conservatism among laymen is not so amazing as is the survival of the will to discover support for ancient superstitions among

[4] Lombroso, Cesare, *Crime: Its Causes and Remedies* (Modern Criminal Science Series), Little, Brown & Company, Boston, 1911.

Although Lombroso was not the first to call attention to atypical physical traits in relation to criminality, his works did focus attention on the study of the individual offender. See Lindesmith, Alfred, and Levin, Yale, The Lombrosian Myth in Criminology, *Amer. J. Sociol.,* 1937, **42,** 635–671.

[5] A recent attempt to revive the psychophysical theory in psychology is found in Sheldon's work. See *The Varieties of Human Physique* by William H. Sheldon in collaboration with S. S. Stevens and W. B. Tucker, Harper & Brothers, New York, 1940.

contemporary scholars. In *Crime and the Man,* published in 1939,[6] Hooton has given specious credibility to the Lombrosian theory. Reviewing Hooton's work, E. H. Sutherland has shown it to be faulty in the sample of criminals used, the insignificance of the differences noted, the inadequacy of the sample of noncriminals, the arbitrary and indefensible assignment of superior and inferior traits, the confusion of traits that are inherited with those that are not, and failure to consider differences in laws and enforcement policies in different jurisdictions.[7]

Perhaps the basic fallacy in all attempts to relate criminality to physical characteristics of the criminal is the implication that the individual's social behavior can be directly caused by the possession of a physical trait or combination of traits without reference to the part that trait may have played in the development of his social attitudes and habits. The reasons for these are to be found largely in the history of the *responses of others to him* that are *related by him* to the trait or traits in question. There is also the problem of explaining the behavior of those who possess the trait but do not become criminals. There is yet to be found any single physical trait or combination of traits that is discovered exclusively in criminals.

A further difficulty is faced in the fact that changes in the physical traits of individuals are not correlated with changes in group attitudes and laws that make the offender a criminal. Take the case of a naturalized Italian who spent his youth in a society where making and selling wine was as morally right as producing and selling buttermilk is in the United States. When the Prohibition Amendment was passed he became a criminal. When it was repealed he was an honest man once more. But throughout this series of changes in the definition of crime his hereditary endowment remained unchanged, and probably his physical, mental, emotional, economic, and social conditions did not change in any way that could be causally related to his temporary criminality.

PERSONAL FACTORS

Students of criminal behavior who examine research evidence objectively are in agreement that *criminals are made and not born.* They behave as they do primarily because they have been subjected during their lifetime "to influences which encourage criminal behavior."

The range of criminal acts is so great and the variation in the specific combination of the personal and environmental factors, as they are discovered in each act, so vast that any statistical summary of the

[6] Hooton, Earnest A., *Crime and the Man,* Harvard University Press, Cambridge, Mass., 1939.

[7] *J. Crim. Law Criminol.,* April, 1939, pp. 911–914.

traits of convicts can be only suggestive in throwing light on the problem of understanding any specific act of crime. Case studies like *Brothers in Crime,* edited by Clifford Shaw,[8] describe actual patterns of factors in individual cases. While it must be recognized that neither the case study nor the statistical summary gives satisfactory evidence on which to generalize, each has value when used with critical understanding.

It is important to remember that any descriptive factor, as age, sex, or marital condition, may be important in one act of crime and irrelevant in another; it may be tied in with other factors in one situation but may have no significance in another; and for the same individual, it may have one significance in the etiology of a murder and a different value as a causal factor in a theft. It is evident, then, that the percentage of all convicted persons, of a given age, who are found guilty of murder does not indicate the importance of age in any one case of murder. Nor can it be used, without supporting evidence, in comparing murder with other crimes. The causal pattern in each criminal act is unique. In the statistical table age units have been taken out of context and thrown together as if they were all of equal significance. The data presented in the following paragraphs give what Professor Gillin has called "the physiognomy of crime"—the profile of crime, not the diagnosis of any one crime.

Age of Criminals. Data on arrests and commitments to penal institutions indicate fairly accurately the age distribution of the criminal population. The United States Bureau of Census regularly compiles statistics on prisoners in State and Federal prisons, and the Federal Bureau of Investigation collects similar data for persons arrested.

Age at commitment, of course, represents a time lag of several months (in some cases, years) following arrest. Arrest data, on the other hand, are corrupted by the large numbers of "suspects," arrested in police "drag nets." When a serious crime is committed the police, lacking definite leads, "pick up" all persons who have police records of former arrests for the type of crime under investigation. After appearing in a "line-up," where witnesses of the crime attempt to identify suspects, nearly all, if not all, such "arrested" persons are released. They may be reported, however, in arrest statistics.

The median age of all felons received from court in State and Federal prisons reported in 1946 was 26.6, compared with 28.0 years in 1942.[9] The intervening years showed a slight but regular decline. This

[8] Shaw, Clifford (Ed.), *Brothers in Crime,* University of Chicago Press, Chicago, 1938.
[9] *Prisoners in State and Federal Prisons and Reformatories, 1946,* p. 22, Bureau of the Census, Washington, D.C., 1948.

trend may reflect the influence of the war on the type of prisoners received by the Federal prisons (draft dodgers and deserters). Commitments in 1946 were concentrated in the age group twenty to twenty-four years (see Table 11–1). In this group were 27.6 per cent of all

Table 11–1. Felony Prisoners Received from Court, by Age and Sex, for the United States, 1946
(Per cent distribution)

	Male	Female
All ages.................	100.0	100.0
Under 15 years...........	0.1	0.1
15–19....................	16.3	15.3
20–24....................	27.6	29.4
25–29....................	18.4	18.5
30–34....................	12.6	11.9
35–39....................	9.3	10.7
40–44....................	6.2	6.3
45–49....................	4.3	4.2
50–54....................	2.4	1.9
55–59....................	1.4	0.9
60–64....................	0.7	0.3
65–69....................	0.4	0.5
70 years and over........	0.3	

males, and 29.4 per cent of all females. The crime rate decreases rapidly in the age groups over twenty-five years. Convicts of all ages over thirty-five years total only 24.9 per cent of all prisoners. This is less than the proportion in the 5-year modal group (27.7 per cent) who are twenty to twenty-four years of age.

The median age of misdemeanants in 1942 was 38.9 years while that of felons was only 28.0 years. Misdemeanors include such offenses as disorderly conduct, drunkenness, and vagrancy. All prisoners committed for less than 6 months are here classed as misdemeanants. The more serious crimes, frequently involving personal violence, are characteristics of younger offenders. Older criminals, most of whom have served one or more sentences, are physically and emotionally less adapted to commit the more daring types of crime. Many, failing to make good adjustments in the community and being unwilling to risk being involved in more serious crimes, resort to "panhandling" or some form of petty larceny.

The concentration of female misdemeanants in age group fifteen to nineteen includes a large group of females committed for sex offenses. Of all male misdemeanants, 57.0 per cent were committed for disorderly conduct and vagrancy. Ages of the jail population are somewhat older than the prisoners in State and Federal institutions.[10] This is because juvenile delinquents are excluded by law from jails in many jurisdictions and a large part of the jail population is made up of older vagrants, beggars, "dopers," and "plain drunks" who are committed for short periods.

It has been the custom to consider children exempt from the degree of responsibility exacted of adults before the law. Under common law a child under seven, being incapable of criminal intent, could not commit a crime. He was assumed to be fully responsible after age fourteen. The courts commonly based their decisions on the degree of *mens rea* (guilty mind) supposed to be involved in cases of children between the ages of seven and fourteen. Table 11–2 shows how the age of responsibility varies from country to country. Children are considered mature at earlier ages in more of the southeastern European countries with milder climates than in those of northwestern Europe.

Table 11–2. Minimum Age of Responsibility by Countries*

9th year	10th year	12th year	14th year	15th year	16th year	21st year
Spain	Bulgaria Greece Austria Poland Uruguay	Switzerland Hungary	Germany Denmark Norway Czechoslovakia	Finland Sweden	Belgium	California

* Elmer (Strong), Anna June, *The Relative Occurrence of Specific Crimes in Various Age Groups*, Master's Thesis, University of Pittsburgh (1937), p. 6, quoting G. von Mayr in *Statistick and Gesellschaftslehre*, Handwörterbuch der Kriminalogie, p. 23, Leipzig (1932).

In general, crimes in which violence or the threat of violence is involved are committed by young offenders. Prevalent are robbery, burglary, larceny, and auto theft. Drunkenness, disorderly conduct, and petty larceny are found at all ages. The crime rate declines rapidly after the age of forty. Older offenders are usually implicated in cases of embezzlement and fraud, while a disproportionate number of men over fifty are charged with sex offenses.

While there is evidence that many "official" juvenile delinquents (those problem children having juvenile court records) continue their antisocial behavior in adulthood (become criminals), it is also true that many adult criminals are not known to have records as juvenile offenders. This does not mean that they are known not to have been juvenile delinquents. The apparent contradiction in the two statements

[10] Wood, Arthur E., and Waite, John B., *Crime and Its Treatment*, pp. 229–230, American Book Company, New York, 1941.

may result from the fact that the statistics are incomplete. We do not know how many serious juvenile behavior problem children "outgrew" their delinquency without being referred to the juvenile court. Similarly, we do not know how many adult criminals qualified as delinquents when they were children but were never referred to a court or were not officially recorded as "juvenile delinquents." Many cases are handled by many courts, "unofficially."

A further possibility is that they may have had juvenile "records" not available to prison authorities at the time of their admission to prison. Few histories on file in our prisons include a complete record of the childhood of the prisoner. The statistics are so inconclusive that it is impossible to say what proportion of all juvenile delinquents become criminals or, of all criminals, were juvenile delinquents.[11]

Sex as a Factor. For every female prisoner in State and Federal prisons for a felony, in 1946, 18 males were committed. Males and females are about equal in number in the general population. The overrepresentation of men in prison is largely the result of cultural differences in the social roles of men. and women. Men are supposed to be aggressive, competitive, and sensitive to challenges to their honor and to defend it, if need be, by manly resort to physical violence. Theirs is the role of provider. A good man may be expected to steal, if necessary, to feed his family. Men compete for the favor of women by lavishing them with gifts and entertainment. Much of the crime committed by men is motivated by the desire to please or impress women.

When compared with those of females, male crimes are proportionately higher for robbery, burglary, auto theft, embezzlement and fraud, rape, and violating liquor laws. Offenses ranking higher among women than men include murder, manslaughter, aggravated assault, receiving stolen property, commercialized vice and other sex offenses, violation of drug laws, and nonsupport and neglect.[12]

Men commit more crimes than women, but when women do run afoul of the law it is usually for highly emotionally motivated offenses, frequently involving physical violence. This is a natural consequence of the relatively repressed role required of them. There is no evidence that female crime is different in emphasis from that of males because of any inherent or biological differences between the sexes, except those that give them a different place in our society.

Juvenile offenders in the younger age groups show little evidence of difference in the types of offenses reported for boys and girls. Hart-

---

[11] *Cf.* S. Glueck and E. T. Glueck, *One Thousand Juvenile Delinquents*, p. 151, Harvard University Press, Cambridge, Mass.; N. Bodin, Do Problem Children Become Delinquents and Criminals? *J. Crim. Law Criminol.*, 1937, **27**, pp. 545–559.

[12] See Table 32 in *Prisoners in State and Federal Prisons and Reformatories, 1946*, Bureau of the Census, Washington, D.C., 1948.

shorne and May[13] have found deception rates about equal for boys and girls in a study of school children. Juvenile court records indicate that boys and girls under age sixteen years have approximately the same rates for shoplifting and petty theft. The rate for all offenses for boys is about four times as high as the rate for girls.[14] All such evidence points to the conclusion that the male and female delinquency and crime rates are not biologically determined. They result, rather, from differences in the opportunities, suggestions, and obligations presented in our culture as it defines the roles of the sexes. Culture-imposed differences become more pronounced as boys and girls approach maturity.

Mental Characteristics. *Feeble-mindedness.* During the second decade of the present century students of criminology were greatly concerned with feeble-mindedness as a cause of crime. Mental tests that had been devised and standardized for school children were applied to adult convicts. The testers not only did not standardize their tests for adults, but they made the same mistake in method that Lombroso had made. They failed to test a control group from the general population. They concluded that mental deficiency was "the greatest single cause of delinquency and crime"[15] and that nearly all, if not all, criminals were of low-grade mentality.

Significant surveys of mental test studies of delinquents and convicts have been made by Sutherland,[16] Zelaney,[17] and Chassell.[18] Sutherland concludes that variations in the methods used by the testers probably reflect more that is significant about attempts to do this kind of testing than they do about the intelligence of criminals. Delinquents are not significantly different from those of the general population. The feeble-minded do not show a disproportionate amount of delinquency, and feeble-minded prisoners cause no more disciplinary problems than others. Feeble-minded convicts on parole are about as successful as others and they become recidivists about as frequently as other convicts. He concludes that the relationship between crime and feeble-mindedness is, in general, very slight.

Zelaney equated the procedures of the testers and arrived at a ratio of 1.2 to 1.0 when the appraisals of the intelligence of delinquents and the general population were related. Chassell found correlations of .10

[13] Hartshorne, H., and May, M. A., *Studies in Deceit,* p. 180, The Macmillan Company, New York, 1928.

[14] *Juvenile Court Statistics,* Children's Bureau, Statistical Series No. 8, p. 4, 1951.

[15] Goddard, H. H., *Human Efficiency and Levels of Intelligence,* p. 74, Princeton University Press, Princeton, N.J., 1920.

[16] For a review of these studies, see Sutherland, *op. cit.,* pp. 103–105.

[17] Zelaney, L. D., Feeble-mindedness and Criminal Conduct, *Amer. J. Sociol.,* 1933, **38**, 564–578.

[18] Chassell, Clara F., "The Relation between Morality and Intellect," *Teach. Coll. Contr. Educ.,* 1935, No. 607, Part III and Chaps. 3–8.

to .39 of morality with intellect, a relationship she thinks is positive, but low. She did, however, report delinquency rates among the feeble-minded unusually high. Carl Murchison gave the Army Alpha tests to a group of white convicts and discovered that the convicts scored slightly higher than the soldiers.[19]

While the evidence presented here indicates little, if any, statistical relationship between feeble-mindedness and crime, we should not get the impression that it is not an important factor in specific cases of criminal behavior. Where it is associated with such factors as criminal suggestion and the absence of good family, school, and neighborhood influences that establish habits of law obedience, feeble-mindedness may be a very important factor in the explanation of individual cases of criminal behavior. The feeble-minded, per se, are suggestible, not bad.

Mental Disorders. Every discussion of the traits of criminals mentions psychoses. Every author of such a discussion hastens to call attention to the confusion among the authorities in the definition of the several forms of mental disorganization, the arrays of diagnostic symptoms, and the research methods used in relating mental illness to criminal behavior. The psychoses are regarded as the most severe types of mental disorder but of relatively infrequent occurrence (1 to 5 per cent) among prisoners admitted to penal institutions.[20] Prison psychosis, which develops after incarceration, is correlated positively with length of sentence,[21] indicating the ineffectiveness of present methods of treating criminals. Types of mental disorder most frequently found in criminals are the syphilopsychoses, psychoses in combination with mental deficiency, those related to the use of alcohol and drugs, dementia praecox, manic-depressive psychosis, and psychopathic inferiority.[22]

Neurotics, constitutional psychopathic inferiors, and *epileptics* are discovered in varying numbers among criminals. Neurotics, unable to compete satisfactorily in society, *may* resort to crime. The social scientist may regard society, itself, as neurotic and the neurotic criminal as "merely a person acting naturally in a neurotic society."[23] The psychopathic inferior, an unbalanced egocentric, is variously estimated to be responsible for much or little crime. When psychiatrists can get together on their diagnoses, we may have more consistent, if not more

[19] Murchison, Carl, American White Criminal Intelligence, *J. Crim. Law Criminol.,* 1924, 15, 239.

[20] Sutherland, *op. cit.,* p. 107.

[21] See Wood and Waite, *op. cit.,* p. 273.

[22] Parsons, A. P., *Crime and the Criminal,* p. 99, Alfred A. Knopf, Inc., New York, 1926.

[23] See Devereux, George, Maladjustment and social Neurosis, *Amer. Sociol. Rev.,* 1939, 5, 845; Horney, Karen, Culture and Neurosis, *Amer. Sociol. Rev.,* 1936, 2, 222–224.

substantial, evidence on the importance of psychopaths in the etiology of crime. Some psychiatrists consider the fact of conviction of crime evidence of a psychopathic personality. Therefore, all criminals are psychopaths, and, stated in reverse, psychopathic personality becomes an important cause of crime. In a study of psychopaths in the Western State Penitentiary in Pennsylvania, 21 per cent of those so diagnosed were convicted of murder, while among nonpsychopaths, only 12 per cent were murderers.[24] The implication here is that psychopathic criminals are involved in a disproportionate number of violent crimes. Wilson and Pescor think not more than a fifth of the prison population is psychopathic.[25] Whatever the frequency of psychopathic personality among prisoners may be, the fact remains that many more psychopaths exist in the noncriminal population, and the psychopathic criminal must be the product of his psychopathy *and something else*.

At the most only a small proportion of crime can be related to epilepsy. Estimates range from 1 to 6 per cent, in the earlier studies, to 0.25 per cent in C. L. Anderson's study in Michigan.[26] He found 0.21 per cent in the general population. Here again, not all epileptics are criminals. But although epilepsy is found only infrequently among prisoners, it is, in combination with other factors, thought to be contributory to a number of serious crimes.

Mental illness seems to be significant in the etiology of crime, for the most part, in three ways: (1) where delusions of persecution lead the individual to attack his imagined persecutor; (2) where the psychosis has the effect of excluding the patient from relationships that give status, for which he compensates by attention-getting behavior; and (3) where the psychosis is a substitute for crime, in an intolerable life situation—a flight from reality as an alternative to criminal outbursts.

The crimes of the insane are "good copy" for newspapers. The public reads of the bizarre details with relish; circulation of the newspapers increases; and the public gets an exaggerated idea of the importance of mental disorders in relation to all crime. It goes without saying, however, that all dangerous psychotics should be isolated. The contemporary scene reveals a situation in which inadequate diagnosis, corruption of the judicial process, the determinate sentence (which never should be imposed on the insane criminal, but sometimes is), incompetent or dishonest parole boards, and insufficient facilities for treating the criminal insane are operating to make it possible for considerable

[24] Wholey, Cornelius C., Psychiatric Report of Study of Psychopathic Inmates of a Penitentiary, *J. Crim. Law Criminol.*, 1937, **28**, 57.

[25] Wilson, J. G., and Pescor, M. J., *Problems in Prison Psychiatry*, p. 30, Caxton Printers, Ltd., Caldwell, Idaho, 1939.

[26] Anderson, C. L., Epilepsy in the State of Michigan, *Ment. Hyg., N.Y.*, 1936, **20**, 441–462.

numbers of dangerous psychotics to move about in their communities without official restraint.

Nationality and Race. In proportion to their number, the part of our population who are native-born commit more crimes than those who are foreign-born. Studies of crime rates of *the children of foreign-born parents* indicate that they have higher rates than the native-born in industrial cities and, especially, in those where most of the foreign-born are of the "new immigration." For example, Donald A. Taft reports that in 1933 they had higher rates in nine states, while in 26 states the reverse was true.[27] The clue to the social maladjustment of this group is to be found in their unsatisfactory economic and social situation in the community.

Most frequent among charges for which the foreign-born are convicted are violations of immigration laws, and behavior resulting from ignorance of American laws and customs or failure to understand how we enforce and interpret them. They have relatively high rates for violations of drug laws, burglary, and larceny. Murder and manslaughter rank approximately the same (thirteenth and fourteenth) when the rank order of all offenses of the native-born and the foreign-born are compared.

Negroes, with 33 per cent of all admissions to penal institutions in 1946, had nearly four times the rate their proportion of the total population would indicate that they should have. Of all Negro offenses (felonies), burglary ranked first, with 20.7 per cent of the total; larceny second, with 17.2 per cent; robbery third, with 11.8 per cent; and aggravated assault fourth, with 11.0 per cent. Rape had the same rank order position (sixth) for Negroes as for Whites. For the Negro group in the state penitentiaries, it constituted only 4.1 per cent of all offenses, while for the White population it was 4.7 per cent.

Many factors contribute to the relatively high Negro crime rate. They are arrested where others would be warned, "bawled out," or ignored by the police. When arrested they are more frequently held for trial and convicted. When convicted they are given more severe sentences. Fewer Negroes than Whites, when arrested, are able to pay fines as an alternative to commitment to an institution.

The difference between the crime rates of Negroes and Whites would be less if the Negro's status in our society were such as to give him security and self-respect. Unstable home and family life,[28] exposure to

[27] Taft, Donald A., Nationality and Crime, *Amer. Sociol. Rev.*, 1936, **1**, No. 5.
[28] Elmer, M. C., *The Sociology of the Family*, p. 352, Ginn & Company, Boston, 1945; see S. Glueck, and E. Glueck, *Unraveling Juvenile Delinquency*, p. 287, Harvard University Press, Cambridge, Mass., 1951, for a discussion of the place of the family and the "home atmosphere" in the development of "personality and character."

criminal influences in the slum areas he is forced to occupy, and exclusion from responsibility for public administration of the social controls have deprived the Negro of social and psychological influences that operate to make the White population less in danger of arrest and conviction of crime.[29]

Marital Status. Census reports of the prison population, when analyzed in relation to the general population, indicate the importance of marital status as a selective factor in adult crime. Divorced, single, widowed, and married rank in the order named in relative frequency of commitment to prison. Divorced females twenty to twenty-four years of age have the highest rate.

Table 11–3 shows the divorced to be overrepresented for both male

Table 11–3. Felony Prisoners Compared with the General Population by Marital Status and Sex, for the United States, 1946*
(Per cent)

Marital status and sex	Prisoners, 1946	General population†	
		1940	1950
Male, total.	100.0	100.0	100.0
Single.	48.8	33.2	26.2
Married.	41.8	61.2	67.8
Widowed.	2.1	4.3	} 5.9
Divorced.	7.2	1.3	
Female, total.	100.0	100.0	100.0
Single.	28.5	25.8	20.3
Married.	54.6	61.0	65.5
Widowed.	7.3	11.5	} 14.1
Divorced.	9.6	1.7	

* Adapted from *Prisoners in State and Federal Prisons and Reformatories: 1946*, Table 19.

† From U.S. Census, *Population*, 1940, and Table 1, *Preliminary Reports*, April, 1951.

and female prisoners. Single males are much more overrepresented than are single females. Obviously marriage reduces the crime rate of men more than of women. Professor Gillin compared 172 prisoners with their noncriminal brothers. He found the criminals, with greater frequency than their brothers, were single or divorced, given to quarreling with wife, and differed from wife in nationality, religion, educational,

[29] See E. Franklin Frazier, *The Negro Family in the United States*, pp. 362–368, University of Chicago Press, Chicago, 1939, for a discussion of the Negro family in relation to delinquency and crime.

and economic status.[30] Failure on parole was reported to be associated with marital discord by the Gluecks.[31]

Responsibilities, when voluntarily accepted, become stabilizers in human personalities. The husband and wife who accept their obligations in marriage, adopt a routine that fits the requirements of their roles, and find ego satisfaction in successful day-to-day achievements become conditioned to a program that leaves little time or opportunity to respond to criminal suggestion. In time the routine itself becomes a part of their habit systems, providing satisfaction of itself, and restlessness and frustration when it is interrupted. Any suggestion of criminal activity is resisted because it carries the implication of disruption of the familiar, satisfying routines and loss of the security they have provided.

Single persons, who have never married, lack the added stability which a well-ordered routine in married life provides. They may or may not have developed adequate adjustment techniques to make reasonably orderly living possible. The widowed, on the other hand, have known the stabilizing influence of marriage and the security it provides. Having lost these with the death of the spouse, the resulting personal disorganization may make them, on becoming widowed, more responsive to criminal suggestion. Many of the divorced are likely to have had poorly adjusted personalities before marriage. When their broken marriages add to their basic instability a sense of failure and defeat, self-pity, desire for revenge, economic insecurity (in many cases of women who are divorced), and disrupted social and friendship patterns, divorcees may be susceptible to influences that may lead to crime. The statistics indicate the divorcee is likely to be more unstable than the single, married, or widowed.

ENVIRONMENTAL FACTORS

Failing to find the cause of crime in the individual, many investigators have sought it in his environment. The home, neighborhood, culture conflict, poverty, unemployment, economic exploitation, poor housing, inadequate schools, playgrounds, and churches, bad companions, mobility, commercialized recreation, movies, radio, press, and even civilization have been blamed with causing crime. Many of these alleged factors in the etiology of crime have been shown to be statistically related to criminal behavior.

Statistical studies of environmental factors producing crime present grave difficulties of method and interpretation. As suggested above, a

[30] Gillin, John L., Backgrounds of Prisoners in the Wisconsin State Prison and of Their Brothers, *Amer. Sociol. Rev.*, 1936, 2, 204–212.

[31] Glueck, Sheldon, and Glueck, Eleanor T., *500 Criminal Careers*, pp. 268–270, Alfred A. Knopf, Inc., New York, 1930.

statistical item, identified and added to a tabulation, takes on a value undifferentiated from all other items in its class. This neglects the unique value or weight of any given factor, in any specific act of human behavior. To illustrate, a schoolroom from which two delinquent boys are habitually absent is not the same environment for each of them when he is present. In one case the boy may come from an impoverished home and be so shabbily dressed that he feels humiliated in the schoolroom where all the other children are well dressed. He stays away from school to avoid the unpleasant experience. Having accepted the role of truant, he is defying the authority of ordered society. He is now against those who represent constituted authority. Seeking social justification and the feeling of security that group membership gives, he identifies himself with a delinquent gang. In the other case the boy of a well-to-do family has a slight impairment of hearing. His teacher seated the pupils alphabetically, putting him in the rear of the room where he had difficulty in hearing directions given by the teacher. Failing to discover his handicap, the teacher interprets his poor responses as a form of deliberate rebelliousness and punishes him. This he considers unjust. To escape what, to him, is an unfair and intolerable situation, he becomes a truant and adopts delinquent habits. In a statistical table in a study including these cases, that schoolroom might be counted twice as "inadequate school environment," without any indication that its place in the two causal patterns of the delinquency of the two boys was not identical. Once buried in the statistical table, it is impossible for the person making the study, or one who reads the report, to see any difference in the contribution of the school as a factor in the environment in these two cases.

Environment, then, is what one responds to. It is not a place or a set of conditions apart from the socially conditioned habits and attitudes of the person for whom it is environment. Doubtless the environmental factors mentioned above are related to the criminal behavior of *some criminals*. But no such factors have been discovered to cause those exposed to them to become criminals *without exception*. The relationship, where it does exist, is neither clear nor direct. Each case needs to be analyzed individually.

Statistics can be presented to show that most of those convicted of conventional crime come from the lower economic classes, but most of the total population also belong to the lower economic classes. To make the problem more difficult, statistics on income are inadequate and difficult to relate to social behavior.

Approached from another direction, such factors as income, schooling, child labor, and recreation have been greatly improved in many communities in recent decades. But improvement in these aspects of the environment has not produced a commensurate improvement in the crime and delinquency rate.[32]

Much of contemporary crime is committed in cities by city people. Moreover, the crime rate increases with the size of the city. Rural rates include a larger proportion of crimes against the person.[33] The city gives the potential criminal suggestions and opportunities for crime not present in the country where there is relative cultural, economic, and moral homogeneity. The crowded streets, teeming with hurrying strangers who have neither interest in nor a sense of responsibility for those about them, present the opportunity for the criminal to pick pockets, shoplift, rob a bank, or murder a member of a rival gang and lose himself quickly in the crowd. Intense competition producing severe nervous tension, social pressure to keep up with the Joneses (live beyond one's means), the reduced influence of the city family, the mobility of city populations with relatively large numbers unmarried or temporarily away from home, the clash of culture of the nationality groups and of children of the foreign-born with the cultures of their parents, the moral cynicism, bred in a social atmosphere of business ethics and political corruption, which is revealed in the expression, "everything is a racket," the get-rich-quick complex, the presence of commercialized vice and gambling and of "shady" forms of commercialized amusement, and the availability of safe "hide-outs"—in short, impersonal, urban society, lacking the social controls of the primary (face-to-face) rural community, presents the suggestions and opportunities for crime. On the other hand, many great ethical leaders have been born, and have lived their lives, in the city.

Environmental conditions may afford the means and the suggestions for crime; they never determine that one must be a criminal. Behavior emerges out of attitudes and habits that predispose one to respond in certain ways to the environment. Most of one's social attitudes grow out of association with a small group of intimates. The chance pattern of associations the individual develops, then, becomes a crucial factor in his environment as it influences him to react in ways that are either criminal or law-abiding. To know what kind of people his intimate associates are, however, is not enough. To understand the criminogenic process it is necessary to know the entire sequence of interacting factors that produced the personality that formed the associations contributing to the development of his antisocial attitudes.

Statistical summaries of the characteristics of criminals are useful in indicating the relative frequency of the presence of certain factors

---

[32] Cf. Vold, op. cit., pp. 272–276.

[33] Barnes, H. E., and Teeters, N. K., New Horizons in Criminology, p. 147, Prentice-Hall, Inc., New York, 1943.

in the pattern of criminal behavior. They do not help us to know why a certain offender committed a certain crime. The median age of criminals is about twenty-seven years. It is approximately 10 years younger for felons than for misdemeanants. Most serious crimes involving violence are the acts of younger offenders—in the early twenties. Children under a certain age are not regarded as fully responsible under the law. This age varies from country to country and from state to state in this country. Male convicts have a ratio, to the general population, greatly in excess of that for female offenders. This is due largely to cultural rather than biological differences. The foreign-born are not responsible for a disproportionate amount of crime. Their children do have high crime rates, especially those derived from the new immigration and those who live in industrial cities. Ample evidence demonstrates the causes of the high Negro crime rate to be cultural rather than biological. Divorced, single, widowed, and married rank in that order in relative frequency of rates of commitment to prison. Divorced women and single men are particularly overrepresented among convicts. Feeble-mindedness and insanity are not independent causes of crime. The feeble-minded are suggestible to good or bad suggestion; the mentally ill may commit crimes that have a logical relationship to their delusions. Environment may predispose to crime but no environment alone is reponsible for the criminal behavior of any offender. The slums of our cities are the locale of much conventional crime. Rural communities do not present, to the same extent, either the suggestions or the opportunities for crime.

APPREHENSION OF OFFENDERS

The treatment process and protection of the public from harm and the fear of harm cannot be realized unless criminals are identified and apprehended by the police. Apprehended and convicted they can be legally treated as criminals. Some European courts act on the assumption that the burden of proof is on the accused. In American law the accused is presumed to be innocent until he has been proved guilty.

Having narrowed the field of possible suspects by logical use of such evidence as they may have, the police are under pressure, when a serious crime has been committed, to arrest the most likely suspects. The local police feel this pressure more than do State and Federal police officers because the press, radio, and public are closer to them and reflect a vital, personal, sometimes almost hysterical interest in the speedy arrest of the guilty.

During the few hours that intervene between arrest and a preliminary hearing, the police question the accused to clarify the probability of his guilt or innocence. Believing him to be guilty, they attempt to get a confession together with a narrative of the crime. In this way they may discover facts that will have significance in apprehending and convicting accomplices as well as additional evidence useful in convicting the arrested suspect or convincing him to plead "guilty." This evidence has further value in aiding the judge in passing sentence, and probation and parole officers in functioning intelligently.

METHODS OF DETECTING DECEPTION

Police interrogation is one of the crucial steps in our method of dealing with criminals. Its usefulness depends on the truth of the responses made by the individual questioned.[34]

Psychology has made important contributions to enable the police and the courts to get truthful reports from defendants and witnesses. Tests for deception are derived from the principle that consciousness of guilt engenders a vague fear reaction. This fear or psychological pressure induces in the suspect one or more reactions—psychological, emotional, physical (acts of omission or commission), or evasion of questioning—that may indicate deception. While research evidence is available in abundance to support this proposition, the tests are not infallible because (1) other fears, not related to the crime being investigated, may cause the suspect to respond as if he were lying when, actually, he is telling the truth in response to the question asked of him; (2) conditions other than fear may produce the same physical and emotional responses; and (3) some individuals do not make the kind of responses to fear which are recorded in the tests, or the quality of their responses is not normal.

The recognition of psychological pressure as a device for detecting deception is not a recent discovery, nor is it limited to any one culture. The ancient Hebrews, Chinese, and Egyptians are known to have recognized its significance and applied it crudely in testing the truth of assertions. King Solomon established the maternity of a child by noting the extreme fear of the actual mother when he threatened to sever the child's body. The ancient Chinese made suspects hold dry rice powder in their mouths for a few minutes. They were told that the powder had magical power to identify the guilty. Any suspects who showed evidence of subnormal salivation were considered guilty.[35]

Fear of torture was used in the medieval courts to induce the accused to confess. Modern "third degree" methods, sometimes used by police officers who lack the skill to employ less crude methods, are in

[34] It is also true that some instances of attempted deception during police interrogation can be interpreted by the police to aid them in discovering the truth.

[35] Inbau, Fred, *Lie Detection and Criminal Investigation,* 2d ed., p. 109, The Williams & Wilkins Company, Baltimore, 1948.

the medieval tradition. Confessions obtained under such duress are usually worthless in getting convictions.

The products of scientific research in the areas of systolic rhythm and blood pressure, respiration, electrodermal responses, eye movements, brain waves, free association, muscular tensions and body movements, and reaction to certain drugs have been utilized in attempts to devise methods of detecting deception.

Blood Pressure. A study was reported in 1917 by W. M. Marston[36] in which he noted the rise of blood pressure when he questioned subjects about a fictitious crime. Using an ordinary stethoscope (the kind employed by physicians) attached to an inflated armband, he recorded observations at intervals during the interrogation. He reported a correct diagnosis of 98 per cent of more than one hundred cases. The method has been incorporated in the Keeler polygraph with refinements that make it possible to get a continuous reading throughout the examination of a suspect. Other investigators, using Marston's method, have obtained lower scores of accuracy in laboratory tests, but none has made less than approximately 70 per cent of correct determinations of "guilt."

Breathing Records. A series of experiments in which breathing records were used to indicate deception was reported by Vittorio Benussi, an Italian, in 1914. The ratio of the time of inspiration to expiration (the I/E ratio) increased after the subject told a falsehood. When Burtt repeated Benussi's work, with certain variations, he failed to get results that would establish the I/E ratio as the infallible symptom of deception the Italian assumed it was.[37] While laboratory tests indicated only 73 per cent of the cases could be accurately diagnosed, police investigators have used breathing records in association with other types of evidence to get useful results. They have noted that unusually deep breathing and irregular respiration following falsehood are significant.

Electrodermal Response. From physiology and physics come the knowledge that perspiration, as a conductor of electric current, can be used to measure fluctuations in the secretion rate of the sweat glands in response to changing emotional states. Variations in the electrodermal response (also referred to as the "psychogalvanic reflex") are measured by a sensitive galvonometer. They are affected by body tensions and emotional changes.

Critics of the method refer to its "extreme delicacy." Others contend this characteristic is its chief advantage. When the tests are made not

[36] Marston, W. M., Systolic Blood Pressure Symptoms of Deception, *J. Exp. Psychol.*, 1917, 2, 117–163.

[37] Burtt, H. E., Inspiration Ratio during Truth and Falsehood, *J. Exp. Psychol.*, 1921, 4, 1–23.

only fear but anger, embarrassment, surprise, or expectancy may produce changes in the readings. Much depends on the control the operator exercises over the examining situation. He must make sure that extraneous factors will not corrupt the record. Sudden noises or interruptions in the questioning may produce variations, or the subject may conceal a dishonest response by thinking of some exciting experience immediately before answering a "harmless" question.

Geldreich has been able to get almost perfect results under laboratory conditions by first "fatiguing" the electrodermal response by a long list of questions, all of which produced the same type of response, and then administering the actual test.[38] The practical application of the method in the field by police officers has not been entirely satisfactory. Its extreme responsiveness to irrelevant stimuli has made the burden of control of the testing situation and interpretation of results too great for confident utilization under crime laboratory conditions.

Eye Movements. When eye movements of subjects were tested in detecting a "laboratory crime," Berrien reports,[39] six judges made diagnosis ranging in accuracy from 64 to 77 per cent. By using consensus of the judges, accurate determinations were made in 80 per cent of the cases. The "guilty" subjects were betrayed by the greater steadiness of their gaze during a "silent period," after a short rest which followed the actual interrogation. The method has not been generally adopted in crime detection laboratories.

Brain Waves. When minute electrical currents generated (particularly in the occipital area) in the brain are amplified and passed through an oscilloscope they have two notable characteristics. A relatively slow rhythmical current is observed which has been named the "alpha" wave. Superimposed on the alpha wave is a much faster oscillating current which has been called the "beta" wave. Experimenters have noticed that the alpha waves tend to disappear during states of emotional agitation. Oberman was able to apply this reaction as a device for detecting deceit with accuracy ranging from 39 to 50 per cent of his cases.[40] The average percentage of accuracy in detecting guilt by this method is approximately 48. It needs refinement to have practical utility in the field of criminalistics.

Narcosynthesis. For more than two decades psychiatrists have used drugs such as *scopolamine* to induce mental states conducive to recall of unpleasant latent memories. Introduced in 1929 by Dr. R. E. House,

[38] Geldreich, E. W., Studies of the Galvanic Skin Response as a Deception Indicator, *Trans. Kan. Acad. Sci.*, 1941, **44**, 346–351, reported by F. W. Berrien, *Practical Psychology*, p. 446, The Macmillan Company, New York, 1945.

[39] Berrien, *op. cit.*, pp. 449–450.

[40] Oberman, C. E., The Effect on the Berger Rhythm of Mild Affective States, *J. Abnorm. Soc. Psychol.*, 1939, **34**, 84–95.

the method had extensive use during the Second World War in the treatment of "battle fatigue." Crime investigators have adapted it to their purposes to gain "leads" to material evidence helpful in solving crimes. In France a number of tests have been made of psychonarcosis in police work.[41] Results were inconclusive in approximately 60 per cent of the cases. The device "failed to penetrate strong ego protection." Some field investigators in this country feel that it has value in inducing psychological pressure on the suspect who is invited to take the test and reminded that he has the constitutional right to refuse to submit but is also told that refusal will have incriminating significance when his case is tried in court.[42] Fearing what he may disclose during the test more than he fears telling "the truth," in his own way, while in full possession of his mental functions, the theory is that he will elect to confess, if he is guilty. "Truth serum" (the drug employed) has not been validated by laboratory evidence as a reliable agent to induce truthfulness.

Combination of Methods. The practical application of research findings useful in detecting deception has produced techniques that involve a combination of methods. The device for testing truth most widely used by crime investigators is the Keeler psycho-polygraph (the lie detector). It makes recordings of blood pressure and pulse fluctuations, respiration, and electrodermal records on a strip of ruled paper. The polygraph was developed by Leonard Keeler and his associates between 1935 and 1938 in the Crime Detection Laboratory at Northwestern University. Such accuracy was achieved in its employment by skilled operators that over two thousand cases were examined with only twelve erroneous diagnoses.

While the polygraph has made irrefutable contribution to improved crime detection, it is not a "foolproof" automaton that can be relied on to give unmistakable answers when operated by untrained examiners. Skill in its use can be attained only after extensive experience under the guidance of competent operators.

Improved models of the polygraph include a manometer that indicates muscular contraction sometimes used by criminals, with some knowledge of the polygraph techniques, to falsify recording of blood-pressure changes.[43]

[41] Gagnieur, J. P., Magistrate, Judicial Uses of Psychonarcosis in France, *J. Crim. Law Criminol.* 1949–1950, **40,** 372–380.

[42] In *Commonwealth v. Yeager,* tried in Allegheny County, Pennsylvania, September, 1949, refusal to give an answer to a question that presumably might have been incriminating was admitted in evidence.

[43] Reid, John E., Simulated Blood Pressure Responses and the Lie Detector and a Method for Their Detection, *J. Crim. Law Criminol.,* **36,** 201–214, Northwestern University School of Law, Chicago; also see Inbau, *op. cit.,* pp. 54–66.

Good police work in the use of scientific methods of detecting deception depends on skill in assembling and analyzing as many kinds of evidence of dishonesty as can be made available. Crime investigators are being trained to "condition the suspect in preparation for his interrogation.[44] This includes suggesting "lie detector" and "truth serum" tests with a somewhat detailed explanation of how the mechanisms of the polygraph work when the subject tells a falsehood. The explanation "establishes the validity of the instrument in the mind of the suspect," convinces him of the futility of resistance, and stimulates fear of detection. The attendant neuroglandular responses prepare him to make more definitive records when the polygraph is used. Often, this explanation and the presence of the instrument are enough to produce a confession. If the suspect refuses to cooperate he is told that his silence indicates guilt and will go far to convict him before a jury.

Other uses of the polygraph have demonstrated its value in saving time and expense of police investigation of the innocent,[45] and in screening employees in commercial establishments. Bonding companies, banks, and retail stores have used it to improve the honesty of their employees and reduce losses. While polygraph records are not generally admitted in evidence by the courts, there is growing interest in the possibility of developing scientific methods of establishing truth with such validity as to be recognized by the courts.

ESTABLISHING GUILT

Traditional attitudes of the legal mind include superstitious confidence in the testimony of a witness—almost any witness, it would seem—in preference to "circumstantial evidence." Science postulates the validity of sensory evidence, but only when (1) it has been acquired under the most exacting conditions, (2) it has been acquired by those best qualified to observe (trained specialists), and (3) a sufficient number of different observers have reported the same observation under conditions that will test every conceivable relevant variation of the phenomenon under observation and the conditions under which the observation can be made. Having met these requirements, the scientist accepts the net results, *tentatively,* as the most credible approximation to reality, unless or until more meaningful observations are made.

Credibility of Witnesses. Scientists, as a class, do not consider the testimony of a witness valid merely because he says, under oath, that he "was there when it happened and saw it." He may be "truthfully"

[44] Nevin, W. L., *Keeler Polygraph Operation and Techniques,* a paper read before an institute on criminal investigation, Pittsburgh, Apr. 26, 1950.
[45] Keeler, L., The Lie Detector Proves Its Usefulness, *Pub. Management,* June, 1940, pp. 163–166.

reporting what he believes he saw. But he may have been influenced in his observation of a crime by "stereotypes,"[46] sensory defects, emotional factors, diffused attention, by factors related to age, experience, and intelligence, and by his position when he witnessed the crime. His "honest" account of what he saw may be further perverted by inaccuracy of recall.

Psychologists have made extensive researches dealing with the *accuracy of remembering*. They have discovered that what has been experienced may be recalled with distortions and omissions that are related to such factors as the time interval involved, prejudice and antipathy, the age and health of the rememberer, suggestions, inhibitions, and the repetition of fictitious accounts of the experiences.

Experiments in recalling nonsense syllables reveal a rapid decline in ability to remember during the first hour, after which the rate of forgetting levels off. What is forgotten during the week that follows is approximately equal to the decline in ability to recall during the first hour. Comparable experiments in which stories or expository materials having meaning for the subject are used show that the significant elements in the part that has meaning are remembered with considerable accuracy for relatively long periods of time while insignificant details are quickly forgotten as in the case of nonsense syllables.[47] Criminal lawyers frequently make inferences based on the assumption that the witness cannot actually remember accurately the significant parts of his testimony because he has been confused in recalling meaningless details. Or, a jury may discount the value of the testimony of a witness who relates an enormous number of details glibly, because "his story is too pat." In this instance, the witness may be one of those unusual individuals with a "photographic mind" (capacity for eidetic recall), and he may be giving an extremely accurate report.

Trial by Jury. Following the pioneer studies of Hugo Münsterberg,[48] psychologists have produced mountains of evidence that demonstrate the anachronism of trial by jury. The difficulties of prosecuting a criminal case through the maze of complexities of procedural "red tape" have led prosecutors to avoid bringing to trial most cases in which there is not preponderant evidence of guilt and a plea of "guilty," making a jury trial unnecessary. Consequently there has been a sharp decrease

[46] Lippmann, Walter, Chapter on Stereotypes in *Public Opinion*, Harcourt, Brace and Company, Inc., New York, 1922; see M. R. Cohen, and E. Nagel, *An Introduction to Logic and Scientific Method*. Harcourt, Brace, and Company, Inc., New York, 1934, for a discussion of "how we get our beliefs."

[47] Newman, E. B., Forgetting of Meaningful Material during Sleep and Waking, *Amer. J. Psychol.*, 1939, **52**, 65–71.

[48] Münsterberg, Hugo, *On the Witness Stand*, Clark Boardman Company, Ltd., New York, 1925.

in frequency of the use of the petit jury in criminal trials. Defense lawyers, in some cases, advise clients to waive trial before a jury.

Laws in more than half the states permit the defendant to wave a jury trial. The alternative is for a judge or panel of judges to hear the evidence. The jury is used in only 1.7 per cent of criminal cases in the superior courts and 13.6 per cent of felony cases tried in the district courts.[49] The average is probably no more than 5 per cent.

Early forms of the jury were composed of country gentlemen and burghers, presumably able men. They knew intimately the defendants and the conditions involved in the local incidents they interpreted. In our modern urban society, jurors usually are not the more able members of the community; they do not have intimate personal knowledge of the defendants, and they are likely to be confounded by the complex problems and technical matters they are asked to consider. They are further confused by the prejudicial and conflicting arguments of the prosecutor and the defense counsel. Jurors are likely to be the kind of people who are especially susceptible to suggestions supported by prejudice. Our methods of selecting jurors eliminate most of the able and educated.

A further criticism of the jury system derives from the inability, even of trained and superior audiences, to note and retain significant details of a presentation in involved, redundant, verbose, legal language with the intermittent interruptions and delays that characterize taking of testimony in a jury trial. The "typical juror" does not assimilate even a small fraction of it.[50]

Psychologists studying changes in jury opinion conclude that the persuasiveness of evidence depends on its context, hence, the importance of the order in which it is presented. There is a "psychological moment" when a fact or an assertion may have great influence on jury opinion. Presented at another time, its effect may be lost or minimal.[51] Women, as jurors, perform in ways that are not significantly different from those of men. The opening and closing statements of prosecutors and defense counsels are discovered to have more influence on the verdict than all the ritualistic, time-consuming, technical procedure that intervenes.[52] Most of the presentation of evidence would seem to be pure waste of time and the taxpayer's money.

Criticisms such as these have led such organizations as the American

[49] Barnes and Teeters, op. cit., p. 364.
[50] Ibid., p. 362.
[51] Weld, H. P., and Roff, M., A Study of the Formation of Opinion Based upon Legal Evidence, Amer. J. Psychol., 1938, 51, 609–629.
[52] Weld, H. P., and Dauzig, E. R., A Study of the Way in Which a Verdict Is Reached by a Jury, Amer. J. Psychol., 1940, 53, 518–536.

Law Institute to recommend critical modification of the trial-jury system in criminal cases, if not its abolition. The American Bar Association and the national associations of medical doctors and of psychiatrists have passed resolutions urging that psychiatric service in pre-sentence clinics be provided.

A California law of 1944 (Section 5079 of the Penal Code) provides that the Director of Corrections shall establish a psychiatric and diagnostic clinic to make a scientific study of each prisoner. His life history, the casual sequence of his criminal behavior, and recommendations for his care, training, and employment, in reference to his reformation and the protection of society, are to be considered.

Authoritative opinion has suggested that a board of criminologists be substituted for the jury, to go beyond the California law and determine whether a defendant is to become a prison inmate, go free, or accept treatment, outside the prison, under the supervision of the board. Such a board should include a lawyer (specialist in criminal law), a psychologist, a psychiatrist, a sociologist, and a social worker. This would, of course, necessitate changes in constitutional and statutory laws, which, in turn, could be accomplished only if the public were convinced of the advisability of such changes.[53]

DISPOSITION OF THE CONVICTED

Before nineteenth century humanitarianism and twentieth century social science began to have their effect on our thinking, the criminal was believed to be possessed of a devil or of the freely-arrived-at will to do wrong. Basing penal policy on this belief, it seemed reasonable to try to change his will to commit crime or, failing in this, to eliminate him. But the situation was complicated by other implications of the doctrine of moral responsibility.

Being free to choose good or bad ways of behaving, the criminal was thought to have chosen deliberately to offend. He therefore owed society a debt of restitution in proportion to the injury his crime had done. Where actual material injury was involved, restitution was reasonable; but this was not enough. Having made society suffer, he must suffer in payment of the debt. Pain was the agent (1) to drive out the evil spirit or will to do wrong, (2) to even the score, and (3) to cause other potential criminals to suppress their evil tendencies because of the fear inspired by the frightful example of suffering of those who were punished.

Humanitarians, prominent among whom were the Quakers, armed

---

[53] See J. E. Nordskog, Psychiatry in Criminal Trials, pp. 425–433 in J. E. Nordskog. E. C. McDonagh, and M. L. Vincent, *Analyzing Social Problems, The Dryden Press*, Inc., New York, 1950, for a presentation of this point of view.

with the argument that torture, mutilations, and floggings neither reformed nor deterred criminals, began to agitate for a new penology. They succeeded in eliminating most of the worst penal barbarities, substituting solitary confinement in a penitentiary for physical punishment. Their belief was that the offender, when isolated in a cell, would review his evil past, become penitent, and be converted. Meanwhile, loss of freedom was a form of payment of his debt to society.

In response to this new theory, penitentiaries were built. Laws were modified to eliminate torture, and crimes were standardized (reduced to a few simple categories) and weighted so that length of the period of incarceration was made commensurate with the supposed degree of severity of the offense. Buildings to house criminals were constructed for security with little thought of the health or welfare of the prisoners. Prison administration frequently was taken over by politicians and the prison personnel were selected for their supposed efficiency (brutality) as guards.

A century of treating offenders in penitentiaries has demonstrated the failure of the method.[54] Few who are committed are reformed. Instead of being converted to morality and good citizenship, the first offenders usually leave the prison embittered, vengeful, and educated in crime by contact with older, more experienced criminals. About half of all admissions to prisons today are recidivists who have been convicted of one or more previous offenses. Follow-up studies show that few who are released from prison ever make good adjustments in the community.

One of the first reforms attempted by modern penologists was classification of prisoners. In the eighteenth century prisons, all classes, ages, and sexes of problem people were herded together. One important type of classification was by age.

Since children less than seven years of age under common law were not capable of committing crime, they could not be classed with older offenders. Regardless of the nature of a child's offense, then, it was not reasonable to house him with habitual criminals. This line of reasoning led to the emergence of the modern distinction between juvenile delinquency and adult crime and eventually to the establishment of special juvenile courts to handle child offenders. In the United States the age limit for juvenile cases varies from sixteen to twenty-one.

The juvenile court in theory is set up as a social agency equipped with trained specialists competent (1) to investigate the total child-in-his-situation (physical, mental, pathological, and emotional traits of

---

[54] Sanford Bates, in Paul W. Tappan *et al., Contemporary Correction,* foreword, p. vii, McGraw-Hill Book Company, New York, 1951, says "the policy of vengeance and repression" characterizing our use of prisons has failed.

the child, and his playmates, school adjustment, home, and neighborhood conditions); (2) to diagnose his case in a conference of all persons qualified to contribute usefully to the analysis; and (3) to plan and administer a program for his adjustment.

The attempt is made to avoid the social stigma of arrest and conviction. The child is not charged with a crime and tried at a public hearing with lawyers for the prosecution and defense debating the issue of his guilt or innocence. The judge does not limit his methods in conformity to traditional juristic procedure. Once convinced that the child needs the service of the court, he proceeds from the incident that brought the case to his attention to study the child and his total environment, together with the history of the case, to determine developmental factors in the child's background. The aim is to understand and to assist the child, not to convict and punish him. Where institutional commitment is employed, it is thought of as treatment, not punishment. This, in brief, is the theory underlying the juvenile court.

In practice, the juvenile court has made a record little better than that of the penitentiary. Although approximately half of its cases are also repeaters, its failures are due in part to failure of the public to understand the requirements and urge the provision of adequate facilities for the treatment of juvenile cases. In many jurisdictions criminal court judges alternate in criminal and juvenile court service. Monday through Friday they sit in a *traditional* criminal court applying traditional procedure—based on outmoded assumptions of moral responsibility and uniformity (not recognizing the unique pattern of every human act) within the several categories of crime. On Saturday morning they hear juvenile cases—in a situation that duplicates all the faults of the trial court for adults. They preside over what are juvenile courts in name only. Other inadequacies have to do with insufficient and untrained staffs of assistants, inadequate appropriations, and particularly in rural counties, the unavailability of adequate service agencies in the community to supplement the work of the court. Failure of the citizenry to understand the aims and methods of the court and, hence, to cooperate further weakens the service it can give.

More fundamental is the criticism that the socially unadjusting personality of the problem child develops long before the juvenile court makes contact with him. Society needs social machinery to prevent the development of delinquent personalities and the situations in which they are produced.

Criminologists today insist that the principles now recognized in juvenile court theory are equally applicable to *the treatment of adult offenders*. Trends in the treatment of adult convicts include the gradual disuse of the jury trial (only about 5 per cent of arrests now result in jury trials), the increasing use of scientific aids in detection and the presentation of testimony, and greater judicial discretion in the disposition of convicted persons with increasing use of the suspended sentence and probation, the indeterminate sentence, and parole. Prisons continue to fail either to punish or to give socially readjusting treatment to the criminal.

Needed reforms in our treatment of adult offenders that have been suggested are as follows: (1) Two public agencies should be substituted for the trial court to deal with arrested persons; one, a *disinterested* council composed of specialists in detection and the law, to apprehend and appraise the legal status of the accused; the other, composed of trained specialists (psychologists, psychiatrists, medical doctors, and persons trained in social service) to investigate, diagnose each case, and plan and supervise the treatment determined. (2) A new kind of institutional program is needed that will include individualized study of each case and a trained staff housed in a variety of smaller, specialized buildings equipped to give the wide range of services the individual needs of prisoners may require. Only the small minority of hopelessly degenerate and incorrigible convicts need to be confined in maximum security type buildings. Even these can be housed in cottages and confined in an enclosure of charged wire with less expense, and with as great security as the traditional prison provides. (3) Some kind of follow-up program is needed, for persons who are to be released from institutions, that will *begin during institutionalization* and, hence, provide the basis for generating in the convict the belief that he can reconstruct his life pattern and make good in the community. (4) Also important is the re-education of the public to support the program and assist the problem adult in finding a place in the economic and social life of the community.

CRIME PREVENTION

Discussions of the prevention of crime include such items as preventing delinquency by helping the near-delinquent, mobilizing existing community resources by coordinating agencies that treat social problem situations that contribute to criminal behavior, and reducing the frequency and intensity of all types of personal and community disorganization.

Those who view the problem realistically see crime, in part, as a function of the number and complexity of laws—the more laws there are, the more laws will be broken. They also see civilization, itself, with its internal inconsistencies and the frustrations it imposes on the many, so much less fortunate than the few, as a fundamental cause of crime. In a highly competitive pecuniary culture, wherein high-pressure advertising urges us to believe *we have a right* to things we cannot afford, and wherein the conviction exists that status comes with a show of wealth, economic crimes are natural consequences. Among people who believe "everything is a racket," "only suckers work for a living," "no rich man ever made his money working," "to get anywhere you have to have a pull," and "anything (crime) can be fixed if you have the right connections," crimes that are attempts to equate the conditions of competition are not surprising. In a polyglot society of people of many discordant religious, political, and cultural backgrounds, conflict between culture groups and attendant violation of "one law for everybody" is implicit. In a civilization wherein the necessity for making quick decisions, complex interrelationships, exaggerated social competition, and changing ethical standards produce unbearable emotional tensions and interpersonal conflicts, murder and mayhem are to be expected. We cannot hope ever to prevent all crime.

Mankind must face the problem of eliminating the greatest of all crimes against society, war. The atomic bomb has brought us face-to-face with the alternatives—world order under international law, or oblivion.

SUMMARY

Modern penology is a revolt against the use of physical punishment to reform and deter criminals and satisfy an outraged public. By confinement in penitentiaries, it was thought, the convict would contemplate his evil ways, become penitent, and hence be reformed. His loss of freedom was a form of payment of his debt to society. Leading penologists today regard the penitentiary as a hopeless failure and question the validity of the entire system of criminal jurisprudence that has evolved from medieval superstitions and the procedural development of criminal-court practices. An early attempt to reform modern penology was the introduction of the juvenile court, which operates as a behavior clinic, staffed by specialists who think of the court as an agency to give treatment to children who need help—not to punish them. While the juvenile court has eliminated most of the abuses and stupidities of the conventional criminal court, it has failed in its purpose, largely because (1) in practice it has not lived up to good juvenile-court theory, and (2) it takes the child long after the unadjusting personality traits that have made him delinquent have been established. Leaders in penology are now urging the abolition of the traditional trial court and judicial deposition of convicts and the substitution of service agencies for the apprehension, study, and treatment of adult criminals. For the penitentiary, they would substitute an agency equipped to rehabilitate and retrain all but the small minority of incorrigibles who should be isolated securely and inexpensively, but humanely. Some kind of after-prison program is badly needed that will help the released convict to become wholesomely reintegrated into society outside. The success of any program will depend on the degree to which the public is educated and motivated to give it support.

Crime prevention should include helping the near-delinquent to keep out of trouble, bringing all social agencies to bear on social problem situations that predispose to crime, and eliminating personal and social disorganization generally. Much crime will never be prevented while our civilization continues to motivate behavior that, at the same time, it prohibits.

RECOMMENDED SUPPLEMENTARY READINGS

Alexander, Franz, and Healy, William: *Roots of Crime,* Alfred A. Knopf, Inc., New York, 1935.

Alexander, Franz, and Staub, H.: *The Criminal, the Judge, and the Public,* trans. by G. G. Zillboorg, The Macmillan Company, New York, 1931.

Barnes, H. E., and Teeters, N. K.: *New Horizons in Criminology,* 2d ed., Prentice-Hall, Inc., New York, 1951.

Bromberg, Walter: *Crime and the Mind,* J. B. Lippincott Company, Philadelphia, 1948.

Burtt, H. E.: *Legal Psychology,* Prentice-Hall, Inc., New York, 1931.

Giardini, G. I.: Psychology in Criminology, Chap. IX, in J. Stanley Gray (Ed.), *Psychology in Use,* Part II, American Book Company, New York, 1941.

Giardini, G. I.: The Place of Psychology in Penal and Correctional Institutions, *Federal Probation,* April–June, 1942.

Glueck, Sheldon, and Glueck, Eleanor: *Unraveling Juvenile Delinquency,* Harvard University Press, Cambridge, Mass., 1951.

Karpman, Benjamin: Milestones in the Advancement of Knowledge of the Psychopathology of Delinquency and Crime, *Orthopsychiatry:* 1923–1948, pp. 100–189, American Orthopsychiatric Association, Inc., 1948.

Porterfield, A. K., and Stanley, Clifton C.: *Youth in Trouble,* The Leo Potishman Foundation, Fort Worth, 1946.

Reckless, Walter C.: *The Crime Problem,* Appleton-Century-Crofts, Inc., New York, 1950.

Sanford, R. N.: Psychological Approaches to the Young Delinquent, *J. Consult. Psychol.,* 1942, **7,** pp. 223*ff.*

Stromberg, E. T. (Ed.): *Crimes of Violence,* University of Colorado Press, 1950.

Sutherland, E. H.: *White Collar Crime,* The Dryden Press, Inc., New York, 1949.

Swanson, G. E.: The Disturbances of Children in Urban Areas, *Amer. Sociol. Rev.,* October, 1949, pp. 675–678.

Tappan, Paul W.: *Contemporary Correction,* McGraw-Hill Book Company, Inc., New York, 1951. For psychological services—testing, research, therapy—in correctional institutions.

Chapter 12

PSYCHOLOGY IN INDUSTRY—
WORK AND EFFICIENCY[1]

It is often said that human beings want to get as much as they can for as little as possible. This bargain-seeking attitude may be observed in the field of work as well as in other areas of human enterprise. It does not seem surprising, therefore, to find that, when men work on their own, or when they employ other men to do their work, they

[1] This chapter was written by Dr. Alfred G. Dietze, Associate Professor of Psychology, Michigan State College.

330

want all that they can get for their investment of time, effort, or money. This, in essence, is the goal of efficiency that our present-day civilization prizes so highly. In the interest of this goal many modern industrial firms employ experts to investigate the conditions that influence the work output of their employees and to install practices and devices to improve the quality as well as the quantity of their product per unit cost of work.

THE NATURE OF WORK

It is appropriate to begin our discussion with a brief consideration of the nature of work and variations in the course of work under certain conditions. Our knowledge in this area derives chiefly from the laboratory and may, for that reason, be considered by some as abstract and remote from the field of our present applied interest. It should be remembered, however, that basic principles are put to the test in the laboratory and that controlled experimental findings give insight into some of the fundamental problems that are involved in the human affair of daily work. Let us examine, therefore, first some of the basic concepts in this general area and then some of the experimental findings that pertain to the course of work.

Basic Concepts

Many of the concepts we use roll off the tongue or pen with such glib finality that we tend to take for granted, without questioning, that we know exactly what they mean. However, so often these terms are used so imprecisely and with such varied meaning that it seems necessary to define the more important ones that are to be used in that context.

Work. The physicist thinks of work in terms of a force displacing an object in space at a given rate; thus it would be measured in terms of mass times distance divided by time. This idea of energy applied to bring about a change underlies our present use of the term "work." Physiologically work is a matter of rate of energy consumption, involving metabolism, at which level it may be measured in terms of such metabolic by-products as heat production or oxygen consumption. From this point of view, although our interest lies primarily in the use of energy to bring about useful results, work is not basically different from other activities, e.g., activities having a recreational, or non-utilitarian, function, such as play. The difference between work and play is a matter of attitude toward rather than nature of the activity.

Human work is sometimes classified as physical and mental. When a man is lifting a load he is said to be doing physical work; when he is adding numbers, or solving business problems, he is said to be doing mental work. An examination of the definitions for these alleged types of work, however, reveals no clear-cut basis for this distinction. Whether one lifts a weight, or performs an act of reasoning, the sensori-neuro-muscular processes that are involved require the same kind of energy for their consummation. One task may, of course, use more the larger muscles of the back, trunk, and legs; while the other may bring into play more the finer muscles of the throat and vocal cords. This is a difference of degree rather than of kind, and there seems to be no reason for assuming that different principles govern them. There is, of course, justification for considering differences in the course of work for different tasks, or utilizing different muscle systems, but not because there is a basic difference in type requiring different explanatory concepts.

Measuring Work Output. We have already suggested the variables that go into the physical equation for work, *viz.*, mass, distance, and time. We have also noted the changes in the physiological cost of work in terms of accompanying metabolic changes. In considering human work, however, still other concepts become meaningful. These are *amount, excellence,* and *difficulty*,[2] in terms of which we also tend to evaluate work. Since each of these may vary independently, it becomes necessary to measure them separately under constant conditions of the other variables. In terms of these three variables plus time, there result four methods of measuring the effect of various experimental conditions on work output. These are (1) measuring the time required for producing a given amount of change under constant conditions of excellence and difficulty; (2) measuring the amount of change that can be produced in a given period of time under constant conditions of difficulty and excellence; (3) measuring changes in excellence (*e.g.*, in terms of accuracy, or number of errors) that take place under uniform conditions of the other three variables; and (4) measuring the difficulty of a task that can be performed under stated conditions of the other three variables. The last of these variables is the only one that presents considerable difficulty in measurement, but the general meaning will be clear enough to the reader so that we shall not go into the technicalities involved.

Efficiency. Engineers measure the efficiency of a mechanical device by the ratio of energy production to energy consumption. An application of similar notions to human work may be found in Poffenberger's[3] definition of efficiency as "the production of the maximum output of the highest quality in the shortest time, with the least expenditure of energy and the maximum satisfaction." Into the numerator of such an

[2] See Bills, A. G., *General Experimental Psychology,* p. 415, Longmans, Green, & Co., Inc., New York, 1934.

[3] Poffenberger, A. T., *Principles of Applied Psychology,* p. 364, Appleton-Century-Crofts, Inc., New York, 1942.

equation would have to be put everything that we get in return for work, *e.g.*, quantity of the product, its quality, and the various satisfactions it brings to consumer and producer; in the denominator belong all expenditures of materials, time, energy, health, and sacrifice of workers' satisfaction.

In practice it becomes quite impossible to devise methods for taking all these factors into account. Efficiency is relative. However, this definition should be kept in mind so as not, in our eagerness for rich returns, to lose sight of the human factor in work: work has effect upon the worker as well as upon the product. Many such effects are intangibles that do not lend themselves to ready measurement, such as values, personal satisfactions, and the like; but regarding their reality and essential importance there can be no reasonable doubt. For technical purposes and laboratory experimentation variations in efficiency are revealed as changes in the several variables described in the section above on Measuring Work Output, or physiologically as changes in the energy cost of work.

Fatigue and Impairment. It is well known that a machine doing work uses up energy in the form of fuel, and the machine also wears out. These phenomena result in less effective performance and lower output. Work similarly affects the human worker, using up energy stored in the muscles and impairing the organism. In both cases fuel can be replenished, and in a more limited way worn-out parts can be replaced or repaired. In the case of the human worker, however, there is alleged to be a special, temporary kind of interference with performance that results from work, called "fatigue."

Fatigue is a term of confused meaning. It has been used to refer to decline in work output, to the wearing-out process, to subjective feelings of aversion to work, to depletion phenomena, etc. Bartley and Chute[4] have subjected this term to semantic and critical scrutiny. Following these authors, we shall regard fatigue as "an experimental pattern arising in a conflict situation in which the general alignment of the individual may be described as aversion." In this state the individual feels limp and uncomfortable and interprets these feelings as signs of inadequacy for further activity. For physiological changes in tissues and organs that reduce the organism's ability to function, the term "impairment" is suggested. Impairment is observable only through methods of physiology and biochemistry, and reduction in the ability of the total organism to perform is not a criterion of impairment. A third term, "work output," that we have already used above, needs also to be distinguished. It refers to all activity of the organism and

[4] Bartley S. H., and Chute, Eloise, *Fatigue and Impairment in Man*, McGraw-Hill Book Company, Inc., New York, 1947.

may be measured either in the laboratory or in industry by methods already described.

VARIATIONS IN WORK OUTPUT

From what has gone before it appears that we dare not press too far the analogy between human efficiency and the efficiency of an inanimate machine. The analogue neglects many important facts about the complexity and adaptability of the human organism. As we have seen, during work not only is the objective situation changed in the sense of

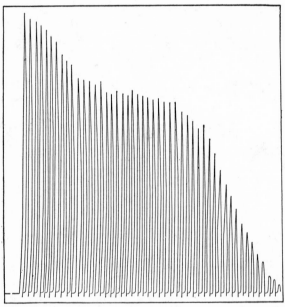

FIG. 12–1. Ergograph record of the flexors of the middle finger of the right hand. (*From Howell, W. H., A Text-book of Physiology. W. B. Saunders Company, Philadelphia.*)

shifts in space and alterations of substance, but the worker himself is undergoing change. Quite other than in the case of the machine, some of this change is in the nature of reversible impairment and recovery. Even more of it is in the nature of shifts in level of integration, for any of the organ systems of the human being can be used in many different ways and for many different purposes. All these changes feed back to affect the quality and quantity of the work being done. Two opposite effects may be noted: as a result of practice the organism learns and his work improves; as a result of fatigue and impairment a decrement may appear in the work output. Learning as a psychobiological phenomenon was treated in Chap. 4 and will be treated again in Chap. 14 in regard to its control and guidance in industry. Here we turn to a consideration of factors that appear in the course of work that are related to the other factors.

The Course of Work. The course of work is graphically represented in work curves, where performance is often plotted against time, as in Figs. 12–1 and 12–2. Figure 12–1 is the record of a subject lifting a weight of 1 kg. at the rate of one pull of maximum extent every other second and relaxing on the odd second. The original record was made by means of an instrument called the "ergograph," or "work recorder." The distance from the base line of each vertical stroke represents the extent of a pull, and there is one such stroke for every 2 seconds during

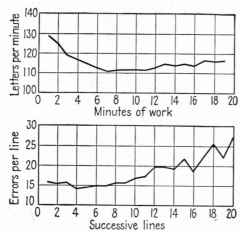

Fig. 12–2. Work curves for rate and accuracy in typing letters of the alphabet. (*Adapted from Robinson and Bills, Two Factors in the Work Decrement, J. Exp. Psychol., 1926, 9, 415–443.*)

which the work was performed. Variations in the height of the strokes therefore represent proportionate variations on the course of performance. The two curves in Fig. 12–2 were obtained in a somewhat different manner for a different type of task. The upper curve represents the number of letters typed by a subject during successive minutes of work; the lower curve depicts changes in the number of errors made by a subject under similar conditions.

The General Decrement. The most common feature found is the general work decrement. This has also been called the "fatigue effect," on the assumption that it is produced by physiological fatigue, *i.e.*, temporary impairment resulting from the work activity. The general decrement represents a decline in the rate or quality of performance when a task is sufficiently prolonged and continuous. The decrement appears in almost every type of activity if continuously performed, as in weight lifting at a constant rate, the daily and hourly output of industrial workers, typing, and the implicit operations of arithmetic.

The curves delineated in Figs. 12–1 and 12–2 clearly show work decrement. There seems to be, however, considerable variation in the manner in which this effect appears. Thus in Fig. 12–1 we note a gradual decline at the beginning of the record, followed by an extended period during which the worker was able to maintain a steady output somewhat lower than his initial level, which finally is followed by a rapid drop to a point where it is no longer possible to continue the performance until the capacity of the muscle is again restored through rest. In other cases, however, the subject may be able to continue at his initial level, or even a higher level, for a long time, and then either gradually or rapidly drop to a point where he can no longer continue. Many other patterns occur, and investigations have shown that they

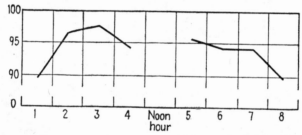

Fig. 12–3. Production during an 8-hour day. (*Adapted from Pub. Health Ser. Bull.,* 1920, *No.* 106, 74.)

are rather stable characteristics of individual performers. It seems that, no matter what muscle group is used or what the task may be, individuals will tend to show a work decrement of the same general type.

The Warming-up Effect. Figure 12–3 represents a production curve for a group of industrial workers during an 8-hour day. Production is expressed as per cent of maximum output of which the plant is capable. While the general decrement effect is apparent in the curve, a more striking feature of the curve is rise in production during the first 3 hours of the forenoon from an initial 89 per cent to a peak of 97 per cent. Such a rise in the work curve appearing before a decrement sets in is known as the "warming-up effect." This phenomenon is frequently observed not only in industrial output, but also in laboratory experiments.

The explanation usually offered for the warming-up effect is that it is due to a general stimulating effect of the metabolic by-products of exercise upon the efficiency of the muscles involved. The work decrement, on the other hand, is thought to be the result of the toxic effects of an excess of these same metabolites interfering with muscular performance. Be that as it may, the warming-up phenomenon is well known to athletes and other skilled performers, *e.g.*, a baseball pitcher could hardly pitch a game without first putting his muscles into proper condition by appropriate warming-up exercises.

The warming-up effect seems to appear in the early part of a somewhat discontinuous activity. In the case of continuous, uninterrupted work the immediate appearance of a work decrement is more commonly found. This fact is well illustrated in an experiment by Robinson and Heron,[5] the results of which are shown in Fig. 12–4. Subjects recited the alphabet backward as rapidly as possible under three different con-

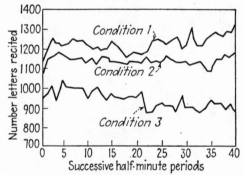

Fig. 12–4. Warming-up effect in reciting letters of alphabet backward. (*From Robinson, E. S., and Heron, W. L., The Warming-up Effect, J. Exp. Psychol.,* 1924, **7,** 81–97.)

ditions: (1) continuous recitation for 20 minutes, (2) alternating 30 seconds of recitation with 15 seconds of rest until a total of 20 minutes of work was performed; (3) alternating 30 seconds of recitation with 30 seconds of rest for a total of 20 minutes of working time. The results are in line with the explanations offered above. Since industrial work is often of such an interrupted nature, a rise in production during the early part of a working day may be widely expected; however, it should also be taken into consideration that the initial low level in the daily output curve may be incidental to such extraneous factors as time spent in getting tools ready, oiling the machinery, and other preparatory activities that consume time, instead of being an inherent feature of the course of work itself.

Work Spurts. Work curves invariably have an irregular zigzag appearance. This reveals considerable unevenness in the rate of performance during the work period. Such peaks are known as "spurts."

[5] Robinson, E. S., and Heron, W. T., The Warming-up Effect, *J. Exp. Psychol.,* 1924, **7,** 81–97.

Several types of spurts have been described, the most common being the initial spurt and the end spurt.

The initial spurt manifests itself in the work curve as an unusually high peak at the beginning. This effect is nicely shown in Fig. 12–5 from an investigation by Chapman and Nolan.[6] It represents the record of the number of columns of figures added by a subject in successive 30-second intervals for a total of 16 minutes of working time. A plausible explanation of this effect is that subjects tend to overshoot their ability for sustained performance at the beginning of the working period and, being unable to keep it up, drop down to a more comfortable pace that they can easily maintain for a considerable time.

The end spurt manifests itself at the close of the work period. It seems to appear when workers become aware of the approach of the end of the workday or work period. This suggests the possibility of its

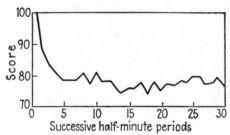

FIG. 12–5. Initial spurt in addition. (*After Chapman, D. C., and Nolan, W. J., Initial Spurt in a Simple Mental Function, Amer. J. Psychol., 1916, 27, 256–259.*)

being a motivational effect. The fact is extremely noteworthy that such a spurt may occur at the end of a long period of exhausting effort and after the subject had already dropped down to a very low level of performance. The organism, therefore, seems able under certain motivational sets to mobilize what appears to be a reserve of energy even after apparent exhaustion, a fact already noticed by William James[7] and often referred to as "second wind."

The Physiological Cost of Work

We have already seen that the work decrement, like other features of the work curve, has no simple explanation. The older explanation in terms of fatigue leads to confusion, for decreasing output is not invariably associated with fatigue in the sense in which we have defined it, or with physiological fatigue (impairment). It is not possible to infer

[6] Chapman, D. C., and Nolan, W. J., Initial Spurt in a Simple Mental Function, *Amer. J. Psychol.*, 1916, 27, 256–259.

[7] James, William, The Energies of Men, in *Memories and Studies*, Longmans, Green & Co., Inc., New York, 1911.

an inner condition of the worker from the work decrement and other signs of waning efficiency with any degree of certainty. Instead, we may investigate (1) the effects of work upon the worker in terms of physiological and psychological cost, and (2) the effect of various conditions surrounding work that affect the welfare of the worker and, perhaps, secondarily affect his efficiency. In the following paragraphs we shall examine the first of these problems.

The Energy Cost of Work. Human work involves metabolism, the transformation of energy within the body. Such energy transformation is measured by the amount of heat liberated by the organism during work. The unit of measurement used for this purpose is the large calorie, equal to the amount of heat required to raise the temperature of one kilogram of water one degree centigrade. Therefore the difference in the amount of heat liberated by the organism at work in excess of its heat production while at rest serves as a measure of the energy cost of work.

The human organism, in performing work, actually generates more energy than it transforms into mechanical work. This represents wasted energy. Fenn[8] has shown that an average man running at maximum speed generates about 13 hp. Of this, 2.94 hp. are used in useful work, the rest being wasted. This is a mechanical efficiency of 22.6 per cent. According to Hill,[9] a steam engine without a condenser possesses an efficiency rating of 7½ per cent; gas engines have a rating of 14 to 28 per cent; and diesel engines vary in efficiency from 29 to 35 per cent. Thus the human machine may be said to be mechanically more efficient than the steam engine, but less efficient than a diesel engine.

It is interesting to compare the energy demands of different kinds of tasks. The striking differences that appear are well illustrated in Table 12–1, which summarizes the hourly energy expenditures of a man of average weight while performing certain common motor work activities. Note the wide differences in the energy requirements of the different activities listed. If we assume a basal metabolic rate equal to the energy consumed while asleep, even sitting quietly in a chair raises the energy consumption by 55 per cent. Light household tasks, such as dishwashing or ironing, require another 60 per cent or more. Slow walking takes twice as much energy as sitting in a chair, while the task of walking upstairs at a normal speed uses up more than five times as much energy as ordinary walking and fully eleven times what is expended when sitting at rest. Walking upstairs is twice as energy-depleting as swimming or running at the rate of 5.3 miles per hour.

[8] Fenn, W. O., Mechanical Energy Expenditure in Sprint Running as Measured by Moving Pictures, *Amer. J. Physiol.*, 1929, **90**, 583.

[9] Hill, A. V., *Living Machinery*, p. 69, Harcourt, Brace and Company, Inc., New York, 1927.

Table 12–1. Energy Expenditures at Various Common Tasks*
(For a man weighing 70 kg.)

Task	Calories per Hour
Sleeping..	65
Awake lying still....................................	77
Sitting at rest......................................	100
Dressing or undressing..............................	118
Singing...	122
Typewriting rapidly.................................	140
Ironing, dishwashing................................	144
Walking slowly (2.6 miles per hour)..................	200
Carpentry, metal working, industrial painting............	240
Walking moderately fast (3.75 miles per hour)...........	300
Severe exercise.....................................	450
Sawing wood.......................................	480
Swimming..	500
Running (5.3 miles per hour)........................	570
Walking upstairs....................................	1,100

* From Table 23 in Sherman, Henry C., *Chemistry of Food and Nutrition* (6th ed: p. 185, The Macmillan Company, New York, 1941.

These facts in themselves are sufficient reasons for organizing the routine of work at home or in the shop so as to minimize the need for climbing stairs.

Since students actually and proverbially complain about the exhaustive nature of "mental" work, we may appropriately ask, what is the evidence? A number of studies bear upon this problem. Benedict and Benedict[10] required their subjects to add numbers without the use of paper and pencil. This activity required only 3 to 4 per cent more energy than lying at rest! The energy that was consumed was due to whatever muscular movements and tensions occurred during the performance. An experiment by Goldstein[11] forced this author to conclude that, when the effects of muscular tensions are eliminated from the effects of "mental" activity, any residual effects caused by supposed brain actions are not detectable by biochemical means. Indeed it has been said that the number of calories contained in a salted peanut will run the brain machinery in thinking for a whole day! These findings will not, of course, convince the student who is certain that he is ruining his health and due for a collapse as a result of his strenuous studying.

Much of the energy wasted in human performance is the result of improper management of muscles. Too many muscles are used, and

[10] Benedict, F. G., and Benedict, C. G., *Mental Effort in Relation to Gaseous Exchange, Heart Rate, and Mechanics of Respiration,* Carnegie Institute of Washington, Publication 446, 1933.

[11] Goldstein, H., A Biochemical Study of the Metabolism of Mental Work, *Arch. Psychol., N.Y.,* 1934, No. 164.

these encounter unnecessary resistances from opposing muscle groups. The fact that well-trained athletic and other skilled performers expend much less energy than a novice doing the same task is ample evidence for this generalization. With proper training it would be quite possible to learn how to economize considerably on the energy cost of work. This holds true also of mental work, where the fatigue encountered is caused more by worry, lack of interest, aversion to the task, and the like, than to thinking.

Physiological Breakdown. Work makes demands upon the circulatory and respiratory systems to provide the muscles with oxygen and fuel, to remove toxic by-products of metabolism, and to dissipate heat. Many things may go wrong, too, during strenuous muscular activity: the heart may fail, the muscles may utilize their energy in defective ways, and the physiological equilibrium may be strained to the breaking point. Such things as specific chemical lacks may develop, causing distress, anxiety, and even death. Investigators have studied blood-sugar depletion during heavy work but do not find so great a change in workers accustomed to heavy manual labor as might be expected.[12] More important than sugar depletion in bringing about symptoms of exhaustion in workers doing heavy labor under conditions of high temperature is the loss of salt through perspiration. Excessive salt depletion results in extreme symptoms and may be fatal, the effects being similar to heat stroke, including cramps, fatigue, heart distress and extreme palpitation, and depression.[13] Fortunately this lack may be easily and effectively counteracted by taking salt in the drinking water or in the form of salt tablets, a practice that has become common in heavy industries.

Neurological Effects. In an investigation of the effects of fatigue on muscular control in ergographic work, Ash[14] found that, as the work decrement becomes more and more evident in the performance of the middle finger, the adjacent index and third fingers make abortive contractions of increasing intensity. It appears, therefore, that, as the muscles become exhausted for a particular load, a neural overflow into adjacent muscles occurs. That this increases the energy cost of work and reduces efficiency is clear. A similar tendency to wasteful energy overflow has been observed to accompany the work decrement in everyday tasks. An analogous effect was found by Davis[15] to occur during "mental" performance. Since many jobs in modern industry require high-

[12] Dill, D. B., Bock, A. V., Edwards, H. T., and Kennedy, P. H., Industrial Fatigue, *J. Industr. Hyg. Tox.*, 1937, **18**, 417–431.

[13] Bartley and Chute, *op. cit.*, pp. 133–134.

[14] Ash, I. B., Fatigue and Its Effects upon Control, *Arch. Psychol.*, 1914, No. 31.

[15] Davis, C. R., Patterns of Muscular Activity during Mental Work and Their Constancy, *J. Exp. Psychol.*, 1939, **24**, 451.

speed precision performance, the above results would indicate that it is important not to pace work so fast that lost precision will seriously affect the quality of the product.

"Fatigue Transfer." We may consider here also what has been called "transfer of fatigue."[16] It has been found that, under certain circumstances, a decrement manifesting itself in a given type of performance will be accompanied by a decrement in other performances as well, as if there were a transfer of fatigue. This effect seems to take place according to a gradient along the dimensions of distance and time. The nearer the affected organ system to the system that has been focally active, the greater the effect; also the nearer the affected act is in time to the one that has just been functioning, the greater the effect. This is another example of the fact that sensori-nuero-motor systems never function in isolation but that the organism acts as a whole. What affects the parts affects the whole. Another interesting effect of prolonged and continuous work in this connection has been observed by Wickwire and Burge.[17] They found that the strength of a stimulus that will elicit the knee jerk becomes greater at the end of a workday than it was at the beginning and that strenuous work during the day gives a more pronounced effect of this type than lighter work. This may, of course, be interpreted as another indication of general organismic loss that temporarily results from work.

Effects on Sensory Processes and Attention. It is not farfetched to expect that work may affect sensory acuity and the discriminative functions in general. Older attempts to measure supposed decline in sensory acuity by means of the two-point cutaneous threshold, or by means of sensitivity to faradic stimulation, etc., have not been very successful, perhaps because these reactions are influenced by too many other variables that are difficult to control. Ferree and Rand[18] consider the ability to maintain maximal visual acuity over a period of 3 minutes, and the speed of accommodation for near and distant objects to be more promising criteria. Bartley and Chute[19] discuss the results of five different approaches to the assessment of so-called "visual fatigue": (1) sensory methods, (2) ergographic methods, (3) symptomatic methods, (4) ease of seeing method, and (5) conflict methods. Since so many modern occupations, e.g., aviation, make great demands on visual acuity, this area deserves as much attention as it can get.

---

[16] See Bills, op. cit., pp. 468ff. for a review of studies on this phenomenon.

[17] Wickwire, G. C., and Burge, W. E., The Threshold Stimulus of the Knee Jerk as an Index of Physical Fitness, Amer. J. Physiol., 1936, 116, 161.

[18] Ferree, C. F., and Rand, G., Lighting in Its Relation to the Eyes, Proc. Amer. Phil. Soc., 1918, 57, 440–478; Human Factor in Airplane Crashes, Arch. Ophthal. N.Y., 1937, 18, 789–795.

[19] Op. cit., Chap. 9.

Hollingworth[20] has revived the attempt to measure decline in efficiency by means of the ability to control attention. He found that, when subjects feel fatigued or have worked continuously for a period of time, their ability to control attention declines, as shown by an increasing rate of spontaneous reversals when looking at such an ambiguous figure as the transparent cube in Fig. 12–6. Such alternation is related to feelings of strain, blocking, diurnal variations in work speed, etc. These findings may have a significant bearing upon such matters as accident-proneness after prolonged periods of labor.

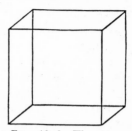

FIG. 12–6. The transparent cube: a reversible figure.

In conclusion it may be said that the relative significance of and relations between the various criteria of the physiological cost of work above described, and many others that have been described elsewhere, have not as yet been determined. However, that the organism pays a price for its own activity has been amply illustrated.

THE HYGIENE OF PERFORMANCE

In the preceding sections we discussed in brief detail the course of performance during a work spell and the effects of work upon output and upon the worker. Equally important are various factors about the management of work and the conditions that affect work that influence the welfare of the worker as well as his efficiency in production. We shall consider, in particular, the management of rest to ensure adequate recovery, maximum output, and increased worker satisfaction; the protection of worker health through industrial hygiene and safety programs; certain problems that relate to the functioning of the sensory and perceptive powers in the guidance of work; the influence of surrounding atmospheric conditions; and the effects of environmental disturbing influences.

REST AND RECOVERY FROM WORK

We turn now to a consideration of the problem of the management of the workday in such a way as to ensure adequate recovery from work and to maintain the highest level of productivity that is consistent with the interest and wefare of the worker. This brings up first the concept of a margin of safety in work.

The Margin of Safety. In considering the construction of a bridge or other mechanical device the factor of safety must be taken into ac-

[20] Hollingworth, H. L., Perceptual Fluctuations as a Fatigue Index, *J. Exp. Psychol.*, 1939, **24**, 511–519.

count. This has been defined as the ratio of the greatest load capacity of the device to the maximum load that it is designed to bear. Safe construction requires a margin of safety at least three times this factor.

A similar concept may be applied to human work, where the safety factor may be reckoned as the ratio of the greatest potential increase in metabolic rate to the observed increase in work. Here the margin of safety should also be at least three times the safety factor. When such a sufficient reserve of energy is available tasks are carried out easily and with little awareness of exertion. The hygiene of work requires the maintenance of this minimal margin plus a sufficient additional reserve that the worker may invest in the enjoyment of activities of his own choosing at the end of the working day without seriously encroaching on the reserve allowed for the margin of safety.

In protecting the margin of safety, it must be remembered that productivity and recovery from work are dependent upon a complex set of factors. Because of the limitations of language these can be discussed only one at a time, but in actuality in constant simultaneous interaction. What may be true of one set of conditions, therefore, may no longer be true if even a single factor is changed. It is not possible to prescribe a set of ideal rules for avoiding the undesirable effects of work and ensuring peak efficiency. For instance, rest pauses introduced into a 10-hour day may be quite different in effect from similar pauses introduced into a 6-hour day. Each type of work is different and must be studied in relation to the conditions that are peculiar to it. The general fact, however, that when work is continued beyond a certain point the physiological cost becomes rapidly excessive and efficiency declines has been amply illustrated by industrial investigations.

Length and Distribution of Rest Pauses. The question arises as to where in the working day rest pauses may be most effective, how frequent they should be, and how long. No categorical answer can be given. Shepard,[21] in an experimental situation, had 12 college men work continuously with a chest weight machine for 8 hours at a stretch. He introduced rest pauses of varying duration at various points of the day, during which the men were required to lie down and relax completely. He concluded that a worker doing light muscular work in an 8-hour shift cannot give his maximum output unless he rests at least 16.6 per cent of the time during working hours. Vernon and Bedford[22] studied the effects of introducing rest pauses into the work schedule of light industry. In one of their investigations they compared the hourly output without rest pauses during a 2-week interval of girls employed

[21] Shepard, G. H., Effect of Rest Periods on Production, *Person. J.*, 1928, 7, 186–202.

[22] Vernon, H. M., and Bedford, T., The Influence of Rest Pauses on Light Industrial Work, *Industr. Fatigue Res. Bull.*, 1924, No. 75.

at labeling with the output when they were given a 10-minute rest in the middle of the forenoon. In spite of the resulting 2 per cent loss in working time occasioned by the rest pauses, production increased 13 per cent. Another investigation of theirs showed a 13 per cent gain in production of girls assembling bicycle chains when they were allowed to rest 5 minutes at the end of each hour of work.

In adopting practices in regard to duration of rest pauses the aim should be to allow sufficient time to overcome the deleterious effects of a previous work period without interfering with the continuity of work or introducing production slumps from which the worker must recover by a warming-up period. Investigations seem to indicate that a rest pause of 10 minutes' duration will accomplish this end for most industrial work, and frequent rests of 2 to 5 minutes per hour for mental work. The frequency of rest pauses must, of course, not be great enough to cut down the working time so much that the gain in efficiency will be at the expense of total daily production.

In regard to the question of location of rest pauses, investigators seem agreed that rest is most effective if it comes at or just after the peak of the work curve. This position would, of course, have to be determined for each job. In theory, if the rest pauses are introduced at this point, production should be maintained at a high level and a work decrement should not appear.

Rest pauses deserve much more attention than they have received. The type of work in which they are most beneficial would be work that is repetitive and unvaried, involves uninterrupted physical exertion, calls for strict attention, requires the maintenance of tiring postures, and involves exposures to extremes of temperature, humidity, etc.[23]

Rest pauses may be voluntary or formal. The latter are introduced in accordance with supervisor policy. However, when workers are left to their own devices, they often take rest pauses of their own. These are usually not authorized. Such voluntary pauses often take the form of migrations to the lavatory, where a cigarette may be smoked and a few minutes of conversation with fellow workers may be indulged in. It is questionable whether workers derive the greatest benefit from rest under these circumstances, but it must be admitted that in many plants the lavatory is the only place of respite without fear of direct censure.

It would seem that authorized formal rest periods are more effective than these furtive escapes from the tedium of work. Relative to this point, McGehee and Owen[24] observed the occurrence of unauthorized

---

[23] *Cf*. Bartley and Chute, *op. cit.*, p. 181.

[24] McGehee, W., and Owen, E. B., Authorized and Unauthorized Rest Pauses in Clerical Workers, *J. Appl. Psychol.*, 1940, 24, 605–614.

rest pauses among clerical workers in government offices, and the relation of these to production, and compared the results with those obtained when authorized pauses were introduced. They found that less time was spent in unauthorized rest under the latter conditions and that daily output showed considerable improvement.

How may workers best spend their rest pauses? Should they be left entirely to their own devices, or should the nature of the "rest" be prescribed? Rest periods are most often spent in the workroom and are used for the consumption of refreshments. Shepard in the previously cited study required his subjects to relax while lying down. Wyatt[25] reports a study in which the following uses of rest periods were effective in the order listed: complete resting in a chair, with a gain of 9.3 per cent; uncontrolled rest, with a gain of 8.3 per cent; listening to music, with a gain of 3.9 per cent; having tea, with a gain of 3.4 per cent; and walking about, with a gain of 1.5 per cent. In the case of mental work, Bills[26] believes that complete relaxation is apt to bring about an undesirable reduction in tonicity that would make resumption of work difficult. He feels that a more active use of rest pauses is to be preferred.

The following principles serve to summarize the conclusions of extensive industrial researches in regard to rest pauses:

1. Duration of rest pauses should not be less than 10 minutes.
2. Two 10-minute rest periods are more effective than one 20-minute period.
3. The noon lunch hour should not be considered a rest period.
4. The rest period should not be an "earned" privilege, but a pause for rest granted to everyone.
5. Control of rest periods in regard to relaxing activity should provide best results.

Length of Workday. The question regarding the optimal length of the workday was once a hotly disputed issue. Before the introduction of the 8-hour day in industry it was not unusual for men to work as many as 100 hours a week and 15 to 16 hours a day! Now it is generally recognized that the 8-hour day excels not only from the point of view of worker attitude, but in superior production and fewer accidents. Thus the shorter workday fortunately serves the needs of both workers and management. Only as an emergency expedient during times of national crisis and manpower shortage are longer hours justified, and then only on the basis of extra reward in the form of overtime pay. Prior to the Second World War there was the beginning of a tendency toward the adoption of a 6-hour day in many places. This gives rise to new problems, since under the 6-hour plan men are re-

[25] Wyatt S., Rest Pauses in Industry, *Industr. Fatigue Res. Bull.*, 1927, No. 42.
[26] Bills, A. G., *The Psychology of Efficiency*, p. 124, Harper & Brothers, New York, 1943.

quired to work continuously without rest pauses. Worker reaction to the 6-hour day on the part of workers who had also had experience with the 8-hour day was reported by Best.[27] Two hundred and eighty mill workers were divided in opinion as follows: 23 per cent thought the 6-hour day less fatiguing; 42.5 per cent reported no difference; and 35.5 per cent thought the 6-hour day more fatiguing.

VISUAL REQUIREMENTS

Modern living imposes a heavy load on the visual functions from the earliest years and throughout life. Almost every job involves the ability to see, and many industrial jobs require specialized seeing skills. Some jobs require the worker to see accurately at close range, as in the case of inspectors and hosiery loopers; others require keen distance vision, as in the case of bus drivers and aviators; still others require the ability to distinguish differences of color, as in the case of textile workers and operators of color-printing presses. Industry is paying increasing attention to the visual requirements of various jobs and the visual qualifications of workers.[28]

Modern optometry and ophthalmology, in their efforts to aid men to see more comfortably, have advanced far beyond the diagnosis and correction of structural and pathological conditions of the eye. There is an increasing recognition of the fact that seeing is an act of the whole organism and that faulty habit patterns may interfere with accurate visual performance as much as refraction. Seeing is a function of the nervous system as well as of processes taking place within the eye itself. Its hygiene cannot be restricted to the latter, and modern methods of eye training often accomplish what the mere fitting of glasses cannot do.

Among the factors involved in comfortable and efficient seeing, the following are among the most common:

Visual Acuity. Visual acuity can no longer be presumed to be properly measured by separate determination of the acuity of each eye, for functional seeing involves the cooperation of two eyes. It not infrequently happens that an individual will have high visual ability in one eye while the other is covered, but very poor acuity when the two eyes are used together.[29] Acuity must also be considered relative to the distance at which the eyes are to be used. There is no high correlation between acuity in near and far vision. Tiffin[30] presents evidence for an

[27] Best, E. L., U.S. Dept. of Labor, *Reports*, 1934, No. 116.

[28] See Tiffin, J., *Industrial Psychology*, Chap. 6, Prentice-Hall, Inc., New York, 1942.

[29] See Betts, E. A., *The Prevention and Correction of Reading Difficulties*, p. 148, Row, Peterson & Company, Evanston, Ill., 1936.

[30] *Op. cit.*, pp. 139–140.

inverse relationship between visual acuity tested at 20 feet and production in the case of hosiery loopers, the operators with the poorer vision being the more productive. However, when tested at a distance of 13 inches these workers had such good vision that the tests employed failed to discriminate between them. In view of such findings it becomes essential that workers be placed in jobs to which they are visually suited; or that they be outfitted with seeing aids that enable them to be proficient; or finally, that they be trained to use their eyes in the way their jobs demand.

Postural Coordination. Pronounced inability in convergence, known as squint, seriously interferes with depth perception. Minor deviations, known as phorias, may or may not interfere with efficient seeing, depending upon the extent to which the individual is able to compensate for them. Such deviations may be due to faulty habits or to organic conditions; and they often impose a severe strain on the seeing mechanism, giving rise to serious inaccuracies of perception that, as Tiffin has shown, may influence efficiency on the job.

Stereopsis. Faulty stereopsis, or depth perception, is often produced by the habit of suspension, the image of one eye being disregarded so that vision becomes essentially monocular. Such habits result in misjudgment of distances, an important function in the skillful operation of rapidly moving vehicles, etc. Stereopsis can be improved through orthoptic training.

Color Vision. It is said that approximately 4 or 5 per cent of men are partially color deficient, the most common type being the confusion of red and green with yellow or gray. We have already indicated certain fields in which this ability is essential. Defective color vision is considered congenital and not subject to correction; however, its presence or absence in workers must be determined by appropriate tests to ensure efficiency and safety.

Provisions for Greater Visual Efficiency. This is not the place for an exhaustive treatment of modern methods of eye care and the science of seeing, but a number of practices are listed that, under competent direction, foster better vision and greater efficiency on the job. These include

1. Optometry to determine an individual's visual characteristics.
2. Corrective methods for mechanical defects, including lenses and corrective exercise.
3. Orthoptic training for increasing ocular efficiency, especially in regard to stereopsis and convergence.
4. Job placement with respect to visual aptitudes of applicants and the visual requirements of the job.

5. Simplification of tasks to reduce the number and complexity of visual operations required of the worker.
6. Optical aids on the job, *e.g.*, magnifiers, projectors, gauges, etc., that obviate eyestrain in the making of judgments of size, direction, quality, etc.; also occupational spectacles that adjust the focus for close work. Figure 12–7 shows the improvement of production resulting from the use of occupational spectacles by hosiery loopers.

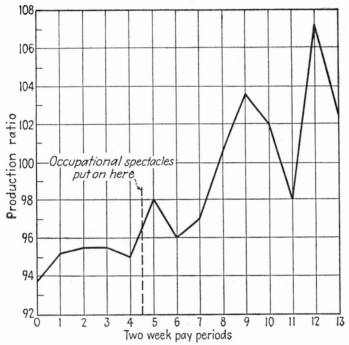

FIG. 12–7. Increase in production of hosiery loopers after putting on occupational spectacles. (*Adapted from Tiffin, Joseph, Industrial Psychology, Prentice-Hall, Inc., New York, 1942.*)

7. Devices to protect against dusts, splash, chips, etc.
8. Adequate illumination.
9. Periodic check-up and measures to maintain visual efficiency.
10. Education in eye care.

Illumination. Seeing, as Luckiesh says, is a "partnership of vision and lighting," and one of the most direct ways to improve efficiency is to provide adequate illumination at the workplace in accordance with the requirements of the visual tasks to be done. The effect of improved illumination is brought out in Fig. 12–8, which shows the effect of increasing illumination from 8 to 60 foot-candles, by means of supplementary lighting fixtures, on the rate of production and of error in a key-punching operation. Production began to increase and errors to diminish as soon as the new equipment was installed, the production level ultimately reaching a point 60 per cent higher than under the previous conditions of low illumination.

How much light is required for different tasks is still a somewhat debatable question, depending upon standards of different investigators. Requirements vary with respect to individual differences in sensitivity to light. Ferree and Rand[31] found the upper limit of light intensity conducive to comfortable reading varying over a wide range from below 5 to above 40 foot-candles in a group of persons ranging in age

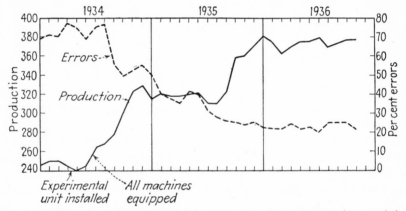

Fig. 12–8. Effect of supplementary lighting on production and errors in a statistical key-punching operation. (*Adapted from Luckiesh, M., and Moss, F. K., The Science of Seeing, p. 275, D. Van Nostrand Company, Inc., New York, 1937.*)

from ten to seventy-seven years. About half these people found their upper limit for comfort in the range from 10 to 20 foot-candles.

Luckiesh recommends much higher lighting values than most other investigators, but in view of his lifelong research in this field his recommendations are given in Table 12–2. Judged by these standards many of the tasks performed by workers in the factory, in offices, and in the home are accomplished under conditions of illumination definitely too low, and Luckiesh's reference to a "half-seeing world" appears to be more than a figure of speech.

Glare. An important requirement of adequate illumination is that the visual field be evenly lighted. When contrasts of brightness exist, the worker will experience discomfort from glare. Examples of intense glare

[31] Ferree, C. E., and Rand, G., Good Working Conditions for the Eyes, *Person. J.,* 1936–1937, **15**, 339.

Table 12–2. Conservative Foot-candle Recommendations on a Rational Basis of Characteristics of the Visual Task and Requirements of Performance*

Foot-candles Required	For Tasks Such As
100 or more	Very severe and prolonged tasks such as fine needlework, fine engraving, fine penwork, fine assembly, sewing on dark goods, discrimination of fine details of low contrast as in inspection.
50–100	Severe and prolonged tasks such as proofreading, drafting, difficult reading, watch repairing, fine machine-work, average sewing and other needlework.
20–50	Moderately critical and prolonged tasks such as clerical work, ordinary reading, common benchwork, average sewing and other needlework on light goods.
10–20	Moderate and prolonged tasks of office and factory and, when not prolonged, ordinary reading and sewing on light goods.
5–10	Visually controlled work in which seeing is important, but more or less interrupted or casual, and does not involve discrimination of fine details or low contrasts.
0–5	The danger zone for severe visual tasks and for quick and certain seeing. Satisfactory for perceiving larger objects and for casual seeing.

* Adapted from Luckiesh and Moss, The Science of Seeing, Table LVIII, p. 345, D. Van Nostrand Company, Inc., New York, 1937.

are the reflections of the sun from brightly polished surface, or the existence of a bright light source within the visual field, as when light is placed directly in front of the worker's eyes. Lower brightness differences commonly encountered are due to uneven illumination, deep shadows, etc. These are also glaring and interfere with proper seeing.

Responsible for visual interference and discomfort from glare is first the fact that the retina of the eye cannot adjust to greatly disparate brightnesses, and the result is glare. There is, further, a reflex tendency of the eyes to turn to the brighter of two light sources, distracting vision away from the task at hand and reducing the quality of visual performance. The inhibition of these movements requires the opposition of antagonistic muscles, causing strain. Finally there may be continual fluctuation between the glare spot and the task, imposing intolerable strain on the eye muscles. These glare effects often result in feelings of general fatigue, nervousness, and even nausea and visceral upset.

Freedom from glare is difficult to achieve with artificial illumination since the light source must be close to the worker's eyes. It is not uncommon to find glare spots as much as a million times the light intensity of the darkest spots in the room. The worst lighting is found when there is a bare light source within the visual field. The best is indirect lighting, with no lighting units within the field of view, the light being reflected from the ceiling and walls. Unfortunately, this form of lighting is expensive. The cost of indirect illumination may be reduced by combining direct and indirect lighting, keeping the light source out of the visual field of workers as much as possible. When lights occur in the field of view, either they should be shaded or the workers should wear eye shades to shield the eyes from glare. Such shades should be opaque and should have a light, not a dark, lining, since the contrast of a dark lining with the surrounding field of illumination would introduce another source of glare. One of the most efficient methods of lighting is the controlled mixing of natural sunlight from large windows and artificial light in such a way that the illumination is kept at a constant level automatically.[32]

ATMOSPHERIC CONDITIONS AFFECTING EFFICIENCY

Chief among the conditions of the surrounding atmosphere that influence the health and efficiency of men are sunlight, the composition of the air, and cooling power of the air.

Sunlight. Sunlight is one of the essentials of organic life without which men cannot live for long. Insufficient light results in degenerative diseases, increased susceptibility to infection, and lassitude. In many industries men labor in semidarkness in places where the sun cannot penetrate. Workers in offices and factories, too, get insufficient exposure to sunlight during the working day. Even the smoke pall that hangs over industrial cities cuts down the effective sunlight by 40 per cent or more, particularly in the winter. This constitutes a serious threat to the health of thousands of city dwellers.

Industry, to be sure, cannot make sunshine where the sun will not shine. The only remedy for inadequate exposure to sunlight in the interest of health and efficiency is to give workers sufficient time off during daylight hours. Daylight saving time, introduced first as a war conservation measure, has become a widespread practice that enables workers to arrive home early enough to enjoy several hours in outdoor activity. The industrial hygiene program should encourage workers in the practice of spending some time daily in outdoor pursuits.

The Atmosphere. Pure air contains 78.14 per cent nitrogen, 20.93 per cent oxygen, 0.90 per cent argon, and 0.03 per cent carbon dioxide. In addition, the atmospheric air contains water vapor and many impurities in the form of fumes, vapors, dusts, etc. These may be harmful to man in certain concentrations.

Oxygen is an absolute necessity for organic life. Lack of it will cause death in a few moments. Fortunately the proportion of oxygen in the atmosphere where men live and work is very constant, rarely varying beyond the limits of 20 and 21 per cent. Thus lack of oxygen is not a problem under the usual conditions of shop and office. The recent

[32] See Ferree, C. E., and Rand, G., The Effect of Mixing Artificial Light with Daylight, *Trans. Illum. Engng. Soc.,* 1926, **21,** 588–609.

development of high-altitude aviation, however, presents problems in which oxygen want plays a more prominent role. Although the percentage of oxygen at high altitudes is the same as near the surface of the earth, the air is more rarefied because of decreased pressure, so that an equal space contains less in absolute amount of the gas than at sea level. Thus at an elevation of 5,000 ft. above sea level the amount of oxygen is cut down 17 per cent, and at 10,000 ft. by as much as 32 per cent. Under these conditions less oxygen is taken into the lungs by each breath, and this must be compensated for by more rapid breathing and heart action.

Reducing the amount of oxygen in the air being inhaled results in a series of psychological disturbances that have been investigated by McFarland[33] and others. The first disturbance to appear as a result of oxygen want is a loss of critical capacity and self-criticism. Subjects show mental confusion and faulty judgment. They may become emotionally upset but do not ascribe their emotional state, or their failure in tasks attempted, to the effects of reduced oxygen intake. This fact is now so well known in aviation that pilots are required to turn on their oxygen supply at a definite altitude whether they think they need it or not. Such disturbances are usually accompanied by feelings of exhilaration resembling those in mild alcoholic intoxication.

At a later stage of oxygen depletion both simple and complex psychological functions are impaired. High-speed coordination, attention, concentration, choice reaction time, speed and accuracy in arithmetic computation, etc., show marked decline in efficiency.[34] Still later, motor and habitual sensory processes become affected. Handwriting becomes illegible because of tremor and ataxia; letters are omitted or reversed in order and undergo a change in size. Vision is disturbed. The eyes fixate longer and make more frequent fixations per line of print in reading,[35] and dark adaptation is affected.[36] When the oxygen concentration of the cerebral blood supply falls to below 24 per cent, consciousness is lost and muscular spasms occur. These and related findings are of especial importance for the development and safety of air navigation at high altitudes.

[33] McFarland, R. A., Psycho-physiological Studies at High Altitudes in the Andes, *J. Comp. Psychol.*, 1937, **23**, 191–258; **24**, 147–220; The Psychological Effects of Reduced Oxygen Pressure, *Res. Publ. Assoc. Ner. Ment. Dis.*, 1939, 19, 112–143; The Internal Environment and Behavior: I. Introduction and the Role of Oxygen, *Amer. J. Psychiat.*, 1941, **97**, 858–877.

[34] Barach, J. E., McFarland, R. A., and Seitz, C. P., Effects of Oxygen Deprivation on Complex Mental Functions, *J. Aviat. Med.*, 1937, 8, 1–11.

[35] McFarland, R. A., Evans, J. N., and Halperin, M. H., Ophthalmic Aspects of Acute Oxygen Deficiency, *Arch. Ophthal., N.Y.*, 1941, **26**, 886–913.

[36] McFarland, R. A., and Evans, J. N., Alterations in Dark Adaptation under Reduced Oxygen Tension, *Amer. J. Physiol.*, 1939, **127**, 37–50.

Carbon dioxide is given off into the air as a product of animal metabolism. It serves also to stimulate breathing. Excess CO_2 concentration is usually not a problem under conditions normally encountered in work. In the worst-ventilated office, factory, or school, its concentration does not rise above 0.5 per cent, at which level it is harmless. Even a concentration of 2 per cent will cause no discomfort, although breathing will be accelerated about 10 per cent. Concentrations beyond this level rapidly increase the rate of breathing. A concentration of 6 per cent brings great distress, with headache, perspiration, and flushing, though no immediate danger to life. CO_2 does not act as a poison, even in large concentrations. Its effects are due to the displacement of the oxygen in the blood, thus producing a kind of anoxia.

Nitrogen becomes a problem only under conditions of high atmospheric pressure. In submarines, tunneling operations, and deep-sea diving, men work under intense pressure, running as high as 50 lb. per sq. in., or more than three times the normal pressure at sea level. High atmospheric pressure is not uncomfortable to the worker after a brief period of adaption; but under intense pressure nitrogen becomes more soluble in the blood and when the worker undergoes decompression small nitrogen bubbles may form in the body tissues. This is the condition feared by deep-sea divers, which they refer to as "the bends." When decompression is too rapid there is extreme discomfort and pain, and under certain circumstances death may result. It is important that workers at high-compression jobs breathe air as free from carbon dioxide as possible, since the latter stimulates excess breathing, thus increasing the amount of gases taken into the body to be dissolved in the blood.

Fumes, vapors, and dusts are impurities in the air sometimes present in harmful concentrations. Under such conditions they may threaten health and efficiency. Some of the substances resulting from industrial operations are extremely toxic, while others merely bring discomfort and distract the worker. Adequate devices for carrying away noxious substances and pouring fresh air into the worker's environment must be provided, or gas masks and other protective devices must be worn when the impurities themselves cannot be removed rapidly enough.

Vile odors, too, are present in some industries. Unless these are associated with toxic substances, they act more as psychological distractions than in a directly harmful manner. Since, however, distractions interfere with performance, unpleasant odors should be counteracted by introducing fresh air into the workroom. People differ widely in their tolerance for unpleasant odors, some finding it almost impossible to adapt to them.

Cooling Power of the Air. Work generates heat. The human machine, therefore, like any other machine, must be cooled in order to function smoothly. The temperature of the human body must be maintained at a level near a mean of 98.6°F., a regulatory function depending upon most delicate physical adjustments under the varying conditions to which it is exposed. Most of the excess heat generated by the body as a result of activity is dissipated into the surrounding air. Since the latter is subject to great irregularity, the chief problem of ventilation is that of maintaining the cooling properties of the air at an optimal level for health, comfort, and efficiency. Factors involved in cooling the body are temperature, relative humidity, and the movement of the air. In general, however, the results of research show that a temperature of 68°F. at 50 per cent relative humidity is optimal for moderate physical work and for mental activity. Above and below these conditions discomfort will be experienced that may be sufficient to affect efficiency under otherwise normal working conditions, although under test conditions these effects may be counteracted by extra effort of motivated subjects.

The Working Environment

There are other factors that affect work for better or worse besides the ones we have thus far discussed. In addition to ventilation, illumination, physiological states, and the like there are many sights, sounds, odors, pressures that at all times compete for attention. Efficiency is a resultant of *all* the forces that during a given time influence behavior, some of them serving as motivators or accelerators, others as disturbances. Psychologists interested in "human engineering" have of late been giving more attention to these incidental factors that do not enter directly into the tasks in which men are engaged. Thus the influence of disturbers, of boredom, of noise, of music, and of other conditions has been investigated.

Distractions. Distractions may be defined as any stimuli that interfere with performance and disturb the worker. They may be external in source, such as loud noises, unusual sights, and foul odors; or they may be due to internal states of boredom, dissatisfaction, or emotional conflict. Thus a distraction is not a unique form of stimulation but simply a matter of paying attention to stimuli that are foreign to the task one is supposed to be doing. Certain attributes of stimuli have a peculiar advantage in attracting attention and therefore are distracting if they are unrelated to one's task. They include such factors as intensity, sudden change, movement, unusual quality, and duration, or persistence.

Effect of Distractions on Performance. The results of investigations regarding the effects of distractions are not unequivocal. On the one hand, it is common observation that workers are disturbed by the occurrence of unusual or intense incidental stimuli; and on the other hand experimental laboratory studies show little, or no, detrimental effects of so-called "distractors." Indeed, the effect may under certain circumstances be beneficial.

In an experiment on the effects of distraction on thought processes Hovey[37] equated two groups of college students on the Army Alpha test. Six weeks after the initial test both groups were again tested with another form of the Alpha, the experimental group being exposed during the testing to severe distraction. Bells, buzzers, shrill whistles, organ pipes, and other noisemakers were sounded, while a phonograph played lively music. Spotlights were continuously flashed off and on in utter confusion, while assistants were constantly going in and out with a great deal of ostentation in manner and garb. In spite of these unusual conditions, the experimental group performed nearly as well as the control group, making a score of 133.9 as compared with 137.6 for the controls. This is a loss of only 3.7 points ascribed to the distractions.

In a classic experiment Morgan[38] tested the effects of noise on the performance of subjects engaged in code substitution, by means of a typewriterlike apparatus that also automatically recorded the strength of the subjects' responses. Work was first performed under conditions of quiet; then the distractions were introduced, followed by another 10 minutes of quiet. The distractions were in the nature of loud and unpleasant noises. The subjects improved in the task throughout the experiment, although at the onset of the distracting conditions there was some temporary slowing up of the work. Most subjects, however, regained their previous speed quickly and went on to further improvement during the period of distraction. When the noises ceased there was again a brief slump, so that it appears that cessation of noise is also distracting once subjects have become accustomed to it.

Morgan points out that subjects tend to overcome distractions by putting forth extra effort, this extra effort being in excess of that needed to overcome the disturbing influences. Hence, paradoxically, distractions may have a facilitating effect on work under these conditions. Similar conclusions were reached by Ford,[39] who investigated the effect of noises on the performance of intellectual tasks.

[37] Hovey, H. B., Effects of General Distraction on the Higher Thought Processes, *Amer. J. Psychol.*, 1928, 40, 585–591.

[38] Morgan, J. J. B., Overcoming of Distractions and Other Resistances, *Arch. Psychol.*, 1916, No. 84.

[39] Ford, A., Attention-automatization: An Investigation of the Transitional Nature of Mind, *Amer. J. Psychol.*, 1929, 41, 1–32.

It seems, then, from the above considerations that the effects of distractions are closely related to motivation. The motivated subject overcomes the deleterious effects of unfavorable temperature, unfavorable atmospheric conditions, foul odors, and distracting noises. He does this by putting forth extra effort, which in Morgan's experiment was shown by harder pressure exerted by the subjects on the keys of the apparatus during distractions than during periods of quiet. Other experimenters have shown that negative adaptation to distraction sets in rapidly if the distraction continues or is repetitive. Thus the extra effort, or excess energy cost of work, under distracting conditions

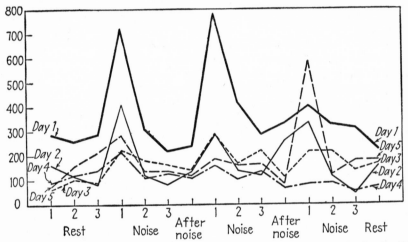

FIG. 12–9. The effects of distraction on muscle tension. (*From Davis, R. C., The Muscular Tension Reflex and Two of Its Modifying Conditions, Ind. Univ. Pub., Sci. Ser., 1935, No. 3.*)

finally becomes negligible. This is apparent in an experiment by Davis,[40] the results of which are illustrated in Fig. 12–9. This study investigated the effort expended by a group of subjects during periods of quiet and of noise. The subjects did no work but sat in a chair during the experiment, and action potentials from the forearm were recorded. Following an initial 5-minute period of quiet, three cycles alternating 2 minutes of noise and 2 minutes of quiet were studied. This was done on 5 successive days. It will be noticed that on the first day of the experiment a sharp increase in action potentials occurred at the onset of noise in each instance but that on successive days this effect became less and less pronounced. This type of adaptation takes

[40] Davis, R. C., The Muscular Tension Reflex and Two of Its Modifying Conditions, *Ind. Univ. Pub., Sci. Ser.,* 1935, No. 3.

place in a variety of distracting circumstances and presents an excellent illustration of the adaptive capacity of the human organism.

Boredom. Most baffling among the many types of distractions are certain subjective conditions to which workers are prone, outstanding among these being boredom, or lack of zest for work. Although the bored man's muscles do not ache from fatigue, and although he has not infringed upon the margin of safety, he nevertheless shows a work decrement. This is clearly illustrated in Fig. 12–10, which depicts changes in the output of a worker assembling bicycle chains under conditions in which he reported boredom compared with a similar period in which he felt free from boredom. Boredom set in after about 5 minutes of work, at which point the two curves diverge, the work

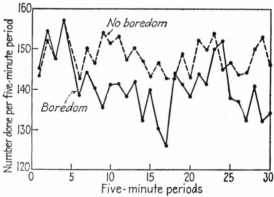

Fig. 12–10. Effect of monotony in an assembly task. (*Adapted from Wyatt, S., and Fraser, J. A., The Effects of Monotony in Work, Industr. Fatigue Res. Bd.,* 1929, No. 56, 10.)

under the condition of boredom showing a sharp decrement. At the end of 100 minutes of work this worker believed the end of the distasteful work period to be near, and his production curve rose accordingly for a while. When the quitting signal did not occur, however, the work level dropped again. In Fig. 12–11 is shown the diurnal curve of output of an industrial worker who reported boredom usually about the middle of a working spell. Note the sharp drops in output correlated with these periods.

The causes of boredom are to be discovered in the worker rather than in the objective conditions of work, although it is frequently associated with monotony or sameness of the tasks performed. The subjective nature of boredom is evident from the fact that activities that are very interesting to some people may create boredom in others. A concert that will thrill one person may be considered uninteresting by another. It is generally agreed that boredom occurs when an individual must attend to things because of duty although he wants to attend to something quite different. This conflict between subjective desire and duty sets up tensions that bring about a state of general weariness and loss of zest.

According to Poffenberger, workers are most apt to show boredom in simple, highly repetitive, and rapidly repeated operations. Hence in industrial jobs boredom can be reduced by providing variety in the tasks performed, reducing the work tempo to a tolerable pace, providing for frequent rest pauses, and allowing for social intercourse during the workday. Some men, it should be observed, like monotonous work requiring repetition of the same task over and over again. For

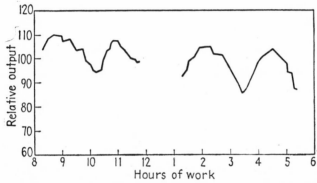

Fig. 12–11. Relation between output and boredom in industrial work. Worker reported feeling of boredom about the middle of the forenoon and again about the middle of the afternoon. (*Adapted from Wyatt, S., and Fraser, J. A., The Effects of Monotony in Work, Industr. Fatigue Res. Bd., 1929, No. 56, 13.*)

some people such work seems simpler than work requiring varied activity, and for others it gives time for thinking about other things. The tendency to daydream must, however, be guarded against in jobs requiring strict attention.

ENGINEERING ASPECTS OF EFFICIENCY

It should be apparent that human efficiency is conditioned by every conceivable factor surrounding behavior. A complete treatment of the subject would be coextensive with the whole of psychology and much of physiology. The dependence of performance on individual differences in intelligence, special aptitudes, training, age, sex, etc., is discussed in other chapters of this book. The effects of mental health, diet, and drugs have also been discussed. There remain for treatment certain principles for economizing effort and time in the persuance of a job through work methods and equipment design. This important field may be labeled "efficiency engineering."

WORK METHODS

Wasteful methods of work and the utilization of energy result in a tremendous loss of time and energy in industrial operations and in everyday life. Noting this fact led F. B. Gilbreth, the father of scientific management and efficiency engineering, to propose finding the easiest and most economical ways of doing a task as a first step in reducing waste and production costs. He and his wife developed a system of procedures that they called "time-motion study."[41] They classified all movements into a number of fundamental classes, called "therbligs" (Gilbreth spelled backwards). The names of these units of movements are as follows:

1. Searching	9. Inspecting
2. Finding	10. Transporting load
3. Selecting	11. Prepositioning
4. Grasping	12. Releasing load
5. Positioning	13. Transporting (empty)
6. Assembling	14. Waiting (unavoidable)
7. Using	15. Waiting (avoidable)
8. Taking apart	16. Resting

By means of special graphic devices the Gilbreths recorded the course of movements during the performance of any task being studied; they developed special cameras for recording movements, and the use of a stop watch for timing them. By means of their methods they analyzed in great detail the movements of workers on the job, and on the basis of such analysis taught them how to eliminate unnecessary motions. Their aim was to develop for each job the *one best way* of doing it. In the case of bricklaying, for instance, Gilbreth found that the number of movements made by a skilled workman could be reduced from 18 to 5 for each brick laid, thereby increasing the number of bricks that could be laid from 120 to 350 an hour. In other industrial jobs he was similarly able to increase production from 50 to 150 per cent or more.

Seashore[42] has extended the concept of work methods to cover skills in sensory, affective, and intellectual processes. Other areas of application may also be found.

Although time-motion study has contributed greatly to the improvement of industrial efficiency, certain cautions are nevertheless to be

---

[41] Gilbreth, F. B., and Gilbreth, L. M., *Fatigue Study,* The Macmillan Company, New York, 1919.

[42] Seashore, R. H., Work Methods: An Often Neglected Factor Underlying Individual Differences, *Psychol. Rev.,* 1939, **46**, 123–141.

kept in mind. In many of the reports of increased production resulting from improved techniques no study has been made of the energy cost of such methods, or of the satisfactions derived by workers. There is the need to supplement time-motion study with parallel studies of nerve-muscle changes and of psychological effects. As will be recalled, these are important factors in any acceptable definition of human efficiency. The assumption that there is a single "one best method" for doing a job may also be questioned. What may be best for one individual may not be at all good for another. Individual differences in strength, size, and other physiological and psychological characteristics may require different combinations of movements for different individuals even though analysis may seem to point to a theoretical one best way.

Some of the principles characterizing efficient movements may be summarized as follows:

1. Successive movements should be so made that one movement ends in a position that leads easily and without lost effort into the next.
2. Movements should be so organized that little change in direction is required in passing from one movement to the next.
3. Movements should be so organized that an easy rhythm can be established that will result in the development of a single automatic act.
4. Movements should be smooth and steady. There should be no sudden shifts in direction or speed.
5. The number of movements that make up a job should be kept at a minimum.
6. Both hands should be used together, their movements synchronized. An idle hand wastes work opportunities.
7. A stroke should be delivered, if possible, at the point of maximal momentum of movement.[43]

Tool and Equipment Design

An important requisite for efficient performance is the use of suitably designed tools and equipment, and the arrangement of the work space for the greatest economy of movement. An early investigation by Frederic Taylor[44] is instructive in this connection. He found, on observation, that skilled shovelers in a plant lifted loads varying between 3½ lb. in moving rice coal to 38 lb. in moving ore. He set out to determine what load would permit a skilled man to move the most material in a day. Starting with a large shovel, he gradually reduced the size of the shovel from day to day until he discovered that a load of

[43] See Myers, C. S., *Industrial Psychology in Great Britain*, pp. 87ff., Jonathan Cape, Ltd., London, 1926.

[44] Reported by R. M. Barnes, *Motion and Time Study*, p. 11, John Wiley & Sons, Inc., New York, 1940.

21½ lb. enabled the worker to move the maximum amount per day. He redesigned the shovels used for different purposes so that in every case men would move 21½ lb. of material on a fully loaded shovel, with a resulting increase in output in the neighborhood of 300 per cent, and a reduction in handling cost of fully 50 per cent.

Industry is constantly striving to improve the design of tools and equipment to permit greater efficiency in their use. This has traditionally been a responsibility of engineers, whereas the selection and training of workers has been a responsibility of psychologists. However, although engineers competently design equipment from the point of view of mechanical efficiency, they often disregard the characteristics and limitations of the human operator that will use the devices. The need to design equipment with the human operator in mind became a keen problem during the Second World War, when a great deal of intricate fighting equipment was designed and men had to be trained quickly to use it. This led to the participation of psychologists in the design aspects of equipment development.[45]

Engineering psychology deals with the behavior of human beings in complex continuous tasks. Such tasks frequently require great skill in rapid interpretation of instruments and signal displays, and in the controlling of sources of extraneous power. The field is too extensive for exhaustive treatment here but demands detailed study by the serious student of human efficiency. Among problems of engineering psychology are the design of visual, auditory, tactual, and other displays and signals so that they can be quickly interpreted and easily discriminated to serve as cues for action; the arrangement of controls for speedy and least effortful manipulation, the pacing of machines to accord with the reaction potentialities of workers (reaction time, most efficient reaction system, etc.); and the most effective layout of work space and job.

A feature of machine operations deserving special mention is the adjustment of the machine to the rhythm of the worker. It has been found that machine pacing of work results in greater efficiency than the irregular and sporadic movements that workers adopt when left to their own devices. However, it is extremely important that for every type of work and individual worker the optimum tempo be found in order to gain the greatest benefit in terms of production, energy economy, comfort, and personal satisfaction. As Wyatt and Langdon[46] report, if the speed of the machine exceeds the natural speed of the worker, the work will be irregular and fatiguing to the worker. On the

[45] Stevens, S. S., Machines Cannot Fight Alone, *Amer. Scientist*, 1946, **34**, 389–400.
[46] Wyatt, S., and Langdon, J. M., The Machine and the Worker, *Industr. Health Res. Bd. Report*, 1938, No. 82.

other hand, if the speed is below the worker's capacity, dissatisfaction and boredom will result. It follows that an adjustment of the machine to the average speed of a group of workmen will be too fast for some and too slow for others. It would, therefore, be desirable to provide a variable adjustment for each machine so that each worker can adjust it to suit his own needs.

SUMMARY

Modern industry demands streamlined methods of production. At every hand it seeks the largest possible return for its expenditures. This chapter undertook to summarize some of the problems relating to the elimination of waste in human work.

Work was defined in terms of human energy applied to the bringing about of useful, or at least desired, results. Physical and mental work were shown to be essentially similar in nature, and the chief techniques for measuring efficiency at work were outlined. This was followed by a study of work-curve phenomena and the problem of fatigue, or, stated more exactly, the physiological cost of work. The effects of work on the body were found to result in certain deleterious metabolic changes as well as other disturbances interfering with optimal performance.

Since the satisfaction and personal welfare of the worker are important outcomes of work, they must be included in the numerator of the efficiency equation. Thus the problem of the hygiene of work beomes important on humanitarian grounds as well as economic. Some of the conditions that are capable of manipulation to reduce the untoward effects of work were outlined. These include the proper use of rest pauses and the distribution of effort, the hygiene of the sense organs, especially those for sight, and the control of the worker's environment to provide optimal conditions of illumination and the surrounding atmosphere. The extent to which it is possible to draw upon individuals' energy reserves through special motivation without threatening their health is at present an unanswered problem. A brief section at the close of the chapter emphasized the fact that much can be gained in efficiency through discovering and mastering good work habits and using tools that are ideally suited to the tasks to be performed.

RECOMMENDED SUPPLEMENTARY READINGS

Bartley, S. H., and Chute, E.: *Fatigue and Impairment in Man,* McGraw-Hill Book Company, Inc., New York, 1947.

Bills, A. G.: *The Psychology of Efficiency,* Harper & Brothers, New York, 1943.

Bray, C. W.: *Psychology and Military Proficiency,* Princeton University Press, Princeton, N.J., 1948.

Fitts, P. M.: Engineering Psychology and Equipment Design, Chap. 35, in S. S.

Stevens (Ed.), *Handbook of Experimental Psychology*, John Wiley & Sons, Inc., New York, 1951.

Gilbreth, F. B., and Gilbreth, L. M.: *Fatigue Study*, The Macmillan Company, New York, 1919.

Gray, J. S.: *Psychology in Use*, rev. ed., American Book Company, New York, 1950.

Gray, J. S.: *Psychology in Industry*, McGraw-Hill Book Company, Inc., New York, 1952.

Poffenberger, A. T.: *Principles of Applied Psychology*, Appleton-Century-Crofts, Inc., New York, 1942.

Seashore, R. H.: Work and Performance, Chap. 36, in S. S. Stevens (Ed.), *Handbook of Experimental Psychology*, John Wiley & Sons, Inc., New York, 1951.

Tiffin, J.: *Industrial Psychology*, Prentice-Hall, Inc., New York, 1934.

Viteles, M. S.: *Industrial Psychology*, W. W. Norton & Company, New York, 1932.

Viteles, M. S.: *Science of Work*, W. W. Norton & Company, New York, 1934.

Chapter 13

PSYCHOLOGY IN INDUSTRY— EMPLOYMENT METHODS[1]

THE EMPLOYMENT PROBLEM

The world works for a living. Nearly all adults spend a major portion of their waking hours at work for pleasure or profit. If psychology is pertinent to practical human affairs, then it must have something to contribute regarding this significant segment of human behavior.

In approaching the problem of employment the first need is to comprehend the great size, diversity, and instability of the labor force. In earlier days the world of work was relatively simple in that a few basic occupations such as agriculture, husbandry, fishing, and weaving accounted for most of man's work activities. In present days of specialization and technical development, however, work areas have been broken down into successively smaller portions. A representative ex-

[1] This chapter was written by Stanley E. Seashore, Assistant to Director, Institute for Social Research, University of Michigan.

ample is seen in the iron and steel industry, which once was a single occupation, one man doing all the necessary operations, while today there are about 5,000 separate occupations in this industry alone.[2] A Dictionary of Occupational Titles,[3] published in 1939, lists 17,452 separate occupations, yet the introduction to this volume asserts that the list is by no means complete. The things people do for a living are truly strange and varied.

Some comprehension of the size of the employee population can be gained from an examination of Table 13–1, which shows that in 1949

Table 13–1. Total Employment, Termination Rate, and Accession Rate for Nonagricultural Civilian Establishments in the United States*

Date	Total employment (000,000 omitted)	Termination rate, % per month	Accession rate, % per month
August, 1949............	51.2	4.0	4.4
August, 1947............	50.6	5.3	5.3
August, 1945............	44.5	17.9	5.9
August, 1943............	43.9	8.3	7.6
August, 1941............	41.5	4.1	5.4
August, 1939............	34.9	3.0	5.1

* Data from *Monthly Labor Review*, November issue of years indicated.

over 50 million persons were gainfully employed in nonagricultural, civilian establishments in the United States. The instability of this work force is shown in the termination rates and accession rates in the same table. From these data it appears that in August of 1949, well over two million of these people secured new employment. Extended to an annual basis, it appears that there were approximately 24 million job changes in this work force, not including promotions, transfers, and other internal job changes. The effective selection and placement of this number of people in such a way as to fill the economic and psychological needs of both employee and employer is a problem of great magnitude.

COST OF FAULTY PLACEMENT

Many of the millions of persons annually employed on new jobs are victims of faulty placement in that they fail to suit the employer or fail to gain from their new jobs the satisfactions that they are seeking. There are several sources of evidence pointing to this conclusion.

The termination data mentioned above are based upon terminations for a variety of reasons, including discharge, voluntary quitting, mili-

[2] *Job Descriptions of the Iron and Steel Industry,* 25 vols., American Iron and Steel Institute, New York, 1943.

[3] U.S. Employment Service, *Dictionary of Occupational Titles,* Government Printing Office, Washington, D.C., 1939.

tary leave of absence, and lay-off for lack of work. According to Department of Labor reports for representative years, the proportions are as shown in Table 13–2. While some terminations are involuntary (lay-off and military leave of absence), a substantial percentage are voluntary and represent instances where performance has been so grossly inadequate as to warrant discharge or where the employee is dissatisfied with the conditions of his employment. Inadequate employment methods and faulty placement figure largely in these causes of occupational maladjustment. The employer bears the high cost of training for replacements while the terminated individuals bear the heavy cost of periodic unemployment and of major readjustments in family, social, and personal way of living.

Table 13–2. Causes for Termination of Employment

Cause	1949, %	1947, %	1945, %	1943, %	1939, %
Discharge........................	7	8	4	8	4
Quit............................	45	76	35	71	25
Lay-off.........................	45	15	59	8	71
Other (including military leave)....	3	2	2	13	—

* Data are for month of August for years indicated. From *Monthly Labor Review.*

Not all faulty placement leads to termination of employment, for it is customary in American business and industry to continue the employment of some workers whose productivity is below a profitable level. In one group of experienced typists, for example, all working on similar materials, production records show that the slowest typist produced 60 per cent of an arbitrary standard while the best typist produced 102 per cent of this standard amount. Both typists received the same pay yet the cost to the employer per finished sheet was nearly double for the poor operator. This is a hidden cost of faulty placement. Table 13–3 shows the ratio of productivity between best and poorest workers for a few other types of employment. These figures suggest that among experienced workers in typical occupations the best worker is likely to produce about twice as much as the poorest worker. Among inexperienced or inadequately selected groups these differences are, of course, much greater. For those who are on piecework or other types of incentive pay plans, these differences are reflected in actual earnings.

Data such as these suggest the amount of financial gain that employers and employees can achieve through proper selection and placement. Such data also raise questions about the welfare of the marginal worker who continues indefinitely at his work, insecure from both a psychological and economic point of view. The records of mental hospitals and of criminal and domestic courts bear out the thought that

Table 13–3. Comparison of Productivity between Best and Poorest Workers in Various Occupations

Occupation	Production best	Production poorest	Ratio	Source
Hosiery looping..	7 doz. per hr.	3.25 doz. per hr.	1:2.15	Tiffin, Joseph, *Industrial Psychology*, p. 6, Prentice-Hall, Inc., New York, 1942.
Electrical fixture assembling.	1 4 5 % o f average	60% of group average	1:2.4	Tiffin, p. 4.
Planer operation.	.9 hr. to complete standard job	3.6 hr. to complete standard job	1:4	Original study
Drill press operation.	.5 hr. to complete standard job	2.1 hr. to complete standard job	1:4	Original study
Ironing shirts....	213 sec. per shirt	279 sec. per shirt	1:1.3	Laird, D. A., *The Psychology of Selecting Employees*, p. 37, McGraw-Hill Book Company, Inc., New York, 1937.
Machine bookkeeping.	140 "production score" based on standard time allowance	94 "production score"	1:1.5	Hay, E. N., Predicting Success in Machine Bookkeeping, *J. Appl. Psychol.*, 1943, **27**, 492.

many serious personal maladjustments have their origin in part in occupational maladjustment. The objectives in applying psychological techniques to the employment problem are, accordingly, to reduce unnecessary job changes, to ensure the placement of workers in jobs they can perform effectively, and to ensure placement in jobs that may provide necessary personal satisfactions.

TYPES OF EVIDENCE IN EMPLOYMENT

Many business and industrial firms follow a fairly standard procedure in the employment of new personnel. A typical procedure is likely to include all or some of the following steps:

1. The applicant applies for work and is given a brief preliminary interview.
2. The applicant fills out a detailed form presenting his personal characteristics and background.
3. The applicant may be given appropriate vocational tests.
4. The applicant is given a more thorough interview.
5. The applicant may be referred to a prospective supervisor for further interview.

6. A physical examination is given.

7. The applicant is registered as an employee and is scheduled to work.

The first six of the above steps are designed, through varying methods, to get information about the applicant. The employer goes to great length to secure the evidence that will determine his decision to employ or reject the applicant. If several positions are open, the employer will go to equally great length to determine the type of work in which the particular applicant can best be utilized. The interviews, the personal-history record, and the tests, both vocational and medical, provide the evidence on which an applicant is accepted or rejected. How adequate is this evidence? How dependable is it in the important business of employment? The following pages discuss some of the psychological methods and experiments that have contributed to our understanding and improvement of the employment process.

THE EMPLOYMENT INTERVIEW

The interview is without question the most fundamental part of the employment procedure. Usually an interview is the basis for a decision with respect to an applicant's capabilities and personal qualities and is the basis for a final decision with respect to job placement. Because interviewing is used universally in this way critical thought should be given to the dependability of the employment interview and to improvements in procedure that may enable the interviewer to do his task with greater accuracy.

Employment interviews are conducted for a variety of reasons and in a variety of ways, determined by the circumstances in which interviewing takes place. The most common purpose is to obtain personal data about the applicant and to inquire in detail about general facts that have been noted on an application blank. Other purposes are to inform the applicant regarding the nature of the work available and to form an estimate of personal qualities that are not ordinarily revealed through means other than personal contact.

The actual conduct of the interview is not standard. Some of the variations that have appeared in the experience of employment interviewers are noted below:

1. Some firms provide not a single interview but a series including, possibly, (a) a very brief preliminary interview during which the obviously unqualified or disinterested applicants are rejected, followed by (b) one or more intermediate interviews, somewhat more thorough, during which a decision is made regarding employment, and after the new employee is signed up, there is often (c) a final interview during which the new employee is given additional details with respect to work procedure, responsibilities, place of work, and other items necessary for a new employee.

2. While most employment interviewers confine their investigation to superficial aspects of the applicant's personal characteristics or personal history, others make an attempt to get at fundamental motives and attitudes which are not evident in the ordinary interview and which may be of critical importance in the occupational success of the applicant.

3. Some interviewers have a standard sequence of questions which they follow more or less rigidly to permit a better comparison of applicants, while others avoid artificial control or direction on the theory that the use of standard questions tends to destroy the spontaneity and flexibility that they regard as the essential characteristic of the interview.

4. The duration of the employment interview varies considerably. Periods ranging from 3 to 40 minutes are not uncommon, depending upon the time available and the type of position to be filled.

5. The manner of reporting and recording interview results permits much variation. Some interviewers keep no record whatever, while others maintain a narrative report or a summary rating.

6. Most interviews are conducted individually; *i.e.*, two people discuss the matter mutually. On the other hand, some are conducted by a committee of interested persons.

Several methods have been devised for the systematic study of interview methods and interview results. One of the earliest and most frequently used methods was to have applicants interviewed by a number of interviewers in order to determine how well they could agree in their conclusions. Others have attempted to estimate the accuracy of employment interviews by comparing the interviewer's judgment with some objective evidence of subsequent success or failure on the job.

These methods for checking the reliability and validity of interviewing are illustrated in the pages that follow.

AGREEMENT AMONG INTERVIEWERS

One of the earliest studies of the interview was carried out by Scott, Bingham, and Whipple in 1916.[4] This study gave clear-cut and somewhat startling results and consequently it will be presented here in some detail. The cooperation of 23 interviewers was secured, 20 of these men being sales managers regularly engaged in the interviewing and selection of new employees. Twenty-four applicants for sales positions presented themselves to each of the 23 interviewers. The interviewers were permitted to use any method of their own choosing and were required only to rank the applicants in order with respect to their probable success at selling. Through this method it was possible to secure the judgments shown in Table 13-4, as to the relative qualifications of 24 applicants according to the views of 23 typical interviewers.

[4] Described in W. V. Bingham, and B. V. Moore, *How to Interview*, pp. 100–103, Harper & Brothers, New York, 1941.

Table 13–4. Showing Rankings Assigned to 24 Candidates for Selling Positions by Each of 23 Interviewers*

Appli-cants	Interviewers																							Av.	Range
	a	b	c	d	e	f	g	h	i	j	k	l	m	n	o	p	q	r	s	t	u	v	w		
A	13	14	12	11	18	7	3	19	1	4	4	8	5	5	18	5	16	22	10	11	1	5	19	10	1–22
B	2	8	7	7	12	7	3	·	6	1	2	2	3	3	7	1	3	2	10	11	4	12	4	2	1–12
C	23	22	17	2	11	20	20	13	12	7	15	12	11	24	23	12	19	11	10	5	24	11	7	15	2–24
D	18	21	8	8	9	9	14	·	18	2	15	14	17	2	19	15	15	6	5	24	7	10	17	13	2–24
E	22	19	16	24	24	17	23	22	18	22	23	19	20	17	18	19	23	18	23	17	22	15	23	24	15–24
F	20	23	15	23	14	15	9	22	21	24	15	9	23	22	14	21	22	23	16	21	15	20	20	21	9–24
G	11	15	13	14	13	4	18	16	24	12	15	23	22	22	12	22	17	17	16	21	10	18	21	19	10–24
H	15	24	24	20	23	23	23	22	23	23	15	19	24	7	23	10	24	24	10	23	20	24	22	23	7–24
I	16	11	6	18	15	20	23	11	20	9	23	15	13	18	7	20	20	20	·	17	14	19	14	17	6–23
J	12	17	21	19	19	17	14	22	6	15	15	23	15	15	18	24	21	19	23	15	13	23	9	20	9–24
K	10	9	20	21	21	22	14	14	3	·	15	5	9	19	3	15	5	21	10	17	17	14	15	14	3–23
L	7	5	9	3	16	11	3	10	8	·	15	12	8	3	3	19	12	4	21	15	2	9	13	6	2–19
M	14	7	2	9	10	14	18	3	·	12	15	12	14	9	18	3	13	5	10	2	11	16	5	12	2–21
N	24	12	23	2	21	24	20	19	21	15	23	19	21	22	23	23	9	15	21	7	17	22	24	22	12–24
O	8	6	1	6	3	4	14	16	14	4	4	5	4	12	3	9	9	3	1	21	11	7	11	3	1–16
P	21	13	18	17	16	19	3	12	15	12	15	19	10	16	15	12	14	8	21	5	17	21	18	16	8–21
Q	9	18	3	4	4	1	9	1	9	18	7	8	18	22	11	2	·	7	2	3	6	5	10	5	1–18
R	5	16	11	14	5	6	9	9	12	2	2	2	2	10	12	·	9	10	10	6	4	5	3	8	1–22
S	4	4	4	10	7	3	14	7	17	15	15	19	19	13	7	10	9	1	16	14	3	1	3	7	1–19
T	17	20	22	15	21	10	3	16	7	20	7	8	16	1	18	15	1	14	19	21	22	17	6	18	6–22
U	3	1	10	5	6	5	9	2	4	7	2	5	6	13	13	6	3	9	5	11	20	2	2	1	1–20
V	5	2	5	11	1	2	14	5	10	9	15	2	1	10	3	3	9	16	10	7	17	3	1	4	1–16
W	1	3	19	13	2	12	14	4	5	18	15	8	9	7	9	8	9	13	5	4	8	8	12	9	1–18
X	19	10	14	·	8	17	7	7	·	20	7	8	9	7	9	8	·	·	2	·	8	13	16	11	2–20
	.77	.69	.70	.82	.76	.78	.81	.76	.76	.59	.69	.83	.72	.55	.69	.74	.81	.67	.63	.69	.55	.85	.69		

* Small letter at top of each column indicates an interviewer; large letter at left of each line indicates an applicant: columns at right show average rankings of the applicants and the range of rankings given to each applicant. Bottom line shows coefficient of correlation between each column and the average column.

This table reveals a wide range of opinion among the interviewers with respect to any given applicant. Applicant A, for example, was considered the best by one interviewer and was ranked 22 by another interviewer. On some applicants, however, the range of opinion was considerably less; *e.g.*, applicant E's ranking ranged from 15 to 24. This seeming lack of agreement, however, is balanced by the fairly close correlation between individual interviewers' judgments and the average ranking. Interviewer *v* produced rankings that correlated .85 with the average ranking, whereas interviewer *u* produced rankings that correlated only .55, indicating relatively low agreement with the judgment of other interviewers. From these data it can be concluded that interviewers will disagree in individual cases yet some of them, presumably more skilled, will show remarkable agreement with the group judgment.

Similar studies have been carried out by several other experimenters. In some cases the results are essentially similar although the experimenters' interpretations varied somewhat; in other cases a much lower degree of agreement among interviewers was obtained.

AGREEMENT BETWEEN INTERVIEWERS AND SUPERVISORS

Some have contended that results such as those just described are faulty in that the consistency found in interviewers' judgments may be due to the interviewers having stereotyped attitudes, possibly erroneous, about the ideal characteristics required by the job to be filled. One possible check on this criticism is to compare the interviewer's judgment with actual job performance. One such study has been completed in connection with the employment of clerical workers in a large steel company.

In this situation three interviewers were engaged in employing women for a variety of typical office positions such as file clerk, typist, messenger, stenographer, and calculator operator. These interviewers had no special training other than familiarity with the company's business and some experience on their job. Brief interviews were allotted to each applicant, the interviews ranging from 3 minutes to 15 or 20 in accordance with the interviewer's judgment. At the conclusion of an interview the applicant was rated with respect to her suitability for each of the jobs for which she was to be considered. Following the interview and rating, these applicants were given vocational tests and further interviews prior to employment. Those actually employed were rated after 90 days by their immediate supervisor with respect to their ability, performance, cooperativeness, and initiative.

A comparison of the interviewer's ratings with the supervisory rating produced the results shown in Table 13–5. In this table each horizontal line represents a group of employees, group A being those receiving "average" ratings from the interviewer and Group E being those receiving the highest possible rating from the interviewer. (Employment was granted only to applicants rated "average" or better.) Each group is divided to indicate "superior," "average," or "unsatisfactory" performance after 90 days of employment. It is evident from this table

Table 13–5. Relationship between Interviewer's Prediction of Success
and Supervisor's Report of Success
(99 women clerical workers)

Interviewer's rating	Supervisor's rating		
	Per cent unsatisfactory	Per cent average	Per cent superior
Group A (average rating).............	3	66	31
Group B...........................	0	65	35
Group C...........................	0	47	53
Group D...........................	0	31	69
Group E (highest possible rating)......	0	0	100

that applicants rated most favorably by the interviewer have a substantially higher probability of superior performance than those with average ratings. The only unsatisfactory performance ratings were assigned to individuals in group A who were given "average" ratings by the interviewers. The agreement between the interviewer's judgment and the supervisor's rating is shown by a correlation coefficient of .62. This compares favorably with the predictions achieved by other employment devices and suggests that the interview, whatever its weaknesses may be, is in this instance functioning in a useful way.

STANDARDIZING THE INTERVIEW

Some experimenters have attempted to improve the interview by establishing a standard series of questions and a standard method for evaluating the responses given by the applicant. One of the most thorough attempts along this line was carried out by Hovland and Wonderlic in connection with the selection of employees for the Household Finance Company.[5] Based upon a preliminary experiment, a Diagnostic Interviewer's Guide was developed with a series of questions of proved value in differentiating the better applicants from the poorer ones. The questions were grouped into four sections, viz., work history, family history, social history, and personal history; and spaces were provided for recording responses to each of the 37 questions. Fol-

[5] Hovland, C. I., and Wonderlic, E. F., Prediction of Industrial Success from a Standardized Interview, J. Appl. Psychol., 1939, 23, 537–546.

lowing each section of the guide was a series of questions that the inter-- viewer could answer to rate the applicant. On the basis of these ratings an interview score was calculated.

The reliability of this guide in use was estimated in one instance by having a group of applicants interviewed and rated separately by differ- ent interviewers. A correlation of .71 was obtained with 23 cases. On a larger number of cases, the reliability was checked by calculating the internal consistency of the records. This method gave a coefficient of .57 for the work-history section, .46 for personal history, and .25 for each of the remaining two sections, with a total reliability index of .82. Reliability of this degree is considerably higher than that ordinarily expected from an interview and compares favorably with the reliability of other psychological instruments that have been widely accepted.

The validity of the Diagnostic Interviewer's Guide has been checked in two ways. In one instance the scores of 100 individuals remaining in employment were compared with the scores of 100 individuals who had been dismissed. A statistically significant difference in total score was shown between the averages of the two groups. The other test of validity was made by examining the records of 300 individuals sub- sequent to employment. Interview scores were divided into five cate- gories, and the percentages of those still on the job, those resigned, and those dismissed were examined for each of the five categories. The results indicated a progressive increase in the percentage of satisfactory employees corresponding to increasingly higher interview scores.

TRAINING INTERVIEWERS

It is believed by many that interviewers can increase their skill and their accuracy of judgment substantially by experience and special training. One significant attempt to study this question was made by the Industrial Relations Association of Philadelphia during 1940–1941 under the direction of Driver.[6] For this research a special observation room was provided that resembled an ordinary interview room but had a one-way screen permitting observers to hear and see the pro- ceedings without themselves being seen or heard. A group of employ- ment managers and others interested in the problem devised a list of traits to be observed during interviews and also devised a method for rating each applicant who was interviewed in this experimental situa- tion. A group of applicants, unaware of their being observed, were then each interviewed by one of these experienced personnel managers while the others observed the course of the interview and rated the applicant on the basis of facts brought out or observed in the interview.

[6] Driver, R. S., *Research in the Interview*, pp. 20–31, American Management Asso- ciation, No. 112, Office Management Series, 1944.

Under these conditions improvement was observed in the consistency of ratings given by the various persons participating. In the course of the experiment the deviation of individual ratings from the group average was reduced 36 per cent. This presumably indicates that the controlled practice and group discussion of interviewing problems provided a clearer terminology and more thorough interviewing method that resulted in greater uniformity of judgment.

The applicants were rated on a number of individual qualities that proved unlike in the consistency with which they could be rated. While the results were inconclusive there is evidence for believing that interviewers in general are better able to judge those qualities for which objective data are brought out in the interview. For example, such qualities as "ability to learn abstract material" and "ability to deal with other individuals" were rated with greater agreement than such qualities as "dominance" and "self-confidence."

The third significant observation developed from this experiment concerns the inability of most of the interviewers, in spite of their practical experience and special training, to describe the basis on which their judgments were formed. Employment interviewing, it appears, is still an unsystematic, intuitive function for many personnel managers.

PERSONAL DATA IN EMPLOYMENT

A person applying for work is very likely to be confronted with an application form. It is almost universal practice among organizations regularly employing new personnel to have a questionnaire on which the applicant may state the type of work he prefers, his qualifications, and his personal history. These forms range from brief registration cards to formidable multipaged forms.

There appears to be little uniformity in the information required in application blanks. Some of the most frequently used items are given in Table 13–6. Most forms have, in addition, a number of items that are of special importance to the firm in question or are believed by the employment manager to be of some special significance in the evaluation of an applicant's qualifications. Many of the questions are used primarily to identify the applicant and to aid the mechanics of employment (*e.g.*, name, address, social security number); others are included primarily to accommodate legal and company policy limitations in employment (*e.g.*, age, citizenship, relatives in company); the remaining items are designed primarily to serve as indicators of the applicant's probable success on some job (*e.g.*, previous employment, education, physical impairments). Some items, of course, may serve all three purposes.

With an application blank, the employment manager can collect a

Table 13–6. Questions Most Frequently Asked on 40 Representative
Application Forms*

Item	Frequency	Per cent
Present address...........................	40	100
Date......................................	39	98
Marital status............................	39	98
Age and date of birth.....................	37	93
Education.................................	37	93
Telephone.................................	37	93
Where previously employed.................	34	85
Signature.................................	33	82
Place of birth............................	32	80
Work desired..............................	32	80
List dependents...........................	30	75
Height and weight.........................	28	70
Reason for leaving previous jobs...........	28	70
Relatives in company......................	25	63
Social security number....................	25	63
Physical impairment.......................	24	60
Salary on previous jobs...................	23	57
Citizenship...............................	21	53
Employed here before.....................	20	50

* Adapted from *Employment Procedures and Personnel Records*, pp. 22–23, National Industrial Conference Board, Studies in Personnel Policy, No. 38, New York, 1941.

large amount of personal data about each applicant in a fairly easy manner. The manner is so easy, in fact, that he may collect more data then he can use and much more than the applicant wishes to give, for, to the industrial applicant with limited schooling, the filling out of an application blank is a difficult task. One employment manager hiring young women for unskilled and semiskilled factory work reported the average time required to fill out his application blank to be more than 1 hour and that additional time was needed to check and complete the record since a majority of the applicants were unable to perform the task correctly. On the whole, however, the applicant can provide reasonably accurate data and with strange patience will even record seemingly irrelevant facts such as the model of his automobile, the birth dates of his six children, or the maiden name of his mother.

EVALUATION OF PERSONAL DATA

Ordinarily the employment manager draws from his own experience and his knowledge of living and working conditions to evaluate the various items of information. Often he has the aid of the prospective supervisor, who will state his judgment as to the traits desired in the new employee. As might be expected, the opinions of such experienced judges are often correct and in the long run are probably quite satisfactory. There are many occasions, however, when experience is incomplete, when opinions differ, or when apparent bias exists. Such occasions require a systematic review of personal data with reference to a specific job or general type of employment in order to establish the most effective interpretation.

Various methods have been used in analyzing or validating personal data. All these methods involve a careful examination of the job performance of a group of employees and of their personal traits at the time of their employment. If it is discovered, for example, that superior welders tend on the average to have completed more years of school than a group of inferior welders, then it can be stated with some confidence that additional schooling is a trait predictive of success at welding. On the other hand, if the facts show that welders with little schooling perform as well as those with greater amounts of schooling, then it is established that this item of personal data is of no value in predicting success. If a number of traits are studied in this way, those that prove to be significant may be assembled to form a composite index of probable success on the job. To illustrate the method, a study will be described below of the traits that characterize successful women steel-mill workers.

Analysis of Personal Data—Manual Occupation

A large steel company during a certain year employed several thousands of women for various types of unskilled and semiskilled jobs, mainly involving heavy physical work and permitting only short training periods. The basis for selection had varied widely from plant to plant and among the several departments in each plant according to the hunches, prejudices, or personal experiences of those in charge of hiring. Some, for example, preferred older women, some younger; some insisted on high school education while some preferred applicants with limited education—the less the better; some preferred applicants who were tall and heavy, while other used rather strict standards of moderate size. A study was made to determine whether these factors could be shown objectively to be related to successful performance on the job. Other similar factors were also studied. Since the conditions of hiring did not permit determination in advance of the job to which the new employee would be assigned, the analysis was made without differentiating among the various kinds of work.

For several groups of women who had been on the job for 3 months or longer, ratings were secured from their supervisors to separate those who were considered to be "superior" from those who were "fair" or "poor." These groups were then compared with respect to each of the items of personal data available from the application blanks filled out at the time of employment.

The main finding was that very few of the factors which one or another of the employment agents depended on as a basis for judging the applicants' qualifications could be shown to be predictive of success on the job. Such items as religious preference, nationality, marital status, having relatives working for the company, and many others showed no important relationship with success. The three items of personal data which most consistently "came through" were age, weight, and schooling. Table 13–7 shows for one department how these

Table 13–7. Probability of "Superior" Job Performance for Various Levels of Age, Weight, and Schooling
(202 women steel-mill employees)

Age	% rated superior	Weight	% rated superior	Years schooling	% rated superior
–19	33.3	–109	36.0	7 or less	26.7
20–23	47.2	110–129	40.7	8	40.4
24–27	46.0	130–149	57.2	9	51.8
28–31	64.0	150–169	52.0	10	44.7
32–35	44.3	170–189	20.0	11	48.0
36 and over	44.4	190 and over	24.0	12	47.4

three items are related to success ratings and illustrates the kinds of relationships which can be found. Such information can be of considerable value in reaching a rational basis for the evaluation of applicants and in avoiding the arbitrary rejection of applicants for reasons which have no bearing on their probable success.

AN INDEX OF EMPLOYABILITY

The evaluation of personal data in a systematic way can be carried out with reference to any occupation or any group of occupations. An interesting application of the method has been made by Newer,[7] whose object was to predict the employability of public-relief clients.

A survey of opinion among business, industrial, and United States Employment Service personnel workers provided Newer with 16 factors that were commonly believed to be significant in determining a relief client's employability. These factors (see Table 13–8) were arranged into a convenient scale and were weighted in accordance with the survey of expert opinion, so that a rating, or score, could be calculated

[7] Newer, Bernard S., An Employment Expectancy Rating Scale, Master's Thesis, Syracuse University, Syracuse, N.Y., 1942. Reported also by Casety, M. A., An Index of Employability, Occupations, 1944, 22, 477–483.

for any individual. The scale was then applied in the spring of 1942 to a random sample (206 cases) of the persons seeking relief benefits in January, 1939, at the Onondaga County, New York, Department

Table 13–8. Factors Used by Newer in an Index of Employability Scale

Age	Physical defects
Experience	Education
Unemployment	Previous wages
Nationality	Prison record
Dependency	Reason for leaving previous work
Race	Sex
Religion	Personality
Citizenship	Home conditions

of Public Welfare. A comparison of the calculated index of employ-ability with the actual number of months of employment that each individual obtained during a subsequent 40-month period showed that the index had a fairly high validity, in that individuals with high indexes tended to secure more frequent or more permanent employ-ment than individuals with low indexes. The coefficient of correlation between the indexes and actual employment was .72.

As a further check on the value of personal data in predicting an individual's probability of being employed, studies were made of the composition of the personnel still on the relief rolls in January, 1943, and February, 1944. As shown in Table 13–9, the 1939 clients included

Table 13–9. Comparison of Index of Employability Scores for Public-relief Clients in 1939, 1943, and 1944*

Index of employability	January, 1939 (N 206)	January, 1943 (N 741)	February, 1944 (N 163)
85–	10%	0.5%	
75–84	28	2.5	
65–74	23	5	4%
55–64	23	25	24
45–54	11	33	35
–44	5	34	37
	100%	100%	100%
Total number of clients from which sample was drawn.....	7,500	1,200	950

* Adapted from Newer.

a fairly even distribution of employability scores throughout the range, while in 1943 and 1944, as the relief clients were absorbed into the in-creasingly available jobs, individuals with high indexes disappeared from the relief rolls and the rolls became heavily loaded with low-index individuals.

The author suggests several possible practical applications of such an index of employability: (1) It can be used as a diagnostic aid for the public-relief case worker since an unemployed individual with a high employability index probably is a victim of some personal malad- justment rather than of general economic depression, (2) future accept- ance of public-relief clients could possibly be tempered by a knowledge of the applicant's employability in order that the more employable individuals might be kept in competition for the available jobs, and (3) in employment agencies, the acceptance of clients could be based upon an employability index in order to concentrate the agency's efforts on those clients for whom results can be expected with a minimum of cost.

ANALYSIS OF PERSONAL DATA—SALES OCCUPATION

A number of investigations have been reported dealing with the personal data predictive of success in the sale of insurance. One of these, which illustrates typical methods and results, was carried out by Russell and Cope.[8] An analysis of the records of 500 salesmen resulted in the data of Table 13–10, from which a score for any applicant can be calculated by summing the chances for success for all items that correspond with the applicant's personal data. The score totals may range from 579, in the case of an individual with all the less favorable traits, to 732, for one who has all the more favorable traits.

The value of such a systematic study of personal data is indicated by the figures in Table 13–11, which show the percentage distribution of scores for successful as compared with unsuccessful salesmen. None of the successes scored below 640, while a majority scored over 670. In contrast to this, the failures were distributed quite evenly over the entire range of scores. By eliminating the applicants who scored below 640, this company could have avoided the costly employment of 31 per cent of the failures with a corresponding increase in the average success of those who remain.

An interesting sidelight on this method of evaluating personal data is given by a subsequent study of the salesmen employed by the same firm between 1927 and 1935.[9] Again various personal data items were correlated with actual records. A majority of the items found to be significant in the earlier study were also significant in 1935. Certain items were found to be no longer significant (*viz.*, offices held, number of investments owned, elapsed time since leaving school, and home ownership); some new items were added to the significant list (*viz.*,

[8] Russell, W., and Cope, G. V., A Method of Rating the History and Achievement of Applicants for Positions, *Public Personnel Studies,* 1925, **3**, 202–219.

[9] *Selecting the Successful Salesman,* The Phoenix Mutual Life Insurance Company, Hartford, Conn., 1937.

Table 13–10. Relationship between Personal Data and Success of 500 Life Insurance Salesmen*

Item	% Chances for Success	Item	% Chances for Success
Age:		Marital status:	
23 years and less	49	Married	59
24–32	58	Single	49
33–38	64	Club memberships:	
39–44	53	1 or less	43
45 and over	50	2	58
Selling experience (life insurance):		3 or 4	62
		5 or more	68
None	66	Schooling:	
Less than 3 years	69	15 years and under	68
3–6 years	86	16 years and over	54
Over 6 years	90	Out of school:	
Offices held:		9 years or less	60
Less than 3	59	Over 9 years	73
3 or more	83	Home conditions:	
Dependents:		Rent or board	52
None or 1	49	Own home	63
2 or more	63	Life insurance carried:	
Number of investments:		None	47
1	46	Some	59
2	54		
3 or more	74		

* Adapted from Russell and Cope.

previous income, previous occupation, minimum living expenses, length of residence in community, and duration of negotiation for employment). The shift in items may be assumed to reflect (1) the introduction of job tenure as an additional factor in determining success,

Table 13–11. Distribution of Scores on Personal Data Scale for Successful and Unsuccessful Insurance Salesmen*

	579–640	641–670	671–732
Successful salesmen	0	24	76
Unsuccessful salesmen	31	42	27

* From Russell and Cope.

and (2) an actual change in the diagnostic value of items because of elapsed time and changing conditions. These changes illustrate the need for maintaining a continuous appraisal of the factors that are to be considered in employment.

SOME LIMITATIONS OF THIS APPROACH

The three studies reported above are given as examples of an approach to the evaluation of personal data in employment. Many other occupations have been studied in the same way, and, in fact, it is becoming routine practice to include such material in occupational analyses.

It is a frequent protest of supervisors and employment managers that the results of such studies are unrealistic and violate common sense because they establish the validity of only a small number of simple factors and do not deal effectively with the unusual or the complex factors that in the actual employment situation may be of critical importance. It is true that some factors do not lend themselves to statistical study because they occur too infrequently. For example, poor health is rarely *proved* to be a valid reason for rejecting an applicant, because a group of employees being studied rarely includes enough individuals with definite evidences of ill health to establish the point. This, however, does not deny the probability that on certain jobs ill health would be a detriment to performance. Similarly, items that are insignificant alone may in relation to other items assume importance. For example, years of schooling as a separate item may be of no significance; yet when considered in relationship to the applicant's age or family economic background it may be of great significance in that it reflects adherence to popular educational standards and reflects full utilization of one's opportunities. Such considerations make it evident that systematic evaluation of personal data, while of value as evidence in employment, does not always convey the entire picture and in practice must be supplemented by other methods of appraisal.

EMPLOYMENT TESTS

Employment tests have been in common use for many years among business and industrial firms in America. A survey by the National Industrial Conference Board[10] of 462 firms showed that, in 1940, 111 (24 per cent) were using trade tests for manual jobs while 76 (16 per cent) were using tests for the selection of clerical workers. The same survey showed that, of 40 larger firms, 22 (55 per cent) were using tests to some extent. More recent surveys[11] indicate that the use of tests is increasing rapidly, especially among the larger, more progressive firms. These data are somewhat difficult to evaluate as they deal with selected firms and because some may be making very limited use of tests. It is clear, however, that there is a widespread acceptance of the idea of using employment tests and that their use is increasing.

[10] *Employment Procedures and Personnel Records,* p. 38, National Industrial Conference Board, Studies in Personnel Policy, No. 38, New York, 1941.

[11] *Personnel Testing,* California Council of Personnel Management, San Francisco, Calif., 1946.

BASIC IDEAS IN EMPLOYMENT TESTING

The ideas in employment testing are not so new or so complex as many believe. The job tryout is an employment practice of long standing and is, in a sense, a crude, relatively inaccurate, and costly form of an employment test. The typical employment interview also is, in some ways, similar to an employment test in that both are ways of observing the applicant's behavior in order to predict the later performance of the applicant on the job. The test differs mainly in being more carefully controlled and in being aimed at specialized, limited aspects of the applicant's qualifications.

The typical employment test consists of a brief sample of an applicant's performance on a task that is related to the actual job for which he is being considered. By control of the conditions during the test, one may learn in a few minutes what otherwise might take days or even months to learn under conditions of lesser control. There are three fundamental characteristics of an employment test that should be noted. (1) A test is standard, e.g., a printed series of questions to be answered or a standard task to do; the test is thus the same for all applicants. (2) An employment test provides some type of objective record of the applicant's performance. This important feature makes it possible for tests to be used by different examiners and makes it possible to use statistical methods for verifying the value of the tests. (3) An employment test provides norms, based upon experience, that permit the interviewer to determine how an applicant compares with other applicants or with established job requirements.

TYPES OF EMPLOYMENT TESTS

The tests used for employment in business and industry are of many kinds to suit the many special needs of various firms and various occupations. In general, the tests fall into three categories—aptitude, achievement, and personality, as described in Chap. 5. These are used as follows:

1. *Tests of Aptitude*—to determine to what extent the applicant has the capacity to learn and to perform the job quickly and efficiently.
2. *Tests of Achievement*—to determine to what extent the applicant has already acquired the knowledge or skills required by the job.
3. *Tests of Personality*—to determine to what extent the applicant is suited for the job in terms of interests, mental health, and capacity for personal adjustment to the working conditions.

A few of the tests widely used in employment are indicated in Table 13–12. Additional information on these tests or on the many other tests

Table 13–12. Some Tests Used in Personnel Selection

Name	Description	Purpose	Source
Otis Self-Administering Test of Mental Ability	A series of multiple choice questions dealing with vocabulary, analogies, opposites, syllogisms, arithmetic problems, etc.	To aid in estimating potential occupational level, learning aptitude, capacity for intellectual work	World Book Company
Thurstone Examination in Typing: Form A	Preparation of typed material from rough copy, preparation of a typed table, and a short spelling test	To measure speed and accuracy in the use of the typewriter	World Book Company
Minnesota Vocational Test for Clerical Workers	Comparison of pairs of numbers and pairs of names for similarity	To measure speed and accuracy in routine clerical work	Psychological Corporation
Bennett Test of Mechanical Comprehension: Form AA	A series of illustrated questions regarding practical mechanical problems	To measure the understanding of basic physical relationships encountered in every day living	Psychological Corporation
Minnesota Rate of Manipulation Test	A board with blocks and round holes; applicant is required to place the blocks in the holes or (alternative use) to turn over the blocks in position	To measure the rapidity of hand and forearm movements	Educational Test Bureau, Inc.
Tweezer Dexterity Test	A small board with holes and metal pins to fit; applicant is required to insert pins in holes using tweezers as tool	To measure speed and accuracy of finger and wrist movements	Human Engineering Laboratory
Bernreuter Personality Inventory	Series of questions regarding the subject's interests and attitudes	To measure the following aspects of personality: neurotic tendency, self-sufficiency, introversion-extroversion, dominance-submission, confidence, sociability	Stanford University Press
Minnesota Multiphasic Personality Inventory	Series of questions regarding the subject's interests, attitudes, experiences and beliefs	To measure the subject's tendency toward certain clinically isolated mental disorders such as paranoia, schizophrenia, hysteria, etc.	University of Minnesota Press
Strong Vocational Interest Blank	Series of questions revealing subject's attitude toward various occupations, school subjects, amusements, activities, peculiarities of people, etc.	To establish a comparison of individual's interests with those of successful persons in specified occupations	Stanford University Press

available can be secured from the sources shown in the suggested readings list at the end of this chapter.

Evaluating Employment Tests

One of the main findings from research on employment problems is that tests, to be effective, must be selected or designed specifically for the situation in which they are to be used. Tests which are useful in one situation may not be so in another even though the situations appear on the surface to be similar. This is a result of the fact that human abilities tend to be specific rather than general (*e.g.*, superior ability on one manual task does not necessarily imply superiority on another) and of the fact that each occupation tends to have its own characteristic set of critical requirements. As a consequence, many hundreds of different employment tests have been developed, each having specific uses and specific limits of usefulness.

With such a variety of possible tests to consider, the first problem in setting up a testing plan is that of making an appropriate choice. As experience grows in the field of testing it becomes increasingly possible for an experienced person to make an adequate choice on the basis of a familiarity with the employment problem, the kinds of applicants to be appraised, the job requirements, and a knowledge of the characteristics of various available tests. Usually, however, it is desirable or even necessary to resort to some procedure of trial or experimentation to determine which tests, if any, will prove to be effective. Such a "validation" procedure normally includes these steps:

1. Examine the employment problem to determine whether improved selection is likely to be of help.
2. Study the occupation to determine the critical psychological factors which appear to be related to success or to failure on the job.
3. Select or design some criterion of employee performance which will distinguish between better and poorer employees.
4. Choose or develop a series of tests which appear to measure the critical characteristics required by the occupation.
5. Give these tests to a number of employees whose performance on the job can be measured by the above criterion.
6. Compare the job performance and test scores for each individual to estimate the potential value of the tests separately and in various combinations for predicting performance.
7. Make a final selection of tests and of required standards of test performance in order to get maximum predictive power with a minimum of testing time and cost.

The above procedure is simple in outline but quite complex in its detail. In the following pages will be described a few instances in which such validation methods have been applied to practical problems of employment.

TESTS FOR CLERICAL OCCUPATIONS

Employment tests are used most widely and most effectively for the clerical occupations. The reasons for this are apparent when one considers the nature of clerical work, which lends itself to experiment with paper and pencil job-sample tests, and when one considers the uniformity of clerical work from one industrial or business firm to another. These factors encouraged early research and permitted the rapid spread of employment testing with a minimum of original research.

Following some preliminary trials with a variety of tests, the following battery was finally adopted for regular use by one large company:

1. A verbal test of mental ability (12 minutes).
2. A clerical test requiring the checking of pairs of names and pairs of numbers for identity (15 minutes).
3. A typing test requiring accuracy and speed in reproduction of copy (10 minutes).
4. A shorthand test scored for the rate at which the applicant can take shorthand notes and the accuracy and speed with which the notes are transcribed (about 20 minutes).

The first two tests were given to all applicants for office employment, while the latter two were given only to applicants claiming to be skilled in typing or shorthand.

After these tests had been in use for some time a study was made of the relationship between the employment test scores and later job performance. As a criterion of actual performance, ratings were obtained from the supervisor after the employee's first 90 days of service; these ratings reflected the performance, ability, cooperation, and initiative of the new employee and are known to have a fairly high reliability. For this analysis, the employees were divided into upper, lower and middle thirds according to their test scores; and the percentage of employees receiving "average," "above average," and "superior" ratings was calculated for each group. Table 13–13 presents the results. The first column, titled "Mental Ability Test," shows that the percentage of "superior" employees decreased from 77 per cent among the high-scoring applicants to 24 per cent among the low-scoring applicants. The clerical test also proved to be somewhat effective, the percentages being 57, 50, and 31. In the third column is shown the relationship between the typing-test scores and the supervisory ratings. In this case, the table represents only those new employees who were employed for positions requiring typing skill. Of those whose typing scores were in the upper third, 90 per cent proved to be "superior" employees while those scoring in the lower third produced only 27 per cent "superior" ratings. The shorthand-test scores show similar results.

Table 13–13. Relationship between Employment Test Scores and Probability of "Superior" Performance
(Women clerical workers)

Performance on tests	Per cent of new employees rated "Superior" after 90 days			
	Mental ability test (N 126)	Clerical ability test (N 126)	Typing test (N 92)	Shorthand test (N 48)
Applicants in upper third on test	77	57	90	87
Applicants in middle third on test	38	50	31	82
Applicants in lower third on test	24	31	27	47

It was concluded from this study that the tests originally selected were actually functioning in this type of employment situation and that they provided a convenient and useful aid in the selection of better clerical workers.

TESTS FOR MECHANICAL OCCUPATIONS

A large percentage of the employed people of America are engaged in work of a manipulative or mechanical nature. It is not surprising, therefore, that a great amount of research has been carried out on the use of employment tests for the placement of people in those occupations. One such study was made by Bennett and Fear[12] on the selection of machine tool operators.

A group of 40 experienced operators, some known to be excellent operators, others known to be relatively incompetent, were given the five tests listed below:

1. Revised Beta. (A paper and pencil, nonlanguage test of mental ability.)
2. Mechanical Comprehension Test (see Table 13–12).
3. Two-hand Coordination Test. (A test requiring coordinated operation of two screw mechanisms.)
4. A Hand-Eye Coordination Test. (A test requiring the following of a moving target with a small pointed instrument.)
5. Hand-Tool Dexterity Test. (A test requiring use of common tools to disassemble and assemble nuts and bolts.)

The check with 40 operators showed that all five tests served to identify the better as compared with the poorer operators. However, an analysis of the results showed further that two of the tests in combination,

[12] Bennett, G. K., and Fear, R. A., Mechanical Comprehension and Dexterity, Person. J., 1943, 22, 12–17.

namely, tests 2 and 5, would be most effective, and these two were given to all machine tool operators employed during subsequent months.

About 12 months after this program had been initiated, ratings were obtained of the performance of the new workers. According to these ratings some employees were considered excellent on the job, some good, others average, below average, or poor. The percentage of individuals, divided according to their employment test scores within each of these rating categories, is shown in Table 13–14. This demon-

Table 13–14. Relationship between Performance Ratings and Employment Test Scores for Machine-tool Operators

Rated performance	Combined ratings on mechanical comprehension and dexterity tests				
	A, per cent	B, per cent	C, per cent	D, per cent	Total per cent
Excellent on job...............	50	41	9	0	100
Good on job....................	31	44	21	4	100
Average on job................	18	36	36	10	100
Below average on job...........	0	43	19	38	100
Poor on job..................	0	25	25	50	100

stration of the close relationships between test scores and actual performance resulted in the acceptance for subsequent employment of only those applicants who scored *A* and *B* on the tests.

Tests for Unskilled Workers

The nature of American industry is such that the unskilled, routine, manipulative jobs tend to predominate over others. It is significant, therefore, that psychological testing methods have also contributed substantially to the improvement of selection for this type of work. Representative of experiments in this field are those reported by Cook.[13] Table 13–15 summarizes the results obtained through experiments on two occupational groups, coil winders and solderers

The first portion of the table shows the relationship between scores on a special coil winder's test to the actual performance of a group of 113 coil winders as evidenced by their incentive earnings. The job in this case consisted of winding fine wire around a core, inserting insulators, splicing wires, and attaching leads. The test designed for this occupation consisted of a semicircular double row of pegs on which the applicant was required to wind a cord in a predetermined pattern. When a time score established by experience was taken as the dividing

[13] Cook, D. W., *Psychological Tests for Unskilled Jobs*, pp. 18–29, American Management Association, Personnel Series, No. 50, New York, 1941.

Table 13–15. Relationship between Employment Test Scores and Performance
on Unskilled Jobs

A. Coil Winders (Special Job-sample Test)

	Per cent failing test	Per cent passing test	Total per cent
High-earning group...............	8	92	100
Low-earning group................	72	28	100

B. Solderers (Otis, Monotony, and Finger Dexterity Tests)

	Per cent below average performance	Per cent above average performance	Total per cent
Above average on tests.............	18	82	100
Below average on tests.............	100	00	100

mark between passing and failing employees on this test, it was found
that 92 per cent of the high-earning group passed the test, while 8 per
cent failed. In contrast to this, of the lower earning group 28 per cent
passed and 72 per cent failed. The advantage to the company in employing applicants scoring above the critical mark is evident.

In the case of solderers somewhat similar results were found. In this
job girls were required to attach colored wires to terminals according to
a simple print, cut off excess wire, and then solder. Three tests proved
to be of value in employment for this occupation: the Otis S-A Test
of Mental Ability, a Monotony Test in which the subject is required
to tap a stylus through a series of small holes without touching the
metal rim of the holes, and a Finger Dexterity Test in which small
metal pegs are placed rapidly into a series of holes in a wood block. It
will be seen from the table that girls above average on the three tests,
with very few exceptions, were considered to be above average in job
efficiency, whereas those scoring below average on the combined tests,
without exception, were considered to be below average in job performance.

TESTS FOR INSPECTION OCCUPATIONS

The inspection occupations in industry vary greatly as to their critical requirements. For some types of inspection, good performance
seems to depend upon technical knowledge and judgment, while for
others the critical factors may relate to manual skills or perceptual
skills. Since a great many inspection operations involve visual inspection, it is not surprising that vision tests have often proved to be useful as employment aids.

In Table 13–16 are shown the results of validation experiments for three inspection occupations, using visual skills tests. In all three cases, the tests were made with an instrument (Bausch and Lomb Ortho-Rater) designed to provide scores on 10 different aspects of visual skill such as sharpness of vision, color discrimination, and depth perception. In each case the results shown in the table indicate that the vision tests, if used as a basis for selection, would have increased significantly the proportion of superior employees.

Table 13–16. Validity of Visual Skills Tests for Inspectors

Occupation	Tests	Evidence of validity
Lens inspectors (99 cases)*	Vertical and lateral phoria (muscular imbalance)	Of 32 long-service employees, only 1 failed the tests; of 67 employees who terminated within 8 months, 25 failed the tests
Piston-ring inspectors (170 cases)†	All 10 tests	Of those meeting the visual standards, 72% were rated A or B (high) on productive efficiency as compared with 54% for the total unselected group
Assembly inspectors, electronic devices (125 cases)‡	All 10 tests	Of those meeting the visual standards, 50% were rated "good" or "excellent" as compared with only 34% for the total unselected group

* Kephart, N. C., Visual Skills and Labor Turnover, *J. Appl. Psychol.*, 1948, **32**.
† Tiffin, J., Vision and Industrial Production, *Illumination Engineering*, 1945, **40**.
‡ Coleman, J. H., and Feinberg, R., Vision Tests for Inspectors Insure Good Placement, *Factory Management and Maintenance*, 1945, **103**.

Tests for Semiprofessional Occupations

Ordinarily a person who has received extensive training or experience in one of the technical or professional occupations has given so much time and energy in this training that his entry into some other field can hardly be considered. Furthermore, the problem of survival during a competitive intensive training period tends to eliminate persons who lack adequate capacities in the field. Nevertheless, several firms have found it possible and worth while to establish batteries of tests for use in the employment of semiprofessional personnel.

One such study has been made by a large company in connection with the employment of industrial engineers and assistants, for miscellaneous duties that included the making of time and motion studies analysis of production data, and the analysis of production and control procedures. A group of 66 individuals engaged in this work were given a trial series of nine tests. This series included tests of mental ability, clerical aptitude, elementary arithmetic, mechanical comprehension, practical judgment, and a personality questionnaire. The experimental group was selected from a larger group of men so as to include representative "good" engineers and representative "poor" engineers according to the supervisor's judgment.

Analysis indicated that three of the tests in combination would provide a significant index for use in future employment. These three tests were those for mental ability, arithmetic, and mechanical comprehension. When these three tests were combined into a single predictive index the results shown in Table 13–17 were found. The first group

Table 13–17. Relationship between Performance Ratings and Performance on Employment Tests
(66 industrial engineers and assistants)

Combined score on 3 tests	Per cent rated "poor"	Per cent rated "good"
15 or higher (20 cases)..........	10	90
10–15 (18 cases)...............	44	56
5–10 (15 cases)................	47	55
5 or lower (12 cases)...........	83	17

represents 20 men scoring 15 or higher on the combined tests. In this group 90 per cent were "good" employees, 10 per cent were relatively "poor." At the other extreme were 12 men scoring below 5 on the combined tests. In this group 17 per cent were considered "good" employees, 83 per cent were considered "poor." It is evident that the company, by rejecting applicants scoring below 5, can thereby eliminate men who are very likely to be "poor" engineers.

TESTS FOR SUPERVISORS

One of the occupational categories which has been most resistant to successful testing is that of supervision. A number of studies have been made, but few have demonstrated any significant relationship between the tests used and performance on the job. One might surmise that this is due to the fact that the critical requirements in supervision are in the area of personality characteristics—an area in which adequate measurement is very difficult.

One of the few studies reporting significant results was made on 297 supervisors (foremen, assistant foremen, job setters, and group leaders) in three aircraft-engine and propeller plants.[14] These supervisors were rated as to their performance and were divided into "superior" and "average" groups. Three tests were given to these supervisors, and an analysis was made to determine the increase in per cent of "superior"

[14] Shuman, J. T., Value of Aptitude Tests for Supervisory Workers, *J. Appl. Psychol.*, 1945, 29, 185–190.

supervisors that would have been obtained if those scoring in the lowest one-fourth on the tests had been rejected. The results, shown in Table 13–18, indicate that all three tests are predictive of rated success on the job.

Table 13–18. Gain in Per Cent of Supervisors Who Are "Superior" Resulting from Rejection of Those Scoring in Lowest Fourth on Tests

Test	Per Cent Improvement
Bennett Test of Mechanical Comprehension, AA	20
Otis S-A Test of Mental Ability, A	17
Paper Form Board, Revised	17

It should be noted that the "supervisors" in this study are at the lowest levels of supervision and include men who presumably spend a good part of their time on production work rather than on supervision, as such. The prediction is, in fact, better for job setters and group leaders (more involved in direct production work) than for foremen and assistant foremen. This raises a question as to whether the successful prediction relates to the productive aspects of the job or to the supervisory aspects.

SUMMARY

The psychological factors in employment are considered to be significant because of (1) the economic advantages to be gained through proper matching of job requirements and employee abilities, and (2) the social and personal advantages to be gained through the job security and job satisfaction that accompany proper placement. Data on individual differences in productivity, on turnover rates, and employment rates suggest that the problem is one of great scope and importance.

In the typical employment situation three primary sources of evidence are used in determining an applicant's fitness for a given position. These are (1) an interview, (2) a record of personal data, and (3) employment tests. The purpose of this chapter has been to discuss methods used to check the utility of these employment aids and to discuss some representative studies in each area.

Studies of the employment interview suggest that the average interviewer falls far short of perfection in his appraisal of applicants yet is able to predict an applicant's probable success with a significant degree of accuracy. Standardized procedures in conducting the interview, in recording the interview, and in evaluating the content appear to produce worth-while gains in the reliability and validity of the interview. Interviewers vary greatly in their competence, primarily for want of systematic training in the interviewing skills.

In checking the value of personal data as evidence in employment it appears that, for many occupations, certain objective facts about an applicant's physical, educational, social, and economic history may be of definite value in differentiating the better applicants from the poorer ones. These items vary from one occupation to another; they may vary from time to time; they are not easily identified without the use of a statistical evaluation of past experience. Factors can be identified that predict, not only general employability, but also an individual's probable success on any specific job.

Tests as an aid to employment are used on a small scale relative to their potential application, yet they have a firm acceptance among the more enterprising organizations. Their applicability to nearly all types of occupations has been verified beyond serious question.

The scientific methods for studying the psychology of employment are used by business and industry for the purpose of economy. They are used mainly because they lead to reduced cost in hiring, training, supervising, and producing. The employment aids discussed in this chapter do not provide for the perfect placement of new employees but are expected when used in combination, each supplementing the others, to effect an improvement over the results achieved without systematic study.

RECOMMENDED SUPPLEMENTARY READINGS

Bellows, R. M.: *Psychology of Personnel in Business and Industry,* Prentice-Hall, Inc., New York, 1949.

Bennett, C. K., and Cruikshank, R. M.: *A Summary of Manual and Mechanical Ability Tests,* Psychological Corporation, New York, 1942.

Bennett, G. K., and Cruikshank, R. M.: *A Summary of Clerical Tests,* Psychological Corporation, New York, 1949.

Bingham, W. V., and Moore, B. V.: *How to Interview,* Harper & Brothers, New York, 1941.

Blum, M. L.: *Industrial Psychology and Its Social Foundations,* Harper & Brothers, New York, 1949.

Dorcus, R. M., and Jones, M. H.: *Handbook of Employee Selection,* McGraw-Hill Book Company, Inc., New York, 1950.

Fear, R. A., and Jordan, B.: *Employee Evaluation Manual for Interviewers,* Psychological Corporation, New York, 1943.

Gray, J. Stanley: *Psychology in Industry,* McGraw-Hill Book Company, Inc., New York, 1952.

Harrell, Thomas W.: *Industrial Psychology,* Rinehart & Company, Inc., New York, 1949.

National Industrial Conference Board: *Experience with Employment Tests,* NICB Studies in Personnel Policy, No. 32, New York, 1941.

Super, D. E.: *Appraising Vocational Fitness,* Harper & Brothers, New York, 1949.

Tiffin, J.: *Industrial Psychology,* Prentice-Hall, Inc., New York, 1942.

Uhrbrock, R. S.: The Personnel Interview, *Person. Psychol.,* 1948, 1, No. 3.

Wagner, R.: The Employment Interview: A Critical Summary, *Person. Psychol.,* 1949, 2, No. 1.

Chapter 14

PSYCHOLOGY IN INDUSTRY—
TRAINING AND MORALE[1]

In our industrial and commercial society, with about a third of the population so employed, there is naturally a great deal of concern about people in relation to their work. This concern has focused in part upon the problems of efficiency and productivity, and in part upon the problem of the motivations and satisfactions which people have in relation to their work. The contributions of scientific psychology in this area have been varied and substantial. In Chap. 5 there was presented a discussion of the psychology of vocational choice; in Chap. 12 there was a discussion of psychophysiological factors in work efficiency; in Chap. 13 specific attention was given to the matching of individual aptitudes and abilities to the job. In Chap. 15 you will read of wage determination as one factor of psychological importance in the work situation. The present chapter will be concerned with the development of individual competence in work performance, *i.e.*, training, and with the provision of optimum motivation and satisfaction in one's work, *i.e.*, morale.

TRAINING

Of the many personnel problems confronting the manager of a firm, the development of job skills is one of prominence. In a typical firm the

[1] This chapter was written by Stanley E. Seashore, Assistant to Director, Institute for Social Research, University of Michigan.

major item of expense is the amount paid for the services of employees, and it is apparent that a successful enterprise must be based upon the ability of the members to carry out the details of their work accurately and economically. In addition, there is a constant need for maintaining skills that have once been acquired, and a need constantly to develop the new skills required by changes in the work and by the promotion of people to positions of successively greater skill and responsibility. One indication of the magnitude of the training problem can be gained by considering the data shown in Chap. 13 regarding the occurrence of job changes. Each of these job changes, about 2 million per month, represents a training problem because some new skills or work methods must be learned. In addition, each time an employee is transferred or promoted and each time a new process or work method is introduced it is necessary to train the personnel affected. It is for these reasons that many firms have extensive formal training programs and maintain staffs of specialists who are concerned with research and administration in the field of training.

Systematic training for business and industrial personnel is given in a variety of forms to correspond with the variety of occupational demands characteristic of our time. One of the oldest and most commonly recognized training systems is the apprenticeship plan, in which a complex trade is taught over a period of several years, during which the trainees serve as helpers to tradesmen, receive instruction, and gradually gain experience in increasingly difficult phases of their trade. Bricklayers, machinists, painters, pipefitters, and carpenters are among those who normally learn their trade through an apprentice program.

In addition to apprentice programs, a variety of other types of training programs have been developed. "Learner training," for example, has been widely practiced in recent years, such programs usually being similar to apprenticeship but of shorter duration and providing a more limited range of skill and knowledge. In "vestibule training" specific job skills and related information are taught in a shop or school set apart from the regular working place; new employees are trained briefly before being introduced to the actual job. Many firms arrange courses, usually called "vocational" or "extension" courses, in subjects related to the work done by the firm so that employees may voluntarily prepare themselves for advancement. Special training for supervisors and administrators is often offered. This training usually takes the form of periodic classes or conferences for new or for experienced persons to inform them of company policies and procedures and to give instruction or exchange of ideas on various matters relating to their work. Most training, of course, is given not through such formal programs as these but on the job by the supervisor in the course of his daily contacts with his subordinates. A detailed discussion of these and other types of training is given by Dodd and Rice.[2]

In all the above types of training, the purpose is to impart a more or less extensive group of related skills or items of knowledge. They differ in the nature of the instruction given and the manner in which the material is organized, but in all cases there is an essential similarity. This similarity lies in the fact that each training program is compounded of many smaller units of instruction which, if they are to be taught effectively, must be taught in a manner consistent with known principles common to all complex learning. An electrician apprentice, for example, must learn the large number of specific items (tasks or jobs) required for his trade. Similarly a new supervisor or clerical worker must learn specific tasks no more mysterious or vague than those making up the electrician's trade. The problem in business and industrial training is to apply sound psychological principles to each item of job instruction, as well as to the over-all plan of training.

A Job Instruction Plan

One of the most simple and practical presentations of sound instruction method is embodied in the Job Instructor Training Program developed in the early months of the Second World War by the Training Within Industry branch of the War Manpower Commission.[3] This program, popularly called "JIT," was presented to assist supervisors and other persons responsible for wartime training to carry out their task with a minimum of waste time and effort. Under this program, many thousands of persons were given a 10-hour course in how to give job instruction.

The success of this program is evident from the speed and ease with which persons with little or no industrial experience were drawn into war-production actitivies and contributed to the most intensive production program the world has known. The JIT program was successful because it provided for the application of psychological principles to the problem of how to teach a man to do a job. The following pages present some of these principles and discuss their application.

Some Psychological Principles in Job Instruction

The basic ideas of the JIT program are simple enough to be summarized on a pocket-size reminder card bearing the information shown in Fig. 14–1. Side 1 presents the things to consider in preparation for the actual instruction, and Side 2 presents the four steps that normally

[2] Dodd, A. E., and Rice, J. O. (Eds.), *How to Train Workers for War Industries,* Harper & Brothers, New York, 1942.

[3] War Manpower Commission, *Job Instruction Training Manual,* Government Printing Office, Washington, D.C., 1942.

ensure quick and thorough learning. Although the steps are phrased with reference to manual jobs, the same ideas can be adapted to other kinds of jobs as well.

Selecting a Training Unit. The first problem in teaching a man to do a job is the selection of a unit of training that is psychologically

SIDE 1	SIDE 2
How to Get Ready to Instruct	**How to Instruct**
Have a Time Table—	Step 1—*Prepare the Worker*
how much skill you expect him to have, and how soon.	Put him at ease.
	Find out what he already knows about the job.
Break Down the Job—	Get him interested in learning job.
list principal steps.	Place in correct position.
Pick out the key points.	
	Step 2—*Present the Operation*
Have Everything Ready—	Tell, Show, Illustrate, and Question
the right equipment, materials, and supplies.	carefully and patiently.
	Stress key points.
	Instruct clearly and completely,
Have the Work Place Properly Arranged	taking up one point at a time—but
just as the worker will be expected to keep it.	no more than he can master.
	Step 3—*Try Out Performance*
	Test him by having him perform the job.
	Have him TELL and SHOW you; have him explain key points.
	Ask questions and correct errors.
	Continue until you know HE knows.
	Step 4—*Follow Up*
	Put him on his own. Designate to whom he goes for help.
	Check frequently. Encourage questions. Get him to look for key points as he progresses.
	Taper off extra coaching and close follow-up.

FIG. 14–1. War Manpower Commission job-instructor reminder card.

appropriate. For example, in teaching a person to operate an automobile, one might teach the entire task including starting the motor, engaging the gears, steering, control of speed, reversing, parking, observation of driving conventions, and so on, all as a single operation. An alternative method would be to impart a mastery of each step before combining them. A third possibility, the method considered most effective, would be to teach a minimum of each step and then to perfect them together as a single job unit under actual driving conditions. It is known, for many jobs, that proper selection of the unit of training will greatly facilitate learning.

The JIT plan requires that a job breakdown be made as a guide to the selection of a training unit. Figure 14–2 shows a typical breakdown for a milling machine operation, Part A being a breakdown for a mill dovetail, Part B being an elaboration of one step (Step 4) in this

Part Slide Base 235310	Operation Mill Dovetail
Important steps in the operation	Key Points—knacks, hazards, "feel," timing, special information
1. Select cutter	Small—minimize chatter
2. Select holder parallels	Narrow—yet to give good hold
3. Place piece in vise	Check with tissue
4. Rough cut	Start by hand—1″—Check for finish stock and location
5. Trial finish cut	Check—make correction
6. Finish cut	Finish without stopping
7. Remove from vise	
8. File burrs	
9. Check	

An experienced workman in a machine shop made this breakdown in 6 minutes. This instructor uses this breakdown "as is" for workers who have had other milling-machine experience. For green men each of these steps might constitute an "instructing unit" by itself and require a separate detail breakdown. Figure 14–2B shows the detailed breakdown for Step 4, above, Rough cut.

FIG. 14–2A. Job breakdown sheet for training man on new job.

operation. Such a breakdown not only provides a guide for the instructor, but it enables the selection of functional units that may be isolated for training purposes and enables the combining of those smaller units into larger units. In the absence of a clear definition of the steps to be taught either in written form, as a job breakdown, or in the mind of a skilled instructor, there often occurs an illogical sequence of training or the inclusion of irrelevant matters that tend to complicate and interfere with the learning process.

One problem that deserves attention in preparing a job breakdown and in selecting a suitable training unit is ensuring that any given series of steps, if taught separately, are the same alone as they would be in the normal work sequence. The applicable principle appears to be that the best training units are the smallest units that can be isolated without thereby changing their character or losing their integration with preceding, following, or otherwise related units. This matter, as well as other aspects of the selection of the training unit, is discussed in some detail by Viteles.[4]

Transfer of Training. In Chap. 4, a discussion of transfer of training was given with reference to formal education and the general conclusion drawn that transfer appears to occur mainly when there are identical elements in the learning and performing situations. The JIT program accordingly emphasizes that training should be given in a place and with equipment and materials as similar as possible to the actual working situation.

Part_____Slide Base 235310_____Operation Rough cut for Milling Dovetail

Important steps in the operation	Key Points—knacks, hazards, "feel," timing, special information
1. Run up table by hand	Slow when nearing cutters
2. Feed 1″ by hand	
3. Stop machine and run back table	Never run table back while cutters are in use
4. Check cut	Location and finish
5. Set feed	
6. Start machine	
7. Finish cut	
8. Check	

FIG. 14–2B. Job breakdown sheet for training man on new job.

A study by Woodward[5] made in this connection indicates the relatively little transfer that may occur in the learning of a motor task. For this experiment two similar groups of trainees were taught to perform a simple assembly task. The control group received an original standard period of training followed after a lapse of time by a standard final period of training. The experimental group received similar training on the first task, assembly of a loom, plus an intervening period of training on a second task that was superficially different but essentially the same as the original task. The results shown in Table 14–1 indicate that the intervening practice on the similar task resulted in an insignificant advantage for the experimental group over the control

[4] Viteles, M. S., *Industrial Psychology*, pp. 317–342, W. W. Norton & Company, New York, 1932.

[5] Woodward, Patricia, An Experimental Study of Transfer of Training in Motor Learning, *J. Appl. Psychol.*, 1943, 27, 12–32.

Table 14–1. Transfer of Training in an Assembly Task

Trials (in groups of three)	Mean score control group	Mean score experimental group	Difference	Critical ratio
First............	360.6	348.2	12.4	1.77
Second..........	324.6	317.1	7.5	1.25
Third...........	308.3	294.3	14.0	2.74
Fourth..........	295.2	281.2	14.0	2.86

group. This difference, occurring under conditions highly conducive to transfer of training, amounted in practical terms to a maximum advantage of about 5 per cent, and there is reason to believe that even this advantage would have disappeared had the experiment been continued for a longer period. This experiment appears to demonstrate that transfer of training may occur for manual tasks under certain favorable circumstances but that this transfer is probably of little real value compared with the improvement shown by direct training on the task to be learned.

It is common knowledge in industry that any new or transferred employee must receive training, no matter how extensive his former experience and no matter how similar his former and new jobs may seem. It is even true that a man being transferred from one lathe to another must learn the special features of the new machine and the knacks required to use it most effectively. The JIT plan is therefore psychologically sound in its provision for training *on the job* whenever possible.

Even though each job is to some extent unlike all others, there are many jobs or groups of jobs having elements in common that permit a person trained in one to adapt his knowledge and skill easily to another. These job families (see Chap. 5) are now being identified by means of comparative job descriptions in order that persons who must change their work may select new jobs that will utilize their former training.

Motivating the Learner. Step 1 in the JIT plan properly emphasizes the need to get the learner interested in learning the job. This is based on the psychological principle mentioned in Chap. 4 to the effect that the amount and speed of learning depend in part upon the trainee's intention and active desire to learn.

Most new business and industrial workers have their chief incentive in the fact that they must learn to do their work in order to keep their jobs. This financial incentive is often refined as an aid in industrial training by having the amount of pay increased in accordance with the progress made in training, or by having a beginner's rate of pay, lower than the regular rate, which the trainee must accept until he has learned enough to meet the performance standard of experienced workers. While the financial incentive is not the only source of motivation and while it is not always the most effective motivation, it is one that is widely recognized and relatively easy to use.

Among the other sources of motivation for trainees that have been shown to be effective are the knowledge of a definite goal to be achieved and the knowledge of the usefulness of the task being learned. The JIT plan recognizes these, first, by providing a previously determined schedule for learning that the trainee is challenged to meet and, second, by providing at the beginning of the training period an explanation of the purpose of the task, its importance, and its place in the over-all function of the firm.

A typical experiment illustrating another type of motivation was carried out by Ross.[6] In this instance, students were allowed practice on a simple task of penciling short lines, four vertically and one diagonally, as rapidly as possible. Three groups were selected on the basis of equivalent average initial performance and then 10 practice, or learning, periods were allowed each group. Group 1 were informed of their progress daily, group 2 were given partial information, and group 3 were given no information about their progress. At the end of the experiment the three groups, formerly equal, had average corrected scores of 57.4, 54.3, and 53.2, respectively. Apparently the simple device of informing trainees of their progress serves in some circumstances as a definite motivating factor for efficient learning.

Interference. One of the most striking features in learning a new task is the ease with which improper work methods may be acquired and the difficulty experienced replacing them with correct work methods. Once learned, a routine task may become so automatic that a positive effort to unlearn a method must be made before a better method can be substituted. This interference, or negative transfer of training, can be avoided only by learning the task correctly in the first instance.

Any person who has learned to operate a typewriter using visual rather than kinesthetic senses to locate keys and who has then undertaken to learn the touch system is aware of the interference encountered in learning the newer work method. In industry also, learning periods are often prolonged unnecessarily by a change of work method during the training. Gilbreth[7] was among the first to observe this as a result of his detailed study of the bricklayers' trade. He found that bricklayer trainees originally instructed at a slow pace were required to learn a different set of motions when the pace was increased to normal work-

[6] Ross, C. C., An Experiment in Motivation, *J. Educ. Psychol.*, 1927, **18**, 337–349.
[7] Gilbreth, F. B., *Motion Study*, p. 116, D. Van Nostrand Company, Inc., New York, 1911.

ing speed. Not only was the original instruction largely wasted, but it retarded the speed of later learning of the correct method.

Steps 2 and 3 of the JIT plan, emphasizing systematic, step-by-step demonstration, description, and practice and also the preparation of the job breakdown, are intended to ensure that the trainee has no opportunity to learn inefficient or unsafe methods. In addition, the JIT plan places responsibility for training in the hands of one person rather than several persons, thereby preventing the new worker from receiving contradictory instruction in work methods from instructors who may have developed individual knacks that are not standard.

Emotion. The emotional state of the learner is known to be an important factor in facilitating or retarding the learning process. In general, moderate excitement such as that arising from high degrees of interest or motivation appears to aid learning. On the other hand, excess emotionality tends to distract the learner, reduce attention, and inhibit learning.

This is a matter of importance in industrial training, because much of the training is given under conditions that are likely to be unfavorable. A new or transferred employee usually feels strongly the stress of being in a new and strange situation. He often has just been through the confusing details of an employment procedure and is often more concerned with getting to know his new supervisor and the men with whom he is to work than he is with learning his new job. It is proper, therefore, that the first phase of Step 1 in the JIT plan is "put the learner at ease."

Comprehension vs. Drill. Some psychologists[8] distinguish between thoughtful learning, or comprehension, and blind learning based on repeated practice. The difference can be illustrated by the learning curve for a typical. industrial task that involves both comprehension and motor skill. Table 14–2 shows the learning progress of three green planer operators who were learning to perform a standard operation on steel armor plate. All three individuals show the poor initial performance characteristic of new workers, followed by a rapid improvement while "thoughtful" learning is taking place, and then a period of slower improvement based upon the perfection of manual skills and individual knacks.

It is believed that a majority of business and industrial jobs are being simplified and made repetitive to such a point that comprehension can be imparted during an initial formal training period, with subsequent slower improvement in performance being achieved by practice on the job. This characteristic of a growing majority of jobs

[8] Pear, T. H., *Skill in Work and Play,* Methuen & Co., Ltd., London, 1924; Cox, J. W., *Manual Skill,* Cambridge University Press, London, 1934.

Table 14–2. Progress of Planer Operator Trainees during Successive Two-week Periods

Period of training	Per cent improvement over mean performance during initial period		
	Operator 1	Operator 2	Operator 3
Initial period..................			
Second period.................	37.0	49.0	29.5
Third period..................	6.6	6.0	5.4
Fourth period.................	11.3	10.3	5.4
Fifth period..................	9.4	5.3	1.0

emphasizes the advantage of systematic training for comprehension, and correspondingly it de-emphasizes the role of extended practice in the development of skill. The comprehension of a job is the aspect of skill that most easily and most profitably can be influenced by systematic training methods. The JIT plan is therefore psychologically sound in requiring careful *explanation* of the job to the trainee, *demonstration* of how it is performed, and finally a *verification* of the trainee's comprehension by requiring him to perform the task early in the training process and to explain it verbally to the instructor.

RETRAINING THE EXPERIENCED EMPLOYEES

While the value and necessity of systematic training for new employees is apparent it is often surprising to observe the results that can be obtained from the retraining of experienced workers. It would appear that the best of initial training does not guarantee optimum performance nor does it prevent the later acquisition of inefficient, unsafe, or costly working methods.

Table 14–3. Improvement in Performance of Open-hearth Furnace Crews during a Retraining Program

Five-week Periods	Net Tons per Furnace per Operating Hour
Before retraining...............	11.82
Second period..................	12.40
Third period...................	12.72
Fourth period..................	12.92
Total improvement.............	9.4%

Table 14–3 illustrates the improvement in performance resulting from the retraining of experienced crews operating open-hearth steel furnaces. When selected superior crew members were trained in job instruction methods and assigned to give individual instruction to each

of the other crew members, the result was an increase in average output for the furnaces, a decrease in fuel consumption, and a related decrease in operating delays or interruptions of work due to mechanical failure. For this open-hearth department, during the fourth period, nearly 3,000 additional tons of steel were produced per week as compared with the average production before institution of the retraining program.

During recent years many firms have established programs for periodic retraining of certain employee groups in recognition of this tendency for men in some circumstances to experience a loss of skill even though regularly engaged in the work.

MORALE

A foreman once hired a crew of men for temporary help in unloading bricks from railroad cars. The new crew was put to work and the foreman went off to other duties. When he returned some hours later the men were sitting about loafing. They had unloaded the first car in about half the time considered "standard" by the regular crews.

In another plant there were rumors of dissatisfaction among the men. The manager brushed the rumors aside. "I know these men and I know their families. Most of them I've known for years. If there is anything wrong, they'll come and tell me about it. They know they have the highest wages and best conditions around here. . . . " Two weeks later the plant was shut down. The men had gone on strike.

Incidents like this remind us of how little we know about the forces which motivate men. The management policy sincerely intended as a generous gesture may be seen by the men as a threat; the "impossible" job may be accepted by the workers as a welcome chance to show what they can do; a man may voluntarily leave a "good" job to take one that pays less and offers less favorable working conditions; a new foreman may succeed in increasing production without any change in his crew or his work methods. To understand such things, we must go beyond the "objective" situation to examine the way men see the situation and the satisfaction and motivations they get from it. This is sometimes called the study of "morale."

What Is Morale?

People concern themselves with the problems of morale in work groups for a number of different reasons. The manager of a factory may have as his objective the development of a level of morale which is optimum in terms of productivity and efficiency. He may be sincerely concerned with the personal values which workers gain from having a job which they see as being stimulating and satisfying. He may be concerned with building an organization which has high morale in the sense of being able to withstand drastic changes or extremely unfavorable conditions without becoming disorganized and ineffective. Whatever the motivations of those who study morale, it seems probable that they are concerned with a common problem and that they will ultimately find that they can share the same methods in reaching their different objectives.

The different purposes which people have in dealing with morale are reflected in the variety of meanings given to the term. There is no satisfactory definition of what morale "really is." Most of those who attempt to define it end by saying that high morale in a work situation is the condition that exists when people:

1. Are motivated toward high productivity
2. Are satisfied with their jobs
3. Want to remain with the organization
4. Act effectively in a crisis
5. Accept necessary changes without resistance or resentment
6. Actively promote the interests of the organization

While such statements do not clarify much the meaning of the term, they do provide a basis for going ahead with studies of the factors which influence morale. They name some kinds of behavior which can be observed and measured and which can be used as indexes reflecting the underlying level of morale.

METHODS FOR STUDYING MORALE

The scientific study of morale is relatively new, and it is not surprising to find that the subject remains largely unexplored. In any field of study there is a necessary early period characterized by crude efforts to define the problem to be solved, to determine the major underlying factors at work, and to develop and perfect the instruments and methods needed to measure these factors. We now have progressed to the point where some of the critical aspects of morale have been identified and a few useful measuring instruments have been devised.

In the next pages we shall describe a few studies which represent different ways of investigating morale. The first section will be concerned with the direct questioning of various groups of workers as to the sources of satisfaction which they see in jobs. The second section will deal with a study of broader scope designed to compare plants with high and low morale and to form some preliminary ideas as to the critical factors which are associated with differences in morale. A third section will present a portion of two studies aimed at a specific kind of causal factor in morale, viz., the practices of supervisors. The final section will describe an experiment in which high and low morale conditions were produced by the introduction of changes in a working situation.

WHAT WORKERS WANT IN A JOB

During the past decades a number of studies have been made to discover the factors that workers consider to be most important in a job. The procedure has often been simply one of presenting a list of job characteristics and having respondents indicate their relative importance.

A study of this kind by Chant[9] is representative in its methods and results. He secured the judgments of 100 male department-store employees and of 150 men in miscellaneous occupations. They were shown a series of pairs of job factors and were asked to choose the "most important" of each pair. A study related to this one was made by Wyatt and Langdon,[10] who used a similar list of factors and secured judgments in a similar way. Their study was made with a group of 325 female factory workers. The results of these two studies are shown in

Table 14–4. Rank Position of Factors Important in a Job

Factors	100 department-store workers, male (Chant)	150 miscellaneous workers, male (Chant)	325 factory workers, female (Wyatt and Langdon)
Opportunity for advancement.......	1	1	5
Steady work.....................	2	2	1
Opportunity to use your ideas.......	3	3.5	7
Opportunity to learn a job..........	4	3.5	8
Good boss.......................	5	5.5	4
High pay........................	6	7	6
Opportunity to be of public service..	7	5.5	
Good working companions..........	8	8	3
Comfortable working conditions.....	9	9	2
Good hours......................	10	11	9
Clean work......................	11	10	
Easy work.......................	12	12	10

Table 14–4, in which the factors are ranked in accordance with their importance as judged by the various groups of respondents.

A more recent study of the same kind was made by Jurgensen,[11] who

[9] Chant. S. N. F., Measuring the Factors That Make a Job Interesting, *Person. J.*, 1932, 11.

[10] Wyatt, S., and Langdon, J. N., Fatigue and Boredom in Repetitive Work, *Indust. Health Res. Bd. Repts.*, 1937, No. 77.

[11] Jurgensen, C. E., What Job Applicants Look for in a Company, *Person. Psychol.*, 1948, 1, No. 4.

prepared a list of 10 job factors and had nearly 4,000 persons judge their order of importance. He was able to show the average rank given to each of the 10 factors by various categories of respondents. Thus he could compare the judgments of men and women and those of persons in several contrasting occupational categories. The subjects were applicants for employment in a large public-utility company. The same list of job factors and the same procedures were also used in a subsequent study of department-store employees.[12] The results of these two studies are shown in Table 14–5.

Table 14–5. Average Ranks Assigned to Job Factors by Various Groups
(1.0 indicates maximum importance; 10.0 indicates minimum importance)

Factor	Male applicants		Female applicants (378)	Department-store employees	
	Clerical (259)	Manual (2252)		Male (62)	Female (139)
Security................	3.2	2.9	4.6	3.3	3.8
Advancement...........	3.2	3.6	4.6	3.8	5.5
Type of work............	3.1	4.0	2.8	4.1	3.8
Company...............	4.7	4.9	5.4	6.9	6.8
Coworkers..............	6.3	6.0	5.4	6.9	5.8
Supervisor..............	6.4	6.1	5.4	6.1	5.0
Pay....................	6.0	6.3	6.4	4.8	5.3
Hours..................	7.2	6.8	6.1	5.4	5.3
Benefits................	7.8	7.2	8.2	6.9	7.3
Working conditions.......	7.1	7.2	5.8	6.4	6.6

Such surveys of factors considered important in a job tend to show that there is some agreement among various groups as to the kinds of factors that are most important. In the four surveys reported here, for example, there is a consistent finding that such factors as opportunity for advancement, security of job, and kind of work are seen as more important than such factors as good working conditions or favorable benefit programs; the factor of high pay seems to have a middle position of importance. In some surveys important differences appear between various groups of respondents in their judgment of the factors. In Table 14–5, for example, it is shown that women tend to be interested more than men in short-range or temporary factors that increase the pleasantness of work as compared with the long-range factors that relate to lifetime economic support. In Table 14–5 it is shown that factory workers give much greater emphasis to "comfortable working conditions" than do department-store workers.

[12] Hardin, E., Reif, H. G., and Heneman, H. G., Stability of Job Preferences of Department Store Employees, *J. Appl. Psychol.*, 1951, **35**, No. 4.

Data of this sort have two kinds of utility. First, they have stimulated a reconsideration of the idea, predominant in business-management thinking, that high pay and good working conditions are the only or primary considerations in judging a job. Second, they have been useful to particular companies in connection with planning to provide the kinds of jobs that employees want to secure and keep. Such surveys, on the other hand, represent only a beginning effort toward understanding the wants and motivations of workers. It may be that what workers *say* is important depends upon the dissatisfactions they are experiencing in a particular situation rather than upon some underlying system of a job values. Furthermore, there is reason to believe that what a worker *does* (in choosing a job, for example) may not always be consistent with the considerations he says are important.

FACTORS RELATED TO MORALE

While surveys of the kind described in the previous paragraphs are of some value in approaching the problem of morale, it is clear from common observation that what a worker wants in a job is only a part of the complex set of factors which determine his level of morale. A number of studies have been designed to secure more extensive information about morale in relation to worker's expectations, attitudes, satisfactions with specific aspects of the job, and objective conditions of work, as well as their wants. We shall describe one such study which was concerned with the morale and motivation of shipyard workers.[13]

The study had its origin in the fact that five large shipyards engaged in similar work showed great differences in productivity. The best shipyard required only 57 days to produce a certain type of vessel while, at the other extreme, the least productive shipyard required 207 days, or nearly four times as long. The study was planned to provide some information as to the human factors which might help to explain these great differences. Three kinds of data were obtained: (1) worker satisfactions and dissatisfactions with many specific aspects of the working situations, (2) information as to actual conditions at the several plants, and (3) reports concerning out-plant factors of living conditions such as housing and transportation. This information was obtained by intensive interviewing of a sample of workers from each plant as well as from observations and records.

The results show that worker morale varied greatly from shipyard to shipyard and was correlated with the productivity of the yards. However, there appeared to be no simple patterns of relationships among

[13] Katz, D., and Hyman, H., Morale in War Industries, in T. N. Newcomb, and E. L. Hartley (Eds.), *Readings in Social Psychology*, Henry Holt and Company, Inc., New York, 1947.

the factors studied, and each yard presented its own complex of determinants of morale.

Shipyard B enjoyed good worker motivation in spite of poor community living conditions. Identification with the yard's success in turning out ships plus good earnings made up for the daily frustrations of getting to and from work.

Shipyard A had the advantage of relatively better community conditions for its workers and the advantage of a longer established plant, as well as an excellent earning situation due to a seven-day week. Its workers took pride in producing ships but the morale situation was complicated by rumors of a cut-back in work-week and wages and a change in type of craft to be produced. The uncertainty about company policy led to anxiety and insecurity among employees.

At the other end of the scale was Shipyard D struggling under a miserable out-plant situation, with inadequate housing, bad sanitary conditions, and poor recreational facilities. Moreover, the in-plant pattern was on the debit side, with resentment over a cut in work-week and wages, poor production, and poor labor-management relations.

Two of the shipyards, C and E, were in adjoining areas of the same New England city and thus were similar with respect to the out-plant factors. These two plants differed greatly in both productivity and morale. Table 14–6 summarizes some of the finding for these two plants

Table 14–6. Comparison of Two Shipyards on Productivity, Situational Factors, and Worker Satisfactions and Dissatisfactions

	Shipyard E	Shipyard C
Average number of days to turn out a ship	207	76
Per cent of employees living within 1 hour travel time to plant	54	52
Per cent of employees with weekly earnings of $55 or more	39	65
Per cent of employees thinking about quitting	56	38
Per cent of employees who are satisfied with:		
Wages	47	83
Length of workday	83	96
Length of work week	60	55
Shift worked	83	73
Working conditions	74	87
Promotional policy	50	70
Productivity of plant	31	70
Use of worker's skills	56	66
Use of worker's time	49	60

and illustrates the consistently unfavorable picture which was obtained of plant E in comparison with plant C.

The authors draw three principal conclusions from this study: (1) There seems to be a circular causal relationship between morale and productivity so that low productivity leads to low morale and this in turn leads to still further reduction in productivity. On the other hand, increased productivity gives men a feeling of accomplishment which leads to increased effort. (2) Worker morale seems most directly related to immediate psychological and physical factors in the work situation, and when the factors associated with the job itself are favorable, the out-plant factors appear to have relatively little influence on morale. (3) The significance of any particular factor in relation to morale must be interpreted with consideration for the specific plant and community situation. It is difficult (except for the plant in question) to identify factors as being "most important" or "least important."

SUPERVISORY PRACTICES AND PRODUCTIVITY

The relationship between the supervisor and his men has long been an area of great interest to those concerned with the problems of morale and motivation in work. Recent research has tended to confirm the importance attributed to this relationship and has begun to throw some light upon the conditions and practices of supervision which are effective in promoting both worker satisfaction and high levels of productivity. The importance of supervisory practices stems not only from the fact of day-to-day personal relationships between supervisor and worker, but also from the fact that in most organizations the supervisor is a person of considerable authority through whom the policies and programs of the organization are brought to bear on the worker. In a sense the supervisor *is* the company as far as the experiences of the worker are concerned. The supervisor is in a position to determine to a large extent the attitudes, opinions, and behavior of the men in relation to their work and to the company.

While there are many aspects to the problem of supervision, we shall consider here only that of the relation between supervisory practices and productivity. Several studies have been directed toward this problem. We shall refer to two studies which were specifically designed to investigate productivity, one among clerical workers in an insurance company office, and the other among railroad-track maintenance workers.[14]

Both studies were planned to take advantage of situations in which there were a number of sections of workers engaged in similar work

[14] Katz, D., Maccoby, N., and Morse, N. C., *Productivity, Supervision and Morale in an Office Situation*, 1950; and Katz, D., Maccoby, N., Gurin, G., and Floor, L. C., *Productivity, Supervision and Morale among Railroad Workers*, 1951, University of Michigan Press, Ann Arbor, Mich.

and having similar working conditions. In the insurance company as in the railroad company, some of the work sections were known to be more productive than others, and it was possible to compare the "high-production" sections with the "low production" sections. In all the groups information was gathered regarding the objective working conditions and the attitudes and opinions of both the workers and the supervisors. The analysis of these data was planned to determine, among other things, whether differences in supervisory practices might account for some of the differences in productivity. The following summary of some of the results of these two studies is taken from the 1951 report on the railroad study.

The effective supervisor is able to differentiate his role as a leader from his role as a section employee, to remove himself occasionally from the actual operations of the group, and to spend his time planning the work, directing his employees and performing specific, highly skilled tasks. The less effective supervisor perceives himself less as a leader and more as a worker just like the rest of the men in the section.

At the same time, the effective supervisor appears to take a personalized approach to his employees, is concerned with problems of motivating them and is sensitive to their needs. . . . The men in high sections of the railroad see their foreman as more interested in the men's off-the-job problems, more helpful in training them for better jobs, and constructive rather than punitive in attitudes towards the men's mistakes. . . . Heads of high sections (in the clerical situation) are more often "employee oriented" than heads of low sections and tend to regard employees as "human beings" rather than as "people to get the work out."

In both studies, first-line supervisors of high and low producing sections differ in their attitudes towards their jobs as supervisors. In the clerical situation heads of high sections emphasize personal dealings with employees as the most important part of their jobs while heads of low sections emphasize production and technical aspects. In the railroad situation, foremen of high sections tend to like their jobs as foremen for "employee oriented" reasons and foremen of low sections for "work oriented" or "self oriented" reasons.

In the area of close-versus-general supervision, however, the relation to productivity is not consistent in the two studies. In the clerical study, the heads of high producing sections exercise a somewhat general, non-detailed sort of supervision over their employees while heads of low sections exercise close, detailed supervision over their sections. In the railroad study, questions about how closely they supervise their sections show little difference between high and low foremen.

Table 14–7 presents one set of comparisons from these studies to illustrate the kind of data supporting the findings. Effective supervisors tend to spend a substantial part of their time on duties which are dis-

Table 14–7. Relation to Group Productivity of Time Spent by Group Head on Supervisory Activities

	Number of supervisors reporting they spend their time*	
	Half or more on supervision	Less than half on supervision
Clerical work groups:		
High production...........	9	2
Low production............	4	7
Railroad work groups:		
High production...........	20	11
Low production............	9	22

* In response to a direct question asking proportion of time spent on supervision and proportion spent on production work.

tinctly "supervisory" in character and less times doing productive work similar to that of their subordinates.

OVERCOMING RESISTANCE TO CHANGE

The studies described in the preceding pages all depended upon interviews or questionnaires as their main source of information about worker's and supervisor's attitudes, opinions, beliefs, and satisfactions. It is also possible, although more difficult in many respects, to investigate the determinants of morale and motivation by actual "experiments" in which changes are introduced into the working situation and the effects of the change are observed.

Such an experiment was carried out in a clothing factory. The purpose of the experiment was to determine the effect upon productivity of different ways of introducing changes in work procedure.[15]

It had been the experience in this plant that whenever a change in work procedures was introduced a period as long as 8 weeks or more was often needed to get the productivity of the work group back up to standard. This was due in part, of course, to the loss of productivity while learning the changed job. It was felt, however, that other factors accounted for the remaining discrepancy and that the attitudes of the workers toward the change in work would be found to be a critical factor.

The experiment in question involved introducing changes into the jobs of four separate work groups. These changes were comparable in

[15] Cech L., and French, J. R. P., Overcoming Resistance to Change, *Hum. Relations*, 1948, 1, No. 4.

their importance, as judged from time studies of the operations, and there was no reason to expect that the four groups would respond to the changes differently than such groups had in the past or that they would be much unlike one another in their progress toward standard levels of performance on the changed jobs.

The experiment consisted of introducing the job changes with different degrees of participation by the group members in planning the change. One group, called the "control" group, was treated just as such groups had been treated in the past; they were informed of the change and the reasons why it was necessary, the new basis for wage calculation was explained, and their questions were answered. A second group, called Experimental Group I, received a more thorough explanation of the change, were asked for suggestions on how the operation should be set up, and had a chance to suggest and approve a procedure for making the change; certain special workers were selected as representatives of the group to participate in a preliminary tryout of the changed job. The remaining two groups, Experimental Groups II and III, were given a still more extensive opportunity to understand the contemplated change, to make suggestions both about the change itself and about how best to introduce it; all members were given the preliminary training and observation in connection with setting up the new piece rate for wage calculation.

Records of the productivity of the four groups were kept for periods preceding and following the changes in work method. Figure 14–3 shows the results obtained.

The control group dropped to a relatively low level of productivity and made no progress toward improvement during the 32 days represented. The group which participated through representation (Experimental Group I) had an initial loss of productivity but regained their former level of production within 2 weeks. The two groups having total participation in planning the change (Experimental Groups II and III) recovered their normal productivity within a few days and then proceeded to produce at an even higher rate. There were also observed some important differences among the four groups as to feeling of satisfaction with the change and as to the number of workers who quit their jobs, the Experimental Groups II and III being best on both these factors.

It is not to be concluded from this experiment that participation in planning of changes is "the best" method for motivating workers or that this will improve productivity in all situations or over long periods of time. It does illustrate an additional method for investigating morale, and it appears to show that when workers are given opportunity to participate in decisions which affect them additional sources of motivation may be tapped and additional satisfaction with the working situation may result.

SUMMARY

Many of the problems confronting the management of a business or industrial concern are directly related to the effective use of the capabilities of the workers and to the provision of conditions which result in effective relations among the members of the organization. Much

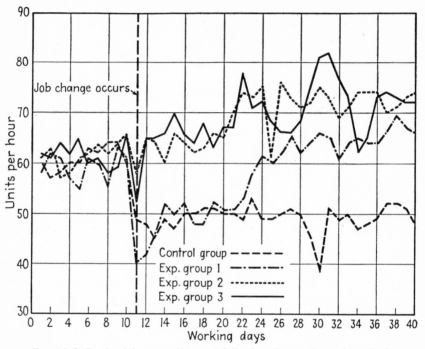

FIG. 14–3. Productivity preceding and following changes in work methods.

attention has been given in recent years to the systematic study of these personnel problems toward the end that psychological principles may be more fully utilized in their solution.

One persistent problem which has yielded to psychological investigation is that of employee training. Studies dealing with the conditions necessary for learning have been transferred to the industrial situation and have led to important changes in our understanding of what can be accomplished through training and our understanding of effective training methods.

A beginning has been made in the area of worker morale. Studies have been made which serve to outline the major factors contributing to high morale and which give some clues as to the steps which can be taken to gain a further understanding of the perceptions, satisfactions, and motivations of people in relation to their working situation.

RECOMMENDED SUPPLEMENTARY READINGS

Blum, M. L.: *Industrial Psychology and Its Social Foundations,* Harper & Brothers, New York, 1949.

Dodd, A. E., and Rice, J. O. (Eds.): *How to Train Workers for War Industries,* Harper & Brothers, New York, 1942.

Gray, J. S., *Psychology in Industry.* McGraw-Hill Book Company, Inc., New York, 1952.

Halsey, G. D.: *Training Employees,* Harper & Brothers, New York, 1949.

Hartmann, G. W., and Newcomb, T. (Eds.): *Industrial Conflict,* The Cordon Company, Inc., New York, 1940.

Hoppock, R.: *Job Satisfaction,* Harper & Brothers, New York, 1935.

Houser, J. D.: *What People Want from Business,* McGraw-Hill Book Company, Inc., New York, 1938.

McMurry, R. N.: *Handling Personality Adjustment in Industry,* Harper & Brothers, New York, 1944.

Chapter 15

PSYCHOLOGY IN INDUSTRY— WAGE DETERMINATION

Wages are determined by a multiplicity of factors—economic conditions, profits, attitude of stockholders, prevailing community wages, as well as the worth of the job and the worth of the man on the job. It is these two last factors which interest the industrial psychologist. Given a total payroll, large or small as determined by other factors, what is the most equitable distribution of that payroll among a given group of employees? What portion of the payroll dollar should go to each employee? The industrial psychologist believes that he can determine this in a systematic and accurate manner.

Two procedures are involved in an equitable distribution of the payroll dollar—a determination of the worth of a job, and a determination of the worth of an employee. Each procedure is discrete and does not involve the other. The first is called "job evaluation" and the second is called "employee merit rating." Needless to say, both are performed whenever there is an employer-employee relationship, although they may not be accurately determined.

JOB EVALUATION

The worth of a job can be determined entirely aside from any consideration of the worth of the employee on the job. In fact, jobs can be evaluated in new industries and pay rates determined before a single employee goes to work. Job evaluation may be defined as a systematic procedure of determining the worth of jobs by comparing them with

416

each other or with standardized "bench mark" jobs. This comparison may be made with whole jobs or with discrete job factors followed by a summation of factor values. In either case, it is a systematic procedure of determining the comparative worth of jobs themselves irrespective of the customary wage rate. A job is evaluated for what it is rather than for what it has been, or for what influence the employees on the job may exert. It is not a question of increasing or decreasing the total payroll. All the jobs may be underpaid or overpaid. Job evaluation is a systematic determination of the relative value of jobs in relation to each other. It will reveal the jobs that are not getting a fair share of the payroll, as well as those that are overpaid in relation to other jobs on the same payroll. Job evaluation has nothing to do with raising or lowering wages except within the limits of the present payroll.

The first step in job evaluation, regardless of the method used, is *job analysis* or a study of what the job consists of and the conditions under which it must be performed. This may involve observation of the job and interviewing the workman, or an actual performance of the job, or a questionnaire inquiry. However obtained, it consists of information about *what* a worker does, *how* he does it, *why* he does it, and the skill involved in the doing. Job evaluation can be done accurately only by those who know the jobs being evaluated as thoroughly as the workmen who perform them. The importance of thorough job analysis in job evaluation cannot be overemphasized.[1]

There are many ways or procedures of job evaluation, which will be described later, but all of them attempt to determine the value of jobs in relation to other jobs which come under the same payroll. This is just as important for jobs on incentive pay, or piece rate, as it is for the hourly paid jobs. Base rates and hourly rates can be determined only by some sort of job evaluation. Unfortunately, this is frequently a prevailing rate which either developed like Topsy, or was a result of bargaining which confused the worth of the workman with the worth of the job. As early as 1871, the U.S. Civil Service Commission made preliminary steps to evaluate jobs by systematic procedure. However, it was not until about 1925 that the point system of job evaluation was developed by Kingsbury,[2] Lott,[3] and others.

Then, during the Second World War, the Wage and Salary Stabilization Law required that all increases be justified, and the War Labor Board usually interpreted this to mean by job evaluation. At any rate,

[1] See *Training and Reference Manual for Job Analysis*, Department of Labor, U.S. Employment Service, 1944.

[2] Kingsbury, F. A., Grading the Office Job, *Management and Administration*, 1923, pp. 73–78.

[3] Lott, M. R., *Wage Scales and Job Evaluation*, The Ronald Press Company, New York, 1926.

job evaluation is now an accepted and widely used procedure of wage determination.

Job Ranking and Grading

Perhaps the oldest method of job evaluation is *job ranking*. The more difficult jobs are ranked higher than the less difficult ones, and these get higher than the easy ones. Pay rates then depend on how high a job ranks. Job ranking is usually done by a committee which studies the jobs carefully, though formal job analysis is seldom a preliminary step. Few companies use job ranking in spite of its simplicity (and accuracy if carefully administered).

Job grading is a procedure of classifying jobs in previously determined and defined grades. When used properly, it is preceded by careful job analysis and the classification is done by a committee of specialists in job evaluation. One of the best examples of this method is that of Westinghouse Electric Corporation for salaried employees.[4] The grades are defined as unskilled, skilled, interpretative, creative, executive, and administrative.

Group I—Unskilled

Storekeeper	Switchboard tender
Shipping clerk	Storeroom attendant
Schedule clerk	File clerk
Order stock checker	Duplicating-machine operator
Record clerk	Office boy (girl)
Transcribing clerk	

The job is the accomplishment of assigned tasks in an established routine fashion. To function in these jobs, accuracy and dependability are necessary but neither experience nor training is required.

Group II—Skilled

Production clerk	Second (power-plant) engineer
Detail draftsman	Secretary-stenographer
Assistant buyer	Interviewer
First (power-plant) engineer	Ledgerman
Process demonstrator	Stenographer
Statistician	Typist

These are the jobs of skilled workers. The tasks require discrimination and choice, technique of hand or brain, and often artistry. (Both experience and training are prerequisite.)

[4] *Salary Administration, Position Analysis and Classification,* Westinghouse Electric Corporation.

GROUP III—INTERPRETATIVE

Foreman	Secretary
Assistant foreman	Time and motion analyst
Shipper	Chief clerk (chief of clerical section)
Police sergeant	Layout draftsman
Buyer	Inspector
Office manager	

The function of jobs of interpretation is to meet, classify, and cope with situations clearly recognized as within the scope of the established system. These things are done by applying the standards created in the higher groups. Those who function in this group must clearly see the situation in hand and fit it into the established pattern. The work may involve supervisory executive responsibility for the control of the efforts of large or small groups of workers.

GROUP IV—CREATIVE

Supervisor, general works staff	Maintenance engineer
Supervisor, works manager's staff	Tool (design) engineer
Division staff supervisor	Plant layout engineer
Assistant division staff supervisor	Test engineer
Manufacturing engineer	

The creation of material values calls for familiarity with techniques and a breadth of conception of their application and withal the ability to discriminate and choose or reject. Creative employees observe phenomena by study of a manifold of situations and collect data for the construction of patterns for use in formulating general procedures, thereby establishing standards of practice. Their influence extends downward in the organization, carrying with it the tone of superiors and upward to those superiors influencing the tone and character of the executive instructions that are promulgated in those higher groups to set policy in action. Under their technical leadership, the operation of the creation of things is carried out by the hourly paid workers, the integrated result of which effort is to be recognized on this level. However, the individual hourly paid jobs are of the skilled and unskilled groups. The function of the staff superiors and engineers of this group is the accomplishment of that integration.

GROUP V—EXECUTIVE

Superintendent	Assistant superintendent
Captain of police	General foreman

The function here is translating plan into action, by the control of the direction in which those of the lower groups will apply their efforts, and the interpretation to them of the meaning or intent of the policy or procedure. Executives advise with superiors on policy and procedure reflecting to them broad knowledge of and experience with operating conditions.

GROUP VI—ADMINISTRATIVE

General works manager	Works manager
Director, general works staff	Assistant works manager

The administrator has the broad manufacturing responsibility, universally or within a prescribed division of the manufacturing organization. By negotiation and arbitration, he brings into harmonious arrangement individual and divergent interests; he promulgates general rules and procedures for the manufacturing organization as a whole, or within the limits of jurisdiction; he shapes broad plans and applies them. The position involves executive responsibility of the first order for large or small groups of subordinates depending upon the sphere of activity.

Each grade classification carries its own wage range. While some progress is possible within the grade, major progress necessitates passing to the next higher group. Job grading is adequate for some companies and is definitely better than no method at all, but it is inferior to the more systematic job-evaluation methods described below. It is a simple procedure of making a rough approximation of the worth of a job.

Sometimes job ranking and job grading are combined. Jobs are classified in grades (each grade carrying a wage range) and then ranked within the grade to determine the specific wage. This is probably better than either method used alone and, if carefully administered, may not be inferior to other procedures of job evaluation, especially for clerical and skilled jobs. There has been no study of job grading and job ranking in comparison with the point systems and money value systems of job evaluation described below. It is the opinion of the author that they may be satisfactory when used (1) in combination as suggested above, (2) after very careful job analysis, and (3) by evaluators who are thoroughly familiar with the procedures of job evaluation.

MONEY VALUE SYSTEMS

Job ranking and job grading are often criticized because they evaluate jobs as a whole and do not afford a breakdown of job values. The so-called "factor comparison"[5] system evaluates jobs on the basis of

[5] See Benge, E. J., *et al., Manual of Job Evaluation*, Harper & Brothers, New York, 1941.

"five critical factors" which are alleged to be present in all jobs. These are: mental requirements, both inherent and acquired; skill requirements, including job knowledge; physical requirements; responsibilities of various kinds; and working conditions.

The procedure of this system is to select 15 or 20 "key jobs" within a company (1) that are representative of all those to be evaluated and (2) that already carry wage rates acceptable to both labor and manage-

Table 15–1. Ranking of Key Jobs on Job Factors

	Factors				
	Mental	Skill	Physical	Responsi- bility	Working conditions
Delivery man 7-C-8	4	4	1	4	1
File clerk 9-C-2	4	4	3	4	2
Typist (copy) 3-C-18	3	3	4	4	4
Stenographer 7-C-23	2	2	4	2	4
Secretary 1-C-4	1	1	2	1	4

ment. These are then ranked on each of the five job factors, as shown in Table 15–1. The next step is to apportion the wages of each key job to each of the five factors. This is shown in Table 15–2. These key

Table 15–2. Money Value of Key Jobs for Each Job Factor

Jobs	Wage rate (month)	Factors				
		Mental	Skill	Physical	Responsi- bility	Working conditions
Delivery man 7-C-8	145	20	20	55	30	20
File clerk 9-C-2	120	20	20	35	30	15
Typist (copy) 7-C-33	140	35	35	30	30	10
Stenographer 7-C-23	175	50	40	35	45	10
Secretary 1-C-4	230	65	45	50	60	10

jobs are then used as "bench marks" for evaluating all other jobs by comparison on each of the five factors. This explains the label "factor comparison."

This system has both advantages and disadvantages over the ranking and grading systems. An advantage is that it is diagnostic. It breaks jobs down into discrete factors and evaluates each separately. This affords information as to *why* some jobs are evaluated higher than some other jobs. A second advantage is that it provides criteria or standards with which to compare jobs being evaluated. If the key jobs are properly evaluated (and the accuracy of this step is fundamental) it is easier to evaluate other jobs by comparison than it is to evaluate them without such standards. The key jobs are "bench marks" which facilitate the accuracy of evaluation judgments. A disadvantage is that the factors are inflexible. Useful factors are those which are variables between jobs. Constant factors are useless in evaluation. For example, if working conditions are the same for all jobs being evaluated, the wage rate for that factor should be the same for all jobs. Conversely, a variable factor may be ignored because it is not one of the five used in this system. For example, social intelligence is an important variable when receptionist and sales jobs are being evaluated with other jobs not requiring this factor. It is a job specification which should carry money value to the degree that it exists. A second disadvantage of the factor comparison is the fact that jobs are evaluated in dollars and cents. Currently paid rates unfortunately influence the judgment of evaluators when jobs are evaluated in money units. It is easier to evaluate jobs impartially when money value is not considered.

POINT SYSTEMS

Point systems of job evaluation rate jobs on discrete "factors" which have varied "point values" according to the "degree" of the factor. Table 15–3 reproduces a simplified manual used in evaluating clerical jobs. The point values for various degrees of each factor are also shown. Jobs are evaluated on each factor separately, and these are then added to determine the total value of the job. A typical job evaluation is shown in Table 15–4. The total value of this job is 225 points, which justifies a monthly salary of between \$186 and \$239 ($225 + 200 = 425 \times 0.50 = 212.50 \pm 12\frac{1}{2}$ per cent), depending on the merit of the workmen on that job. Most evaluation manuals for point systems are not so simple as this one and define both factors and degrees more elaborately.

Note that the justifications in Table 15–4 necessitate a thorough understanding of each job. Careful job analysis must precede the use of point systems of job evaluation.

Table 15-3. Manual for Evaluating Routine Office Jobs

Factors		I		II		III		IV		V
						Degrees				
Education—Formal schooling or equivalent	(15)	High school Filing clerk Copy typist	(30)	High school plus 1 year secretarial training Simple bookkeeping	(45)	2 years college Simple accounting Secretary	(60)	College graduate Some administration function	(75)	Graduate training Specialist—CPA
Experience—Training time	(20)	30 days or less Simple filing Copy typist	(40)	1 to 4 months Minor secretarial	(60)	4 months to 7 year Secretary to official	(80)	1 to 3 years Minor supervisor	(100)	More than 3 years Assistant to a major official
Initiative—Number and importance of necessary decisions	(15)	Work patterned, closely supervised	(30)	Supervision available. Minor decisions Simple filing Copy typist	(45)	Tasks varied. All decisions with precedents Ordinary secretarial	(60)	Many and varied decisions with precedent and/or supervision Major secretary	(75)	Decision making major function Office manager Supervisor
Attention—Necessary with interruptions and confusion	(10)	Quiet environment. Few interruptions	(20)	Usual office traffic. Other employees Assistant secretary	(30)	Active office, much detail Secretary	(40)	Varied duties and much office traffic Head secretary in busy office	(50)	Office manager or assistant to official
Responsibility—For records and reports	(10)	Practically none except for routine messages	(20)	Simple records such as appointment schedule	(30)	Records kept under close supervision	(40)	Records kept under remote but available supervision	(50)	Entire time spent in keeping records. No supervision
Responsibility—For contacts with others	(10)	None except with supervision	(20)	Only with other employees in same office	(30)	Necessary contact with other departments	(40)	Receptionist	(50)	A public relations job
Responsibility—For confidential information	(10)	Practically none except as required by good office practice	(20)	Access to semi-confidential information	(30)	Access to but not responsible for confidential information	(40)	Responsible for confidential information to a limited degree	(50)	Access to *all* information of highly confidential nature
Responsibility—For supervision of others	(10)	No supervision duties	(20)	A head employee works full time and directs work of assistant	(30)	Works part time and supervises part time	(40)	Full-time supervisor	(50)	Office personnel manager. Supervisor of supervisors

Evaluate job and add points. To this total add a base of 200 points. Multiply this total by 0.50 or ½. This will be the mean monthly salary recommended. A plus and minus range of 12½ per cent is allowed for each job. An employee's actual salary within this range is then determined by merit rating.

Table 15–4. Job Evaluation—Clerical Jobs

Code ___1-C-74___   Class _____

Job Name Secretary   Department X _____

Job Purpose General secretary to X——

Factors	Value	Justification
Education	30	Need high school level of education to comprehend nature of work. Commercial training needed for dictation and typing
Experience	40	Work is routine. Can be learned in 4 months or less
Initiative	45	Minor decisions regarding transcribing, mimeographing, telephone messages, etc., with remote supervision
Attention	30	Average variability in duties performed and average office traffic
Responsibility for records and reports	30	Keeps records as directed. All patterned and with precedent. Does necessary filing
Responsibility for contacts with others	30	Routine contacts with personnel, both within and without department. No contacts with general public except by telephone
Responsibility for confidential information	10	None
Responsibility for supervision of others	10	None
Total value	225	

After jobs have been tentatively evaluated, a table can be made of these (see Table 15–5) and then analytically studied. Jobs can be compared with each other on each factor. If a job is overevaluated or underevaluated in comparison with other jobs, the error is more obvious. Note job 1-C-76. This was originally rated 20 for *experience*. When it was considered with the other jobs, this rating was raised to 40. At the same time, job 1-C-45 was raised from 40 to 60. This vertical comparison of jobs on each factor results in greater accuracy.

There are many point systems of job evaluation. Usually they are designed for use in specific industries and for jobs of specific type. The system developed by the National Electrical Manufacturers Association (and also used by the National Metal Trades Association) has been widely used for evaluating plant production jobs in electrical and steel fabricating industries. The 11 factors used in this system and their degree weights are shown in Table 15–6. Other well-known point systems of job evaluation are General Foods with 10 factors, Revere Cop-

Table 15-5. Summary of Evaluations for 10 Clerical Jobs

	Education	Experience	Initiative	Attention	Responsibility				Total
					Records and reports	Contacts with others	Confidential information	Supervision of others	
1-C-74 Dept. X, secretary......	30	40	45	30	30	30	10	10	225
1-C-107 Dept. X, secretary......	30	40	45	30	30	30	20	30	255
1-C-108 Dept. X, secretary......	30	40	45	30	30	30	40	20	265
1-C-45 Dept. X, secretary......	30	60	45	40	40	30	10	30	285
1-C-80 Dept. X, clerk-typist...	30	40	30	20	20	20	10	10	180
1-C-76 Dept. X, clerk-typist...	30	40	30	20	10	30	10	10	180
2-C-15 Dept. Y, secretary......	30	60	45	30	40	30	10	20	265
2-C-18 Dept. Y, secretary......	30	40	45	30	30	30	20	30	255
2-C-32 Dept. Y, typist.........	30	20	30	30	10	10	20	10	160
2-C-47 Dept. Y, file clerk......	15	40	30	10	10	20	30	10	165

per and Brass with 11 factors, U.S. Steel with 15 factors, and Wright Aeronautical with 13 factors.

While Stigers and Reed[6] recommend the use of 36 factors in evaluating jobs, Lawshe and his associates[7] have found that the same results can be obtained by the use of only three factors. In fact, "overall value to the company" seems to be the only factor necessary for adequately evaluating jobs when a more analytical breakdown is not needed.

More important than the number of factors used is the relative weight in points given them. Worker qualifications (education, experience, aptitudes) usually carry greater weight than any other group of factors. These carry 35 per cent of the total in the system shown in Table 15-1. In systems for evaluating production jobs, this percentage is even greater (National Electrical Manufacturers Association is 50

[6] Stigers, M. F., and Reed, E. G., Theory and Practice of Job Rating, McGraw-Hill Book Company, Inc., New York, 1944.
[7] Studies in Job Evaluation, J. Appl. Psychol., 1944-1950.

Table 15–6. Factors and Degree Values for the National Metal Trades System of Job Evaluation

Factors	Degrees				
	1	2	3	4	5
Skill:					
1. Education..........................	14	28	42	56	70
2. Experience.........................	22	44	66	88	110
3. Initiative and ingenuity...............	14	28	42	56	70
Effort:					
4. Physical demand.....................	10	20	30	40	50
5. Mental and/or visual demand..........	5	10	15	20	25
Responsibility:					
6. Equipment or process.................	5	10	15	20	25
7. Material or product...................	5	10	15	20	25
8. Safety of others......................	5	10	15	20	25
9. Work of others......................	5	10	15	20	25
Job conditions:					
10. Working conditions...................	10	20	30	40	50
11. Unavoidable hazards..................	5	10	15	20	25

per cent, U.S. Steel is 45 per cent, Westinghouse is 60 per cent). Effort, as indicated by such factors as initiative and attention, carries 25 per cent of the total in Table 15–1, only 15 per cent in the N.E.M.A. system, 16 per cent in the U.S. Steel system, and 22 per cent in the Westinghouse system. Responsibilities carry 40 per cent in Table 15–1, 20 per cent in N.E.M.A. system, 24 per cent in the U.S. Steel system, and 14 per cent in the Westinghouse system. Working conditions (including danger hazards) are not used as a factor in Table 15–1, but carry 15 per cent in the U.S. Steel system and 4 per cent in the Westinghouse system. This difference between the Table 15–1 system and others is explained in part by the difference in type of jobs for which they are used. The Table 15–1 system is for clerical jobs only and the others are for production jobs.

"Ready-made point systems of job evaluation" (such as those mentioned above) are appropriate when:

1. Job evaluators are relatively inexperienced.
2. The jobs to be evaluated are of the same type as those for which the system was designed.

Unfortunately, jobs are frequently so different from those for which a ready-made system of evaluation is designed that they are misevaluated by the system. The system is not valid for all situations. If the job evaluator is adequately trained for this work, it is often advisable to prepare a "custom-made" system to fit the specific jobs being evaluated. This involves rather extensive and complicated research which is justified only when a ready-made system is definitely inappropriate. No system of job evaluation is appropriate unless the factors are *variables* in the jobs being evaluated and weighted according to the degree of that variability. For example, working conditions are variable in production jobs but not usually in clerical jobs. They constitute an appropriate factor when evaluating the former, not when evaluating the latter. Often several factors on ready-made systems of job evaluation are constant for all jobs being evaluated. Conversely, variables between jobs being evaluated often are not factors on the system of evaluation being used. For example, in one plant some jobs were really combinations of several jobs and required great versatility in their performance. Other jobs were short-cycle routines which required little or no versatility. The system of job evaluation being used did not have a factor to cover this variable. Factors in job evaluation should be the variables that actually exist between the jobs being evaluated.

By summary and implication from the systems just considered, we may state four basic principles of job evaluation that should guide efforts along this line.[8]

1. Jobs should be evaluated on the basis of those factors which are significant in the jobs themselves, rather than on the basis of factors which are significant in other jobs in other situations.
2. Jobs should be evaluated in terms of points which can later be translated into dollar values rather than in terms of dollar values directly.
3. In spite of certain disadvantages, it is better to evaluate jobs in comparison with standard jobs (referred to above as key jobs) which are typical of those being evaluated.
4. Factor and degree weights in points should be adjusted until they fit the key jobs. This means that a job-evaluation system should be "custom-built," evaluated in points (which can be translated into dollar values), and be adjusted to fit those key jobs that are already properly paid.

Custom-fit Systems

To satisfy the four principles of job evaluation just stated, it is possible to construct a system which fits the peculiarities of the jobs to be evaluated. It will contain no factors which are not significant variables and it will not omit any significant variables as factors. Furthermore, the weight of each factor variable will be in accordance with its significance as a variable. The procedure of developing such a custom-fit system of job evaluation may be stated in five procedure steps.

[8] See Gray, J. S., *Psychology in Industry*, p. 171, McGraw-Hill Book Company, Inc., New York, 1952.

1. First, it is necessary to have a local job-evaluation committee composed of intelligent individuals who are well acquainted with all jobs to be evaluated. Both labor and management should be represented on this committee. There should not be more than seven members, each chosen on the basis of his intelligence, his acquaintance with the jobs, and his willingness to work hard and cooperate with others. The success of the procedure depends largely on the caliber of this committee.

2. The second step (the first act of the committee) is to select 15 or 20 key jobs. (It is assumed that all jobs have been analyzed and job descriptions and specifications carefully prepared. If not, this is a prerequisite to further progress.) The key jobs must be representative or typical of the rest of the jobs in the company. If the jobs are highly varied—some clerical, some production, and some professional—one system of job evaluation cannot be made to fit. (Of course, if there are less than 50 jobs in each category, it is not feasible to develop a custom-fit system either. It is better to adopt the money-value system or one of the ready-made point systems described above.) Clerical jobs and production jobs should be evaluated as separate units, using different job factors and different weights.

Also, the key jobs should carry wage rates, which, in relation to the size of the total payroll, are accepted by all members of the committee as unquestionably fair. This is fundamentally important. If the wage rates of the key jobs are not fair, in relation to the wage rates of all other jobs under the same payroll, the custom-fit system of job evaluation cannot be fair. The key jobs are the criteria for determining the fitness of the new evaluation system. It is sometimes possible for the committee to agree on a theoretical fair wage for a key job when the actual wage is considered unfair. A fair theoretical wage is as useful in constructing a custom-fit system of job evaluation as a fair actual wage.

3. The third step is to discover the variables that exist in the various jobs to be evaluated and the magnitude of those variables. Only the major job variables can be used as evaluation factors. Each factor as well as each step degree of that factor must be carefully defined. This constitutes the "manual" and is illustrated in Table 15–3.

4. A determination of the job factors is then followed by a determination of their value or weight. Important factors should carry more value than less important ones. It is easier to decide the per cent value of each factor. If there are 8 factors, the per cent value of each may be distributed as illustrated in Table 15–3. If there are 11 factors, they may be weighted as in Table 15–6. The value of each degree beyond

the first is obtained by multiplying the value of the first by the number of the degree. Each degree should then be carefully defined to conform with its weight or value.

When tentative factor and degree weights are thus determined, their accuracy and appropriateness can be checked by a test evaluation of the key jobs. If the key jobs are evaluated accurately, it is assumed that the weights are appropriate. If not, the weights must be changed until the key jobs are accurately evaluated. Thus, the key jobs are used as criteria for validating the new evaluation system.[9]

5. When the evaluation system has been so adjusted that it evaluates the key jobs accurately, the next step is to evaluate all the jobs in the company. This procedure is no different from that described above under Point Systems and illustrated in Table 15–4.

The advantage of using a custom-fit system of job evaluation after it is constructed is that it determines job values more accurately than is possible in any other way and it is simple and easy to use. The disadvantage is that it requires so much time, effort, and technical training to construct it that it is impractical for small companies.

WAGE SCALES

After jobs have been evaluated, it is important then to translate the point values into dollar values. Note the directions at the bottom of Table 15–3, "Evaluate job and add points. To this total add a base of 200 points. Multiply this total by 0.50 or ½. This will be the mean monthly salary recommended. A plus and minus range of 12½ per cent is allowed for each job. An employee's actual wage within this range is then determined by merit rating." This is probably the most simple and easy way of translating point values into wage rates.

Another procedure is to establish "labor grades" or value classifications. For example, the value classifications used with one system are shown in Table 15–7. Here the classification carries a range, instead of each individual job as suggested in Table 15–3. Note that each class overlaps in salary so that trial transfers can be made without affecting salary.

After all jobs in an establishment have been evaluated, a scattergram will show the number of jobs in each classification that are overpaid, accurately paid, and underpaid. Table 15–8 shows the status in one company before wage adjustments had been made. Note that, while 9 jobs are overpaid, 23 are underpaid according to the evaluations. Obviously, salary adjustments should be made if job evaluation is to

[9] This procedure involves statistical procedure too complicated to be discussed here. See Gray, *op. cit.,* pp. 179–183.

Table 15–7. Employment Classifications Showing Evaluation-point Value and Salary Value

Evaluation point range	Class	Yearly salary range
150–174	1	$1,500–$1,800
175–199	2	1,700– 2,000
200–224	3	1,900– 2,200
225–249	4	2,100– 2,400
250–274	5	2,300– 2,600
275–299	6	2,500– 2,800
300–324	7	2,700– 3,000
325–349	8	2,900– 3,200
355–374	9	3,100– 3,400
375–399	10	3,300– 3,600

have any significance. Ideally, the 23 underpaid jobs should be raised and the 9 overpaid jobs should be reduced in salary. Practically this is not advisable. While company morale would be raised by increasing the underpaid jobs, it would be adversely affected if the overpaid jobs were lowered. It is better to give the employees on the overpaid jobs an opportunity to transfer to jobs that are in higher salary brackets so they will not need to take a reduction in salary. Then, the salary rate can be reduced when a new employee goes to work on the overpaid job.

Table 15–8. Relation of Present Salary to Evaluation Points for 59 Clerical Jobs

	EVALUATION POINTS									
	150-174	175-199	200-224	225-249	250-274	275-299	300-324	325-349	350-374	375-399
Yearly salary, dollars	1	2	3	4	5	6	7	8	9	10
3300 - 3600										
3100 - 3400										1
2900 - 3200								1	1	2
2700 - 3000						2	3	2		
2500 - 2800				1	1	5	1	1		
2300 - 2600				2	4	1				
2100 - 2400			1	4	3	1				
1900 - 2200		1	2	2	1	1				
1700 - 2000	1	5		1						
1500 - 1800	3	2	1							
	1	1								

The wage rate of a job class or grade should be rigorously adhered to if a salary structure is to have functional value.[10]

MERIT RATING

Merit rating is a systematic procedure of evaluating the worth of a workman. It is similar to job evaluation in that it is a judgment procedure. It is a determination of worth by judgment.

Merit rating deals, or should deal, with *subjective* factors of worth. Objective factors such as amount of production and absenteeism are evaluated by objective procedures—counting, measuring, ascertaining facts. Judgment is not necessary. As the degree of subjective factors cannot be counted or measured, they must necessarily be determined by judgment. It is a mistake to attempt to judge the merit of a workman on intelligence, for example, when this can be measured accurately with a test. It is not too wrong to say that merit rating is a procedure of determining the degree of those subjective factors of worth that cannot be determined more accurately in some other manner.

Consequently, merit rating is a necessary procedure. When workmen are employed, they have degrees of worth to the company aside from the measurable amount of their production. This degree of worth is determined by judgment—either carefully and systematically, as described in the following pages, or uncritically and perhaps even uncaptiously. The problem is not whether or not to merit-rate, but whether or not to merit-rate with care and system, or hastily, indiscreetly, and even with bias and prejudice. Systematic merit rating is better than unsystematic methods of determining human worth.

There are various procedures of merit rating which have varied worth in different situations. All are better than nothing, and yet none are very good. They are briefly described in the following pages with advantages and disadvantages indicated.

TRAIT SCALES

Degree scales of separate traits are one of the oldest methods of merit rating. Table 15–9 illustrates one of these scales. Originally, the degrees were not described but merely named as high, above average, average, below average, and low. It was found that careful definitions of each trait and of each degree of each trait raised the low reliability of the procedure. Metrical values are usually assigned to each trait and to each degree of each trait so that a meriting-rating score can be obtained. For example, in Table 15–9 the "superior" degree may carry a weight of 6, the "above-average" degree a weight of 4, the

[10] For more detailed discussion of wage and salary schedules where jobs are formally evaluated, see J. L. Otis and R. H. Leukart, *Job Evaluation,* Chaps. 11–16. Prentice-Hall, Inc., New York, 1948.

Table 15–9. Scale for Rating Workmen

Workman's name_____Department_____Date_____

Check opposite each trait the degree which most accurately fits this workman

Trait	Degree			
	Superior	Above average	Ordinary	Unsatisfactory
Knowledge of job	( ) Thorough and competent	( ) Good but not the best	( ) Adequate	( ) Superficial—not adequate
Job performance	( ) Excellent, one of best	( ) Very good	( ) Satisfactory	( ) Slow and inaccurate
Judgment	( ) Sound and practical	( ) Occasional error in judgment	( ) Decisions uncertain	( ) Generally wrong in judgment
Initiative	( ) Makes his job bigger	( ) Very alert	( ) Follows directions adequately	( ) Must be carefully directed
Attitude toward responsibility	( ) Seeks it	( ) Will accept it	( ) Tries to avoid it	( ) Fails when given responsibility
Dependability	( ) Never fails his obligations	( ) Occasionally slips	( ) Must be checked	( ) Usually fails his obligations
Cooperation	( ) Helps others at every opportunity	( ) Good team worker	( ) Fair team worker	( ) Cannot work with others
Leadership	( ) Others seek to follow him	( ) Attains some influence	( ) Rarely influences others	( ) Has no influence on others

"ordinary" degree a weight of 2, and the "unsatisfactory" degree no weight at all. Thus, a workman rated superior in all 8 traits would be given a value of 48.

The trait-scale method of merit rating is perhaps more widely used than any other method. However, the reliability has been found to be low and the weighting is arbitrary. There is no justification for assuming that all the traits in Table 15–9 have equal value or that the step between "ordinary" and "above average" is equal to the step between "above average" and "superior." Superior initiative, for example, may be worth many times as much as superior cooperation, or vice versa. The trouble with substituting varied weights to traits and degrees is that no way has yet been devised for determining the validity of any system of weighting. This handicap applies to all forms of merit rating.

MAN-TO-MAN COMPARISON

When departments are small, each workman can be compared with each other workman. Usually, the merit rater is merely asked to judge which of *two* workmen is superior in "over all worth to the company." A form for such rating is shown in Table 15–10. This procedure is called "paired comparison." The rating score is then the number of workmen who are exceeded. For example, in Table 15–10, if Swede

Table 15–10. Form for Comparing Workmen with Each Other on Over-all Value to the Company

Rating Form

Rater_____Department_____Date_____

The men under your supervision are listed in the form below. Compare each man listed in the vertical column at the left with each man listed horizontally across the top. If he is superior to the man listed at the top in over-all worth to the company, put a plus sign in the square below. If he is inferior to him, put a minus sign in the square. If you think the two are equal in over-all worth to the company, put an equals mark.

	Bill Smith	Swede Carlson	Jack Green	Hank Smith	Dick Melby	Tom Carter	Nick Wilson	O. M. Black	Ed Thomas
John Jones									
Bill Smith									
Swede Carlson									
Jack Green									
Hank Smith									
Dick Melby									
Tom Carter					·				
Nick Wilson									
O. M. Black									

Carlson is rated as superior to every other workman, his score is 8. If he is superior to only 4 other workmen, his score is 4. While this procedure is difficult to use when departments are large, it is still widely used in both business and industry.

WEIGHTED CHECK LISTS

Some companies rate workmen by having supervisors check a specified number, often five, of a list of statements which best characterize a workman. He chooses the statements from a list of weighted statements which range from very commendable to very unsatisfactory. A list of such statements is shown in Table 15–11. Each of these state-

Table 15–11. Check List for Merit Rating Employees

Employee's Name_____Dept._____

Rater's Name_____Date_____

Check *five* statements (no more, no less) from those listed below which are most characteristic of this workman.

_____ 1. His accuracy in work is average.
_____ 2. He justifies utmost confidence.
_____ 3. He does not cooperate with others.
_____ 4. His knowledge of his job is good but not the best.
_____ 5. He has few followers. Limited leadership qualifications.
_____ 6. He accepts and handles responsibility well.
_____ 7. He has much initiative. Makes his job bigger.
_____ 8. He has poor judgment. Decisions too frequently wrong.
_____ 9. He knows his job thoroughly.
_____10. Other people like him. They accept his opinions.
_____11. He never fails an obligation.
_____12. He is considered to be generally dishonest.
_____13. He is very original. Fertile with new ideas.
_____14. He is a good team worker.
_____15. He is not dependable. All his work must be checked.
_____16. He follows directions adequately but does no more than told.
_____17. He has only superficial knowledge of his job.
_____18. He is overcritical of everyone.
_____19. Fellow workmen seek his advice.
_____20. He is a trouble maker.

ments has a value or weight. If statements 2, 7, 9, 11, and 19 are checked, the merit score is 27.6. If statements 5, 8, 12, 15, and 18 are checked, the resulting score is only 6.3. Superior workmen get high merit scores while inferior workmen get low scores. The check list is not widely used but, if carefully constructed and weighted, it is easily and quickly administered. Little is known of its reliability.

CORRECTION OF MERIT-RATING FALLACIES

Studies show that merit rating is a very unreliable form of measurement. Repeat ratings seldom correlate with original ratings higher than .50, which is much too low for reliability. Tiffen[11] found that the cor-

[11] Tiffen, J., *Industrial Psychology*, p. 348, Prentice-Hall, Inc., New York, 1946.

relations between pairs of raters were below .50 on every trait of a rating scale, although the agreement on the scale as a whole was .55. These data are shown in Table 15–12. Other studies show that, when

Table 15–12. Reliability Coefficients in a Merit-rating Scale

Trait	r
Safety	35
Knowledge of job	46
Versatility	47
Accuracy	45
Productivity	46
Over-all job performance	46
Industriousness	47
Initiative	48
Judgment	45
Cooperation	37
Personality	39
Health	36
Total scale	55

a large number of raters are used, half the raters correlate with the other half high enough to be satisfactory. In other words, five raters will correlate with five other raters higher than will a pair of raters.

A factor that causes low reliability in merit rating is the difference in pattern of distribution of ratings. One rater will tend to rate everyone too high (the leniency error); another will tend to rate everyone near the average (the central-tendency error); and another will tend to rate everyone too low (the acrimony error). This can be corrected by "forced distribution" or requiring that a specified number of ratings be given to each degree of each trait. For example, raters may be instructed when using the rating form shown in Table 15–9 to place 15 per cent of all ratings under "superior," 35 per cent under "above average," 35 per cent under "ordinary," and 15 per cent under "unsatisfactory." In this way, the patterns of distribution of all ratings would be directly comparable.

Another error of rating distribution that causes low reliability is the "halo" error, or the tendency to rate a workman on all traits according to a justifiable rating on one trait. For example, if Jones is unquestionably superior in "knowledge of the job," there is a tendency to rate him superior on all other traits whether he deserves it or not. This error can be reduced by rating Jones on but one trait at a time. The transfer, or carry-over, from one trait to another is not so great if there is at least a day interval between rating on each trait. The longer the interval between trait ratings, the less the halo effect.

Three suggestions are implied in the above discussion for raising the reliability of merit rating.

1. Use as many qualified raters as possible.
2. Require a specified distribution of ratings in all degrees on all traits.
3. Rate but one trait at a time and allow at least a day interval before rating on another trait.

SUMMARY

Wages and salaries are usually determined by custom instead of by analytical and systematic procedures. The "prevailing wage" is often interpreted to be the fair wage. Systems have been developed for more carefully evaluating both jobs and workmen. The former is called "job evaluation" and the latter "merit rating."

Job evaluation is a careful analytical study and judgment of the value of jobs in comparison with other jobs. This latter step may be of "jobs as a whole" or of analyzed factors of jobs. It may be in terms of money or dollar value or it may be in terms of points which are later translated into dollar values. *Job ranking* and *job classification* are methods of evaluating jobs as a whole. They are simple to interpret and valuable if used carefully and critically. *Money value* or *factor comparison systems* rate jobs on isolated factors and in terms of dollars for each separate factor. Key or "bench mark" jobs are chosen as criteria for judging the worth of other jobs. *Ready-made point systems* are used more widely than all other systems combined. If the jobs to be evaluated are like those for which the system was devised, they may be evaluated accurately. Too often a ready-made system was devised for evaluating jobs in one industry and is not appropriate for use in any other. This situation justifies the development of a *custom-fit system* which is altered until it is appropriate. This also necessitates the use of key jobs which are both typical and fairly paid.

Whatever system of job evaluation is used, its validity should be checked by trying it out on jobs that are generally recognized as "fairly paid." If the evaluation system rates these jobs in accordance with their pay rates, it may then be said to be valid.

Merit rating is an analytical and systematic procedure of evaluating workmen. This may be done by rating the workman as a whole (overall value to the company) or on a number of traits separately. While the whole-man method is accurate and easily used, it is unsatisfactory when men want to know why they are rated high or low. Analytical merit rating is no more accurate and is more difficult to use, but it is more valuable in bringing about self-improvement and man development.

RECOMMENDED SUPPLEMENTARY READINGS

Benge, E. J., *et al.*: *Job Evaluation,* Harper & Brothers, New York, 1941.
Gray, J. S.: *Psychology in Industry,* Chaps. 6, 7, McGraw-Hill Book Company, Inc., New York, 1952.

Johnson, F. H., *et al.: Job Evaluation,* John Wiley & Sons, Inc., New York, 1946.

Lytle, C. W.: *Job Evaluation Methods,* The Ronald Press Company, New York, 1946.

Otis, J. L., and Leukart, R. H.: *Job Evaluation,* Prentice-Hall, Inc., New York, 1948.

Patton, J. A., and Smith, R. S.: *Job Evaluation,* Richard D. Irwin, Inc., Chicago, 1950.

Smyth, R. C., and Murphy, M. J.: *Job Evaluation and Employee Rating,* McGraw-Hill Book Company, Inc., New York, 1946.

Tiffen, J.: *Industrial Psychology,* Chap. 10, Prentice-Hall, Inc., New York, 1947.

Chapter 16

PSYCHOLOGY IN MARKETING
AND ADVERTISING[1]

One of the most interesting applications of psychology to the solution of practical everyday problems is concerned with the determination of the kinds of things which people will buy and with the best means by which to acquaint them with these things. These coordinate areas of study are intimate aspects of marketing and advertising.

In practice, marketing and advertising are studies requiring the efforts of specialists of many fields: economists, sociologists, artists, and journalists, as well as psychologists. Each specialist has his part to play, and quite often teams of specialists work together on the solution of interdisciplinary problems.

The main emphasis of this chapter will be on the applications of psychology to problems concerned with: the preferences of consumers for products having varied characteristics (*e.g.*, uses, color, size); the appeal of these products for consumers who differ in demographic aspects (*e.g.*, age, sex, geographic location); and influences which affect consumer preferences (*e.g.*, advertising and salesmanship).

[1] This chapter was written by Martha (Blosser) Noggle and revised by William R. Myles, Assistant Professor of Business Administration, Alabama Polytechnic Institute.

MARKETING AND ADVERTISING RESEARCH

Marketing research is composed of three main areas of investigation. These areas are product analysis, consumer research, and distribution research. Psychological principles can be applied to each of these areas in some degree. The areas or fields are closely interrelated. The answers to problems in one field, for example, consumer research, will have an important impact on problems in the other two fields—product analysis and distribution research. Moreover, the areas in marketing research are not discrete; they overlap and blend into each other.

Product Analysis

Product analysis deals with the product, its uses, and its performances, in order that it can be modified or described to fit the consumer's wishes. The product analyst is concerned with finding answers to the question, what types of products will people buy? His investigations lead him to inquire about the usefulness of products. Just what is the product used for; does it, or will it satisfy an existing want? Does the shape of the product appeal to the consumer; what about the package? Is the product made in a convenient size; should we build larger or smaller pianos? What about the weight of the product; should it be made heavier or lighter? Do people want polka-dotted automobiles; what colors will appeal to them most? Can last year's dress styles be used this year; are they still in style? There can be little doubt that if the analyst can come up with the answers to these questions the product will be satisfactory to the consumer.

Lack of psychological facts and statistics, such as would be revealed by the answers to the above questions, has been responsible for the failure of many a "would-have-been" manufacturer and for the failure of many costly advertising campaigns. Bradford reports an instance in which a new company failed because the board of directors refused to accept the findings of a marketing research agency.[2] A company that proposed producing a new product for waterproofing shoes asked the marketing analysts of an advertising agency to determine if the product was satisfactory, effectively named, packaged properly, priced properly, and if it was being put on the market at the correct time. The result of the agency's research indicated that the product and its price were acceptable but that the package detail looked like a worm crawling around the can. In addition, they advised the company of an impending business recession. The board of directors rejected these findings and continued with its original plan. The product did not sell,

[2] Bradford, Ernest S., *Marketing Research*, p. 14, McGraw-Hill Book Company, Inc., New York, 1951.

and a short time later a business recession forced the company out of business.

There is the case of the talcum powder magnate who spent thousands of dollars on literature glorifying purity, smoothness, and antiseptic qualities. *Then* he made an investigation. Ninety-five out of every hundred women bought his powder because they liked the *odor*. The other five bought because they liked the little can.

The appeal to a human want is basic to the design of a new product and to the discovery of new uses for an old product, as well as being the basis upon which rests the pulling power of advertisements. Generally, wants are divided into three classes: primary—those that are basic, unlearned, and individual; secondary—those that are learned but are universally learned; and tertiary—those that are individual and idiocentric. For example, a want for food is a primary want; a want for steak is a secondary want; a want for steak smothered in onions is a tertiary want.

A summary of an investigation of a nationally distributed product—raisins—will show some of the values of analyzing the product.[3] Sample questions were:

Do you buy raisins in bulk or package?
In what ways do you use raisins?
What do you like most about raisins?
With what brands of raisins are you familiar?

Seven hundred Boston housewives took part in the survey. (For a national survey, investigations should be carried on in 6 to 10 typical sections of the country. An adequate and reliable sampling has been obtained only when the results are not changed by adding more cases.) Answers to the questionnaires were tabulated and commented on. Some of the conclusions of this survey were:

Raisins are bought almost entirely in package form.
Brand names are well established. (Nearly 60 per cent of sales were Sun-Maid.)
The average family uses 20 to 25 lb. a year.
There is considerable seasonal difference in sales.
Raisins are most frequently used for puddings, cakes, pies.
Thirty-five per cent of the housewives used more raisins than they did the year before.
Strongest appeals were:
  "Taste good"
  "Make delicious dishes"
  "High food value"
  "Good for health"

[3] Starch, D., *Principles of Advertising*, Chap. 8, McGraw-Hill Book Company, Inc., New York, 1923.

Weakest appeals, in order, were:
"Contain iron"
"Easily digested"
"Relieve fatigue"
"A beauty food"

The value of such facts to the raisin industry is obvious.

Quite often it is possible to gain a clearer understanding of the product by asking people about what they do not want or like rather than about what they do want or like. A study of the dislikes of businessmen regarding American hotels, carried out by the Market Research Corporation of America, is shown in Table 16-1.[4]

Table 16-1. What Businessmen Dislike

	Per Cent
Unreasonable rates	27
Poor furnishings	19
Indifference and "too impersonal" service	17
Food	11
Room size	11
"Too independent"	9
Lack of conveniences	9
Lack of cleanliness	9
"Unfavorable in every respect"	9
Assigning poor rooms when good rooms are available	7
Discourtesy	7
Poor lighting	6
Noise	6
Old	6
Lack of radio	4
Laundry price	4
Elevator service	3
Lost laundry or clothes	3
Unsatisfactory adjustment of stolen property	2
Poor convention rooms	2
Special charge for conference rooms	1
Loaded telephone charges	1
Poor blackboard in conference room	1

The relative strength of appeals to various wants has been studied frequently. In one study, made by the Gallup Research Bureau, 29,000 representative readers of 46 issues of 20 different Sunday newspapers living in 16 cities were interviewed. The results of this study indicate the effectiveness of basic advertising themes; they are presented in Table 16-2.[5] The way in which the appeal to a want is applied to an

[4] Market Research Corporation of America, What Do Sales Executives Like and Dislike about American Hotels? *Sales Management,* Oct. 1, 1936.

[5] Reported by H. W. Hepner, *Effective Advertising,* pp. 215-216, McGraw-Hill Book Company, Inc., 1949.

Table 16-2. Reaction of Sunday Newspaper Readers to Basic Advertising Themes

Copy appeal	Readers per inch	
	Men	Women
News features	0.653	1.007
Sex allure	0.377	1.027
Social advancement	0.476	0.837
Narrative technique (both strip and straight copy)	0.318	0.695
Characters from the product's radio program	0.388	0.541
Reason-why copy	0.316	0.563
Contests	0.162	0.414
Testimonials	0.200	0.356
Scare appeals	0.139	0.407
Smartness and newness	0.271	0.251
Health appeal	0.218	0.272
Product's reaction under test	0.276	0.263
Price reductions and values	0.262	0.167
Premiums	0.167	0.256
Service given with product	0.083	0.321
The product alone	0.232	0.073

Table 16-3. Rank of Basic Appeals

Appeal	Rank by advertisements	Rank by men	Rank by women
Economy	1	8	9
Efficiency	2	9	9
Emulation	3	4	4
Novelty	4	4	8
Quality	5	1	3
Fear	6	3	6
Health	7	10	4
Ambition	8	7	7
Sex	9	2	1
Vanity	9	6	2

advertisement is illustrated by Allen[6] in Table 16-3. The results of a survey by Gallup of the relative strength of basic appeals, determined by number of advertisements and by vote of readers, is shown in Table 16-4.[7] This study was based on the attention value of full-page black-and-white ads in four leading weekly magazines.

The effectiveness of appeals is influenced by external conditions and

[6] Allen, C. N., A Psychology of Motivation for Advertisers, *J. Appl. Psychol.*, 1941, **25**, 378.

[7] Hotchkiss, G. B., *An Outline of Advertising*, p. 232, The Macmillan Company, New York, 1950.

by the product being advertised. In prosperous times, appeals to comfort and luxury rank higher than appeals to economy; in depression the ranks are reversed. The age of the reader is a factor also. Appeals to the welfare of loved ones, or to sex, increase as children grow older. Occupation and social position of the reader also influence the effectiveness of appeals. Although the motives of the individual differ, there are common characteristics. The best advertising aims at the most com-

Table 16–4. Examples of appeals used in Advertising Headlines and Slogans

Primary Wants	Appeals to Primary Wants
Appetizing food	"Meat on the Table"
Thirst-quenching drinks	"The Pause that Refreshes"
Comfortable surroundings	"See the kitchen 'Good Housekeeping' likes"
Escape from pain and danger	"Feel that Knot of Pain fade away"
Sex companionship	"Cigars Needn't Interfere with Kisses"
Welfare of loved ones	"My Daddy's Smart" (Frequently used in insurance advertisements)
Social approval	"Now that's what I call good coffee"
Superiority over others	"How to win friends and influence people"
Mastery over obstacles	"Are you flying blind?" (I.C.S.)
Play	"Play Winter Sports in Winter Sportswear"
Secondary Wants	Appeals to Secondary Wants
Universality	"Around the corner from everywhere"
Health	"Join the 'Regulars' with Kellogg's All Bran"
Efficiency	"More Free Time for Mothers"
Convenience	"No Need to Shift or Use the Clutch"
Dependability, quality	"Strong as the Rock of Gibraltar"
Economy, profit	"Clipping this coupon saved him $17.92"
Style, beauty	"Make your figure lovelier the easy way"
Cleanliness	"Banish 'Tattle-tale Grey'"
Curiosity	"What can a Man Believe In?"
Information, education	"What do you know about sheets?"

mon characteristics. The product is a chief consideration in determining the appeal. For instance, the health appeal is near the top of the lists in persuasiveness, yet beauty is a more effective appeal in the sale of mouth washes. For years Listerine used an appeal to health with only moderate success. By switching to the desire for social approval, with the halitosis campaign, sales increased rapidly. Formerly, bank advertising emphasized saving for security in old age; now such advertising stresses saving as a means to future pleasures, such as travel. Until recently shoe manufacturers stressed style and price in their advertisements. Then Bostonian Shoes found that most men are far more interested in comfort. Shoe advertising changed emphasis from style to feel. Here the two appeals are theoretically approximately equal in strength—yet the appeal to comfort is more effective than style in shoe advertising. The most powerful appeal for shaving cream was found to be "cool and refreshing." For study lamps, the strongest appeal is "reduction of eyestrain," while "low price" was fifth, "beauty of design" sixth, and "quality of construction" seventh.[8] These data suggested that among the most powerful advertising appeals are sex, social advancement, vanity, ambition, quality, love of family, and health. In short, the appeal must suit the individual product.

The Union Trust Company of Detroit tested the color preference for booklets by having one booklet printed in 10 different colors. Booklets of each color were on display in the lobby of the bank for 14 days.

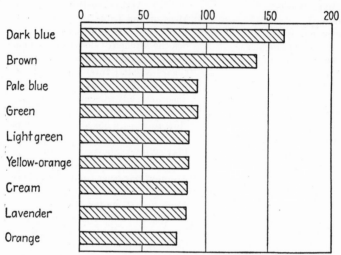

Fig. 16–1. Number of various colored booklets selected. (*From Hepner, H. W., Effective Advertising, p.* 464, *McGraw-Hill Book Company, Inc.,* 1949.)

The color of the booklet was the only variable. The number of booklets of each color taken is shown in Fig. 16–1.

Consumer Research

In a message to stockholders, Alfred P. Sloan, Jr., president of General Motors, emphasized the importance of consumer research as follows:

As a result of large-scale operations and world-wide distribution, producer and consumer have become more and more widely separated, so that the matter of keeping a business sensitively in tune with the requirements of the ultimate consumer becomes a matter of increasing importance.

Through Consumer Research, General Motors aims to bridge this gap.[9]

The size and complexity of modern business result in an ever increasing distance between manufacturer and consumer. Consumer research is

[8] Sandage, C. H., *Advertising, Theory and Practice,* pp. 295–297, Business Publications, Inc., Chicago, 1936.

[9] Brown, L. O., *Marketing Research and Distribution Research,* p. 20, The Ronald Press Company, New York, 1949.

the producers' method of keeping in touch with the wants and needs of the customers.[10]

Strong[11] suggests that the following topics be considered in a consumer analysis:

1. Who is the customer? the potential customer?
   a. Location
   b. Characteristics—income, social class, age, sex, occupation, education, nationality, religion
   c. Buying habits—frequency of purchase, amount purchased, when purchased, use of trade name in purchase, relation of price to consumption
2. Why do people buy
   a. Wants which product satisfies and uses of product
   b. How are the wants satisfied without the purchase of the product
   c. Factors preventing sales—products and services rendered by competitors, lack of income
3. Where are the most advantageous markets

Table 16–5. Variations in Buying Preferences

| City | Per cent of families buying the product | | | |
	Instant coffee	Graham crackers	Shaving cream	Prepared cake flour
1. Milwaukee..............	19.7	87.6	33.5	67.6
2. Omaha.................	12.2	66.0	29.7	62.9
3. Philadelphia............	42.4	38.1	52.3	46.5
4. Indianapolis............	26.7	*	33.1	52.2
5. St. Paul...............	9.6	76.0	37.0	73.7
6. Columbus, Ohio.........	35.4	61.1	46.0	51.0
7. Fresno, Calif...........	19.2	57.7	39.2	63.6
8. Seattle................	17.7	60.9	39.7	71.7
9. Birmingham............	13.6	*	43.4	30.1

* Not given.

A market consists of people with money to spend and a willingness to spend it. It is a trading area which may be nationwide, regional, or local. Table 16–5 gives some indication of the variation in buying preferences which is to be found in nine cities in the United States.[12]

[10] "Consumer research will uncover fundamental human desires. Product analysis will provide a basis for shaping the product to harmonize with existing human desires. Market analysis will locate and measure the ability of consumers to buy the product." Sandage, *op. cit.*, p. 126.

[11] Strong, E. K., Jr., *Psychological Aspects of Business*, pp. 177–178, McGraw-Hill Book Company, Inc., New York, 1938.

[12] Kleppner, Otto, *Advertising Procedure*, 4th ed., p. 534, Prentice-Hall, Inc., New York, 1950.

The market for particular products depends to a large extent on the money which people have to spend. Table 16–6 shows the distribution of income to individuals in the United States according to how they earned their income.[13] A geographic distribution of income of wage earners is shown in Table 16–7.[14] The importance of changing trends in consumption patterns should not be neglected in consumer research.

Table 16–6. Distribution of Income in the United States for 1950

	Billions of Dollars
Total national income	$236.2
Wage earners	152.2
Business and professional	23.2
Farmers	13.0
Rental income	7.4
Corporations	35.5
Interest on securities	5.0

Victor Lebow, reporting a study made by the Bureau of Labor Statistics, writes that at the depth of the depression (1932) 38 per cent more pairs of silk stockings were bought by women than in the prosperous year of 1928. In addition, at each lower income level the proportion spent for silk stockings increased.[15]

Table 16–7. Gross Earnings of Production Workers for Selected States

State	Average weekly earnings, November, 1951	Average weekly earnings, December, 1951
Alabama	$49.72	$50.50
California	72.84	74.49
Connecticut	68.80	69.88
Georgia	46.26	48.48
New York	66.08	67.20
North Carolina	45.96	47.25
Oklahoma	63.94	65.56
Pennsylvania	64.49	65.66
Rhode Island	55.62	59.31
South Carolina	46.14	47.56
Vermont	55.95	58.91
Wisconsin	69.74	72.67
Wyoming	70.94	71.45

A study by Marketing Publications, Inc., shows the importance of differences in sex for various products.[16] A carefully selected sample of

[13] Economic Report of the President Transmitted to the Congress, by the Council of Economic Advisers, January, 1951.

[14] Monthly Labor Review, March, 1952, 74, No. 3, 361–366.

[15] Lebow, Victor, New Outlooks for Marketing, J. Business, University of Chicago, July, 1949, 22, No. 3, 160.

[16] Marketing Publications, Inc., Tell Magazine, November, 1948.

2,000 families were asked questions regarding the selection of products. It was found that men were relatively unimportant in the purchase of aspirin, laxatives, and vacuum cleaners but that more men than women purchase women's watches. The influence of women was almost as great as the influence of men in the buying of men's ties and sport shirts (see Fig. 16–2).

Kleppner reports a study by *Modern Magazines* which shows the peak ages at which women buy 51 different toilet articles.[17] Combs, tooth paste, and sunburn remedy are bought most often by teen-agers between the ages of fifteen and nineteen; cake rouge, shampoo, and deodorant by women between twenty and twenty-four; eyewash and bath soap by women between thirty and thirty-four; bath salts, hand

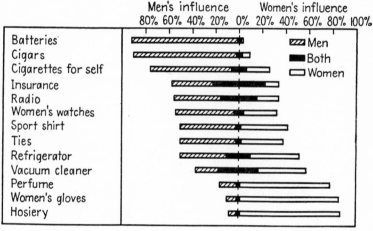

Fig. 16–2. Influence of men and women and combined influence in selecting various products.

cream, and vanishing cream most often by women between fifty and fifty-four.

The surveys reviewed above were general and resulted in many facts about the products being investigated. Consumer surveys are also used to determine the answer to one specific question about one product.[18] This type of survey, summarized in Table 16–8, was used to set the selling price of a brand of soap.[19]

Obviously, consumer research contributes to business success by keeping business in touch with customers, developing new sources of profits by discovering new products and new markets, and avoiding

[17] Kleppner, *op. cit.,* p. 533.
[18] Marketing research is the study of markets in a broad general way. Market analysis, on the other hand, is a study of markets and marketing methods for a specific product.
[19] *Drug Trade News,* May, 1932, p. 31.

Table 16–8. Market Analysis Used to Set the Selling Price of Soap

Selling price per cake	Number of cakes sold	Total sales made	Cost of goods	Gross profit	Variable expense	Fixed expense	Net
$0.10	600	$60.00	$40.00	$20.00	$3.60	$10.00	$ 6.40
0.09	800	72.00	48.00	24.00	4.32	10.00	9.68
0.08	1,200	96.00	66.00	30.00	5.76	10.00	14.24
0.07	1,300	91.00	71.50	19.50	5.46	10.00	4.04

unanticipated changes that may make a product obsolete. Market analysis is used to determine who buys the product, why they buy, who uses the product, shopping habits, brand preference, how much can be sold, and type of product that should be produced, and to determine future trends and conditions by studying past conditions.

METHODS USED IN MARKETING AND ADVERTISING RESEARCH

Laboratory Methods. Many advertising problems can be investigated in the laboratory under controlled conditions. The tachistoscope, for example, has been used by Hotchkiss to determine how much of a full-page advertisement can be grasped when the advertisement is exposed for only 1 second.[20] A psychogalvanometer was used by Eckstrand and Gilliland to test the effects of advertisements. They found the rank order correlation between this method and the controlled-recognition method to be .51.[21] The "program analyzer," developed by Lazarsfeld and Stanton, is used to keep a continuous record of the likes and dislikes of a radio audience. It is essentially a modified polygraph having 11 sets of pens. Of each set, one pen is connected to a red button and one pen is connected to a green button. The experimenter plays a transcription of a program and the subject pushes the red button to indicate the portions of the program which he dislikes, and the green button to indicate the portions of the program which he likes. After playing the recording, the subject's responses are further investigated by asking questions to determine specifically why he liked or disliked portions of the program.[22]

Motion pictures of the eye have been used by Karslake and Tiffin to determine which parts of an advertisement attract attention.[23]

An instrument, developed at the Massachusetts Institute of Technology, called the "audimeter" was used by Stanton to determine the

[20] Hotchkiss, *op. cit.*, p. 23.

[21] Eckstrand, G., and Gilliland, A. R., The Psychogalvanometric Method for Measuring the Effectiveness of Advertising, *J. Appl. Psychol.*, 1948, **32**, 415–425.

[22] Peterman, J. N., The Program Analyzer; A New Technique in Studying Liked and Disliked Items in Radio Programs, *J. Appl. Psychol.*, 1940, **24**, 728–741.

[23] Karslake, J. S., The Purdue Eye Camera: A Practical Apparatus for Studying the Attention Value of Advertisements, *J. Appl. Psychol.*, 1940, **24**, 417–440.

times at which radios are tuned in.[24] The audimeter is a device attached to the receiver in the homes of a selected audience. A record of the time the family turns the radio on and off is made on a tape which the cooperating family mails to the experimenter. The instrument ejects a 25-cent reward when the tape is removed at the proper time.

General Methods. Many marketing and advertising problems do not lend themselves to carefully controlled laboratory tests, nor are they susceptible to repeatable tests. It is then necessary to rely on methods which effectively can make use of subjective judgments and which give a "reasonable" degree of reliability to the answers obtained. These methods include:

1. *Sales Tests.* Several advertisements or samples from proposed advertising campaigns are used in a limited area and measured in terms of effect on sales. The study by Stanton, reported later, is an example of the sales-test method. This method if properly carried out probably gives as good results as any other one method of testing. The catch is, of course, in properly controlling all the variables. Some of these almost impossible to control variables include: competition of other brands, selection of comparable areas, abilities of salesmen, reader interest, buying power of consumers, dealer cooperation, and the length of time for the advertisement to take effect. The results achieved by the sales-test method can usually be secured by one of several simpler and less costly methods.

2. *Coupon or Inquiry Test.* Effectiveness of the advertisement is measured by the number of inquiries received. Hattwick reports the results of an inquiry test made by the *Chicago Tribune* in 1945.[25] Above a picture showing Christmas cookies, the reader was asked to send for recipes. Requests for the recipes came in as follows:

Date	Replies
Dec. 1	1,521
Dec. 3	2,178
Dec. 4	1,427
Dec. 5	749
Dec. 6	338
Dec. 7	343
Dec. 8	392
Dec. 10	396
Dec. 11	283
Dec. 12	244
Dec. 13	513
Dec. 14	246
Total	8,630

[24] Stanton, F. N., Checking the Checkers, *Advertising and Selling*, Dec. 19, 1935, 25, 42.

[25] Hattwick, M. S., *How to Use Psychology for Better Advertising*, p. 290, Prentice-Hall, Inc., New York, 1950.

This, according to the *Tribune,* illustrated the pulling power of the paper.

3. *Consumer-attitude Surveys.* Such surveys are based on questionnaires which are designed to determine what people want or like. The study of the likes and dislikes of men and women, in Table 16–11, is an example of a consumer survey. One of the most popular methods of making consumer surveys is the consumer panel or jury. A group whose members are carefully selected to include representative samplings of the population are asked questions ranging from judgments on a piece of copy to habits of use of products.

4. *Unaided-recall Test.* This test measures whether or not the advertisement is remembered. One example of this technique is that of the "triple-associates" question developed by Henry C. Link. Questions are phrased to bring out an unaided response by associates. The researcher might ask, "What cigarette is advertised by 'It's Toasted'?" The associates are then: cigarette company, "Its Toasted," and the correct answer, "Lucky Strike." Hepner reports that one company's advertising may be so ineffective that only 1 or 2 per cent of the people know the theme or slogan. Advertising of other companies may be so effective that 70 per cent can answer with the third associate.[26]

5. *Recognition Test.* Many varieties of the recognition method have been used. In one study two groups of women were interviewed, one group who had not read a particular issue of the *Ladies' Home Journal,* and a second group who had read it. A record was made of those women who said that they had seen or recognized the advertisements. The results of the study are presented in Table 16–9.[27]

Table 16–9. Percentage of Women Recognizing Various Advertisements

Advertisement for	Group A had read magazine, %	Group B had not read magazine, %
Ipana	57	36
Jell-O	57	29
Woodbury	45	32
Squibb	38	32
Swift	66	38
Wheaties	59	48
Shredded Wheat	52	36
Rinso	67	53
Hot Point	31	6
Sealtest	33	5

[26] Hepner, *op. cit.,* p. 182.
[27] Advertising Research Foundation, *Copy Testing,* pp. 45–50, New York, 1939.

ADVERTISING

Advertising in the United States has developed into an annual 5 billion dollar business. Expenditures of advertisers on various media in 1949 were distributed as shown in Table 16–10.[28]

Newspaper	$1,905,000,000
Outdoor	131,000,000
Radio	633,800,000
Television	63,000,000

Table 16–10. Expenditures of Some of the 100 Leading Advertisers on Advertising Media in 1950*

(In thousands of dollars)

Advertiser	Total	General magazines	Network radio	Network TV
Procter & Gamble Co	$27,023	$ 4,574	$18,357	$ 570
General Foods Corp	18,418	6,619	7,506	1,128
General Motors Corp	16,878	11,700	660	1,063
American Tobacco Co	9,678	3,883	4,091	951
Westinghouse Electric Corp	3,020	1,863	152	673
Nash-Kelvinator	2,653	1,938	....	563
U.S. Steel Corp	2,412	860	1,437	

* Adapted from Publishers Information Bureau compiled by Leading National Advertisers, Inc.

That it costs to advertise is indicated by the preceding data; but that advertising results in increased profits for business, and increased savings for the consumer is not so well understood. The following chart (Fig. 16–3), which demonstrates the relationship between the price and sales for electric refrigerators, should dispel any doubts of the savings which follow effective advertising.[29] In 1922 the cost of electric refrigerators was over $500 and fewer than 100 were sold; by 1936 the price had dropped to $164 and over 2,200 were sold.

A school principal, intelligent and well educated, was once heard to say that he didn't allow nationally advertised products to be used in his home. By avoiding advertised brands, and therefore any advertising costs, this man believed he was buying better quality for less money. In theory, at least, advertising, by increasing consumption, lowers production costs. "The ordinary, logical sequence is: The more a product is efficiently and truthfully advertised, the more it is consumed; the

[28] Zeisel, H., U.S. Advertising Volume Passes 5 Billion, Hits New High, *Printers' Ink*, June 16, 1950, **231**, 28–30.
[29] Adapted from data reported by Hepner, *op. cit.*, p. 21, from J. De Jen, who utilized data from *Electrical Merchandising*.

greater the quantity consumed, the greater the quantity produced; the greater the quantity produced, the lower the cost of production per unit."[30] For example, a certain clothing manufacturer was doing a business of $3,500,000 yearly, with a selling expense equal to 8 per cent of total sales. He began a national advertising program, and in a few years his sales were $14,000,000 annually, with a selling cost, including advertising, of 5 per cent. By spending $10,000 for advertising, a retail shoe store increased annual sales from $100,000 to $168,000.

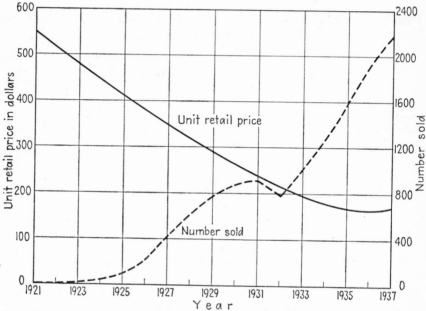

Fig. 16–3. Sales and price of electric refrigerators 1921 to 1937. (*From Hepner, H. W., Effective Advertising, McGraw-Hill Book Company, Inc.,* 1949.)

They reduced the price of shoes 25 cents a pair, and at the same time made a slightly larger profit on each pair of shoes sold. Money spent for advertising benefits both producer and consumer.

FACTORS OF THE ADVERTISEMENT

The individual parts of the advertisement—illustrations, copy, type, color, headlines, position, size, etc.—have been carefully studied and evaluated.

Color. In a Sears, Roebuck and Company catalogue there were two pages of skirt ads, one in color, the other in black and white. The style,

[30] Rowse, E. C., and Fish, L. J., *Fundamentals of Advertising,* p. 26, South-Western Publishing Company, Inc., New York, 1937.

quality, and price were identical. The colored page drew ten times more returns than the black-and-white.[31] Face powder in a blue box sells more quickly than that in a green; tan cars are more popular in the West, black in the East; green is the most popular color for fountain pens; "white eggs in a blue box sell 30 per cent faster" than in a box of any other color; sales for Woodbury soap increased when the wrapper was changed from green and ivory to blue.[32] Color is assumed to be even more important in advertisements of products such as wallpaper and paint, linoleum, tile, bath towels—products in which color is an intrinsic part of the goods.

A two-color ad costs about 17 per cent more than a black-and-white ad of the same size, and a four-color ad costs about 44 per cent more than a black-and-white ad. Rudolph, in a study of 2,500 advertisements which appeared in *The Saturday Evening Post,* shows that advertisements in two colors have only 0.9 per cent more attention value than black-and-white advertisements.[33] The attention value of a four-color advertisement is approximately 54 per cent greater than either the black-and-white or two-color ad. After considering the added cost of the four-color, Rudolph concludes that its net attention value is approximately equal to 7 per cent.

Color preferences are influenced by culture and by age. The Chinese like red, but blue is lacking in favor; Africans like blue (to them, a symbol of peace) and dislike red, which they believe symbolizes war. A young child prefers red, blue, white, green, and brown, in that order. The most popular color with London school children is blue followed by red, yellow, and green. Vassar college students prefer blue, red, green, yellow, and orange. A comparison of the color likes and dislikes of men and women is shown in Table 16–11.[34]

Color is used chiefly because of its attention value. It also aids in the recognition of trade-mark or package, gives a better picture of the style and texture of the product, and conveys an attitude or emotion.[35]

Size. Does a large advertisement receive more attention than a small one? Is the attention value in direct proportion to the size? Are several small ads more effective than one large ad? The most comprehensive study of the problem of size was made by Starch, using the inquiries

[31] Starch, *op. cit.,* p. 583.

[32] Color for Sales, *Modern Packaging,* April, 1938.

[33] Rudolph, Harold J., How Are Size, Color, Bleed Related to Attention and Readership? *Printers' Ink,* Nov. 14, 1947, p. 44. See also *Attention and Interest Factors in Advertising,* Funk & Wagnalls Company, in cooperation with *Printers' Ink,* 1947.

[34] Hollingworth, H. L., *Advertising and Selling,* p. 101, Appleton-Century-Crofts, Inc., New York, 1925.

[35] Some meanings of colors are given in Color for Sales, *Modern Packaging,* April, 1938, p. 30.

Table 16–11. Color Preferences of Men and Women

Color	Per cent of men who like it	Per cent of men who dislike it	Per cent of women who like it	Per cent of women who dislike it
Red.........	22	7	42	8
Orange......	5	25	8	31
Yellow.......	2	32	5	8
Green.......	7	15	9	21
Blue.........	42	12	9	23
Violet.......	19	8	19	9
White.......	3	1	8	0

received by 98 companies from 2,339 magazine advertisements.[36] Table 16–12 summarizes his results. From this evidence Starch concluded that "advertisements brought replies very nearly in proportion to their size, although the smaller sizes had a slight advantage." A recent study by Rudolph tends to substantiate this study by Starch. Rudolph found the half-sized ad to be about 60 per cent as effective in attention values as the full-sized ad.[37]

In a study of the relationship of attention value and size of advertisements in *The New York Times,* Franken found the results shown in

Table 16–12. Relation of Size of Advertisement to Inquiries Received

Size of space	Size ratio	Number of replies per 100,000
Full page..............	100	225.3
Half page.............	50	120.4
Quarter page..........	25	71.8
Sixth page............	17	38.9

Table 16–13.[38] The square-root theory, first suggested by Hollingworth, is used to determine the theoretical ratio. Hollingworth explained it: "The number of inquiries tends to increase as the square root of the amount of space used. That is to say, use four times the space and you double the returns; use nine times the space and you treble the returns." For example, if a quarter-page ad received 100 replies, a full-page ad would receive 200 replies; if inquiries were in direct proportion to the size of the ad, and a quarter-page ad drew 100 replies, a

[36] Starch, D., An Analysis of Over 3,000,000 Inquiries Received by 98 Firms from 2,339 Magazine Advertisements, quoted by Hepner, *op. cit.,* p. 471.

[37] Rudolph, *op. cit.,* p. 44.

[38] Franken, R. B., as quoted by Hotchkiss, *op. cit.,* p. 214.

full-page advertisement would receive 400 replies. The larger ad draws more attention than the smaller, but the attention is not in direct proportion to the size of the ad.

Table 16–13. Relation of Size of Advertisement to Attention Value

Average size in column, in.	Number of advertisements	Size ratios	Experimental attention ratios	Theoretical attention ratios
3.4	22	1.00	1.00	1.00
7.6	17	2.24	1.48	1.49
14.4	17	4.25	1.83	2.06
22.7	13	6.70	2.10	2.58

Cuts and Illustrations. The chief purposes of illustrations have been listed as follows:[39]

1. To attract attention
2. To beautify the advertisement
3. To direct attention toward the product
4. To suggest a story
5. To enforce and supplement the text
6. To show the appearance of the product
7. To show the use of the article
8. To appeal to the instincts or emotions
9. To dramatize the use of the product

The type of picture used is regulated by its purpose in the advertisement. The results of a survey show that advertisements without pictures averaged 83 per cent less attraction for women, and 44 per cent less for men, than did those advertisements with pictures.[40] When a soap manufacturer ran a picture of a baby in six women's magazines and offered the picture, "suitable for framing," upon request, there were 235,000 replies.[41] A famous example of the effectiveness of a cut is shown by an independent corporation full-page ad of several years ago. When the advertisement, for a memory course, was set in 8-point type, the sales cost was $1.50 to $2.25. By adding a small cut and using 6-point type, the sales cost was reduced to $1.00.[42] The rotogravure section of the Sunday newspaper, made up almost entirely of pictures,

[39] Rowse and Fish, *op. cit.*, pp. 156*ff*.
[40] Blumberg, R., and Rheinstrom, C., How Advertising Techniques Are Rated by Gallup Survey, *Printers' Ink*, Mar. 24, 1932, pp. 117*ff*.
[41] Burtt, H. E., *Psychology of Advertising*, p. 270, Houghton Mifflin Company, Boston, 1938.
[42] Rheinstram, C., Keyed Copy, *Advertising and Selling*, Mar. 7, 1928.

is read by 90 per cent of the people getting the paper—a figure unequaled by any other section of the paper.[43]

Pictures of people draw more attention than pictures of objects. In one study, with outdoor poster boards as the medium, 67 pictures of people were recalled, compared with 39 pictures of objects; 48 pictures of people were recognized, compared with 37 pictures of objects.[44] Readers of Sunday rotogravures prefer pictures of children, then, in order, photographs of groups of adults, sports scenes, animals, and natural scenery.[45] Pictures irrelevant to the product being advertised draw more attention, but relevant pictures increase the memory value for the article or trade name being advertised. For example, a soap manufacturer used three different pictures in an advertising campaign—the first, completely irrelevant; the second, partially irrelevant; the third, relevant. The cost of the ad for every 1,000 women who saw it and knew the brand of soap advertised was[46]

For the irrelevant ad	$34.85
For the partially irrelevant	26.60
For the relevant	7.10

In another study of the relation of attention value to the subject of illustrations Rudolph found that illustrations of the result of not using the product were most effective and that illustrations of the results of using the product were least effective. Following in order from most to least effective were the testimonial, product in use, irrelevant, and pictures of the product.[47]

Headlines. The headline, called the "most important part of an advertisement,"[48] is an introduction to the rest of the advertisement. "The best headlines are those that appeal to the reader's self-interest—headlines that offer the reader something he wants." Examples are

Another $50 Raise
Quit Work at 55

The next best type of headline gives news, such as

New features of the Ford truck
New Frigidaire gives you Hydrator

[43] Hepner, *op. cit.*, p. 506.
[44] Burtt, *op. cit.*, p. 271.
[45] Survey of Gallup Research Bureau, reported in Hepner, *op. cit.*, p. 508.
[46] Hepner, *op. cit.*, p. 513.
[47] Rudolph, H. J., How the Subject of the Illustration Is Related to Attention Value, *Printers' Ink*, Dec. 5, 1947, p. 44.
[48] Caples, J., *Tested Advertising Methods*, p. 13, Harper & Brothers, New York, 1947.

Another type of headline arouses curiosity.

> Lost: $35,000
> Are you playing fair with your wife

Types of headlines, classed according to function by Glim,[49] include

1. Label headlines—state the name of the article or summarize the copy.

Examples:

> TEA to Tempt an Empress
> Hay Fever

2. Message headlines—give information, often the article's main selling point.

Examples:

> Cash for Old Coins
> Give Your Face That "Air-Conditioned" Feeling

3. Provocative headlines—novel, stimulate the reader without revealing the copy.

Examples:

> How high is an 8-foot fence?
> It'll Lead You Astray—and You'll Like It

Table 16–14. Relation of Title to Yearly Sales of the "Little Blue Books"

Old title	Sales	New title	Sales
1. Ten O'Clock	2,000	1. What Art Should Mean to You	9,000
2. Pen, Pencil, and Poison	5,000	2. The Story of a Notorious Criminal	15,800
3. Fleece of Gold	6,000	3. Quest for a Blond Mistress	50,000
4. The Mystery of the Iron Mask	11,000	4. The Mystery of the Man in the Iron Mask	30,000
5. "Patent Medicine" and the Public Health	3,000	5. The Truth about "Patent Medicine"	10,000
6. Addison and His Times		6. London Life in Addison's Time	7,000
7. Art of Controversy		7. How to Argue Logically	30,000
8. Life of Tolstoy	2,500	8. Life of Tolstoy: Russian Novelist	6,500
9. Essay on Shelley	2,000	9. Shelley: Idealistic Dreamer	8,000
10. Casanova and His Loves	8,000	10. Casanova: History's Greatest Lover	22,000
11. Poems of Evolution	2,000	11. When You Were a Tadpole and I Was a Fish	7,000
12. Apothegms	2,000	12. Terse Truths about the Riddle of Life	9,000

[49] Glim, A., 3 Types of Headline Exist, *Printers' Ink,* Apr. 9, 1931, p. 12.

4. Others—headlines which do not fall into the three preceding classifications, such as the question headline (Wouldn't You Spend a Dollar on a Good Book?) or the selective headlines (To All Housewives).

The drawing power of book titles, similar in form to headlines, is shown by an analysis of the sales of "The Little Blue Books." These books sold for a nickel each and were advertised in leading magazines by title only, with no other description. Results of the change of title upon sales are shown in Table 16–14, compiled by E. Haldeman-Julius, the publisher.[50] Mr. Haldeman-Julius found the strongest appeals for his books were (1) sex, (2) self-education and improvement, (3) free thought or skepticism, and (4) entertainment or fun.

The length of the headline has been the subject of a number of psychological investigations. Generally, the longer the headline the less chance it has of being remembered. In one study by Lucas, an inverse correlation of —.80 was found between recall scores and the number of words in the headline.[51] Rudolph found the following relationships between the length of the headline and the percentage of observers who stopped to read the headline.[52]

Length of Headline	Per Cent of Those Stopped Who Read the Headline
1–3 words	87.3
4–6 words	86.3
7–9 words	84.0
10–11 words	82.5
Over 12 words	77.9

ADVERTISING MEDIA

Newspapers. "The newspaper is read universally" by all classes and groups. It is especially effective when the advertising is directed to one locality. Newspaper advertisements are timely—the copy can be changed daily; the sales are immediate. The newspaper is an excellent medium for testing an advertisement. Financially, advertising is the most important part of the newspaper. A paper selling for 5 cents on the street costs the publisher from 15 to 25 cents. Advertising makes up the difference.

An analysis of the influence of the position (in terms of special pages, e.g., sports page) of the advertisement on its observation is reported by Hepner.[53] Part of this study is shown in Table 16–15. From these and other data Hepner concludes that the preferred positions for advertis-

[50] Haldeman-Julius, E., *The First Hundred Million,* Simon & Schuster, Inc., New York, 1928.

[51] Lucas, D. B., The Optimum Length of Advertising Headline, *J. Appl. Psychol.,* 1934, **18**, 665–674.

[52] Rudolph, H. J., *Printers' Ink,* Nov. 21, 1947, p. 46.

[53] Hepner, *op. cit.,* 334–335.

ing in a newspaper are (1) picture page; (2) page 1; (3) news pages 2 to 11; (4) other news pages, in that order for both men and women.

Table 16–15. Influence of Position by Type of Page upon Observation

Type of page	Average observations, per cent	
	Men	Women
Picture..............	71	73
Part 1..............	68	68
News pages 2–11......	49	49
Other news pages......	40	46
Sports..............	40	13
Amusement...........	22	39
Women's.............	10	44

Wiseman summarized newspaper advertising as follows:

The newspaper is a local medium, its editorial content is ephemeral (most of it is "dead" within an hour), reading time is limited to a few minutes, the readers of its advertisements are seeking news about merchandise and prices, and their interest must be engaged at first glance or be lost forever. Studies of newspaper readership reports show that, to get economical attention and reading, newspaper advertisements need not be pretty, or large, or tricky; and that aside from "shopping lists," those which get the highest amount of attention and reading are usually informal, open, even seemingly amateurish. They display price when possible. They contain news headlines. Their texts, while not necessarily short, are written in news style with the essential information in the first few words. . . . Their appeals are made to primary buying motives, money-saving, style, newness.[54]

Magazines. Magazines may be classed in two groups—general and business. There are approximately 600 general magazines, magazines of universal appeal, such as *The Saturday Evening Post, The Reader's Digest,* and *Time.* Also classified under general magazines are those specialized in regard to age, sex, and interests, such as *Vogue, Ladies' Home Journal, American Boy,* and *Popular Mechanics.* There are approximately 1,900 business publications, including industrial periodicals, trade or commercial periodicals, service and professional periodicals, catalogues, and data books.[55] The advertisements in business publications are technical and specific. Page rates run from $100 to $200. Other magazine advertising rates are shown in Table 16–16.[56]

[54] Wiseman, M., Why "National Advertising Copy"? *Advertising and Selling,* January, 1941, p. 21.
[55] Hepner, *op. cit.,* p. 342.
[56] *Ibid.,* p. 348.

Table 16–16. Cost of Magazine Space, July 15, 1947

Magazine	Thousands of circulation	Basic page rate	Rate per page per thousand
The Saturday Evening Post.	3,848	$10,500	$ 2.72
Collier's................	2,803	7,000	2.50
Life....................	5,144	15,225	2.96
Time...................	1,560	5,200	3.33
American...............	2,465	5,500	2.23
National Geographic......	1,455	4,200	2.89
Harper's Magazine.......	152	750	4.94
Vogue..................	261	2,300	8.82
Esquire................	607	3,200	5.27
Fortune Magazine........	215	2,750	12.80
Country Gentleman.......	2,163	6,500	3.00
The Poultryman..........	33	575	17.43
Christian Herald.........	340	930	2.74

Advantages of magazine advertising include:[57]

1. Magazines are more selective of a quality market.
2. Details of placement and circulation are known.
3. The advertisement has a longer life. (A copy of a popular magazine has been in the author's dentist's office for 4 years.)
4. Specific audience appeals may be selected and used in an appropriate magazine.
5. Provides good reproduction of all illustrations on good paper. Color is especially amenable to magazine advertising

Disadvantages of magazine advertising include:

1. Magazine advertisements are inflexible and must be contracted for and planned months before publication.
2. They are costly, averaging from $5,000 to $10,000 a page.
3. It is a disadvantage for the advertiser who does not need national coverage.

Radio and Television. Radio and television are the media most rapidly increasing in importance. Nine out of ten families in the United States own radios, and by 1952 more than 13,000,000 television sets had been sold. Table 16–10 shows the relative importance of radio and television compared with other media in terms of volume of advertising.

A count of 122,000 people in 10 cities showed that 27.8 per cent of them listened to the radio 6 hours or more a day; 59.7 per cent listened

[57] See Lucas, D. B., and Britt, S. H., *Advertising Psychology and Research,* pp. 670–672, McGraw-Hill Book Company, Inc., New York, 1951. Also Wiseman, *op. cit.*

4 or more hours; 91 per cent listened 2 or more hours a day; 99 per cent listened at least 1 hour a day.[58] From 8:00 to 9:00 P.M. is the most popular hour for listening to the radio—47.4 per cent of urban radios are in use then. The next most popular radio hours are 9:00 to 10:00 and 7:00 to 8:00 P.M. The most popular radio hour of the week is Sunday from 8:00 until 9:00 P.M. The percentage of radio time devoted to each type of program is shown in Table 16–17.[59] These results

Table 16–17. Percentage of Time Devoted to Various Types of Radio Programs

Program	Per Cent of Total Time
Musical:	
Popular	36
Light	8
Classical	8
Semiclassical	5
Novelty	3
Religious	1
Nonmusical:	
Script (dramatic, dialogue)	13
Announcements of program content	6
Commercial announcements	5
Educational	5
Special events	4
Functions	3
Political	1
Church programs	1
Humorous	1

are based on the programs of one week heard on stations affiliated with the Columbia Broadcasting System. Popular music and dramatic programs account for 49 per cent of radio time, commercials for 5 per cent.

Radio advertising is more direct and more personal than most types of advertising. Cantril and Allport[60] found that people remember directions, sentences, numbers, advertising trade-marks, facts, and abstract material better when they are heard over the radio than when they are read. On the other hand, radio is an expensive medium—a coast-to-coast broadcast costs from $10,000 to $15,000 an hour for time, in addition to costs of production and talent. Hepner concludes that radio is best adapted to advertising products of "frequent purchase and rapid consumption."

A carefully designed study of the effectiveness of a radio advertise-

[58] Goode, K., Advertising, p. 278, Greenburg: Publisher, Inc., New York, 1941.
[59] Burtt, op. cit., p. 395.
[60] Cantril, H., and Allport, G. W., The Psychology of Radio, Harper & Brothers, New York, 1935.

ment was made by Stanton.[61] Two markets were selected in which all the manufacturer's sales factors were exactly comparable except that the program was broadcast in Market A and not in Market B. Comparisons were made of total retail sales in the two markets, listeners vs. nonlisteners in Market A, regular listeners to determine if they were also regular buyers. Results showed that retail sales were 88 per cent greater in Market A over Market B; that the sale of the brand was 81 per cent greater than the next most popular brand among listeners, but only 7 per cent higher among nonlisteners; and that the sale of the brand was 263 per cent higher than the next most competing brand among regular listeners.

Some advantages of radio and television include:

1. Either local or national advertising can be done on a network basis or with spot programs.
2. The audience is made up of all income groups.
3. Makes possible personalized selling—forceful and dramatic effects may be employed.
4. The program may attract a loyal, continuous following.
5. They are flexible; last-minute changes may be made to take advantage of current events.

Some disadvantages of radio and television are:

1. The message is short-lived. (It only seems that repetitious slogans are never-ending.)
2. Part of the desired audience may be lost because of time changes across the nation.
3. There are a limited number of good listening and good looking spots available.
4. Production and talent costs may run total costs to extremely high amounts.

Other advertising media include direct mail, billboards, posters, electric signs, novelties, catalogues, displays, and exhibits.

SALESMANSHIP

Selling is that division of marketing which has to do with all the numerous activities whereby those individuals or firms possessing goods or capable of rendering services seek to influence others to trade with them. Personal selling is that in which the influence is exerted directly by salesmen or women. Salesmanship is a popular term used to designate the body of arts practiced by sellers in their attempt to influence others to buy.[62]

[61] Stanton, Frank, A Two Way Check on the Sales Influence of a Specific Radio Program, *J. Appl. Psychol.*, 1940, **24**, 665–672.

[62] Barnhard, quoted by H. K. Nixon, *Principles of Selling*, 2d ed., p. 67, McGraw-Hill Book Company, Inc., New York, 1942.

What the Salesman Does

The following job description which was prepared by the Kendall Mills division of the Kendall Company illustrates the duties involved in textile products sales:

1. Calls on customers and prospective users and distributors in the jobbing and retail trades on diapers and nursery products, cotton, mosquito netting, cheese cloth and milk filters, or on industrial consumers who are public health or surgical dressing manufacturers, pharmaceutical concerns, research laboratories, miscellaneous industrial users and manufacturers of clothing, many of whom are working on government contracts for shirts, blouses, uniforms, caps, coats, and shorts.
2. Takes orders for above textile products the servicing of which requires knowledge of grey cloth constructions, finishes, dye processes and put-ups for various uses over and above trade knowledge based on familiarity with the products.
3. Helps plan schedule of shipments of material under an allocation program; helps advise on, put in contract with, or develop product or put-up to fit government contract or bid requirements.
4. Gives information on matters affecting government; shows samples and points out merchandising or manufacturing features for the customer's benefit.
5. Handles complaints in the customer's plants.
6. Makes daily reports of business transactions, keeps expense accounts, studies trade periodicals and keeps his customers informed of price changes, cotton and cloth market conditions.
7. Attends training courses at plant and other conferences to exchange distribution information.
8. Operates within a defined territory under branch office supervision keeping regular contact with customers and prospective users.[63]

Aspley reports a study which was made by the Bureau of Business Research at Ohio State University in 1947 for the members of the National Wholesale Druggists Association, showing the amount of time salesmen spend in various activities. It was found that in the country the average salesman worked $10\frac{1}{3}$ hours a day, of which $6\frac{5}{6}$ hours were spent inside the store, $3\frac{1}{2}$ hours outside the store, and $2\frac{1}{3}$ hours in travel. The country salesman averaged $8\frac{3}{10}$ calls of $52\frac{7}{10}$ minutes each. City salesmen worked only $8\frac{1}{4}$ hours a day, of which $5\frac{1}{4}$ hours were spent in the stores, 3 hours outside the stores, and 2 hours in traveling between stores. He made $9\frac{5}{10}$ calls of $35\frac{9}{10}$ minutes each.[64]

[63] Aspley, John Cameron (Ed.), *The Sales Manager's Handbook,* 6th ed., p. 621, Dartnell, Chicago, 1949.
[64] *Ibid.*, pp. 915–916.

QUALITIES OF THE SALESMAN

The aptitudes and abilities of salesmen must be considered in relation to the sale of product or service and a definite sales job. The qualifications of a competent insurance salesman are unlikely to be the same as those of a good automobile salesman. Personal qualifications must be matched with the duties and responsibilities of the job. A study made by 108 firms of the Northeastern Roofing, Siding, and Insulating Contractors Association demonstrates the need for carefully determining these qualities and applying them to the employment function. These firms determined that it cost them, on the average, $590 for each commission salesman who quit.[65] Between January, 1948, and January, 1949, the firms hired 1,314 salesmen—of these 1,252 quit before the end of the year: 85 per cent lasted 4 months or less. Only 26 companies used an application blank; 6 used some type of interview form; and 7 used aptitude tests. The favored sources of recruitment were newspapers and applicants recommended by other employees.

In order to determine the qualities that make a good salesman, George Todd studied the records of 500 salesmen who had failed or succeeded in selling fraudproof checks and check systems. He found that the average salesman without dependents sold 35 per cent below the average of all new salesmen; married men without children sold 4 per cent more than the average of all new salesmen; married men with up to four children sold 18 per cent above the average (more than four children were too much of an encumbrance); the best new salesmen were between thirty and thirty-five; all better salesmen were high school graduates; college graduates showed a somewhat greater advantage; those who entered college but dropped out before graduating had the lowest average; those who worked while attending school (high school or college) were more successful than those who did not; the best salesmen had several thousand dollars' worth of life insurance.[66] Todd also reports that 65 per cent out of every 100 salesmen now hired by his company are successful.

Rating Scales. An example of the way in which qualifications for selling may be evaluated is found in a study of 10,000 salesmen employed by 11 life insurance companies from 1933 to 1935, made by the Life Insurance Sales Research Bureau.[67] Factors from the personal

[65] Northeastern Roofing, Siding, and Insulating Contractors Association, Careless Hiring and Training: What Does It Cost in Dollars, *Sales Management,* July 15, 1949, pp. 58–59.

[66] Todd, George, 65% of the Men We Hire Now Stick and Succeed, *Sales Management,* Dec. 1, 1947, pp. 99–104.

[67] Canfield, B. R., *Salesmanship: Practices and Problems,* 2d ed., pp. 44–46,

history of successful and unsuccessful salesmen were compared, and the following weights were established:

1. Dependents:
   No dependents...................... 3
   One dependent...................... 4
   Two dependents..................... 6
   Three dependents................... 8
   Four dependents.................... 8
   Five dependents.................... 7
   Six or more........................ 4
2. Occupation:
   Executive, not in retail business.......... 10
   Office worker, semi-executive............ 8
   Salesman of real estate................. 6
   Professional........................... 6
   Salesman of tangibles.................. 4
   Manual work........................... 1
3. Employment status:
   Employed.............................. 6
   Unemployed less than 1 month.......... 8
   Unemployed 1 month................... 7
   Unemployed 4 months.................. 4
   Unemployed 6 months or more.......... 2
4. Time with present employer:
   Less than 3 months.................... 3
   3–8 months............................ 4
   2 years to 3–11 years.................. 6
   8 years or more....................... 9
5. Present membership in organizations:
   None.................................. 3
   One................................... 3
   Two................................... 4
   Three................................. 8
   Four or more.......................... 11
6. Net worth:
   $0 to $999............................ 2
   $1,000 to $5,999...................... 4
   $6,000 to $9,999...................... 6
   $10,000 to $14,000.................... 8
   $15,000 or more....................... 10

An applicant is then evaluated on the basis of these weights. For example, if John Doe were a salesman of real estate, unemployed 1 month, belonged to two organizations, had one dependent, had been with his last employer 2 years 5 months, and had a net worth of $4,500, he would have a weighted score of 31. This score is then interpreted, in terms of age, as "excellent," "very good," etc.

McGraw-Hill Book Company, Inc., New York, 1950; also Canfield, B. R., *Sales Administration: Principles and Problems,* pp. 101–103, Prentice-Hall, Inc., New York, 1947.

The validity of such a system was indicated by the Guardian Life Insurance Company.[68] Using the table of factor weights (shown above) as a basis, they developed a personal rating scale, using seven factors— age, education, marital status, previous experience, financial status, years in the community, and employment. The relationship between average first-year sales and scores on the rating scale is shown in Fig. 16–4.

The values of this method of predicting sales success are pointed out by Viteles: " . . . The relatively simple device of determining experimentally the significance of marital status, number of dependents,

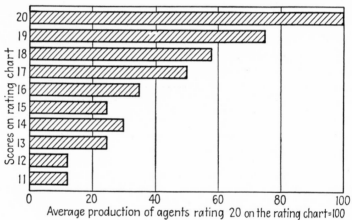

Fig. 16–4. Relation between score on rating chart and average first-year sales.

organization affiliation, and so on, to sales accomplishment has withstood the test of time better than any other single method employed in predicting sales achievement."[69] However, he warns that the specific items and weights, to be valid, must be experimentally discovered by each specific company using the method.

The steps in the analysis of application-blank items, as listed by Rosenstein, Director of Personnel Research Foundation, are[70]

1. Classification of application blanks
   Using four groups—very good, good, fair, and poor—classify each application blank in the group to which the salesman belongs, using the man's status as a salesman as a criterion.
2. Tabulate the data and derive the success percentage.
   Establish a table for each item within each of the four groups.

[68] Chart System for Choosing Salesmen, *Printers' Ink Monthly*, March, 1939, p. 49.
[69] Viteles, M. S., *The Value of Psychology in Selecting Salesmen*, American Management Association, Marketing Series, 1941, No. 45.
[70] Rosenstein, J. L., *The Scientific Selection of Salesmen*, p. 77, McGraw-Hill Book Company, Inc., New York, 1944.

3. Assign values to each item.
4. Develop scores—from the point values derived in step three, establish the range of scores for each of the four groups.
5. Use the scores in selection.

Tests. Tests are becoming increasingly popular as a means of differentiating good salesmen from poor ones. A psychological test is merely a sampling of a man's ability or behavior. Types of tests most frequently used to rate salesmen are mental ability, sales interest and aptitude, personality, verbal ability, and, in some cases, clerical and mechanical ability. By giving a test to present employees and comparing the scores with the individuals' performance records, critical scores can be established.

Mental abilities tests measure general academic intelligence and mental alertness. The most successful salesmen are seldom the most intelligent. Successful salesmen of liquor, tobacco, feed and produce, and health and accident insurance score between the 30th and 70th percentiles on an intelligence test.[71] However, for salesmen who deal with higher executives or who are sales engineers, the 60th percentile is the lower critical score. Table 16–18 shows the relative intelligence levels of various business occupations in terms of raw scores.

Table 16–18. Intelligence Levels of Various Occupations

Occupation	Number in group	Range of middle 50 per cent of scores	Median
Major business executive...............	84	90–156	127
Sales engineers........................	94	110–150	120
College seniors........................	100	100–137	118
School superintendents and special subject teachers...........................	97	100–119	109
Business executives (general group).......	78	82–116	102
Real estate sales......................	25	80–115	102
Office speciality sales..................	111	60–112	95
Insurance sales........................	326	60–110	86
Office clerks..........................	267	55–105	84
Routine sales.........................	191	41–94	71
House-to-house sales...................	160	30–95	65
Policemen (all grades).................	147		42
Retail sales clerks....................	52	20–50	33

Many lists of traits have been compiled, and much has been written about the personality of the salesman. A hearty handshake and "hail-fellow-well-met" attitude are no longer considered to be the only neces-

[71] *Ibid.*, p. 160.

sary personality characteristics of the salesman. Dodge,[72] using the Bernreuter Personality Inventory, found that successful salespeople

1. Are less moody and worry less
2. Are more self-confident and self-sufficient
3. Are more aggressive and willing to assume responsibility
4. Are more social
5. Are less self-conscious
6. Are less desirous of telling others of personal fortune
7. Are less resentful of criticism or discipline
8. Tend to report themselves as more radical or unconventional

The personal qualities of the salesman considered most important by professional buyers—the purchasing agents of seven large corporations—are shown in Table 16–19.[73] One hundred and forty-one salesmen

Table 16–19. Personal Qualities of Salesmen, as Rated by Purchasing Agents

Quality	Rank	Rating (possible 100)
Sincerity	1	82
Courtesy	2	82
Enthusiasm	3	80
Self-confidence	4	79
Self-control	5	77
Alertness	6	77
Appearance	7	76
Tact	8	75
Use of English	9	74
Aggressiveness	10	73
Voice quality	11	69

Table 16–20. Relationship between Salesmen's Scores on Interest Inventory and Rating by Manager

Score on interest inventory	Rating by managers (per cent)		
	Outstanding success	Success	Failure
+6	25	53	22
+4 and +5	16	56	28
+3 to −2	11	47	42
−3 to −5	8	39	53
−6	4	20	76

[72] Dodge, A. F., What Are the Personality Traits of the Successful Salesperson? *J. Appl. Psychol.*, 1938, 22, 229–238.
[73] Canfield, *Salesmanship: Practices and Problems*, pp. 54, 55.

were rated, 74 of whom were successful, and 67 unsuccessful. Professional buyers prefer professional salesmen—those who are sincere, courteous, enthusiastic, self-confident, self-controlled, and alert.

Because interest is an important factor in success, interest tests are being used more and more widely. The Strong Vocational Interest Test, made up of items concerning occupations, school subjects, activities, types of people, and personal characteristics, is most widely used. The testee indicates the items he likes, is indifferent to, and dislikes. The

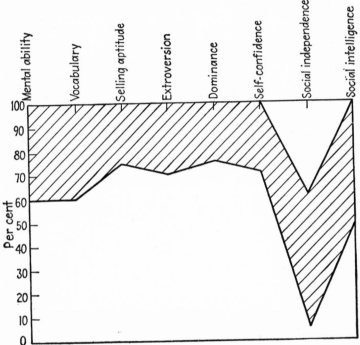

FIG. 16–5. General profile of high-level salesmen. (*From Rosenstein, J. L., Scientific Selection of Salesmen, p.* 242, *McGraw-Hill Book Company, Inc.,* 1944.)

results are then compared with the interest profiles of successful men in many different occupations. The test is based on the assumption that, if a man has interests corresponding to the interests of successful men in a given occupation, he is likely to succeed in that field.

That the interest inventory can be used successfully in the selection of salesmen is indicated by a survey made by the Aetna Casualty and Surety Company. While attending a school conducted by the company, 588 men filled out the inventory. A year later they were rated by their managers on their degree of success. Scores on the test ranged from +6 to —6. The relationship of the interest inventory to the manager's ratings is shown in Table 16–20.[74] Although the interest inventory is frequently unreliable in individual cases, it is significant for groups. For example, Strong[75] reports that life-insurance salesmen with $B+$ on the life-insurance interest ratings earn twice as much as those with C ratings; men with A ratings earn almost three times as much as those with C scores. (He found the average annual paid-for

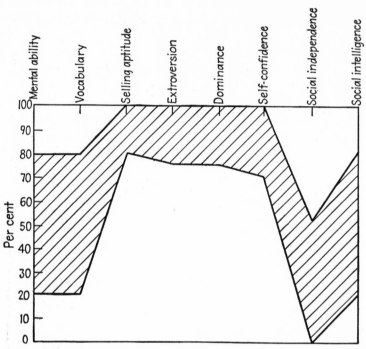

Fig. 16–6. General profile of lower-level salesmen. (*From Rosenstein, J. L., Scientific Selection of Salesmen, p. 243, McGraw-Hill Book Company, Inc., 1944.*)

production of men with a C rating to be $62,000; for men with a $B+$ rating, $127,000; A rating, $169,000.)

A summary of the scores of high-type salesmen and lower-type salesmen on the various tests is shown in Figs. 16–5 and 16–6. Figure 16–5 is the "general profile within which high-type salesmen fall. It was drawn as a composite of the records of salesmen in pharmaceutical manufacturing, dairy machinery, office-form machinery, truck and trailer manufacturing, casualty insurance, economic service, stock, bank extension, steel products, and display advertising sales." Figure

[74] Bills, M. A., Relation of Scores on Strong's Interest Analysis Blanks to Success in Selling Casualty Insurance, *J. Appl. Psychol.*, 1938, **22**, 97–104.

[75] Strong, E. K., *Vocational Interests of Men and Women*, p. 491, Stanford University Press, Stanford, Calif., 1943.

16–6 shows the range "within which lower-level salesmen fall and is a composite of the profiles of salesmen in distillery sales to taverns, tobacco to retailers, feed and produce, furnace and household appliances, roofing and siding, and used automobile sales."[76]

It must be remembered that there are extreme variations among sales jobs and, therefore, among the traits and characteristics of the man who is successful on the job. A large electrical corporation may require that its salesmen be graduate engineers, yet wholesalers of feed and produce may find that salesmen above the 80th percentile in mental ability are unsuccessful in that selling situation. The traits of the successful salesman vary with the product being sold and with the buying public.

Summary

Psychological methods are essential to the proper conduct of research in the field of marketing. They have been used to a large degree for determining the factors which affect the product, for determining the factors which affect the wants and needs of consumers, and for determining the factors which influence consumers' preferences. Research in the subfields of marketing is interrelated and of an interdisciplinary nature.

Some of the factors which condition the product are its uses, shape, package, size, weight, color, and style. The product must satisfy a human want, either basic, secondary, or tertiary.

Among the many factors that are important in determining the wants and needs of consumers are their geographical location, income, desire for change, sex, and age. Consumer research is used to keep the producer informed of the wants and needs of consumers.

The purpose of advertising and salesmanship is to influence consumer preference. The effectiveness of printed advertisements depends largely on the color, size, cuts, illustrations, and headlines, and on the medium which is used. The salesman's effectiveness is related to his personal characteristics. These may be determined by psychological research and applied to the use of rating scales and tests. The average successful salesman is sincere, self-confident, and socially adaptable and has a high degree of selling aptitude and interest.

RECOMMENDED SUPPLEMENTARY READINGS

Aspley, John Cameron (Ed.): *The Sales Manager's Handbook,* 6th ed., Dartnell Corp., Chicago, 1949.

Benge, Eugene, J.: *Manpower in Marketing,* Harper & Brothers, New York, 1945.

Bradford, Ernest S.: *A Survey and Directory of Marketing Research Agencies in the United States,* Bureau of Business Research, City College School of Business, New York, 1947.

[76] Rosenstein, *op. cit.,* pp. 242–243.

Bradford, Ernest S.: *Marketing Research,* McGraw-Hill Book Company, Inc., New York, 1951.

Breen, G. E., Thompson, R. B., and West, Harry: *Effective Selling,* Harper & Brothers, New York, 1950.

Canfield, B. R.: *Salesmanship: Practices and Problems,* 2d ed., McGraw-Hill Book Company, Inc., New York, 1950.

Canfield, B. R.: *Sales Administration: Principles and Problems,* Prentice-Hall, Inc., New York, 1947.

Caples, John: *Tested Advertising Methods: How to Profit by Removing Guesswork,* Harper & Brothers, New York, 1947.

Goode, K. M.: *Advertising,* Greenberg: Publisher, Inc., New York, 1941.

Hepner, H. W.: *Effective Advertising,* 2d ed., McGraw-Hill Book Company, Inc., New York, 1949.

Hotchkiss, G. B.: *Advertising Copy,* 3d ed., Harper & Brothers, New York, 1949.

Hotchkiss, G. B.: *An Outline of Advertising,* 3d ed., The Macmillan Company, New York, 1950.

Kleppner, Otto: *Advertising Procedure,* 4th ed., Prentice-Hall, Inc., New York, 1950.

Lucas, D. B., and Britt, S. H.: *Advertising Psychology and Research,* McGraw-Hill Book Company, Inc., New York, 1951.

Metz, Herbert (Ed.): *Opportunities in Selling,* Government Printing Office, Washington, D.C., 1947.

Nixon, H. K.: *Principles of Selling,* McGraw-Hill Book Company, Inc., New York, 1942.

Pederson, C. A., and Wright, M. B.: *Salesmanship: Principles and Methods,* Richard D. Irwin, Inc., Chicago, 1951.

Rosenstein, J. L.: *Scientific Selection of Salesmen,* McGraw-Hill Book Company, Inc., 1944.

Rowse, E. C., and Fish, L. J.: *Fundamentals of Advertising,* South-Western Publishing Company, Inc., New York, 1937.

Rudolph, Harold J.: *Attention and Interest Factors in Advertising,* Funk & Wagnall Company in cooperation with *Printers' Ink,* 1947.

Sandage, C. H.: *Advertising Theory and Practice,* rev. ed., Chicago Business Publications, Inc., 1939.

Simmons, Harry: *Practical Sales Management,* Prentice-Hall, Inc., New York, 1946.

Tosdal, H. R., and Carson, Waller: *Survey of Salesmen's Compensation,* National Sales Executives, New York, 1951.

Chapter 17

MILITARY PSYCHOLOGY[1]

PSYCHOLOGICAL NATURE OF WARFARE[2]

The applications of psychology in military affairs are old in origin and wide in scope. Modern warfare has extended them, refined them, experimented with them, and utilized them with scientific precision. Our generation cannot claim credit for the introduction of psychology into warfare, but it can claim credit for increasing scientific applications of psychological principles. Not all applications can be encompassed in this chapter; many have counterparts, often identical, in civilian life, which have been treated in other sections of this book.

The military psychologist is not obligated to theorize about causes of war. He is one element of society's cutting edge concerned with the most effective prosecution of the war and must operate on the assumption that war is, or will be, a *fait accompli*. He does need to understand the human fighting machine to know that men will suffer and die while preferring to live in comfort, that they will accept regimentation as a means of fighting for individuality, that they will make supreme sacrifices for one group of men while trying desperately to annihilate

---

[1] This chapter was written by Dr. George L. Fahey, Associate Professor of Psychology in the University of Pittsburgh; formerly, Major, AGD.

[2] References cited in this chapter are from nonmilitary or unclassified military publications. Opinions stated are those of the author and are not to be construed as reflecting Defense Department policies.

another group of apparently similar men. Such paradoxical behavior is not different, except in its frequency and intensity, from the behavior problems any psychologist encounters among men facing conflicts.

War is a violent expression of a conflict, a method of problem solving aimed at destruction of the adversary. It is as old as human history and by no means limited to human beings. It is derived from basic urges for self-expression, self-preservation, and, undoubtedly, in some degree from the psychoanalytically described urge for self-destruction. It differs only in complexity from Cain clubbing Abel to death because Cain experienced a conflict (which he blamed on Abel) and which he thought to relieve by the extinction of Abel. "Only in complexity," however, is not a phrase to be passed over lightly. Wars are made and fought and won by numerous Cains and Abels who show certain peculiarities in their collective behavior that they often do not reflect individually.

Traditionally war has been made a sort of tribal fetish, surrounded with glamour and ideological infusion of divine guidance, and in some cultures it has become a goal rather than a means to an end. The world wars of the twentieth century (some historians say there has been only one war, long continued) have stripped many of the gaudy trappings from war and shown it to be dirty business, infamously conceived and foully conducted. Yet enough of the glamour remains to make it continue to appear a convenient panacea for national or international distress.

Resort to war among primitive peoples is commonly aggression for economic gain or resistance to such real or imagined aggression. As cultures are enriched the causes of war are multiplied and wars arise from motives other than physical occupation of territory or custody of cattle. Struggle for self-expression, to impose a creed or culture, to gain *Lebensraum*, to inflate national ego by enslaving a neighbor, to divert internal contention, and other conflicts unite with economic frictions to produce wars between civilized nations. Often the basic causes are so obscured by verbalized ideologies that only the historians can unravel them.

Increased transportation and communication facilities have given war an increased global significance. One cannot say that modern war is more deadly than the survival and extermination struggles recorded in the Old Testament, but the perimeters of battlefields are now unlimited and the citizen remote from combat can no longer find security in distance.

Despite this broadening of war's scope, the military psychologist must not lose sight of a concept fundamental to his work. Nations fight but nations themselves are incapable of fighting. Marble halls do not throw stones; documents do not tear one another to shreds; the Statue of Liberty is not a flame-thrower. Individual human beings make the wars and fight them. The social psychologist seeks to discover why; the military psychologist accepts war as a fact and capitalizes on the strengths of his own forces and the weaknesses of his enemies. How to fight most effectively is the problem of the military strategist and the military psychologist alike.

The contributions of psychologists to the over-all effectiveness of a nation's fighting forces are made through specific functions performed on many different planes of the all-out war configuration. Selection and assignment; orientation to the services; development of training aids, conduct of training, and improvement of training methods; development and dissemination of indoctrination and propaganda materials; analysis of attitudes; espionage and counterespionage; prevention, diagnosis, and treatment of psychological casualties; preparation of the civilian soldier, crippled or well, for readjustment to civilian life are some of these planes.

THE ROLE OF THE PSYCHOLOGIST IN THE MILITARY SERVICES

The use of psychological knowledge in warfare is by no means new. Troy was captured by a handful of Greeks who understood principles of human behavior and bent them to their own use. The aborigine who daubed his face with awe-inspiring colors and bedecked himself to resemble an inhuman horror was applying a knowledge of human emotions to increase his enemy's fear and bolster his own courage.

The First World War made the first use of professional psychologists identified by that name. The U.S. Army commissioned one small group in the Adjutant General's Department for work in testing and classification. A few others were commissioned in the Sanitary Corps (the unit carrying many specialists attached to the Medical Department). In the Second World War psychologists were utilized by all the services and for a wide variety of tasks.

In the rapid mobilization years of the early 1940's, men with civilian training in psychology were "rare birds." As they entered the services they were usually directly assigned to units or schools in the specialty. Such sorting of civilian backgrounds did not furnish an adequate number, and training schools for various types of psychological duties were operated, as the AGD school courses for personnel technician, classification specialist, and the like. Many others were given on-the-job training in functioning units.

During these early years the demand for psychologists was chiefly in connection with classification and assignment. Later those needs were routinized or passed and the demand was greatest in connection with separation counseling, and it was especially acute for clinical psychologists in hospitals, rehabilitation centers, and disciplinary units. Throughout the Second World War there appeared to be a gradually increasing demand for psychologists capable of aiding and advising commanders in morale problems. In the peace years following the war the need continued for clinical psychologists, but the relative proportion of military psychologists increased greatly. Their number was supplemented by many civilian psychologists working on full or part-time military research projects. Many of these workers had wartime military service.

Obviously there can be no one description of a military psychologist. Varying duties require varying levels of academic training, professional experience, personal qualities, related training and experience, and military experience. Illustrative job descriptions follow from which both duties and qualification requirements of some of the specialties may be inferred.

Personnel Psychologist (2230)[3]

Advises commanding, staff, and line officers on personnel matters of a psychological nature. Administers or supervises administration of psychological tests to military personnel for classification and assignment purposes; determines type of test to be given, such as individual or group tests of intelligence, educational achievement, vocational aptitude, special skill, interest, and adjustment; administers or supervises administration of tests, prepares reports of test ratings and recommends classification and assignment in accordance with approved personnel management policies and procedures.

Advises on the selection, method of training, assignment and reassignment of illiterates and other personnel who are slow to meet military requirements and makes recommendations regarding their disposition; advises on classification and assignment of individuals with special abilities, and in the selection of personnel for specialized assignment or training.

Interviews or supervises interviewing of individuals concerning occupations, educational courses, or military occupational specialties appropriate to interests, needs, and abilities, and advises regarding vocational, educational, avocational, or personal problems of military personnel who do not have neuropsychiatric or psychological disabilities; provides vocational and educational guidance to military personnel being separated from the service; refers personnel with indications of mental or emotional disturbance to the proper neuropsychiatric agencies.

Advises on general and special personnel problems, on the development of techniques in personnel administration, and in the analysis of factors affecting morale and general welfare of the troops.

Must have a Doctor's degree based in part upon a psychological disserta-

[3] Officer Classification; Commissioned and Warrant, *War Department Technical Manual,* 12-406, Change 3, October, 1949.

tion conferred by a graduate school of recognized standing or must have been certified in a field of professional psychology by a specialty board acceptable to the Department of the Army.

RESEARCH PSYCHOLOGIST (2231)[4]

Plans, formulates, supervises, or conducts psychological research pertaining to a wide variety of military problems, such as procurement, selection, classification, assignment, and training of personnel; design and use of training aids and military equipment; measurement and evaluation of performance and achievement; measurement and control of morale; and surveys of opinions and attitudes.

Employs available tests, rating scales, questionnaires, and other devices which will aid in the solution of these problems. Develops various types of psychological measuring devices, such as written and performance tests of aptitudes and proficiency; personality inventories; rating scales; standardized interviews; and questionnaires. Develops experimental apparatus or equipment needed to conduct necessary research. Employs experimental and statistical techniques; collects data relevant to the specific problems, such as test scores and personal data; prepares reports and recommendations.

Must have experience in experimental psychology, developmental psychology, social psychology, physiological psychology, psychometrics, statistical methods, or related branches of applied psychology.

Must have a Doctor's degree based in part upon a psychological dissertation conferred by a graduate school of recognized standing or must have been certified in a field of professional psychology by a specialty board acceptable to the Department of the Army.

CLINICAL PSYCHOLOGIST (MOS 2232)[5]

a. General. As a member of the neuropsychiatric team in any station dealing with the problems of military personnel having disabilities of a psychological nature, performs one or more of the duties described in the following paragraphs:

b. Duties.

(1) Applies psychological principles and techniques as aids to the diagnosis and treatment of individuals; administers and interprets projective and other psychological tests, including those of personality, intelligence, motor coordination, achievement, vocational aptitude, and interests.

(2) Carries out remedial therapy in cases of aphasia, speech, hearing, visual, habit, and motor defects; counsels on educational and vocational problems, and on changes in military occupational specialty for military personnel having neuropsychiatric or other psychological disabilities; assists in or carries out psychotherapy under neuropsychiatric supervision.

[4] *Ibid.*

[5] Military Clinical Psychology, *Department of the Army Technical Manual,* 8-242; *Department of the Air Force Manual,* 160-45, July, 1951, pp. 187–188.

    (3) Performs experimental research as related to the evaluation of current and proposed methods of therapy and diagnosis, the dynamics of normal and abnormal behavior and problems of personality development.

    (4) Provides instruction and training in the principles and practices of clinical psychology to appropriate members of the neuropsychiatric staff and others; assists in the program of orienting officers and enlisted men in personal adjustment problems.

    (5) Recommends revision of policies to improve use of clinical psychology personnel; serves as liaison officer in clinical psychology between other military and civilian agencies.

c. Prerequisites.

    (1) Must have a Doctor's degree based in part upon a psychological dissertation conferred by a graduate school of recognized standing, or

    (2) Must have been certified in clinical psychology by a specialty board acceptable to the Department of the Army.

CLINICAL PSYCHOLOGY TECHNICIAN (MOS 2289: GRADES E-5 AND E-6)[6]

a. Summary. Assists clinical psychologist in administering standard individual or group psychological tests, in obtaining psychiatric information pertinent to individual cases, and in helping individuals to carry out instructions of the professional staff.

b. Duties.

    (1) Administers prescribed psychological tests. Makes individual feel at ease prior to administration of test to establish necessary rapport. Gives individual instructions in test procedure in accordance with test manual. Notes answers, either verbal or performance depending on test, and obtains time required for each answer if such time is to be recorded. Observes and records behavior of individual during test. Records responses on answer sheet as required. Computes score in accordance with test instructions. Prepares report for clinical psychologist indicating results obtained.

    (2) Obtains identifying and other prescribed information. Interviews individual regarding personal habits, behavior, attitudes, and other factors pertinent to development of a case history. Attends group sessions and serves as recorder. Obtains previously prepared military records of individuals, including medical and social histories, and such other information as will assist clinical psychologists in an understanding of an individual's psychiatric disturbance.

    (3) Helps individual to carry out instructions of professional staff. Explains purpose and reasons for referral. Attempts to interest individual in recreational, occupational, and informational programs provided as part of treatment. Conducts, or assists individual in conducting, prescribed remedial treatments for educational and

[6] *Ibid.*, pp. 189–190.

vocational handicaps. Assists in re-education of habits and sensory or motor disabilities. Stimulates participation and observes behavior in group psychotherapy sessions.

c. Qualifications. Must be able to perform the duties described above, be fully acquainted with the duties of neuropsychiatric technician (3403), grade E-4, and possess the following special qualifications:

(1) Must know techniques of standard psychological test administration.
(2) Must know techniques of conducting interviews.
(3) Must be familiar with factors underlying behavior mechanisms and mental illness in relation to individual adjustment.
(4) Must know scope and mission of neuropsychiatric service.

PERSONNEL MAN (PN)[7]

The Navy has a great variety of jobs and schools for which its members must be classified and assigned in accordance with their backgrounds, interests, abilities, and aptitudes. Only by careful classification, and occasional re-classification, can personnel be utilized to the highest degree of satisfaction and efficiency to the individuals as well as to the Navy itself. Personnel Men work under Personnel Officers in doing this important work. They assist Educational Service Officers in educational guidance, and aid in the solution of personal problems.

Duties and Responsibilities. Personnel Men recommend school and job assignments in the Navy on the basis of background as determined by interviews, aptitude tests, and previous records. They analyze, evaluate, and classify naval jobs. Personnel Men counsel personnel in respect to Navy jobs, educational opportunities in the service, training for different jobs, promotion requirements, various benefits provided, and personal matters. They are adept in recognizing maladjustments and taking corrective measures. Keeping personnel records and making personnel reports are part of the work.

Some of the more specific duties and responsibilities of Personnel Men are:

(1) Interviewing: Conduct interviews with Navy personnel for the purpose of collecting information relative to educational background, interests, and abilities; post information obtained on records. Counsel personnel in regard to selection, classification, training, and duty assignments. Evaluate the qualifications of personnel after interviews, taking into account education, occupational background, and test scores.

(2) Recommendations: Make recommendations for the selection, classification, assignment, training, and enlistment of Navy personnel.

(3) Tests, Scoring Methods and Aids, and Tabulations: Administer, score, and interpret such tests as General Educational Development, end-of-course, subject, aptitude, interest, and psychological.

---

[7] *United States Navy Occupational Handbook,* 1950 ed., Bureau of Naval Personnel.

(4) Lectures: Prepare and give informational lectures to groups of personnel concerning ratings, schools, jobs, and opportunities and benefits of a naval career.

(5) Job Analysis: Analyze Navy jobs to determine tasks performed, job relationships, occupational families, convertibility to civilian jobs, and the qualifications required to perform the job in terms of mental and physical abilities, education, experience and training.

In addition to these jobs, Army and Air Force manuals describe duties and qualifications of related military occupational specialties. These include:[8] Instructor, Military Psychology and Leadership (2715), Psychological Assistant (2239), Psychiatric Social Worker (3605), Social Work Technician (2263), Recruiting Specialist (1935), Personnel Administrative Specialist (4816), Personnel Management Specialist (3290), and Personal Affairs Consultant (1274).

Britt and Morgan[9] have reported results of analysis of the questionnaire returns of 968 military psychologists in service in July, 1945. Of this number, 35.5 per cent were in Army Service Forces, 26.7 per cent in Army Air Forces, and 25.1 per cent were in the Navy. Others were distributed through Army Ground Forces, Marines, Public Health Service, Coast Guard, and Maritime Service. The model age group in each of the three services utilizing most psychologists was twenty to twenty-nine. Ninety-five per cent of the psychologists reporting from the Navy were officers while only 63 per cent of those reporting from the Army were commissioned. Functions performed showed few differences according to rank except for increased administrative responsibility with increased rank. Over 70 per cent of the total group were spending more than half their time in psychological duties. Questions concerning favorable and unfavorable aspects of military life as compared with civilian life showed the majority of the group anticipating return to civilian life. Heaviest concentration of prior education was at the M.A. or Ph.D. levels with rank attained somewhat proportionate to extent of civilian education.

By far the greatest number of psychologists working in the military services have been assigned to classification and assignment or clinical duties. Others have made important contributions in other areas, such as in the Military Intelligence Corps with research or operational duties in the conduct of psychological warfare. Their work has been in analysis of enemy propaganda and in preparation and dissemination of materials for morale building among the troops, on the home front, and for the resistance forces in enemy-occupied territory. Some have

[8] SR 615-25-15, Department of the Army, Washington, D.C., 1950.

[9] Britt, Steuart Henderson, and Morgan, Jane D., Military Psychologists in World War II, *Amer. Psychol.*, 1946, 1, 423–437.

worked with the FBI in detection and control of subversive activities at home.

Each of the services has utilized specialists, chiefly experimental and educational psychologists, in the development of improved training procedures. These researchers have made intensive studies of military jobs and built courses of study with a wide variety of accompanying sensory aids to facilitate most rapid and effective attainment of training objectives.

Another small group of psychophysiologists are making valuable contributions to knowledge related to such problems as the psychological effects of various injury and disease processes, climatic conditions, frostbite, pressure and vibration conditions, and the like. Of special importance are the psychophysical problems of airmen traveling at phenomenal rates of speed, at very high altitudes, over excessively long periods of time, and in unnatural body positions necessitated by aircraft design. Some psychologists have been engaged in research on human behavior related to atomic and radiation warfare.

CONDUCT OF PSYCHOLOGICAL WARFARE

The use of psychological principles and devices in warfare is as old as the history of conflict. The savage daubed his face to terrorize his enemy. "Divide and conquer" techniques are recorded in the Old Testament. Modern warfare has developed few new procedures but has greatly systematized and expanded the old ones. The expressed credo of those who make psychological warfare has been quoted by Colonel Hall[10] as follows: "The body of the enemy may be broken without breaking his spirit but the warrior who captures the spirit of the opponent can simply walk in and take over."

Basically the techniques of psychological warfare (variously abbreviated as "psychwar," "psywar," or "sykewar") or propaganda take two directions: assault upon the fears, suspicions, and weaknesses of one's enemy; and the cultivation of one's own strengths with correction or concealment of weaknesses. The psychological attack upon the enemy is often referred to as "war of nerves" while the self-strengthening endeavor is known as "morale building."

WAR OF NERVES

Psychological assault may precede conflict or accompany it. History of recent years shows such preparation for the wars of the twentieth century began years before open fighting with the dissemination of propaganda designed to cultivate sympathy for the have-not nations.

[10] Hall, Col. Donald F., Psychological Warfare Training, *Army Information Digest,* January, 1951, 6, 40–46.

Nazi Germany proved especially adept at such propagandizing. Planning for the world-wide spread of communism appears to have been initiated in the nineteenth century.

Various techniques are employed, more or less subtly disguised. Chief among them have been:

1. Data gathering in the enemy territory to learn his strengths and weaknesses.

2. Cultivation of trust and confidence so as to facilitate such data gathering and allay suspicion. More specifically, one of the most popular devices has been the initiation of movements for world peace and disarmament.

3. Spreading of rumor in the enemy territory. For example; peace may be secured by head-hiding gestures (isolationism) rather than by constant vigilance; cultivation of local dissensions, even by the committing of overt acts to cast disfavor on a government, party, race, or religion; cultivation of internal dissatisfactions, excessive self-criticism, or defeatism. A review of our own history during the interim period between the First World War and the Second World War will show how we very earnestly suscribed to isolationism, misguided peace and disarmament programs, national cynicism, disrespect for institutions and traditions, and related strength-sapping fallacies. Often these were motivated by man's most beautiful ideals but nevertheless served our potential enemies better than ourselves.

Only the naïve student would credit all these activities to the direct efforts of enemy agents. In the conduct of psychological warfare, the psychologist need not attempt to create new distrusts, arouse new suspicions, or turn hatred upon the well-beloved. Instead, he capitalizes on existing fears and purposes. In any nation he has but to fan certain flames and smother others to make the fire burn where he wants it, the fuel being supplied locally. Even heaven in its early days apparently had a group of local citizens whose inner hostilities could be channeled into a revolt against the prevailing culture.

4. Fostering of defeatism, disillusionment, despair, weariness, and cynical appraisal of war aims and of the contributions of allies.

5. Utopian promises to potential collaborators. These need not be realistic. It is only necessary that they appeal to the wants of the proposed recipients; as, abundant food supply, or correction of old injustices.

Psychological warfare became an increasingly definitive mode of attack during the Second World War. The "weapon" now has Special Staff status in the Army with Tables of Organization and of Equipment resembling those of familiar line units. As might be expected of a new service its organization is subject to revision. Currently, the Army utilizes a Radio Broadcasting and Leaflet Group with a Group Head-quarters Unit, Reproduction Company, and Mobile Radio Broadcasting Company. Subunits include publication platoons, propaganda platoons, and loudspeaker platoons.

These units are concerned with preparation and dissemination of propaganda to the enemy at the front lines. Printed matter is distributed by means of specially designed aerial bombs or artillery shells. Word-of-mouth messages are transmitted by radio broadcasts and by loudspeakers. Their functions include analysis of and counterpropaganda against that distributed by the enemy. They utilize various sources of military intelligence, including interrogation of prisoners, to direct propaganda most effectively against enemy weak spots.

Necessarily, the personnel of these units must possess skills concerned with printing, broadcasting, writing, and the like but their major value is dependent upon effective use of psychological principles. According to Colonel Hall,[11] "The hypothetically 'perfect' psychological warfare officer would be a diplomat, historian, publisher, geo-politician, advertising expert, soldier-strategist, and academic psychologist."

Morale Building

Psychological warfare seeks to divert the enemy from his purpose. It also seeks to bolster national zeal at home and at the front. "Morale is the capacity to stay on the job—especially a long, hard job—with determination and zest. It is the opposite of apathy."[12]

Troops with low morale fight poorly, quit readily, and experience relatively more casualties than troops with high morale. The development of morale is a problem for the military psychologist depending upon a great many factors, some of which are intangible and seemingly immeasurable, at least in their proper proportion. Basically it appears to depend most heavily on the factors of vitality, motivation, and self-confidence.

The National Research Council Committee on Psychology for the Fighting Man stated that morale building is a primary task of leadership and offered the following rules to military leaders:[13]

1. Make each man feel he is needed by his unit, that his job in it is important.
2. Never let a man forget that he is a soldier and that a soldier of the Army of the United States is an important and respected person.
3. Make it clear that the unit has its own important function in winning the war.

[11] *Ibid.*
[12] *Psychology for the Fighting Man,* p. 240, National Research Council, Washington, D.C., 1943.
[13] *Ibid.,* pp. 242–243.

4. Encourage the expression of pride in the achievement of the unit.
5. Give commendation and encouragement when it can be sincerely and appropriately given, for fair appreciation usually works better than condemnation.
6. Never belittle or humiliate a man in front of others except when a military emergency, as in battle, may require quick correction. When a rebuke is necessary, do it in private, and make it clear that it is the act that is punished, not the man.
7. Keep idleness at a minimum, but make recreation possible.
8. Train each man in every useful task and action that actual combat will require and teach him that these habits will reduce his fear when combat comes, as well as make him a trained and able fighter.
9. Let men work together in groups whenever possible, because the social relation increases effectiveness.
10. Let the soldier on isolated duty feel that he is an indispensable man, not a forgotten one.

Underlying this kind of leadership are more basic factors. The fighting man must be fit to fight; possessed of a spirit of adventure, physical stamina, freedom from fatigue, disease, and boredom; and as comfortable as possible under the circumstances. He must also be motivated to fight by an understanding and appreciation of the war issues and the stakes involved in victory or defeat. Despite pious protests to the contrary, he must hate his adversary if he is to fight to the death. The fighting man must also possess a high measure of confidence in himself, his unit, and his nation. The ideal soldier believes, is certain, that he "belongs to the best unit in the best service, of the best nation." He knows his weapons are the best, his equipment unexcelled, and his leaders wholeheartedly devoted to him as a man and to the nation. Insofar as he doubts any of these values, his fighting spirit is deadened.

Military psychologists have sought to inculcate the proper motivation, vigor, and self-confidence by such means as

1. Repeated emphasis upon issues of the war and necessity for total defeat of the enemy.
2. Deliberate and planned counterpropaganda to combat that issued by the enemy. Interestingly, the naïve character of some enemy propaganda has been so obvious that its uncensored release without comment has been convincing evidence of its violent distortion of the truth.
3. Provision of the best equipment and weapons, and exhaustive familiarization training in their use.
4. Explanation, insofar as possible within the limits of security from espionage, of military plans and procedures. Commanders who were able to brief men fully in advance of missions as compared with those who, from choice or necessity, led combat teams uninformed as to their

mission, secured such strikingly better morale that the War Department directed such briefing be afforded whenever possible.

5. Provision of the best possible accommodations for men in the form of food, clothing, shelter, mail delivery, entertainment, and post-exchange privileges. Mess and mail have often been called the most important factors in individual morale.

6. Correction so far as possible of grievances raised by soldiers and a sympathetic reaction to those uncorrectable.

7. Time scheduling so that each man's day is filled with work or recreation, that boredom and inactivity are at a minimum.

8. Appreciation of the soldier's natural desire to escape the service periodically, thereby providing a liberal pass and furlough policy.

9. Justice in the trial and punishment of offenders, defense of the unjustly accused, and opportunity for the nonchronic offender to rehabilitate himself.

10. Provision of the most comprehensive and efficient medical service possible for the sick and wounded.

11. Maintenance of as democratic relationship as possible between officers and men.

12. Provision of opportunities for promotion, commendation, awards, and decorations for personal initiative, sacrifice, and valor.

13. Provision of counseling and assistance in personal affairs or legal matters.

14. Recognition of interests and capacities as well as military necessity in classification and assignment.

15. Assistance to individuals in their adjustment to military life by extensive orientation, preventive mental hygiene, and individualized attention.

Extensive research was conducted during the Second World War by Stouffer[14] and others to discover attitudes of soldiers bearing chiefly on their morale. Attitudes toward many factors of military life were investigated, including attitudes toward food, clothing, war issues, leadership, military practices, interrace relations. Results were frequently utilized in modifications of existing military practices ranging from the packaging of rations to the selection of personnel for military courts-martial. Following the Second World War similar research featuring the "critical incident" technique has been carried on by Flanagan and others in the American Institute for Research. Of special interest in such studies has been the use of such validation criteria as combat performance.

Adjustment to Military Life. Military life has certain advantages and

[14] Stouffer, S. A. *et al., The American Soldier,* Vol. I, Princeton University Press, Princeton, N.J., 1949.

disadvantages when compared with civilian life. These factors combine in each individual recruit with his past experience and personality traits to make his transition easy or difficult.

Most commonly cited advantages of military living include security, in the form of assured food, clothing, shelter, orderliness, and system, and the protection of institutional membership. Other advantages are, according to the motives of the individual, freedom from responsibility; opportunity for advancement; increased income for some men; abundant companionship; travel and excitement mixed with periods of routine activity; assurance of masculinity; and, for older men, recaptured youth; opportunity for heroism and martyrdom; release from unhappy marriage or family ties or from monotonous jobs; freedom from certain puritanical standards not exacted by the realistic code of the Articles of War. There is also in war for the psychopath or potential homicide a psychic release not available in peacetime.

On the opposite side, military life has corollary disadvantages including destruction of established securities in family, profession, and civilian society; loss of individuality and privacy; forced association with large numbers of strangers possessing widely differing interests; curtailment of luxuries and privileges; enforced discipline; limited income, for most men; enforced cooperation and group action as opposed to competitiveness on the individual level; plus the many irritations of waiting in line, uniform regulations, bed check and reveille, "KP," saluting, eating from a mess kit, sleeping on the ground, carrying a heavy pack, wearing G.I. shoes, and the undemocratic aspects of RHIP (Rank Has Its Privileges) or, in the language of the soldier, "chicken." Above all, there is in wartime the constant threat of injury or death.

In such a pattern of pros and cons the recruit is certain to experience confusion. Most men effect a satisfactory transition through a limited number of unhappy experiences and come to accept military life with reservations. Some find it to be their preferred career. Others find adjustment impossible and, in spite of the preinduction psychiatric examination, demonstrate traits of maladjustment necessitating their release or, if they revolt too belligerently, commitment to a penal installation or mental hospital.

Each service recognizes in its training that recruits experience transition problems and the early weeks of training are devoted primarily to learning and practicing military life. The haste of wartime mobilization makes extended programs of orientation and indoctrination impossible. The most rapid adjustment seems to come when the recruit is obliged, from the beginning, to live the life of a soldier, sailor, or marine. He follows a rigid schedule under strict discipline; his reactions are closely observed by officers and noncoms adept at picking out those failing to conform. Along with military living, lectures, demonstrations, and other means teach him what is expected of him.

UTILIZATION OF MANPOWER FOR WARFARE

Traditionally the United States depended upon a small professional army and navy to be supplemented by the militia in emergency. A small minority of the militia maintained some military organization in the National Guard, Officers Reserve Corps, Naval Reserve, and the like. The regulars were a token force used for incidents or as training cadre in case the militia was called. In this century, the militia concept was restructured into selective service. Current planning in terms of universal military service differs markedly from the post-Revolution plan for rapid mobilization of the young male population under the banners of the separate states.

This difference may not be correctly interpreted, however, as merely a trend in political thinking. In the early days of our history many men lived a life that allowed them to become soldiers in a relatively short time. As soldiers, their duties were simple and their weapons familiar. In recent years the pattern of civilian living has become distinctly less rigorous. Concurrently, military operations and equipment have become so complex that the modern fighting man must be a specialist as well as able to live under adverse conditions. As a result, it is now highly necessary to select men carefully for military service and place them at the tasks they best fit.

PSYCHOLOGICAL EXAMINING OF SELECTEES[15]

Psychological screening was a specific mission of the Armed Forces Induction Stations where the process of eliminating the mentally, emotionally, and morally unfit received increased emphasis during the war period. The psychological, as distinguished from the psychiatric, examination at these stations was a screening, not a grading process. The objective was the segregation of those who could not read and write and the elimination of those of that group who would not be able to learn those skills in a reasonable length of time. Evidence that a man had graduated from an English-speaking high school or had been employed in an occupation requiring functional literacy was adequate

---

[15] Procedures described here are aspects of a constantly changing scene. Those described were utilized during the great mobilization, service, and separation periods of the Second World War. So far as possible, subsequent unclassified changes in principles or broad practice are included. The structure is that which might be expected to prevail in another period of large-scale mobilization. For example, as this is written, schools for illiterates are not essential. They exist, however, in blueprint stage for speedy reactivation if all-out war should again necessitate them.

to establish his literacy. Lesser training or experience necessitated the use of a short minimum literacy test consisting of some material to read and some questions based on it to be answered orally. Failure to pass this test was considered evidence of illiteracy. For military purposes, literacy was defined as ability to read and write as well as the average fourth-grade child. That level was considered as the minimum skill necessary for the man to cope with various classification tests to be taken later, to read bulletins and orders that might pertain to him personally, and to keep up correspondence with his family.

Nonlanguage tests were employed to determine if an illiterate had sufficient mental ability to justify sending him to a special training unit. Illustrative of these nonlanguage tests, successor to the Army Beta Test of the First World War, was the Visual Classification Test (VC and VC1A). In this test the subject is confronted with a series of pictorial items in groups of five. Of each five-item group, four are somehow alike but the fifth is different. The examinee crosses out the one that is not like the other four. Several sample items are given for demonstration by the examiner. The test proceeds with a minimum of verbalization but with much emphasis on ability to comprehend and follow directions, an important function for the soldier.

Illiterates who showed sufficient intelligence to justify literacy training were inducted, and others were rejected. Suspected malingerers were detected, if possible, and referred to the military psychiatrists. It is probable that very few men malingered their way out of the service on the grounds of illiteracy or mental defectiveness. The simulation of such defects is usually recognized with ease by the trained examiner.

Experiences early in the Second World War thoroughly exposed the fallacies of two popular notions—first, "Anyone who isn't smart enough to get along in the world is good enough for the Army," and second, "The Army will either make a man or break him." Specialized warfare has no place for the mentally defective or for the generally maladjusted individual. A circular letter from the Surgeon General's Office[16] clearly stated Army policy on this matter.

The army is one of the elements of national defense and its present mission is one of preparation for an offensive-defensive type of warfare. It is in no sense a social service or a curative agency. It is to be considered neither a haven of rest for the wanderer or shiftless, nor a corrective school for the misfits, the ne'er-do-wells, the feeble-minded or the chronic offender. Furthermore, it is neither a gymnasium for the training and development of the undernourished or underdeveloped, nor is it a psychiatric clinic for

---

[16] Circular Letter, No. 19, Surgeon General's Office, War Department, Mar. 12. 1941, as quoted by James W. Layman, 1st Lt. S.C., AUS, Utilization of Psychologists in the General Hospitals of the Army, *Psychol. Bull.,* 1943, **40**, 212–216.

the proper adjustment to adult emotional development. Therefore, there is no place within the army for the physical or mental weakling, the potential or prepsychotic, or the behavior problem. If an individual is a behavior problem in the civilian community, he will certainly become a more intensified problem in the army.

Although accomplished by psychiatrists rather than psychologists, another major type of psychological screening took place at the induction stations. This was the elimination of the emotionally unstable, immature, psychotic, prepsychotic, or perverted selectee.

According to Ebaugh,[17] the military misfit is one who lacks capacity to meet or stand the stress of prolonged military experience because of structural or functional defects. Men who temporarily show the strain of severe fighting can be easily helped; those who are easily upset are not wanted in a crisis. They are a dangerous source of weakness. Not only are they suffering, but they readily and unknowingly disturb others and by suggestion destroy the morale of their associates.

Eight categories of such men were listed by the Surgeon General's Office:

I. Persons below minimum literacy (shown by a score of 9 in the Army Information Sheet)

Persons below minimum mentality (shown by a score of 35 in the Visual Classification Test)

(Standards of literacy and mentality as determined by psychological tests and usually corresponding to fourth-grade educational level)

II. Psychopaths having shown persistent misbehavior or a poor work record

III. Inductee previously hospitalized for a mood disorder, or one who shows evidence of markedly impaired judgment during mood swings

IV. Psychoneurotics showing any of the following patterns:
   a. Inefficiency in work or school
   b. Long periods of inactivity or hospitalization
   c. Excessive drifting from place to place, job to job, or doctor to doctor

V. Pre-psychotics, post-psychotics or schizophrenics presenting:
   a. A previous history of psychiatric hospitalization
   b. A definite picture of oddness or peculiarity after a three to six minute examination

VI. Alcoholics showing any of the following:
   a. Excessive drinking resulting in the loss of jobs
   b. Repeated arrests
   c. Reliable history of hospitalization for excessive drinking
   d. Narcotic and sedative addicts

[17] Ebaugh, F. G., Misfits in Military Service, *Diseases of the Nervous System*, 1943, **4**, 3–8.

VII. Persons with any type of syphilis of the nervous system

VIII. Inductees showing an existent organic disease of the brain, spinal cord, or peripheral nerves

Inductees showing residual effects from nervous system disease that would prevent moderately efficient day to day work and a regular routine of living

Cases giving a reliable history of convulsion, fainting, treatment for epilepsy, "black-outs," fits, spasms, or "falling out spells," regardless of etiology

Military psychologists and psychiatrists working separately or as teams carry the responsibility of preventing the induction of individuals predictably unsuited on psychological grounds for military service. In the foreseeable future, such prediction is liable to error because the variables operating are numerous and complex. They are often vastly different variables from those that can be available at the time of prediction.

CLASSIFICATION AND ASSIGNMENT

Modern classification has gone far from the system of the apocryphal Boer War Colonel who touched each man with his riding crop as he came down the gangplank, announcing, "You're a cook," "You're a rifleman," "You're an orderly," etc. Modern militarists find a less arbitrary system imperative. They depend instead upon objective testing criteria, conversion tables for transposing civilian jobs into military ones, tables of attrition, tables of organization, and many other impedimenta of classification.

The Staff in the Personnel Research Section of the Adjutant General's Office has reviewed the history of Army classification procedure.[18]

No provision was made for the placement of recruits in the First World War until after mobilization had begun in 1917, but the place of scientific tools in the personnel system of the Army was well established by Armistice time.

Testing and classification were the functions of two agencies in 1917 and 1918, because of the fact that mental testing was at first considered merely as a reliable method of eliminating mental incompetents who would be altogether unable to learn the performance of even the simplest military tasks. The services of the men who devised the Army Alpha and Beta tests were therefore offered to the Surgeon General; and the Division of Psychology of the Medical Department continued in charge of this work until the end of the war, although the Division's functions, as they developed, departed radically from the narrow field originally envisioned.

[18] Staff, Personnel Research Section, Classification and Enlisted Replacement Branch, The Adjutant General's Office, Personnel Research in the Army: I. Background and Organization, *Psychol. Bull.*, 1943, 40, 129–135.

Some of the tests and methods devised during the First World War, although changed, are still in use; for example, the general classification test, the grade system for indicating degrees of relative ability to learn, and trade tests.

During 1917 and 1918 and in the years following, very little attention was paid to the question of efficient classification and placement. After 1918 Army Regulations called for a shortened form of the Stanford-Binet to be administered to recruits. With the exception of the Army Air Corps and the Signal Corps, little use was made of the test in classification and selection. This disinterest was to be expected with the rapid demobilization and the maintenance of a small peacetime Army in the following years.

Concurrently, the utilization of classification and assignment procedures in business, industry, and government service expanded greatly. Transfer of these procedures enabled psychologists and personnel technicians to adapt quickly to their enormous task in the Second World War. Many new devices had been developed in selection and testing, and a large group of men with both training and experience in the field of personnel work were available almost immediately to the Armed Forces.

A special agency to deal with Army test construction was organized in the spring of 1940 and an advisory committee was set up on the Classification of Personnel in the Army with Dr. Walter V. Bingham as chairman.

During the summer of 1940 an Army Regulation (Enlisted Men Initial Classification) was drawn up establishing the Army classification policy and making provision for a complete testing program. The first trial forms of what became known as the Army General Classification Test, the AGCT, were constructed. For illiterates or those men whose language was other than English, nonlanguage tests were prepared; also, the first forms of the clerical and mechanical aptitude tests were devised. By the time of the passage of the Selective Training and Service Act in September, 1940, the tests were in process of standardization and validation. Early the next year all those men who had come from the Regular Army and National Guard were classified on the basis of the new tests and procedures.

With the advent of the Selective Service Act, new problems presented themselves to those concerned in Army Personnel Classification. According to the Personnel Research Section,[19] the factors responsible were as follows: "(a) sudden influx of large numbers of men, (b) increase in the range of mental ability and type of background of soldiers, (c) need for the selection of more officer candidates, and (d) need for

[19] *Ibid.*

rapidly and accurately determining degrees of skill and aptitude as a basis for special selection or training." Additional professional personnel were obtained and reorganizations effected to meet the growing demands of the arms and services for tests used in selection problems.

With special selection programs of the various arms and services, an increasing number of tests measuring specific achievement, aptitude, or knowledge was developed. Selection for Officer Candidate Schools called for the construction of an examination that would better differentiate between the abilities of men in the Army grades I and II. Tests for Warrant Officer candidates were drawn up in 1941 for approximately 30 specialties.

The Reception Center. Reception centers located at strategic points received all men inducted into the Army, introduced them to the service, began their classification, made their initial assignment, and provided a brief introductory training. The average soldier will recall the Reception Center as a place where he received a heavy measure of "housekeeping detail," such as kitchen police and area police (picking up cigarette butts and candy wrappers), and sore feet from G.I. shoes; but the initiation of his classification was the most important thing that happened.

His classification began with the AGCT (Army General Classification Test, replaced in 1951 by the Armed Forces Classification Test which is of the same type but uniform for all services and administered at the Armed Forces Induction Stations). The test yields a score indicative of his ability to learn as compared with other soldiers. Raw scores were transmuted to standard scores for record purposes and also into grades. These scores and grades were entered on his Qualification Card (Form 20), which accompanied him throughout his term of service. Retests were possible for cases considered to be unreliably measured, and in 1944 the Army Individual Test was introduced and administered as an individual examination standardized against the AGCT. Similarly, the inductee also took the Mechanical Aptitude Test and usually the Radio-telegraph Operator Aptitude Test. These tests were designed to assist in the selection of men for critically needed specialist training in mechanical jobs or in the highly important skill of radio operation.

The next important classification step at the Reception Center was the interview. Trained specialists interviewed each inductee at length, using as a guide and record sheet the Soldier's Qualification Record, Form 20. Interviews were informal and conversational in nature but aimed directly at the determination of a suitable assignment. Test scores were usually available for the interviewer to use in conjunction with previous military experience, hobbies and special interests, civilian occupations, knowledge of language, and record of physical condition.

All this information was utilized by the assignment officer in recommending an assignment. Theoretically, assignments were made to replacement training centers, but they were also made to specific jobs or to field units. Inductees with highly developed skills useful to the service were often assigned directly from the Reception Center to jobs. Other men, especially early in the war, were often assigned to field units for training rather than to replacement training centers. All men were assigned to a basic arm: Infantry, Cavalry, Armored, Field Artillery, or Coast Artillery, or to one of the services: Quartermaster Corps, Engineers, Medical Department, and the like.

Assignment was based on three factors—what had a man done? what was he capable of doing? and where was he needed most? The first two questions were answered by the tests, the interview, and his physical condition; the third, by requirement rates. Each reception center was allotted quotas by the War Department upon a daily or weekly basis. Every week so many men per 1,000 had to be sent to the Infantry, to the Air Forces, or to other arms or services. In addition, "rare birds" were held out and specially assigned. Irregular requisitions often came for excesses of certain types, as 50 additional cooks for Fort Knox or the next 20 radio repairmen to Fort Monmouth. The needs of the service proved to be fluctuating and often exasperating to the classification officer. To the insistent demands of quotas most stories of misassignment may be traced; thus, John Jones was trade-school trained as a refrigerator mechanic, but the Army made him a truck driver; while Bill Smith, who drove trucks for 10 years, was trained to be a medical technician. Undoubtedly, there were errors in assignment in the haste and waste of mobilization, but most such cases arose from the fact that when Bill Smith came up for assignment there was a priority on medical aid men while the refrigerator mechanic hit a period of demand for drivers. Largest of all these demands, of course, was for the combat rifleman; and lawyers, farmers, pharmacists, and all others with sound bodies stood subject to that assignment unless they happened to fall into the "rare birds" categories; i.e., those inductees who brought into the Army rare and valuable civilian occupational training or experience. Radar technician is a good example while another is psychologist, which, in fact, was in many cases rare enough to yield a commission.

An exception to the above process was the illiterate who was forwarded to a Special Training Unit for training and then returned to the Reception Center for processing.

The Soldier's Qualification Record, WD AGO Form No. 20, was developed with a view of furnishing a record form that combined the features of continuity, accessibility, and comparability. It was initiated at the Reception Center and followed the man throughout his Army career. Each unit commander under whom he served was responsible for maintenance and entry of accumulative data on the man's card. The form was always readily accessible to the unit commander and others concerned with the soldier's training and duties. In some units it was kept in the company, where it had utmost accessibility to those most directly concerned. In other units it was kept in the battalion or other higher echelon, where it was available to the company officers and also could be used for classification and assignment within the larger unit. The card is highly standardized, had few and only slight revisions throughout the war, and allows comparison of the man with any other man whose record is available regardless of location in the Army. Similar forms, WD AGO Forms No. 66-1, 66-2, and 66-3, were used for officers.

For purposes of classification and assignment in divisions, corps, service commands, or other high echelons, machine record forms were kept for rapid sorting of many cards on the basis of all pertinent and recorded data. Such records involved the use of complex machines and skilled operators and were less useful at lower levels, where cards were sorted by hand.

Replacement Training Center. From his assignment to a service branch at the Reception Center, the recruit usually moved within a week to a Replacement Training Center, where he was trained as a replacement to fill a vacant position in a field unit. The course combined training in skills necessary to all soldiers, such as physical conditioning, use of rifle, map reading, etc., and individual training for a particular Army job. In most cases he left the RTC after 13 to 17 weeks with a military occupational specialty (MOS) and was assigned to a field unit for further training or for duty in that specialty.

During the entire process, he was subject to reclassification and reassignment as his special strengths and weaknesses were evidenced in tryout experiences. Even in combat, classification was a continuous process and men shifted jobs with the loss of other men. Most illustrative were the battlefield commissions for enlisted men who demonstrated exceptional leadership qualities.

Except in combat, the ever-present tool of continuous classification was the Soldier's Qualification Record with its information concerning test scores and background experience. New data were cumulatively added indicating service schools attended, duties performed, and appropriate dates and rating on manner of performance in terms of "skilled," "semiskilled," or "potential." On the basis of recorded scores and experience background a man might be assigned directly to a military job, considered for Officer Candidate School, or college training in the Army Specialized Training Program. He might be sent to one of the many specialist schools in radio, auto mechanics, meteorology, ordnance, personnel administration, and the like. Some individuals found inadequate could be sent to Special Training Units or, in some large camps, to special developmental battalions from which grossly inept ones were discharged to civilian life.

Nearly all Army tests are similar in nature but differ in content and purpose. Objectivity and simplicity of instructions are the rules, with items based as often as possible on military problems and situations. Most tests were designed for administration to large groups by examiners who were trained for the test but were usually not professional psychometricians. Standard scores based on a mean of 100 were obtained for nearly all tests.

The best known test in the Army was the AGCT, administered to all literate recruits at reception centers. All forms required about 1 hour for instructions and examining and were usually machine scored. They covered areas of vocabulary, arithmetic, and block counting and were arranged in ascending order of difficulty with a very high ceiling. Raw scores were transmuted into standard scores as follows: (TM 12–425, Par. 19)[20]

Standard scores	Army grade	Qualitative level
130 and above......	I	"Men in this grade possess a high level of mental ability."
110–129............	II	"Nearly all of these men are capable of performing the skilled administrative and technical work of the Army."
90–109.............	III	"This is the largest group in the Army. These men are of average mental ability."
60–89.............	IV	"These men are below average in their ability to learn new tasks and somewhat slow in their grasp of situations."
59 and below........	V	"Although these men are very slow learners, and not quick at grasping situations, they can perform adequately on many jobs."

The second most widely used Army classification test was the Mechanical Aptitude Test. Several forms consisting of three parts were developed measuring understanding of mechanical movements, surface development (patterns and forms), shop mathematics, mechanical

[20] Personnel Classification, *War Department Technical Manual*, 12-425, 1944.

information, mechanical comprehension, and tool recognition. Raw scores were converted into standard scores, and Army grades corresponding to the distribution on the AGCT were given.

All men who scored above 60 (later raised to 85) on the AGCT were given the Radio-telegraph Operator Aptitude Test (ROA). The test was reproduced by phonograph records, and examinees were required to determine and check whether pairs of numbered sounds were identical or different.

Special Problems in Classification and Assignment. Unfortunately, not all men inducted were capable of ready classification and assignment. As indicated earlier, illiterates, if they were reasonably intelligent, were inducted. Men with histories of psychosis, prepsychotic tendencies, psychopathy, enuresis, immaturity, or psychoneuroses sometimes slipped through the induction screening (and some made valuable soldiers). Some who had shown previously no obvious traits of maladjustment broke under the strains of Army life. All these complicated the work of fitting men into most suitable military jobs. Those who proved incapable of adjustment were discharged as unsuited for training. Many were placed in special training units, developmental battalions, rehabilitation centers or similar training commands that combined military training, academic training, and psychotherapy.

The Special Training Unit in the Army was designed to bring educationally, physically, or emotionally handicapped men to a high enough level to absorb necessary training and perform certain Army jobs. As described by Seidenfeld, these units conditioned many men for soldiering.[21]

Within the military services there are a sizable number of men who are moderately physically handicapped, some who are on the dull side mentally, and still others whose learning is retarded due to lack of acquaintance with the English language. Such men, however, are capable of giving a great deal of useful military service provided they are trained to execute the duties assigned to them. This means that each man in these categories must be given some specialized form of training prior to, or concurrent with, his regular military instruction. Obviously, such training requires more time than normally allocated to basic military instruction within the Army. This additional time for training and the special program of instruction is provided by the establishment of an educational program designed specifically for Special Training Units. Men assigned to such units, in addition and prior to regular training, take from eight to thirteen weeks special training during which halftime is devoted to academic instruction in the fundamental subjects of reading, writing, and arithmetic, and the remain-

[21] Seidenfeld, Morton A., Lt. Col., AGD, The Special Training Units of the Army, *Psychol. Bull.*, 1943, **40**, 279–281.

ing half to that instruction in the basic military subjects. . . . The evidence indicates that with present techniques about 95 per cent of all men sent to special training successfully complete their instruction and go on to regular training.

Special Training Units concentrated primarily on illiterate inductees. Mental hygiene units for the emotionally maladjusted were developed at a number of installations. In most cases they were directed by a psychiatrist who worked in cooperation with psychologists and others. Ebaugh has described such a unit.[22]

Psychiatric services were set up in replacement training centers where inductees go for basic training after they have been inducted and have spent several days in reception centers being classified and tested to determine correct placement and service. The replacement training center afforded much opportunity for excellent preventive mental hygiene work, in addition to elimination of those unstable soldiers not rejected at induction centers.

Ebaugh reported neuropsychiatric functions at the replacement training center conducted by psychiatrists working with psychologists, psychiatric social workers, chaplains, judge advocates, military police, and classification and orientation officers. Treatment and diagnosis were afforded to ambulatory patients and referrals made to the rehabilitation unit. Group psychotherapy was afforded by talks to troops on such subjects as fear, discipline, sex, war issues, drinking, recreation, fatigue, anxiety, and officer-soldier relationships.

A common example of effective work in RTC's was the treatment of homesickness evidenced either by a depression in which the men affected were aware of the cause, or by apathetic behavior by preoccupied men showing no emotional disturbance and appearing satisfied but continually thinking of home with no idea of how these thoughts prevented their adjustment. Such men were absent-minded, slow, inefficient, careless, untidy, and unreliable. Usually, one interview sufficed to correct the problem, and in all cases a better adjustment appeared after a few such interviews.

Lipkin[23] summarized his work as Personnel Consultant in a rehabilitation center, which was, as the name implies, a military installation designed to rehabilitate men who had failed to adjust to Army life. Men sent to rehabilitation centers have been convicted of general court-martial offenses but were considered capable of rehabilitation. Lipkin's duties included the following activities:

[22] *Op. cit.*
[23] Lipkin S., The Personnel Consultant in an Army Rehabilitation Center, *Psychol. Bull.*, 1944, **41**, 524–531.

1. Conducting a program of group psychotherapy to
   a. Reduce emotional tensions present among the rehabilitees.
   b. Develop social and personal values more akin to those of the average soldier.
   c. Assist rehabilitees to a better understanding of self and others.
2. Carrying on a program of personality testing to
   a. Enlighten both the Personnel Consultant and his enlisted assistants as to the nature and types of personality difficulties and personality structures possessed by rehabilitees.
   b. Measure changes in attitudes and anxieties resulting from the program of group psychotherapy at the center.
3. Acting as Personnel Consultant to the Commandant and other officers of the Center on matters pertaining to group and individual rehabilitee morale and development.
4. As Classification Officer carrying on duties common to all Classification Officers but with the major function of recommending assignment when rehabilitees are considered ready for restoration by the administration.
5. Scheduling a lecture program for guard and custodial personnel to give them a better appreciation of the problems they face in their relationships with rehabilitees as well as means to solve these problems.

Specialist Training. As might be expected, many men came into the services endowed with more than average abilities, qualities of leadership, and other favorable traits. To exploit these was a more critical objective than the upgrading of the unfavored. Several opportunities were available to exceptional men: to receive training as highly skilled specialists, as in the radar training program of the Navy; to pursue officer-candidate courses leading to commission; or to work toward either of these ends through the Army Specialized Training Program or the Naval Reserve Training Program.

Numerous service-conducted specialist courses were set up by each of the services ranging from a few days' refresher training to accelerated courses requiring months to complete. Most common were courses for mechanics, cooks and bakers, radio operators and technicians, and in aircraft maintenance.

Officer-candidate schools selected outstanding volunteers who aspired to commissions. Their programs were of varying length beyond the minimum of the "ninety-day wonder." Training was an exaggerated basic training combining required leadership abilities with specialized training in the weapons or instruments of the service. Men selected for Army OCS were required to have an AGCT score of 110 or better and be recommended by individuals and boards of officers who examined them on attitudes, information, and personal qualities.

Selection played a large part in the determination of eligibility for the Army Specialized Training Program or Navy Reserve Training Program, both at the college level. The Army required an AGCT score of 115 or better, high-school graduation, and recommendations of merit. Naval units required similar standards, even more rigid, as the Navy program led to a commission, while the ASTP did not necessarily do so.

In all these special educational opportunities, including that of the Air Force described above, eligibility was based on ability of individuals to profit from training and, in return, to render more valuable service thereby. Selection was determined by previous training, aptitude, preference, personality factors, and the needs of the service. Most important, however, was aptitude.

In certain specialist areas, measurement and prediction have not been very effective in the past. Notable among these is the factor of leadership ability. Above-average scores on such a test as the AGCT are frequently associated with ability to size up a situation, plan an appropriate course of action, and then elicit the cooperation of a group of men in the conduct of that action. Yet, some individuals with high AGCT scores seem woefully deficient at such tasks. Other men have demonstrated leadership ability although their test scores classify them as mediocre or inferior. Current research attempting to define, measure, and predict traits involved in leadership ability may lead to improved methods of selection and training of future officers and noncoms. Illustrative of such research is that being done for the Navy at the University of Rochester by Launor F. Carter and others.[24]

In 1946, General Eisenhower, then Army Chief of Staff, directed the inclusion of a course in applied psychology in the curriculum at West Point. A Department of Military Psychology and Leadership was created, and instruction in psychology has been distributed over the 4-year course.[25]

Special problems of classification and assignment are presented by the reservist called back to duty. When he was first inducted he was given a military occupational specialty on the basis of his civilian education or experience or was assigned to training for a military job. Sometimes this may have been a succession of jobs. When he was released from active duty he may have continued work similar to his military occupation. More likely, he returned to his preservice work or entered other civilian work. Possibly he went to school and became an engineer, lawyer, accountant, or other kind of civilian specialist.

[24] Carter, Launor F., Meirowitz, Beatrice, and Lanzetta, John, The Behavior of Leaders and Other Group Members, *Amer. Psychol.*, July, 1951, **6**, 323–324 (abstract).

[25] Gee, Col. Samuel E., Leadership at West Point, *Army Information Digest*, September, 1951, **6**, 58–60.

On his return to service, classification and assignment personnel have the complex task of evaluating this training and experience. This must be done in terms of the needs of the service and, so far as possible, the interests of the individual.

To aid in this process, as well as in the placement of recruits, various trade tests prove useful. The Navy has utilized such tests for a number of years in the selection and promotion of personnel in its many specialized jobs. At a rather elementary level, the Oral Trades Questions of the U.S. Employment Service have been available as an aid in military classification. The Air Force has developed a series of similar tests particularly for its specialists but useful for similar work elsewhere. As this is written, 147 Air Force Job Knowledge Tests (AFJKT) have been prepared under conditions of carefully controlled experimental test construction. These tests measure job information and are valuable aids to classification since they give more objective evidence of knowledge of a job than may be accurately inferred from reported numbers of months' experience.

PSYCHOLOGICAL AFTERMATH OF WARFARE

Veterans' hospitals are filled to overflowing with the casualties of the wars of the twentieth century. An increase rather than decrease in the burden on society and on the individuals concerned seems inevitable. Wounded men with residual physical disabilities are potential public charges. Equally so are the psychiatric casualties who retain mental or emotional handicaps. In large measure, those men represent only an exaggeration of the problems experienced by every returned serviceman.

ADJUSTMENT PROBLEMS OF THE RETURNED SERVICEMAN

Transition from civilian to military life has been described as filled with difficulties. No less so is return to civilian life. Profound changes occur in the serviceman who spends many months away from home and in combat. Profound changes have also occurred in the environment to which he returns. Rogers[26] has listed some of the psychological problems faced by the returned serviceman or woman.

1. Vocational readjustment
2. Hostilities
3. Disturbances of self-esteem (sense of adequacy, loss of status, and labels of "psychoneurotic," and the like)
4. Uncertainty of purpose
5. Combat residuals (restlessness, disturbed sleep, hyper-emotionality)
6. Marital and family adjustments
7. Adjustment to handicaps

[26] Rogers, Carl R., Psychological Adjustments of Discharged Service Personnel, Psychol. Bull., 1944, 41, 689–696.

More specifically, these problems include transition from active, outdoor life to a comparatively stable indoor life; transition, for many men, from adventurous, exciting living to monotonous jobs (as the fighter pilot who became a letter carrier), and for others, leaving monotonous, routine assignments to perform duties requiring new learnings and mental activity and skill; transition from military cooperation and teamwork to competitive individualism; loss of the security of position, assurance of life necessities, and the corollary threat of unemployment; discontinuance of the personal welfare interests and responsibilities assumed by officers and military agencies; loss for many men, especially young officers, of posts of responsibility and relatively high wages; return to home situations where the family has learned to live independently and where working wives have often contributed to a joint income greater than the husband might ever reasonably expect to earn alone.

Colonel Evans,[27] formerly Chief, Classification and Replacement Branch, Adjutant General's Department, reported the military appreciation of the problems of the returning serviceman and the intent to discharge him with as much aid in transition as possible.

Each of the services released its personnel through separation units or hospitals. As part of the processing, group and individual counseling was afforded with respect to benefits available to the veteran. Advisement was given on civilian occupational opportunities currently available and suggestions made for the conversion of skills learned in the service to skills of civilian importance. A qualification record was furnished for each individual. This he might show to prospective employers as evidence of his military training and experience. The United States Armed Forces Institute (USAFI) cooperated with the American Council on Education and others in the establishment of means for evaluating military training in terms of civilian educational requirements. They also made available the Tests of General Educational Development by means of which many veterans established the equivalence of a high school education or, in some schools, received college credits.

Problems of readjustment to civilian life have probably existed for ex-servicemen in all eras of history. The sharp contrast between the veterans of the First and Second World Wars may be viewed as evidence of an increasing social appreciation of these problems. Men discharged in 1918–1919 received few benefits unless they were disabled. After a bitter struggle and some violence they extracted a bonus for their military service. It was paid with considerable reluctance by a society which had toasted its veterans as heroes but expected them

[27] Evans, George R., *Preparing the Soldier for His Return to Industry*, pp. 8–12, American Management Association, Personnel Series, No. 85, New York, 1944.

to make their own readjustment. Some portion of the lawlessness of the 1920's has been attributed to these veterans and the observable cleavage between the ex-soldier and the civilian.

Veterans of the Second World War received a much different welcome home. Early in the war, their return and their problems were anticipated and a Bill of Rights, Public Law 346, 78th Congress, assured them protection of employment where reasonably possible, opportunity to borrow money for home or business, and opportunity for education proportionate to their service time. While other variables have clearly had an influence, veterans of the Second World War appear to have bridged the gap from citizen-soldier to citizen-ex-soldier with much less conflict than their fathers did after the earlier war. We must note, of course, that many individual men discharged in 1918–1919 made the transition with no outward demonstration of conflict. We should also note that these men in large measure were the civic and social leaders who developed the system of benefits made available to their sons in the second quarter of the century.

Closely related to military psychologists are those who work with veterans' affairs. Subsequent to the Second World War, the Veterans' Administration experienced an enormous expansion and found critical need for clinical psychologists in several specialized areas. Chief of these was for clinical psychologists assigned to hospitals and mental hygiene clinics. Duties varied for such workers but, in general, they have worked with psychiatrists and psychiatric social workers in the making of diagnoses, especially through the use of psychological test results. They have also played an increasingly important role in individual and group psychotherapy.[28]

Another large group of psychologically trained specialists employed by the VA included those concerned with educational and vocational counseling under the provisions of Public Law 346 (the G.I. Bill of Rights) and Public Law 16 (the Vocational Rehabilitation Act). Such counseling activities were carried on in VA hospitals, regional offices, and by contract units at nearly all universities and colleges.[29]

As the postwar years passed the need for counseling specialists decreased. The need for clinical psychologists has remained acute. This need gave rise to the VA training program for clinical psychologists continuing in a number of graduate schools whose training facilities have been approved. The program, based on a careful screening process, has featured graduate study leading to the Ph.D. in psychology, combined with supervised practice in VA hospitals and clinics.[30]

[28] Miller, James G., Clinical Psychology in the Veterans Administration, *Amer. Psychol.*, 1946, **1**, 181–189.

[29] Scott, Ira D., and Lindley, Clyde J., The Advisement and Guidance Program of the Veterans Administration, *Amer. Psychol.*, 1946, **1**, 190–200.

[30] Miller, *op. cit.*

Numerous other agencies, Red Cross, veterans' organizations, Community Chest affiliates, and the like have contributed to the readjustment of the ex-serviceman. Their services have usually been of an advisory nature and have not featured the work of professional psychologists.

PSYCHOLOGICAL PREPARATION FOR PEACE

The responsibility of the military psychologist has been defined as participation in the conduct of warfare. As any other citizen and member of his profession, he is interested in peace and aspires for greater human endeavors than efficient destruction of fellow men.

Experience in military psychology indicates that the millennium of peace will be speeded or retarded in its coming by our world-wide ability to accomplish certain basic objectives. These include international concern for assurance of freedom throughout the world, rather than for racially, geographically, or politically distinct segments, and the development of means for settlement of international conflicts on a level less violent than the savagery of war.

To lead to this objective, there falls on the professional psychologist the task of further developing and refining principles and techniques by which human energies may be turned most efficiently to the procurement of goods and spiritual values that satisfy basic human longings. More specifically, the psychologist should secure data demonstrating the dignity of all races and the fallacies of supermen obsessions. He should assist in the discovery and evaluation of conflicts and their resolution before they reach the emotional peak culminating in war. It is interesting to speculate on how recent history might have been written had a free press had access to an unprejudiced fact-finding poll, such as the American Institute for Public Opinion, in the Axis countries during the 1920's. Psychologists of the future must persist in the measurement of the will of the people.

The psychologist must further continue to concern himself with principles and devices for the analysis of human capacities and the most efficient manner to relate these capacities with the work of the world. New developments in personnel control, assignment, administration, and training should be available to the armed forces in such a way that they may be quickly and efficiently utilized should another period of rapid mobilization ever occur.

SUMMARY

The use of psychological technique in warfare is as old as the history of conflict. During the twentieth century, these techniques have been refined and expanded on a scientific basis. Psychological assault upon the enemy through carefully planned propaganda campaigns increases his fears and diverts his energies to internal dissensions and defeatism. Men called to military service are classified and assigned to military occupations according to experimentally validated testing and interviewing methods, so that natural and acquired aptitudes are most fully utilized. Modern warfare exacts a heavy psychological toll from the individuals who conduct it. Many cases of neurosis and psychosis occur in war that probably would never have occurred without the shock of battle. Indoctrination for conflict and subsequent care for the psychologically exhausted are major responsibilities for the military psychologist.

RECOMMENDED SUPPLEMENTARY READINGS

Boring, E. G. (Ed.): *Psychology for the Armed Forces,* Infantry Journal, Washington, D.C., 1945.

CBS Assessment Staff [Murray, H. A. (Ed.)]: *Assessment of Men,* Rinehart & Company, Inc., New York, 1948.

Curtis, I.: *World War: Its Cause and Cure,* Oxford University Press, New York, 1945.

Davis, Frederick B. (Ed.): *The AAF Qualifying Examination,* AAF Reports, Report No. 6, Government Printing Office, Washington, D.C., 1947.

Davis, Frederick B.: *Utilizing Human Talent: Armed Services Selection and Classification Procedures,* American Council of Education, Washington, 1947.

DuBois, Philip H. (Ed.): *The Classification Program,* AAF Research Reports, Report No. 2, Government Printing Office, Washington, D.C., 1947.

Flanagan, John C. (Ed.): *The Aviation Psychology Program of the Army Air Forces,* AAF Research Reports, Report No. 1, Government Printing Office, Washington, D.C., 1947.

Flanagan, John C., and Berger, Dorothy: Research for and by the Armed Forces, *Rev. Educ. Res.,* 1948, **18,** 615–641.

Guilford, J. P. (Ed.), *Printed Classification Tests,* AAF Research Reports, Report No. 5, Government Printing Office, Washington, D.C., 1947.

National Research Council, Committee on Underseas Warfare, Panel on Psychology and Physiology: *A Survey Report on Human Factors in Underseas Warfare,* National Research Council, Washington, D.C., 1949.

National Research Council, Committee on Underseas Warfare, Panel on Psychology and Physiology: *Psychology for the Fighting Man,* Infantry Journal, Washington, D.C., 1943.

National Research Council, Committee on Underseas Warfare, Panel on Psychology and Physiology: *Psychology for the Returning Serviceman,* Infantry Journal, Washington, D.C., 1945.

Stouffer, S. A., *et al.: The American Soldier: Adjustment during Army Life,* Vol. I; *The American Soldier: Combat and Its Aftermath,* Princeton University Press, Princeton, N.J., 1949.

Stuit, Dewey B.: *Personnel Research and Test Development in the Bureau of Navy Personnel,* Princeton University Press, Princeton, N.J., 1947.

Thorndike, Robert L.: *Personnel Selection,* John Wiley & Sons, Inc., New York, 1949.

PSYCHOLOGY IN MUSIC AND ART[1]

Music and art are branches of aesthetics and are usually considered to be entertaining, enjoyable, "highbrow," but useless, impractical, and above all unscientific. Musicians and artists are stereotyped as "peculiar" and highly emotional. Fortunately, there is ample evidence that both music and art are entertaining and enjoyable to be sure, but also useful, practical, and very scientific. No branch of physics is more exact than the frequency, the force, the resonance, of sound. No branch of chemistry is more exact than the composition of color, and no phase of engineering is more important than that of design. This

[1] This chapter was written by Dr. Gunborg Berglund-Gray, former Assistant Professor of Speech in the University of Georgia.

chapter will review some of the uses psychology has made of these two great fields of aesthetics.

PSYCHOLOGY OF MUSIC

While music is as old as civilization itself, it is only in comparatively recent years that it has been the object of scientific investigation. Musicians have traditionally considered music to be an art that is so intangible that it cannot be studied by scientific procedures. However, the trend now is to consider music to be composed of quantitative and measurable sound waves that have both quantitative and qualitative effects on its hearers. Methods have been developed for measuring sound waves and reducing them to scientific simplicity. Progress has been made in analyzing feeling and interpretative reactions to the extent that measurement would seem to be a future probability. In other words, the art of music is slowly becoming the science of music.

PSYCHOLOGICAL PRINCIPLES OF MUSIC

Seashore[2] has stated 20 basic principles of the psychology of music that are worth careful consideration.

1. The only medium by which music can be conveyed from the musician to the listener is the sound wave.
2. Sound waves have four characteristics that are variable and measurable. They are frequency, intensity, duration, and form. All can be traced to variables in vibration at the point of origin of the sound waves.
3. The psychological equivalents of these four characteristics of sound are pitch, loudness, time, and timbre. Combinations of these make up harmony, volume, rhythm, and tone quality.
4. There are illusions in hearing as well as in seeing, and the sounds we hear are not always in accordance with the sound waves that have been produced. The nature of the ear is such that certain characteristics of sound waves are selected and others are subdued. The sound heard is often more pleasing than it would have been if all characteristics had functioned equally. For example, the vibrato as heard is considerably reduced in intensity from its existence in sound waves.
5. Musical art is not the production of sounds that are fixed and regular. Rigid pitch, uniform intensity, pure tone, and perfect harmony do not make musical art—that which people enjoy hearing. It is variation from the mechanically perfect that listeners acclaim as pleasing music.
6. There is a basic starting point (zero) in the measurement of each of the four components of sound waves. Intensity begins with silence, form with pure tone, duration with zero duration, and frequency with an arbitrary tone.

[2] Seashore, C. E., *Psychology of Music,* pp. 28–32, McGraw-Hill Book Company, Inc., New York, 1938.

7. Understanding the physical and psychological elements of sound makes it possible to define each element accurately. Ambiguous and meaningless terminology can thus be eliminated from the field of music.

8. Pitch, intensity, and time can be represented graphically in a musical pattern score that has both musical and scientific meaning. Since timbre is of more complex nature it is recorded in a series by itself in the form of tonal spectra.

9. It is possible to set up norms of musical performance in terms of objective measurement.

10. Better music can be produced because of scientific research and experimental procedures.

11. All theories of musical aesthetics can be scientifically analyzed and experimentally studied.

12. It is likely to be found that music has therapeutic value in clinical psychology.

13. It is now possible to study the objective measurement of musical talent in relation to the measurement of other aptitudes in the total personality, in solving such problems of musical guidance as "the musical medium, the extent of proposed training, and the object served in the musical pursuit."

14. In giving musical guidance, it is necessary to supplement scientific measurement with adequate audition, case history, consideration of personality traits, and the recognition of human resourcefulness.

15. While all musical performance depends on the mastery of fundamental skills that were isolated and learned as definite techniques, in artistic performance these habits must be so integrated that they are a part of the whole and do not stand out as separate skills or techniques.

16. To promote the acquisition of musical techniques, instrumental aids may be used. For example, frequency, intensity, duration, and form can all be quantitatively indicated at the time the tone is made.

17. With the use of scientific measurement in music, the composer and the performer alike will be faced with new problems constantly. "The listener will always be expecting something new."

18. Public school music must be the first to adopt the scientific approach and adjust its methods of teaching accordingly.

19. The psychology of music is not apart from fundamental psychology but a part of it. It is merely an adaptation of the psychological principles of sensation, perception, learning, thinking, feeling, and action, to the production and enjoyment of music.

20. A nonmusical psychologist can record cold musical facts, but only a musician with scientific training can interpret them.

Tests in Music

The Seashore Measures of Musical Talent are perhaps the best known music tests. They appeared first in 1919 and were revised in 1939. There are two series, each testing the same talents. Series A is designed for use with unselected groups and is more of a general screening test. Series B is intended for use where greater diagnosis is desired. The tests measure accuracy in judgment of variations in pitch, loudness, time, rhythm, timbre, and tonal memory. The variations are recorded on phonograph records. In giving the test for pitch discrimination, for example, the examiner says

> You will hear two tones in rapid succession. The second tone is either higher or lower in pitch than the first. You are to mark on the test blank in the proper column whether the second tone is higher or lower than the first.[3]

Thus, in measuring the sense of pitch, pitch is the only variable. All other components are kept constant. Likewise, in measuring the sense of time, two notes of the same pitch but differing in length, or duration, are sounded. The testee is asked to indicate whether the second note is longer or shorter than the first.

It is advisable, if possible, to repeat the test at least once. This gives a more reliable score. In all cases, the score is the total number of correct judgments.

Reliability correlations range from .69 to .89. When the odd-numbered items were correlated with the even-number items (and the Spearman-Brown prophecy formula applied) the results for Series B were as follows:

Pitch................ .78
Loudness............. .77
Time................ .70
Timbre.............. .72
Rhythm............. .72
Tonal Memory........ .89

The validity of these tests is indicated in a study by Stanton[4] at the Eastman School of Music. Entering students were given the Seashore music tests and an intelligence test. On the basis of both tests they were rated in five classifications—*safe*, or likely to succeed in music school; *probable*, or those who will likely make satisfactory musical progress if conditions are favorable; *possible*, or those who might succeed in music but the odds are against them; *doubtful*, or those who will not "carry the work of the course with sufficient credit or satisfaction to warrant the effort involved"; and *discouraged*, or those who "are obviously not fitted to carry on the regular course work in a music

[3] Seashore, C. E., Lewis, D., and Saetveit, J. G., *Manual of Instructions and Interpretations for the Seashore Measures of Musical Talent*, Radio Corporation of America, 1939.

[4] Stanton, H. M., The Measurement of Musical Talent, *Univ. Ia. Stud. Psychol. Music*, II, 1935.

school." Of 565 students who graduated within 4 years, "the percentages graduating from the groups classified as discouraged, doubtful, possible, probable, and safe were 17, 23, 33, 42, and 60 respectively." Obviously, the tests were predictive.

More recently Manor[5] studied the relation of musical aptitude in fourth-grade children, as measured by the Seashore tests, to musical achievement. He found that the highest correlations with achievement were for pitch (.49), tonal memory (.32), rhythm (.21), and tonette scores (.41). The relationships were not considered to be of value in guidance.

However, the manual of instructions states that: "As measuring instruments they are fully adequate, but the use of them requires tact, skill, ability to motivate, favorable atmosphere, and wisdom in interpretation."

The Kwalwasser-Dykema Musical Tests, like the Seashore tests, use phonograph records and measure various forms of music discrimination. There are 10 parts or tests in the battery: Tonal Memory, Quality Discrimination, Intensity Discrimination, Tonal Movement, Time Discrimination, Rhythm Discrimination, Pitch Discrimination, Melodic Taste, Pitch Imagery, and Rhythm Imagery.

In the quality discrimination test two tones are sounded twice, sometimes on the same instrument and sometimes on different instruments. If two instruments are used, the quality between the two soundings is sufficiently different to reveal the fact to one who has keen quality discrimination.

The tonal movement test "measures the ability to judge the tendency of a succession of tones to proceed to a point of rest." There are 30 patterns of four tones each, all incomplete without a fifth tone. The testee must decide whether the fifth tone should be higher or lower than the fourth tone to complete the melodic progression.

In the melodic taste test the opening phrases of two short melodies are identical but the closing phrases are different. The testee chooses which of the closing phrases makes the best melody.

Neither the reliability nor the validity of these tests is mentioned in the manual. However, Manzer and Marowitz[6] gave the battery to 101 college sophomores and juniors and then repeated it a few days later. They computed the coefficients for each of the subtests between the two testings and found the following reliability correlations: tonal memory, .73; quality discrimination, .32; intensity discrimination, .05;

[5] Manor, H. C., A Study in Prognosis: The Guidance Value of Selected Measures of Musical Aptitude, *J. Educ. Psychol.,* 1950, **41,** 31–50.

[6] Manzer, G. W., and Marowitz, S., The Performance of a Group of College Students on the Kwalwasser-Dykema Tests, *J. Appl. Psychol.,* 1935, **29,** 331–346.

time discrimination, .43; and rhythm discrimination, .48. Except for tonal memory, these are all too low for effective measurement.

Weiner[7] gave the Kwalwasser-Dykema tests to 100 students in the High School of Music and Art in New York City. One year later he repeated them and computed the correlations. For tonal memory the coefficient of correlation was .56, for quality discrimination it was .40, for intensity discrimination .21, for rhythm discrimination .08, and for time discrimination .50.

The low validity of the test is indicated in a study by Bienstock,[8] who correlated the scores on five of the Kwalwasser-Dykema tests (tonal memory, quality discrimination, intensity discrimination, time discrimination, and rhythm discrimination) with the classroom marks made in music by 80 students in a music school. The correlations ranged from —.15 to .43 with an average of .14.

The Drake Tests of Musical Talent[9] are in four parts—test of musical memory, test of interval discrimination, test of retentivity, and test of intuition. The first two are best known and have highest reliability and validity.

The musical memory test consists of 24 two-measure melodies each of which is repeated with four possible variations—same with no change, change in key, change in time, and change in note or notes. The testee records on an answer sheet whether the repetition is the same (S), or different in key (K), or different in time (T), or different in note (N). The standard or base melodies increase in difficulty and the variations of each increase in number up to seven. The author claims a reliability coefficient (by test repetition) of .93 and a validity coefficient (with teachers' estimates) of .67.

The interval discrimination test requires that the testee choose the longer of each of 80 pairs of intervals. The first interval is always between tones that are below middle C and the second is between tones higher in pitch. In the first half of the test, the intervals become progressively shorter, and in the last half they become longer. For example, in Trial 1 the first interval is 11 half steps and the second is 4 half steps; in Trial 40 the first interval is 16 half steps and the second is 15 half steps. A reliability coefficient of .83 (split-half method) is claimed for the test and a validity coefficient of .35 (with teacher estimates).

The retentivity test is intended to measure the more elemental factors

[7] Weiner, M., The Effects of Home Practice on Music Ability as Measured by Five of the Kwalwasser-Dykema Tests, Master's Thesis, No. 374, School of Education, College of the City of New York.

[8] Bienstock, S. F., A Predictive Study of Musical Achievement, *J. Genet. Psychol.,* 1942, **41,** 135–145.

[9] Drake, R. M., Four New Tests of Musical Talent, *J. Appl. Psychol.,* 1933, **17,** 136–147.

of melody. It developed primarily as a test of absolute pitch, or memory for isolated tones. It is really a memory test for interval, rate (given by a metronome), and three tones. The reliability is .76 for the entire test and .61 for the tone part alone (absolute pitch). When compared with teachers' estimates, the correlation is .47 for music students.

The intuition test is supposed to measure "expression and feeling for musical form," which is assumed to be innate and unaffected by musical training. It is a measure of the ability to distinguish between a proper and an improper answer to an unfinished musical theme. In the test, two musical phrases are given (or played); the testee decides whether or not the second is a proper complement of the first. There are 72 such pairs of phrases. Both the coefficient of reliability and the coefficient of validity are low (below .40).

The Drake tests are not presented on the phonograph but on the piano. Obviously, the test administrator must be skilled in playing various parts of the test and even then he introduces a possible additional variable.

Drake[10] made a careful study of the reliability and validity of a number of music tests using several groups of English school children as subjects. The validity and reliability correlations for the three batteries discussed above are given in Table 18–1. As Drake concludes, only three tests of the three batteries have sufficiently high reliability and validity coefficients to make them useful instruments of measurement. These have been starred in Table 18–1.

The Whistler-Thorpe Musical Aptitude Tests.[11] In these tests the examiner plays the scores from the manual and the children (grades 4 to 10) answer questions regarding rhythm recognition, pitch discrimination, and the discrimination of chords. The reliability of the entire test is .93 while that of separate parts is somewhat lower. The correlation with teachers' estimates of musical aptitude ranges from .56 to .37, or .78 to .52 when corrected for attenuation. There are percentile norms for grades 4 to 10 based on 2,000 cases.

The Lundin Musical Ability Test. Because of the low validity, and therefore reduced usefulness, of other musical aptitude tests, Lundin attempted to construct a battery of musical tests which measure "a number of acquired behaviors built up through a process of interaction of the individual with musical stimuli over a period of time."[12] There are five separate parts measuring (1) interval discrimination, or ability to recognize two musical steps as being the same or different;

[10] Drake, R. M., The Validity and Reliability of Tests of Musical Talent, *J. Appl. Psychol.*, 1933, **17**, 447–458.

[11] Published by the California Test Bureau, Los Angeles, Calif.

[12] Lundin, R. W., The Development and Validation of a Set of Musical Ability Tests, *Psychol. Monogr.*, 1949, **63**, No. 10.

Table 18–1. Coefficients of Validity and Reliability for Three Music Tests

Tests	Validity			Reliability
Drake tests:				
*Musical memory..................	.671,	.546,	.660	.93, .91, .85
Interval discrimination..............	.585,	.421,	.770	.74, .83, .43
Retentivity........................	.546,	.387,	.520	.76, .73, .53
Intuition.........................	.361,	.355		
Seashore tests:				
*Pitch...........................	.270,	.315,	.534	.72, .84
Intensity........................	.051,	.143,	.157	.85, .88
*Tonal memory...................	.334,	.418,	.114	.94, .86
Time.............................	.149,	.383,	.414	.68, .70
Rhythm..........................	.084,	.367		.68, .48
Consonance......................	−.030,			.30
Kwalwasser-Dykema tests:				
Quality..........................	.171,	.241		.66, .39
Melodic taste.....................	−.132,	−.108,	−.089	.61, .40
Pitch............................	−.239,	−.003		.39
Tonal memory....................	.417	.255		.55, .57
Tonal movement..................	.155	.238,	−.027	.85, .73

* Starred tests have satisfactory reliability and validity.

(2) melodic transposition, or the ability to recognize a melody when it is transposed to a different key; (3) mode discrimination, or the ability to recognize chords of the same harmonic structure; (4) melodic sequences, or the ability to recognize a fourth melody as the same or different from three (all the same) preceding it; and (5) rhythmic sequences, or the ability to recognize a fourth rhythmic pattern as the same or different from three (all the same) preceding it. The tests were all phonograph records. The first four were recordings of a Hammond electric organ and the fifth was a recording of a piano.

The reliability of the total test was .89 when administered to a group of musicians, and .85 when administered to an unselected group. When correlated with music teachers' ratings, the validity was .69 for the entire test. The critical ratio of the difference between the mean score (147.68) of the musician group and that of the unselected group (118.43) was 21.51. This test has a low correlation with intelligence (.15) and also with the Seashore and the Drake musical tests.

Musical Achievement Tests. The tests discussed above are supposed to test aptitude or capacity to learn musical function readily. There are also tests of musical accomplishment. They answer the question, how much musical function (singing, playing and instrument, sight reading, etc.) has already been learned.

The Knuth Achievement Tests in Music are on three levels—for grades 3 and 4, for grades 5 and 6, and for grades 7 to 12. They are all multiple choice in form. The test administrator plays a few measures on the piano from one of four musical scores on the test. The student then checks the melody played. There are 40 such exercises at each test level and the score is the total number right.

The *McCauley Examination in Public School Music* is for grades 4 to 9. It measures sight and oral identification of melodies; information about musical compositions, instruments, terminology, and famous musicians; and ability to identify notes, rest values, keys, and chromatics. The test is timed and takes 100 minutes to administer.

The *Gildersleeve-Soper Musical Achievement Test* is for grades 4 to 8 and measures knowledge of musical terms, musical notations, musical symbols, familiar melodies, types of compositions, and composers. Centile norms are based on 3,000 cases.

The *Providence Inventory Test in Music* is in 10 parts—Naming Notes, Placing "Do," Naming Note Values, Naming Key Signatures, Naming Measure Signatures, Naming Rest Values, Naming Syllables, Naming Melodies, Naming Syllables (Bass Staff), and Naming Symbols. The total test takes but 28 minutes. The content and method of scoring are both objective.

TYPICAL STUDIES IN THE PSYCHOLOGY OF MUSIC

Scientific research must always follow in the wake of scientific measurement. As more accurate tests are developed, more accurate and significant research will be performed. The following studies are the results of the development of the musical tests reviewed above.

Ross[13] studied the relation of musical talent to general intelligence and scholastic achievement on both the elementary and high school levels. He gave 1,541 pupils in grades 5 to 12 the Seashore Tests of Musical Talent, the Terman Group Test of Mental Ability, and the Stanford Achievement Tests.

There were low but positive relationships between musical talent and intelligence. The correlations between intelligence and the musical tests were as follows: pitch, .25; intensity, .12; time, .17; consonance, .21; tonal memory, .26; and rhythm, .16. The correlations indicated no relation between musical talent and reading and arithmetic abilities. The composite achievement scores correlated with the sense of pitch .20, with intensity .25, with consonance .26, and with tonal memory .31.

It was found that those pupils from the eleventh and twelfth grades who elected music had a mean I.Q. of 110, which was three points above the average for the entire group in these two grades.

[13] Ross, V. R., Relationship between Intelligence, Scholastic Achievement, and Musical Talent, *J. Juv. Res.*, 1936, 20, 47–64.

In the elementary grades, the upper 10 per cent on the Seashore tests were found to equal or excel 79 per cent of their classmates in reading, 77 per cent of them in arithmetic, and 80 per cent on the whole achievement test battery. The lowest 25 per cent on the musical tests were found to be low on both the intelligence test and the achievement tests.

Drake[14] administered a battery of music tests selected from his own, the Kwalwasser-Dykema, and the Seashore batteries to a group of 163 thirteen-year-old English boys. He then correlated the resulting scores with intelligence. The r's ranged from .03 to .27. In another experiment he administered his own test of musical talent and the Otis Higher Examination to a group of 158 American college women. The correlation was .28. The music test scores correlated .16 with college grades.

Hollingworth[15] studied the amount of musical talent among intellectually superior children. She found that children who are in the upper centile on intelligence tests are no better than a random sampling of children of the same chronological age on the Seashore music tests. The superior children had mean centile scores on the music tests as follows: pitch 46.7, intensity 50.0, time 58.0, consonance 47.9, and tonal memory 52.3. (Norms appropriate for their chronological age, eight to eleven, were used.)

Sward[16] studied the percentage of Jewish people in symphony orchestras in the United States. In 12 of the best-known symphony orchestras he found that 34 per cent of the string section and 51 per cent of the first-violin players were Jewish. In 11 of the 12 cities where these orchestras were located, Jews made up only 16 per cent of the population. Of the solo artists who appeared with the Boston, Chicago, New York, and Philadelphia orchestras for 12 seasons (1920 to 1933), 47.5 per cent of the violinists and 35.4 per cent of the pianists were Jewish. See Table 18–2 for these data.

Gundlach[17] made an interesting study of the relation of musical structure to its effect on hearers. He played 40 selected fragments (recorded) from classical piano solos and orchestral compositions to 102 auditors (54 were advanced music students). The listeners reported what mood they believed the composer was trying to express in each fragment. He then analyzed the music on the basis of seven structural characteristics—loudness, tempo, average pitch, rhythm,

[14] Drake, R. M., The Relation of Musical Talent to Intelligence and Success in School, *J. Musicol.*, 1940, **2**, 38–44.

[15] Hollingworth, L. S., Music Sensitivity of Children Who Test above 135 I.Q., *J. Educ. Psychol.*, 1926, **17**, 95–107.

[16] Sward, K., Jewish Musicality in America, *J. Appl. Psychol.*, 1933, **17**, 675–712.

[17] Gundlach, R. H., Factors Determining the Characterization of Phrases, *Amer. J. Psychol.*, 1935, **47**, 624–643.

Table 18–2. Jewish Musicians in Symphony Orchestras

	Number	Jewish	Per cent
Symphony players:			
String section..............................	664	226	34.0
Wind section...............................	167	16	9.6
Brass section..............................	151	16	9.4
Percussion section.........................	46	11	23.9
Total.................................	1,048	269	25.7
Solo artists:			
Violinists.................................	59	28	47.5
Pianists..................................	65	23	35.4
Violincellists.............................	21	3	14.3
Total.................................	145	54	37.2
Jews in:			
General population.........................	.....	...	3.58
Eleven symphony cities.....................	.....	...	16.1

Table 18–3. Moods Most Frequently Associated with Certain Structural
Characteristics of Music

Structural Characteristics	Moods
Tempo:	
Fast.......................	Animated, glad, uneasy
Slow.......................	Dignified, tranquil, somber, delicate, melancholy, mournful
Rhythm:	
Smooth....................	Brilliant, animated, glad
Rough, irregular.............	Uneasy, grotesque
Intensity:	
Loud......................	Triumphant, animated, brilliant
Soft.......................	Delicate, tranquil, sentimental, melancholy
Pitch:	
High.......................	Brilliant, sentimental, whimsical
Low.......................	Mournful, somber, dignified
Melodic range:	
Wide......................	Brilliant
Narrow....................	Mournful, somber
Orchestral range:	
Wide......................	Uneasy, animated
Narrow....................	Tranquil, delicate, dignified
Melodic steps:	
Large......................	Triumphant, exalted, glad
Small......................	Uneasy, mournful

melodic range, orchestral range, and variety of step widths between successive notes.

The results indicated (see Table 18–3) that musical structure tends to produce certain characteristic moods or feelings with fair uniformity, regardless of the musical training of the listeners. Thus, Handel's

Harmonious Blacksmith produced a mood of dignity while the scherzo from Dvorak's *New World Symphony* produced an animated mood. The former is predominantly slow in tempo while the latter is fast.

The effects of jazz and dirge music on typewriting were studied by Jensen.[18] He checked the words and errors per minute made by a group of eleventh- and twelfth-grade pupils during periods of no music, jazz music, and dirge music. He found that the average speed was 33.64, 31.06, and 32.93 words per minute for the three periods. The errors were .937, 1.21, and .907 per minute. Jazz music decreased speed and increased errors, while dirge music decreased speed and also errors.

These and other studies seem to justify the conclusion that when musical cadence is just slightly faster than the tempo of the activity being performed, the activity is increased. If the music is of varied tempo or just slightly slower than the activity, it then tends to reduce the speed of the activity.

Music in Industry. Music is now recognized as having a significant effect on feelings of boredom in performing short-cycle jobs in industry.[19] Wyatt and Langdon[20] studied the effects of phonograph music in industry on the production of paper snappers, a short-cycle job that takes only 30 seconds. Production was carefully noted for 30 days without music, then for 40 days with phonograph music distributed throughout the day in various ways, and again for 25 days without music. Music definitely increased production from 2.6 per cent to 6.0 per cent, depending on the time of day it was played.

The effect of amplified phonograph music on scrappage in the manufacture of radio tubes was studied by Humes.[21] He found that in a 3-week period of no music there was a mean hourly scrappage of 3.97 per cent. When slow music (63 to 80 beats per minute) was introduced for an hour and 15 minutes per day there was a mean hourly scrappage of only 2.84 per cent. When fast music (104 to 152 beats per minute) was played for the same period there was a mean scrappage of 2.88 per cent per hour. Then, when programs of familiar, new, and subtle music were arranged and played for an hour and 15 minutes each day, the mean hourly scrappage was 3.46 per cent. The differences in scrappage between the three music periods and the no-music period were all statistically significant. (Critical ratios were 7.24, 8.46, and 3.21, respectively.)

[18] Jensen, M. B., The Influence of Jazz and Dirge Music on the Speed and Accuracy of Typing, *J. Educ. Psychol.*, 1931, 32, 458–462.

[19] See Gray, J. S., *Psychology in Industry*, Chap. 10, McGraw-Hill Book Company, Inc., New York, 1952.

[20] Wyatt, S., and Langdon, J. N., *Fatigue and Boredom in Repetitive Type Work*, Industrial Health Research Board, London, 1938, No. 77.

[21] Humes, J., Effects of Occupational Music on Scrappage in the Manufacture of Radio Tubes, *J. Appl. Psychol.*, 1941, 25, 573–587.

Smith[22] studied the effects of varied amounts of music on employee attitude, production efficiency, and accidents, in radio assembly. More than one thousand employees (most of them women) took part; 58 per cent of the employees were between the ages of twenty and thirty. The experiment lasted 8 weeks. The program of music was arranged so that one day in each week there was no music; one day there was 1 hour of music; one day there were 2 hours of music; one day there were 3 hours; one day 4 hours; and one day 5 hours. The arrangement rotated every week so that Monday was a no-music day one week, a 4-hour music day the next week, a 1-hour music day the next week, etc.

Employee attitude toward this music was very favorable. The music was "extremely pleasant" to 74 per cent of the employees; it was "quite pleasant" to 22 per cent; it was "mildly pleasant" to 2 per cent; and 2 per cent did not care for it at all. The "no-music" day of the week was always the most unpopular day. About half the employees asked for music "all the time."

On the music days average production exceeded that of the no-music days 17.3 per cent for the night shift and 7.2 per cent for the day shift. Table 18–4 shows the gains in production due to music and the con-

Table 18–4. Production Gains Due to Varied Amounts of Music and Confidence Level of Gains

Hours of music	Production gain		Confidence level, per cent
	Amount	Per cent	
Day shift:			
1	9.5	12.0	2
2	8.4	10.6	4
3	3.0	3.8	25
4	5.4	6.8	15
5	3.1	3.9	25
Night shift:			
1	8.0	13.2	10
2	12.0	19.8	1
3	9.6	15.8	5
4	14.9	24.5	0.3
5	8.1	13.3	2

fidence levels of those gains. There were more effects of music on the night shift than on the day shift, but this may have resulted from boredom being greater at night than in the daytime. Smith thinks that, since the level of day production was higher than that of the night

[22] Smith, H. C., *Music in Relation to Employee Attitude, Work Production and Industrial Accidents*, *Appl. Psychol. Monogr.*, 1947, No. 14.

shift, there was less room for improvement in the day production. Production of the day shift without music was still greater than night-shift production with music. Average hourly production for the two shifts with and without music was as follows:

Shift	No music	Music
Day..........	79.1	84.8
Night.........	60.7	71.2

The study did not show such definite effects of music on accidents. One shift had a slight increase in accidents on music days (a difference significant at the 5 per cent level of confidence), but the influence of music on accident frequency for all three shifts was exactly zero.

PSYCHOLOGY IN ART

The average person does not realize that art functions in every phase of daily existence. Too often, art is regarded as that which is displayed in the galleries of museums and on the walls of some public buildings. Actually, art is found in every phase of modern life. (1) It is displayed in paintings and reproductions traditionally designated as "art." (2) It is an essential part of all display advertising, whether pictorial or in show windows. (3) It is obvious in the design of all manufactured articles, from flat irons to public buildings. (4) It is a part of the design and color of all clothing, from footwear to milady's headdress. (5) It is the acme of all human behavior, because by definition *art is the product of superior skill*.

The mediums of artistic expression are many—sculpture, painting, drawing, design, in fact, whatever may be one's field of specialty. *Excellence in behavior is art* regardless of the nature or the product of the behavior.

FACTORS COMPOSING ART ABILITY

Artistic ability, like any other ability, is composed of an inherited capacity, or faculty, and learning, or development. The latter is, of course, limited by the former, yet superior artistic capacity is useless without development. Artistic ability is both inherited and acquired.

Meier explains that there are at least six significant factors in artistic ability.[23] Three of these are believed to run in families or are "probably involved in stock heredity," but the others are probably more dependent on environmental development. While these overlap with each other, they do indicate the complexity of artistic ability.

[23] Meier, N. C., Factors in Artistic Aptitude, *Psychol. Monogr.*, 1939, **51**, 140–158; and *Examiners' Handbook: Meier Art Tests*, University of Iowa, Iowa City, 1942.

Craftsmanship aptitude is evidenced in early life in traits of patience, pride in doing things well, good eye-hand coordination, and a tendency to acquire skills easily. Persons with such traits are likely to have ancestors with craftsmanship ability, such as cabinet making, weaving, wood carving, watch and instrument making, engraving, drafting, etc. Evidence for this statement is shown in Table 18–5. Note that the aver-

Table 18–5. Craftsmen in the Ancestry of Students and Artists

Group	N	Per cent with no known craftsmen in ancestry	Average number of craftsmen per person in ancestry
Unselected college students..............	153	36	2.05
Unselected high-school students.........	23	35	1.61
Total..........................	176	35.8	2.00
Artists.............................	58	15	3.59
Art students, art schools..............	282	9	4.74
Art students, colleges.................	230	13	3.98
Art students, high school and normal school...........................	43	13	4.07
Art staff, engraving firm..............	31	6	5.64
Total..........................	644	11.02	4.37

age number of craftsmen in the ancestry of artists and art students is more than twice that of unselected high school and college students.

Volitional perseveration is the "self-initiated desire to carry on sustained planning and assiduous effort leading to the accomplishment of a product satisfying to the craftsman ideal of work." In other words, there is motivation to turn out a product of superior nature. Whether in child or adult, there is a dissatisfaction with accomplishment that does not meet a high standard of excellence. The person with artistic talent is not satisfied with sloppy work. He is a severe critic of his own accomplishments. He perseveres until his high standard of work is reached. He does not have to be forced to turn out better work. He desires excellence.

Aesthetic intelligence is the ease with which the person with art capacity can "assimilate experience which has potential significance for present or future development in a work of art." It is the ability to organize vivid experiences and understand their significance. It consists of segments of general intelligence that are significant in art. The superior artist is usually superior in general intelligence.

Perceptual facility is the "ease and readiness with which the individual responds to and retains experience, particularly that of a visually experienced type." It is the ability to see more and retain it longer. A trip through the country is an exciting adventure for an artist. The ordinary person looks at a tree and sees merely an object that produces shade. The artist looks at the same tree and sees a poem, or a painting, or an object of beauty. The artist does not have to hunt for perceptual meanings; he is always seeing them. For him, life is full of interest. He has habits that "feature adequacy and completeness in examining everything of interest." Details do not escape his notice.

Creative imagination is the ability to select certain significant parts of past experiences and recombine them into a "composition having aesthetic character." A work of art, regardless of the medium, is always an expression of the experiences of the artist—not as they occurred but as they have been recombined and synthesized to portray something of the artist himself. The new is always composed of parts of the old. It is not a duplication of the old but the old in new relationships. Unless the old is shown in new clothing, there is no art. An unretouched photograph is not art. Creative imagination is to select some things for emphasis and other things for omission. The artist is creative when he puts an object in a new setting.

Aesthetic judgment is the ability to discern those relationships that are in accordance with universal principles of all good art. It is the perception of the functioning of aesthetic principles. Whether a drawing be produced by a prehistoric caveman or by a modern artist, if it shows proportion and balance it will meet the approval of all those who have aesthetic judgment. It is "not the application of a series of rules but is something which the individual acquires on the basis possibly of some innate neuro-physical constitution."

These six factors are not equally significant in the production of all art but certainly they are all important. They constitute a basis for further scientific study of artistic behavior.

ART TESTS

The Meier Art Judgment Test[24] is perhaps the best-known test in the field of art. It consists of 100 pairs of pictures, one of each pair differing from the other in some significant detail. The testee chooses which of each pair he prefers. The better picture of each pair was determined by the opinion of 25 art experts. The score is the number of accurate choices plus added weight for certain pairs that have been found to be especially discriminating. Percentile norms are given for adults, senior high school, and junior high school levels.

The reliability of this test is in the high seventies (range .70 to .84), which is regarded as satisfactory. However, the author promises to publish two supplementary tests (on Creative Imagination and Aesthetic

[24] This test was originally known as the Meier-Seashore Art Judgment Test.

Perception) which, when combined with the Art Judgment Test, will measure artistic talent with much greater accuracy. The validity of the test is indicated by the fact that those with known art ability score significantly higher than average individuals. Art school teachers score higher than art school students, and they score higher than senior high school students. Furthermore, art-judgment scores correlate very low with general intelligence (range —.14 to .28), at least indicating that this test is not measuring general intelligence. One research reports a correlation of .46 between test scores and subsequent grades in art classes for 50 students.

The McAdory Art Test[25] is another prominent test of the same nature. This consists of 72 plates, each illustrating some subject in four different ways. The testee ranks all four variations in order of his preference. The subjects are from a wide variety of objects in everyday life, such as furniture, utensils, clothing, architecture, and painting. Some are in black and white, and some are in color. The correct ranking, or the key, has been determined by the consensus of rankings of a large number of experts. Norms are available for each grade from 3 through 12 and for adults.

Reliability coefficients range from .59 to .93, which is high enough for use by trained testers. The correlation with intelligence is low, as are the correlations with scores made on the Meier test. The correlations between scores on this test and subsequent art school grades are also low. In general it is regarded as inferior to the Meier test.

The Lewerenz Visual Art Tests[26] are designed to measure art abilities in the public schools. There are norms for grades three to twelve inclusive. The test has nine subtests that are arranged as follows:

Part I:
   Test 1. Recognition of Proportion
   Test 2. Originality of Line Drawing
Part II:
   Test 3. Observation of Line and Shade
   Test 4. Knowledge of Subject Matter Vocabulary
   Test 5. Visual Memory of Proportion
Part III:
   Test 6. Analysis of Problems in Cylindrical Perspective
   Test 7. Analysis of Problems in Parallel Perspective
   Test 8. Analysis of Problems in Angular Perspective
   Test 9. Recognition of Color

A reliability correlation of .87 is reported for 100 pupils in grades 3 to 9. The validity of the test is indicated by a correlation of .40 between

[25] Published by Teachers College, Columbia Univeristy, New York, 1929.
[26] Lewerenz, A. S., Tests in Fundamental Abilities of Visual Arts, California Test Bureau, Los Angeles, 1927.

scores on the test and marks in art classes for a group of Los Angeles school children.

The Design Judgment Test by Graves consists of 90 items which are designed to measure the appreciation of designs having varied degrees of artistic merit.[27] The art factors involved are unity, dominance, variety, balance, symmetry, proportion, and rhythm. A large number of paired and triple designs were administered to two groups—one consisting of art teachers and students and the other of non-art students. Each individual was asked to select the best design of two or three shown together. Ninety pairs (and triplets) that received the greatest agreement among the art group, and the greatest disagreement between the art group and the non-art group, were then chosen as permanent test items. A score on the test consists of the total number of right selections. The reliability was found to be .83.

The Horn Art Aptitude Inventory[28] consists of three parts—the scribble exercise, the "doodle" exercise, and the imagery test. In the latter, key lines are given and the subject completes a drawing. The scoring is done by comparing with samples, and judgment. Independent scorers correlate as high as .85. The test was found to correlate .53 with grades after an art course was completed.

There are many other tests of artistic ability, but those just mentioned are typical. The Knauber Art Ability Test measures the effects of art training and has norms for grades 7 to 16. The same author also has an Art Vocabulary Test, which has been found useful in school situations. There are a number of art information tests, especially in such over-all survey tests as the Cooperative General Culture Test and the Graduate Record Examination. There are also a number of drawing scales that can be used to rate drawings by children. McCarty and Thorndike have constructed such scales.

INTELLIGENCE AND DRAWINGS

A number of attempts have been made to infer the level of intelligence from the quality of drawings. Binet included two drawings in his famous intelligence scale (a square in the fourth year and a diamond in the seventh). Two intelligence tests have been devised and standardized that consist entirely of drawings. Both are unique and worth brief review.

Miller Drawing Test. Miller[29] took his cue directly from the Binet test and devised a scale of 20 drawings of increasing difficulty (see Fig.

---

[27] Graves, M., *Design Judgment Test*, Psychological Corporation, 1948.

[28] Horn, C. A., and Smith, L. F., The Horn Aptitude Inventory, *J. Appl. Psychol.*, 1945, **29**, 350–355.

[29] Miller J., Intelligence Testing by Drawings, *J. Educ. Psychol.*, 1938, **29**, 390–394.

18–1). The testee is asked to copy the figures as they are shown to him, one at a time, on white cardboards 11 by 15 in. There is no time limit and the size of the copy is disregarded. Norms were obtained for grades 4 to 12, inclusive.

A reliability correlation of .87 was found when the test was read-ministered to 300 children. It correlated with scores on the Pintner-Cunningham Primary Mental Test .75, with children in kindergarten and first grade as subjects. The Otis Primary Test was used in grades

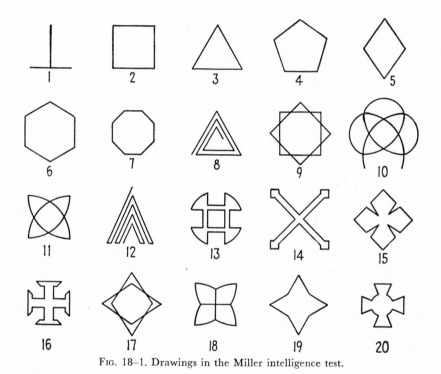

Fig. 18–1. Drawings in the Miller intelligence test.

2 to 5, and the correlation was .72 for 400 children. The Henmon-Nelson Test of Mental Ability was used in the upper grades, and the correlation was .69. All the children tested were in Wilkes-Barre, Pennsylvania. When the test results were compared with teachers' judgments of pupils' intelligence, a correlation of .85 was found for the kindergarten and first grade, .75 for the second grade, and .73 for the third grade.

This test is easily administered and quickly scored. The correlations with other tests seem too high in light of the reliability correlation of .87, but further research is now in progress.

Goodenough Draw-a-man Test. A more prominent test of intelligence by drawings is by Goodenough.[30] She believes that "the changes in children's drawings that take place from age to age as well as the difference between the drawings of children of the same age have been shown to be far more closely related to general intelligence than to special artistic talent in children under the age of ten or eleven years."[31]

Fig. 18–2. Drawings and their mental-age equivalents.

Consequently, she has developed a test in which children are instructed to "make a picture of a man. Make the very best picture you can. Take your time and work very carefully." Then the drawings are scored according to very objective instructions, and the mental age determined from a table for ages four to twelve inclusive. Typical drawings and the mental ages they indicate after being scored are shown in Fig. 18–2.

The reliability was originally reported by Goodenough to be .94 on

[30] Goodenough, F. L., *Measurements of Intelligence by Drawings,* World Book Company, Yonkers, N.Y., 1926.

[31] Goodenough, F. L., *Developmental Psychology,* p. 333, Appleton-Century-Crofts, Inc., New York, 1934.

retest and .77 by the split-half method. However, Williams[32] has since found that the scoring is not entirely objective and there is a discrepancy when different scorers rate the same drawing. He found that correlations between separate ratings ranged from .80 to .96. McCarthy[33] found that scorers do not agree with themselves when they rerate a drawing. Such discrepancies amounting to a year or more in mental age were found in 12.4 per cent of the cases. She found a split-half reliability of .89, but only .68 on retest.

Like the Miller test, the validity of the Goodenough test is surprisingly high. As originally reported by Goodenough, the correlations with the Stanford-Binet Test were as follows: fourth grade, .86; fifth grade, .70; sixth grade, .83; seventh grade, .72; eighth grade, .56; ninth grade, .73; tenth grade, .85; average for all grades, .76. On the whole, these correlations are substantiated by later studies.

It must be emphasized that drawing tests, such as the two just discussed, are not indicative of artistic ability. Superior drawings indicate superior intelligence but not superior art ability. Goodenough even doubts that children under twelve, except in rare instances, ever possess special artistic talent. She says, "In spite of careful search, both in connection with this study and during a year spent as field worker in the Stanford University gifted-children survey, the writer has been unable to locate a single child under the age of twelve years whose drawings appeared to possess artistic merit of a degree at all comparable to the musical genius occasionally shown by children of this age."[34]

TYPICAL STUDIES IN THE PSYCHOLOGY OF ART

There have been a large number of significant investigations in the field of art that cannot be reviewed in this chapter. Some of them are pure research and deal with such problems as color vision, conditioning, and design perception. Others are in the applied field and have already affected the nature of advertising and design.[35]

Using his visual art tests, mentioned above, Lewerenz[36] studied *sex differences* among school children in Los Angeles. He found that the girls were superior in only two of the nine abilities measured—originality of line drawing, and recognition of color (see Fig. 18–3).

[32] Williams, J. H., Validity and Reliability of the Goodenough Intelligence Test, *Sch. & Soc.,* 1935, **41,** 653–656.

[33] McCarthy, Dorothea, A Study of Reliability of the Goodenough Drawing Test of Intelligence, *J. Psychol.,* 1944, **18,** 201–215.

[34] Goodenough, F. L., *Measurements of Intelligence by Drawings,* p. 53, World Book Company, Yonkers, N.Y., 1926.

[35] Studies of the significance of color in advertising are reviewed in Chap. 16.

[36] Lewerenz, A. S., Sex Differences on Ability Tests in Art, *J. Educ. Psychol.,* 1918, **19,** 629–635.

Brandt[37] has devised a camera that records eye movements and fixations while the subject is looking at a picture. By the use of this apparatus such problems are studied as the following: areas of primary attention, effect of color on identical layouts, effects of mass on the attention value of various units, types of pictures that attract greatest interest, etc. It is probable that research with this device will make the commercial use of art so objective that in the future it will be used only in the manner that is most effective.

Michaels[38] studied color preferences among school children at various ages. Except for age six, there was high agreement for blue and red as favorite colors and for green and yellow as the colors least favored.

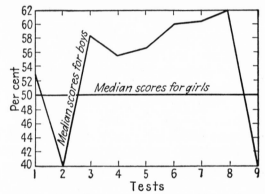

Fig. 18–3. Comparison of median scores for boys with median scores for girls on the Lewerenz tests in visual art.

Violet and orange were the intermediate colors, and the agreement was less reliable (see Table 18–6).

Katz[39] studied the preferences of school children for traditional and modern paintings. He constructed a test of 64 pairs of paintings, one of which was an accepted painting (chosen from Italian, Dutch, Flemish, French, German, and American art), and the other a modern painting (chosen from the schools of impressionism, expressionism, and cubism). The traditional pictures had all been recommended for study in the New York City elementary schools, while none of the modern pictures had been so recommended. The test was given to 2,437 boys and girls in grades 2 to 6. Each pupil chose the picture in each pair that he liked better. At all grade levels, there was a preference for traditional paint-

[37] Brandt, H. F., of Drake University and *Look* magazine. See also Taylor, E. A., *Controlled Reading*, University of Chicago Press, Chicago, 1937.

[38] Michaels, G. A., Color Reference According to Age, *Amer. J. Psychol.*, 1924, **35**, 79–89.

[39] Katz, E., *Children's Preferences for Traditional and Modern Paintings*, Thesis, Teachers College, Columbia University, New York, 1944.

Table 18–6. Six Colors Ranked According to Preference at Various Age Levels

Age	N	Colors					
		Violet	Green	Blue	Yellow	Orange	Red
6.0 years	27	4	3	5	1	6	2
7.2 years	52	5	3	1	6	4	2
8.1 years	62	4	6	1	3	5	2
9.2 years	58	3	6	1	5	4	2
10.3 years	88	4	6	1	5	3	2
11.2 years	64	2	6	1	5	3	4
12.4 years	84	2	6	1	5	3	4
13.4 years	65	3	5	1	6	4	2
14.3 years	57	5	6	1	4	3	2
15.4 years	18	5	2	1	4	6	3

ings, although this preference decreased in the upper grades and became of less statistical significance. The mean score for traditional pictures was 39.82 and for the modern pictures it was 24.18.

SUMMARY

This chapter reviewed the applications of psychology to two of the major fields of aesthetics—music and art. Seashore's basic psychological principles of music were reviewed and then various tests of musical ability were briefly described. While none of them are sufficiently reliable and valid to be used for more than rough screening, they have been carefully standardized and used for various research purposes. A few typical studies in the psychology of music were reviewed to illustrate the nature of research in this field. Some of the uses of music in industry were indicated.

Meier's diagnosis of art ability was briefly discussed. While art tests do not measure all six of his factors, they are notable steps toward reducing this field of aesthetics to an objective science. Color in advertising and "streamlining" in design are indications of the wide practical uses now being made of art.

RECOMMENDED SUPPLEMENTARY READINGS

Benson, B. E.: *Music and Sound Systems in Industry,* McGraw-Hill Book Company, Inc., New York, 1945.

Farnsworth, Paul Randolph: Musical Taste and Its Measurement and Cultural Nature, Stanford University Publication, *University Series,* No. 1, 1950, Vol. II.

Kerr, Willard A.: Effects of Music on Factory Production, *Appl. Psychol. Monogr.,* 1945.

Lowenfeld, Viktor: *Creative and Mental Growth,* rev. ed., The Macmillan Company, New York, 1952.

Meier, N. C.: Factors in Artistic Aptitude, *Psychol. Monogr.*, 1939, **51**, 140–158.

Meier, N. C.: *Art in Human Affairs,* McGraw-Hill Book Company, Inc., New York, 1942.

Read, Herbert Edward: *Education through Art,* Pantheon Books, New York, 1945.

Schoen, M.: *Psychology of Music,* The Ronald Press Company, New York, 1940.

Seashore, C. E.: *Psychology of Music,* McGraw-Hill Book Company, Inc., New York, 1938.

Seashore, C. E.: *In Search of Beauty in Music,* The Ronald Press Company, New York, 1947.

Soibelman, Doris: *Therapeutic and Industrial Uses of Music, A Review of the Literature,* Columbia University Press, New York, 1948.

Wyatt, Ruth F.: Improvability of Pitch Discrimination, *Psychol. Monogr.*, 1945, **58**, No. 2.

Chapter 19

PUBLIC OPINION AND PROPAGANDA[1]

PUBLIC OPINION

The behavior of the individual is controlled by the facts as he sees them. If I have been bitten by a dog, new dogs will look dangerous to

[1] This chapter was written by Dr. Ross Stagner, Professor of Psychology at the University of Illinois.

me, and my actions toward them will be protective or hostile. If I have been told that labor unions are dangerous, my opinions of them may likewise be unfavorable. A man who sees Negroes as dirty, Mexicans as untrustworthy, and Russians as cruel will behave toward persons of these groups in terms of his perception. What must be emphasized vigorously is that, in all these instances, it is perception, not physical reality, which governs. The same country looks friendly to one observer, inimical to another. Each behaves in accordance with his own perception.

This analysis means that we are pursuing a vain hope when we talk optimistically about settling social conflicts on the basis of "the true facts." Facts are not independent of the observer. Engineers may agree that Germany is building a new railway, but political observers may

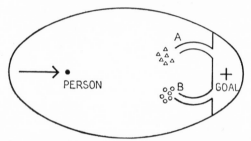

FIG. 19–1. Perception as a guide to a goal. In striving toward a desired goal, the person must choose between various courses of action. Whether he selects *A* or *B* will depend on the attractive or threatening appearance of such acts. Public opinion defines certain policies as valuable or harmful and so guides decisions of leaders in various fields.

see it as a threat to Russia, as a device for bolstering the economy, or as a sop to a political pressure group. What is the "real" fact? Such determinations are virtually impossible.

Social behavior, like individual behavior, consists of effort toward a goal (Fig. 19–1). Motives impel us to seek certain situations and to avoid others. In trying to attain a goal, such as wealth, power, fame, or security, one must choose between alternative courses of action. His choice will depend upon how he perceives these activities.

Purely individual perceptions depend upon one's unique personality, his individual frame of reference. However, we also have shared frames of reference. All Catholics, Methodists, or Moslems have certain religious standards in common, which guide their perceptions of religious events. All Republicans have certain views in common, a shared way of looking at specific political questions. The differences between the British Labor party members and the Conservatives reduce to the fact that men in one group perceive issues in a way which differs from that of the other group.

The existence of a frame of reference makes possible the holding of opinions. If someone asks me what I think of Freud's psychological theories, I can give a coherent answer because I have a frame of reference for viewing this problem. The existence of shared frames of reference makes possible *public opinion*. To the extent that people have standards for judging the Communist party, or the Arab-Israeli conflict, or the high cost of living, opinions can be collected from large numbers of individuals and these opinions tabulated to give us a picture of group trends, the "climate of opinion" on this issue. It should be remembered at all times, of course, that no group holds an opinion. Only individuals have opinions, attitudes, and frames of reference; public opinion is a statistical construct.

Public opinion is nevertheless a powerful factor in decisions by business leaders and government officials. Law enforcement is all but impossible in the face of adverse public opinion; a democratic foreign policy must be acceptable to public opinion; even in a totalitarian state, policy must at least be rationalized as being in line with public opinion, and an elaborate secret-police mechanism is used to report on public feelings. Government policy on many issues (such as the nationalistic tone of Russian propaganda for domestic consumption during the Second World War) is regulated to get the best results in terms of the climate of opinion. Many large corporations now make "market surveys" to determine what features should be built into a new product or what to stress in the advertising program. Even pricing and labor policies are said to be affected somewhat by public-opinion findings.

Public opinion on domestic and foreign policies has a profound bearing on the future welfare of the American people. The approval given to high tariffs and economic nationalism will significantly affect the prospects for enduring peace. On such issues as publicly owned enterprise, social security, and other economic policies, public opinion may well decide for or against dependable prosperity. Even if a majority, by inaction, allows a minority effectively to control national affairs, the majority is to some extent responsible for the failure to take a decisive stand.

In a democracy, this role of public opinion has long been recognized. Even George Washington bowed to, or tried to modify, the opinions of his citizens. George Fort Milton has recently called attention to the great powers of the President as "Chief of Public Opinion." And it is true that a vigorous President can play an important role in leading the people. On the other hand, many of our chief executives have accepted policies personally distasteful to them because convinced of the public demand for such acts.

This serves to emphasize a key point in this chapter: *viz.*, that it is vital to obtain measurements of public opinion by the best scientific methods. Traditionally, Congressmen have talked with their constituents; diplomats have sounded out opinion abroad; straw votes have been cast. But these methods far too often have led to hopelessly inaccurate data. Congressmen usually talk to friends; diplomats move only in upper-class circles; straw votes are subject to a variety of errors.

Public-opinion measurement is rapidly approaching the status of a mature science, based upon modern sociology and social psychology. Naturally we can give only a brief sketch of scientific methods of opinion study in this chapter, but some consideration of methodology is essential to an understanding of the psychological problems which are our primary concern.

METHODS OF STUDY

The basic problems in public-opinion research have been the selection of questions, the method of presenting questions, and the selection of persons to answer the questions. To some extent all these are still controversial. The following summary emphasizes the points on which the experts are in agreement. Let us consider first the problem of choosing the members of the public who are to tell us about their opinions.

Stratified Sampling. To get a perfect picture of opinion on any issue, it is theoretically necessary to interview every person affected by it. This is clearly impossible on topics affecting thousands and millions of individuals. We then turn to the task of obtaining a truly *representative sample* that will give us the trend for the entire population within a specified margin of error. This is the same problem that faces a democratic society; our representative system of government is based upon geographic sampling. Each senator or congressman represents all the citizens of a given area.

Now opinions do differ geographically. Southerners disagree with Northerners, and the Middle West with New England. But differences within regions are greater. Workers and employers, for example, usually have sharper disagreements than characterize regional differences. Persons of little education see public affairs in a manner quite at variance with that of the college graduate.

The science of sampling develops from simple facts such as these. If men and women are found to disagree on many topics, then future polls must represent the sexes proportionately to get a balanced result. If the wealthy, middle-class, and poor people have divergent views, each stratum must be represented in numbers proportional to the number in the whole population. Thus, the well-to-do must be a minority of the group polled rather than a majority, as in the ill-fated Literary

Digest poll of 1936. Racial groups must be allowed a voice proportional to their total size, and so on.[2]

There are four major agencies making opinion surveys in the United States today on the basis outlined, known as *stratified random sampling*. They are the American Institute of Public Opinion, headed by Dr. George Gallup, whose books[3] give a clear, popular account of how the polls work; Fortune Survey, conducted by Elmo Roper; Office of Public Opinion Research, headed by Dr. Hadley Cantril, author of some technical contributions[4] on the science of polling; and the National Opinion Research Center, headed by Dr. H. H. Field. AIPO[5] is financed by the sale of columns to newspapers, and Fortune Survey is handled by *Fortune Magazine*. So far no evidence has appeared to indicate any biasing of either survey by financial domination. OPOR is loosely affiliated with AIPO and also with Princeton University. Both these last two organizations are privately financed and professionally staffed.

The exact layout of the scientific cross section of the American population, used as a basis for national poll results, differs in detail but not in principle for each of the four agencies. As a type we cite the standard NORC sample, which, based on 2,500 people, can identify American opinion trends with a probability of 997 in 1,000 that the margin of error will be less than 3 per cent. Of these 2,500 people, 46 per cent will be male, 54 per cent female; 91 per cent White, 9 per cent Negro; 15 per cent upper economic level, 53 per cent middle, 32 per cent lower; 18 per cent college, 39 per cent high school, 43 per cent grade-school trained; 27 per cent will live in New England, 32 per cent in the Middle West, 29 per cent in the South, and 12 per cent Far West. They will also be properly distributed as to size of city, type of occupation, etc. (These figures are periodically corrected to allow for population changes, *e.g.*, reduction in percentage of men during the war.) Very precise instructions to interviews result in meeting these proportions with very few errors.

For such simple problems as the forecasting of a presidential elec-

[2] If a primary aim of the poll is to predict the outcome of an election, then groups must be balanced on the basis of probable voting. Thus, Southern Negroes encounter voting restrictions which make it necessary to give them reduced representation in a national sample.

[3] Gallup, G., *Guide to Public Opinion Polls*, Princeton University Press, Princeton, N.J., 1948; also (with S. F. Rae) *The Pulse of Democracy*, Simon and Schuster, Inc., New York, 1940.

[4] See, for example, Cantril, H., *Gauging Public Opinion*, Princeton University Press, Princeton, N.J., 1944.

[5] For convenience the polls of the various agencies will hereafter be identified by initials: AIPO is American Institute of Public Opinion; OPOR, the Office of Public Opinion Research; and NORC, the National Opinion Research Center.

tion, the stratified sampling technique is virtually the only new development necessary to ensure dependable results. Public opinion, however, is of great importance on a variety of issues other than the actual choice of candidates.[6] In connection with more complex issues, the polling agencies have grappled with, and are beginning to solve, such questions as the following:

How Should Questions Be Phrased? One of the trickier aspects of opinion surveys has been that of phrasing the item so that it does not predetermine the results. In the early days, opinion polls were often deliberately slanted by loading the question. An advertising man in a frank moment once referred to them as fishing expeditions: "We knew what we wanted and went after it with a poll."

Today the elimination of bias due to faulty question construction seems in the main successful. Double-barreled items are rarely seen nowadays; prestige-bearing terms are mostly weeded out; and unusual words are either eliminated or carefully defined.

A fundamental procedure of all agencies now is to pretest their questions on small groups to see if the meaning is clear. The results of such tests are sometimes startling. Even simple words may carry different meanings for different interviewees. Consider the following OPOR question: "After the war is over, do you think people will have to work harder, about the same, or not so hard as before?" This item looks clear and impartial, yet there are three words that created confusion in the results. It was found that "people" meant "everybody in the United States" to 60 per cent of the persons questioned but meant limited groups to the rest; "harder" meant "longer hours" to 15 per cent, "more carefully and accurately" to 25 per cent, and "against stiffer competition" to 12 per cent. "Before" meant "prewar times" to 50 per cent, "earlier in the war" to 37 per cent, and so on. Before a question is through its pretesting, an attempt is made to iron out all these misunderstandings.

Another problem in phrasing questions arises in providing fair alternatives. Some questions are like, "Have you stopped beating your wife? Answer yes or no." It is not even possible in some cases to decide how many alternatives ought to be shown. NORC once asked the question, "Do you think we ought to start thinking now about the kind of peace we want after the war?" Eighty-one per cent answered in the affirmative. Later they used this form: "Which of these seems better to you: for us to win the war first and then think about the peace, or to

[6] Compare Cantril, H. (Ed.), *Public Opinion 1935–1946* (prepared by Mildred Strunk), Princeton University Press, Princeton, N.J., 1951. In this volume are summarized literally thousands of polls which bear on the intelligent conduct of public affairs in a democracy.

start thinking now about the kind of peace we want after the war?" In this case only 41 per cent endorsed the proposal to start thinking now, because the question implied that such thinking is in contradiction to vigorous effort on behalf of winning the war. Should this alternative be presented or ignored?

This question must also be considered in the light of the fact that a certain number of people manifest what might be called the "yes" tendency; *i.e.*, they tend to agree with whatever proposition is positively presented. Thus some individuals will express themselves as favoring both a high tariff and a low tariff; national isolation and collective security, etc., if these propositions are presented positively and not too close together. So the opinion poller usually tries to correct for this, by reversing his question with half the group or by requiring a choice between two alternative answers.

Early opinion surveys were often loaded with emotional terms and implied arguments. That such loading is highly effective can be demonstrated with the following three versions of the same idea, circulated as an experiment by Fortune Survey:

A	B	C
Do you think that the government should or should not forbid labor in defense industries the right to strike about working conditions?	Because every man is entitled to safe and healthy working conditions, labor (in defense industries) should be allowed to strike for them.	Because working conditions in this country are the best in the world, labor (in defense industries) should not be allowed to strike about them.

The percentage approving a ban on defense strikes was as follows: *A*, 59 per cent; *B*, 45 per cent; *C*, 74 per cent. Obviously, phrasing of items can seriously distort survey results. While the above were intentional and flagrant violations of good presentation, it is possible for an apparently impartial item to be subtly loaded and to give misleading results. Alleged facts about public opinion must never be accepted without a consideration of this possibility. Pressure organizations representing a small group of people are especially anxious to create the appearance of having a wide backing. Surveys not conducted by any of the four agencies mentioned above are thus open to suspicion, although they may be properly set up and handled in good faith.

Do Interviewers Bias Poll Results? The mail ballot has been discarded from opinion-survey work because only the more educated segments of the population, or those with axes to grind, will answer. The use of personal interviews raises another question; does the interviewee tend to give the answers he thinks the interviewer wants or expects?

The facts to date indicate that different interviewers do get results that are biased in certain ways. Most important seems to be appearance and status of the interview. An extreme case was found in an NORC study of Southern Negro opinions, as reported respectively to Negro and White interviewers. It seemed unquestionable here that the Negroes had given biased answers to the interviewer of the dominant race.

How do you think Negroes would be treated if the Japanese conquered the U.S.A.?	Negro interviewer	White interviewer
	Per cent	Per cent
Better...........................	9	2
Same as now.....................	32	20
Worse...........................	25	45

To some extent, interviewers bring back answers loaded in favor of their own views; thus, Republicans err by overestimating the vote for their party; interventionist interviewers found more people agreeing with them, while isolationist interviewers found a larger proportion of isolationists in the population, in the heated days of early 1941; and middle-class interviewers turn up more antilabor attitudes than do working-class interviewers.

The only controls devised so far on this point are, first, to train interviewers to conceal their own views;[7] and second, to use interviewers from varying social and economic groups so that any systematic errors will cancel each other in the final result.

It may be that, if interviewers are allowed to pick their own respondents, they pick people like themselves—perhaps their own friends and neighbors. To control this, some organizations now use *area sampling* (properly stratified, of course), in which the interviewer must go to preselected houses rather than have any personal freedom to choose persons he will question. This method is more expensive than *quota sampling,* which simply requires the interviewer to obtain certain percentages of males, females, Republicans, etc. It is said, however, to give more precise results than the quota sampling procedure.

In some experiments, the interviewer has been ruled out entirely by having the respondent mark a ballot, which is then folded by him and placed in a locked box. This secret voting method encounters difficulties in a population of limited literacy. It does, however, reveal some

[7] In this connection see the standard instructions given all interviewers for NORC: Williams, D., Basic Instructions for Interviews, *Publ. Opin. Quart.*, 1942, 6, 634–641.

hidden attitudes that would be subject to social disapproval if expressed to the interviewer directly; *e.g.*, anti-British or anti-Jewish prejudices. The best future, nonetheless, seems to lie in better training of interviewers rather than in developing the secret-ballot technique.

Who Selects the Question to Be Asked? If opinion polls are to fill their rightful place in a democratic society, they must cover all issues on which public opinion is divided. Yet those selecting poll issues may ignore problems on which they do not care to have light cast; or, more dangerous still, they may be forbidden to ask certain questions. To take some random examples, nobody has asked the people of Russia how they feel about the atom-control controversy. And as far as we know, no one has asked a sample of Americans this question: "In view of General Motors' net profit of $565,000,000 in 1950, do you think O.P.S. should grant them a price increase?" Aside from the ban on polling soldiers, the American government has apparently been fairly careful to avoid arbitrary restrictions on the topics covered by polling agencies. This question of over-all control of the polls can be posed, but the answer goes beyond the limits of this chapter.

Some Special Techniques. The basic technique of current opinion study is the personal interviewing of single individuals, selected by chance but in accordance with fixed sampling rules, on specific questions with specified alternative answers. In recent years the limitations of this procedure have induced the development of a variety of special techniques, each of which is useful for certain purposes. Some of them will be sketched here very briefly.

Follow-up Questions. A bare yes or no answer to a question of a general character may not be very revealing. Some pollsters prepare a battery of follow-up questions to clarify details. NORC conducted a survey on world organization, for example, in which those who wanted to see measures of this type taken for the maintenance of peace were asked to indicate what functions the world organization should have. It was then found that the average American would accept international government if it meant such sacrifices as continued rationing of food, paying more taxes, and keeping part of our army as a sort of international police force; but a majority opposed giving up our armed forces entirely, opposed giving up reparations, and opposed free trade with other countries in the organization. This gives a much clearer picture than the bare statement of approval of a union of nations.

Open-end Interviews. For nationwide sampling purposes, it is necessary that respondents be required to pick one of a fixed set of alternatives. If each person were allowed to answer freely, the tabulation of a national trend would be virtually impossible because of the shades of difference expressed by these varied responses.

There are, however, circumstances under which the free answer or open-end interview is desirable. One is the case in which a question is too complex for the preparation of a reasonable limited number of alternatives. Another arises when the presentation of answer choices might be expected to prejudice the result. A third is found in studies seeking to determine the causal background of opinion.

Open-end interviews must necessarily be conducted by skilled psychologists, as opposed to the average interviewer who is trained only in a specific method. The casual or apparently irrelevant remarks of the interviewee may have considerable meaning for the expert. Suppose, for example, that a man stated vehemently that he would vote for Stevenson against Eisenhower, arguing that a military man is likely to become a dictator. Then he began talking about how autocratic his own father had been. A listener sensitive to emotional reactions could form a pretty accurate judgment on the spot as to the likelihood that the political reaction was merely a displacement of latent hostility toward the father.

This method has been used extensively in studies of nationalist attitudes,[8] morale,[9] and other problems. It is often used at the beginning of a study, to clarify possibilities that may be put into the customary objective form; it is equally valuable as a follow-up to extensive interviewing with the usual technique, in that it gives an opportunity to check theories that may have developed during an investigation.

Panel Studies. When Dr. Gallup reports that there has been an increase in support for reciprocal trade agreements, he means only that the current sample shows a higher proportion in favor than was found earlier. The second sample does not include any of the individuals interviewed on the first occasion. The policy of getting an entirely new group of each survey is a good one, because repeated questioning might introduce a vitiating factor into the situation.

It may, however, be desirable to find out how specific persons change from time to time. During a political campaign, for example, it would be interesting to know the effects of a big mass meeting, a radio speech by a presidential candidate, or exciting world events upon the momentary choices of the electorate. To gain such information psychologists have developed the panel technique. A panel is composed of a carefully selected sample, representative of the general population, each member of which is interviewed regularly.[10]

[8] Fromme, A., On the Use of Certain Qualitative Methods of Attitude Research, *J. Soc. Psychol.*, 1941, **13**, 429–459.

[9] Reported in Cantril, *op. cit.*

[10] To control the possibility that this regular questioning may in itself change opinions, it is customary to set up two or more equated panels, only one being interviewed on every occasion. Compare the Erie County study described on pp. 551–554.

Intensive Spot Survey. Instead of trying to get a fair sample of the national population, it may be deemed better to question practically everybody in representative areas. Thus the Department of Labor gathers consumer statistics by intensive checks in a few typical urban, small-town and rural communities. Because Erie County, Ohio, has a long history of agreeing closely with the national presidential vote, it has been studied carefully to trace the evolution of political opinions. The spot check makes possible the use of fewer interviewers, hence is more economical. It cannot be used where regional controls are needed.

Mass-Observation. Before the close of this section on technical problems in opinion surveys, it is desirable to mention the "Mass-Observation" organization that has for several years been "taking the public pulse" in England.[11] "Mass-Observation" includes such methods as listening to conversations on street corners, in taverns, and at sporting events; asking questions informally; counting the number and types of people doing certain things (praying in public, attending brutal sports events); collecting spontaneous essays, diaries, etc. These procedures have certain features to commend them: direct observation, freedom from verbal concealment. On the other hand, many will be displeased with the idea of deliberate eavesdropping, as the main method might be described. It is even more distressing, to those familiar with the pitfalls of public-opinion study, to note how casually the problems of stratified sampling, question phrasing, and other controls have been approached.

As far as the United States is concerned, it seems safe to predict that the development of polling will continue along lines already laid down: interviews rather than mail ballots; improved stratified sampling; formal rather than open-end questions, except for special studies; continuous statistical analysis to ensure that the obtained results are the most reliable possible.

VALIDITY

We can check the results of one poll against another, or of one type of question against another, to see that the answers agree. This is a measure of the extent to which the surveys are *reliable*. But one might still ask, "Do people act that way? Are the results valid?"

It could be argued that, if a person says he dislikes communism, that is automatically a valid index of his personal opinion, since we cannot go behind his statement. But, as has been found since V-E Day in Germany, the most ardent Fascist can say he always disliked Fascism. The validity of a remark, therefore, ought to be measured by checking it against action.

[11] Madge, C., and Harrisson, T., *Britain by Mass-Observation,* Penguin Books, Ltd.; Harmondsworth, Middlesex, 1939.

Insofar as voting is concerned, the validity of the scientific polls is amply proved. The margin of error on most recent elections has been small. It appears that, if a person says he is going to vote Democratic, or Republican, or Socialist, this can be accepted as a valid datum. There are, however, a certain number who prefer to say, "Undecided," and it was this group which caused the error in prediction of the 1948 election.

On issues where personal prestige might be involved (opinions about which emotion is quite strong), the findings are not so satisfactory. Schanck[12] reported that his subjects gave quite different opinions, speaking as private citizens, from those they put forth when speaking as church members. Apparently we get a great deal of this in governmental circles, when a man admits privately that the official administration policy seems foolish to him, yet defends it in public. In these cases we should have to distinguish between *public* and *private* opinions.

On matters where self-respect is involved, the results of opinion polls are also likely to err. Hyman[13] reports two significant observations. From war-plant payrolls he got names of recent absentees, and, in the course of an opinion poll about such issues, worked in the question, "Have you missed work recently?" A considerable percentage (up to 23 per cent in one group) replied falsely. Using a list of names of people who had redeemed war bonds, he contrived to ask, "Have you found it necessary to cash any bonds?" The results show an interesting pattern.

Of those above average in economic status, 43 per cent said no.
Among those of average status, 25 per cent said no.
Among the poor group, only 7 per cent said no.

In this case, it seems clear that those in the better economic categories did not wish to confess that they had redeemed bonds, whereas the poorer citizens saw no reason to deny their plight. Poll results probably are not valid where the giving of a specified response would expose the respondent to an accusation, or even a feeling, that he had lowered his personal status by so doing.

In most instances, by the very nature of *public* opinion data, such answers are not involved. Thus, the evidence favors the view that surveys not relating to an election are about as valid as the surveys that predict election returns so accurately. The British Institute of Public Opinion, for example, could have foretold the 1945 general election in Britain rather accurately by a study of poll data on such questions

[12] Schanck, R. L., Study of a Community and Its Groups and Institutions Conceived of as Behaviors of Individuals, *Psychol. Monogr.*, 1932, No. 195.
[13] Hyman, H., Do They Tell the Truth? *Publ. Opin. Quart.*, 1945, 8, 557–559.

as housing, nationalization of natural resources, and the like. And in elections involving a referendum vote by the public on a specific issue, the opinion polls have given very accurate forecasts.

With a few exceptions, therefore, it seems possible by modern scientific methods to obtain in a few days a reliable and valid index of public opinion on any topic that has been widely discussed. It is not reasonable to conclude from this that opinion polls should replace Congress as a means of deciding national policy. Elected officials are expected to study issues carefully and thus to be better informed than the electorate. They should consider the opinions of the public, as revealed through orthodox polls, and be influenced but not blindly led by the results. This, interestingly enough, is the belief of the average citizen[14] and of elective officials.[15]

DETERMINANTS OF OPINION

To what extent does the widespread questioning of individuals by the polling process throw light on the real determinants of opinion? Each person is likely to assert that his opinions are based on his own personal experience, contacts with friends, and reasoning. As psychologists we are well aware of the uniqueness of the individual. How, then, can statistical averages give valid information about these opinions? For every opinion must be held by an individual; the public exists only statistically.

The facts seem to answer unequivocally. Regardless of the assertion by each individual that his opinion represents his reasoned conclusion (or words to that effect), it is clear that such factors as the amount of economic security he has, the amount and kind of education he received, the section of the country he inhabits, and other items have profound influences upon his opinions. These factors are not matters of reasoning. But they do affect the manner in which we reason, the arguments we accept, the conclusions we endorse.

Education. The most consistent group differences on opinion polls are those found when respondents are classified by educational level. Persons with some college training differ most sharply from the general trend. Those limited to grammar school, in general, are more nationalistic, more traditional, in their public opinions than the average. College-trained citizens are much quicker to accept the need for a world organization; they are less deceived by the theory that war is inevitable; they are more critical of harsh peace terms. In a comparison with experts on the causes of war, the college-educated came

[14] Goldman, E. F., Poll on the Polls, *Publ. Opin. Quart.*, 1945, 8, 461–467.
[15] Hartmann, G. W., Judgments of State Legislators Concerning Public Opinion, *J. Soc. Psychol.*, 1945, 21, 105–114.

closest to endorsing the program set up by the experts as a means for
approaching permanent peace.

It is easy to see why these differences in opinion would develop. Not
only does the person of higher education have more facts upon which
to base his judgment; he also has a different background of experience
with reality. He has grown up (on the average) in a protected environment; he comes most often from a well-to-do family; and he has been
less forced to concentrate on the day-to-day job of earning a living. Add
to this the superior intelligence of the average person going to college,
and the result necessarily is a different point of view on public issues.
Breadth of vision, a consideration of factors beyond the immediate
present, is a major consequence. Opinions of the college-trained allow
more for the needs and wishes of people in other countries—not necessarily less selfish but more realistic about such international relationships. An example is the following question asked by NORC in 1945:

If some kind of world organization is formed, which one of these things would you like to see?	College, per cent	High school, per cent	Grade school, per cent
The United States has the most to say about running it..	12	21	37
Britain, Russia, and the United States together have the most to say about running it......................	27	18	16
All the countries in the organization have about the same amount to say about running it....................	47	52	34

Such findings of opinion polls suggest that, despite all the legitimate
criticisms of our colleges, one end product of college education is a
more intelligent and enlightened public opinion.

Economic Status. Our daily lives are to a very substantial extent
filled, to the exclusion of other interests, by economic activities. The
need to earn a living is a major motive in the personality of the average
adult. Thus, it is natural to expect—and find—significant differences
between economic groups as to opinions. Such differences are of two
kinds: occupation and income. It is generally found that businessmen,
farmers, and domestic servants have very conservative views on economic issues; professional, skilled, and unskilled laborers being more
to the left on such questions. Similarly, general economic status—
having a high or low standard of living relative to the community average—determines many opinions.

It is easy to understand the millionaire's preference for sales taxes
as against higher income-tax rates. Nor are we surprised when beef
stockmen favor free trade in the abstract but want Argentine beef
barred from the American market. Such opinions represent crude self-

interest. It is more difficult to comprehend the housemaid's angry opposition to labor unions, or the bookkeeper's feelings on the subject of excess-profits taxes.

An adequate explanation of these instances in which whole groups of individuals express opinions clearly opposed to their personal economic welfare depends on more subtle psychological considerations. A majority of white-collar workers seem unconsciously to assimilate the attitudes of top management and to repeat opinions expressed by these successful businessmen. One mechanism involved probably is that of *identification:* the clerk adopts the mannerisms, style of dress, and ideas of the boss. This presumably serves the need for a feeling of success, if only through fantasy. Another factor may be *unconscious learning:* the office employee must carry out certain policies to keep his job, and he inevitably begins to think of these as the right policies. (This is the basis of the success of much totalitarian propaganda.)

OPINIONS BY ECONOMIC LEVEL

UPPER	28%	72%
MIDDLE	48%	52%
LOWER	71%	29%

FIG. 19–2. Opinions on government control of business as related to economic status. As income decreases, endorsement of postwar controls on business increases. (*Reproduced through Courtesy of National Opinion Research Center.*)

Economic status, in the more general sense of standard of living, also is a potent influence upon opinion. This is particularly apparent in the case of public issues relating directly to economic conditions, as illustrated in Fig. 19–2. These results were in response to the question— When we *do* get back to peacetime conditions, do you think the American people will be better off if the government has *more* control or *less* control of business than it had before?

It is noticeable, however, that in many instances there are differences between economic groups on questions of no immediate economic significance. A Fortune poll on postwar treatment of Germany, for example, showed a decidedly greater proportion of poor people favoring very severe policies toward the Germans. One possible interpretation of this is that it reflects the greater degree of frustration—and, presumably, aggressive tension—among people at lower economic levels.

Marked changes in economic level, or in economic security, may be expected to produce drastic shifts in opinion. In 1928 Herbert Hoover was elected President by a landslide; in 1932 he was defeated by an even greater sweep. Admittedly the major intervening change was the economic collapse of 1929. Opinions about individual enterprise, social security, and related topics were completely revised under the impact of this catastrophe. A change of even greater significance for history was simultaneously taking place in Germany. In Fig. 19–3 is charted the growth of the Nazi party in members and in votes. From an insignificant minority in 1928 it changed to a powerful bloc, though never a majority, by 1932.

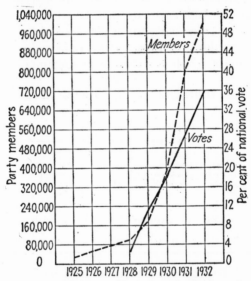

FIG. 19–3. Effect of the depression on Nazi strength. From an insignificant minority in 1928 the Nazis rose to the point of polling approximately 40 per cent of the total vote in the last free elections in 1932.

Cultural Area. Inasmuch as this discussion is restricted primarily to opinions of the American public, no attempt will be made to consider geographical factors as they influence world opinion generally. It is worth noting, nontheless, that opinion breaks sharply as we cross national frontiers. Americans customarily believe their nation to be the greatest and finest in the world, whereas Frenchmen prefer to reserve such adjectives for France, Germans for Germany, and Russians for the Soviet Union. Such cleavages, it is unnecessary to remark, are due purely to training, not to heredity.

Even within the United States, differences according to area are of considerable significance. One example is the so-called "Solid South," which has been characterized by marked race prejudice, by relatively militaristic attitudes, and by general economic conservatism. Another is the traditionally isolationist Middle West, where suspicion of "foreign entanglements" and particularly of England is widespread. The Pacific Coast and New England likewise have characteristic patterns of public opinion.

It is easy to understand that a child reared in a wealthy home unconsciously absorbs the attitudes and opinions of his elders, which in turn are determined largely by economic self-interest. Much of the child's learning is preverbal; much of it is based on imitation of admired adults. The scornful tone of voice, the smile of approval, the shrug of indifference are potent influences on opinion but are rarely if ever recognized as such.

In the same manner, prejudices and taboos that are regionally distributed are handed down from parent to offspring. Horowitz,[16] in his excellent study of prejudice against Negroes in the South, found that these antagonistic attitudes were largely indoctrinated by unconscious teaching and learning. Parents denied telling their children that Negroes were bad in any way; yet the children stated that parents did not want them to play with Negro children. Horowitz found compelling evidence that the parents unconsciously communicated prejudice through facial expressions, tones of voice, and other nonverbal mechanisms. The children thus acquired an unfavorable opinion of the Negro race without being deliberately taught this.

The developmental history of this traditional attitude is instructive as a starting point for understanding other established opinions, such as nationalism, occupational preferences, religious and political faiths. Horowitz found race prejudice to be very rare before the age of five years. In the early school grades, prejudice is likely to be an all-or-none reaction and is verbalized as "Negroes are bad, cruel, no-good." In adolescence, the White children reveal the customary stereotype of the Negro, in which a certain number of good traits (humor, music, etc.) are ascribed along with less desirable features.

These observations fit rather closely with those on the development of other attitudes on public issues.[17] It would appear permissible to conclude that, in a class or area in which certain opinions are held by the majority of adults, these opinions are passed on to children through these mechanisms. The earliest stage in the development of an opinion regarding any psychological object would seem to be a generalized reaction of approval-disapproval. Later, this undiscriminating response becomes differentiated into judgments on separate aspects of the object.

[16] Horowitz, E. L., Development of Attitude toward the Negro, *Arch. Psychol. N.Y.*, 1936, No. 194.

[17] See, *e.g.*, Horowitz, E. L., Some Aspects of the Development of Patriotism in Children, *Sociometry*, 1940, 3, 329–341.

In many cases, of course, even this later stage is merely blind parroting of established views rather than a thoughtful evaluation of the situation. Education has by no means solved the problem of inducing thoughtful consideration of all major issues. In some cases the adult community even imposes legal restrictions[18] on the freedom of educators to carry out this responsibility.

Emotion. An adequate prediction of the average man's opinions on any public issue can be made, based on such objective considerations as his economic level, his schooling, his religious affiliation, and the region in which he spent his childhood. Such predictions might at present attain an accuracy of 90 per cent on widely discussed issues.

Nevertheless, there are exceptions. Some wealthy young men become Communists. Some Southerners crusade for job equality for Negroes. Sons of flag-waving patriots occasionally become ardent internationalists. In these cases we look for emotional determinants.

It has been shown by Lasswell,[19] and confirmed by many investigators, that the boy's attitude toward his parents may be a decisive influence on his public opinions. All of a group of labor agitators studied by Lasswell had intense antagonisms to their fathers; in many cases this hostility was unconscious. Studies of college students have revealed a tendency for boys with close relationships to their parents to be nationalistic; those who felt relatively distant from their parents were more international-minded. In such cases we find evidence that the parent is a sort of symbol of authority, of the power of the nation. Rejection of parental authority may lead to rejection of the economic or political system that the parents represent.

Under our present setup, an overwhelming majority of the public have their ideas determined for them by accidents of birth, occupation, and education. A few reflect accidents of family emotional conflict. The man who has reached a position on any public issue by pure logic and reasoning is rare indeed.

PROPAGANDA

In the foregoing discussion, nothing has been said about the power of propaganda to mold public opinion. This omission was deliberate. Actually, the power of propaganda has often been overrated. Following the First World War there was a period during which propaganda was rather hysterically blamed for exaggerated evil deeds.

[18] Thus the state of Tennessee once forbade the discussion of the theory of evolution in the schools; and teachers in the District of Columbia once were forbidden to mention the word "communism" in class. Even more numerous are the unwritten taboos that teachers must observe to keep their jobs.

[19] Lasswell, H. D., *Psychopathology and Politics,* University of Chicago Press, Chicago, 1930.

There are two circumstances in which propaganda is a true determinant of opinion: one, when a new issue arises for which family tradition or economic self-interest offers no obvious judgment; and two, when crisis conditions have destroyed our emotional adherence to traditional opinion.

When a situation is not clearly structured—when a person does not have, either from personal experience or from his training, a clear interpretation of what is happening—propaganda has an excellent opportunity. Thus, *e.g.*, propaganda about the bestial qualities of our enemies in the Second World War was highly successful, since few of us had acquaintances in the enemy nations, and the other side of the story was suppressed by censorship. But propaganda against inflationary buying and trading with the "black market," which ran counter to crystallized opinions regarding economic self-interest, was not nearly so potent.

There are certain emotional factors that help along such hostile propaganda as that just mentioned. In wartime, the civilian has many aggressive tensions bottled up that cannot be released in action. Thus he is particularly predisposed to accept propaganda that helps him project this aggressiveness onto others and see them as full of deadly designs on him. If he has any guilt feelings about the destruction rained on the enemy by his own nation, the guilt is alleviated by overstressing the horrible character of the enemy people.[20]

Another common human characteristic that facilitates this functioning of propaganda is a need to avoid uncertainty. Tense situations with unpredictable outcomes make us uncomfortable. A complex catastrophe such as the great depression may be understood only in terms of numerous conditions, but minds of limited intelligence and education are not satisfied by such ambiguous explanations. A clear, simple formula is needed. Thus the success of propaganda placing the blame on Wall Street, inventors, the Communists, the capitalists, and so on. In Germany the Nazis sold the idea that the depression was caused by the Versailles Treaty, the Jews, and the Communists. In times of uncertainty, propaganda can be effective in controlling opinion.

A second type of situation making propaganda effective is that in which traditional opinion has been proved unreliable. Such is the revolutionary situation that arose in Russia in 1917. Belief in the sovereignty of the Czar, the rights of private property, and the necessity for

[20] It is probable that the differences in opinion between educated and uneducated groups (see above) are due in considerable measure to the greater susceptibility to propaganda found among poorer, illiterate people. An instructive analysis of this problem was made in connection with the famous radio broadcast of a Martian invasion, which threw a not inconsiderable number of persons into panic. Susceptibility was found closely connected to low economic and educational status and presence of emotional tension. See Cantril, H., *The Invasion from Mars,* Princeton University Press, Princeton, N.J., 1940.

waging war against the Germans led the Russian people only to defeat, hunger, and despair. Under these conditions a wave of anger and disillusionment brought above the rejection of traditional attitudes. The Bolsheviks, with a well-planned propaganda campaign, deflected public opinion into a revolutionary channel. The same thing happened in Germany in 1918, but the Social Democrats did not exercise the iron censorship and continuous propaganda that enabled the Russian regime to keep power.

Even in the absence of such intense emotional crises as those mentioned, propaganda probably successfully molds opinion if there is no counterpropaganda and if it it fits in with childhood conditioning. The Communists built up a tremendous propaganda machine precisely because they were not sure public opinion was with them. By barring all conflicting ideas and hammering home certain statements continually, they built favorable opinions or prevented hostile opinion from crystallizing.

PROPAGANDA AND THINKING

If we are to understand the nature of public opinion, both as shaped by early childhood experiences and as patterned by propaganda, we must inquire into the nature of the thought processes that determine it. Public opinion today reflects in varying degrees the impact of two kinds of thinking: realistic and animistic.

Realistic thinking is based on observable facts and scientific principles of logic. Most of our opinions about the physical world are formed in this manner. We are reasonably certain that automobiles run because gasoline is exploded inside the cylinder by an electric spark. When the desired results do not appear, we do not blame mysterious supernatural forces or the malice of our enemies. Instead, we examine the fuel and ignition systems.

Animistic thinking is primarily emotional and subjective. Many of our opinions about political and economic institutions, as about human behavior in general, are determined animistically. No one would imagine that we could cure an automobile of defective performance by putting it in jail, but this irrational method of dealing with human beings is utilized daily. Scientists would not presume that the controversy between the wave theory and the quantum theory of light meant that advocates of one were a menace to the advocates of the other. But advocates of communism and capitalism automatically assume that each is a threat to the other; and in so thinking they tend to make this tragic assumption a reality!

We have progressed past the stage of thinking about wind, lightning, and rain in terms of spirits. But we have not achieved a similar level in our consideration of economic cycles, immigration, international trade and similar human interactions. Propaganda that seeks to appeal to animistic thinking about foreigners, persons who threaten our comfortable existence, or anything strange and unknown, may be effective.

Public opinion, of course, is always a composite of both realistic and animistic thinking. Opinions of Whites about Negroes (and vice versa) are partly realistic, mostly animistic. Public approval of the new international organization to preserve peace is partly realistic, but in considerable degree it is purely wishful thinking. When issues arise requiring the sacrifice of treasured American prerogatives, much of this approval may fade away. If based upon a sounder appraisal of real conditions, it might survive such blows.

This leads to the suggestion that there are two kinds of propaganda, one seeking to stimulate realistic thinking, the other appealing to animistic tendencies. (Any given bit of propaganda may of course do both.) Insofar as science recognizes good and bad phenomena, we may say that propaganda based on realistic analysis of conditions is good, while that which seeks to explain a situation in terms of spirits, human malice, and similar intangibles is bad. A careful analysis of the tangible conditions existing in Japan just prior to the bombing of Pearl Harbor would prove highly beneficial in forming a realistic public opinion about the Japanese people; whereas an analysis in terms of alleged inherent brutality and similar intangibles can lead only to desperate confusion.

Other Psychological Mechanisms. It has been pointed out that propaganda is more effective if it appeals to certain psychological needs, such as that for the release of aggressive tension in wartime or for a simple formula to explain a complex situation. To round out this discussion, it is worth while to mention some other psychological mechanisms that may be involved.

In a competitive world, most of us develop a need for success, in the form of wealth or power. Failing to achieve this through personal effort, we may be encouraged to *identify* ourselves with a powerful nation or with a political movement. (Some of Adolf Hitler's speeches are excellent applications of this principle.) Much propaganda is subtly calculated to develop this identification of self with a particular group.

Propaganda that seeks to establish opinions of a socially disapproved character (*e.g.*, advocating violence in some form) may make use of the tendency to *projection*. The propagandist points out that the enemy is about to resort to violence against us; we project our own hostile impulses onto him and see that he is really worse than we; and therefore it is permissible to attack him. This is readily observable in capital-labor conflicts, as well as in the field of international relations.

Many of us have impulses to act along socially disapproved lines but are kept in check by childhood training and conscience. By furnishing a plausible *rationalization* for acting, the propagandist may influence our opinions and behavior. Many German businessmen wanted to profit by seizing competing Jewish businesses. The Nazi propagandist furnished an excuse with his fabrication of a Jewish plot against the welfare of the nation.[21]

EFFECTIVENESS OF PROPAGANDA

The statement has already been made that it is easy to overestimate the effectiveness of propaganda. We should not wish on that account to swing to the opposite extreme and underestimate its importance. We have shown that, on issues that are confused and confusing to the average man, the suggestions he receives from press and radio may decide his opinions for him. There are many such issues these days. We have also pointed out that special emotional factors may predispose a varying number of persons to act on propaganda for a given policy. At times this number may be sufficient to influence the course of history.

Unfortunately, the experimental studies on the influence of propaganda are entirely inadequate to demonstrate the exact extent and limitations of its effects. Most of the investigations have been conducted in classrooms, by having students listen to a prepared speech or read a statement on a given topic. Only a single presentation is customary, in contrast to the barrage encountered in real life. Little use has been made of emotional approaches, whereas human emotion is the basic raw material of the skilled propagandist. An exception to this general criticism is the well-planned study by Hartmann[22] on the emotional and rational appeals in propaganda. Carefully prepared leaflets were distributed to selected wards of a Pennsylvania city during an election campaign. Lack of finances and the handicap of running under a Socialist label prevented the study from obtaining very striking results, but a slight difference suggested the superiority of the emotional approach.

Various studies, such as that of Annis and Meier[23] and one by

---

[21] For a further development of the role of emotions, motives, and unconscious mental mechanisms in determining the receptiveness of the individual to a propaganda message, see R. K. Merton, *Mass Persuasion,* Harper & Brothers, New York, 1946. This book deals with the war bond sales campaign of Kate Smith; while it probably overestimates the actual effectiveness of the propaganda materials, the interviews with people who bought bonds nevertheless provide valuable insights into the dynamic aspects of propaganda reception.

[22] Hartmann, G. W., Field Experiment on the Comparative Effect of "Emotional" and "Rational" Political Leaflets in Determining Election Results, *J. Abnorm. Soc. Pyschol.,* 1936–37, **31**, 99–114.

[23] Annis, A. D., and Meier, N. C., Induction of Opinion through Suggestion by Means of "Planted Content," *J. Soc. Psychol.,* 1934, **5**, 65–81.

Chen,[24] reveal that significant differences in opinion can be produced by single items of propaganda.[25] The Annis and Meier technique, involving the preparation of faked editions of the student newspaper, was worthy of better application. An interesting observation by Bode[26] was that different types of propaganda might have the same effect. Bode showed adult groups two films on labor problems, one from the conservative and one from the liberal viewpoint. Both films produced greater liberalism on the questions involved! An interestingly parallel finding comes from Remmers'[27] work with high school students. Material favoring more government control of farming produced the expected change in opinion of city children but had a negative effect on attitudes of farm children in the same school. Propaganda, therefore, does not always follow the intent of the propagandist.

In contrast to these very small-scale studies, we have in the United States at periodic intervals an opportunity to study the effects of propaganda on a relatively enormous scale. In every national election campaign, the voters are deluged with a variety of appeals presented through an assortment of techniques. It might appear fairly easy to study these campaigns and determine the effectiveness of the various methods.

Unfortunately, any such investigation requires a great deal of money and a staff of well-trained investigators. Therefore, not many have been made. The best to date is that by Lazarsfeld and associates[28] on the 1940 presidential campaign. As it exemplifies the panel-type study excellently, the technique is given here in some detail.

In May, 1940, a staff of interviewers contacted some adult in every fourth house in Erie County, Ohio. This procedure assured the nearest possible to a true random sample completely representative of all districts. From the 3,000 interviews obtained, four panels of 600 each were prepared, equalized for economic, educational, political, and religious composition. One of these groups was reinterviewed in July, another in August, and a third in October, regarding their changes in voting

[24] Chen, W. K., Influence of Oral Propaganda Material on Student Attitudes, *Arch. Psychol. N.Y.*, 1933, No. 150.

[25] A suggestion that a single Roosevelt "fireside chat" may have influenced opinion significantly is contained in one AIPO report. On Dec. 29, 1940, the President broadcast to the nation on the "lend-lease" idea and America's stake in the European conflict. Of those who, interviewed a few days later, said they heard this speech, 71 per cent thought we should help England even at the risk of war, whereas the percentage of support for that alternative among Roosevelt voters a week earlier was only 62. An increase of 9 per cent would be quite significant.

[26] Bode, B., An Experiment in Propaganda, *J. Adult Educ.*, 1941, **13**, 365–374.

[27] Williamson, A. A., and Remmers, H. H., Persistence of Attitudes Concerning Conservation Issues, *J. Exp. Educ.*, 1940, **8**, 354–361.

[28] Lazarsfeld, Paul F., Berelson, B., and Gaudet, Hazel, *The People's Choice*, Duell, Sloan & Pearce, Inc., New York, 1944.

intention. The fourth group, the main panel, was reinterviewed six times, about once a month, from May until after the election in November. A total of about 8,400 personal interviews was required.

The above procedure gives a base line showing the political intentions of the people prior to the beginning of the campaign. Lest frequent repeat interviews cause some to become self-conscious about politics and thus not act normally, the three control panels were given only one additional interview. The main panel provides the majority of the data, however, since detailed records could be obtained on speeches heard, magazines read, meetings attended, and so on.

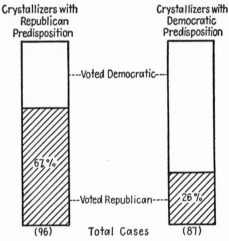

FIG. 19–4. Predisposition to be influenced by propaganda. The same socioeconomic factors which distinguish Republicans from Democrats can be used to identify, generally with marked accuracy, those "undecided" voters who will be influenced by the campaign to vote Republican or Democratic. (*Reproduced through Courtesy of Duell, Sloan & Pearce.*)

It is striking to note that 49 per cent of these people reported no change in voting intent at any time. Their minds were made up before the candidates were nominated; the oratory of the campaign left them unmoved; 28 per cent changed from "no choice" in May to a definite preference, 14 per cent Democratic, 14 per cent Republican. A group of 15 per cent fluctuated in preference but eventually voted for their precampaign preference, leaving only 8 per cent of the people interviewed who actually switched their vote as a result of the campaign. This finding suggests that even a heavy barrage of propaganda need not necessarily be effective; an observation immediately qualified by noting that Democratic and Republican propagandas may have canceled each other.

Even more striking, in the Lazarsfeld data, is the fact that the reaction of the undecided voters to partisan material can be predicted in advance. The authors demonstrate this as follows: in the original (May) interviews, it was found that Republican votes were concentrated among farmers, people of upper economic status, and Protestants; Democratic, among urban dwellers, lower economic status, and Catholics. By setting up point scores for these factors, they could compute an index of predisposition toward Republican or Democratic affiliation.

Now they computed this index for the 183 persons who were undecided in May. From this index, they could predict correctly the final

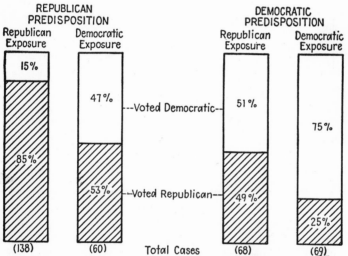

FIG. 19–5. Effect of a relative monopoly of propaganda. When, by chance, a person is exposed almost exclusively to propaganda favoring one party, he is likely to be influenced in that direction despite the presence of factors predisposing to a vote for the other ticket. (*Reproduced through courtesy of Duell, Sloan & Pearce.*)

vote of 70 per cent (see Fig. 19–4)! The same held true for an analysis of those changing party. Most of the party-changers moved to a position more in harmony with their occupation or economic standing.

This means that *in general* partisan propaganda, presented in this kind of situation, activates latent dispositions rather than inducing people to vote against their established habits. But if, for some reason, a person is subjected almost entirely to propaganda from one side, then the chances are he will vote that way (see Fig. 19–5). Thus we must still make allowances for such situations as that in Soviet Russia where one variety of propaganda has a monopoly. "Freedom for competing propagandas" is probably an essential of an intelligent public opinion.

The authors confirm another generally accepted maxim by pointing out that their Republicans systematically avoided Democratic propaganda, and vice versa. Thus, part of the ineffectiveness of propaganda is due to the fact that it is heeded most by those already believing in it.

Propaganda and the Learning Process. Lazarsfeld found that, when people are free to choose their reading and other material, they select items favorable to their established convictions and avoid that which might impel a change in opinion. Several recent investigations of the memory process, using material of a propagandistic nature, show that the mind may unconsciously accomplish the same function.

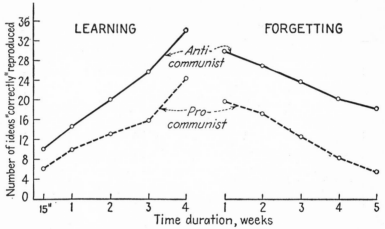

FIG. 19–6. Learning and forgetting of controversial material. At each learning session, a paragraph strongly critical of communism was read twice by each subject. After a 15-minute wait, he attempted to reproduce it. Successive sessions were one week apart. Forgetting sessions were identical except that no opportunity was given to re-read the paragraph. (*Reprinted from J. Abnorm. Soc. Psychol., by permission.*)

Edwards[29] tested students for attitude to the New Deal. He later presented to them a memorized speech carefully prepared to present an equal number of pro- and anti-New Deal statements. On a memory test, however, the students who disliked the New Deal remembered mostly critical statements, whereas those favoring the Roosevelt regime recalled the laudatory remarks. Further, there was a considerable amount of distortion, in that the speaker's words were twisted to fit the beliefs of the listener.

Levine and Murphy[30] required their subjects deliberately to attempt to memorize paragraphs favorable to and critical of the Soviet Union.

[29] Edwards, A. L., Political Frames of Reference as a Factor Influencing Recognition, *J. Abnorm. Soc. Psychol.,* 1941, **36**, 34–50; Rationalization in Recognition as a Result of a Political Frame of Reference, *ibid.,* 224–235.

[30] Levine, J. M., and Murphy, G., Learning and Forgetting of Controversial Material, *J. Abnorm. Soc. Psychol.,* 1943, **38**, 507–517.

Half the subjects were active Communist sympathizers, the other half vigorously anti-Communist. The learning and forgetting curves for the paragraph hostile to the U.S.S.R. are shown in Fig. 19–6. It is clear that the material is learned most readily and remembered longest by the group liking it. The same observation can be made on learning and forgetting the material favorable to the Russians.

In the light of the preceding analysis, it will be seen that public opinion is a product of learning but that, in trying to have people learn his material, the propagandist is working against considerable odds. Most of the learning (on major issues) takes place in early childhood; people select their reading and radio material to get propaganda they already believe; and the chances are good that they will distort conflicting propaganda to make it seem to reinforce their established attitudes. To meet these handicaps, there have been developed a considerable number of propaganda tricks that merit our attention.

PROPAGANDA DEVICES

It is necessary for the propagandist, in seeking to change opinion, to attract the attention of the person being propagandized and to make the changed opinion palatable to him. The problem of attracting attention is handled through the orthodox advertising techniques as worked out for newspaper advertising, radio, billboards, and the like. The task of making the proposed new idea acceptable is somewhat akin to the situation in advertising, but there are obvious differences relating to the intangible nature of the commodity being offered for sale. The techniques employed are therefore somewhat different. It is possible to classify them in many categories, but the following simple schema may be useful. It is the one developed by the Institute for Propaganda Analysis and therefore rather widely publicized before the war.[31]

Name Calling. One of the simplest and commonest devices is that of attaching unpleasant names to those who disagree with your views. Those who criticize labor unions are often denounced as "Fascists," while those who venture to defend human rights against property rights are called "Communists." This is substantially the same method as the "unpleasant smell" device in advertising.

That name calling is effective is proved by the experiments of Menefee[32] and Hartmann.[33] Menefee asked his subjects to check a list

---

[31] For an excellent introduction to the work of this Institute, see Violet Edwards, *Group Leader's Guide to Propaganda Analysis,* Institute for Propaganda Analysis, Inc., New York, 1938.

[32] Menefee, S. C., Effect of Stereotyped Words on Political Judgments, *Amer. Sociol. Rev.,* 1936, 1, 614–621.

[33] Hartmann, G. W., Contradiction between Feeling-tone of Political Party Names and Public Responses to Their Platforms, *J. Soc. Psychol.,* 1936, 7, 336–357.

of opinions with which they were to agree or disagree. Some weeks later the same opinions were presented, but on this occasion each statement was preceded by the label "A Fascist statement," "A Communist statement," etc. In this case people changed their answers to get away from approval of items called Fascist or Communist but increased their endorsement of "liberal" and "democratic" opinions. Hartmann found that 55 per cent of Pennsylvania adults approved of a majority of the planks in the Socialist platform, but very few of them liked "Socialist" as a name for a political party. He interpreted this as meaning that the label might deter many potential Socialist voters.

Transfer. Transfer is employed when completely irrelevant pleasant or unpleasant ideas are introduced into propaganda in an attempt to have their influence spread to adjacent suggestions. Just as the beautiful girl has nothing to do with the quality of the cigarette advertised, so God, home, and the Star Spangled Banner have nothing to do with the average politician's speech. Nevertheless, it is presumed that both tricks are effective.

Glittering Generalities. The effectiveness of the use of glittering generalities depends basically upon transfer. A writer who opens his article with a belief in the rights of man and concludes that we must reduce the excess-profits tax on corporations is using glittering generalities. The attitude of approval that is set up by the broad generalization will, it is hoped, carry over to the specific opinion suggested later.

Testimonial. The testimonial makes use of the prestige value of a person who has been cured by the patent medicine, or of someone who is alleged to be an expert on the topic at issue. Thus George Washington was quoted freely by both isolationists and interventionists in 1941. Often the expert has no qualifications whatever in the field under examination. A cosmic-ray expert is no authority on the validity of Socialist theory, and a mathematical genius is not an authoritative source of information about life after death. Nevertheless, famous names are used by propagandists everywhere for their testimonial value.

Several experimenters[34] have shown the value of this technique. The method involves obtaining the subject's opinions on one occasion, then later presenting the same statements of opinion with their alleged authors' names attached. The amount of shift to agree (or disagree) is a measure of the author's prestige value. On some items, the amount of shift is substantial.

Split ballots on opinion polls[35] have shown that the inclusion of a

[34] Compare Lurie, W., Measurement of Prestige and Prestige-suggestibility, *J. Soc. Psychol.*, 1938, 9, 219–225.

[35] A split ballot is used when half the people interviewed get a question in one

specific person's name changes the poll data somewhat. Ascribing a proposal to the President increases the percentage of approval. During the Lend-Lease controversy in 1941, ascribing statements to Senator Burton Wheeler caused more people to reject them. The opponent of peacetime military training who quoted Adolf Hitler as the outstanding exponent of this idea was making use of reverse prestige or a negative testimonial.

Plain Folks. Another technique that is quite similar to transfer is the plain folks device. The attempt is to make the idea pleasant by setting it in a familiar, "homey" context. Presidential candidates often have their pictures taken in fishing clothes or pitching hay. Because of some overuse of this device by his publicity staff, Wendell Willkie was ironically referred to as "Wall Street's barefoot boy." If any insincerity is detected in this type of material, it is likely to do more harm than good.

Card Stacking. The distortion of facts by presenting only those harmonizing with the propagandist's purpose is known as card stacking. Wartime censorship always aids the corruption of public opinion by stacking the cards in one direction. However, even in normal times, the system of control of newspaper and radio now in effect in this country stacks the cards on many issues. Newspapers have refused to sell advertising to consumer cooperatives and to advertise a labor union's views on a strike.

Card stacking may involve leaving out certain facts, stressing some while glossing over others, or outright falsification. With increasing public alertness, propagandists seem to have moved in the direction of less bald falsehood, more discreet evasion of inharmonious facts. It is, however, literally impossible for the average man to be competently informed on all major issues of national and international importance. And there is still some evidence to support Hitler's statement, "The bigger the lie, the easier to get people to accept it."

Bandwagon. The last of these seven propaganda devices is that of the bandwagon. This is known in experimental psychology as the effect of majority opinion. Allard[36] polled students on various issues, then presented fictitious majorities from "national opinion surveys." Substantial numbers of students changed their minds to agree with the reported majority.

Most of us like the feeling of social approval that comes from going along with the majority. So, when the speaker shouts, "Jones will win by a landslide; vote for Jones!" many will go along. There does not

---

form, the others receiving a slightly different wording: *e.g.,* "Do you agree with the proposal . . . " vs. "Do you agree with the President's proposal . . . "

[36] Allard, W., Test of Propaganda Value in Public Opinion Surveys, *Social Forces,* 1940, **20**, 206–213.

seem to be much logic in voting for a candidate you dislike, merely because he is sure to win; nevertheless, many people confess to having done just that. No doubt the desire to avoid embarrassment in post-election conversations also plays a part in this behavior.

Composite Appeals. Few pieces of propaganda will show just one of these devices. All or most of them are likely to appear in any substantial barrage for or against a particular object. Borland[37] points out the diversity of appeals used in the attack on national health insurance, which has been debated often in Congress. Some of these appeals run into conflict with each other; one speaker, for example, on the floor of Congress, pointed out that government-sponsored medical care is a feature of Soviet Russian life, thus, automatically, "Communistic" and "bad." This is the familiar name-calling technique. Then he went on to assert that the proposed legislation was part of a Communist plot to bankrupt the United States and ruin the medical and dental professions (transfer). Now this would logically lead to the conclusion that the Communists were plotting to bankrupt Russia and ruin the medical and dental professions there. It is unlikely that recipients of this propaganda broadside noted the inconsistency; once an unfavorable way of perceiving a given object is established, it may be seen as having all sorts of "bad" features, even those which are logically incompatible. The emotions play a relatively larger part than intelligent thinking in the formation of public opinion.

The purpose of propaganda is to induce a certain way of perceiving an object of public concern. This means that the propagandist will use all the devices listed above, and others unclassifiable. He will appeal to strong motives (security, recognition, greed) and emotions (fear, hostility, nationalistic pride). He will try to fit his material with already existing perceptions, so that he will benefit from positive transfer. (Hence, conservative propaganda always has an advantage.) The more of these dynamic factors he can mobilize, the stronger and more permanent will be the resulting opinion changes.

MEASURING THE PROPAGANDA ENVIRONMENT

In a certain sense, propaganda pervades all our media of public communication. Much of the material in our newspapers and on the radio is placed there deliberately for the purpose of influencing opinion, and perhaps even more fulfills the same function without deliberate intent.

This is not inherently an undesirable condition. Any attempt to shape opinion, whether for desirable or for undesirable ends, may be

[37] Borland, L. R., The National Health Insurance Bogey, *Etc., Review of General Semantics,* 1949, **6**, 213–217.

called propaganda. One essential of a democratic society is freedom of minorities to attempt by persuasion to convert the majority to their way of thinking. Freedom of propaganda is therefore an often-ignored but necessary freedom. Furthermore, as long as alternative opinions get reasonable representation, the public seems to do an independent job of making up its mind. It will be remembered that in the 1936 and 1940 elections the newspapers of this country were against Mr. Roosevelt by an overwhelming majority. The electorate was not swamped by this flood of Republican propaganda.

With regard to such questions as foreign affairs and novel or radical innovations in institutional practice, the question of adequate representation for all points of view may be far more important. On such topics we may have a virtual monopoly of propaganda, in that only a nationalistic or a conservative view is ever presented. The misrepresentation of the United States in the press of many foreign nations should be a warning to us that we probably are not getting a fair picture of our international neighbors.

Harold Lasswell has been most vigorous in urging the accumulation of systematic data on the direction and quantity of propaganda dealing with significant social problems. He and his associates have published a number of papers[38] outlining techniques for this purpose. Basically, the idea of a world attention survey would be to tabulate the major ideas being held before the public of the greater nations, and to show if these ideas were treated positively or negatively. Such a survey might choose such basic concepts as democracy, communism, fascism, nazism and socialism; the frequency of references to each in newspapers of wide circulation in the United States, Britain, Mexico, Argentina, etc., and the proportion of approving and disapproving remarks on each, would be tallied. The result would give us a realistic picture of the propaganda being presented in each nation.

An earlier and more limited example of the same type is the study by Russell and Wright[39] of newspaper editorials referring to specific foreign countries. One of their charts, reproduced here (Fig. 19–7), shows the relative approval of Germany and France in various newspapers in this country, 1910 to 1929. Only during the war years is there a real preponderance of propaganda.

Such an analysis of Russian and German newspapers in 1939 gives forewarning of the Nazi-Soviet pact of August, 1939, which was such

[38] Lasswell, H. D., World Attention Survey, *Publ. Opin. Quart.*, 1941, 5, 456–462; Janis, I. L., Fadner, R. H., and Janowitz M., Reliability of a Content Analysis Technique, *ibid.*, 1943, 7, 293–296; Lasswell, H. D., and associates, Politically Significant Content of the Press: Coding Procedures, *Journalism Quarterly*, 1942, 19, 12.

[39] Russell, J. T., and Wright, Q., National Attitudes on the Far Eastern Controversy, *Amer. Pol. Sci. Rev.*, 1933, 27, 555–576.

a surprise to the Western democracies. It may be that a continuing project of this type would give the public (and the government) a sounder basis for predicting developments in international affairs. To the United Nations, such techniques seem to offer a necessary first step toward the detection and control of war-breeding propagandas anywhere in the world.

The Lasswell technique is limited to a determination of the proportion of positive to negative propaganda on any given issue and aims at extensive determination of such facts. White[40] has expanded this general approach by developing a method for the intensive analysis of specific propaganda materials (e.g., Hitler's speeches). White has pre-

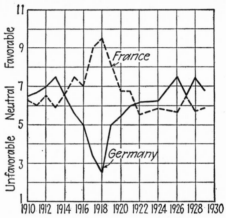

Fig. 19–7. American newspaper editorials on France and Germany, 1910 to 1929. (*Reproduced from American Political Science Review.*)

pared a list of 125 basic value words, covering pretty adequately every human value to which a propagandist could appeal. He then has analyzed propaganda relating to a specific concept (e.g., Russia) in terms of the frequency of reference to the various value words, the kind of relationship asserted or implied, and so on. This procedure would clearly be too cumbersome for broad propaganda surveys but might be highly informative in analyzing books, specially selected speeches or articles, and such items being circulated in our own or some other country.

Exposure Frequency. A complete survey of the propaganda environment will have to include some estimate of exposure. We need to know what is being set before the people and also how many perceive it. Cantril and Lambert[41] found that only 43 per cent of the readers of a

[40] White, R. K., Value-analysis: A Quantitative Method for Describing Qualitative Data, *J. Soc. Psychol.*, 1944, 19, 351–358.

[41] Cantril, H., and Lambert, G. B., Increasing Public Understanding of Inflation, *J. Abnorm. Soc. Psychol.*, 1944, 39, 112–117.

small-city daily newspaper noticed a full-page advertisement dealing with the causes of inflation, and only 10 per cent read it carefully. Different papers have different kinds of audiences, and, of course, a given audience will prefer one type of approach to another.

The quantitative aspect of propaganda exposure should also include a methodical study of the effects of repeated exposure to material slanted in a given direction. It is reasonable to assume that repetitions of propaganda will have a cumulative effect, just as people learn more about history or chemistry or psychology by taking more courses. On the propaganda front, however, the most important quantitative factor may prove to be that of monopoly. If—as was the case in Nazi Germany and is still the policy of Soviet Russia—only one viewpoint is allowed representation in newspapers and other media, there is no chance for a competing perception of controversial situations to be built up, and for public awareness of governmental errors. For this reason scientists deplore the tendency to punish expression of unpopular views in the United States.

An experimental study by Dietsch and Gurnee[42] seems to support the view that monopoly is more important than repetition in itself. They did an opinion study of a campus group on the controversial issue of subsidies for college athletes. Then they arranged for part of their group to be exposed to leaflet propaganda against subsidies. Some subjects received only one leaflet, others two, and others three, while a fourth (control) group received none. The results were measured by repeating the poll:

	Per Cent
Pretest: favoring subsidies	49
Posttest:	
After one leaflet	16
After two leaflets	11
After three leaflets	17
Control group	42

These findings suggest that a single exposure to a planned presentation of the arguments against subsidies is about as effective as two or three similar leaflets. It should be noted that, in the absence of a campaign in favor of subsidies, even one such item has a truly striking effect.

In a culture such as that of the United States where most propaganda is still free and competitive, the main determinant of frequency of exposure is the person's pre-existing opinion. This means that persons with a Republican political preference will read Republican newspapers, listen to Republican speeches, etc., while those of a different attitude cling to their own preferred sources. Thus, in effect, a vast

[42] Dietsch, R. W., and Gurnee, H., Cumulative Effect of a Series of Campaign Leaflets, *J. Appl. Psychol.*, 1948, **32**, 189–194.

quantity of propaganda is wasted because it is perceived only by those persons who are already convinced.

The study by Star and Hughes[43] of the "Cincinnati plan for the UN" illustrates this point effectively. The Cincinnati plan involved an intensive effort to get news about the UN into the papers, on the radio, etc. It was, very sensibly, preceded by an opinion survey of attitudes toward and information about the UN. After 6 months of vigorous publicity, a follow-up survey was carried out. The results were disappointing; most of the people who reported seeing newspaper stories or hearing radio broadcasts about UN activities were those already favorably disposed; the neutral and antagonistic citizens apparently just *did not see* the published materials.

Channels of Exposure. Is it more effective to present propaganda by way of the newspapers, the radio, the movies, or television? There are many small studies on this point, but no one has done a really comprehensive comparison of the effectiveness of the major media in changing people's perceptions of a public-opinion issue. Since there seems good reason to hold that, for the most part, human thinking is organized around a visual frame of reference,[44] it might be assumed that pictorial material would be maximally effective. However, the printed word has high prestige in our culture and might therefore be expected to function as a potent propaganda medium.

A study by Wilke[45] compared the effect on opinion of propaganda materials presented in a personal speech, in a speech heard by radio, and in mimeographed form. The relative potency, as judged by opinion changes, was in the order given. Seeing and hearing the speaker was more effective than listening to him over a loudspeaker, and this was more influential than merely reading the arguments.

The rising importance of television in our society makes this issue of great potential significance. If the illusion of personal contact which now becomes possible really makes propaganda appeals as effective as many psychologists fear, the "propaganda menace" may become a real and terrifying one. When we consider the high cost of TV programs, it becomes obvious that groups with strong financial resources may "sell" their ideas to the rest of the population by getting a monopoly of propaganda on this very potent medium.

The problems of the propaganda environment thus include the objects about which propaganda is disseminated, the emotional loadings which are applied to these objects, the frequency of presentation of

[43] Star, Shirley A., and Hughes, Helen M., Report on an Educational Campaign—The Cincinnati Plan for the UN, *Amer. J. Sociol.,* 1950, 55, 389–400.

[44] See Stagner, Ross, and Karwoski, T. F., *Psychology,* particularly Chaps. 6, 11, McGraw-Hill Book Company, Inc., New York, 1952.

[45] Wilke, W. H., Comparison of Speech, Radio and Printed Page as Propaganda Devices, *Arch. Psychol. N.Y.,* 1934, No. 169.

such biased materials, the frequency of reception by the people at whom the propaganda is directed, and the relative potency of the different channels over which propaganda comes. All these questions raise important issues about freedom of propaganda in a democratic society.

PUBLIC OPINION IN A DEMOCRACY

There is no reason to suppose that opinion polls either will or should take the place of legislative bodies in our society. While there is a certain specious appeal to the idea that a majority of the public must be right, countless independent thinkers from Christopher Columbus on have proved that the majority is often wrong. On many issues, a public-opinion poll is at best a tallying of ignorance, misinformation, or prejudice. Nevertheless, each of those ignorant, misinformed, or prejudiced persons has a right to express his opinion, and that opinion ought to be considered by lawmakers as a significant fact.[46]

Inasmuch as the bandwagon effect has proved to be a reality, the question of deliberate manipulation of poll data is often raised. Actually there has been surprisingly little evidence to indicate that anything of the sort has been attempted by the established polling agencies. There seems to be a good basis here, nevertheless, for opposing a poll conducted by the government. The method adopted in this country in the Second World War of employing private poll organizations to collect certain data, using their own established procedures, seems inherently safer. In the long run, of course, there is no guarantee against such manipulation except an alert and enlightened electorate—the same sole guarantee against all other political malfeasance.

The use of opinion and propaganda surveys suggests the possibility of certain improvements in the functioning of democracy. These would include publication of the fact that an excessive amount of propaganda along certain lines was appearing in a given medium, analysis by social scientists of the implications and probable results of such propaganda, and opinion polls on the topic. By enforcing freedom of propaganda, the government could ensure to the people the right to make up their own minds after hearing alternative views on a given issue. Intensive studies of individuals who issue (or who accept) antidemocratic propaganda could lead to suggestions for child training and educational techniques leading to a reduction in the number of such persons.[47] These and many other applications will be developed as social psychology continues to make an ever wider contribution to our democratic civilization.

[46] *The Journal of Social Issues* (May, 1946, 2, No. 2) has a series of excellent articles on the use of opinion polls in government as a device for fostering the intelligent conduct of a democratic society.

[47] See, for example, *The Authoritarian Personality*, by T. W. Adorno *et al.*, Harper & Brothers, New York, 1950.

SUMMARY

Public opinion is composed of the opinions held by individuals on matters of common interest. While public opinion has always been important to government, whether democratic or totalitarian, it is only with the development of stratified random sampling that accurate estimates could be quickly made. Such surveys confirm the belief that public opinion is generally based on nonrational bases; early emotional conditioning seems to be very significant. It is encouraging to find that persons of higher education are more realistic in their thinking and that the educational factor outweighs other determinants of opinion.

Propaganda may be an effective influence on public opinion when (1) the situation is confused so that traditional prejudices do not determine the public reaction, or (2) a crisis has destroyed faith in traditional values. Propaganda is more likely to be effective if it (1) offers an outlet for repressed emotion, (2) offers a simple explanation of a confused situation, (3) fits in reasonably well with traditional symbols, and (4) promises gratification to strong motives.

While propaganda is not a major determinant of public opinion in normal times, it may influence a decisive group of people, or in time of crisis it may bring about acceptance of new social ideas—either very desirable or very harmful to the community. A general understanding of propaganda and practice in analyzing it is thus socially valuable.

RECOMMENDED SUPPLEMENTARY READING

Public Opinion

Blankenship, A. B.: *Consumer and Opinion Research,* Harper & Brothers, New York, 1943.

Bogardus, E. S.: *The Making of Public Opinion,* Association Press, New York, 1951.

Cantril, H.: *Gauging Public Opinion,* Princeton University Press, Princeton, N.J., 1944.

Doob, L. W.: *Propaganda and Public Opinion,* Henry Holt and Company, Inc., New York, 1948.

Gallup, G.: *Guide to Public Opinion Polls,* 2d ed., Princeton University Press, Princeton, N.J., 1948.

Irion, F. C.: *Public Opinion and Propaganda,* The Thomas Y. Crowell Company, New York, 1950.

Lasswell, H. D.: *Democracy through Public Opinion,* George Banta Publishing Company (The Collegiate Press), Menasha, Wis., 1940.

Propaganda

Blanco White, A.: *The New Propaganda,* Victor Gollancz, Ltd., London, 1938.

Freeman, Ellis: *Conquering the Man in the Street,* Vanguard Press, New York, 1940.

Merton, R. K.: *Mass Persuasion,* Harper & Brothers, New York, 1946.

Miller, C. R.: *The Process of Persuasion,* Crown Publishers, New York, 1946.

Appendix

FUNDAMENTAL STATISTICAL CONCEPTS

Psychological data, like those of any science, are usually expressed in statistical terms. It is impossible to read and comprehend psychological literature without understanding statistical concepts. The following pages explain as briefly as possible most of the statistical terms used in this book. No attempt is made to explain methods of calculation except when this is essential to a comprehension of meaning. An illustrative calculation is given in Table A.

Table A. Illustrative Calculation

Name	Height (x)					Weight (y)					
	1 in.	2 dev.	3 d^2	4 σ value	5	6 lb.	7 dev.	8 d^2	9 σ value	10	11 $dx \cdot dy$
John	52	-1	1	$-\,.28$	94.4	64	-3	9	$-\,.33$	93.4	3
Bill	46	-7	49	-1.94	61.2	50	-17	289	-1.87	62.6	119
James	55	2	4	.56	111.2	64	-3	9	$-\,.33$	93.4	$-\,6$
Dexter	58	5	25	1.4	128	75	8	64	.88	117.6	40
Marvin	48	-5	25	-1.4	72	60	-7	49	$-\,.77$	84.6	35
George	54	1	1	.28	105.6	63	-4	16	$-\,.44$	91.2	$-\,4$
Tom	53	0	0	0	100	72	5	25	.55	111	0
Sam	52	-1	1	$-\,.28$	94.4	66	-1	1	$-\,.11$	97.8	1
Hal	58	5	25	1.4	128	86	19	361	2.09	141.8	95
Ken	54	1	1	.28	105.6	70	3	9	.33	106.6	3
											$+296$
											$-\ 10$
Total	530	28	132	......	.....	670	70	832	......	.....	286

1. $M_x = 530 \div 10 = 53 \qquad M_y = 670 \div 10 = 67 \left(\dfrac{\Sigma \text{ scores}}{N}\right)$

2. $\text{A.D.}_x = 28 \div 10 = 2.8 \qquad \text{A.D.}_y = 70 \div 10 = 7 \left(\dfrac{\Sigma d}{N}\right)$

3. $\text{S.D.}_x = \sqrt{132 \div 10} = 3.6 \qquad \text{S.D.}_y = \sqrt{832 \div 10} = 9.1 \left(\sqrt{\dfrac{\Sigma d^2}{N}}\right)$

4. $\text{S.E.}_{mx} = 3.6 \div 3 = 1.2 \qquad \text{S.E.}_{my} = 9.1 \div 3 = 3 \left(\dfrac{\text{S.D.}}{\sqrt{N-1}}\right)$

5. $r = \dfrac{286}{10(3.6 \times 9.1)} = .87 \left(\dfrac{\Sigma dx \cdot dy}{N(\text{S.D.}_x \cdot \text{S.D.}_y)}\right)$

6. $\text{P.E.}_r = .055 \left(\dfrac{.6745(1 - r^2)}{\sqrt{N-1}}\right)$

7. Weight predicted when a boy is 51 in. tall:

$.87(9.1 \div 3.6)(51 - 53) + 67 = 62.65 \text{ lb.} \left[y = r\dfrac{\text{S.D.}_y}{\text{S.D.}_x}(x - M_x) + M_y\right]$

8. $\text{S.D.}_{est.} = 9.1 \sqrt{1 - .757} = 4.5 \;(\text{S.D.}_y \sqrt{1 - r^2})$

565

THE MEAN OR AVERAGE

The term "mean" is generally used in psychological literature instead of "average." It is calculated by adding all the cases or scores and dividing by the number.

DEVIATIONS FROM THE MEAN

"Deviation" refers to *how far* above or below the mean a score may be (see Table A, columns 2 and 6). This distance is expressed sometimes in terms of a fraction of the *average* deviation (the sum of all deviations divided by the number) but usually in terms of a fraction of the *standard* deviation, sometimes called "sigma." The standard deviation is more stable than the average deviation. It is calculated by squaring each deviation, adding the squares, dividing by the number of cases, and taking the square root of this quotient (see calculation in Table A). Each score (usually referred to as a "raw score") can then be expressed in terms of its "sigma value," *i.e.*, the distance the score is above or below the mean in terms of a fraction of the standard deviation. This fraction is calculated by dividing the score deviation by the sigma (standard deviation). Negative sigma values can then be eliminated by transmuting to a positive scale called a "standard score." For example, in Table A, the sigma values in columns 4 and 9 were transmuted to standard scores (columns 5 and 10) by arbitrarily fixing the mean or zero sigma at 100 and allowing each full sigma value to be 20. Since the first sigma value in column 4 was —.28, the standard score value would be $100 - (.28 \times 20) = 94.4$. The value of transmuting raw scores into sigma values and standard scores is that they can be added, subtracted, or averaged. Inches value can now be added to pounds value.

RELIABILITY OF THE MEAN

It is always important to know how reliable or accurate the mean is. Would investigation of other samples give the same results? How typical are the height and weight of the boys in Table A of ten-year-old boys in general? This accuracy can be determined by calculating the standard error of the mean. This is the standard deviation divided by the square root of the number of cases. It means that the true mean is probably (68 chances in 100) between the range of one standard error. In Table A, the true mean height is probably 53 ± 1.2 in., and the true mean weight is probably 67 ± 3 lb. It could be stated with greater certainty (96 chances in 100) that the true mean is between the range of two standard errors, *i.e.*, the height is 53 ± 2.4 in. and the weight is 67 ± 6 lb.

THE SIGNIFICANCE OF A DIFFERENCE BETWEEN AVERAGES

Suppose that a group of ten-year-old girls averaged 51 ± 1.0 in. in height. Is this average significantly lower than the average for the boys in Table A? In other words, is this difference of 2 in. a true difference or merely due to chance? This is determined by dividing the difference by the standard error of the difference. The standard error of a difference between two averages is calculated by taking the square root of the sum of the squares of the standard errors of the two averages. The standard error of the average height of the boys in Table A is 1.2, while the standard error of the average height of the group of girls mentioned above is 1.0. The square root of the sum of the squares of these standard errors is 1.56 (that is, $\sqrt{1.44 + 1.0} =$ 1.56). The difference in means divided by this standard error of the difference is 1.3 (that is, $2 \div 1.56 = 1.27$), which is not very significant. In fact, there are 10 chances in 100 that this difference is not a true one. If this "critical ratio" had been 2.3 instead of 1.3, there would have been only 1 chance in 100 that the difference was not a true one. Table B shows the significance of critical ratios of different sizes.

Table B. The Significance of Critical Ratios in Terms of Chance

$D/\text{S.E.}_d$	Chances in 100	$D/\text{S.E.}_d$	Chances in 100
.00	50	1.60	94
.10	54	1.70	96
.20	58	1.80	96
.30	62	1.90	97
.40	65	2.00	98
.50	69	2.10	98
.60	73	2.20	98.6
.70	76	2.30	98.9
.80	79	2.40	99.2
.90	82	2.50	99.4
1.00	84	2.60	99.5
1.10	86	2.70	99.7
1.20	88	2.80	99.7
1.30	90	2.90	99.8
1.40	92	3.00	99.9
1.50	93		

THE COEFFICIENT OF CORRELATION

It is easy enough to compare two variables—John is 52 in. tall and weighs 64 lb. It is more difficult to compare *two series of variables.* For example, what is the relation of the height to the weight of *ten* boys (see Table A). The statistical procedure for calculating the degree of relationship between two series of variables is called the "coefficient of correlation." It is expressed in decimal fractions ranging from —1.00, a perfect negative relationship, through .00, the complete absence of relationship, to 1.00, a perfect positive relationship. Another way of saying it is that —1.00 and 1.00 indicate the complete absence of chance while .00 indicates pure chance. However, the relation of the size of a coefficient of correlation and chance is *not* an arithmetical one. A correlation of .50 does not indicate a relationship 50 per cent better than chance but only 13 per cent better. Table C shows the significance of various coefficients of correlation in terms of chance. (These values are calculated by the formula $1 - \sqrt{1 - r^2}$.)

The reliability of a coefficient of correlation is affected by its size and the number of cases involved. This is indicated by the "probable error."

The formula for calculating this is $\dfrac{.6745\,(1-r^2)}{\sqrt{N-1}}$. In the problem shown in Table A, the P.E. is .055, which means that the chances are even that the true correlation (adequate sampling) between the height and weight of ten-year-old boys is between .925(.87 + .055) and .815(.87 — .055). (In one study of 1,127 cases, the correlation between height and weight was .96.)

Table C. The Significance of Coefficients of Correlation of Different Sizes

r	Prediction, Per Cent Better Than Chance	r	Prediction, Per Cent Better Than Chance
.00	00	.80	40
.10	00.5	.85	47
.20	2	.90	56
.30	5	.93	63
.40	8	.95	69
.50	13	.97	76
.60	20	.98	80
.70	29	.99	86
.75	34	1.00	100

PREDICTION FROM COEFFICIENT OF CORRELATION

The usefulness of a coefficient of correlation is that it can be used to predict the score of one series when the score of the other is known. For example, if it is known that the height of a new boy is 51 in., his weight can be predicted by further calculation of data given in Table A. This is calculated by the "regression equation." A weight of 62 lb. is predicted for a height of 51 in. This procedure is quite useful in industrial situations when the correlation between an employment test and merit rating is known. The success of prospective employees can be predicted from their test scores.

Predictions made in this way are not always accurate, but the degree of inaccuracy can be calculated. This is called the "standard error of estimate." It is calculated by multiplying the standard deviation of the estimated series by the square root of one minus the correlation squared. As shown in Table A, this is 4.5. This means that there are 68 chances in 100 that the new boy's true weight is between 58 lb. (62.5 — 4.5) and 67 lb. (62.5 + 4.5).

NAME INDEX

SUBJECT INDEX